Cyber Crime and Cyber Terrorism

Fourth Edition

Cyber Crime and Cyber Terrorism

Robert W. Taylor
University of Texas at Dallas

Eric J. Fritsch
University of North Texas

John Liederbach
Bowling Green State University

Michael R. Saylor
University of Texas at Dallas

William L. Tafoya
University of New Haven

 Pearson

330 Hudson Street, NY NY 10013

Vice President, Portfolio Management: Andrew Gilfillan
Portfolio Manager: Gary Bauer
Editorial Assistant: Lynda Cramer
Field Marketing Manager: Bob Nisbet
Product Marketing Manager: Heather Taylor
Director, Digital Studio and Content Production: Brian Hyland
Managing Producer: Jennifer Sargunar
Content Producer: Rinki Kaur
Manager, Rights Management: Johanna Burke

Operations Specialist: Deidra Smith
Creative Digital Lead: Mary Siener
Managing Producer, Digital Studio: Autumn Benson
Content Producer, Digital Studio: Maura Barclay
Cover Designer: Studio Montage
Cover Images: Scanrail1/Shutterstock
Full Service Project Management: Ranjith Rajaram
Composition: Integra Software Services, Ltd.
Text Printer/Bindery: LSC Communications, Inc.
Cover Printer: Phoenix Color/Hagerstown
Text Font: TimesLTPro-Roman

Library of Congress Cataloging-in-Publication Data

Names: Taylor, Robert W., 1951- author. | Fritsch, Eric J., author. | Liederbach, John, author.
Title: Digital crime and digital terrorism / Robert W. Taylor, University of Texas at Dallas, Eric J. Fritsch, University of North Texas, John Liederbach, Bowling Green State University.
Description: Fourth Edition. | Hoboken : Pearson, [2017] | Revised edition of the authors' Digital crime and digital terrorism, [2015]
Identifiers: LCCN 2017038219| ISBN 9780134846514 | ISBN 0134846516
Subjects: LCSH: Computer crimes. | Cyberterrorism. | Hackers. | Computer crimes—Investigation—United States. | Computer crimes—United States—Prevention.
Classification: LCC HV6773 .T39 2017 | DDC 364.16/8—dc23
LC record available at https://lccn.loc.gov/2017038219

2013047759

1 18

ISBN-13: 978-0-13-484651-4
ISBN-10:   0-13-484651-6

CONTENTS

Section IV   The Future of Cyber Crime and Cyber Terrorism: Prevention and Trends

Chapter 14   INFORMATION SECURITY AND INFRASTRUCTURE PROTECTION   359

PREFACE

NEW TO THIS EDITION

Each chapter includes new pedagogical features to aid students and instructors in comprehending the complex subject matter discussed in each chapter. These include the following:

Chapter Objectives at the beginning of each chapter identifying the core elements students need to learn.

Boxes throughout the chapters highlight interesting topics that are relevant to the chapter subject matter. In many cases, these box items highlight case studies or examples of the subject matter under discussion in the chapter.

Quick Facts boxes provide unique tidbits of information related to the chapter topics and enhance student learning.

Summaries are organized around chapter objectives and provide a clear and concise discussion of each chapter subject matter.

Review Questions at the end of each chapter pose a series of questions to test students recall of the chapter information.

Critical Thinking Exercises at the end of each chapter require students to go further and think on the analytic level. Most of the exercises involve our research and discussion.

It is the authors' shared experience that there is little in the way of introductory textbooks covering the issues of cyber crime and cyber terrorism. We have found numerous books covering the details of the technical side of these issues and others that cover the legal side. However, there are very few works that attempt to provide a summary introduction and overview of these issues. In this vein, we have tried to approach the various topics covered in this book in a nontechnical and nonjargon style. Criminal justice students and practitioners will find the technical components quite readable and understandable. Computer science students and practitioners will find the criminal justice material bereft of jargon and written in a readable and understandable style as well. In sum, we specifically tried to bridge the gap between criminal justice knowledge and competence and the technical issues that arise during investigations of the crimes and acts we cover. It is our fervent hope that the techie will get as much out of this book as the criminal justice student.

Cyber Crime and Cyber Terrorism is written for students and practitioners with a beginning interest in studying cybercrimes, cyberterrorism, and information warfare committed using computer and computer network technology. The text is written in a user-friendly fashion, designed to be understandable by even the most technologically challenged reader. Issues addressed in the book include descriptions of the types of crimes and terrorist acts committed using computer technology; theories addressing hackers and other types of digital criminals; an overview of the legal strategies and tactics targeting this type of crime; and in-depth coverage of investigating and researching cyber crime, cyber terrorism, and information warfare. Readers will find a conversational tone to the writing designed to convey complex technical issues as understandable concepts and issues. Additionally, upon completion of the text, readers should find themselves better prepared for further study into the growing problems of crime, terrorism, and information warfare being committed using computer technology.

The first section of the book covers the etiology of the cyber crime, cyber terrorism, and information warfare problem. The focus in this section is on the types of crimes, acts of terrorism and information warfare that are committed using computers, networks, and the Internet. Additionally, the reasons why offenders commit these types of crimes are examined in relation to current criminological theories and explanations. As the reader will find, applying criminological theory to cyber crime, cyberterrorism, and information warfare is a relatively recent endeavor. This section includes a chapter dedicated to hackers, and concludes with a new chapter focused on threats from sophisticated cybercriminal organizations. Chapter 1 provides an introduction and overview of computer crime. In particular, a categorization of computer crimes is presented. Chapter 2 provides a definition and overview of two key areas of concern in regard to computer crimes, specifically "information warfare" and "cyberterrorism." Chapter 3 reviews criminological theories that can explain cyber crime. Since few theories have been applied directly to cyber crime, this chapter focuses on the criminological theories that can be applied to cyber crime. In other words, the theories explained in this chapter were developed to explain crime in general, not cyber crime specifically. Chapter 4 presents an overview of hackers. Finally, Chapter 5 focuses on new threats from sophisticated cybercriminal organizations operating in a worldwide venue.

The second section of the book details the various types of crimes that are committed using digital technology. Chapter 6 describes the ways in which the computer revolution has altered the techniques used to commit some of the most common white-collar offenses, including embezzlement, corporate espionage, money laundering, and fraud. In addition to these traditional white-collar offenses, the chapter provides an overview of the emerging area of identity theft crimes. Chapter 7 discusses viruses and other types of malicious code. The chapter takes an etiological approach with an emphasis on the description, examples, and categorical analysis of these various threats. Chapter 8 focuses on crimes against persons committed over the Internet, including exploitation, stalking, and obscenity. The chapter goes into detail on the etiology of these types of offenses and the offenders who commit them. Finally, Chapter 9 provides the reader with an introduction to the issues surrounding the growth of the Internet and the dissemination of extremist ideologies over the World Wide Web.

The third section of the book discusses the law, law enforcement, and investigation of cyber crime and cyber terrorism. Chapter 10 reviews the law and legislation as it applies to the collection of evidence and prosecution of cyber crime. First, search and seizure law for digital evidence is discussed, including searches with warrants and numerous searches without warrants. Second, the major federal statutes governing the collection of digital evidence, especially electronic surveillance law, are discussed along with federal criminal statutes that forbid certain types of computer crime. Third, issues related to the admission of digital evidence at trial, including authentication and hearsay, are reviewed. Finally, significant U.S. Supreme Court cases in the area of cyber crime are discussed. Chapter 11 then discusses the primary role of the many federal agencies involved in detecting and enforcing computer crimes. The chapter continues with a discussion concerning the role of local agencies, with an emphasis on detailing the myriad of limitations associated with the local agencies' response to computer crime. Chapter 12 highlights the role that investigators play in the enforcement of cyber crime laws. Techniques for acquiring investigative information are presented in this chapter, along with conceptual tools that allow an investigator to communicate with computer experts. Finally, Chapter 13 reviews the collection of evidence and evidentiary issues related to cyber crime and terrorism.

The final section of the book covers prevention of cyber crime and terrorism and an overview of what the future might hold in these areas. Chapter 14 presents the problems associated with information security and infrastructure protection. The chapter discusses at length the problems and prospects presented by the USA PATRIOT Act as well as other laws designed to protect the information infrastructure. The concluding chapter of the book, Chapter 15, uses research developed by Carter and Katz as a framework to present an analysis of what the future of cyber crime, cyber terrorism, and information warfare might look like. The results of the research led to the development of eight forecasts for the future. Each prediction is accompanied by examples, trends, and analysis of what the future may hold.

CHAPTER 1 INTRODUCTION AND OVERVIEW OF CYBER CRIME AND CYBER TERRORISM

- Reorganization of text throughout the chapter
- Updated text, scholarship, and statistics on the costs of cybercrime
- Updated and new text on the classification of computer crime including extensive overviews of more recent computer crime classification schemes
- New material on recent major distributed denial-of-service attacks
- New material that underscores how the emergence of dangers regarding online victimization influenced popular culture during the dawn of the twenty-first century

CHAPTER 2 CYBER TERRORISM AND INFORMATION WARFARE

- New material on Low-Level Cyber war including discussion on *Stuxnet* and *Flame*
- Update material on Viruses and Worms with new material on the Global "WannaCry" malware infections of 2016–2017
- New box items throughout the chapter, including new material on the encryption of terrorist iPhones, recruitment videos from the Islamic State, and the burgeoning cyber threats stemming from hackers in North Korea

CHAPTER 3 THE CRIMINOLOGY OF COMPUTER CRIME

- Updated theoretical research relating to computer crime
- Significant update to routine activities theory
- Added new and modern box items throughout the chapter

CHAPTER 4   HACKERS

- New material on hacker subculture, the classification of hackers, and their views on the role of prosocial hacking in the protection of consumers and businesses in the fight against computer crime
- New material that describes and identifies the Internet of Things as a prime target of hackers, computer criminals, and cyber terrorists
- New material on hacktivism and the continued prominence of the hacktivist group Anonymous

CHAPTER 5   SOPHISTICATED CYBER CRIMINAL ORGANIZATIONS

- Updated statistical data throughout the chapter
- New case material on espionage
- New and more contemporary box items throughout the chapter
- Updated material on the "Deep Web" or Tor Network

CHAPTER 6   WHITE-COLLAR CRIMES

- Updated statistics and cases throughout the chapter
- New material on the problem of intellectual piracy and the origins of these crimes within American history
- New section on proposed strategies to mitigate identity theft and the concept of "fractured identities"

New text regarding the largely ignored phenomenon of Trade Based Money Laundering and how this crime threatens global international trade and commerce.

CHAPTER 7   VIRUSES AND MALICIOUS CODE

- New statistical information throughout the chapters
- Updated material on ransomware, viruses, worms, Trojan horses, and other malware
- New discussion on viruses and malicious code attacks, with updated information regarding attack trends, vulnerability trends, malicious code trends, and spam trends

CHAPTER 8   SEX CRIMES, VICTIMIZATION, AND OBSCENITY ON THE WORLD WIDE WEB

- New material on the role of social media as a facilitator of cyberstalking with detailed discussion of the threats posed by child predators using "Snapchat" and other online social media software platforms
- Updated case studies on cyberstalking victimization and updated statistical data throughout the chapter
- New material on the size and scope of child pornography on the Internet
- Updated material on laws and legislation protecting children online
- New material on prostitution and the sex trade online with discussions relating to the "Ashley Madison" scandal, unique online sites that review sex workers

("providers"), massage parlors, new types of porn sites, such as webcams and streaming services that focus on a world-wide audience
- New material on online dating scams (ODS) and the tragedy of child sex trafficking

CHAPTER 9   ANARCHY AND HATE ON THE WORLD WIDE WEB

- Updated references and material throughout the chapter
- Expanded the section on "U.S. Intelligence Weaknesses"
- Added new material on the Dark Web; updating other material in Chapter 5 on the "Deep Web"
- Augments and distinguishes "Black Market" and other "Fake Trade" discussed in Chapters 6 and 15
- Added new material on WikiLeaks
- Added new material on "Fake News"

Updated discussion of right-wing hate groups

- Updated coverage of the Earth Liberation Front (ELF)
- New section on the Reauthorized PATRIOT Act (2011)

CHAPTER 10   DIGITAL LAWS AND LEGISLATION

- Significant revision and update of federal statutes applicable to cyber crime and cyber terrorism
- Added new and modern box items throughout the chapter
- New coverage of recent U.S. Supreme Court cases

CHAPTER 11   LAW ENFORCEMENT ROLES AND RESPONSES

- New material and box items throughout the chapter
- Revision and update of federal law enforcement agencies tasked with the investigation of cyber crime and cyber terrorism

CHAPTER 12   THE INVESTIGATION OF COMPUTER-RELATED CRIME

- Updated material and references throughout the chapter
- Added new commentary on the current state-of-the-domain of computer crime investigation
- Add new material that distinguishes "corporate security" from "private police"
- Augmented the landmark case *Frye v. United States*
- Augmented the landmark case *Daubert v. Merrell Dow Pharmaceutical* hence, updating "the *Daubert* Test"

CHAPTER 13   DIGITAL FORENSICS

- Minor update of this strong chapter focusing on the art and science of digital forensics with new material on digital forensics and mobile devices operating outside the Windows operating systems, such as cell phones, PDAs, and tablet devices

- Updated and new material on addressing mobile devices using Android OS, Apple's iOS, and Windows Mobile systems
- New material on commercial forensic packages used by law enforcement to analyze digital evidence for the arrest and prosecution of suspects
- New material on the use of technology in solving high-profile cases, including the infamous BTK (Blind-Torture-Kill) serial murder case in Kansas

CHAPTER 14 INFORMATION SECURITY AND INFRASTRUCTURE PROTECTION

- Minor update on this chapter focusing on information security and infrastructure protection
- Updated material on deep packet inspection (DPI), DPI firewalls, and RSA SecurID
- Updated section on the evolution of cyberattacks discussing how cyberattacks have become more sophisticated, polymorphic, and multi-vector in their approach to defeating security, presenting challenges to both the home user and the advanced cybersecurity professional

CHAPTER 15 CYBER CRIME AND TERRORISM: A FORECAST OF TRENDS AND POLICY IMPLICATIONS

- Updated statistical information and new research regarding patterns and trends in computer crime and cyber terrorism
- Added new material on big data trends, cyber threat trends, ransomware, electro-magnetic pulse (EMP), the Faraday cage, drones, and artificial intelligence
- Updated new policy implications relating to the growing need for transparency in cybercrime investigations, particularly at the international level

INSTRUCTOR SUPPLEMENTS

Instructor's Manual with Test Bank. Includes content outlines for classroom discussion, teaching suggestions, and answers to selected end-of-chapter questions from the text. This also contains a Word document version of the test bank.

TestGen. This computerized test generation system gives you maximum flexibility in creating and administering tests on paper, electronically, or online. It provides state-of-the-art features for viewing and editing test bank questions, dragging a selected question into a test you are creating, and printing sleek, formatted tests in a variety of layouts. Select test items from test banks included with TestGen for quick test creation, or write your own questions from scratch. TestGen's random generator provides the option to display different text or calculated number values each time questions are used.

PowerPoint Presentations. Our presentations offer clear, straightforward outlines and notes to use for class lectures or study materials. Photos, illustrations, charts, and tables from the book are included in the presentations when applicable.

To access supplementary materials online, instructors need to request an instructor access code. Go to www.pearsonhighered.com/irc, where you can register for an instructor access code. Within 48 hours after registering, you will receive a confirming email, including an instructor access code. Once you have received your code, go to the site and log on for full instructions on downloading the materials you wish to use.

ALTERNATE VERSIONS

eBooks. This text is also available in multiple eBook formats including Adobe Reader and CourseSmart. CourseSmart is an exciting new choice for students looking to save money. As an alternative to purchasing the printed textbook, students can purchase an electronic version of the same content. With a CourseSmart eTextbook, students can search the text, make notes online, print out reading assignments that incorporate lecture notes, and bookmark important passages for later review. For more information, or to purchase access to the CourseSmart eTextbook, visit www.coursesmart.com.

ACKNOWLEDGMENTS

First and foremost, we want to thank our wives, significant others, children, extended family, and friends for their support and patience with all of us as we compiled the fourth edition of this book. As is the case with many of these types of projects, we locked ourselves in our offices, missed family functions, worked during vacations, delayed retirement, and, in general, put out our loved ones while writing this book. Thank you for your love, patience, and support during these times.

Since our first edition, time has presented us with a new set of authors. Dr. D. Kall Loper has left academia to pursue a career as an expert in digital forensics, a field that he helped found and develop. And quite sadly, our good friend and colleague Dr. Tory J. Caeti was killed in a terrible traffic accident in August 2006 while serving as a consultant with Bob Taylor to the U.S. Department of State Anti-Terrorism Assistance Program in Kenya. Tory and Bob were to present material to the Kenyan National Police on digital terrorism. We miss Tory, and he will be forever in our thoughts. Dr. Tom Holt joined us for the second edition, but has subsequently moved on to focus his work on cybercrime. For this edition, we are fortunate to have the services of Mike Saylor, from the Cyber Defense Labs located on the campus of the University of Texas at Dallas as a valuable coauthor. Further, retired-FBI agent Bill Tafoya now professor, and a long-time friend and colleague, has also joined us as a coauthor for this edition. As the "father of police futuristics," Bill was an early participant in defining and recognizing digital crime and digital terrorism as major threats to the future of our society. To a great extent, our understanding of the threats posed by cybercrime and digital terrorism were first discussed in the early years of the development of the *Society for Police Futurists International* (PFI), an organization started by Bill back in the early 1990s. Bob was one of the first educators to join Bill in presenting at the first "International Symposium on the Future of Law Enforcement" at the FBI Academy in Quantico (April, 1991) featuring Alvin Toffler as the keynote speaker. It was Bill's hard work that began serious study on the future of policing, and Bob's early paper presented at this conference that became the first outline for this book. We also express our sincere appreciation and a heartfelt "thank you" to several graduate students who have assisted us on this project. Specifically, Jennifer Davis-Lamm worked tirelessly for Dr. Taylor in researching various aspects of the cyberworld. Alexandra Jones assisted Dr. Fritsch in compiling recent theoretical research applicable to computer crime. Dr. Tafoya expresses a special thank you to Meredith Emigh and Gabriella Palmeri for their dedication unearthing the many current references used in this book, and pays a heartfelt homage to Dr. Richard H. Ward (deceased) for his vision and contribution to the discipline of Criminal Justice. Thanks too, to Bernard "Bud" Levin and Shawn Henry for their important insight into several chapters of this edition. We would like to thank Tamara Lynn, Fort Hays State University and Priscilla Montagna, Bunker Hill Community College for reviewing the fourth edition of this book. We would also like to thank the hundreds of students in our classes who have purchased and used previous editions of the book. Their suggestions on text revisions have been invaluable, and have been incorporated within this most recent edition of the text.

Finally, we would like to thank our editorial staff at Pearson. Gary Bauer's guidance and assistance was instrumental in getting this book to press. We also want to thank all other Pearson staff involved in this project. They epitomize patience and understanding in dealing with slow academics who take forever to return phone calls and e-mails.

Introduction and Overview of Cyber Crime and Cyber Terrorism

CHAPTER OBJECTIVES

After completing this chapter, you should be able to

- Describe the current issues, trends, and problems in cyber crime and cyber terrorism.
- Understand estimates on the costs of cybercrime.
- Understand the intended audience, purpose, and scope of this text.
- Discuss the developmental perspective on the problem and changes to cybervictimization.
- Describe the scheme for classifying computer crimes.

INTRODUCTION

Scenarios that depict the rising problem of cyber crime and cyber terrorism are numerous and impossible to ignore—data destroying viruses that shut down the Internet, computer thieves stealing credit card and Social Security numbers, identity theft victims that number into the millions, terrorists laundering money and using the Internet to steal billions of dollars in an instant, and nation-states launching cyberattacks to destroy their enemies in ways more lethal than the famous amphibious assaults of the last century's world wars. The situation is worsened by public perceptions that law enforcement and governmental officials are ill-equipped to deal with these crimes. Cyber crimes inspire fear in consumers and lead to a lack of trust in the security and safety of e-commerce and online business transactions. Fears of imminent and crippling attacks to our society and infrastructure are the direct result of our reliance on computers and networks for a host of societal functions, including military operations, finance, communications, utilities, and mass transit.

In 2013, details emerged regarding the work of a sophisticated global network of thieves who stole $45 million from automated teller machines (ATMs) located within 27 different nations.[1] A decade earlier, the public viewed images of thousands of people walking home from work due to a power problem that began in Canada and quickly spread to the United States. The disaster led many to believe that terrorists had attacked the nation's power grid. Recent descriptions of both Chinese and Russian hacker intrusions into power grids in the United States continue to concern citizens and governments alike. To be sure, the scope and nature of cyber crime and cyber terrorism sometimes creates misperceptions and fear that exceed the identifiable threats; however, the dangers posed by cybercriminals and terrorists *are* real and present unique and difficult challenges to law enforcement and other governmental officials.

The transformation of the digital infrastructure and information technology over the course of the last three-quarters of a century has been nothing short of astonishing. The first electronic computer was completed in 1945, and the first long-distance electronic communication on the Internet was sent in 1969.[2] Until the creation of the personal computer, computers and the Internet were the exclusive tools of society's scientific elite and the military and were housed at major university campuses, military bases, and corporate research parks. In fact, the coming "information society" would become increasingly dependent on computers and networks to keep our society operational. Computers are now fixtures of everyday life, and almost every form of interaction, business, and communication between people relies on computers and network systems in some fashion. The Internet has truly made the world a smaller place. Students can register for or drop classes in real time from their homes while sitting in front of a keyboard. Individuals are able to swiftly and conveniently withdraw money from bank accounts at any time by using ATMs. Friends use satellite transmissions linked across vast computer networks to instantly communicate with one another. Social networking Web sites like Facebook, Myspace, Instagram, Pinterest, and Twitter allow individuals to connect, communicate, and instantly update the world about their attitudes and activities. Stock transactions, flight schedules, reference libraries, e-commerce, the latest news, and innumerable other resources are *all* available with a few clicks of the mouse.

The advancement of computer technology and networking rapidly expanded communications and information markets, but this progress has also come with enormous social and economic costs. The same technology that provides useful services has also been perverted for criminal and terrorist purposes. Technological progress in the areas of computing, networking, communications, and e-commerce provides criminals and terrorists with an unbelievable array of new tools and opportunities to perpetrate their crimes. The Internet is, in essence, a lawless frontier where bullies, deviants, criminals, and terrorists can roam freely with reckless abandon. The rapid advancement of computers and networks occurred without adequate regulation or monitoring, and produced a scenario where the "law of the jungle" often prevails. Lawmakers and law enforcement personnel alike are still trying to play catch-up.

New Threats to the Information Age

Computers are currently used to perform many traditional criminal acts, most prominently the production and distribution of child pornography, financial crimes, information and corporate espionage, exploitation, stalking, and identity theft. The openness of the Internet has expanded the scope of criminal opportunities and has spawned whole new categories of crimes and criminals, including "hackers," who seek to invade our computer networks, and virus writers, who develop tools that can damage and destroy computer systems. The number of Internet-connected devices—including traditional computers, mobile devices, and newer technologies—is currently estimated to exceed 8.7 billion.[3] The expansion and sheer amount of Internet traffic has already exceeded the estimates predicted by experts and commentators a few years ago. The opportunities to commit computer crimes and the technical competence of the criminals have clearly expanded more quickly than our efforts to control them. Perhaps the most feared online crime is the interception of privileged information, such as credit card numbers or passwords leading to identity theft. Abuses associated with the issuance of credit have reached epidemic proportions. One recent case, for example, occurred in 2013, wherein

18 individuals were charged in one of the largest credit card fraud schemes ever prosecuted by the federal government. The wide-scale conspiracy involved the creation of more than 7,000 fake identities to obtain tens of thousands of fraudulent credit cards.[4]

Theft of intellectual property ranging from trade secrets to illegal reproduction of copyrighted consumer materials such as music and movies has an incalculable cost. The Motion Picture Association of America (MPAA) reported fiscal losses upward of $6 billion from movie piracy in the United States alone. Over 40 percent of these reported losses were argued to be a result of university students in the United States.[5] These are the most recent publicly available data on the costs of movie piracy. There can be no doubt that the costs of this type of online piracy are much higher now, nearly a decade after the publication of the MPAA data. One more recent study estimates that at least 45 percent of U.S. citizens pirate movies, including upward of 70 percent of younger viewers.[6] The 2014 Academy Award–nominated film *The Wolf of Wall Street* is estimated to be one of the most pirated films of all time, with over 30 million illegal downloads.[7]

While identity theft is probably the most feared online crime, it is not the only threat to Internet consumers. The other category of cyber crime that inspires the most fear and disdain is virus writing and other types of malicious software, or malware. Any time an average user has a problem with his or her computer, the person is likely to have a knee-jerk response, blaming the problem on a virus. The virus protection industry is now a multimillion dollar business, selling and proffering security online. Consumer fear is, however, not unfounded, as a study by the security company PandaLabs found: Almost 25 percent of personal computers with some sort of protective software around the world were infected with malicious software, compared to 33.2 percent of systems without protection.[8] Beyond these dangers, threats from would-be terrorists and politically motivated "hactivists" threaten the functioning of our government, commerce, and military operations. Recent studies indicate that many corporations, government agencies, and utility companies are highly vulnerable to computer attacks from "outsiders," who in some cases may be able to seriously affect large segments of the population through a single organization's computer system. This threat cannot be taken lightly, and the Federal Bureau of Investigation (FBI) and the Department of Homeland Security both conclude that the potential exists for serious harm emanating from attempts to tamper with the information infrastructure.

Purpose and Scope of This Book

This text is primarily intended to be an introduction to the problems of cyber crime and cyber terrorism. A special emphasis is placed on being decidedly nontechnical in our writing and explanations; however, some technical terms and issues are inevitable in this field of study. We hope that we have described the technical jargon in sufficient detail such that the casual reader will not be lost in the shuffle. The intended audience is anyone interested in learning more about the etiology of cyber crime and cyber terrorism. The average criminal justice student may have a solid knowledge of the law, criminology, and criminal justice systems, yet possess little knowledge of the complexities of cyber crime and victimization. Computer science students well versed in the technical aspects of computers and networks may have little knowledge of the legal aspects of their field and issues of criminality and victimization. Furthermore, practitioners in both the criminal justice field and the computer science field typically have limited knowledge of each other's occupations. Finally, many students and casual readers may simply wish to become better educated in this area. This text is written with all of these groups in mind.

The ambition of the authors was to bring aspects of both of these fields together in a readable, nontechnical text designed to increase knowledge about the problems of cyber crime and cyber terrorism. Anyone with a little knowledge about computers and the criminal justice system should find merit in the topics covered in this text. We have also consciously focused on common cyber crimes and common computer systems, as these will be most familiar to the neophyte. The text is decidedly focused on Microsoft-based systems, common Internet systems, and the most typical types of cyber crime and cyber terrorism. As such, certain types of cyber crimes and certain operating systems/software are beyond our scope and intent. Again, a decided effort was made to explain the more technical parts of this book in a "user-friendly" tone; however, readers who know very little about computers might have some difficulty with some of the details and level of description.

The first section of this book covers the etiology of cyber crime and cyber terrorism and includes a discussion of the criminology of these types of crimes and potential offenders. Who are the cyber terrorists and cyber hackers, and why do they commit their crimes and acts of aggression? The second section addresses the various types of cyber crimes and covers the nature, extent, and offender groups in each of the chapters. Chapters on white-collar crime, viruses and malicious code, exploitation, and hate are all covered in this section. The third section covers the law, enforcement, and investigation of cyber crimes and terrorism. Included in this section are chapters on the laws and legislation covering cyber crime and cyber terrorism, the agencies charged with enforcing these laws, and the investigative and forensic aspects of this area. Finally, the book concludes with chapters on preventing these types of crimes and threats and discusses what the future might hold.

Defining the Terms

As in any new area of study and exploration, the terms often change to match industry-wide jargon or innovative style. For instance, the authors use the terms "cyber crime" and "cyber terrorism" to encompass the myriad of crimes committed within the vast fields of information technology and computer networks. The prefix of "*cyber*" has now been introduced into our social vocabulary to mean almost anything "real" or "virtual" attached to a computer or network. For instance, we now refer to cybertalk, cyberspace, and even cybercafés, as a prefix to meaning that the following word is computer or computer network related. Hence, *cyber crime* can easily be called *cybercrime* or *computer crime* since the terms refer to the same types of activity, or *cyber terrorism* can be referred to as "cyberterrorism." Interestingly, classic works on computer crime by Donn Parker[9] are absent the "cyber" prefix as well as early legal constructs developed to initiate legislation against criminality involving computers. *Malware* is another new term to the computer crime world. Malware includes computer viruses, worms, Trojan horses, spyware, adware, or any other destructive software aimed at disrupting normal computer network services, collecting sensitive information, or gaining access to private computers, systems and/or networks. Short for *malicious software*, malware is often referred to as "*computer contaminant*" and is a legal terminology by statute in several U.S. states.[10] Clearly, the discipline has matured rapidly over the past few years, and this book attempts to keep pace using these terms interchangeably.

OVERVIEW

Cybercrime has increased dramatically in recent years. Indeed, both the character and nature of these offenses and their frequency of occurrence have changed notably since about 1995, when the Internet experienced explosive growth.[11] One simply needs to search the phrase "computer crime" or "cybercrime" on Google or any other Internet search engine to find a plethora of incidents and commentaries on the problem. The question of how much computer crime occurs is simply unknown given the scope and variety of the problem. Not only is there significant inconsistency in defining computer crime offenses, there is an absence of any attempt to collect offense data systematically. Offenses vary in character from clear criminality (e.g., theft, fraud, or destruction of data files) to acts where criminal culpability is less clear, such as violations of privacy (e.g., unauthorized access to credit reports or medical records). Similarly, types of criminal behavior by computer users also vary (e.g., pornography, extortion, cyberstalking, or gambling). This situation is complicated by the global character of networking offenses—transactions and behavioral interactions can occur between people worldwide from their homes with no scrutiny by immigration, customs, or other government entity.

Given these complexities, our broad overview of cyber crime and cyber terrorism provided in this chapter covers a wide range of issues, including an introduction to what we refer to as a "developmental perspective" on these problems, the realities of increased victimization, a discussion on ongoing changes to the character of cybervictimization and the emergence of cyber terrorism as an important concern, and an overview of studies designed to estimate the exponential costs of cyber crimes. The chapter concludes with a section that introduces the reader to a widely recognized system for classifying the various types of computer crimes. This section provides an organizational framework for discussions on the various types of cyber crimes and forms of cyber terrorism covered in the remainder of the text.

A Developmental Perspective on a Growing Problem

Personal computing and the Internet have grown substantially since the introduction of the microcomputer. Technological development including memory capacity, processing speed, software capabilities, and remote communications via computer (i.e., networking) grew geometrically. Similarly, there has been rapid integration of computing, telecommunications, multimedia, and information archiving technologies. With the public's embrace of the Internet and its staggering growth since the mid-nineties, the need for network security became obvious. Certainly there were some early efforts to explore the idea of computer crime and recognition of the technological transformation as a potential crime problem that required significant attention; however, these early efforts to control computer crime largely reflected the groundbreaking but limited technology of the day.

One of the earliest commentators on the problems associated with computer crime was Parker.[12] Parker recognized the potential for computer-related criminality even in systems that were by today's standards archaic. His early work underscored how easily criminals could misuse information that is now much more easily accessible. In the late 1970s, the Bureau of Justice Statistics highlighted the emergence of computer crime through a series of publications that included an overview of important issues,[13] computer security,[14] and crimes related to electronic fund transfers.[15] These monographs focused on the potential for cybercriminality and considered issues of law, investigation, case development, and possible criminal strategies. This ground-breaking research employed methodologies that still apply to many operational aspects of security and crime control today. Yet, the reports contain very limited documentation of actual criminality and do not include discussion of cybercriminals, per se. In the 1980s, a few more publications emerged on the topic, mostly dealing with logistical issues associated with computer-related criminality. Several publications discussed methods to prevent computer crimes.[16] Others explored practices for effectively investigating and prosecuting a computer crime case.[17]

As research developed on the problems of computer crime, several common themes emerged. Some research offered classification schemes for the emerging crime problems.[18] Scholars also began documenting cases of computer-related fraud within government agencies, nearly all of which were cases of trust violations.[19] Others outlined the work of hackers during the early days of Bitnet, or the predecessor of the modern-day Internet.[20] Some researchers began to call for the creation of dedicated computer crime units.[21] Publications and a new line of products were introduced as part of an entire new industry designed to provide security against these new computer criminals, including firewalls, encryption systems, operations security, virtual private networks, physical security, access controls, and biometric security developments. Nearly all of the publications employ the same methodology: describe the security issue, offer options for a solution, and provide technological procedural alternatives for each potential solution. Behavioral approaches and descriptions of problems and trends are virtually nonexistent within these publications. One exception is Icove et al.,[22] who not only comprehensively focus on security and investigation but also offer some interesting insights about motivations and behaviors. While their work provided some guidance to the emerging field of cybersecurity, the research was limited because it was based on a small number of investigations.

Other publications about cybercrime are found in the popular press. Case studies such as *The Cuckoo's Egg*[23] and *Takedown*[24] look at specific instances of network incursion. Stoll[25] documents the case of a computer hacker from Germany who penetrated a wide range of U.S. academic and military computers seeking information to steal and sell on the global national security market. Shimomura[26] describes the investigation, arrest, and prosecution of Kevin Mitnik, perhaps the most well known of all hackers, who was released in early 2000 from federal prison for computer crime violations. Both publications provide interesting and unique insights about the capacity to commit cybercrimes as well as the difficulty of investigating these offenses. However, as case studies, they offer information about specific offenders, not generalizations about trends in cybercriminality or patterns of offending.

A great deal of effort continues to be dedicated to all forms of computer security because of the growth in the problems of hacking/cracking and the use of malicious software. These efforts include firewalls, encryption technologies to control computer access, and virus control. Ironically, rapid growth in the computer security industry has largely occurred *without* adequate research on the nature of cybercrimes and criminals. The majority of research in this area focuses on the mechanisms and techniques used rather than on the etiology of the offenders and the offenses they commit. According to Parker, the lack of attention paid to computer crime historically is no accident, mostly because researchers had concluded that the problem was not worthy of specific research efforts. The result was that cybercrime and the massive problems associated with these new forms of criminality were largely ignored by policy makers and scholars. Parker underscored how wrong-headed these views were given the eventual reality of substantial losses.[27] The irony is that Parker's observations were made more than a decade ago, yet there is little substantial progress in understanding and addressing the problem from criminological and investigative perspectives. Even more troubling is that fact that Parker's comments were made during a period in which computing was dominated by big business, government, and researchers. Today, personal computing has changed the entire face of the computer industry and has exponentially increased the risk of computer crime victimization to the ordinary citizen.

The Reality of Increased Cybervictimization

Two trends clearly drive the reality of increased cybervictimization. The first trend involves the increased use of computers by virtually every citizen. Cybervictimization will clearly continue to increase as more and more people utilize the Internet and computers become further ingrained in our everyday lives. These trends have been obviously influenced and accelerated by the dissemination and ownership of smartphones—devices that are much more a "computer" than a "phone"—since they are mobile devices that perform many of the functions of a computer through Internet access. Among adults in the United States, 77 percent now own a smartphone.[28] So, roughly three-fourths of all American adults carry and use a personal computing device during virtually all of their waking hours—devices that provide ongoing opportunities for cybervictimization.

There seems to be a connection between the movement toward industrialization and increased commercial activity, related increases in Internet connectivity, and the ongoing rise in cybervictimization. For example, a study comparing reporting of cybercrime victimization in eight industrialized nations across the globe found that computer security incidents were on the rise, particularly in Canada, Australia, the United Kingdom, and the United States.[29] In fact, the United States had the highest victimization rate overall, followed by the United Kingdom and Japan. These findings would suggest that the risk of victimization increases with time and the penetration of computers and the Internet within any particular society.

The second clear trend driving increased cybervictimization is the increased availability of technical information on virus creation and computer hacking techniques that enable more and more technically savvy computer criminals. This information is available to both organizational "insiders" and "outsiders," and there is an ongoing debate as to which of these groups poses the largest threat to potential victims. In the mid-1980s, Van Duyn suggested insider threats were far more serious than outsider threats because insiders are much more familiar with the data and how they are processed.[30] In short, "insiders" know exactly where to look for vulnerable information, and if they are in any doubt "can reference the systems documentation which usually includes programming specifications, file and record layouts, a data element dictionary, and so on."[31]

As a result of these situations, many experts conclude that vulnerability from within an organization is the most dangerous and poses the most serious threat. In fact, one study estimated that 90 percent of economic computer crimes were committed by employees of the victimized companies. A study conducted in North America and Europe in 1995 found that 73 percent of the risk to computer security was from internal sources, while only 23 percent was attributable to external sources.[32] Unlike "outsiders" attempting to break into a system, "insiders" are oftentimes able to more easily circumvent safeguards, reducing their chances of being detected. Moreover, if the employee has authorized access to the information, but chooses to steal or destroy it, then detection is even more difficult. The argument in favor of the dangers posed by "insiders" clearly still has merit, but the dangers posed by "outsiders" have more recently increased due to the emergence of networking, expansive growth in user-friendly Internet protocols, and adaptable databases integrated within Web pages. Exponential growth in the e-commerce realm and the number of financial transactions conducted online has also increased the threats posed by "outsiders." Whether the greatest threats are posed by "insiders" or "outsiders," the parallel trends involving increased computer use and the availability of information to potential computer criminals virtually ensure that the number of cybercrime victims will substantially grow well in the future.

Changes to Cybervictimization and the Emergence of Cyber Terror

To this point, the focus of much of the research and attention in this area has been cyber crime and the individual victimization of private citizens, or the use of computers as criminal instruments. Barrett[33] however offers insights about the wide range of cybercriminality that can occur and a description of behaviors that range from acts best described as "crimes" and those more likely to be thought of as forms of "terrorism." In this way, Barrett provides a foundation about the capacity of computers to be used as *both* criminal instruments and instruments of warfare. The point is that the dynamics and processes involved in the production of cyber crime *and* cyber terrorism are virtually the same, and that the rise of cyber terrorism poses at least as grave a threat as cyber crime.

Inferences from the reports of the National Infrastructure Protection Center (NIPC) can be utilized to demonstrate that cyber crime and cyber terrorism are on parallel tracks. The NIPC guides the national effort to manage risks to the nation's critical infrastructure that provides essential societal functions including commerce, energy, communications, and national defense. The most recent National Infrastructure Protection Plan (NIPP, 2013) explicitly defines *both* "acts of terrorism" *and* "cyberthreats" as among the most important evolving threats to critical infrastructures.[34]

The point on the convergence of digital acts that can be referred to as "crimes" and those that can be defined as acts of "terrorism" has repeatedly been made clear as part of ongoing international relations and threats posed by foreign adversaries. During the latter 1990s, the U.S. Department of Defense began to commonly confront coordinated attacks on computer systems that originated in Russia. Similar tactics were used by Russian organized crime groups against banks.[35] The point is that Russian groups were perpetrating acts that were similar in terms of tactics and the utilization of digital resources that could be defined as both "crimes" in the traditional sense and acts of "terrorism." Other attacks, such as those perpetrated by Chinese hackers, utilize the same techniques and tools as in coordinated attacks against private citizens and financial industries.[36] Closer to home, the United States and Israel recently developed and deployed a computer worm dubbed as "Stuxnet," which has been described as "the world's first precision guided cybermunition."[37] Stuxnet was designed to undermine Iran's nuclear program. Elements of the program became public in 2010. The advent of the Stuxnet virus and its use against Iran raises issues in regard to the vulnerability of national critical infrastructures that rely on the functioning of computer networks around the globe. The advent of international national warfare centered on the use of digital tactics is clearly upon us. Indeed, the central themes of this book lie at the intersection of the parallel concerns of cyber crime *and* cyber terrorism, and the goals of increasing awareness about these issues.

The Costs of Cybercrime

One goal since the emergence of computer crime as early as the 1980s has been to calculate the costs associated with these offenses, mostly in order to underscore the importance of the problem and garner the resources necessary to fight it. Cyber crime and cyber terror are in many ways different than more traditional "street crimes" such as murder, robbery, and assault; therefore, scholars and business executives and law enforcement officials needed to be convinced—at least during the initial decades of the computer revolution—about the tremendous costs of computer crimes and the need to dedicate significant resources to combat the problem. The initial attempts to calculate the costs of cybercrime focused strictly on the measurement of monetary costs in dollars.

Among these early studies, the American Bar Association (ABA) found that 24 percent of government agencies and corporations surveyed claimed to have been the victim of a computer-related crime in the preceding 12 months.[38] The estimated losses from these crimes ranged from $145 million to $730 million. Another study during the 1980s conducted by the Florida Department of Law Enforcement (FDLE) surveyed 898 public and private sector organizations. The survey found that 25 percent of the responding organizations had been victimized by computer criminals.[39] Perhaps the most comprehensive early study designed to calculate the costs of cybercrime was conducted by the U.N. Commission on Crime and Criminal Justice in 1991. The commission surveyed 3,000 sites utilizing networked computer servers in Canada, Europe, and the United States. Almost three-fourths of the respondents (72%) reported that a security incident had occurred within the previous 12 months, and 43 percent reported that the incident had been criminal in nature.[40] By far the greatest security threats came from employees or people who had legitimate access to the computers; however, a number of external security breaches from hackers telephoning into the systems or accessing via networks were also reported. The earlier ABA and FDLE studies scarcely mentioned this "external threat" and gave little attention to it as a growing problem. This is not surprising, since networking in the late 1980s was comparatively limited. However, the U.N. study suggested that external threats via remote access were a problem that would grow in the years to come—a prediction that has certainly proved to be accurate.

QUICK FACTS

Facebook concedes that roughly 600,000 user accounts are illegally hacked by "outsiders" every day during user's log-on protocols.

Source: Michael Jaccarino, "Facebook Hack Attacks Strike 600k Times per Day." *New York Daily News* (October 29, 2011).

Studies conducted later during the 1990s further demonstrated the scope of the cybercrime problem but struggled to define the exact monetary costs of cybercrime. Carter and Katz[41] during this period showed a trend of victimization that increased significantly over previous studies, with 98.5 percent of the respondents reporting they had been victimized; 43.3 percent of those same respondents reported being victimized more than 25 times. While these numbers seem dramatic, security professionals stated they were surprised at the frequency of admitted victimization, not *actual* victimization. One respondent specifically questioned whether anyone understood or was willing to publicly admit to the enormous scope of the problem. The 1998 joint survey by the FBI and Computer Security Institute found that for the third year in a row, corporate security directors reported an increase of computer system penetration by "outsiders." This represented a 20 percent increase of successful system incursions since 1996.[42] Collectively, these data provide empirical support for the anecdotal evidence: Not only was unauthorized access to and theft from computer systems increasing, but also the number of system incursions committed by "outsiders" and presumably the true monetary costs of computer crime more generally were clearly on the rise.

Studies during the 1980s and 1990s were mostly successful in "sounding the alarm" on the significance of the cybercrime problem and alerting authorities to do something—anything—to recognize and fight the problem. But, it also became clear that the calculation of exact monetary costs associated with cybercrime would be difficult or nearly impossible. Perhaps more troubling, the numbers derived from these estimates could be more misleading than accurate. First, "cybercrimes" can be difficult to distinguish from more traditional crimes since the digital revolution and the penetration of computers and online networks into the everyday lives of most citizens. When you are trying to calculate monetary costs, where do you draw the line between traditional crimes and cybercrimes? This is one reason why cost estimates in these early studies—and even more recent studies—vary so widely. Second, we've now come to recognize the problems of under- and overreporting the costs of cybercrime depending on who you ask about the problem. Some government and law enforcement officials tend to underreport or underestimate these costs in order to manage public perceptions and potential fears about the problem. Business executives and corporations also have an interest in not disclosing cases of cybercrime that could influence the buying decisions of potential customers. Who wants to do business with a company who admits they have data security problems? Others within the business of providing computer security and some law enforcement executives have an interest in overestimating the costs of cybercrime in order to garner more customers and increase spending to protect computer systems and/or apprehend cybercriminals. For all of these reasons, students interested in understanding cyber crime and cyber terrorism need to be wary of published figures on the exact monetary costs of cybercrime. Students should perhaps be more concerned with the *problems and limitations* of these studies rather than the memorization of exact monetary figures on the reported monetary costs of cybercrime.

Still, there is value in trying to identify general monetary costs so that the public is aware of the problem and authorities can develop and monitor the success of strategies to mitigate the problem. Scholars have developed research methods to control for the tendency to over- and underreport costs and measure costs in terms of different types of cybercrime. In 2012, Anderson and his colleagues published research that more accurately measures the monetary costs of cybercrime and distinguishes those costs across several different categories of computer crime, including (1) traditional crimes that are now "cyber" because they are conducted online, (2) transitional crimes that have changed with the advent of the Internet, (3) new crimes that have been originated since the advent of the Internet, and (4) crimes that facilitate other crimes through the misuse of computers.[43] They calculate costs associated with each type of computer crime in terms of costs in anticipation (e.g., antivirus software), direct losses and indirect costs, compensation paid to victims, and general indirect costs (e.g., reputational damage, loss of revenue). Examples of some of their global estimates in regard to the annual costs associated with various types of computer crime include the following:

- Online banking fraud (e.g., phishing, malware) $1.69 billion
- Copyright infringement (software, music) $172 million
- Online credit card fraud $4.2 billion
- Online tax fraud $125 billion
- Advance fee fraud $1 billion
- Stranded traveler scams $10 million
- Cost of cybercriminal infrastructures $24.8 billion

The more advanced research methods used by Anderson and his colleagues resulted in calculations on the direct monetary costs of cybercrime that are probably more accurate than those of previous studies covered earlier in this section of the text. Other recent studies and commentaries on the costs of cybercrime look beyond the calculation of direct monetary costs and discuss additional ways in which cybercrimes more indirectly "cost" governments, businesses, and citizens alike.

These indirect costs are in many ways more stunning than the direct monetary costs of cybercrime because they have not traditionally been considered in the calculation of costs. For example, people generally recognize some of the nonmonetary indirect costs associated with street crime victimizations like burglary. Burglary victims are out money, but also experience anger and other negative emotions associated with feeling "cheated" and personally "violated" by the burglary. Victims of cybercrime and particularly online thefts also experience these feelings that amount to largely uncalculated indirect costs of computer-related crimes.[44] The negative emotions associated with victimization occur whether you are victimized physically or digitally. So too, victims of identity theft experience a loss of individual privacy that is difficult or impossible to calculate in monetary terms. The latest reports from computer security and antivirus software firm McAfee also identify some of the indirect costs of cybercrime including damages to international trade, competitiveness, innovation, and global economic performance.[45] These indirect costs ultimately relate to money; however, they encompass much more than the figures that are included in any accounting report—they are what economists refer to as "opportunity costs," wherein companies fail to realize other economic goals because of more direct losses due to cybercrime. Finally, any consideration of the true costs associated with cybercrime should include expenditures on mitigation strategies, particularly money spent on antivirus software and digital firewalls; digital monitoring; and other information technology outlays related to specifically identifying, catching, and punishing cybercriminals. Worldwide annual spending on information security was estimated to be $75 billion in 2015. The global market for cybersecurity is expected to be worth $170 billion by 2020.[46] No one can deny the staggering costs of cybercrime considering both the direct and indirect costs associated with these phenomena.

QUICK FACTS

Cybersecurity Ventures, a leading researcher and publisher covering the global cyber economy, predicts that cybercrime will continue to rise and cost businesses globally more than $6 trillion annually by 2021.

Source: Cybersecurity ventures (2017). "Cybersecurity Market Report." Available at http://www.cybersecurityventures.com

---

CLASSIFICATION OF COMPUTER CRIME

Classification in general involves the process of arranging or assigning things into classes or groups that share some common characteristics. Students are no doubt familiar with these processes since they commonly confront them within the assigned texts of almost every type of academic class. Criminal justice students, for example, are exposed to various classification schemes within criminology courses focused on the major theories of criminal motivation, including "learning" theories, "control" theories, and "social structure" theories. These courses more generally categorize traditional "street crimes" into the categories of "property" offenses and "violent" offenses.

The emergence of computer crime as a major problem several decades ago forced scholars and law enforcement officials to rethink these traditional classification schemes and come up with ways to organize these newer forms of criminality. Where do computer crimes fit among crimes in general? How can we meaningfully discuss the wide variety of different types of computer crimes without confusing important issues related to determining causes and/or the motivations underlying different types of cyber crime? The classification of computer crimes serves to further define the topic of study and keep those of us who are interested in understanding it "on the same page" conceptually. The classification or grouping of computer crimes also provides more opportunities to demonstrate the topic through specific and noteworthy examples. Finally, classification should ultimately fulfill the needs of law enforcement. The classification of computer crimes can be used to understand the criminal motivations of perpetrators of different types of computer crime in order to help in apprehension. These groupings should ultimately be used to develop specific and effective strategies to mitigate unique types of computer crime.

This section reviews three separate systems for the classification of computer crime. Carter (1995) developed one of the earliest systems to classify computer crime. This scheme is widely known and exists in some form or another within almost every introductory text on computer crime, but Carter's scheme is now approaching 25 years of age. This section also covers two other systems that were developed to classify computer crime: one identified by Gordon and Ford (2006) and the other by Anderson and his colleagues (2012)—the classification scheme used to derive estimates of the costs of computer crime covered in the previous section. These two classification schemes address significant changes in the nature and scope of computer crimes that have occurred over the last 25 years—particularly the too-obvious-to-ignore fact that the Internet now serves as the context for the perpetration of most forms of computer and cyber crimes.

Carter's Classification of Computer Crimes

Carter (1995) developed his classification of computer crimes just prior to the emergence of the Internet as *the* widely available and utilized medium for global communications and the sharing of digital information.[47] His scheme as a result refers to the various categories of computer crime as they would be perpetrated within local hardware or networks rather than within the global system of interconnected computers we now refer to as the "online" or "connected" environment. Carter's scheme retains some appeal because it has been widely disseminated and used to understand the varieties of computer crime. His scheme also marks some of the more fundamental divisions within the large subset of offenses referred to collectively as "computer crime," and here we attempt to demonstrate his various categories through the use of more up-to-date examples. His scheme also is among the most significant in terms of defining how scholars began to organize the "new" forms of criminality within what was then the emerging "digital age."

Carter's classifies computer crimes into four types including crimes in which the computer serves as (1) the target of the crime, (2) the instrument of the crime, (3) incidental to the crime, and also (4) crimes associated with the prevalence of computers.

THE COMPUTER AS TARGET   Crimes where the computer itself is the target include the denial of expected service. This type of crime seeks to deny the legitimate user or owner of a computer system access to his or her data or computer. The denial of service (DoS) is a straightforward intentional criminal act. Although any resource may be denied to the rightful user, the most prominent example of this crime targeting the computer is the network DoS attack, commonly referred to as a "DoS attack." More recent and significant DoS attacks occur over the Internet and involve a multitude of computers that launch simultaneous attacks referred to as a "distributed denial of service" (DDoS) attack.

The significance of DoS attacks was previously demonstrated in a recent conflict between Russia and Estonia, which was caused by the removal of a Russian war monument from a memorial garden in Estonia.[48] Russian citizens in Estonia and elsewhere were enraged by this action, leading to protests and violence in the streets of both Estonia and Russia. Computer-based attacks quickly ensued against government and private resources in both nations by computer hackers and citizens alike. In particular, Russian hackers so severely limited access to Estonian government and financial systems that the government had to temporarily host files on servers in the United States to continue business without interruption.[49] The damage the DoS attacks caused to the Estonian economy was so severe that the country was temporarily crippled as a result. DDoS attacks more recently have at times dominated the news cycle. Several Web sites and organizations affiliated with the 2016 Summer Olympics in Rio de Janeiro, Brazil, were victimized as part of a massive DDoS attack that lasted for several months. Web sites affiliated with the 2016 presidential campaigns of both Donald Trump and Hillary Clinton were also the subject of significant DDoS attacks.[50] Box 1.1 lists what have arguably been the largest or most "successful" DDoS attacks thus far.

BOX 1.1

The Largest DDoS Attacks in History?

Scholars and commentators often disagree as to what specific DDoS attacks have been the "largest" and/or "most successful" in history; however, a cursory search provides a "short list" of some of the most commonly recognized large-scale DDoS attacks:[1]

- The 2008 DDoS attack against the Church of Scientology
- The 2014 DDoS attack against the Hong Kong Democracy Movement
- The 2015 DDoS attack against the British Broadcasting Corporation
- The 2017 "DDoS of Things" attack reached critical mass as bad actors used Internet-connected devices to build botnets that attached hundreds of thousands of systems from large service providers and enterprises to gaming services, media, and entertainment companies, resulting in roughly 3,700 DDoS attacks per day with the cost of each attack ranging from $14,000 to $2.3 million per incident.[2]

_____

[1] _See, e.g.,_ Buntix, J.P (2017). "Top 4 Successful DDoS Attacks." _The Merkle_. Available at http://themerkel.com; _CyberDefense-Hub_ (2017). "3 Famous DDoS Attacks." Available at http://www.cyberdefensehub.com.

[2] Seals, T (March 10, 2017). "IoT DDoS Reaches Critical Mass," _Infosecurity Magazine_. Available at https://www.infosecurity-magazine.com/news/iot-ddos-reaches-critical-mass/.

Crimes where the computer itself is the target also include computer network intrusions that involve the alteration of data. Network intruders target the server and may cause harm to the network owners or the operation of their business. When intrusion is discovered, it often requires the owner or administrator of the affected system to question the integrity, accuracy, and authenticity of data on the network. Although the legitimate user of the system and data is not denied access to either, there is no reasonable certainty of the data's security in the system. Security measures often require the removal of Web-based resources and restoration of data from, hopefully, unaffected backup copies. Finally, computer "vandalism" also falls under the category of crimes where the computer is a target. These acts involve the simple defacement or alteration of a particular Web site. When an intruder removes valuable information from a computer system, the intruder denies the legitimate user or owner access to that information. This could represent a substantial loss of expected revenue as well as public embarrassment depending on the type of defacement.

THE COMPUTER AS INSTRUMENT   Unlike crimes targeting the computer, using the computer as the instrument of the crime means that the computer is used to achieve some other criminal objective. In other words, a burglar uses crowbars and lock picks as the instruments of crime in a fashion similar to the cybercriminal using computers and networks for crimes including theft, fraud, exploitation, and threats or harassment. Some thefts specifically involve theft of service. Although many services available on the Internet are free, some data and services are considered proprietary. This means the users must pay to use the data or service. The use of these proprietary services without payment is theft.

Computers can also be used as instruments to commit fraud. Computer-facilitated fraud exploits the trust, which is guaranteed by law, in a business transaction. The buyer, seller, or peer in a transaction can perpetrate fraud. The most highly publicized form of computer fraud has likely been online auction fraud perpetrated through large commercial Web sites operated by global commercial firms such as ebay, a leader of global online commerce with 169 million active buyers that generates approximately $80 billion in annual gross merchandise volume.[51] Scholars have recognized fraud as an ongoing problem for online auction participants, in particular buyers.[52] The most common complaints of online auction buyers are late shipments, no shipments, or shipments of products that are not the same quality as advertised. The average reported loss per online auction complaint is just over $600.[53]

Other varieties of fraud found online are simply high-tech variants of older methods. Old scams have found entirely new audiences of victims on the Internet. Pyramid schemes have found a new source of legitimacy with professional-looking Web sites and official-sounding Web addresses. In fact, virtually every tired bunko scheme has found new life through the Internet. Perhaps the most common one recently is the Nigerian bank scheme, where unsuspecting victims send their bank account numbers overseas with the dreams of getting millions in return. New forms of whole cloth fraud have also developed online, such as phishing. This offense involves victims being tricked into providing their financial information to a criminal through the use of convincing and extremely accurate fraudulent Web sites.[54] Finally, the Internet has proven to be a "perfect" medium to threaten, harass, bully, and/or stalk individuals. We cover these sorts of computer crime in detail in Chapter 8.

THE COMPUTER AS INCIDENTAL   Carter characterized the computer as incidental to other crimes when "a pattern or incident of criminality uses a computer simply for ease in maintaining the efficacy of criminal transactions."[55] In this category, the computer is not the primary instrument of the crime; it simply facilitates it. Computers appeal to criminal enterprises or businesses for many of the same reasons they appeal to others: They are quick, reliable, very accurate, and perform many business-related tasks far faster than if done manually. Thus, they are used to support many different types of criminal enterprises, including loan-sharking and drug rings. Carter also discussed within this category a range of widely recognized crimes, including money laundering and the production and distribution of child pornography. Child pornographers have clearly benefited from the computer revolution. The Internet has been the key communication medium for the sale and exchange of child pornography on both international and domestic bases. The Internet has also been used to lure victims to pedophiles. Adult users of chat rooms may use the supposed anonymity of the Internet to pose as teenagers to establish a rapport with their intended victim. Numerous "sting" operations have placed law enforcement officers in these same chat rooms posing as children (See Box 1.2 below). We cover in detail these "incidental" computer crimes, including money laundering, in Chapter 6, and sex crimes, including child pornography and pedophilia, in Chapter 8.

Students will recognize one of the limitations of Carter's categorization scheme in attempts to define some types of computer crimes in terms of whether the computer acts as an "instrument" of the crime or just as "incidental" to the crime. The truth is that there are no definitive "lines" to be drawn between these two categories within Carter's scheme. The difference is one of *degree*. This goal has been complicated since the emergence of the Internet as the most important platform for some crimes such as child pornography and money laundering. Is the computer merely "incidental" to the perpetration of these crimes or has the computer become the primary instrument or means by which to perpetrate them? Students should focus on the degree to which the computer is involved in the perpetration of any particular crime and whether it "fits" most appropriately as an "instrument" or as "incidental" to the crime.

CRIMES ASSOCIATED WITH THE PREVALENCE OF COMPUTERS   The fourth category within Carter's classification scheme recognized that some types of crime have emerged or have been greatly facilitated simply due to the ubiquitous and ever-present

BOX 1.2

Computer Crime Meets Reality TV: The Legacy of *To Catch a Predator*

To Catch a Predator was a reality-based television series that ran from 2004 through 2007 The show featured widely recognized television journalist Chris Hansen leading hidden camera investigations that ultimately exposed and detained male adults who had contacted individuals impersonating underage juveniles (usually girls aged 13–15) over the Internet for sexual liaisons. The suspected perpetrators were lured to meet the "decoy" juvenile within the view of the hidden camera, and then were personally confronted on camera after their suspected crime had been exposed in front of millions of television viewers. The show eventually included on-scene law enforcement officers who made the on-camera arrest of the suspected perpetrator. The show was cancelled after one suspected pedophile—an acting assistant district attorney—shot himself to death following his exposure as a suspected pedophile.[1]

The show was extremely popular, largely because it featured the face-to-face confrontation of suspected pedophiles.[2] The show also underscored the emergence of new potential dangers in the age of the Internet. Pedophilia is not a new crime; however, the advent of the Internet made it much easier for pedophiles to contact and subsequently lure unsuspecting juveniles into criminal sex acts. The show clearly touched a nerve with parents who feared the online victimization of their children, most of whom now spent a considerable amount of time online and away from direct parental supervision. Some critics have argued that the show helped to set off a "panic" that was overblown and not consistent with the real-world sexual exploitation of children online.[3] Despite this controversy, the television series clearly worked to underscore some of the major themes of this text involving the emergence of new forms of cyber crime, the need to confront them, and the large-scale changing landscape of crime and criminal justice in the wake of the digital revolution.

---

[1] *Fair* (2009). "The Online Predator Scare: Profiting from Panic." March 1. Available at http://www.fair.org/extra/the-online-predator-scare.

[2] Woodman, S. (2015). "Chris Hansen Is Back to Catching Predators." *New Republic,* October 18.

[3] *Ibid.*, p. 20.

nature of computers and computing in the everyday lives of citizens. This observation was especially poignant during the early 1990s as it seemed, to many citizens, that computers were beginning to "overrun" our lives in ways that most of us were not then used to. This text covers in detail many of the most widely recognized of these types of crime, including intellectual property violations and corporate espionage (Chapter 6). These and other types of offenses, traditionally referred to as "white-collar crimes," have been greatly altered by the presence and wide-scale dissemination of computer and digital technology. We cover the crime of identity theft as an offense that has largely emerged since the digital revolution as a more recent white-collar offense that has exploded largely because of the prevalence of computers in our everyday lives (see Chapter 6). This text also describes how computer technologies and the prevalence of computers have made the production of counterfeit financial instruments, mostly "fake" cash, exponentially easier (see Chapter 11 and as part of our forecast trends in Chapter 15).

One crime that is obviously due to the prevalence of computers is cell phone theft. Smartphones are essentially computers, and over three-fourths of all American adults now own a smartphone. Sharp increases in the theft of cell phones have mirrored the explosion in cell phone ownership and usage. In 2013, about 3.1 million cell phones were estimated to have been stolen in the United States.[56] A recent survey of cell phone theft victims indicates that about one-third of them would be willing to pay $1,000 to retrieve their stolen phone, and over two-thirds of them would be willing to "put themselves in some sort of danger" to get their phone back.[57] These victims are clearly more concerned with the recovery of personal data on the phone than recovery of the phone itself. The most recent data suggests that newer technologies may be slowing down the growth in smartphone theft with the increasing adoption of "kill switches," or technologies that disable phones and deter thieves from re-selling them on the global market. Apple Inc.'s implementation of kill switch technology within its Find My Phone application in 2013 seems to have recently stemmed from the theft of iPhones.[58]

Other Classification Schemes

Scholars over the last two decades have worked to improve upon earlier classification schemes and structure them to reflect significant changes in the nature and scope of computer crimes that have occurred over the last 25 years. This section outlines two other schemes to classify computer crime: one identified by Gordon and Ford (2006)[59] and the other by Anderson and his colleagues (2012).[60]

Gordon and Ford developed a two-category scheme to classify cybercrimes into (a) Type I offenses and (b) Type II offenses. Students should recognize that these two categories of computer crime encompass a wider variety of crimes than any singular category defined within Carter's scheme and most definitely addresses those committed primarily online. Type I offenses are primarily technological in nature and involve three characteristics:

- The crime is a single or discreet event from the point of view of the victim.
- The crime involves the use of malware including computer viruses, worms, and adware.
- The crime can, but may not be, facilitated by computer software vulnerabilities.

Gordon and Ford identify specific examples of Type I computer crimes including any theft and/or manipulation of data through hacking or the introduction of computer viruses, identity theft, and bank or e-commerce fraud based on stolen credentials. The main feature distinguishing Type I crimes is that they are generally singular events from the perspective of the victim and involve malware. Type II offenses, on the other hand, do not involve malware. Type II offenses also generally involve repeated contacts or events from the point of view of the victim. Specific examples of Type II computer crimes include cyberstalking, harassment, child predation, extortion, stock market manipulation, complex corporate espionage, and many forms of cyberterrorism that do not directly involve malware and/or hacking as the main activity. Type II crimes do usually involve the use of software, but not those forms of software defined as malware. Perpetrators instead use programs commonly used by everybody in their everyday lives. For example, a cyberstalker would utilize social media Web sites or instant messaging (IM) software. More generally, Gordon and Ford present a classification scheme of computer-related crimes that recognizes a continuum of behaviors that ranges from offenses that are primarily "technology crimes" (Type I) and those that primarily "people crimes" (Type II).

The second more recent classification scheme was developed by Anderson and his colleagues (2012) primarily to derive estimates of the costs of computer crime covered in the previous section. This scheme is also useful solely for classification purposes, because it focuses on the role of the Internet as the platform for many computer crimes. This classification scheme has four categories:

- Traditional crimes that are now "cyber" because they are conducted primarily online
- Transitional crimes that have changed with the advent of the Internet
- New crimes that have been originated since the advent of the Internet
- Crimes that facilitate other crimes through the misuse of computers

Traditional crimes that are now primarily cybercrimes include such offenses as tax fraud. Transitional crimes that have fundamentally changed since the advent of the Internet include frauds committed online such as e-commerce fraud. New crimes that have originated since the advent of the Internet include those that involve the introduction of malware, including computer viruses and worms. The fourth category in this scheme is generally a comprehensive "other" category since almost any other form of computer crime that does not readily fit within one or more of the first three categories can be defined as those that are facilitated through the misuse of a computer.

QUICK FACTS

According to a 2017 study conducted by Harvey Nash/KPMG, nearly one-third (32%) of businesses were victims of a major cyber crime attack in 2016, with a worldwide loss exceeding $388 billion dealing with, and recovering from, breaches in cybersecurity. The amount spent on remediating computer viruses alone has reached $55 billion per year.

Sources: Ashley Richardson, "Insiders Often Responsible for $388B Annual Cost of Cyber Security Breaches." *Spohn Consulting, Inc.* (Austin, TX: Spohn Consulting, Inc., June 14, 2017).

Martijn Berbree, "Cybersecurity: Why You Should Fear Insider Threats," *Management Today* (May 23, 2017).

Chloe Albanesius, "Cyber Crime Costs $114B per Year, Mobile Attacks on the Rise." *PCMAG* (September 7, 2011).

Summary

Students should take away from this chapter at least three important points. An understanding of these points should "set the stage" for a more productive study of the wide range of topics covered within the subsequent chapters of this book.

First, students should understand more clearly the purpose of this book and presumably the class for which this text has been adopted. The digital revolution has fundamentally altered the landscape of crime and criminal justice on a global scale. The revolution has altered the nature and character of existing crimes, and has spawned a wide variety of new criminal acts that did not exist in any recognizable form prior to the advent of computers and particularly the Internet. We, as scholars, students, and criminal justice practitioners, must recognize and consider these changes within the context of our attempts to understand crime more generally and devise effective policies and strategies of mitigation in the criminal justice system.

Second, students should recognize the emergence of new threats that we term collectively as "cyber terrorism." The digital revolution has altered not only the context of crime but also the context of war. Nation-states as well as individual perpetra-tors can and will take advantage of computers and digital technologies. Cyber terrorism includes ominous and catastrophic events that potentially cripple our critical infrastructure, threaten national security, and spawn international conflict. In the post-9/11 era, terrorism has become a real threat to our society and to our way of life. We have attempted to secure ourselves through the use of physical searches for weapons, the employment of new technological sensing devices in critical areas, more visible signs of police and security presence, and a stepped-up military offensive against those in foreign countries who may pose threats. Trying to engage the police in the "war on terrorism" may be futile, as the criminal justice system (and particularly the police) is designed to address crime rather than terrorism. The people who pose significant terrorist dangers are often motivated by ideologies that are really not "criminal" in the traditional sense of the word. They seek destruction and devastation as part of war, and computer technologies increasingly provide them the means to do so.

Third, students should recognize some of the difficulties in studying these wide-ranging phenomena. This chapter exposed students to some of these difficulties within the discussions on the costs of cyber crime and the classification of these acts. Subsequent chapters will also discuss complications in many forms, including those related to catching and punishing cybercriminals and terrorists. These topics are not straightforward, and there is room for some informed judgment calls, discretion, and a need to effectively navigate uncertainties. The study of cyber crime and cyber terrorism is not settled but rather emerging. There are areas of "gray" and issues still to be determined. Hopefully, students exposed to these realities become emboldened rather than frustrated, and recognize opportunities within their own experience and perhaps future professional careers to participate in the ongoing fight against cyber crime and cyber terrorism.

Review Questions

1. What factors led to the explosive growth of cyber crime over the past few decades?
2. Describe some of the most common forms of cyber crime.
3. What gaps exist in our understanding of cyber crime? What can be done to address these gaps?
4. Why is the number of cybervictims growing?
5. Why is computer crime sometimes underreported?
6. What are the four categories of computer crime according to Carter? Give examples of the types of crimes that fall under each category.

Critical Thinking Exercises

1. This chapter covered the major ways in which computer crimes can be classified and some of the difficulties associated with that goal. Students should go online and identify at least two publicized recent cases of (a) money laundering and (b) child pornography. Determine whether these crimes should be defined within Carter's classification scheme as an "instrument" of the crime or as "incidental" to the crime. Why did you make this determination in each case?

2. This chapter introduced students to some alarming statistics concerning the costs of cybercrime on the societal level. Students should recall if they have ever been a victim of a cybercrime. If so, to what extent did you or your friends incur personal and/or monetary costs associated with cybervictimization. Could those personal losses be calculated monetarily? How did you or others respond to those losses? In what ways did this victimization mirror the experiences of "street crime" victims?

Endnotes

1. *The New York Times* (2013). "Hackers Steal $45 Million in ATM Card Breach." *The New York Times*, May 10: A1.
2. LEINER, B.M. et al. (February 1997). "The Past and Future History of the Internet." *Communications of the ACM* 40(2): 102–108.
3. SODERBERRY, R. (2013). "How Many Things Are Currently Connected to the 'Internet of Things'?" *Forbes*, Retrieved June 11, 2013, from *http://www.forbes.com/sites /quora/2013/01/07/how-many-things-are-currently -connected-to-the-internet-of-things-10t/#556d9bffbd2d*
4. DARRAGH, T. (2015). "Two Sentenced in Massive $200M Credit Card Fraud Case." *NJ.Com*, December 1.
5. Motion Picture Association of America; see: http:// www.mpaa.org (June 25, 2009).
6. MICK, J. (2015). "Nearly Half of Americans Pirate Casually, But Pirates Purchase More Legal Content." *DailyTech*, April 22.
7. NORKEY, T. (2015). "Film Piracy: A Threat to the Entire Movie Industry." *Movie Plot*, April 26.
8. PandaLabs (2007). "Malware Infections in Protected Systems." Retrieved November 1, 2007, from *http://research .pandasecurity.com/blogs/images/wp_pb_malware _infections_in_protected_systems.pdf*.
9. PARKER, D. (1979). *Crime by Computer.* New York: Charles Scribner and Sons.
10. See the National Conference of State Legislatures (NCSL) Web site for a listing of Statutory Citation by State. References to malware, viruses, and contaminants are listed by state as well. Retrieved August 10, 2013, from *http://www .ncsl.org/issues-research/telecom/state-virus-and-computer- contaminant-laws.aspx*.
11. PARKER, D. (1999). *Fighting Computer Crime: A New Framework for the Protection of Information.* New York: John Wiley & Sons, Inc.
12. PARKER, *Crime by Computer.*
13. Bureau of Justice Statistics (1979). *Computer Crime: Criminal Justice Resource Manual.* Washington, D.C.: U.S. Department of Justice.

14. Bureau of Justice Statistics (1980). *Computer Security Techniques.* Washington, D.C.: U.S. Department of Justice.

15. Bureau of Justice Statistics (1982). *Electronic Fund Transfer Systems and Crime.* Washington, D.C.: U.S. Department of Justice.

16. BEQUAI, A. (1983). *How to Prevent Computer Crime.* New York: John Wiley & Sons; COOPER, J.A. (1984). *Computer Security Technology.* Lexington, MA: D.C. Heath and Company; ROACHE, J.Y. (1986). "Computer Crime Deterrence." *American Journal of Criminal Law* 13(2): 391; CARROLL, J.M. (1987). *Computer Security.* Boston, MA: Butterworth Publishing; GALLERY, S. (ed.), (1987). *Computer Security.* Boston, MA: Butterworth Publishing Company; ARKIN, S. (ed.), (1988). *Prevention and Prosecution of Computer and High Technology Crime.* Oakland, CA: Matthew Bender.

17. ROSTOKER, M. and RINES, R. (1986). *Computer Jurisprudence.* New York: Oceana Publications; ARKIN, *Prevention and Prosecution of Computer and High Technology Crime*; CONSER, J.A., CARSONE, L.P., and SNYDER, R. (1988). "Investigating Computer-Related Crimes Involving Small Computer Systems." In M. PALMIOTTO (ed.), *Critical Issues in Computer Investigations*, 2nd ed. Cincinnati, OH: Anderson Publishing Company; HOLLINGER, R.C. and LANZA-KADUCE, L. (1988). "The Process of Criminalization: The Case of Computer Crime Laws." *Criminology* 26(1): 101; CONLY, C.H. (1989). *Organizing for Computer Crime Investigation and Prosecution.* Cambridge, MA: Abt Associates.

18. BEQUAI, A. (1987). *Technocrimes.* Lexington, MA: D.C. Heath and Company.

19. KUSSEROW, R.P. (1983). *Computer-Related Fraud and Abuse in U.S. Government Agencies.* Washington, DC: U.S. Department of Health and Human Services.

20. LANDRETH, B. (1985). *Out of the Inner Circle: A Hacker's Guide to Computer Security.* Bellevue, WA: Microsoft Press.

21. MCEWEN, T. (1989). *Dedicated Computer Crime Units.* Washington, DC: National Institute of Justice.

22. ICOVE, D., SEGER, K., and VONSTORCH, W. (1995). *Computer Crime: A Crimefighter's Handbook.* Sebastopol, CA: O'Reilly & Associates, Inc.

23. STOLL, C. (1988). *The Cuckoo's Egg.* New York: Bantam Books.

24. SHIMOMURA, T. (1996). *Takedown.* New York: Hyperion Books.

25. STOLL, *The Cuckoo's Egg.*

26. SHIMOMURA, *Takedown.*

27. *Ibid.*

28. *Pew Research Center* (2017). "Demographics of Mobile Device Ownership and Adoption in the United States: Mobile Fact Sheet." Available at http://www.pewinternet.org/fact-sheet/mobile/.

29. HOLT, T.J. (2003). "Examining a Transnational Problem: An Analysis of Computer Crime Victimization in Eight Countries from 1999 to 2001." *International Journal of Comparative and Applied Criminal Justice* 27: 199–220.

30. VAN DUYN, J. (1985). *The Human Factor in Computer Crime.* Princeton, NJ: Petrocelli Books, Inc.

31. *Ibid.*

32. U.N. Commission on Crime and Criminal Justice (1995). *United Nations Manual on the Prevention and Control of Computer-Related Crime.* New York: United Nations.

33. BARRETT, N. (1997). *Digital Crime.* London: Kogan Page.

34. US Department of Homeland Security (2013). "NIPP 2013: Partnering for Critical Infrastructure Security and Resilience." Available at https://www.dhs.gov/publication/nipp-2013-partnering-critical-infrastructure-security-and-resilience.

35. SINURAYA, T. (June 1999). "The Cyber Crime Problem Increases." *Crime and Justice International* 29: 1–10, 32.

36. HENDERSON, S.J. (2007). *The Dark Visitor: Inside the World of Chinese Hackers.* Fort Leavenworth, KS: Foreign Military Studies Office.

37. *PBS Newshour* (October 1, 2010). "Hunting an Industrial Strength Computer Virus around the Globe." Retrieved June 14, 2013, from *http://www.pbs.org/newshour/bb/science-july-dec10-computervirus_10-01/*

38. American Bar Association (1987). *Report on Computer Crime.* Chicago, IL: American Bar Association.

39. Florida Department of Law Enforcement (1989). "Computer Crime in Florida." An unpublished report prepared by the Florida Department of Law Enforcement, Tallahassee, FL.

40. U.N. Commission on Crime and Criminal Justice (1995). *United Nations Manual on the Prevention and Control of Computer-Related Crime.* New York: United Nations.

41. CARTER, D.L., and KATZ, A.J. (1998). "Computer Crime Victimization: An Assessment of Criminality in Cyberspace." *Police Research Quarterly* 1(1).

42. Computer Security Institute (1999). *Issues and Trends: 1999 CSI/FBI Computer Crime and Security Survey.* San Francisco, CA: Computer Security Institute.

43. ANDERSON, R., BARTON, C., BOHME, R., CLAYTON, R., VAN EETEN, M., LEVI, M., MORRE, T., and SAVAGE, S. (2012). "Measuring the Cost of Cybercrime." *11th Workshop on the Economics of Information Security*, Berlin, Germany. June 26, 2012.

44. SHINDER, D. (2010). "Calculating the True Cost of Cybercrime." Tech Republic, September 14. Available at http://www.techrepublic.com/blog/it-security.

45. MCAFEE (2014). "Net Losses: Estimating the Global Costs of Cybercrime." Available at https://www.mcafee.com/de/resources/reports/rr-economic-impact-cybercrime2.pdf

46. MORGAN, S. (2015). "Cybersecurity Market Reaches $75 Billion in 2015; Expected to Reach $170 Billion by 2020." *Forbes*, December 20.

47. CARTER, D. (1995). "Computer Crime Categories." *FBI Law Enforcement Bulletin* 64(7): 21–26.

48. BRENNER, S.W. (2008). *Cyberthreats: The Emerging Fault Lines of the Nation State.* New York: Oxford University Press; JAFFE, G. (2006). "Gates Urges NATO Ministers to Defend Against Cyber Attacks." *The Wall Street Journal.*

49. *Ibid.*

50. BISSON, D. (2016). "The 5 Most Significant DDoS Attacks of 2016." *TripWire*, November 29. Available at http://www.tripwire.com/state-of-security/security-data-protection.

51. eBay Inc. (2017). "*eBay* Inc. Reports First Quarter 2017 Results." Available at http://www.ebay.com.

52. BAUERLY, R. (2009). "Online Auction Fraud and eBay." *The Marketing Management Journal* 19(1): 134–144.

53. *Internet Crime Complaint Center* (2006). "Internet Fraud Crime Report." Available at http://www.ic3.gov.

54. JAMES, L. (2005). *Phishing Exposed.* Rockland, MA: Syngress.

55. CARTER, D.L. and BANNISTER, A.J. (2000). "Computer Crime: A Forecast of Emerging Trends." Presented at the Academy of Criminal Justice Sciences Annual Meeting in New Orleans, LA.

56. Consumer Reports (2015). "Smartphone Thefts Drop as Kill Switch Usage Grows." June 11. Available at http://www.consumerreports.org.

57. EADICICCO, L. (2014). "People Are Willing to Go to Extreme Lengths to Retrieve Their Stolen Smartphones." *Business Insider*, May 7.

58. *Ibid.*, p. 20.

59. GORDON, S and FORD R. (2006). "On the Definition and Classification of Cybercrime." *Journal of Computer Virology and Hacking Techniques* 2: 13–20.

60. *Ibid.*, p. 6.

Cyber Terrorism and Information Warfare

CHAPTER OBJECTIVES

After completing this chapter, you should be able to

- Define the concepts of "cybercrime," "cyberterrorism," and "information warfare."
- List the four categories of attacks that encompass cyberterrorism and/or information warfare.
- Identify various elements of our critical infrastructure that are potentially vulnerable to cyberterrorism and/or information warfare.
- Define and describe an information attack.
- Describe some of the tactics used in cyberspace to share information and promote terrorist ideologies between and within terrorist groups.
- Define the words "steganography" and "cryptography" and relate their use in information warfare and cyberterrorism.
- Discuss the concept of information warfare from the Russian and Chinese perspectives.
- Explain the active role of China and al Qaeda in recent cyberattacks against the United States.

INTRODUCTION

Since the beginning of history, warfare has evolved parallel to the development of tools, weapons, and technology. In the twentieth century, warfare developed from hand-to-hand and small weapons combat to sophisticated air combat, and now to the development of electronic "smart" bombs that are programmed to destroy their targets. Traditional means of warfare have been further distorted through the means of technology and also by the escalating events of international terrorist activity. Before September 11, 2001, few would have considered that America's civil aircraft would have been used as weaponry against America itself. However, al Qaeda operatives did just that, killing over 2,840 people in a few short hours. It should not be a surprise, then, that military and guerrilla offensives could be waged on many fronts, from the skyscrapers of Manhattan to the digital networks that coordinate our critical infrastructure (e.g., the Internet, computer networks, telephone systems, and electricity and water supplies).

In fact, the Internet is a critical tool for political and social movements of all types around the world. Groups have employed a range of tactics depending on the severity of the perceived injustice or wrong that has been performed. Often, these virtual efforts develop in tandem with real-world protests and demonstrations. For example, the native peoples, called Zapatistas, in Chiapas, Mexico, used the Internet to post information and mobilize supporters for their cause against governmental repression.[1] Politically driven groups have also employed hacking techniques to engage in more serious strikes against governments and political organizations.[2] Members of a hacktivist group called the Electronic Disturbance Theater developed an attack tool called FloodNet that overloaded Web servers and kept others from being able to access their services. FloodNet was used against the Pentagon as well as other government and business targets as a means of protest against their activities and policies.[3] Even more historical organized terrorist groups like Sri Lanka's Tamil Tigers have engaged in acts of cyberterrorism to disrupt or damage government computer networks.[4] And more recently, radical Islamic groups such as the Islamic State's "United Cyber Caliphate," "Cutting Sword of Justice," "al-Qassam Cyber Fighters," and the "Syrian Electronic Army" have attacked private banks (Citibank, JP Morgan, Regions Bank, Bank of America, and Wells Fargo); businesses (Saudi Aramco, the BBC, al-Jazeera, Sony, and CBS); and governments (United States, Great Britain, Australia, Saudi Arabia, Bahrain, and Qatar).[5] Indeed, the attack on Saudi Aramco in 2012 by the "Cutting Sword of Justice" destroyed over 30,000 computers and may well have been one of "the most destructive attacks that the private sector has seen to date."[6]

Few among the American population have considered a situation involving an attack on our infrastructure. However, this type of attack became a frightening possibility when the lights went out across the northeastern United States on Friday, August 15, 2003. During the initial hours of the blackout, which affected New York City, parts of Connecticut, Vermont, Ohio, and Canada, confusion reigned, and many newscasters covering the outage speculated that it could be a terrorist act. By evening, that scenario had been ruled out and the outage was eventually traced to a power grid failure in Ohio. Regardless, the American public had now seen a glimpse of the very real consequences of such an attack—the cities affected had ground to a virtual halt, oil prices began to rise almost instantly, and panic among the population was evident, especially in the first hours after the outage. Today, attacks against U.S. businesses and governments are commonplace, with an estimated 100 million attempts each day. The Pentagon and the National Nuclear Security Administration both report a whopping 10 million attempts each day! The numbers have virtually quadrupled in the last two to three years.[7] Which of these attempts might be successful? Which might be the next cyber Pearl Harbor or 9/11? The sheer scale of the problem has produced significant demand to counter the threat. Almost all U.S. government agencies now have cyber security and information security experts on staff, with huge resources within the U.S. Department of Homeland Security and the U.S. Department of Defense focusing on the development of cyber weapons as well as cyber defense. Indeed, the president of the United States has the broad power to order a preemptive strike if the country detects credible evidence of a major cyber attack from a foreign entity. New policies also govern how intelligence agencies can carry out surveillance on foreign and domestic subjects via the Internet, electronic eavesdropping, the use of drones, and satellite spying. The cyber world is "front and center" of our country's newest arsenal on defense. The Pentagon recently announced the development of "CyberCity," a virtual town that enables government hackers to practice attacking and defending computer and information networks that increasingly run our world's infrastructure (e.g., power, water, and transportation systems).[8] As one defense expert reported, "In the future, nearly all military missions will have a cyber component."[9]

DEFINING THE CONCEPTS

Even though the protection of our national infrastructure is a large part of the national strategy for homeland security and defense, most individuals do not understand the jeopardy in which such entities are at risk. We take for granted that such entities are secure. "Information warfare" and "cyberterrorism" are actually very broad concepts that, depending on who is defining them, can encompass a range of activities by a variety of different people. They are also two conceptually different events: Cyberterrorism is a component of information warfare, but information warfare is not necessarily cyberterrorism. For this reason, it is necessary to define these topics as separate entities.

Buzzwords: Information Warfare, Cyberterrorism, and Cybercrime

Information warfare is an overarching concept that actually encompasses cyberterrorism. Essentially, information warfare is the gathering or use of information and technology to gain an advantage over another party. More specifically, John Alger, the dean of the School of Information Warfare and Strategy at the National Defense University, defines information warfare as "those actions intended to protect, exploit, corrupt, deny or destroy information or information resources in order to achieve a significant advantage, objective or victory over an adversary."[10] Still another definition states that information warfare is the "coherent and synchronized blending of physical and virtual actions to have countries, organizations, and individuals perform, or not perform, actions so that your goals and objectives are attained and maintained while simultaneously preventing competitors from doing the same to you."[11]

Information warfare consists of six components: psychological operations, electronic warfare, military deception, physical destruction, security measures, and information attacks.[12] Psychological operations (or psy-ops, in popular military lingo) use information to affect the state of mind of the adversary. This could include propaganda, or the spreading of information intended to convince people to subscribe to a certain behavior, belief, or doctrine. The Internet is a perfect tool for this objective.[13]

Electronic warfare seeks to undermine the quality, accuracy, and availability of an adversary's information, while also inhibiting the adversary's information-collection abilities. This is a tool widely used by terrorist organizations, political hackers, and rival countries via the Internet. Military deception is an age-old attack that generally misleads an adversary about military capabilities or intentions. This type of information warfare does not require that the Internet even exist—it can be carried out by more traditional media, like radio and newspapers.[14]

Physical information warfare involves a physical attack on an information system. Security measures are the methods of protecting an information system in an effort to prevent or mitigate an adversary's attack. Finally, an information attack is the direct corruption of information without actually changing the physical components in which it is located.[15]

This should make it clear, then, that information warfare is not limited to those things that can be done with computers. In fact, information warfare is the exploitation or strategic protection of a number of things: telephones, radio signals, radar, electronic devices—anything that can be manipulated in order to control or influence the actions of a decision maker. A more practical definition is that information warfare is any sort of offensive strike or defensive protective measure against an information system, whatever the means. Implanting a virus into a military computer is an information warfare tactic. On the other end of the spectrum, blowing up a cellular phone tower could also be considered information warfare.

In contrast, terrorism is defined as the actual or threatened use of violence by an individual or group motivated by ideological or political objectives. The goal of terrorism is to intimidate or coerce a government or its people.[16] *Cyberterrorism or digital terrorism*, however, cannot be as concretely defined and has spurred significant debate over exactly what it means. The fact is that the word "cyberterrorism" has been misrepresented in both academic circles and the media at large. A panel of experts on cyberterrorism stated, "Dropping ATM networks and shutting down e-mail is not terrorism. If I can't get to my e-mail for a few days, I am not terrorized."[17] This illustrates the common misperception that a network disruption is an act of cyberterrorism. This would be considered more of an act of information warfare.

Cyberterrorism is also not defined by the group perpetrating it. Terrorist groups, such as al Qaeda or another radical Islamic group, may use the Internet to further their propaganda, hide their secrets, or recruit new members. However, none of this is considered to be inherently terroristic and, again, may be considered more of an act of information warfare.[18] According to one definition, "Terrorism is defined by the nature of the act, not by the identity of the perpetrators or the nature of their cause."[19]

Cyberterrorism is specifically a premeditated, politically, or ideologically motivated attack or threat of attack against information, computer systems, computer programs, and data that can result in violence against civilian targets.[20] According to Barry Collin of the Institute for Security and Intelligence, cyberterrorism is "hacking with a body count."[21] An early assessment by RAND's National Research Defense Institute concluded that cyberterrorism may also include attacks motivated by political or ideological objectives that can cause serious harm, such as a prolonged loss of infrastructure, like electricity or water.[22] A similarly broad definition of cyberterrorism was developed and presented by the National Institute of Justice, recognizing any "premeditated, politically motivated attack against information systems, computer programs and data … to disrupt the political, social, or physical infrastructure of the target."[23] Yet another definition includes severe economic loss as a qualifier for cyberterrorism: If economic loss is harsh enough, a destabilization may occur that can result in serious harm to a society.[24] To muddy the waters even more, a less significant activity designed to protest, "spread the truth," or otherwise emphasize a particular belief or political bent without intentional harm to human life is called "hacktivism." In these cases, mostly involving Web site defacement, the criminal actor is involved much more in vandalism and chaos versus economic gain and destruction—terrorism without the body count.

Cybercrime or digital crime, on the other hand, can be loosely defined simply as the commission of a crime with the use of a computer and a network (e.g., the Internet). Cybercrime has facilitated the expansion of almost every traditional crime, including drug trafficking, black market commerce, money laundering, theft, piracy, stalking, fraud, and espionage. Many of these cybercrimes, but specifically espionage, can now be or have been tied to cyberterrorism and information warfare as either an operational objective or a financial enabler. Through the growth and innovation of technology, crime has evolved into cybercrime, and cybercrime has since begun to enable drug cartels, organized crime rings, and terrorists to perpetrate traditional crime as a source of funding and operational reach to achieve their objectives on a global scale.

Essentially, crime, terrorism, and warfare have evolved into their cyber states through the advent and evolution of technology. As technology continuously improves, criminals, terrorists, and rogue states keep pace with identifying new and innovative ways to incorporate them into their operations, expand their reach from regional to global through the use of the Internet, and enable themselves to grow and mature and even enable each other at a much faster pace.

Because of the obvious semantic problems presented by the misuse of the terms "cybercrime," "information warfare," and "cyberterrorism," it is important to keep these definitions in mind when reviewing the threats that criminals, terrorist groups, or hostile nations pose to the cyber security of the United States. Cybercrime will be discussed much more in future chapters, while this chapter focuses on cyberterrorism and information warfare. Four categories of attacks that encompass acts of cyberterrorism and/or information warfare will be discussed. These categories include *infrastructure attacks*, or those attacks designed to manipulate or destroy a system that includes critical functions and/or data; *information attacks*, or attacks focused on demolishing or altering the content of electronic files or computer systems; *technological facilitation*, or the use of cyber communication to distribute and coordinate plans for a terrorist attack, incite an attack, or otherwise assist in the facilitation of terrorism; and *promotion*, which includes fundraising, solicitation, and recruitment.[25]

BOX 2.1
A Short History of Warfare

In a popular futuristic and thought-provoking book, *The Third Wave,* Alvin Toffler discusses a specific approach to the history of warfare. He describes and explains the development of warfare in three different and separate epochs or waves.

The first, or agrarian, wave produced the first known effective change (or revolution) in the history of humankind. Humans began to settle in specific areas and grow food rather than forage and roam large expanses of the land. During the agrarian wave, societies developed and the production of goods and commerce began. Tools were relatively rudimentary, and weapons were designed more for personal protection against wild animals and hunting, rather than specifically for killing people. The value of the goods and/or the rapidly increasing value of property (soil) created new conflicts among people—the first cause of war.

The second, or industrial wave, marked a significant departure from the manufacturing of simple weapons. Industrial and technological improvement allowed the first weapons for the destruction of multiple persons and buildings (infrastructure). Indeed, this era witnessed the defeat of agrarian-based societies to more advanced industrialized people. Landowners had become industrialized nations. Most importantly, war and defense had become a means for justifying the production of more advanced weaponry, including weapons of mass destruction (e.g., nuclear, chemical, and biological). Arbitrary and loosely defined armies had become well-structured and highly mechanized forces. Nations were now capable of delivering lethal attacks against entire societies of people, leaving behind large expanses of scorched and uninhabitable land.

The third wave, the information wave, reveals societies based on the rapid exchange of vital and critical information. Accurate and timely communication characterizes successful, thriving, and global societies. War also emulates information importance and is focused on the destruction of critical infrastructure within societies, hence *information warfare*. High-tech weapons "invade" computer systems and networks with the aim of destroying the ability of a nation to operate. Interestingly, the large sophisticated armies of the industrial period are relatively useless when communication and transportation systems, logistical support, targeting systems, defense networks, and the like succumb to electronic attack.

Most importantly, the third wave points to the vulnerability of large information-based nations and suggests how a relatively small, unorganized yet knowledgeable group of individuals could wreak havoc on such a society. Quite prophetic, considering that the book was written in 1984!

Source: Based on Alvin Toffler, *The Third Wave* (New York: Bantam Books, 1984).

RISK AND CRITICAL INFRASTRUCTURE ATTACKS

Given that most parts of the world now have access to the Internet, almost any country can fall victim to some form of cyberterrorism or information warfare. In fact, Russian factions have engaged in cyberattacks with Estonia and Georgia, which caused the citizens of these countries to face significant economic harm.[26] These conflicts developed from real-world events, notably the removal of a statue in Estonia and an attempted seccession in Georgia. However, the virtual attacks that ensued forced financial and government Web sites offline in these countries, and the amount of Internet connectivity taken up by malicious Web traffic kept individuals from being able to access regular resources like e-mail. Thus, this chapter and discussion will emphasize events that can or have taken place in the United States, but it is important to recognize that some of the conditions we discuss can apply to many other industrialized nations in the world.

The United States is at a particular risk for cyberattack, whether related to information warfare or cyberterrorism, because of several factors. The first is that the United States continues to occupy a precarious position regarding the Middle East. Several fundamentalist and radical Islamic groups (e.g., al Qaeda, ISIS, Hezbollah, and HAMAS) perceive the United States to be evil. Indeed, much of their radical philosophy attacks modernity itself, characterizing complex communication systems, energy use, and computer networks as threats to fundamental Islam. To make matters worse, recent activities by the United States within the Israeli–Palestinian conflict, in Iraq, since 2003, Syria, and in Afghanistan after the events of September 11, 2001, have all contributed to anti-American sentiment within the radical Muslim world. Many of these groups have significant resources, skills, and experience in launching cyberattacks.[27] Furthermore, the progression of the government of Iran to develop and enrich nuclear material has witnessed the first major exchange of cyberattacks involving the United States and a computer worm named "Stuxnet."

Low-Level Cyberwar

In early 2009, a collaborative effort between Israel and the United States produced a computer worm known as "*Stuxnet.*" The program was jointly developed under the code name, "Operation Olympic Games," under the direction of then President George W. Bush, and expanded under former president Barack Obama.[28] The purpose of the Stuxnet worm was to infect the operating system of specific computers that manage the controller devices (Siemens industrial control systems Programmable Logic Controllers—PLCs) primarily found within the pumps and gas centrifuges used in the Natanz nuclear enrichment facilities in Iran.

Shortly thereafter, in 2012, major attacks against U.S. bank Web sites by the rogue group "al-Qassam Cyber Fighters" significantly escalated, and in August of that year Saudi Aramco was hit by the group "Cutting Sword of Justice," which disabled over 30,000 computer systems using the Shamoon virus—one of the most destructive cyberattacks ever witnessed. Not surprisingly, U.S. investigators linked these supposed terrorist groups operating clandestinely in the Middle East…to Iran.[29]

Later in 2012, another highly destructive and sophistical malicious software program (malware) called "*Flame*" was observed in various countries throughout the Middle East. Most of the attacks, however, were centered on Iran. Unlike Stuxnet, which was designed to sabotage or destroy a specific industrial control (PLC) device, Flame was a large program that was written primarily for espionage and information gathering. The program allowed the attackers to seek out and secure drawings, plans, policies, and other documents stored within a computer or computer network. With the vast majority of targets within Iran, and due to the collaborative development again by the United States and Israel, Flame represents one of the most complex cyber warfare programs ever developed.[30] While the U.S. government has acknowledged the existence and development of cyber weapons, it has officially denied responsibility for any attacks against the country of Iran.

Muslim fundamental and radical groups are not the only threat to the United States' cyber security. Anti-capitalist movements, such as those observed in Russia and North Korea, have also shown their prowess at engaging American targets in cyberattacks. Either type of group could levy a great amount of damage on commercial or government interests using techniques that they have already employed in different cyber realms.[31] Indeed, our country has already suffered very sophisticated attacks from such entities. The question, of course, is whether these attacks were state supported. Is it a single hacker or a group acting alone, or might they have been given some incentive by the military or government? Are they using equipment and resources that they obtained or those that have been provided by a covert military group? What resources are they attacking, and how might they benefit a nation more than an individual? In the often confusing and murky world of cyberterrorism and information warfare, the answers to these types of questions are often blurred, as might be expected when secret agencies and spy services are employed. The problem becomes even more confusing when multinational organized crime cartels join the mix. Chapter 5 attempts to address some of these same questions, with a focus on sophisticated criminal organizations.

Infrastructure Reliance

Another important factor that causes significant concern to the United States is the country's significant reliance upon a national information infrastructure. Information infrastructure is composed of five essential components: communications networks, such as those used for phones, satellites, and cable networks; equipment used for the provisioning of information, including televisions, radios, computers, and phones; information resources, which might consist of educational or medical programs or databases; applications, like those used for electronic commerce or digital libraries; and people.[32]

The United States, which has identified itself as the most infrastructure reliant of any nation on earth, is also possibly the most at risk for an infrastructure attack.[33] Critical infrastructure is a particularly attractive target to terrorists (and foreign governments), due to the large-scale economic and operational damage that would occur with any major shutdown.[34] In the late 1990s, the Clinton administration identified eight areas of infrastructure that constitute a virtual national life support system: telecommunications, banking and finance, electrical power, oil and gas distribution and storage, water supply, transportation, emergency services, and government services.[35] The further developed plan presented by former president George W. Bush in his *National Strategy for Homeland Security* identified and characterized the need for critical infrastructure protection.[36] Many of these areas are interdependent on each other, magnifying the potential effects of a breach of one system.[37] Former President Barack Obama laid out a similar plan arrayed along the same lines in a document referred to as the "Cyberspace Policy Review."[38] This document also suggests a for increased cooperation between the government and private industry in or secure critical infrastructure from cyberattack. President Obama took the first toward this cooperation through a White House executive order that directs U.S. ligence agencies to share the latest information about cyber threats with private c nies operating electric grids, power plants, water stations, railroads, and othe industries to help protect them from digital and other cyberattacks.[39] Furthermo Presidential Policy Directive 21 (PPD-21) on Critical Infrastructure Security Resilience expanded the list of critical infrastructure sectors from 8 to 16. These 16 sectors are chemical, commercial facilities, communications, critical manufacturing, dams, defense industrial base, emergency services, energy, financial services, food and agriculture, government facilities, health care and public health, information technology, nuclear reactors, transportation systems, and water and wastewater systems.

Banking and financial institutions are also vulnerable to infrastructure attack, as they depend heavily on networks. If one system is breached by an attacker, then all connecting systems can be severely impacted. However, most banking or financial networks tend to be private, with little external access, and heavily regulated with regard to cyber security and data protection. This helps to somewhat mitigate vulnerabilities in this sector. At the same time, a severe attack against a resource such as the stock exchange or a mortgage bank could cause significant harm to multiple sectors of the country's economy.

As discussed, electrical power and water supply systems rely heavily on electronic sensors that maintain safe levels of service and aid engineers in shutting off supplies if something were to go wrong. Manipulation of these remote sensors by network intrusion is a threat, especially by those who have legitimately gained access in the past. In fact, "malicious insiders," or those who have been given access to a system for a valid reason, such as employment or research, are the greatest threat to infrastructure. Such an insider would have specialized knowledge of a system, as well as access.[40] However, individual and government-sponsored hackers in Russia, North Korea, Iran, and China have begun to illegally access these systems remotely, emphasizing that the threat goes far beyond that of insiders.[41]

QUICK FACTS

Government-sponsored hackers often focus their attacks on U.S. critical infrastructure, such as financial institutions, transportation hubs, and water/power utilities. In early 2016, hackers with direct ties to Syria compromised a U.S. water treatment plant and were able to infiltrate a water utility's control system; they changed the chemical levels used to treat ordinary tap water. The incident marked one of the first major critical infrastructure attacks in the United States.

Source: Verizon Data Breach Digest. March 2016. Available at http://www.verizonenterprise.com

---

Transportation infrastructure, particularly related to civil air traffic control, is also a concern, particularly after the events of September 11, 2001. The systems used specifically for civil aviation have in the past been largely custom designed, which isolates civil aviation systems from most direct attacks. Today, as more and more tasks, including aircraft maintenance, parts manufacturing, and flight management systems, are slowly being replaced by commercial-off-the-shelf software, civil aviation systems are very well protected.[42] Security for both new and old systems is generally elaborate, with layers of administrative controls that could thwart even the most technologically sophisticated intruder. Furthermore, most civil aviation technology is designed to withstand system failure or breakdown through the use of redundant systems or separate subsystems, which are designed to pick up where the main system left off.[43] The Achilles' heel of civil aviation security is its heavy reliance on other types of infrastructure. Air traffic control centers depend on electricity, communications systems, and government services, such as the Federal Aviation Administration. For example, radar operates through simple, dedicated telephone lines. If those telephone lines were to be compromised, the impact could be catastrophic.[44]

QUICK FACTS

The U.S. Federal Aviation Administration (FAA) was compromised in 2009, allowing hackers to gain access to 40,000 FAA user IDs and passwords used to access mission-support systems. This attack followed a 2006 virus infection at the FAA that forced the administration to shut down a portion of the air traffic control systems in Alaska.

Source: U.S. Department of Transporation, Office of the Inspector General Report (May 4, 2009).

The potential severity of an electronic attack against critical infrastructure has led some individuals to use the term "electronic Pearl Harbor" to refer to such an event.[45] This is a reference to the notion that the attack will take citizens and the government by surprise and devastate the population. However, there have already been attacks against the United States' critical infrastructure involving many of these systems. Until recently in 2013 with the Mandiant report's identification of nation state–sponsored hackers (labeled APT1 or Chinese Army Unit 613898), none were directly linked to or proven to be the act of any terrorist organization or foreign country. Many are juvenile pranksters. For example, in March 1997, a teenager hacked into a telephone company computer that serviced the Worcester Airport, located in Massachusetts. Telephone service to the control tower, the airport fire department, airport security, and various other departments was out for more than six hours. The attack caused a ripple effect of delayed and cancelled flights across the country, leading to serious financial losses to the airport and several airlines.[46]

In another infrastructure attack, a disgruntled former Chevron employee disabled the firm's alert system by hacking into the company computers. The attack was not discovered until the system failed to notify engineers of a release of noxious chemicals into the air at a plant in Richmond, California. This event put millions of people in the western United States and Canada at risk.[47]

These two attacks were potentially deadly and costly, but were perpetrated by people without political or terrorist agenda. One was motivated by ego, the other by pure revenge. It is particularly disconcerting to think of what someone with a deep-rooted ideological hatred for the United States could do if a cocky teenager can shut down an airport for no specific reason. Possibilities put forth in academic literature include the most heinous visions of disaster:[48]

- Penetration of an air traffic control system in order to send misleading signals to aircraft, causing midair collisions.

- Taking advantage of the United States' increasing reliance on telemedicine by intruding into hospital computers and changing prescription dosages, resulting in patient death.
- Entering into computerized commuter and freight train routing systems, causing passenger trains to collide or hazardous materials to be released.
- Destroying government computer systems that process tax returns.

What is the risk of an attack on the U.S. critical infrastructure by a terrorist group or rival nation? Unfortunately, no one really knows how vulnerable our critical infrastructure is. Consider the testimony before the U.S. House of Representatives from Michael Vatis, Director of the Institute for Security Technology Studies at Dartmouth College:[49]

> to say that cyber networks are vulnerable does not mean that the critical infrastructures that rely on those networks—such as electrical power, grids, pipelines, telecommunications switching nodes, hospitals, etcetera—are necessarily vulnerable, or that a cyber attack would have a sufficiently long-lasting destructive impact to achieve a terrorist or nation-state's military or political objectives. We still do not actually know the full extent of our critical infrastructure's vulnerabilities to various types of cyber attacks and the extent of their potential impact.

In her testimony before the same group in October 2001, Terry Benzel, the vice president of Advanced Security Research for Network Associates, Inc., stated that she was unaware of any analysis of infrastructure that identified its weaknesses or even the extent to which systems are codependent. Benzel referenced a 1997 exercise designed to identify vulnerabilities against infrastructure.[50] Using only hacking tools available on the Internet, National Security Agency hackers successfully gained access to a number of military and infrastructure systems. However, specific vulnerabilities were never disclosed—only the assertion that the United States is at risk on some level for such an attack.[51] Benzel recommended an in-depth study and analysis of infrastructure to the House, to culminate in suggestions and solutions to shore up vulnerabilities.[52] Our government has been slow to respond to such threats and risks; however, recent events such as low-level digital warfare with Iran and the discovery of APT1 have begun to impact traditionally slow legislators into action. Fortunately, several departments and agencies like the U.S. Department of Justice, U.S. Department of Homeland Security, and the U.S. Department of Defense have been quicker to respond by designing and planning for potential threats and risks as well as developing tactical offensive cyber weapons to be used in case of an all-out attack against the United States. In addition, annual, national level, critical infrastructure cyber exercises (Cyber Storm exercises) are conducted with collaboration and coordination between government and private sector organizations in an effort to assess the U.S. critical infrastructure security posture and incident response effectiveness.[53]

INFORMATION ATTACKS

Both information warfare and cyberterrorism create a host of scenarios for cyberattacks. Attacks on infrastructure have already been discussed. There are less destructive forms of cyberattack that terrorist groups or adversarial nations could employ to achieve information warfare objectives. These information attacks are focused on destroying or altering content within a system, and while information may be corrupted and temporarily lost, physical and virtual systems are still preserved. This means that the attack is much less destructive and more disruptive in nature. However, such an attack can (and most likely would) cause major economic damage and loss.[54] The following sections present examples of these types of attack.

Web Site Defacement

India and Pakistan have been feuding over a relatively small strip of land known as Kashmir for over half a century. Cyberattacks are a more recent development in the history of this conflict, and the most visible of these attacks have been perpetrated by pro-Pakistan hacker groups. According to the Indian Computer Emergency Response Team, website defacements have increased dramatically in 2015 and 2016 with increases of 16 and 21 percent respectfully. The average number of web defacements India is averaging over 2,500 per month, and many have been either political or highly visible to the public.[55] For instance, sites representing the Indian parliament, television networks, newspapers, and academic institutions have all been defaced at some point. These Web sites have been defaced with anti-India images and slogans, with some automatically redirecting Web traffic to pro-Pakistani sites, or in some cases, to Web sites containing pornographic or generally offensive material.[56] This technique has also been used by both Israeli and Palestinian groups, often coinciding with specific political events in the region.[57] Domestically, the White House and the FBI Web sites have both been attacked by single-issue terrorist groups such as the Earth Liberation Front and right-wing hate groups such as the Aryan Nation.

Private industry has also become a regular target for Web defacements by political or religiously motivated hackers. For example, a Danish newspaper published a cartoon featuring the prophet Muhammad with a bomb in his turban in 2005.[58] This image was deemed offensive by the Muslim community, and the newspapers' Web site was defaced repeatedly along with any other site that featured the cartoon. Thousands of Web sites were hacked or defaced by Turkish hackers, who in turn received a great deal of attention from the press for their efforts.[59]

Cyberplagues: Viruses and Worms

The terms "*viruses*" and "*worms*" are often used synonymously to describe malevolent computer programs that are capable of running and duplicating themselves. However, there is a subtle difference between the two. A *virus* is actually a piece of code that attaches itself to other pieces of computer software, like software application code or e-mail attachments. When the user takes an action to make these host instructions run, the virus starts to run as well. The virus then performs a function and lets the host resume control.[60] Meanwhile, the virus has implanted itself into the memory of the computer, where it searches for new hosts. Each time it finds a new host, it inserts itself and then executes its payload, or function, which may be anything from displaying a smiley face on screen to completely wiping the files from a hard drive or installing the today's most prevalent ransomware.[61] The ILOVEYOU virus, which affected Web development and multimedia files and was spread through Microsoft Outlook address book contacts, hit tens of millions of computer users who opened a seemingly innocuous attachment in their e-mail entitled "Love Letter." The total cost of that virus was over a billion dollars.[62] Ransomware infections cost victims over one billion dollars globally, in 2016.[63] For more detailed information on viruses and malicious code, please refer to Chapter 7.

The ILOVEYOU virus was eventually traced to a college student, but there have been indications that foreign governments have explored viruses as a means of offensive information warfare. A report from the U.S. Defense Intelligence Agency warned that the Cuban military was developing a program to propagate viruses against civilian computers in the United States. And, as we have already learned, China has also developed programs to spread computer viruses through its military hacking unit, dubbed APT1.[64]

A *worm* is a program that reproduces itself over a computer network by breaking into computers much like a virtual hacker. Worms do not need the assistance of an unwitting computer user to be unleashed—rather, they find computers that they are able to penetrate, carry out their attack, and then transfer a replica of their code to the next target.[65] Worms run off of weaknesses in popular software in order to reproduce quickly and can have the results of a virus. However, they generally spread much faster, affecting tens of thousands of computers in as little as two to three hours. Estimated costs of worm attacks parallel those of many viruses, with a 2017 ransomware worm attack (WannaCry) affecting over 200,000 computers in more than 150 countries and causing an estimated one billion dollars in damage.[66] The Code Red worm in 2010 specifically targeted the White House computer systems that were running on commercial off-the-shelf software.[67] Although neither of these attacks were tied to any type of terrorism or specific information warfare agenda, others as noted were.

Viruses and worms are part of a much larger term, malicious software (*malware*), composed of any program or script that attempts to disrupt normal computer operations, steal private data, or illegally enter a private computer or computer system.

Distributed Denial-of-Service Attacks

The distributed denial-of-service (DDoS) attack is an attempt by a cyberattacker to prevent legitimate usage of service. DDoS attacks generally take the following forms: destruction or alteration of configuration information for a system, expenditure of resources needed

MAP 2.1 **Global Wannacry Malware Infections**

for legitimate operation, and the actual physical modification of network elements. The result of any of these three types of DDoS attacks is that a system becomes unavailable for a period of time until the system can be brought back under control.[68]

One of the more common types of DDoS attack is the flood attack. In this type of attack, the attacker starts the process of establishing a connection to another machine. The connection is intentionally never completed on the attackers end, but data structures within the victim computer have been reserved to meet the requirements of that connection. As a result, no legitimate connection may be made while the victim machine is waiting to complete the original phony connection request. The DDoS instigator can take over other computers (or rent previously hacked computers) and use them to establish a simultaneous attack of bogus connections of one victim computer.[69] DDoS attacks have been used against government and defense computers, as well as in the largest attack ever recorded, which focused on disrupting the Internet in general. This attack, in October 2016, targeted the domain name service (DNS) provider Dyn and effectively denied access to over 60 e-commerce clients, including Amazon, PayPal, PlayStation, Netflix, and Starbucks, for nearly a full day. The economic impact of this attack has still yet to be determined.[70] Once again, the attack has not been confirmed to be tied to any terror or political objectives.

In 2006, however, a tool called Electronic Jihad Program was found that easily enables DoS attacks against a variety of targets.[71] The tool is linked with a forum and chat room and coordinates attacks and targets a specific site each day. Using a simple-to-use interface, this resource was used in variety of attacks against Web sites around the world. In 2016, the attack on Dyn utilized a new malware (Mirai) that facilitates DDoS attacks by infecting "Internet of Things" (IoT) devices, like home thermostats and smart TVs. The August 2012 attack against Saudi Aramco and the 2016 attack on Dyn represent two of the most sophisticated attacks claimed by a rogue group. Restoring and replacing these services exceeded hundreds of millions of dollars, but was accomplished in a relatively short period of time. Complete Saudi Aramco services were restored in two weeks and Dyn was back online the same day. Thus, DDoS attacks are an important resource in the terrorist and information warfare community.

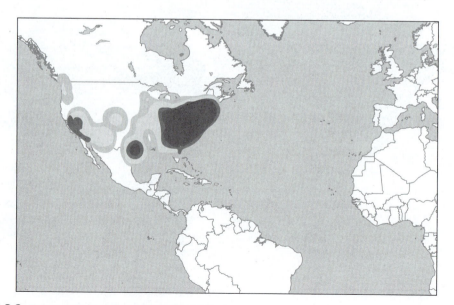

MAP 2.2 Internet Outage during Dyn DDoS Attack

Unauthorized Intrusions

Intrusions can be broadly defined as any set of actions that attempt to compromise the integrity, confidentiality, security, or availability of a single computer or network.[72] Theft of classified government information is of particular interest to terror groups or adversarial nations. The consequences of such an attack could have wide-ranging implications. However, this type of attack is very difficult to identify once it has occurred. Unless data have been altered, or administrators are specifically looking for an intrusion, such an attack may go undetected forever.[73] This is particularly true in advanced and sophisticated cases like those involving the Stuxnet and Flame malware. Both programs were encrypted with commands that destroyed the original program and any file that suggested that the malware had ever been installed. These types of programs are particularly pernicious.

A well-known attack in 1998 exemplifies the issue. A group of hackers composed of people from around the globe announced that they had stolen programs off of U.S. Department of Defense computers that essentially ran U.S. military networks and satellites. The software was stolen from a Windows NT server in the Defense Information Systems Agency within the U.S. Department of Defense. The hackers claimed that the software could be used to virtually shut down U.S. military operations. The group also claimed to have penetrated National Aeronautics and Space Administration (NASA) computers, as well as Pentagon computer systems.[74] The group claimed that their attack was merely an act of public service—a kind of wake-up call for the United States to realize that if a group of simple hackers could gain access to sensitive information, so too could terrorist groups (or rogue nations) willing to use that information to their advantage. Detailed information relating to the event is difficult to acquire, which heightens anxiety and leads to paranoid visions of extreme national vulnerability. The attack was real; however, the U.S. Department of Defense had no knowledge or awareness of the attack and the subsequent loss of information and data.

Similarly, a coordinated series of attacks against private intelligence industry provider, Stratfor, occurred in 2011. The loose-knit hacking movement known as "Anonymous," claimed that it had stolen thousands of credit card numbers and other personal data belonging to the company's clients. Anonymous members posted some of the information on various Twitter and Facebook accounts. While the focus of the attack was unauthorized intrusion and theft of data, the attack was primarily symbolic, attacking an intelligence and security-related company. "Anonymous" is an informal group of hackers, which has become famous for attacking the companies and institutions that oppose anti-secrecy Web site WikiLeaks and its founder Julian Assange. "Anonymous" had previously claimed responsibility for attacks on VISA, Inc., MasterCard, Inc., and ebay Inc.'s PayPal, and this attack was designed to embarrass Stratfor rather than for personal gain. According to several sources, the data were not encrypted. In addition, some files were taken from the company's e-mail system that included a list of written passwords. The failure to protect and secure client information and company e-mail systems was a major fiasco on the part of Stratfor, an intelligence and security-related company based in Austin, Texas.

A series of carefully coordinated attacks on American computer networks and defense systems since 2003, referred to as "Titan Rain," appeared to come from Chinese systems operated by very skilled hackers.[75] Evidence suggests they were able to steal massive amounts of files from NASA, Lockheed Martin, and Sandia National

Laboratories in as little as 10–30 minutes, leaving no traces behind. Though little information is available, this example clearly demonstrates that intrusions are a serious and very real threat to critical infrastructure and networked systems.

CYBER AND TECHNOLOGICAL FACILITATION

These final categories of cyberattack are less a physical attack and more of a tactic in cyberterrorism and information warfare. Facilitation of attack can encompass such things as communication via the Internet by terrorist groups, while promotion of terror might be as simple as recruitment and propaganda.

Facilitation of Attack and Dissemination of Ideology

Information technology has played a great role in the emergence of networked terrorist groups, such as al Qaeda, Jemmah Islamiyiah, and ISIS. Technology has allowed for reduced transmission time in communication, so that members of an organization all over the globe may coordinate their tasks.[76] Information technology has also reduced the cost of communication. In the past, terrorist networks have had to centralize their major activities to reduce detection resulting from direct travel and telephone communication. This made them more vulnerable to discovery, and their operations could effectively be wiped out with just one major raid. However, information technology has allowed these organizations to disperse throughout the world, decentralizing their operations and thereby safeguarding them.[77]

A good example are the myriad of Web sites associated with al Qaeda and the Islamic State that disseminate radical Islamic ideology, appeal for financial support, provide instruction in tactics and weapons, gather intelligence and information about potential targets, radicalize and recruit new members, and support a worldwide communication venue. According to terrorism expert Brian M. Jenkins, "The Internet enables terrorist organizations to expand their reach, create virtual communities of like-minded extremists, and capture a larger universe of more-diverse talents and skills."[78] It is the ability to attract more diverse individuals in the facilitation of an attack that is most alarming. Terrorist operatives can coordinate with each other relatively securely in individual chat rooms and social media sites where they not only embolden each other with rhetoric but also plan and discuss future strategies, attacks, and tactics. The Internet provides a wealth of technical data from weapons manufacturing, arms trafficking, and bomb making (improvised explosive devices—IEDs) to detailed satellite imagery of potential targets and real-time transportation routes for escape.

Developments in information technology have also allowed for more complex information sharing among terrorist groups. Organizations now have access to computer conferencing, chatting, and Web sites that allow for quick and direct communication, such as Facebook Live video streaming.[79] Domestic right-wing groups have historically used Web sites for recruitment and advancement of their philosophies. In fact, a range of Web forums and social networking sites exist for neo-Nazi groups and other racist organizations to connect and discuss their positions.

The emergence of the Internet and cellular communications devices has also engendered the development of so-called *flash mobs* or *smart mobs*.[80] These terms refer to mass formations of individuals in one place and time, coordinated through the use of text or instant messaging, e-mails, and other Web-based communications. This technology enables protests, civil unrest, and violence with some organization. In 2010, for example, the French police were investigating a break-in at a construction site in a largely Muslim and African community, where they found several teenagers.[81] The teens began to run, though it is not clear if they were being chased by police, and climbed into an electrical power substation where two died as a consequence of severe electric shock. These deaths incited local tensions, leading to weeks of rioting, during which buildings and cars were burned, police assaulted, bus stations destroyed, and several killed. The youths involved in these riots are said to have used text messaging and e-mails to coordinate their attacks and avoid law enforcement.[82]

QUICK FACTS

In one of the largest and most unique attacks of its kind, six people were injured, including a police detective in Center City, Philadelphia, in November 2016, as a group of an estimated 20 juveniles started randomly assaulting pedestrians in a specific area. Investigation revealed that all of the suspects communicated via cell phones (text messages) in order to carry out the "flash mob" attack.

Source: ABC News Online, Philadelphia, "2 Arrests, More Suspects Sought in Center Flash Mob Attack." Available at http://6abc.com/news/2-arrests-more-suspects-sought-in-center-city-flash-mob-attack/1604456/

Data Hiding

Also known as steganography, data hiding includes an assortment of methods for secret communication that can conceal the fact that a message even exists at all. Most practically, data hiding refers to the act of taking a piece of information and hiding it within another piece of data, such as an image, sound recording, or word-processing file.[83] Data hiding is based upon two main principles: The first is that files that contain digital images or recordings may be altered without losing their functionality, and second, files may be altered without the effects ever being perceived by the human eye or ear.[84] After the events of September 11, 2001, reports surfaced that revealed that al Qaeda had been transmitting hidden data over the Internet. Hidden maps of terrorist targets and instructions were posted in sports chat rooms and pornographic sites, which could be accessed by anyone with an Internet connection.[85] Data hiding is fairly easy to do, given the availability of free programs on the Internet and commercially available software, and is complex enough that it would take an impossible amount of time and energy to find hidden data in every Internet file. It is for these reasons that data hiding is such a valuable tool for terrorists or adversarial nations.

Cryptography

For the most part, cryptography is discussed as a methodology to secure and protect information from unwanted eyes and unauthorized use. The same technology can be used to secure communication between terrorist groups. Cryptography is generally used in conjunction with data hiding. An encryption program scrambles information in a controlled manner through the use of a cryptographic key. Only those with access to the key can read the encoded material. Couriers for the terrorist group al Qaeda have been intercepted while carrying encrypted diskettes. Ramzi Yousef, convicted of the 1993 World Trade Center bombing, had encrypted plans to destroy 11 American airliners. This was discovered only after FBI agents spent over a year decoding files found in

Yousef's Manila apartment in 1995.[86] Similarly, a tool called Mujahedeen Secrets has circulated among Middle Eastern hacker groups as a means of encrypting e-mail communications with some ease.[87] This free tool was created by Ekhlass Network, Global Islamic Media Front, and allows individuals to encrypt files and messages, compress them, and securely destroy them. More recently, the encryption issue has reached a peak as major computer companies like Apple Inc. and Google Inc. have begun offering encryption programs to secure private data and text messages. See Box 2.2.

PROPAGANDA AND PROMOTION

Terrorist organizations and adversarial nations have also used the Internet for purposes of propaganda and recruitment. The Internet is the best tool available for these purposes, mainly because it remains largely unregulated and has the potential to reach so many. Organizations can influence public opinion and generate funding through the use of Web sites, which can offer even greater control over a message than TV or print, due to the interactive nature of the Internet and the direct link between a group and its webmaster.

BOX 2.2

The Encryption of Terrorist iPhones

In 2013, a classified intelligence leak from former defense contractor Edward Snowden revealed the collection of *all* phone-tracing data from *all* Verizon digital telephone communications under the USA PATRIOT Act. The revelation from Snowden's leak made it clear that at least some (intelligence) agencies had overstepped their power. Telephone companies and Internet service providers (ISPs) like AOL, Verizon, AT&T were spending countless hours and dollars every day trying to fulfill the requests made by police and security agencies under the PATRIOT Act.

In November 2014, in the wake of the Snowden leaks, a civil suit was filed by Twitter, requiring agencies to publish a full transparency report on their surveillance activities. The suit was joined by other entities such as Apple and Google. In early 2015, the Senate failed to block agencies from continuing to collect individual phone records and other data from social media and ISPs. In response, Apple and Google, as well as other companies, began offering encryption programs to secure private data and text messages on mobile devices (especially smartphones). The encryption program renders a locked mobile device (smartphone) impervious to external intrusion without a key, held *only* by the owner of the phone. The issue came to a head in December 2015 with the shootings in San Bernardino, California; the FBI had recovered an Apple iPhone 5C from terrorist suspect Syed Farook, and the FBI needed Apple's assistance to "unlock" the phone. The U.S. Department of Justice file a court order in February 2016, in an effort to require Apple to help the FBI access the contents of the phone; however, that court order was vacated by the courts a month later in March 2016. Then FBI director James Comey, continually warned that such encryption (by Apple and Google) will cost American lives as agencies will not be able to use a variety of tools to track criminals and victims alike, as well as gain valuable intelligence information from terrorist phones. The issue is certainly not over as the United States faces a larger predicament on how to balance the need for intelligence to prevent future terrorist attacks, collect evidence in which to prosecute criminals, and secure our nation from today's threats posed by cybercriminals and cyberspies *with* individual and Constitutionally guaranteed rights of privacy, trust, and security.

Sources: Based on Marjorie Cohn, "The Surveillance State: NSA Telephony Metadata Collection: Fourth Amendment Violation." *Jurist* (January 16, 2014). See: http://jurist.org/forum/2014/01/marjorie-cohn-nsa-metadata.php

National Public Radio, *Morning Edition,* "Encryption, Privacy Are Larger Issues than Fighting Terrorism." (March 14, 2016). See: http://www.npr.org/2016/03/14/470347719/encryption-and-privacy-are-larger-issues-than-fighting-terrorism-clarke-says

Charles R. Swanson, Leonard Territo and Robert W. Taylor, *Criminal Investigation* 12th ed. (New York: *McGraw-Hill, 2017), Chapter 17, Cybercrime.*

Recruitment and mobilization is an important part of terrorist Web presence. Individuals not directly affiliated with a terrorist group, but who support their agenda, may be tapped through the Internet to provide hacking tools, funds, or merely "spread the word." During the al-Aqsa Intifada, Israeli and Palestinian groups each employed this technique to encourage sympathizers to download hacking tools and use them against whichever side they opposed.[88] In addition, a young hacker named Irhabi 007, who was active in a number of Web forums devoted to jihad, or holy war, against the West, hacked into an FTP site operated by the Arkansas Highway and Transportation Department in 2004.[89] He used the site to post 70 terrorist-related files, including audio and video messages encouraging war and hacking methods, and advertised the hacked site in forums across the world to encourage and spread the message of jihad.

Recruiting is made easier by tracking which propaganda is accessed most on a Web site and tailoring messages to fit that particular audience. Terrorist groups can also capture information about those who peruse their Web sites and later contact them. Chat rooms and cybercafés can also serve as forums to recruit interested members of the public, especially the young. It is no surprise, then, that nearly all terrorist groups have an official presence on the Internet. Even the Palestinian Resistance Movement (HAMAS, responsible for literally hundreds of suicide bombings in Israel) can be accessed at *http://en.wikipedia.org/wiki/Hamas.* Hizbollah, a Lebanese Shiite group known best for its involvement in the 1983 bombing of the U.S. marine barracks in Beirut, has a site at *http://english.alahednews.com.lb/.*[90]

Many of the radical Islamic groups have Web sites, but none were more successful than that of American-born cleric, Anwar al-Awlaki. He made numerous YouTube videos, blogged through his own Web site, had a Facebook page, sponsored his own online al Qaeda magazine, *Inspire,* and focused on recruiting "homegrown" terrorists from the United States. He was very successful in developing online relationships with several radical Islamic terrorists who planned and carried out attacks against targets in the United States. Al-Awlaki was in contact with several of the hijackers previous to the 9/11 attacks; he was online with Nidal Malik Hasan, just days before he went on a shooting rampage at Fort Hood, Texas, in 2009; he had contact with Umar Farouk Abdulmutallab, the Nigerian Christmas Day "underwear bomber" in December 2009 who attempted to hijack Northwest Airlines Flight 253; and he had been linked to over a dozen other terrorist plots in the United Kingdom and Canada between 2005 and 2011. His death, as the result of an unmanned drone in Yemen on September 30, 2011, sparked controversy as he was the first American killed by CIA-led drone strikes in the Middle East. Interestingly, even today, his death continues to be a subject of much discussion on several al Qaeda Web sites.

On the domestic front, literally hundreds of sites exist for right-wing hate groups and single-issue terrorist groups. At one point in early 2017, there were over 500 sites dedicated just to the emergence and development of state militia groups.

Funding and Financing Terrorist Groups

Terrorist groups are also engaging in cybercrimes and the use of the Internet as a means of funding their activities. In addition, there are four general categories of direct solicitation, e-commerce, exploitation of online payment tools, and charitable donations. The use of chat groups and spam e-mails to request donations is considered direct solicitation. E-commerce activities include the online sale of goods, including books

BOX 2.3

Recruiting Videos on the Internet

Increased bandwidths and new software have allowed sophisticated terrorists users to develop and disseminate complex information via the Internet. The Islamic State has six different media institutions that focus on Web site development, propaganda, operational communication, and the development of professional quality training and recruiting videos, specifically for the Internet. Some of the videos posted instruct people on how to join the conflict in Syria or Iraq, while others display mechanisms of destruction like suicide bombs and vests. For instance, a recent 26-minute video teaches how to develop a suicide vest and how to use it on a bus.[1] Other videos present information on how to be a better marksman, how to make and set an improvised explosive device (IED), or simply how to conduct morning prayer. The videos are often shot in the field, on the "front lines" with Islamic State fighters and dubbed into several different languages (English, French, Dutch, German, Turkish, and, of course, Arabic).

Many of the propaganda videos are directed at recruiting new and younger members to the cause. Hence, they often romanticize the bonding of brothers in combat, or fighting for one's belief, or living as in the days of old fighting the Crusaders that attacked the Middle East. Most of the videos have strong and forceful passages from the Holy Qur'an, with singing from other members in the background, or fiery speeches by Abu Bakr al-Baghdadi, the leader of IS.

During the initial stages of the IS movement, recruitment of individuals for the cause was an outcry to join the fight in the Middle East (in Iraq, Yemen, Jordon, and now Syria). Indeed, Abu Bakr al-Baghdadi often asked other radical Islamic groups to join the IS movement. However, one of the more dangerous trends in recruitment within the IS today is a concerted focus to "take the attack to Western countries." Certainly since 2015, the numerous attacks in London, Paris, and Brussels support this new trend. Many of the new videos developed by the IS focus on how to accomplish mass carnage in heavily populated European and American cities. Once on the Internet, these videos give the IS a worldwide cyber footprint for training and recruiting. More importantly, they help to accomplish all four organizational tools of the movement: ideology, leadership, recruiting, and publicity, and the accomplishment of these tools suggest that the IS will be a major threat to American and Western ideals for quite some time.

―――――――

[1]Irving Lachow and Courtney Richardson, "Terrorist Use of the Internet." *National Defense University Press*, Issue 45, 2nd Quarter, 2007, p. 100.

Source: Based on Robert W. Taylor and Charles R. Swanson, *Terrorism, Intelligence and Homeland Security*, 2nd ed. (Upper Saddle River, NJ: Pearson, 2018).

Islamic State Training and Propaganda Videos often include speeches from Abu Bakr al-Baghdadi

and recordings that support their cause. Accepting payment through an online payment platform for donations or purchased goods is another funding mechanism for terrorist groups.[91] See Figure 2.1. To counter such activity, *MoneyJihad.com* is a Web site dedicated to, among other things, exposing financial institutions that support or fund terrorist organizations. The Web site lists several banks and financial institutions that maintain relationships with jihadists *(http://moneyjihad.wordpress.com/2013/01/07 /sharia-banks-that-fund-terrorism/)*.

FIGURE 2.1 Screenshot from an Internet site soliciting terrorist funding.

CYBERTERRORISM AS AN ADJUNCT ATTACK

As illustrated previously, not many can agree on exactly what threats cyberterror or information warfare poses to the United States. However, one common theme throughout the literature on this topic is that the threat of cyberterror is at its greatest when considered in conjunction with other terrorist actions. According to testimony of Virginia Governor Jim Gilmore before the House Science Committee in October 2001, "If a cyber attack occurs simultaneously with either a conventional attack or a weapon of mass destruction attack…it can compound and enhance the impact of the original attack."[92]

Cyberattacks are potential force multipliers, which in military terms mean that these types of attacks can increase the impact of a terrorist action when combined with more traditional attacks. This is done without escalating the need for manpower or capital on the terrorists' side. For example, if a terrorist organization bombed a building through conventional means, but coupled it with hacking into and disabling 911 systems, the impact of the attack would be exponentially multiplied, as rescue personnel would not be able to respond effectively.[93]

Al Qaeda, the Islamic State, and Information Technology

Much of the current interest in cyberterrorism and information warfare has sprung from the events of September 11, 2001, and the subsequent discovery of information technology tools used to plan and coordinate those attacks. Al Qaeda, under the direction of Osama bin Laden (and now, Egyptian cleric Ayman al-Zawahri), appears to have a sophisticated system of communication, surveillance, and coordination via computer networks and other information tools. It is widely agreed that members of al Qaeda pose a major threat via the Internet. Al-Zawahri is presumed to be hiding in Pakistan and has released numerous propaganda videos via the Internet since bin Laden's death (in 2011), exhorting followers to violence and "personal jihad."

In a 2002 interview with *Computerworld*, Sheikh Omar Bakri Muhammed, an Islamic cleric with proven ties to bin Laden, said that al Qaeda was actively planning a "cyber jihad," or holy war, against the United States and its allies. Bakri identified the stock market as a major target and described how the fundamentalist Islamic groups are assembling cadres of computer science students sympathetic to al Qaeda's cause in places like Pakistan and Malaysia.[94]

In late 2001, the FBI noted a series of network intrusions into emergency telephone and electrical generation systems, water storage facilities, nuclear power plants, and gas facilities. Each of the probes had been routed through telecommunications centers in Saudi Arabia, Pakistan, and Indonesia—all known operational centers for al Qaeda. In 2002, al Qaeda computers seized in Afghanistan contained information yielded from these probes.[95] And, on May 2, 2011, when Navy SEALS shot and killed bid Laden in his home near Abbottabad, Pakistan, one of their primary targets was the securing of computers and servers used by bid Laden to command and coordinate his organization. The intelligence information derived from these computer systems helps target other individuals as well as thwart planned attacks in the future. Indeed, the destruction of the al Qaeda communication network may not have been as symbolic as the killing of bin Laden, but nonetheless, much more important and effective in actually disrupting the future of al Qaeda as a terrorist organization.

In addition, U.S. officials found evidence on these computers that al Qaeda operatives spent considerable time on Web sites that offer software and programming instructions for the digital switches that run critical infrastructure such as transportation and power grids. Because the switches are not meant for public access, they have few security safeguards built into them. An attack using these switches could yield devastating results. When questioned, some captured al Qaeda operatives admitted that they had large-scale intentions to use that information in attacks on the United States.[96] This information is further confirmed by reports from the FBI (in 2013) that directly point to al Qaeda and the IS targeting of commuter rail and airline systems within the United States.

Simple hacking tools, such as LOphtCrack, were also found on al Qaeda computers. LOphtCrack allows a hacker to run combinations of characters at lightning speed in order to try and replicate a password. Other more sophisticated information technology tools, such as data hiding and encryption, were also a common theme in al Qaeda caches.[97] Additionally, terrorist groups have developed hacker tools to engage in credit card theft and rootkits that would allow hackers to remotely command victim machines. These resources are available for download through a range of Web sites, including a resource titled the "al-Qaeda University for Jihad Studies."[98] This page provides access to propaganda, hacker tools, and instructional materials to train new generations of hackers to continue the mission of this terror network.

Al Qaeda uses this technology so effectively, partly because of the structure of the organization. Bin Laden is part of an inner circle that has reverted to using non-electronic means of communication recently due to the sophistication of U.S. and allied interception. However, outside of this core group exists a loose network of operators who coordinate using the sophisticated information technology already described. These operators are able to participate in the exchange of ideas, information, and plans related to the planning and targeting of attacks against the United States and/or its allies. It is this community of terrorists, residing all over the globe and with varying technological knowledge, that poses such a great threat to the United States.[99]

PERSPECTIVES ON INFORMATION WARFARE

Information warfare is the concept of using information technology to gain tactical or strategic advantage over an opponent during a conflict. This can be intelligence in the sense of knowing the enemy's capabilities, intentions, and dispositions (deployment), or undermining their capabilities and will to fight. Propaganda, disinformation, counterintelligence, deception, and disruption of information infrastructure are all aspects of information warfare. The acronym-obsessed U.S. military currently refers to these capabilities as C4ISR, or Command, Control, Communications, Computing, Intelligence, Surveillance and Reconnaissance. More prudent planners label all these things "information operations." As we have discussed, information warfare is known to be a component and/or objective of cyber or cyber terrorism, and the lines are often blurred as to the exact motivations of each incident and/or actor.

Clearly, the three superpowers—the United States, Russia, and China—have different and varying perspectives on information warfare. These are not rogue states attempting to gain international attention or prowess, but rather the superpowers of the world trying to keep one step ahead of the other. Indeed, the tools of information warfare—*cyberweapons*—may represent the most complex arms race to date. The Pentagon has created a Cyber Command, and information warfare is one of the few parts of the military budget that is expected to grow over the immediate future.[100] The Obama administration has made it perfectly clear that the military can carry out counterterrorism missions in nations where the United States operates under the rules of war or where substantial U.S. interests are threatened. The use of cyberweapons and/or other aspects of information warfare are fair play and have evolved over the last decade as a response to threats against U.S. interests from terrorists rather than specific nations. The final authority for the use of cyberweapons by the United States rests with the President, and like all weapons are to be used narrowly, constituting a reasonable and proportionate force in halting or retaliating against a cyberattack.[101]

The Russian Perspective

Russia's view of information warfare, "informatsionnaya voyna," is a more holistic concept, carrying cyber operations implicitly alongside electronic warfare, psychological operations, and strategic communications and influence. The Russians view cyber capabilities as tools of information warfare, which combines intelligence, counterintelligence, disinformation, electronic warfare, debilitation of communications, degradation of navigation, psychological pressure, and destruction of enemy computer capabilities.[102]

From the Russian perspective, there are considerable similarities between the tactics employed by hacktivism, cyber aggression, and cybercrime. Furthermore, the Russian cyber warrior may employ information weapons such as cybercrime to achieve the technical aspects of a mission and possibly cyberterrorism to address the objectives and motivation of an attack on enemy computer networks.[103] In other words, information weapons, as defined by Russian information warfare expert S.P. Rastorguyev, are "means directed at activating (or blocking) information systems processes in which the subject using the weapons has an interest; being any technical, biological, or social means or system that is used for the purposeful production, processing, transmitting, presenting or blocking of data and or processes that work with the data."[104] Hence, employing cybercrime and cyberterrorism techniques are well within the arsenal of information warfare from the Russian perspective.

QUICK FACTS

The regime of North Korea may be the newest country to join the world of information warfare. Equal in terms of hacking prowess to the United States, China, and Russia, the regime employs an elite squad of 6,800 hackers engaged in full-time fraud, blackmail, and cyberattacks against global businesses and the Western governments. Some of their most infamous attacks were against Sony (2014), and several banks in 2016–2017, including attacks on Anthem, Chase Bank, Bank of the Philippines, Interpark eCommerce, Tien Phong Bank of Vietnam, J.P. Morgan, and the Bangladesh Central Bank, resulting in over $80 billion in loss. North Korea is also a chief suspect in the 2017 WannaCry Ransomware global cyberattack that resulted in over $4 billion in loss.

Source: Charlie Campbell, "Why We Shouldn't be Surprised if North Korea Launched the WannaCry Ransomware Cyberattack," *Time* (May 16, 2017).

The Chinese Perspective

The People's Republic of China is probably not the first threat that comes to mind when discussing information warfare or cyberterrorism. However, tensions between the United States and China remain high, and China is one of the few countries in the world eager to adopt the concept of information warfare. In fact, cyber warfare has been almost totally incorporated into the military lexicon, training, and organization in China.[105] Consider this excerpt from the official Chinese military science handbook:

> In the near future, information warfare will control the form and future of war. We recognize this developmental trend of information warfare and see it as a driving force in the modernization of China's military and combat readiness. This trend will be highly critical to achieving victory in future wars.[106]

Information warfare, as a component of China's national capabilities, is employed as necessary to support their government objectives and strategy. Programme 863, for example, is a Chinese government objective aimed at "making Chinese industry financially independent of foreign technology; China sees cyberspace as a way of compensating for its deficiency in conventional warfare, for example by developing strategies to cripple communication networks."[107] As a result, the Chinese government has assembled special hacker forces to engage the United States in online or cyber warfare and has apparently already used them. In the spring of 2001, a hack into the California power grid was traced back to the Guangdong province in China, where several malicious worms and Trojan horse attacks had also originated. The Department of Defense officials did not think that was a coincidence. Although no proof was ever found that directly implicated the Chinese government or military, conventional wisdom suggests that these attacks had been "ordered."[108] Evidence also emerged in 2009 concerning repeated penetrations into American electrical grids by Chinese hackers.[109] A recent study using covert research methods also found that Chinese computers comprise the largest percentage of machines on the Internet actively scanning for electrical grid communications.[110] This information, coupled with the previously described Titan Rain incidents, suggests that the Chinese are heavily engaged in attempts to access critical infrastructure in the United States.

Furthermore, on April 1, 2001, an American spy plane and a Chinese fighter aircraft collided in midair, leading to the capture of the American plane by the Chinese. The political conflict that followed was accompanied by a wave of attacks on

U.S. Web sites by Chinese hacker groups. Approximately 1,200 sites, including those of the White House, the Air Force, and the Department of Energy, were targeted via defacement or DoS attacks. Again, this was never directly proven to be the work of the Chinese government. However, the attacks were highly visible, and China took no action to sanction those who perpetrated them. The attacks were at least tolerated by the Chinese government; however, given their hard-line stance on crime in China, it seems more likely that the government directly supported such action.[111]

Then, in early 2013, one of the most significant and controversial security reports regarding cyberthreats to the United States emerged from Mandiant, a computer security consulting corporation.[112] Its report documented thousands of cyberattacks aimed primarily against entities within the United States since 2006 from China, and identified a group known as Advanced Persistent Threat One (APT1) as the primary culprit. APT1 is a single organization of individual operators working within China that has conducted one of the most aggressive and sophisticated cyber espionage campaigns ever uncovered. The sheer amount of activity along with the discovery of various sophisticated tools and tactics used by APT1 led the Mandiant to conclude that APT1 is likely a Chinese government-sponsored group with direct ties to the People's Liberation Army (PLA), Unit 61398. Both groups have similar missions, capabilities, and resources and are located in precisely the same building in Shanghai, China. Mandiant believes that indeed APT1 is PLA Unit 61398.[113] APT1's cyberattack infrastructure is composed of over 1,000 servers within a large organizations staffed by hundreds of human operators with direct access to Shanghai communication systems and capabilities. The conclusion that the Chinese government was not only aware of APT1, but now actively involved in the direction and management of group designed primarily to steal digital information and attack Western enterprises sent shockwaves through the international community. The Mandiant report represents the first conclusive evidence that foreign governments do indeed sponsor military-based, cyber activity designed specifically to steal information and disrupt American infrastructure. Awareness of this type of threat has provided the stimulus for billions of dollars dedicated to retaining cutting-edge capability in defending U.S. infrastructure.

Summary

China, Russia, Iran, North Korea, the Islamic State, and al Qaeda, domestic right-wing hate groups, and numerous other terrorist or nation-state entities all have access to the Internet and have the tools to perpetrate a variety of cyberattacks against the United States and/or its allies. By the very nature of these technological attacks, our critical infrastructure is most vulnerable. As a result, a great deal of attention has been focused on the topic. Scholars, government officials, and reporters alike have speculated on the vulnerabilities of the United States to cyberattacks, as well as to the "types" of attacks that may be implemented. As illustrated throughout this discussion, there is a great deal of confusion as to what the threats against U.S. information systems really are.

Clearly, there is a tremendous range of domestic and international terror groups, unfriendly nations, and criminals attempting to or successfully subverting U.S. critical and economic infrastructure. Such attacks could cause untold damage, though it is difficult to document the scope of the problem. It is, however, obvious that the Internet is now a critical component of information warfare and terror activities.

Review Questions

1. Define the concepts of cybercrime, information warfare, and cyberterrorism.
2. What are the six components of information warfare?
3. What are the four major categories of cyberterrorism and/or information warfare?
4. What is "Stuxnet" and "Flame," and how do they relate to low-level information warfare between the United States and Iran?
5. Define critical infrastructure, and give some specific examples of the types of systems vulnerable to cyberterrorism and information warfare within the United States.
6. Name and describe various types of information attacks.
7. What are steganography and cryptography?
8. What has the role of China been in recent cyberattacks against the United States?

Critical Thinking Exercises

1. Global criminal and terrorist incidents are tracked by various organizations around the world. One resource is the Global Incident Map. Explore the site at: https://www.GlobalIncidentMap.com. Why do you think that cyberattacks are not revealed the same as a terrorist bombing or shooting incident?
2. Research the WannaCry Ransomware Cyberattack of 2017 on the Internet. How was it unusual as a cyberattack and unlike other attacks in the past? Who do you think was responsible for the attack?
3. Several scholars have suggested that the next major war will be a cyberwar and that, to some extent, we are already engaged in this war with North Korea, Iran, China, Russia, and various terrorist groups. Discuss this concept as a class—Do you think we are already engaged in information warfare? How vulnerable are we as a country to this type of attack? Do you think we are ready to do "combat" in this area?

Endnotes

1. CERE, R. (2003). "Digital Counter-Cultures and the Nature of Electronic Social and Political Movements." In YVONNE J. (ed.), *Dot.cons: Crime, Deviance and Identity on the Internet*. Portland, OR: Willan Publishing, pp. 147–163.
2. FURNELL, S. (2002). *Cybercrime: Vandalizing the Information Society*. Boston, MA: Addison Wesley.
3. *Ibid.*
4. DENNING, D.E. (2001). "Activism, Hacktivism, and Cyberterrorism: The Internet as a Tool for Influencing Foreign Policy." In JOHN A. and DAVID F.R. (eds.), *Networks and Netwars: The Future of Terror, Crime, and Militancy*. Santa Monica, CA: Rand, pp. 239–288.
5. GROSS, M. (2013). "The Silent War." *Vanity Fair*. See: *http://www.vanityfair.com/culture/2013/07/new-cyberwar-victims-american-business*; MENN, J. (May 18, 2013). "Cyber Attacks Against Banks More Severe than Most Realize." *Reuters*. See *http://www.reuters.com/article/2013/05/18/us-cyber-summit-banks-idUSBRE94G0ZP20130518*.
6. PANETTA, L.E. (October 11, 2012). "Remarks by U.S. Secretary of Defense Leon E. Panetta on Cybersecurity to the Business Executives for National Security, New York." *News Transcript*. U.S. Department of Defense.
7. FUNG, B. (March 8, 2013). "How Many Cyberattacks Hit the United States Last Year?" *Nextgov.com*. See *http://www.nextgov.com/cybersecurity/2013/03/how-many-cyberattacks-hit-united-states-last-year/61775/*
8. O'HARROW, JR., R. (December 2, 2012). "Virtual Town, Virtuous Goals." *The Dallas Morning News*, p. 6A.
9. *Ibid.*
10. SCHWARTEAU, W. (1996). *Information Warfare*. New York: Thundersmouth Press, p. 12.
11. JONES, A., KOVACICH, G.L., and LUZWICK, P.G. (2002). *Global Information Warfare: How Businesses, Governments and Others Achieve Objectives and Attain Competitive Advantages*. New York: Auerbach Publication, p. 5. For further information on definitions, refer to DENNING, D.E. (1999). *Information Warfare and Security*. New York: ACM Press.
12. United States Air Force. (1995). "Cornerstones of Information Warfare." See:http://www.csse.monash.edu.au/courseware/cse468/2006/cornerstones-iw.html (accessed July 1, 2016).
13. See JONES, KOVACICH, and LUZWICK, "*Global Information Warfare*." p. 394.
14. See United States Air Force.
15. *Ibid.*
16. DENNING, *Information Warfare and Security*, p. 68.
17. "Cyberterror Threat Overblown, Say Experts." *Computerworld*, March 14, 2003.
18. EMBAR-SEDDON, AYN. (February 2002). "Cyberterrorism: Are We Under Siege?" *American Behavioral Scientist* 45(6): 1036.
19. THACKRAH, R. (1987). "Terrorism: A Definitional Problem." *Contemporary Research on Terrorism*. Aberdeen, Scotland: Aberdeen University Press, p. 1043.

20. POLLITT, M. (October 25, 1997). "Cyberterrorism—Fact or Fancy?" *Proceedings of the 20th National Information Systems Security Conference*, pp. 285–289

21. GROSSMAN, M. (February 15, 1999). "Cyberterrorism." See: Retrieved July 1, 2016, from *http://www.mgrossmanlaw.com/articles/1999.cyberterrorism.htm*.

22. *Ibid.*, p. 4.

23. STAMBAUGH, H., BEAUPRE, D.S., ICOVE, D.J., BAKER, R., CASSADY, W., and WILLIAMS, W.P. (2001). *Electronic Crime Needs Assessment for State and Local Law Enforcement.* Washington, D.C.: National Institute of Justice. NCJ 186276.

24. DENNING, D.E. (2000). "Cyberterrorism." See: *http://palmer.wellesley.edu/~ivolic/pdf/Classes/Handouts/NumberTheoryHandouts/Cyberterror-Denning.pdf.*

25. BALLARD, J.D., HORNIK, J.G., and MCKENZIE, D. (February 2002). "Technological Facilitation of Terrorism." *American Behavioral Scientist* 45(6): 1009.

26. LANDLER, M., and MARKOFF, J. (2008). "Digital Fears Emerge After Data Siege in Estonia." *The New York Times.* Retrieved May 24, 2007, from http://www.nytimes.com/2007/05/29/technology/29estonia.html.

27. Institute for Security Technology Studies at Dartmouth College (September 22, 2001). "Cyber Attacks During the War on Terrorism: A Predictive Analysis." See: *http://www.ists.dartmouth.edu/docs/cyber_a1.pdf.*

28. SANGER, D.E. (June 1, 2012). "Obama Order Sped Up Wave of Cyberattacks Against Iran." *The New York Times*, p. 1.

29. GORMAN, S. and BARNES, J.E. (October 12, 2012). "Iran Blamed for Cyber-attacks." *The Wall Street Journal.*

30. NAKASHIMA, E. (June 19, 2012). "U.S., Israel Developed Flame Computer Virus to Slow Iranian Nuclear Efforts." *The Washington Post.*

31. *Ibid.*

32. See JONES, KOVACICH, and LUZWICK, "*Global Information Warfare.*" pp. 56–57.

33. *Ibid.*, p. 67.

34. Testimony of JIM G., Virginia governor, before the House Science Committee on October 17, 2001.

35. See DENNING, "Cyberterrorism."

36. See *National Strategy for Homeland Security.*

37. See JONES, KOVACICH, and LUZWICK, "*Global Information Warfare.*" p. 71.

38. MCCULLAGH, D. (2009). "A Cybersecurity Quiz: Can You Tell Obama from Bush?" *Cnet News.* Retrieved May 29, 2009, from *http://news.cnet.com/8301-13578_3-10252263-38.html.*

39. LARDNER, R. (October 20, 2012). "Order Would Inform Industries of Cyberthreats." *The Dallas Morning News*, p 10-A.

40. See Institute for Security Technology Studies, "Cyber Attacks During the War on Terrorism." p. 17.

41. GORMAN, S. (2009). "Electricity Grid in U.S. Penetrated by Spies." *Wall Street Journal.*

42. GOODMAN, S. (2001). "The Civil Aviation Analogy: International Cooperation to Protect Civil Aviation Against Cyber Crime and Terrorism." In A.D. SOFAER and S.E. GOODMAN (eds.), *Transnational Dimensions of Cyber Crime and Terrorism.* Stanford, CA: Hoover Institution Press, pp. 77–80.

43. *Ibid.*, p. 78.

44. *Ibid.*, p. 79.

45. *Ibid.*, p. 2.

46. See DENNING, "Cyberterrorism."

47. *Ibid.*

48. See JONES, KOVACICH, and LUZWICK, "*Global Information Warfare.*" p. 112.

49. Testimony of MICHAEL, A.V., director of Institute for Security Technology Studies at Dartmouth College, before the House Science Committee on April 8, 2003.

50. Testimony of TERRY, B., vice president of advanced security research for Network Associates, Inc., before the House Science Committee on October 10, 2001.

51. See DENNING, *Information Warfare and Security*, pp. 75–76.

52. See Testimony of TERRY BENZEL.

53. U.S. Department of Homeland Security Cyber-Storm. *http://www.dhs.gov/cyber-storm.*

54. ZANINI, M. and EDWARDS, S. (2001). "The Networking of Terror in the Information Age." In J. ARQUILLA and D. RONFELDT (eds.), *Networks and Netwars.* Pittsburgh: RAND, p. 44.

55. Valecha, U. (June, 2017). ".in websites not in safe domain." *The Hindu Business Line*, See: *http://www.thehindubusinessline.com/info-tech/in-websites-not-in-safe-domain/article9731524.ece.*

56. See Institute for Security Technology Studies, "Cyber Attacks During the War on Terrorism." p. 5.

57. *Ibid.*, p. 6.

58. WARD, M. (February 8, 2006). "Anti-Cartoon Protests Go Online." *BBC News. http://news.bbc.co.uk/2/hi/technology/4692518.stm*; DANCHEV, D. (August 25, 2008). "Hundreds of Dutch Web Sites Hacked by Islamic Hackers." *ZDNet. http://blogs.zdnet.com/security/?p=1788.*

59. *Ibid.*

60. See DENNING, *Information Warfare and Security*, p. 270.

61. *Ibid.*

62. See DENNING, "Cyberterrorism."

63. *NBCNews.com.* (January 9, 2017). "Ransomware: Now a Billion Dollar a Year Crime and Growing." Available at *http://www.nbcnews.com/tech/security/ransomware-now-billion-dollar-year-crime-growing-n704646.*

64. See DENNING, *Information Warfare and Security,* p. 275.

65. *Ibid.*

66. CHAN, S. and SCOTT, M. (May 14, 2017). "Cyberattack's Impact Could Worsen in 'Second Wave' of Ransomware." *The New York Times, http://www.newyorktimes.com*; DENNING, *Information Warfare and Security.*

67. See Institute for Security Technology Studies, "Cyber Attacks During the War on Terrorism." p. 10.

68. See JONES, KOVACICH, and LUZWICK, "*Global Information Warfare.*" p. 398.

69. *Ibid.*, pp. 398–399.

70. U.S. Department of Homeland Security, www.dhs.gov (February 16, 2017). "Snapshot: Turning Back DDoS Attacks." See Institute for Security Technology Studies, "Cyber Attacks During the War on Terrorism." p. 11.

71. DENNING, D. (May 15, 2008). "The Jihadi Cyberterror Threat." Paper presented at the UNCC Interdisciplinary Conference on Cybercrime.

72. *Ibid.*

73. *Ibid.*

74. See DENNING, *Information Warfare and Security,* p. 226.

75. THORNBURG, N. (2005). "Inside the Chinese Hack Attack." *Time.*

76. See ZANINI and EDWARDS, "The Networking of Terror in the Information Age." p. 35.

77. *Ibid.*, p. 36.

78. JENKINS, B.M. (2011). *Is al Qaeda's Internet Strategy Working?* Santa Monica, CA: The RAND Corporation. See: *http://www.rand.org/content/dam/rand/pubs /testimonies/2011/RAND_CT371.pdf.* p. 1.

79. *Ibid.*

80. CERE, R. (2007). "Digital Undergrounds: Alternative Politics and Civil Society." In Y. JEWKES (ed.), *Crime Online.* Portland, OR: Willan Publishing, pp. 144–159.

81. *Ibid.*

82. *Ibid.*

83. See JONES, KOVACICH, and LUZWICK, "*Global Information Warfare.*" p. 389.

84. See BALLARD, HORNIK, and MCKENZIE, "Technological Facilitation of Terrorism." p. 996.

85. See JONES, KOVACICH, and LUZWICK, "*Global Information Warfare.*" p. 388.

86. *Ibid.*, pp. 388–389.

87. *Ibid.*, p. 60.

88. See ZANINI and EDWARDS, "The Networking of Terror in the Information Age." p. 42.

89. *Ibid.*, p. 60.

90. See *Ibid.*, p. 43.

91. United Nations. (2012). The Use of the Internet for Terrorist Purposes. United Nations Office on Drugs and Crime. See: *http://www.unodc.org/documents/frontpage/Use_of_ Internet_for_Terrorist_Purposes.pdf.*

92. See Testimony of JIM GILMORE.

93. See EMBAR-SEDDON, "Cyberterrorism." pp. 1038–1039.

94. "Al Qaeda Poses Threat to the Net." *Computerworld,* November 25, 2002.

95. "Cyber-Attacks by Al Qaeda Feared." *Washington Post,* June 27, 2002.

96. *Ibid.*

97. Summarized from Public Broadcasting Station interviews, April 24, 2003. See: *www.pbs.org/wgbh/pages/frontline /shows/cyberwar/interviews/.*

98. *Ibid.*, p. 60.

99. *Ibid.*

100. SANGER, D.E. and SHANKER, T. (2013). "Obama to Hold Cyberauthority." *The New York Times.*

101. *Ibid.*

102. GILES, K. (2011). *Information Troop—a Russian Cyber Command?* Oxford University, UK: Conflict Studies Research Center.

103. *Ibid.*

104. THOMAS, T.L. (2004). *Comparing US, Russian, and Chinese Information Operations Concepts.* Fort Leavenworth, KS: Foreign Military Studies Office. p. 6.

105. HILDRETH, S. (2001). "Cyberwarfare." In J. BLANE (ed.), *Cyberwarfare: Terror at a Click.* Huntington, NY: Novinka Books, p. 14.

106. See JONES, KOVACICH, and LUZWICK, "*Global Information Warfare.*" p. 221.

107. LEYDEN, J. (2011). Hidden Dragon: The Chinese Cyber Menace—Any Decent Government Does Industrial Espionage. *The Register.* See: *http://www.theregister.co.uk/2011/12/24 /china_cybercrime_underground_analysis/* p. 1.

108. "Is China Ground Zero for Hackers?" *ZDNET,* August 28, 2001. See: *http://zdnet.com.com/2100-1107-504010.html.*

109. *Ibid.*, p. 33.

110. KREBS, B. (2009). "Report: China, Russia Top Sources of Power Grid Probes." *The Washington Post.* Retrieved May 1, 2009, from *http://voices.washingtonpost.com / securityfix/2009/04/report_china_russia_top_source.html.*

111. See Institute for Security Technology Studies, p. 8.

112. MANDIANT. (2013). *APT1: Exposing One of China's Cyber Espionage Units.* Alexandria, VA: Mandiant. For more information regarding Mandiant, refer to its Web site at: *www.mandiant.com.*

113. *Ibid.*

The Criminology of Computer Crime

CHAPTER OBJECTIVES

After completing this chapter, you should be able to

- Discuss the tenets of choice theory, including routine activities theory, and its applicability to cyber crimes.
- Describe the assumptions of deterrence theory and its utility.
- Discuss the impact of personality disorders on cyber crime.
- Discuss the major social structure theories that apply to cyber crime.
- Discuss the learning and social control theories that apply to cyber crime.
- Describe the relationship between terrorism and political theory.

INTRODUCTION

This chapter will focus on the causes of cyber crime. There are several theories that have been postulated over the past 100 years to explain crime, and there is an emerging body of research attempting to apply these concepts to cyber crimes. A theory is an attempt to answer the question "Why?" In this chapter, theories will be presented that attempt to answer the question "Why do individuals commit cyber crime?" This chapter will review criminological theories that can explain cyber crime, though it is important to note that these theoretical frameworks were developed to explain crime in general, not cyber crime specifically. As a result, support for some of these theories is mixed and require a great deal of investigation. This discussion will present the existing body of criminological research within a variety of offending and victimization contexts, as well as examples to demonstrate how a particular theory can explain cyber crime.

CHOICE THEORY

According to choice theory, an individual commits a crime because he or she makes a rational choice to do so by weighing the risks and benefits of committing the act. If the risks (e.g., apprehension and punishment) outweigh the benefits, then the person will not commit the act. The opposite is also true. Choice theory became popular among criminologists in the late 1970s for three reasons. First, the positive school began to be questioned. The positive school was based on the belief that crime-producing traits and factors could be isolated, and treatment could be administered to eliminate or control the trait/factor. However, it was being argued at the time that these factors and traits had failed to be identified and isolated after almost 100 years of effort. Individuals became dissatisfied with the positive school and began to offer alternative reasons for why people commit crime.

Second, the reported crime rate in the 1960s and 1970s increased significantly. This was evidence to some that what was currently being done to control crime was not working. Therefore, some began to look for other means to control the crime rate besides treatment and rehabilitation. Third, the practice of rehabilitation came under attack.[1] In 1974, Robert Martinson wrote an article reviewing 231 studies of prison programs aimed at rehabilitating inmates. Martinson concluded that "with few and isolated exceptions, the rehabilitative efforts that have been reported so far have had no appreciable effect on recidivism."[2] This finding, which was picked up by the mass media, was used by critics of prison programs to argue against rehabilitation as a primary justification for incarceration. The results of the article are commonly referred to as "nothing works." Since it appeared that the current efforts had failed, many started to call for a change in judicial policy. Many started to emphasize the need for punishment, not rehabilitation, as the primary reason for incarceration.

Based on these reasons, choice theory and its policy implications became popular. Judicial policy started to change focus, on the offense and not the offender. Choice theory argues that since the offender has made a rational choice to commit the offense, the focus should be on the offense committed, not the offender. Policies such as mandatory sentencing and "three strikes and you're out laws" are popular and are based on choice theory. The idea is that the way to control crime, including cyber crime, is to have offenders fear the punishment and be deterred from committing the act. Since humans are hedonistic (i.e., maximize pleasure and minimize pain), efforts should be placed on making the risks of committing cyber crime higher than any benefit derived from committing the offenses. Those who support the use of punishment to control crime assume that the offender is making a choice to commit the act and can be deterred if the risks outweigh the benefits.

QUICK FACTS

An estimated 17.6 million Americans—about 7 percent of U.S. residents age 16 or older—were victims of identity theft in 2014. Most victims (86%) experienced the misuse of an existing credit card or bank account. About 4 percent of victims had their personal information activity stolen and used to open a new account or for other fraudulent activity. Some victims (7%) experienced multiple types of identity theft during the most recent incident.

Source: Victims of Identity Theft, 2014. Bureau of Justice Statistics, September 2015.

Routine Activities

Routine activities theory is based on rational choice. Routine activities theory was developed by Lawrence Cohen and Marcus Felson. Cohen and Felson argue that the motivation to commit crime and the supply of offenders are constant.[3] Many would argue that changes in the crime rates are due to changes in the number of motivated offenders. However, Cohen and Felson argue that there is always a steady supply of offenders who are motivated to commit crime: Changes in crime rates are due to changes in the availability of targets and the absence of capable guardians.[4]

According to Cohen and Felson, crime occurs when there is a convergence in time and space of three factors:

1. A motivated offender (e.g., a hacker)
2. A suitable target (e.g., a vulnerable computer system)
3. The absence of a capable guardian (e.g., inadequate software protection)[5]

All three factors must be present in order for a crime to occur. In sum, when motivated offenders are present, they make rational choices by selecting suitable targets that lack capable guardianship.

This theory can also account for victimization, as victims, in addition to offenders, are the other people involved in a criminal event. Using routine activities theory as the framework, victimization is most likely when individuals are placed in high-risk situations, are in close proximity to motivated offenders, appear to be attractive targets to criminals, and lack a capable guardian.[6] In addition, victims report higher levels of deviant behavior than nonvictims and share demographic characteristics with offenders.[7] Similarly, individuals who engage in criminal and deviant behavior are at an increased risk of victimization.[8] Some of the tenets of routine activities theory, such as close proximity to motivated offenders, are less applicable for cyber crime than other criminal offenses (e.g., aggravated assault).

This theory is applicable to cyber crime because the rapid expansion of the use of computers and the Internet has increased the number of available targets. The millions of computers online at any point in time are all potential targets for hackers or malicious software writers. In addition, the global nature of the Internet means that an offender in Egypt, for example, could hack into hundreds of computer in the United States without ever leaving home.

In addition, without adequate software protection, there is frequently a lack of capable guardians to protect people from cyber crime. Physical guardians are readily available on computer systems through antivirus software, firewalls, and similar programs.[9] These programs are expressly designed to reduce the likelihood of attacks from viruses, worms, and data loss by either scanning and preventing infected files from being introduced to the system or identifying and removing malicious software if it already has infected the system. Thus, physical guardians in cyberspace work similarly to physical guardians in the real world.

One of the first empirical studies testing this theory conducted by Holt and Bossler found that postulates of routine activities theory can be used to account for online harassment.[10] Specifically, routine computer use, including spending more time in online chat rooms, increased the odds of online harassment. Physical guardianship measures, through antivirus programs and other software, had little influence on the likelihood of being harassed while chatting online. There was also a significant influence that personal and peer involvement in deviance had on the risk of online harassment. Engaging in cyber crime can expose individuals to offenders, thereby increasing their risk of victimization.

A similar test of malicious software infection found that spending more time online engaging in shopping, e-mailing, and chatting did not affect the likelihood of receiving a virus or worm.[11] Individuals engaging in media piracy and viewing pornography were at an increased risk of malware infection, largely because these files are attractive packages that many individuals would want to open. Thus, the findings suggest that the relationship between crime and victimization in the real world may be replicated in online environments. Additionally, computer software that has been created specifically to decrease malware victimization had no significant impact in this study. These findings suggest that there may be some considerable utility in the routine activities framework, though greater research is needed to better understand and assess its applicability to cyber crime.

DETERRENCE THEORY

Deterrence theory flows directly from choice theory. The idea is that offenders, including cyber criminals, commit crime because they make a choice to do so. This choice is based on the perceived risks and benefits of committing the criminal act. If the risks (e.g., apprehension and punishment) outweigh the benefits, then the person will not commit the act. The offender will be deterred from committing the criminal act because of the threat of punishment. There are two types of deterrence: general and specific. **General deterrence** seeks to discourage would-be offenders from committing criminal acts because of the threat of punishment. Therefore, general deterrence occurs when would-be offenders choose not to commit a certain act because they fear the sanction that may be imposed. Sometimes offenders are made an example of in order to keep others from committing the same act. For example, an eighteenth-century judge reportedly told a defendant, "You are to be hanged not because you have stolen a sheep but in order that others may not steal sheep."[12] This is an example of general deterrence. **Specific deterrence** is designed to impose a sanction on a convicted offender in order to prevent him or her from continuing to commit criminal acts in the future. In other words, the sanction should be distasteful to the offender so that he or she does not want to commit any more offenses.

There are several assumptions of deterrence theory. First and perhaps the most important assumption is that individuals are rational actors.[13] In other words, offenders weigh the potential risks and benefits of committing a criminal act and then make a conscious decision about whether to commit the offense. As it applies to cyber crime, it can be argued that many cyber criminals are rational actors, making rational choices to commit a computer crime. Second, offenders must be aware of the penalty for particular crimes.[14] As it applies to computer crime, it is argued that many computer criminals do not know the potential penalties they face for particular crimes. Third, they must view the risks as unpleasant.[15] If a computer criminal does not think apprehension and incarceration is unpleasant or if the criminal does not believe he will be caught, then the criminal will not be deterred. Fourth, in order for deterrence to be effective, it is assumed that the sanction is swift, certain, and severe. The sanction must be imposed quickly to have the greatest deterrent effect, and there must be a high probability that a sanction will be imposed. Most computer crimes remain unsolved so there is a low probability of arrest for these offenses, making deterrence unlikely.

However, it is important to keep in mind that it is not the actual certainty, severity, and swiftness of the sanction that serve as a deterrent but the criminal's perception of the certainty, severity, and swiftness of the sanction. If potential computer criminals believe that the certainty of arrest is high for computer crime, then they will be deterred from committing the offense even if there is little chance of arrest in reality. Likewise, if potential computer criminals perceive prison as a terrible place that they do not want to go to, then they may be deterred from committing offenses. On the other hand, if a computer criminal does not believe that being incarcerated is anything to fear, then the individual is less likely to be deterred. Therefore, if offenders do not believe that the sanctions in court are severe, then they are unlikely to be deterred from committing criminal acts. Likewise, if they do not believe they will be caught, then they perceive a lack of certainty of punishment and thus are likely to commit the crime. The lack of certainty of arrest and punishment is particularly pronounced when it comes to computer crime. There is generally a low risk of apprehension and punishment.

There is minimal evidence to support the argument that the threat of arrest and punishment deters criminals.[16] In fact, evidence supports the contention that informal sanctions from parents and friends serve as more of a deterrent than legal sanctions.[17] In other words, fearing disapproval from your parents and peers for your actions is more likely to keep individuals from committing those acts than the fear of arrest and punishment.

A limited body of research has considered the applicability of deterrence for software and music piracy. Research using samples of college students suggests that the certainty of being caught by an IT administrator or fellow student did not reduce the likelihood of hacking systems without authorization.[18] Severity of punishment, however, helped to reduce the likelihood of hacking activity.[19] The relationship between detection and software piracy is also mixed. For example, one study found that when the certainty of being caught was high, software piracy declined.[20] Though there is not much research in this area, deterrence may have some success in accounting for cyber crimes. Further research is needed to better understand this relationship.

PSYCHOLOGICAL THEORIES

There are several psychological theories that have been applied to criminal activity. This section will explore the impact of moral development and personality disorders on crime. Moral development theories support the contention that there are differences between the moral beliefs of criminals and noncriminals, while personality disorders argue that there are certain personality characteristics that are predictive of crime.

Moral Development and Crime

The relationship between moral development and crime focuses on cognitive development. Cognitive development theory assumes that individuals develop in a sequential

---

BOX 3.1
Hacker Targeted Senior U.S. Government Officials

Justin G. Liverman, 24, of Morehead City, North Carolina, pleaded guilty on January 6, 2017, for his role in a harassment scheme that targeted senior U.S. government officials. Liverman's plea admits guilt to a conspiracy to commit unauthorized computer intrusions, identity theft, and telephone harassment.

According to the statement of facts filed with the plea agreement, beginning in November 2015, Liverman conspired to attempt to intimidate and harass U.S. officials and their families by gaining unauthorized access to victims' online accounts, among other things. For example, Liverman publicly posted online documents and personal information unlawfully obtained from a victim's personal account; sent threatening text messages to the same victim's cell phone; and paid an unlawful "phonebombing" service to call the victim repeatedly with a threatening message. In November 2015, the conspiracy used that victim's government credentials to gain unlawful access to a confidential federal law enforcement database, where Liverman obtained information relating to dozens of law enforcement officers and uploaded this information to a public Web site.

Which theory do you think applies best to this case?

Source: U.S. Department of Justice. (2017). North Carolina Man Pleads Guilty to Hacking Conspiracy That Targeted Senior U.S. Government Officials. Retrieved from: https://www.justice.gov/usao-edva/pr/north-carolina-man-pleads-guilty-hacking-conspiracy-targeted-senior-us-government manner. The individual passes through one step in development, then another step, then another, and so on. Kohlberg argues that there are sequential stages in moral reasoning that individuals pass through as they develop. At each stage, the decision of what is right and what is wrong is made for different reasons. Crime, including computer crime, can be explained by arrested development of moral reasoning at certain stages. People stop at a certain stage and do not progress any further.

Kohlberg stated that there are six stages of moral development. They are as follows:

Stage 1: Punishment and obedience orientation stage—what is right is obedience to power and rules and avoiding punishment

Stage 2: Hedonistic orientation stage—right corresponds to seeing one's own needs met, taking responsibility for oneself, and allowing others to do the same

Stage 3: Interpersonal concordance stage—right is having good intentions and motives and being concerned for others

Stage 4: Law and order orientation stage—right is doing one's duty to society and others and maintaining the rules of society

Stage 5: Social contract, legalistic orientation stage—right is based on upholding the rules and values agreed upon by society, a social contract

Stage 6: Orientation to universal ethical principles stage—right is an assumed obligation to principles such as justice and equality, which apply to all individuals; the individual recognizes the moral rightness of behavior[21]

The first two stages are usually completed by age 7. Stages 3 and 4 are passed through and completed from preadolescence through adolescence, while the last two stages begin in early adulthood. Where do criminals stop in moral development in comparison to noncriminals? Research has found that criminals frequently fall into stage 1 or 2 of moral development, while noncriminals frequently fall into stage 3 or 4.[22] In stage 1, children comply with authority out of fear. Something is viewed as morally right if punishment is avoided. Individuals who did not progress through this stage will think that their criminal behavior is permissible as long as they are not punished for it. Obviously, this stage of moral development does not take into account other people or an obligation to society. In stage 2, children define what is right as that which satisfies their needs. That is why it is referred to as the hedonistic orientation stage. At this stage, children define something as right if they are not punished for it (i.e., stage 1) and it satisfies their needs. It is easy to see why it is argued that many criminals have stopped their moral development at stage 1 or 2. Their only concern with whether something is right or wrong is whether they get punished and satisfy their needs. It is not until stage 3 that children begin to take into account the feelings of others. Development to stage 3 insulates people from crime because they have become concerned about others, not just their own needs. Therefore, it is clear to see that individuals who proceed to stage 3 and perhaps beyond are far less likely to commit criminal acts.

Personality Disorders

Psychologists argue that certain personality characteristics of an individual may influence crime. Personality refers to the emotional and behavioral attributes of an individual. Attempts have been made to provide support for the belief that individuals with certain personality types are much more likely to commit criminal acts. These attempts have focused on identifying differences in the personalities of criminals and noncriminals. One attempt at identifying these personality characteristics was completed by Sheldon and Eleanor Glueck after they compared 500 delinquent and nondelinquent boys. Personality characteristics that were conducive to crime included extroversion, impulsivity, lack of self-control, hostility, resentment, suspicion of others, destructiveness, less fearful of failure, ambivalence toward authority, assertiveness, and feeling unappreciated.[23]

Frequently the term "psychopath" or "sociopath" is used in describing some offenders. These terms technically refer to a condition known as antisocial personality disorder. According to the *Diagnostic and Statistical Manual of the American Psychiatric Association*, "The essential feature of antisocial personality disorder is a pervasive pattern of disregard for, and violation of, the rights of others that begins in childhood or early adolescence and continues into adulthood."[24] Some of the characteristics of antisocial personality disorder are (1) egocentrism; (2) self-esteem derived from personal gain, power, or pleasure; (3) absence of prosocial internal standards associated with failure to conform to lawful or culturally normative ethical behavior; (4) lack of concern for feelings, needs, or suffering of others; (5) deceitfulness, callousness, and hostility; and (6) irresponsibility, impulsivity, and risk taking.[25] It is argued that certain computer criminals satisfy the criteria of antisocial personality disorder. However, it is argued that the prevalence of antisocial personality disorder is lower among computer criminals than among other criminals.

Pedophiles and Psychological Theory

Many people wonder why pedophiles commit the crimes that they do; what combination of factors leads a person to want to commit sexual offenses against a child? Unfortunately, there are no easy answers. As discussed in Chapter 8, pedophiles commit their crimes for a variety of reasons and go on committing their crimes, with little hope of rehabilitation. Most experts agree that pedophiles develop a sexual interest over a long period of time. Furthermore, there is a variety of reasons and factors that relate to developing pedophilia, none of which fully cause or explain the crime. Most commonly, pedophiles are exposed to some type of sexual abuse or trauma during their childhood. Another common factor is that they have had some type of abuse or other related problem during their sexual development and, as a result, develop an interest in children as sexual objects. Interestingly, the advent of the Internet has led to numerous problems in dealing with and detecting pedophiles.

The Internet serves many purposes for the pedophile of today, the least of which is the dissemination of child pornography. This poses a conundrum for theorists: Which comes first—an interest in computers due to existing pedophiliac interests or an interest in pedophilia as a result of viewing these types of images on the Internet? Some of the pedophiles arrested state that they developed an interest in children as sexual objects as the result of seeing such images on the Internet. Others clearly were pedophiles prior to the advent of the Internet and simply learned another technique for obtaining child pornography. In short, the specific reasons why a person becomes a pedophile are not immediately or clearly understood. Nonetheless, psychological theories posit that a person's sexual interests and sexual paraphilias develop in much the same way as other interests and our personalities—through a process of learning, cognitive reinforcement,

BOX 3.2

Online Retailer Sentenced for Largest-Ever Scheme to Import and Sell Counterfeit Contact Lenses

The owner and operator of Candy Color Lenses, a major online retailer of colored contact lenses in the United States, was sentenced to 46 months in prison on January 18, 2017, for running an international operation importing counterfeit and misbranded contact lenses from suppliers in Asia and then selling them over the Internet without a prescription to tens of thousands of customers around the country.

In addition to imposing a prison sentence, U.S. District Judge James C. Mahan of the District of Nevada ordered defendant Dmitriy V. Melnik, 30, of Las Vegas to remit $200,000 in restitution and forfeit $1.2 million in proceeds derived from the scheme as well as property seized during the investigation.

According to the plea agreement, Melnik imported large quantities of colored contact lenses from the People's Republic of China and South Korea that he knew were counterfeit and/or unauthorized by Food and Drug Administration (FDA) for sale in the United States. Many of these contact lenses bore labels with counterfeit trademarks for Ciba Vision FreshLook COLORBLENDS, which are manufactured by Novartis International AG (Novartis).

Melnik further admitted that he sold purportedly "authentic" contact lenses to tens of thousands of customers around the United States without a prescription, adequate directions for use or adequate warnings. After purchasing the contact lenses, many customers complained directly to Melnik about the quality of the contact lenses and questioned Melnik about whether the contact lenses were genuine and FDA approved. Melnik admitted that many of the contact lenses that he sold were substandard, and that some were tested and found to be contaminated with a potentially dangerous bacteria.

As stated in the plea agreement, a substantial part of the fraudulent scheme was committed from outside the United States, and Melnik received at least $1.2 million in gross revenue from this illegal enterprise, including approximately $200,000 alone from the sale of counterfeit Ciba Vision FreshLook COLORBLENDS.

Which theory do you think applies best to this case?

Source: U.S. Department of Justice. (2017, Jan 18). Owner Of Major Online Colored Contact Lens Business Sentenced to 46 Months in Prison in Largest-Ever Scheme to Import and Sell Counterfeit and Misbranded Contact Lenses Prosecuted in the United States. Retrieved from: https://www.justice.gov/opa/pr/owner-major-online-colored-contact-lens-business-sentenced-46-months-prison-largest-ever

and psychological development. Thus, the specific reasons why a person becomes a pedophile are different from case to case, but the process is relatively consistent. The best explanation for this interest is psychological and cognitive in nature.

SOCIAL STRUCTURE THEORIES

The first set of social theories that will be discussed in this chapter can be classified as social structure theories. When originally developed, social structure theories focused on why lower-class individuals are more likely to commit crime than middle- and upper-class individuals. However, modifications and expansions of the original theories have moved away from this distinction and have attempted to explain criminal behavior by all social classes (e.g., general strain theory). This is important in the study of cyber crime because many offenders come from the middle and upper classes. Traditionally, these theories focus on socioeconomic conditions and cultural values as two prominent factors that impact crime. In this section, two major subtypes of social structure theory will be discussed: strain theory and subculture theory.

Strain Theory

One major type of social structure theory is strain theory. Originally, strain theorists saw crime as a result of a lack of opportunity, in particular economic opportunity. Today, modern-day strain theories are much broader than the original theories. At the time of the development of strain theory, it was argued that U.S. society instills in citizens a desire for financial success but does not provide all individuals equal opportunity to achieve that success. Those who do not have an equal opportunity are strained and thus more likely to be criminal. The most prominent strain theory is the one presented by Robert Merton.

MERTON: STRAIN THEORY   There is a unique combination of cultural goals and the means to obtain them in every society. According to Merton, the cultural goal of American society is economic success.[26] It is argued that the primary goal of U.S. citizens is material wealth. This goal is promulgated through a variety of mechanisms, including the media, cultural transmission, and other mechanisms. Along with the goal, there are institutionalized means to obtain the goal, such as education, occupation, and deferral of gratification. However, not everyone has equal access to the institutionalized means to obtain financial success. Members of the lower class have less access to education and good jobs than members of the middle and upper class. Strain theory is sometimes referred to as "blocked opportunity theory." In other words, people are blocked in their ability to access education and a good job. Therefore, there is a discrepancy between a person's desire to obtain economic success and their ability to do so. These individuals suffer from strain.

If an individual is strained, how do they adapt to the strain? Merton developed five modes of adaptation.[27] The modes of adaptation vary in their acceptance or rejection of the cultural goal of economic success and the institutionalized means to obtain the goal. They also vary in the propensity for criminal behavior. The first mode of adaptation is **conformity**. A conformist accepts both the cultural goal of economic success and the institutionalized means to obtain it. A conformist is highly unlikely to commit criminal acts. It is also the most common mode of adaptation.

The second mode of adaptation is **ritualism**. A ritualist rejects the cultural goal of economic success but accepts the institutionalized means to obtain it. One response to strain is to lower your aspirations. This is what a ritualist does. They have lowered their aspiration for financial success but still abide by the means to obtain it, such as employment and education. It is unlikely that a ritualist will commit criminal acts as well.

The third mode of adaptation is **innovation**. An innovator accepts the goal of economic success but rejects the institutionalized means to obtain it. In this instance, the individual engages in innovation to find new means to obtain economic success besides education and employment. One such means is likely to be criminal activity. The innovator may commit such offenses as computer crime, fraud, drug dealing, robbery, burglary, auto theft, bribery, and prostitution, among others in an effort to obtain financial success. This is the mode of adaptation that is most likely to lead to criminal activity and to include computer criminals. Basically, the person wants to be financially successful and will commit criminal acts that help to obtain this goal.

The fourth mode of adaptation is **retreatism**. A retreatist rejects both the cultural goal of economic success and institutionalized means to obtain it. These individuals do not aspire to financial success, nor are they concerned with getting an education and employment. These individuals frequently escape into drug addiction and may commit crimes to support their drug use. Therefore, their strain is reduced by abandoning both the goal and the means to obtain it.

The fifth mode of adaptation is **rebellion**. A rebel rejects both the cultural goal and means but substitutes new goals and means to obtain them. This adaptation is likely to lead to crime and can be represented by some gangs, militias, cults, and countercultures. Criminality is likely to occur with this mode of adaptation, but it will not be as prevalent as criminal activity among innovators.

White-Collar Crime and Strain Theory

White-collar crimes such as money laundering, corporate espionage, and the numerous varieties of Internet fraud schemes described in Chapter 6 fit neatly into the strain theory school of criminology, which suggests that crime and deviance is largely the result of blocked legitimate opportunities. In this sense, individuals who engage in such schemes can be viewed as "innovators" who pursue illegitimate means in order to achieve the conventional goal of material success.

While Merton's original formulation of the theory focused on the blockage of legitimate opportunities experienced predominantly by those in the lower economic classes, contemporary strain theorists have sought to extend strain theory in order to explain the instrumental crimes of middle- and upper-class individuals by defining what they have termed the "relative deprivation" experienced by persons of higher economic status. That is, individuals who already enjoy a certain degree of monetary success may engage in instrumental crimes such as money laundering, espionage, and fraud simply because they *perceive* goal blockage in their attempt to secure ever-increasing wealth. From this perspective, "relative deprivation" offers an explanation as to why crimes such as money laundering and/or corporate espionage are primarily committed by individuals who may already be materially successful.

AGNEW: GENERAL STRAIN THEORY   A more modern version of strain theory is general strain theory. General strain theory was developed by Robert Agnew and tries to explain why individuals who feel stress and strain in their lives are more likely to commit crimes. Agnew's theory does not focus on economic success as the prominent goal in U.S. society, but instead offers a broader explanation of crime than focusing exclusively on the lower class. Agnew argues that crime is due to negative affective states. Negative affective states can include anger, frustration, disappointment, depression, and fear, which are obviously experienced by all classes.[28]

According to Agnew, these negative affective states are caused by several different sources of strain. First, strain can be caused by the failure to achieve positively valued goals. This is similar to the strain discussed by Merton in that it is the result of a disjunction between aspirations (i.e., what one aspires to) and expectations (i.e., what one can expect to achieve). Second, strain can be caused by the disjunction between expectations and achievements. This is different than the first source of strain because it does not focus on aspirations, but on expectations. This disjunction between expectations and achievements frequently occurs when people compare themselves to peers who seem to be doing better than them (e.g., financially or socially). Based on this disjunction, individuals may feel a sense of inequity. Third, strain can be caused by the removal of positively valued stimuli from the individual. This can include the loss of a boyfriend or girlfriend, the death of a relative, the loss of a job, or the divorce of parents, to name a few. Fourth, strain may be due to the presentation of negative stimuli. Examples of negative stimuli include family conflict, school failure, child abuse, and stressful life events. These sources of strain may have a cumulative effect on people in reality. The greater the intensity and frequency strain experiences become for an individual, the more likely the person is to turn to crime.[29]

There are several cyber crimes where general strain theory can be used as an explanation, especially cyberbullying and stalking. Middle and high school students who feel that they are not as popular or pretty as their peers may choose to gossip or make fun of them through social networking sites like Facebook as a means of dealing with the frustration they experience. For example, a young girl named Piper Smith, in Spanaway, Washington, was

BOX 3.3

Hacking/Spamming Scheme Used Stolen E-mail Account

In February 2017, a Florida man was sentenced for his role in a computer hacking and identity theft scheme that hijacked customer e-mail accounts to send bulk unsolicited or "spam" e-mails and generated more than $1.3 million in illegal profits.

Timothy Livingston, 31, of Boca Raton, Florida, was sentenced to serve 48 months in prison. Livingston previously pleaded guilty to one count each of conspiracy to commit fraud in connection with computers and access devices, conspiracy to commit fraud in connection with e-mail and aggravated identity theft.

According to admissions made in connection with his plea agreement, beginning as early as 2011, Livingston operated A Whole Lot of Nothing LLC—a business that specialized in sending spam e-mails on behalf of its clients. Livingston's clients included legitimate businesses, such as insurance companies that wished to send bulk e-mails to advertise their businesses, as well as illegal entities, such as online pharmacies that sold narcotics without prescriptions.

As part of his plea, Livingston admitted that beginning in January 2012, he solicited Tomasz Chmielarz to write computer programs that would send spam in a manner that concealed the true origin of the e-mail and bypassed filters. Livingston also used proxy servers and botnets to remain anonymous and evade spam blocking techniques. Livingston further admitted that he hacked into individual e-mail accounts and utilized corporate mail servers to further his spam campaigns, which enabled him to send out massive amounts of spam without identifying himself as the sender.

Which theory do you think applies best to this case?

Source: U.S. Department of Justice. (February 16, 2017). Florida Man Sentenced for Hacking, Spamming Scheme that Used Stolen Email Accounts. Retrieved from: https://www.justice.gov/opa/pr/florida-man-sentenced-hacking-spamming-scheme-used-stolen-email-accounts

horrified to learn that her sixth-grade classmates posted a cartoon on the video-sharing site YouTube titled "Top Six Ways to Kill Piper."[30] The video featured animated images of girls shooting her and poisoning her, although it is unclear why these girls posted the video. This sort of behavior from Piper's classmates is extreme, but could be a direct response to feelings of anger or frustration toward her.

Individuals who are rejected or jilted by a close friend or romantic partner can feel anger over this and find that the way to cope with this strain is to begin to send mean or threatening messages to get back at this person. For example, a young girl in Missouri named Megan Meier committed suicide as a consequence of receiving hurtful instant messages from a young man she met on the social networking site Myspace. They developed a relationship online, and he terminated it by sending Megan a hurtful message stating that the "world would be a better place without you in it."[31] These messages were actually sent by the mother of Megan's friend named Lori Drew, who created the fraudulent account as a means of getting retribution for slights against her child. This sort of behavior is another extreme example, but demonstrates that cyberstalking and harassment could be a result of strains.

SOCIAL PROCESS THEORIES

Social process theories focus on the relationship between socialization and crime. In particular, social process theories analyze the impact of certain factors such as peer group relationships, family relationships, and failure in school on crime. All of these factors are related to crime. Individuals who associate with criminal peers are at significant risk of committing crime themselves. Likewise, individuals who were brought up in an unnurturing, dysfunctional family are at greater risk of committing crime. Finally, individuals who drop out of school are also at risk for committing crime. Two branches of social process theory will be discussed in this section: learning theory and the social control theory of low self-control.

Learning Theory

According to learning theory, individuals commit crime, including computer crime, because they learn the attitudes, skills, and rationalizations necessary to commit these

---

BOX 3.4

Largest Known Computer Hacking and Securities Fraud Scheme

A Ukrainian hacker was sentenced on May 22, 2017, to 30 months in prison for his role in an international scheme to hack into three business newswires, steal yet-to-be published press releases containing nonpublic financial information, and use that information to make trades that generated approximately $30 million in illegal profits. Vadym Iermolovych, 29, of Kiev, Ukraine, previously pleaded guilty before U.S. District Judge Madeline Cox Arleo to a three-count information charging him with conspiracy to commit wire fraud, conspiracy to commit computer hacking, and aggravated identity theft.

Iermolovych admitted that he was personally involved in the hacks into Marketwired L.P. (Marketwired), PR Newswire Association LLC (PRN), and Business Wire. He admitted to hacking into PRN's network between January 2013 and March 2013. He also admitted that he obtained a set of user credentials of PRN employees stolen from a computer hack into a social networking Web site and then used at least one of those credentials to ultimately gain access into PRN's computer network. Iermolovych also admitted that he sold press releases stolen from the network intrusion into Marketwired, and purchased access into Business Wire's network, all in furtherance of a larger conspiracy to profit from the stolen draft press releases.

As alleged in the indictments, between February 2010 and August 2015, computer hackers based in Ukraine gained unauthorized access into the computer networks of the Victim Newswires. They used a series of targeted cyberattacks, including "phishing" attacks and SQL injection attacks, to gain access to the computer networks. The hackers moved through the computer networks and stole press releases about upcoming announcements by public companies concerning earnings, gross margins, revenues, and other confidential and material information.

The hackers shared the stolen releases with the traders using overseas computer servers that they controlled. In a series of e-mails, the hackers even shared "instructions" on how to access and use the overseas server where they shared the stolen releases with the traders, and the access credentials and instructions were distributed among the traders. The traders created "shopping lists" or "wish lists" for the hackers listing desired upcoming press releases for publicly traded companies from Marketwired and PRN.

The traders generally traded ahead of the public distribution of the stolen releases, and their trading activities shadowed the hackers' capabilities to exfiltrate stolen press releases. In order to execute their trades before the releases were made public, the traders sometimes had to execute trades in extremely short windows of time between when the hackers illegally accessed and shared the releases and when the press releases were disseminated to the public by the newswires, usually shortly after the close of the markets. Frequently, all of this activity occurred on the same day. Thus, the trading data often showed a flurry of trading activity around a stolen press release just prior to its public release.

The traders traded on stolen press releases containing material nonpublic information about hundreds of companies, including Align Technology Inc., Caterpillar Inc., Hewlett Packard, Home Depot, Panera Bread Co., and Verisign Inc.

The traders paid the hackers for access to the overseas servers based, in part, on a percentage of the money the traders made from their illegal trading activities. The hackers and traders used foreign shell companies to share the illegal trading profits.

In addition to the prison term, Judge Arleo sentenced Iermolovych to three years of supervised release and ordered him to pay restitution of $3,004,685.06.

Which theory do you think applies best to this case?

Source: U.S. Department of Justice. (May 22, 2017). Hacker Sentenced To 30 Months In Prison For Role In Largest Known Computer Hacking And Securities Fraud Scheme. Retrieved from: https://www.justice.gov/usao-nj/pr/hacker-sentenced-30-months-prison-role-largest-known-computer-hacking-and-securities acts. Many times this learning takes place in interaction with parents and peers. Criminals are different from noncriminals in the extent to which they have been exposed to definitions and situations that portray criminal acts as appropriate. There are four interrelated learning theories that will be discussed: Sutherland's differential association theory, Akers' social learning theory, Sykes and Matza's techniques of neutralization/drift theory, and subcultural theories.

SUTHERLAND: DIFFERENTIAL ASSOCIATION THEORY   The first learning theory to be presented is Sutherland's differential association theory. At the time of Sutherland's work, social structure theories such as strain were popular. However, he argued that criminal behavior is a function of learning, not the inability to obtain economic success. He presented nine formal propositions that demonstrate that social interaction and learning leads to criminal activity:[32]

1. *Criminal behavior is learned.*[33] Sutherland argued that criminality is not a function of a biological or psychological malady or a function of the social structure, but learning.

2. *Criminal behavior is learned in interaction with other persons in a process of communication.*[34] This communication is verbal and involves interaction with others.

3. *The principal part of the learning of criminal behavior occurs with intimate personal groups.*[35] Learning involves interaction with significant others, such as parents, siblings, and peers. Therefore, families and peers have the greatest influence on learning criminal behavior and attitudes. Sutherland did not see much of a role for movies and newspapers to serve as a medium to learn criminal behavior. However, Sutherland developed his theory prior to the development of television and video games.

4. *When criminal behavior is learned, the learning includes (1) techniques of committing the crime, which are sometimes very complicated, sometimes very simple, and (2) the specific directions of motives, drives, rationalizations, and attitudes.*[36] In the process of learning criminal behavior, an individual will learn how to commit the offense. The individual also learns the attitudes necessary to commit crimes as well as appropriate rationalizations that may justify his or her behavior.

5. *The specific direction of motives and drives is learned from definitions of the legal codes as favorable or unfavorable.*[37] Sutherland argued that an individual may be surrounded by persons who define the legal codes as rules to be observed. In this case, crime is unlikely because the individual believes the law is something to be followed. However, some individuals associate with people whose definitions of the legal code are favorable to the violation of the legal codes. Obviously, crime is much more likely in the latter situation.

6. *A person becomes criminal because of an excess of definitions favorable to violation of the law over definitions unfavorable to violation of the law.*[38] This is the principle of differential association. Sutherland argued that people learn definitions favorable and unfavorable to the violation of the law. When an individual, through association with others, has obtained more definitions that are favorable to the violation of the law than unfavorable, then crime is likely to occur. In other words, the individual has learned to commit certain crimes. This principle is important because it can help explain why criminals may think that some crimes are appropriate while others are not. For example, an individual may think that committing fraud via the Internet is appropriate, but robbery is wrong. How can this be justified? According to Sutherland, the individual has received enough definitions in interaction with others to believe that

committing fraud via the Internet is appropriate. On the other hand, the same individual has not received enough definitions to believe that committing robbery is appropriate as well. Think of definitions favorable to violation of the law on one side of a scale while definitions unfavorable to violation of the law are on the other side. If an individual receives enough definitions favorable to the violation of the law, then the balance will be tipped in favor of committing the crime. The balance can vary from offense to offense and action to action, however.

7. *Differential associations may vary in frequency, duration, priority, and intensity.*[39] Differential association varies on the quality and quantity of social interactions. Therefore, associations with criminal and noncriminal behavior vary in those respects. Frequency and duration mean that more attention will be paid by an individual to definitions obtained in interaction with those with whom they have frequent contact and have had contact with for a long period of time. Priority involves the importance of the relationship to the individual and the importance of criminal or noncriminal behavior to the individual. Intensity involves the prestige of the source of a criminal or noncriminal pattern and the emotional reactions related to the associations.[40]

8. *The process of learning criminal behavior by association with criminal and anticriminal patterns involves all of the mechanisms that are involved in any other learning.*[41] In other words, learning criminal behavior is not different from learning any other behavior.

9. *While criminal behavior is an expression of general needs and values, it is not explained by those, since noncriminal behavior is an expression of the same needs and values.*[42] Sutherland argued that thieves steal in order to obtain money, but workers work to obtain money as well. Therefore, one cannot say that an individual committed a criminal act in order to get money, because that is the same reason why another individual works at a restaurant. In other words, the need for money explains lawful as well as unlawful behavior.

Therefore, Sutherland argued that the accumulation of an excess of definitions obtained in interaction with intimate social groups which say it is OK to commit certain criminal acts leads to criminality.

QUICK FACTS

A "wanna-be-hacker" can find hundreds of Web sites with information and tutorials to learn the techniques and skills of modern-day hacking. In addition to Web sites, there are thousands of YouTube videos on how to hack a variety of electronic devices.

AKERS: SOCIAL LEARNING THEORY   The second learning theory to be presented is Akers' differential reinforcement theory. Sutherland did not apply a learning theory to his theory of differential association. Instead, he stated that criminal behavior is learned like any other behavior. He did not explain how other behavior or criminal behavior is learned.

Akers' social learning model is grounded in four principal components: differential association, definitions, differential reinforcement, and imitation.[43] These concepts are part of a dynamic and interactive process in which the components have effects on each other and reciprocal effects with behavior. The social learning process begins with the relationships individuals have with deviants and nondeviants. Akers defines differential association as "the process whereby one is exposed to normative definitions that are relatively more favorable or unfavorable to illegal or law-abiding behavior."[44] These interactions with others vary in frequency, duration, priority, and intensity, and are the context in which the other elements play a role. The most essential interactions are those involving intimate personal groups, such as family and friends. Secondary and distant reference groups also affect individual behavior by providing context. Individuals are more likely to commit deviant behavior if their patterns of differential association with these groups are involved in deviant behavior.[45]

As individuals are differentially exposed to others, they develop definitions that support or justify their behavior. Definitions are often viewed as an individual's attitude toward and perception of certain behaviors as either acceptable or unacceptable.[46] Definitions can be derived from moral or religious beliefs, from interaction and imitation of others, and through reinforcement of current beliefs. These definitions include justifications and excuses for deviant behavior that neutralize the potential negative ramifications of deviance. In the context of social learning theory, the more neutralizing and positive definitions an individual has toward deviance, the more likely he or she will be to commit deviance when opportunity is provided.[47]

While definitions support involvement in deviance, the balance between past, present, and expected future reinforcements and punishments shapes the likelihood of future deviant behavior. Specifically, behavior is more likely to occur when a reward is given (positive reinforcement) or an unpleasant stimulus is taken away (negative reinforcement). Individuals differentially experience multiple forms of reinforcement and punishment as a consequence of their behavior.[48] Social reinforcements can reward deviance, such as praise and encouragement from peers or changes in social status as a consequence of individual action. Nonsocial reinforcements are also pertinent, encompassing financial gains or losses, legal consequences, and physical harm or gains. Differential reinforcement measures are not frequently included in tests of social learning, though they are related to repeated behavior when measured.[49]

Finally, imitation refers to the commission of behavior after observing someone else committing similar behavior. Whether the person actually imitates a behavior depends on his or her peers, the behavior that he or she observes, and the differential reinforcements observed.[50] Imitation has its strongest role in the initiation stage of behavior and with younger samples. It becomes less influential as the behavior is repeated, as differential reinforcements and definitions play a more important role. Several studies have found strong effects for imitation, though this component is often absent in research due to its narrow role in the learning process and empirical overlap with differential association.[51]

Scholars have applied social learning theory to cybercrime with some success, primarily explaining forms of music or media piracy,[52] as well as a range of offenses including hacking and guessing passwords.[53] In addition, multiple studies have found strong support for a link between having deviant friends, deviant definitions, and cyber crime.[54]

The significance of differential reinforcement and imitation within the social learning model to account for cybercrime is limited. Research has found mixed results for imitation, as its effects vary based on the type of cybercrime committed. Imitation of family members influenced piracy, while teacher encouragement and electronic bulletin boards increased the likelihood of guessing passwords and other deviant acts.[55] These findings suggest that there may be significant value in the social learning theories to account for cyber crime.

SYKES AND MATZA: TECHNIQUES OF NEUTRALIZATION/DRIFT THEORY The third learning theory to be presented is Sykes and Matza's techniques of neutralization/drift theory. Sykes and Matza also argued that the process of becoming a criminal is a learning experience. They posited that most criminals hold conventional values, norms, and beliefs, but must learn to neutralize the values before committing crimes.[56] Most criminals are not committed to a criminal lifestyle and only commit criminal acts on rare occasions. However, these same criminals hold values and beliefs that state that criminal behavior is wrong. How can they commit criminal acts and still hold conventional values? The individuals use techniques of neutralization, which shield them from any sense of guilt. These techniques of neutralization allow individuals to drift into criminality and then back into conventional behavior. That is why this theory is sometimes referred to as drift theory. Sykes and Matza argue that the techniques of neutralization are learned and come before the criminal act. There are five techniques of neutralization:[57]

1. *Denial of responsibility:* This occurs when an individual states that his or her behavior was an accident or resulted from forces beyond his or her control, such as unloving parents, bad companions, or living in a criminogenic neighborhood.[58] Saying "I did not mean to do it" reflects denial of responsibility.

2. *Denial of injury:* This technique of neutralization occurs when an individual denies the wrongfulness of his or her action or believes the offense does not really cause any harm.[59] Saying "I did not really hurt anybody" reflects this technique of neutralization. This technique of neutralization can be applied to many instances of computer crime where the computer criminals do not feel that anybody is truly hurt by their criminal activity. An example can include the propagation of a worm that does not actually damage anything and is more of a nuisance than anything else. The computer criminal may argue that no one really got hurt.

3. *Denial of victim:* This occurs when an individual believes that the victim had it coming or the victim caused the offense to occur.[60] Saying "They had it coming to them" reflects denial of victim. This is certainly reflected in some computer crimes, especially recent malicious attacks on several companies' computers by ex-employees.

4. *Condemnation of the condemners:* This occurs when the individual shifts the blame to others by focusing attention on the motive and behavior of those who disapprove of his or her actions.[61] Basically, the individual is challenging those who are condemning the actions by arguing that the police are corrupt and parents take out their frustrations on their children. Asking "Why is everybody picking on me?" reflects this technique of neutralization.

5. *Appeal to higher loyalties:* This occurs when the individual's peer group takes precedence over the rules of society.[62] Saying "I did not do it for myself, but for my friends" reflects appeal to higher loyalties.

Cressey's classic work, *Other People's Money*, describing the cognitive processes experienced by his sample of convicted embezzlers, compares favorably to Sykes and Matza's attempt to explain youthful deviance in their techniques of neutralization/drift theory. Similar to the "techniques" employed by juveniles in order to escape or "drift" from the norms associated with conventional behavior, Cressey found that many of his sampled embezzlers had successfully "neutralized" their embezzlement prior to committing the actual crime by convincing themselves that they were only temporarily "borrowing" the money, or that he or she was justifiably "owed" the money in exchange for years of underpaid, faithful service to the employer.

Recent research on cyber piracy found that those who have developed definitions that support or neutralize responsibility for piracy behavior are more likely to illegally download media.[63] Data using college samples have found that those who engage in higher levels of piracy report greater acceptance of beliefs of neutralization focusing on denial of responsibility, injury, and victims.[64] For example, those who believe that it is okay to pirate music because they only want one or two songs from CDs (denial of responsibility) or believe that the creators of music are not going to lose any money (denial of victim) are more likely to engage in piracy.[65] Additionally, those who believe that law enforcement and universities do not care about piracy are also more likely to engage in piracy. Finally, those who strongly support the notion that it is acceptable to engage in piracy to provide materials to family or friends or use the resources to complete schoolwork or projects are much more likely to engage in piracy at extremely high levels.[66]

Similar evidence appears to account for the creation of malicious software and virus writing. Once confronted or apprehended because of their virus-writing activity, virus writers use the same justifications and excuses consistent with techniques of neutralization theory. A common statement by virus writers is that it is the computer user's or system's fault that the viruses infected, not the virus writer's (blaming the victim). They state that if the victims had their security up to par, they would not have become a victim in the first place. They also note that such neophytes have no business being online or using their computer if they do not know how to protect themselves. In fact, virus writers tend to show disdain for the average "Internet surfer." Another common theme in the comments of virus writers is that they are not really doing any harm and, in fact, are performing a public service by pointing out the security holes in the software and computer systems (denial of injury/denial of the victim). Some claim that there are not really any victims of viruses, and that such users are simply ill-prepared to conduct commerce or surf online. Another typical justification is that they are really doing good by showing the greed and incompetence of software vendors (especially Microsoft) and other corporations (condemn the condemners). Finally, many virus writers claim that they really did not intend to cause any harm by writing their virus. These techniques of neutralization can be seen in several of the anecdotal items contained in Chapter 7, especially the interview with the Dark Avenger. Taken as a whole, the techniques of neutralization may be significantly useful to account for cybercrimes.

BOX 3.5

Economic Espionage and Theft of a Trade Secret from U.S. Company by Former Employee

On May 19, 2017, Xu Jiaqiang, 31, formerly of Beijing, China, pleaded guilty to economic espionage and theft of a trade secret, in connection with Xu's theft of proprietary source code from Xu's former employer, with the intent to benefit the National Health and Family Planning Commission of the People's Republic of China. Xu pleaded guilty to all six counts with which he was charged.

From November 2010 to May 2014, Xu worked as a developer for a U.S. company. As a developer, Xu enjoyed access to certain proprietary software, as well as that software's underlying source code. The proprietary software is a clustered file system developed and marketed by the company in the United States and other countries. A clustered file system facilitates faster computer performance by coordinating work among multiple servers. The company took significant precautions to protect the proprietary source code as a trade secret. Among other things, the proprietary source code is stored behind a company firewall and can be accessed only by a small subset of the company's employees. Before receiving proprietary source code access, company employees must first request and receive approval from a company official. Company employees must also agree in writing at both the outset and the conclusion of their employment that they will maintain the confidentiality of any proprietary information. The company took these and other precautions in part because the proprietary software and the proprietary source code are economically valuable, which value depends in part on the proprietary source code's secrecy.

In May 2014, Xu voluntarily resigned from the company. Xu subsequently communicated with one undercover law enforcement officer ("UC-1"), who posed as a financial investor aiming to start a large data storage technology company, and another undercover law enforcement officer ("UC-2"), who posed as a project manager, working for UC-1. In these communications, Xu discussed his past experience with his prior company and indicated that he had experience with the proprietary software and the proprietary source code. On March 6, 2015, Xu sent UC-1 and UC-2 code, which Xu stated was a sample of his prior work with his prior company. A company employee later confirmed that the code sent by Xu included proprietary company material that related to the proprietary source code.

Xu subsequently informed UC-2 that he was willing to consider providing UC-2's company with the proprietary source code as a platform for UC-2's company to facilitate the development of its own data storage system. Xu informed UC-2 that if UC-2 set up several computers as a small network, then Xu would remotely install the proprietary software so that UC-1 and UC-2 could test it and confirm its functionality.

In or around early August 2015, the FBI arranged for a computer network to be set up, consistent with Xu's specifications. Files were then remotely uploaded to the FBI-arranged computer network (the "Xu Upload"). Thereafter, on or about August 26, 2015, Xu and UC-2 confirmed that UC-2 had received the Xu Upload. On December 7, 2015, Xu met with UC-2 at a hotel in White Plains, New York. Xu stated, in sum and substance, that he had used the proprietary source code to make software to sell to customers, that Xu knew the proprietary source code to be the product of decades of work on the part of his former company, and that Xu had used the proprietary source code to build a copy of the proprietary software.

Later on December 7, 2015, Xu met with UC-1 and UC-2 at the hotel. During that meeting, Xu showed UC-2 a copy of what Xu represented to be the proprietary source code on his laptop. Xu noted to UC-2 a portion of the code that indicated it originated with his former company as well as the date on which it had been copyrighted. Xu also stated that he had previously modified the proprietary source code's command interface to conceal the fact that the code originated with his former company and identified multiple specific customers to whom Xu had previously provided the proprietary software using Xu's stolen copy of the proprietary source code.

In connection with the economic espionage counts charged in the indictment, Xu stole, duplicated, and possessed the proprietary source code with the intent to benefit the National Health and Planning Commission of the People's Republic of China.

Xu pleaded guilty to three counts of economic espionage, each of which carries a maximum sentence of 15 years in prison, and three counts of theft of a trade secret, each of which carries a maximum sentence of 10 years in prison.

Which theory do you think applies best to this case?

Source: U.S. Department of Justice. (May 22, 2017). Chinese National Pleads Guilty to Economic Espionage and Theft of a Trade Secret From U.S. Company. Retrieved from: https://www.justice.gov/opa/pr/chinese-national-pleads-guilty-economic-espionage-and-theft-trade-secret-us-company-0

SUBCULTURAL THEORIES   A **subculture** is a set of values, norms, and beliefs that differ from the dominant culture. The main tenet of subculture theory is that criminals, including computer criminals, hold values, norms, and beliefs that are in opposition to those held in the dominant culture. These individuals behave in a manner that is consistent with their values, norms, and beliefs, which many times will bring them in conflict with the law. When originally developed, subculture theories attempted to explain gang formation and crime. However, certain types and examples of computer crime can be due to the existence of subcultures. Since there is significant debate over what constitutes a subculture, it may be best to approach the question by determining its main characteristics.

Defined from a broad sociological and criminological perspective, a subculture is any group having certain values, norms, traditions, and rituals that sets them apart from the dominant culture. This includes an emphasis on performing certain behaviors or developing skill sets, like confidence men learning to steal and bilk money from unsuspecting people.[67] Also, subcultural rules or codes of conduct exist that structure how individuals view and interact with different groups. A special argot or slang is present, as well as some outward symbols of membership like tattoos or informal uniforms.[68] These all provide ways to measure an individual's reputation, status, and adherence to the subculture.

This framework suggests membership in a subculture influences behavior by providing individuals with beliefs, goals, and values that approve of and justify particular types of activities, including crime. In the case of offender subcultures, the transmission of subcultural knowledge increases the likelihood of involvement in criminal behavior despite potential legal consequences for these actions. Thus, this is an important perspective to explain how the values and ideas espoused by members of a criminal subculture affect the behavior of its members.

Different types of subcultural frameworks have been developed and vary based on assumptions about the members' adherence to conventional norms and values. For example, Cohen used strain theory to explain the formation and persistence of gangs in the lower classes.[69] Males who could not achieve status through legitimate means in schools felt strained and rebelled against the middle-class values imposed on them. They established an alternative subculture allowing them to achieve status through the use of illegitimate means, including property and violent crime. Cohen's framework suggests that this subculture held behaviors and values in direct opposition to the middle-class values espoused by groups such as the school. As such, this perspective on subculture assumes an outright rejection of conventional norms and values.

Other frameworks do not require members of a subculture to perfectly adhere to its specific values. For instance, Wolfgang and Ferracuti[70] suggested a subculture of violence exists wherein individuals place great importance on their honor and use violence to defend it. According to their theory, this subculture does not require individuals to accept or approve of its norms for their behaviors to be influenced. Anyone may use lethal violence at any time, so all must be willing to respond to this threat in kind.

A similar argument has been made by Elijah Anderson in the book *Code of the Street*.[71] He suggests a code exists in inner-city communities that lead individuals to conform to a pattern of violent behavior on the streets in response to slights against their honor. Regardless of one's involvement in street life and its values, many conform to this code of behavior to navigate through their communities. Thus, a contrasting perspective indicates that subcultures can influence behavior without requiring individuals to adhere to their values.

Hackers and Learning Theories

By rejecting the goals and opportunities of the dominant culture, the hacker subculture provides the context in which hackers situate their actions. It forms their ethics and laws distinct from those of the dominant culture. There is strong evidence of the presence of a social scene, slang, and value system that defines boundaries between hackers and others. For example, the act of hacking is illegal under most conditions, yet the skill and ability needed to perform a hack is highly valued among hackers.[72] In addition, many hackers acknowledge their activities are illegal, but legitimize and justify the actions using various rationales, such as that their actions improve computer security. Thus, hackers place emphasis and value on activities directly contradicting the larger culture.

In addition, hackers have adapted the English language to create a unique slang. There also appears to be a hacker "scene," composed of "inside jokes, real-world meetings (cons), and hacker magazines ('zines)."[73] Understanding this "scene" is part of the enculturation process of hacker subculture, occurring through exchanges with other hackers either in person or online. Referencing these cultural elements permit individuals to measure their status as a hacker against others. Status can also be determined through a great deal of debate over what constitutes a "hacker" as well as motives for hacking, such as curiosity or revenge.[74] These debates create boundaries between hackers, as well as the general computer using public, based on knowledge, skill, and status.[75]

Research on the hacker subculture has found that there are three consistent ideas or values that guide hacker behavior: technology, secrecy, and mastery. One of the most recognized elements of hacker subculture is its relationship to technology. Both the hack and hacker could not exist without technology, and an intimate connection between the individual and technology facilitates the ability to hack.[76] To generate such a connection, hackers must develop "an easy, if not all-consuming, relationship" with computer and communications technology and a willingness to explore and apply it in new ways.[77]

The more closely an individual is connected to technology, the greater his or her ability to understand and perform hacks. Those who can perform "true hacks" have a deep comprehension of computers and programming, allowing them to identify and fix security flaws.[78] Conversely, "derivative hacks" involve the use of prewritten scripts or codes to access flaws without actually understanding how the technology works. Less-skilled hackers, especially those called "script kiddies," are more likely to perform a "derivative hack." Hence, the hacker's relationship to technology can generate status: Those who complete "true hacks" are revered and praised, and the "derivative hack" user is often made fun of or rejected by others.[79]

The importance of technology is also related to the significance of secrecy in hacker subculture. Secrecy is important for several reasons. First, it is a motive for hacking in that many hackers abhor keeping certain types of information private.[80] This fuels many attempts by hackers to remove barriers to certain kinds of information, such as government and technological data. Incidents involving Julian Assange, founder of WikiLeaks, and Edward Snowden, former National Security Agency contractor, are examples of this activity. Second, subcultural members place great emphasis on secrecy because hacking is an illegal act. Hacker activities are kept secret to avoid unwanted attention from various parts of the "establishment," including the criminal justice system.[81] Thus, anonymity is indispensable to the subculture and is the reason hackers create virtual identities online via a screen name or "handle."[82] This protects the hacker's actual identity while engaged in hacking.

However, there is also some ambivalence about secrecy in hacker subculture. Successful hacking creates a desire to brag and share accumulated hacking knowledge. This can help an individual gain status within the hacker community, but places them at risk for law enforcement detection.[83] Hackers tread a fine line between sharing information and keeping certain knowledge private. Those who can successfully navigate this line can also gain some status in the hacker community. Demonstrating a commitment to secrecy is a benchmark for how well one lives up to the image and nature of hacking. True hackers are capable of keeping secrets, creating an ideal for hackers to aspire to; thus, secrecy reinforces and maintains boundaries between hackers.[84]

Status is also tied to another important element of the culture: the idea of mastery. Mastery is a complex element that involves continual learning of new skills that individuals demonstrate to their peers.[85] For example, hackers taunt and challenge the ability of others while online. This frequently leads hackers to use their knowledge and skill to gain control over another individual's system, or take "root" in a system.[86]

Such a demonstration of mastery can increase a hacker's status, as can displays of knowledge of hacker subculture. When communicating with other hackers, especially through Web forums, individuals may refer to the history of hacking, use slang, or reference other important parts of the hacking scene.[87] These references appear to illustrate the intensity of individual connections to hacker subculture and their relative status. The agreed-upon values of the hacker community provide the social context for the hacking activities that violate the standards of the normative culture. The disjunction between the morals of the hacker subculture and the morals of normative society helps to define the activities of "criminal hackers."

Virus Writers and Learning Theories

Social process theories are probably best when used to explain the crimes committed by virus writers and those who propagate and spread viruses. The first empirical observation to take into account when examining the phenomenon of why people engage in virus writing is that there is no common profile of a "typical" virus writer. As discussed in Chapter 7, a common misperception is that virus writers are 13-year-old brainiacs who unleash their wrath on society for no apparent reason. In reality, a virus writer could be that kid or a 35-year-old computer programmer looking to increase his or her salary. This tends to limit the explanatory power of social structure theories, because virus writers can come from many walks of life and are typically wealthy enough to afford the computer machinery necessary to practice their trade. Furthermore, not all virus writers are in it for the money or for the fame. The reasons why virus writers write and propagate viruses can be for money, fame, attention, competition, and simply for a perverse sense of fun.

What is undeniable in the development of a virus writer is that a certain level of technical competency is required. While it is true that virus creation tools exist that make it easier to write viruses, one does not become a virus writer overnight. As such, all virus writers must learn how to write and propagate viruses. The learning process that they go through is similar to any other learning process. The learning includes learning how to write the code necessary to create a virus, but as important is learning how to become a good virus writer. In the world of virus writers, competition and bravado play an important role in conditioning the person, as does learning the tools and tactics of the trade. Some writers do so to prove their computer programming capability. Anecdotal, yet unproven, stories of virus writers who have programmed a "quality" virus and found fame and fortune as the result of their prowess abound. Other virus writers achieve fame because their virus infects a large number of computers and makes it into the media spotlight. However, prior to the fame and supposed fortune of the virus writer, the person goes through a learning and social conditioning process.

When the writer first enters the world of the virus writers, they are treated with disdain and as the newcomer that they are. If they enter chat rooms and exchange information and curiosity about virus writing, they are often ridiculed and subjected to a social conditioning process where they learn the practice through trial and error, and also learn how to be a better virus writer or face ridicule from their peers. Once they have established their reputation, they often engage in banter with other self-proclaimed virus writers. They learn to show their accomplishments and show others how successful their virus is "in the wild." Others receive financial rewards and eventually develop into for-profit virus writers. Still others enjoy the thrill of infecting other people's machines, hacking into secure systems via their Trojan horses, and enjoy reading about their exploits online and in the media.

Nonetheless, they all share a common learning experience in order to ply their trade. This learning experience is unique compared to other forms of criminal learning in that the significant peers who teach them will likely never see them face to face. Most of the learning takes place in chat rooms, on bulletin boards, and via distance learning. As social learning theory posits, the learning is reinforced both positively and negatively over its course, which serves to reinforce the technical competency of the virus writers. Positive reinforcement includes the thrill experienced by propagating the virus and infecting systems; it can also include notoriety and kudos received from their peer group—like graffiti writers, they also love to see their moniker appearing with their work—and, finally, there can be financial rewards. Negative reinforcements include receiving hostility from other virus writers (eventually ending up with an online competition to hack the other's system), receiving ridicule and disdain for their viruses and exploits online, and being sought out by law enforcement. If caught, they may discontinue their activity, but the other forms of negative reinforcement they receive may serve to make them want to become more proficient.

Social Control Theory

Social control theory seeks to answer the question, "Why *don't* individuals commit crime?" Social control theory assumes that people will violate the law. So why don't they? The answer to this question, according to social control theorists, lies in the strength of an individual's ties to conventional individuals and society. Those who have close ties with their families and noncriminal friends as well as those who possess high self-esteem are unlikely to commit criminal acts. These individuals are bonded to the larger society. Individuals who are not bonded to the larger social order are free from constraints to violate the law.

GOTTFREDSON AND HIRSCHI: SELF-CONTROL THEORY   In a later control theory, Gottfredson and Hirschi argue that a person's tendency to commit crime can be found in his or her level of self-control.[88] Self-control involves a person's ability to control his or her own behavior. Basically, they proposed that individuals who commit crime have limited self-control. These people have a tendency to be impulsive, insensitive, and focused on immediate gratification.

What causes people to have limited self-control? Gottfredson and Hirschi argue that lack of self-control is caused by inadequate child rearing.[89] Self-control, according to Gottfredson and Hirschi, is instilled in people by age 8 and is relatively constant thereafter. They suggested that parents must be willing to monitor their child's behavior, to recognize inappropriate behavior when it occurs, and to punish the inappropriate behavior.[90] If this occurs consistently, the child will develop a high level of self-control. Over time, the child will internalize the monitoring by the parents. If the parents are unwilling or unable to do this, then it is likely that their children will lack self-control. When this occurs, criminal activity is likely—however, not guaranteed.

Gottfredson and Hirschi also integrated elements of rational choice theory into the development of their theory. Individuals with low self-control must be presented with the opportunities to commit criminal acts in order for crime to occur. If an individual has low self-control but there is no criminal opportunity, then crime will not take place. On the other hand, if criminal opportunity presents itself to an individual with low self-control, then crime is likely to occur.

Cybercrime scholarship has found that individuals with low levels of self-control are more likely to view online pornography.[91] Additionally, researchers have found a significant relationship between low self-control and cyber piracy in college student populations.[92] This evidence suggests that college students with low self-control cannot resist the temptation of pirating software and music that they are interested in due to the fact that they do not see the consequences of their behavior.

Early research on self-control in the hacker community finds that this theory may have limited applicability. A study using a sample of active hackers at multiple computer security conferences and in a university setting found that both groups had high levels of self-control.[93] In addition, the active hackers had higher levels of self-control than those inside the university. This may be a reflection of the general traits required to become a skilled hacker, including a capacity to learn, diligence, and forethought as discussed in Chapter 4. In turn, their hacks may be more complex, utilizing persistent and unique attacks against specific targets. As a consequence, it may be that computer hackers have higher levels of self-control than both street and cyber criminals.

TERRORISM AND POLITICAL THEORY

The term "terrorism" has been defined in a number of ways by a variety of scholars. For the most part, each definition has yielded a limited understanding of the actual phenomenon. This is particularly true when analyzing the current wave of international and technological situations in contemporary global affairs, such as those occurring in the Middle East and those involving cyber crime and cyber terrorism. In the popular mind, terrorism is viewed as the illegitimate and violent actions of specific groups that violate the authority of rightfully established political entities.[94] Terrorism, in general, always has a political agenda. This agenda may be motivated by various political ideologies, separatist ethnic movements, or radical religious philosophies, but always the purpose of achievement is a specific set of political objectives. Although vague, as to explaining who terrorists are, this definition does provide a conceptual framework concerning what terrorism is.[95] It can be reduced, simply to a choice among violent means—not a choice between violence and nonviolence, but a manifestation of violence against people to achieve a goal.

By extension, terrorists often apply extreme, random acts of violence against the innocent (e.g., attacks on symbolic institutions, such as schools, churches, and synagogues; bombings of common gathering places, such as cafés, shopping malls, and office buildings; and the killing of individuals who represent legitimate governments such as soldiers, police officers, and political leaders), in an attempt to instill fear in the general population. Thus, terrorism is used as a methodology for political action. As Hoffman argues, terrorism is fundamentally and inherently "political." Terrorism is "ineluctably

BOX 3.6

Members of a Cybercrime Organization Net More than $55 Million in Proceeds

On February 10, 2017, Ercan Findikoglu, a Turkish citizen, also known by the online nicknames "Segate," "Predator," and "Oreon," was sentenced to eight years for his leadership role in organizing and carrying out three cyberattacks on the global financial system between 2011 and 2013 that caused more than $55 million in losses. Findikoglu pleaded guilty on March 1, 2016, to computer intrusion conspiracy, access device fraud conspiracy, and effecting transactions with unauthorized access devices. In addition, as part of the sentence, the Court ordered Findikoglu to pay $55,080,226.14 in restitution.

Findikoglu and his co-conspirators used sophisticated intrusion techniques to hack into the systems of credit and debit card processing companies, manipulated network administrator privileges at the victim card processing companies, manipulated account balances of prepaid debit cards to eliminate withdrawal limits on those cards, and stole the personal identification numbers (PINs) associated with the compromised debit cards. Findikoglu and his co-conspirators then disseminated the stolen card numbers and PINs worldwide to trusted associates who encoded magnetic stripe cards with the compromised debit card data. The associates then distributed these cards to teams of cashing crews, who used the cards to make fraudulent ATM withdrawals on a massive scale across the globe. As a result of the effective elimination of withdrawal limits, these cyberattacks were known as "unlimited operations."

Findikoglu organized and carried out three such unlimited operations. In the first operation on February 27 and 28, 2011, Findikoglu's cashing crews withdrew approximately $10 million through approximately 15,000 fraudulent ATM withdrawals in 18 countries. In the second operation on December 21 and 22, 2012, Findikoglu's cashing crews withdrew approximately $5 million through approximately 5,000 fraudulent ATM withdrawals in 20 countries. During this second operation, in New York alone, cashers conducted more than 700 fraudulent ATM withdrawals, totaling nearly $400,000 in losses, at more than 140 different ATM locations over the course of just two and a half hours. In the third operation on February 19 and 20, 2013, Findikoglu's cashing crews withdrew approximately $40 million through approximately 36,000 fraudulent ATM withdrawals in 24 countries. During this third operation, in New York alone, cashers conducted nearly 3,000 fraudulent ATM withdrawals, totaling approximately $2.4 million in losses, over the course of approximately 10 hours.

Findikoglu was paid a significant portion of the illegal proceeds from these unlimited operations.

Which theory do you think applies best to this case?

Source: U.S. Department of Justice. (February 10, 2017). Leader Of Three Worldwide Cyberattacks Sentenced To 8 Years For Computer Intrusion And Access Device Fraud Conspiracies. Retrieved from: https://www.justice.gov/usao-edny/pr/leader-three-worldwide-cyberattacks-sentenced-8-years-computer-intrusion-and-access

about power: the pursuit of power, the acquisition of power, and the use of power to achieve political change. Terrorism is thus violence—or, equally important, the threat of violence—used and directed in pursuit of, or in service of, a *political aim*."[96]

The psychological, economic, strategic, and political consequences of violence associated with terrorism are often much more prominent than the attack itself. Short-term effects of terrorism involve an immediate psychological effect on society, but are relatively benign compared to the long-term impact, which includes a widespread realization of vulnerability. In fact, the consequences of terrorism tend to have a higher value as time goes on.[97] For instance, the economic impact of the September 11, 2001, attack on the World Trade Center buildings was first estimated at a real cost of just over $10 billion. However, looking at the much more involved secondary costs—such as loss of service, impact on the stock market, declining investor sentiment, economic failure of the airline industry, rebuilding of structures, and loss in tourism dollars to the world and, specifically, New York—the estimated cost exceeds $2 trillion.[98] Essentially, the real impact of terrorist events can be measured in the creation of an atmosphere of chaos, fear, and panic in the target population.

No one understood this phenomenon better than Karl Marx. He argued in his early work (in 1887) that political change could not be achieved without conflict.[99] Indeed, he believed that epochs of history changed as groups of people bound by loss of status and class revolted against ruling elites. In Marxist thought, successful revolutionary strategy began with a core group of leading individuals dedicated to the cause. This group, the vanguard, represented the frontlines of violent activity. It was the express purpose of the vanguard to violently confront private property owners and wealthy elites with the opposite elements that maintained their ruling status—replace trust, order, and security with chaos, fear, and panic. To the dedicated Marxist, the vanguard represented contemporary terrorist groups.

Interestingly, a century and a half later, Franz Fanon argued that no government would willingly give up power and wealth; therefore, this power and wealth had to be taken violently. Fanon suggested that the international act of colonization was in itself an act of violence and thus had to be confronted with violence.[100] Accordingly, governments under attack must respond with stricter measures against the general public (the masses). Since there is no clearly identifiable enemy, governments must resort to more harsh and brutal treatment of the indigenous population in order to ferret out the hardcore vanguard members. Constitutional rights become suspended, unwarranted searches become commonplace, torture replaces interrogation, and innocence gives way to presumption of guilt. At the point when the rule of law erodes and the masses react against the ruling government, revolution begins, spurring yet another epoch in human history. To Marx, contemporary terrorists represent the vanguard.[101]

The acts of terrorism aimed at critical information infrastructure (what we call "cyberterrorism" or "cyber terrorism") are simply new tactics to accomplish the same end. The modern and complex societies of today are built on information exchange, global processing, and reliance on computerization and telecommunication. What were supposed to be the hallmarks of advanced societies to increase democratic and free thought have now become huge vulnerabilities. Government and business depend on these critically vital systems, making them prize targets for individuals aimed at destroying normalcy. To compound the problem, these systems have been built by information elites that control them. Government and society have been more than happy to place the burden of development and maintenance of computer systems with a few individuals having narrow educational fields and a keen understanding of complex information systems. Indeed, there has been safety in the fact that few of the masses actually understood much of the critical infrastructure on which our society depended upon for vital existence.

All of that changed, however, as the interconnectivity of systems became commonplace through the marvels of the World Wide Web and the Internet. Heretofore closed and secured systems became vulnerable to outside attack, relatively unsophisticated juvenile hackers could close down business enterprise with seeming ease, and the "experts" were mystified in ways to prevent such attacks. Cyber terrorism has become a reality as sophisticated terrorists understand new tactics that can render airplanes helpless to navigate, force railroads and commuter trains to stop, make electric and water plants idle, and stop local and global communication. In the past, having a tactic that could do so much damage was relatively closed to terrorist groups. Today, they provide some of the most frightful and devastating scenarios relating not only to specific violent actions but also to the extreme vulnerability of our country and our world. Terrorism that attacks our critical information infrastructure may not only attack our country but also attack the world in one massive strike. Retrospectively, Karl Marx may well have been correct. It will be through force that revolution is sparked and accomplished; it is specific acts of violence (and terrorism) that will erode safety, security, and peace and substitute chaos, fear, and panic.[102]

Summary

In this chapter, the major criminological theories that can or have been used to explain cyber crime have been presented. Several different areas of criminological thought can be used to explain cyber crime. First, it can be argued that some computer criminals commit their offenses due to rational choice and a lack of fear of apprehension. Second, it can be argued that restricted moral development and the presentation of a personality disorder may lead a person to commit cyber crime.

Third, strain and subculture theories can be applied to cyber crime. Fourth, learning and social control theories can explain some types of cyber crime as well. Fifth, political theory can be used to explain acts of terrorism. Although little theoretical development has occurred in the area of cyber crime, several current criminological theories have been applied with some success to this phenomenon, including piracy, hacking, cyberstalking, and harassment.

Review Questions

1. According to choice theory, why do individuals commit cyber crime?
2. What are the major assumptions of deterrence theory?
3. Which psychological theories can be applied to cyber crime?
4. What are the five modes of adaptation according to Merton? Which is most likely to lead to the commission of cyber crime?
5. What are the nine propositions presented by Sutherland?
6. What are the four elements of Akers' social learning theory?
7. How does self-control affect cyber crime?

Critical Thinking Exercises

1. Go to the press releases (https://www.justice.gov /criminal-ccips/ccips-press-releases) maintained by the Computer Crime and Intellectual Property Section of the Criminal Division of the U.S. Department of Justice. Go to the current month and click on the title of a press release that interests you. Read the press release and identify the theory covered in this chapter that best explains the cyber crime described in the press release. Be sure to justify your choice of theory with specific facts from the case.
2. Using a search engine, find an article that describes a cyber crime that has occurred in the past month. Read the article and identify the theory covered in this chapter that best explains the cyber crime described in the article. Be sure to justify your choice of theory with specific facts from the case.

Endnotes

1. SIEGEL, L.J. (1992). *Criminology: Theories, Patterns, and Typologies,* 4th ed. St. Paul, MN: West.
2. MARTINSON, R. (1974). "What Works? Questions and Answers About Prison Reform." *The Public Interest* 35: 22–54.
3. COHEN, L. and FELSON, M. (1979). "Social Change and Crime Rate Trends: A Routine Activities Approach." *American Sociological Review* 44: 588–608.
4. *Ibid.*
5. *Ibid.*
6. *Ibid.*
7. SAMPSON, R.J. and LAURITSEN, J.L. (1990). "Deviant Lifestyles, Proximity to Crime, and the Offender-Victim Link in Personal Violence." *Journal of Research in Crime and Delinquency* 27: 110–139.
8. LAURITSEN, J.L., LAUB, J.H., and SAMPSON, R.J. (1992). "Conventional and Delinquent Activities: Implications for the Prevention of Violent Victimization Among Adoles-

cents." *Violence and Victims* 7: 91–108; ZHANG, L., WELTE, J.W., and WIECXOREK, W.F. (2001). "Deviant Lifestyle and Crime Victimization." *Journal of Criminal Justice* 29: 133–143.

9. MELL, P., KENT, K., and NUSBAUM, J. (2005). *Guide to Malware Incident Prevention and Handling: Recommendations of the National Institute of Standards and Technology.* Washington, D.C.: National Institute of Standards and Technology.

10. HOLT, T.J. and BOSSLER, A.M. (2009). "Examining the Applicability of Lifestyle-Routine Activities Theory for Cybercrime Victimization." *Deviant Behavior* 30(1): 1–25.

11. BOSSLER, A.M. and Holt, T.J. (2008). "Examining the Utility of Routine Activities Theory for Cybercrime." Paper presented at the American Society of Criminology meetings, Atlanta, GA.

12. KADISH, S.H. and PAULSEN, M.G. (1969). *Criminal Law and Its Processes.* Boston, MA: Little, Brown, p. 85.

13. WALKER, S. (1998). *Sense and Nonsense About Crime and Drugs: A Policy Guide,* 4th ed. Belmont, CA: West/Wadsworth.

14. *Ibid.*

15. *Ibid.*

16. PATERNOSTER, R. (1987). "The Deterrent Effect of Perceived and Severity of Punishment: A Review of the Evidence and Issues." *Justice Quarterly* 42: 173–217.

17. GREEN, D. (1989). "Measures of Illegal Behavior in Individual-Level Deterrence Research." *Journal of Research in Crime and Delinquency* 26: 253–275.

18. HOLLINGER, R.C. (1992). "Crime by Computer: Correlates of Software Piracy and Unauthorized Account Access." *Security Journal* 2(1): 2–12; SKINNER, W.F. and FREAM, A.M. (1997). "A Social Learning Theory Analysis of Computer Crime Among College Students." *Journal of Research in Crime and Delinquency* 34(4): 495–518.

19. *Ibid.*

20. *Ibid.*

21. KOHLBERG, L. (1969). *Stages in the Development of Moral Thought and Action.* New York: Holt, Rinehart and Winston.

22. HENGGELER, S. (1989). *Delinquency in Adolescence.* Newbury Park, CA: Sage.

23. GLUECK, S. and GLUECK, E. (1950). *Unraveling Juvenile Delinquency.* New York: Commonwealth Fund.

24. America Psychiatric Association. (2000). *Diagnostic and Statistical Manual of Mental Disorders,* DSM-IV-TR, 4th ed. New York: American Psychiatric Publishing, p. 645.

25. America Psychiatric Association. (2013). *Diagnostic and Statistical Manual of Mental Disorders,* DSM-5. Washington, D.C.: American Psychiatric Association.

26. MERTON, R.K. (1968). *Social Theory and Social Structure.* Glencoe, IL: The Free Press.

27. *Ibid.*

28. AGNEW, R. (1992). "Foundation for a General Strain Theory of Crime and Delinquency." *Criminology* 30: 47–87.

29. *Ibid.*

30. HAHN, E. (2009). "Girls Post Online Cartoon on How to Kill Classmate." *MSNBC.* Retrieved June 1, 2009, from *http://www.msnbc.msn.com/id/30881980/*

31. CATHCART, R. (2008). "MySpace Is Said to Draw Subpoena in Hoax Case." *The New York Times.*

32. SUTHERLAND, E.H. and CRESSEY, D.R. (1978). *Criminology,* 10th ed. Philadelphia, PA: J.B. Lippincott Co., pp. 77–83.

33. *Ibid.*

34. *Ibid.*

35. *Ibid.*

36. *Ibid.*

37. *Ibid.*

38. *Ibid.*

39. *Ibid.*

40. *Ibid.*

41. *Ibid.*

42. *Ibid.*

43. AKERS, R.L. (1998). *Social Learning and Social Structure: A General Theory of Crime and Deviance.* Boston, MA: Northeastern University Press.

44. AKERS, R.L. (2001). "Social Learning Theory." In R. PATTERNOSTER and R. BACHMAN (eds.), *Explaining Criminals and Crime: Essays in Contemporary Criminological Theory.* Los Angeles, CA: Roxbury.

45. AKERS, R.L. and JENSEN, G.F. (2006). "The Empirical Status of Social Learning Theory of Crime and Deviance: The Past, Present, and Future." In F.T. CULLEN, J.P. WRIGHT, and K.R. BLEVINS (eds.), *Taking Stock: The Status of Criminological Theory.* New Brunswick, NJ: Transaction Publishers.

46. *Ibid.*

47. *Ibid.*

48. *Ibid.*

49. *Ibid.*

50. *Ibid.*

51. *Ibid.*

52. HIGGINS, G.E. (2005). "Can Low Self-Control Help with the Understanding of the Software Piracy Problem?" *Deviant Behavior* 26(1): 1–24; HIGGINS, G.E. (2006). "Gender Differences in Software Piracy: The Mediating Roles of Self-Control Theory and Social Learning Theory." *Journal of Economic Crime Management* 4(1): 1–30; HIGGINS, G.E., FELL, B.D., and AL. WILSON. (2006). "Digital Piracy: Assessing the Contributions of an Integrated Self-Control Theory and Social Learning Theory Using Structural Equation Modeling." *Criminal Justice Studies* 19(1): 3–22; HIGGINS, G.E., FELL, B.D., and WILSON, A.L. (2007). "Low Self-Control and Social Learning in Understanding Students' Intentions to Pirate Movies in the United States." *Social Science Computer Review* 25(3): 339–357; HIGGINS, G.E. and DAVID A.M. (2004a). "Self-Control, Deviant Peers, and Software Piracy." *Psychological Reports* 95: 921–931; HIGGINS, G.E. and MAKIN, D.A. (2004b). "Does Social Learning Theory Condition the Effects of Low Self-Control on College Students' Software Piracy?" *Journal of Economic Crime Management* 2(2): 1–22; HIGGINS, G. E. and WILSON, A.L. (2006). "Low Self-Control, Moral Beliefs, and Social Learning Theory in University Students' Intentions to Pirate Software." *Security Journal* 19: 75–92;

HIGGINS and WILSON, "Low Self-Control and Social Learning in Understanding Students' Intentions to Pirate Movies in the United States."

53. *Ibid.*, p. 18.

54. *Ibid.*

55. *Ibid.*

56. SYKES, G.M. and MATZA, D. (1957). "Techniques of Neutralization: A Theory of Delinquency." *American Sociological Review* 22: 664–670.

57. *Ibid.*

58. *Ibid.*

59. *Ibid.*

60. *Ibid.*

61. *Ibid.*

62. *Ibid.*

63. For example, see INGRAM, J.R. and HINDUJA, S. (2008). "Neutralizing Music Piracy: An Empirical Examination." *Deviant Behavior* 29: 334–366.

64. *Ibid.*

65. *Ibid.*

66. *Ibid.*

67. MAURER, D.W. (1974). *The American Confidence Man.* Springfield, IL: Thomas.

68. SIMMONS, J.L. (1985). "The Nature of Deviant Subcultures." In E. RUBINGTON and M.S. WEINBERG (eds.), *Deviance: The Interactionist Perspective.* New York: Macmillan.

69. COHEN, A.K. (1955). *Delinquent Boys: The Culture of the Gang.* Glencoe, IL: Free Press.

70. WOLFGANG, M.E. and FERRACUTI, F. (1967). *The Subculture of Violence: Towards an Integrated Theory in Criminology.* London: Tavistock Publications.

71. ANDERSON, E. (1999). *Code of the Street.* Philadelphia, PA: W. W. Norton.

72. THOMAS, D. (2002). *Hacker Culture.* Minneapolis, MN: University of Minnesota Press; HOLT, T.J. (2007). "Subcultural Evolution? Examining the Influence of On- and Off-Line Experiences on Deviant Subcultures." *Deviant Behavior* 28(2): 171–198.

73. LOPER, D.K. (2000). "The Criminology of Computer Hackers: A Qualitative and Quantitative Analysis." Doctoral Dissertation, Michigan State University, *Dissertation Abstracts International* 61-08, Section: A, p. 3362.

74. JORDAN, T. and TAYLOR, P. (1998). "A Sociology of Hackers." *The Sociological Review* 46(4): 757–780.

75. HOLT, "Subcultural Evolution?"

76. *Ibid.*

77. *Ibid.*, p. 93.

78. *Ibid.*, p. 91.

79. *Ibid.*

80. *Ibid.*

81. *Ibid.*, p. 93.

82. *Ibid.*

83. *Ibid.*

84. *Ibid.*

85. *Ibid.*

86. *Ibid.*, p. 91.

87. *Ibid.*

88. GOTTFREDSON, M. and HIRSCHI, T. (1990). *A General Theory of Crime.* Stanford, CA: Stanford University Press.

89. *Ibid.*

90. *Ibid.*

91. BUZZELL, B., FOSS, D., and MIDDLETON, Z. (2006). "Explaining Use of Online Pornography: A Test of Self-Control Theory and Opportunities for Deviance." *Journal of Criminal Justice and Popular Culture* 13: 96–116.

92. HIGGINS, "Can Low Self-Control Help with the Understanding of the Software Piracy Problem?"; HIGGINS, FELL, and WILSON, "Digital Piracy"; HIGGINS and MAKIN "Self-Control, Deviant Peers, and Software Piracy."

93. HOLT, T.J. and KILGER, M. (2008). "Techcrafters and Makecrafters: A Comparison of Two Populations of Hackers." Information Security Threats Data Collection and Sharing 2008. WISTDCS '08.

94. TAYLOR, R.W. and VANDEN, H.E. (September 1982). "Defining Terrorism in El Salvador: La Matanza." *The Annals of the American Academy of Political and Social Sciences* 463: 1.

95. See SCHULZ, R. (Spring/Summer 1978). "Conceptualizing Political Terrorism: A Typology." *Journal of International Affairs* 4: 8; HOFFMAN, B. (1998). *Inside Terrorism.* New York: Columbia University Press.

96. HOFFMAN, *Inside Terrorism*, p. 2.

97. See CRENSHAW, M. (1998). "The Logic of Terrorism: Terrorist Behavior as a Product of Strategic Choice." In W. REICH (ed.), *Origins of Terrorism: Psychologies, Theologies, and States of Mind.* Princeton, NJ: The Woodrow Wilson International Center for Scholars.

98. Institute for the Analysis of Global Security-IAGS, 2004.

99. MARX, K. (1887). *Das Capital.* Moscow: Progress Publishers.

100. See FANON, F. (1963). *The Wretched of the Earth.* New York: Grove Press; FANON, F. (1965). *A Dying Colonialism.* New York: Grove Press.

101. COHEN-AMAGOR, R. (Summer 1991). "Foundations of Violence, Terror and War in the Writings of Marx, Engels, and Lenin." *Terrorism and Political Violence* 1(2): 1–24.

102. MARX, KARL. From his speech at Amsterdam in 1872.

Hackers

CHAPTER OBJECTIVES

After completing this chapter, you should be able to

- Distinguish between computer crime, criminal hacking, and noncriminal hacking.
- Explain why hackers think that the term "hacker" does not refer to criminals.
- Identify hype and exaggeration of hacking incidents found in the media.
- Recognize the role media hype plays in influencing young hackers.
- Classify hackers into broad categories based on activities and expression of ideas in online communication or statements made in person.
- Describe the role of technology that drives the hacker subculture.
- Explain how subcultural status depends on an understanding of technology achieved by the hacker and his or her knowledge of the ethics and values held by hackers.
- Predict hacker actions based on their type.
- Understand how the perceptions of hacking have changed based on shifts in hacker activity over time.

INTRODUCTION: WHAT IS A HACKER?

At this point in most texts, a reader might expect to see a quick definition of a hacker. In some sense, this entire chapter is the definition of "hacker." Originally, the word "hacker" referred to an unorthodox problem solver and master programmer; in fact, these original hackers made the machines and the programs that are vital to modern society.[1] Recognizing this fact, some media sources have championed terms like "computer cracker" and "black hat" to describe criminal hackers. Some sources even directly equate cybercriminals and hackers. The consensus of computer crime experts is that most cybercriminals are insiders to the victim organization, not hackers seeking to gain entry.[2] One thing that is clear is that there is no universal agreement as to the meaning of the word "hacker" or "computer (cyber) criminal." However, there is a *popular* consensus that hackers are bad people who do bad things.[3]

This chapter presents a view of hackers that is intended to assist investigators and law enforcement officer in understanding the way hackers think. Many descriptions of motive and interpretation of hacker actions come directly from hackers (particularly juvenile hackers) themselves. At no time should this chapter be read to condone breaking the law.

Although sympathetic to a hacker's sensibilities, it is not sympathetic to harm caused intentionally or through negligence. Hackers have established their own set of values; these values often conflict with the laws and values of the greater society. Rather than simply reaffirm our distaste for the illegal actions of some hackers, this chapter presents the hacker's understanding of these actions in an attempt to help investigators predict, effectively investigate, and appropriately respond to the intention of the criminal, not media-induced hysteria or uninformed prejudice.

Who and What Is a Hacker?

Hackers break into government and military systems around the world, from the U.S. Department of Defense to NORAD, the North American Aerospace Defense Command.[4] Hackers also electronically steal millions of dollars from major banks.[5] It must be noted, however, that not all hackers engage in illegal activity. Basic First Amendment activities like communication and association are probably the most frequent online activities of hackers.[6] Similarly, not all illegal online activities are hacking. Pedophilia and child pornography draw as much disgust from most hackers as they do from law enforcement. Hackers and the law enforcement community come into conflict over activities like system intrusions and subsequent illegal acts.

When discussing hackers, it is critical to note this distinction and recognize the fact that hacking can be a legitimate and perfectly legal action. In fact, one of the best definitions for a hacker identifies this issue, and thus considers him or her to be "an individual with a profound interest in computers and technology that has used this knowledge to access computer systems with or without authorization from the system owners."[7] Authorization is critical because individuals who hack without it are committing a crime. Those with permission, however, are not technically breaking the law.

The hacker population represents individuals with a broad spectrum of personal motivations, skills, and activities.[8] For example, one of the more inclusive definitions from outside the hacking world is from the Jargon File. This text document, which defines and translates hacker slang, provides eight different definitions for a hacker, including those who "enjoy exploring the details of programmable systems and how to stretch their capabilities, as opposed to most users, who prefer to learn only the minimum necessary" as well as those who are a "malicious meddler who tries to discover sensitive information by poking around."[9] The emphasis on gaining unauthorized access to computer systems is key to the notion of hackers that has been spread in the popular media over the last decade. However, researchers suggest there is no real consensus as to what constitutes a hacker.[10]

BOX 4.1

Phone Phreaks Bring Technology and Attitude to Hacking

- *Telephone technologies (boxes).* Phone phreaks created devices that produced effects on the phone system. The blue box (see below) was used to produce a 2,600-Hz tone, gaining access to the toll network for the placement of calls without charge. The red box simulates the noise of a quarter, nickel, or dime being dropped into a pay phone, allowing free pay phone calls. Other boxes exist or may simply be part

of phreak lore. *Note:* These devices no longer work on the North American phone system, but they did during the days of the bedroom hacker.

- *Counterculture of the 1960s and 1970s.* There was an affinity for political subversives and Vietnam War protestors with the phone phreaks. Many phreaks were members of the youth culture movements of this period. In fact, one famous phreak, Cheshire Catalyst, edited the Technical Assistance Program (TAP) newsletter founded by Abbie Hoffman.[11]

- **Phone company lore.** Phone phreaks did not restrict themselves to the technology of the Phone Company (there was only one back then[12]). This interest was the beginning of social engineering (see below).
- **Paranoia.** Years of hiding from Bell System security and listening in on phone conversations taught phreaks that privacy was an illusion on the phone system. "Ma" Bell heard everything.
- **"ph"onetic spelling.** Phone phreaks regularly replace the letter "f" with "ph." Phonetic spelling may be the basis of "'leet speek," discussed later in this chapter.
- **Blue Boxing.** In 1967, at the age of 19, Ralph R. Barclay invented a device that bypassed direct dialing long distance telephone systems—the blue box. The small rectangular device was composed of dial and numbered buttons that produced tones similar to a telephone, but different, enabling the device to connect directly to telephone lines without a billing number.[13] The early years of *"blue boxing"* are gone as the digital age gave way to stronger security systems, and the young counterculture that helped establish "hacking" grew up to be mature adults often employed as executives in the very companies they attacked. Indeed, the case is often made that these *"phone phreakers"* in the 1960s and 1970s actually helped establish the worldwide communication network that we all enjoy today.[14] By the 1990s, the concept of phone phreaking and blue boxing had come to an abrupt end with the inaugural, widespread use of encrypted (T-1) lines that consisted of 24 separate channels using pulse code modulation (PCM) for data and voice transmission. The blossoming of the Internet gave way to a new environment in which to *"phreak."*

This may be due in part to the range of activities that hackers engage in, and the legality of their actions depends on authorization from the system owners. For example, some hackers engage in phone phreaking, which involves the manipulation, theft, or use of telephone networks for illegal activities. While some have suggested this behavior constitutes a separate category of computer crime, hackers often break into telephone systems to assist in accomplishing hacks. This was a common practice in the 1980s when telephone systems operated through a variety of switching systems. However, most telephone equipment developed in the last 10 years is now indistinguishable from computer networks. Phreakers now operate within these environments, using hacking techniques and tools. Thus, the practice of phreaking has changed but is still an important interest in the hacker community.[15]

Today's Hackers

The same can be said for software cracking, which involves overcoming copy protection devices in electronic media to copy and distribute them.[16] In the 1980s, such materials were called warez or cracks, and the individuals who created the materials were called warez d00dz (pronounced: wârz dōōdz). Initially, warez d00dz actively cracked software and games to quickly and efficiently trade large volumes of what were expensive materials. As computer technology changed, Internet connectivity became extremely common; digital materials like CDs and laser disks developed; and the warez d00dz began to become actively involved in the creation of pirated movies, music, and television. Thus, the contemporary warez scene has expanded to include the following:

- Music, television shows, and movies
- MP3s (volume counts)
- Digitally compressed movies before they are actually released (zero-day release)
- Cable and satellite descrambling
- DVD decoding
- Peer-to-peer (P2P) networking
- Console games

However, most of the warez scene does not pursue technology like other forms of hackers. They focus heavily on tools and materials rather than discovering new problems and weaknesses. Warez groups do intersect with the hacker community today, however, as they support the efforts of hackers through the creation of P2P networking technology that can be used to share files. In particular, pirated materials like Gnutella and programs like BitTorrent allow for file sharing over distributed computers across the Internet.[17]

As with any "download" from the Internet, there are a number of potential security risks using P2P technology. Malware can be bundled with the download that releases personal and/or sensitive data. For instance, in 2009, the actual blueprints to then-President Obama's *Marine One* helicopter were inadvertently released to the public via a breach in a military P2P file sharing site.[18] In more recent years, P2P breaches have been responsible for huge, inadvertent releases of personal identifying information, including names, addresses, dates of birth, Social Security numbers, medical records, and even bank records.[19] Hence, hackers today are responsible for the creation, distribution, and facilitation of modern piracy as well as setting the stage for significant identity theft.

Likewise, writing or programming malware software such as viruses and Trojan horse programs is a growing computer crime problem and is directly tied to hackers. These tools can be used to steal money and data, automate attacks, and control systems remotely. The creation of malicious software can be challenging and requires a good deal of skill to successfully develop.[20] Only a small portion of the hacker community can create these tools, though they are used by a wide range of hackers regardless of their level of skill. The problem of malicious software is detailed in Chapter 7, giving context to this issue.

Hackers also engage in a form of fraud they refer to as "social engineering." This practice was introduced by phone phreaks; the technique is based on the use of the telephone. The idea is to acquire sensitive information from the human running the machine rather than using advanced computer skills to beat the electronic security. Employees reveal passwords, internal information, and even execute the commands for the hacker. Social engineering is essentially a confidence scam. Additionally, hackers will sometimes engage in dumpster diving, or trashing, as a direct way to obtain information. A person enters a dumpster and looks for useful information, which can include technical manuals, notes, technical bulletins, and a plethora of information useful to a phone phreak. Aside from the direct access to phone technology from castoff manuals, even small scraps of office minutia were highly prized (names, schedules, internal information). Such information could be used to further social engineering.

QUICK FACTS

The 2014 PWC U.S. State of Cybercrime Survey found that the FBI informed over 3,000 U.S. businesses that their organization had been hacked during the previous 12 months.

Source: Brian Krebs, "Good Question: How Often Do Hackers Get Caught?" *CBS Minnesota* (December 18, 2014).

THE MEDIA'S POINT OF VIEW: THE DANGER OF HACKERS Since the first public awareness of hackers, a deluge of lurid news stories has blurred the line between hacker and computer criminal. In the 1980s, hackers took control of computer systems and

BOX 4.2

Social Engineering Tactics

Different tactics are used by social engineers. If one technique fails, it is often possible simply to call back and get a fresh start with a new representative from the company and use any information gained from the failed attempt.

Camaraderie: "Hey, this is Joe out here on a pole. I forgot my order sheet. Can you look up the service on this pair? If I have to drive back to the shop, I'll be behind all day."

Bluster: "This is Supervisor Wilson. I need to reset service flags on this account now ... Of course I can't do it myself! I'm up a pole trying to fix what your technicians did to this setup."

Technical detail: "Hello, who am I speaking to? ... Okay Roger, this is Bill at the Tulsa switch. You have a problem with trunk 6. It's okay, we haven't lost calls yet. Go to frame 009 and count up 16 and over 10. That's the bugger as near as we can tell ... Oh—it has a little pen-shaped device on it? That means that it is being monitored. Let's route around it by switching the pair attached. Here's what you do ... "

left taunting messages to legitimate users. Hackers became the focus of fear for a society struggling to come to grips with the nascent information age. The previous generation of hackers largely ignored the upstarts but resented the media's use of the word "hacker" applied to electronic trespassers and vandals. "It was understandable that the journalists covering these stories would refer to the young perps as hackers—after all, that's what the kids called *themselves*."[21] This has continued through today, as the media often focuses on malicious attacks against computer networks and government resources.

There is also a tendency in the media toward publishing the lurid or frightening aspects of crimes, including hacker crimes.[22] When citing worst-case scenarios for hacking or network intrusion, the alteration of medical records always comes up. In a review of "shockers," author Jonathan Littman reported that a Berkeley researcher discovered a medical facility in the San Francisco Bay Area with open telephone lines to medical records. An examination of medical records will show a great deal of personal information, but beyond the threat to privacy, alteration of those records by a single character can be fatal (in the case of blood type). It is easy to understand why the alteration of medical data has received such attention. The problem is that there has never been a recorded instance of a hacker corrupting medical records and killing a person. The lurid nature of the story and the implied threat to readers changes the threat of hackers from a remote curiosity to an immediate threat, and therefore sells. Unfortunately, aspiring hackers often become acquainted with media portrayals of hacking before they begin to interact with actual hackers.[23]

LAW ENFORCEMENT'S POINT OF VIEW: ILLEGAL ACTIONS AND DAMAGE Although the fine points of labeling hacker activities will be covered in more depth later in the chapter, for now, general descriptions will suffice. Hackers explore computers. When the computer belongs to the hacker or when the hacker has legitimate access to the computer, there is no crime. When the hacker does not have permission to use the computer or network, the action is called "system intrusion." Federal statute makes it a crime to knowingly use false credentials or access devices (which include passwords). Virtually any system intrusion requires that use of such a device.[24] Furthermore, federal statute also makes it a crime to illegally access or damage a "protected" computer.[25]

In this case, illegally accessing a computer connected to the Internet is a federal crime. During the process of an intrusion, data may be intentionally or unintentionally altered. Numerous other crimes may be committed, depending on the effects of such data alteration.[26] Worst-case scenarios include damage to financial networks (carrying billions of dollars each day); alteration, deletion, or exposure of health records; and compromise of safety-related systems. The potential for serious economic harm or catastrophic loss of life is very real in computer intrusion when data are altered.

QUICK FACTS

The longest sentence ever handed down to an American for computer crimes is the 20-year prison term of hacker Albert Gonzalez. Gonzalez was convicted and sentenced in 2010 in connection with the theft and reselling of more than 170 million credit card and ATM numbers from businesses including Dave & Busters, TJ Maxx, and Heartland Payment Systems.

Source: James Verini, "The Great Cyberheist." *The New York Times Magazine,* November 20, 2010.

The primary difference between simple network intrusion and data alteration is the intent of the intruder. By reading or "browsing" through confidential files, the intruder actually creates a copy of the file. Thus, mere browsing may be theft, but it does not deprive the owner of the data or the use of the data. To hackers, this makes the distinction between data alteration and intrusion more meaningful. It may be impossible for an investigator to determine if data have been altered. While criminally altered data may be used for fraud, like manipulating stock prices, or simply to deny the expression of the owner's idea, as with Web page defacements, the simple intruder may not cause actual harm. The problem for law enforcement is that it is often hard to determine the intent of an intruder. Substantial effort must be invested in assuring that data have not been altered or that no malicious intent is present. Law enforcement officers and investigators know that malicious intent is not always necessary for a crime to occur. Sometimes simple negligence or innocent mistakes can cause actual harm. Fundamentally, the law does not recognize a hacker's right to explore the systems, confidential data, and computer resources of others. This basic difference in perceptions makes understanding and predicting hacker actions difficult for law enforcement.

THE HACKER'S POINT OF VIEW: PROSOCIAL HACKING   The concept of a hacker subculture was introduced in Chapter 3. Essentially a subculture is a group of individuals within a larger culture. These individuals develop different attitudes and sometimes appearances from the dominant culture. Sometimes members of "deviant" communities define their activities as beneficial or "prosocial."[27] The hacker subculture is a group of like-minded individuals who share a set of values defined in the hacker ethic. It exists through real-world communication but also through common pursuits and common styles in virtual interactions.[28] The subculture's definitions of prosocial hacking define it and differentiate its activities from computer crime. For example, hackers report learning experiences, including creative problem solving and educating others about security vulnerabilities.[29] Hackers understand the crime as a positive action under the "higher" goals supported by the subculture.

The concept of prosocial hacking is perhaps best described by former hackers who are now employed as researchers, educators, and/or cyber security professionals.

Two of those individuals are Ymir Vigfusson and Karen Elazart, who present the concept of prosocial hacking within their individual TEDTX presentations. Vigfusson is an educator and computer security expert who utilizes what he refers to as "hacking contests" in his advanced computer science courses. Students compete in public competitions designed to develop hacking skills. Vigfusson defends the competitions as one of the best ways to teach students the essential skills of cyber security.[30] Cyber security experts must learn how hackers operate in order to stop them, a concept akin to the popular notion that it "takes one to know one." Elazart is a researcher and cyber security analyst who relates her early life experiences as a young hacker. She describes her adherence to many of the hacker subcultural values defined in the latter portion of this chapter. She contends that hackers act as the Internet's "Immune System," whereby non-malicious hacking identifies weaknesses within information systems and can potentially alert cyber security experts before the occurrence of malicious hacks.[31] Here, hacking is defined as a prosocial act that protects users and ultimately strengthens Internet security. These views on various forms of prosocial hacking underscore the fact that there are many different forms of hacking performed by a wide range of individuals. There are no straightforward definitions, but in the next section we outline several different ways in which to define hackers.

DEFINING HACKERS

Although it borders on political correctness for crooks, there is some actual value to understand the distinctions of a name drawn in the hacker community.[32] Perhaps most important, hackers themselves sometimes use these terms to draw distinctions based on fine points of motivation and action that can be valuable to an investigation. Such information may allow an investigator to include or exclude a suspect from an investigation. There are certain actions that a hacker simply would not perform. For example, a malicious attack that serves only to back up an extortion threat would be very unhackerlike. Other hackers would probably be more cooperative in the investigation of such an incident. On the other hand, an attack that demonstrated technical skill in a novel way and embarrassed law enforcement or corporate interests would create solidarity among hackers and great status for the perpetrator.

Cyber criminals Versus Hackers

Although a violation of the law is still a crime, juries may be more sympathetic to the motive of exploration versus personal profit. It is also hard to prosecute a "pure" hacker under federal statutes because the sentencing guidelines are driven by financial damages. These facts alone justify recognizing a distinction; this does not mean excusing an illegal action. It simply means recognizing a fundamentally different reality for investigation and prosecution.

There is little said in mainstream analyses that distinguish hackers from computer criminals.[33] In fact, some well-respected computer crime fighters flatly deny that there is a distinction.[34] Others acknowledge the illegality of the actions, but point to a radically different set of motivations.[35] However, in the underground hacker media, the distinction is a subject of primary importance.[36] Emanuel Goldstein, editor of *2600: The Hacker Quarterly*, has addressed the distinction between hackers and computer criminals in three ways. First, he minimized the criminal damage caused by hacking,

Hacking   Criminal Hacking   Computer Crime

FIGURE 4.1 The relationship between hacking, criminal hacking, and computer crime.

implying that very little actual harm is caused. Second, he defended the criminal actions of hackers based on their motives and adherence to hacker subcultural values, which were not viewed as criminal by him. Third, he disavowed hackers who commit crimes that violate hacker values, such as crimes of financial gain.[37] Thus, it appears that at least some elements of the hacker subculture do not condone what they define as computer crime.

The majority of hacker online actions are perfectly legal; it is hard to imagine committing a crime with every keystroke. Basic activities like communication and information sharing as well as illegal activities all fall within the range of hacker behavior. All of these behaviors can be called hacking. The distinction between hackers who commit crimes and other computer criminals rests upon the attitudes with which a hacker approaches the activity. For various reasons, the hacker subculture accepts actions that violate law. These actions may be called criminal hacking. However, some actions are not accepted by the subculture. These actions and criminal hacking behaviors may be called computer crime. The point of confusion lies in the fact that criminal hacking is considered to be computer crime by law enforcement, but perfectly acceptable hacking by the hacker subculture. Figure 4.1 shows the overlap of these concepts.

CYBERCRIMINALS AND THE INSIDER THREAT   Cybercriminals are often associated with fraud, scamming, and/or embezzlement that follow more traditional lines of criminality—only with the use of a computer. Cybercriminals who are from inside an organization, whether as a member of an organized criminal group or perpetrated individually as a disgruntled employee, present the highest risk for cybercrime and corporate and industrial espionage. Though there are cases where the insider threat was accidental, where an employee or associate had no malicious intent, the criminal definition of the insider threat is a malicious criminal (current or former employee, contractor, or business partner) who has or had legitimate access to an organization's computing environment (network, systems, or data), and has intentionally exceeded or intentionally used access in a manner that negatively affected the confidentiality, integrity, or availability of the organization's information or information systems.[38] The negative impacts to confidentiality, integrity, and availability are often caused by malware infections, disclosure, or exfiltration of an organization's data without permission, manipulation or corruption of an organization's data, and/or denial of services attacks upon an organization's systems. The cybercriminals from inside have or can obtain the knowledge, access, and trust needed to achieve their objectives—which are often malicious destruction or personal gain. This is an inherent threat that can never be fully mitigated, but clearly distinguishes an entirely different set of motives and operations than the hacker who usually attacks an organization from outside via a network.

Insider attacks by cybercriminal were found to occur during normal working hours while on-site and using the attacker's authorized physical and logical access. Attack methods and examples include some of the same techniques used by hackers, but much potentially much more harmful:

- **Social engineering**—The process of deceiving people into giving away access or confidential information.[39] For example, a former multi-level marketing company executive, familiar with the commissions program and processes, convinced his former coworkers to allocate unclaimed customers to his newly established sale representative account, whereby qualifying him for sales promotions, higher commissions, and gifts. See Chapter 2.
- **Authorized use of an organization's systems** —Insiders using the access already provided by the organization to conduct their attacks. For example, call center representatives, with access to customer credit reports, were colluding to sell customer data to an outside organized crime organization for the purposes of identity theft and the creation of fraudulent (disposable) cell phone accounts.
- **Bypassing security and control processes** —When an insider is aware of the organization's safeguards, auditing practices and frequencies, thresholds for approval and alerts, and/or regulatory controls, then he can conduct his crimes under the radar and/or without the additional involvement of organization personnel. For example, an organization's check issuance process required the involvement of two employees as a fraud control; however, both employees in this case were insiders from the same criminal enterprise and would issue fraudulent checks to their conspirators.
- **Compromised accounts** —Obtaining the user ID and passwords of organization personnel to conceal the insider's activity and/or obtain the necessary access for conducting the crime. For example, an insider used passwords stolen from coworkers to conceal the changes he made to credit reporting data in exchange for money, and in support of his conspirator's identity theft activities.

Common objectives for malicious inside cybercriminals include the theft of intellectual property (IP), fraud, and/or sabotage. The Carnegie Mellon University's CERT Insider Threat Database contains over 700 cases (as of December 2012), of which 371 cases were closed with convictions. From the 371 closed cases, CERT categorized them as Intellectual Property Theft—49 cases, Fraud—194 cases, Sabotage—106 cases, and Miscellaneous—22 cases.[40] The majority of these insider-related cybercrimes were perpetrated by lone actors or rogue employees who had the resources, access, and knowledge necessary to commit the crime.[41] However, a connection to organized crime was identified by CERT in a few dozen cases involving collusion between multiple insiders and/or outsiders. All of the cases involving organized crime were found to be motivated by financial gain and the insiders often held low-level positions, were motivated by money, and were recruited by outsiders to commit their crimes.[42] CERT also found that the average damages in cases involving organized crime exceeded $3 million, with some cases exceeding $50 million. Refer to the following Chapter 5 focusing on sophisticated cybercriminal organizations.

There are then significant differences between hackers and cybercriminals. Definitions of computer crime that equate all hacking with criminal behavior are both offensive to hackers and inaccurate. Similarly, definitions that deny that any meaningful criminal action is committed by hackers are absurd to law enforcement and also inaccurate. Hence, the Venn diagram (Figure 4.1) depicts a subset of hacker behavior that is illegal but condoned by the hacker subculture (labeled criminal hacking). The reality of computer crime and obscurity of perpetrator motives makes this abstract system of defining hackers and computer criminals unworkable in the field. As a consequence, less clear-cut labels are often applied.[43]

Crackers

A cracker is a malicious hacker. There is no final authority on who determines when or how a hacker becomes a cracker. There is no clear way to cross the line back to hacker, either.

In response to a computer incident, John Gilmore, cofounder of the Electronic Frontier Foundation, said:

> As usual, the computer underground is doing a service to the country by making it clear just how shallow the government's understanding of computer security is. They are quite curiously refraining from damaging anything in their intrusions but the egos of the bureaucracies involved. As usual, the first response of the Feds is to threaten dire punishment for the messengers. But they are being prodded into actually attempting to keep serious attackers out, a novel idea somewhat overdue for consideration.[44]

Gilmore's recognition of the possible benefit of even vandalous intrusion echoes the hacker community's divergent values. There is no room for this view in the generally accepted concept of property rights, but the hacker community has a different understanding of their actions. Most hackers claim to benefit the systems they intrude upon because they do not destroy data and alert system administrators to security flaws.

Script Kiddies

Script kiddies are often described as a scourge or pestilence on the Internet. A well-administered system with good security policies has little to fear from most script kiddies, but even such a system is vulnerable to a distributed denial-of-service (DDoS) attack launched from a point-and-click program. DDoS attacks use unsuspecting, zombie computers to attack a victim. Persons with inoffensive and frankly uninteresting information on their Web sites may become unwitting accomplices in the script kiddies' attack. Unsecured, home computer systems with cable modems provide easy targets for script kiddies. When equipped with a software program called a client or zombie, the system becomes a weapon to be used against more secure sites.[45]

Script kiddies seem to be primarily concerned with bragging and attacking each other or anyone else who draws their wrath. The attacks are often simple exploits of well-known vulnerabilities, but can disrupt Internet Relay Chat (IRC) channels. Chat rooms are often raided by script kiddies who provoke verbal attacks (a process known as "trolling") and retaliate by "punting" the user out of the chat room. Web page hacking is also a favorite activity of script kiddies and script kiddie groups. The altered Web pages often contain little more than rants, nonsense, or shoutz to friends and insults to enemies and law enforcement.[46]

The term "script kiddie" comes from their use of premade tools or scripts. Script kiddies do not have enough skill to write their own programs or explore new exploits for themselves. They download an attack program and attempt to get it to run. Many such programs exploit long-known vulnerabilities, but some system administrators do not update their software. Internet hackers dismiss the actions of script kiddies as unskilled.[47]

White Hat Versus Black Hat

The current fashion for describing hackers is to use a new set of terminology recognizing the "gray" areas of determining malicious hacking. Thus, "white hat hacker" describes an "ethical" hacker. A "gray hat hacker" is someone who typically behaves in an ethical manner, but sometimes violates accepted ethics. Finally, a "black hat hacker" is a "malicious" hacker (i.e., a cracker or computer criminal using hackerlike methods).

WHITE HAT HACKERS   "White hat" is a term used to describe an ethical hacker. The term "white hat" was needed because so many former or "reformed" hackers entered the computer security field. Eventually, computer science graduates employing hackerlike methods also spurred the need for the term. The reality existed before the label. There was a long and lively debate about hiring "former" hackers. Other examples of white hat hacking include the following:

- Software testing by manufacturers
- Independent verification of software function and security
- Reverse engineering
- Training

"Tiger teams," a term borrowed from the military, described a hacker or team of hackers hired to "test" the defenses of an organization. These white hat hackers follow a strict code of loyalty to their employers. The use of tiger teams is based on the theory that "only a hacker can beat a hacker." There is a great deal of common sense to the notion of testing defenses with the types of attacks used by an enemy. Several computer security/risk management companies have security services units that actually have white hat hackers on their rolls. A short list includes the "A" list of the field: Team CMYRU, KPMG, Kroll, Computer Associates, Gartner, ICSA Labs (antivirus division of Tru Secure), and Cambridge Technology Partners.

GRAY HAT HACKERS   A gray hat hacker is someone who typically behaves in an ethical manner, but sometimes violates accepted ethics. The term "gray hat" came into usage to describe a usually ethical hacker who sometimes indulged in illicit activity. A typical gray hat is a penetration tester who would not attack a client, but hacks and intrudes recreationally. A gray hat may also occasionally violate the hacker ethic against hacking for profit (other than being paid to do penetration testing for a willing client). A typical contemporary interpretation of the hacker ethic usually includes the following elements:

- Do not profit from intrusion.
- Do not intentionally harm a computer system.
- Attempt to inform a system administrator of security flaws.
- Hackers are not bad guys; computer criminals are bad guys.

BLACK HAT HACKERS   A black hat hacker is essentially a cracker or malicious hacker. The term "black hat" does not apply to all computer criminals. Only network intrusion and other "hacker-like" activities committed in conflict with hacker ethics qualify as black hat activities. At first, the term was not used by hackers (malicious or otherwise), but it has since been used by some hackers to describe themselves. In fact, individuals within the hacker community tend to think that a black hat hacker is someone with a good deal of skill over and above that of script kiddies.[48] The general public often thinks of "black hat" hackers as a group of highly clandestine individuals working in the secret world of the Internet. In fact, "black hat" hackers are quite open with their ideas, opinions, and technology. Each year, Las Vegas is host to the "Black Hat" Annual Conference where hackers gather to share ideas, concepts, and even training on new methodologies and tactics for attacking specific systems or spying with new products. The 2013 conference was especially interesting as General Keith Alexander, Director of the National Security Agency, was the keynote speaker. While his speech was greeted with tension and anxiety, most attendees reported that the event heralded a new found respect between the government and "black hat" attendees. It certainly became the subject of numerous blogs on White and Black Hat forums for quite some time.[49]

Hacktivists

Recently, there has been an increase in the political activity of self-identified hackers. Hackers have come together to challenge the treatment of their peers by the government.[50] The common characteristic of hacktivists is the use of hacker skills and attitudes to convey a political message.[51] Because of the emergence of cheap computer technology and Internet connectivity around the world, hacktivists have virtually unlimited access to cheap or free computing power and nearly boundless information. For example, members of a hacktivist group called the Electronic Disturbance Theater developed an attack tool called FloodNet that used a DoS attack method. This tool was used against the Pentagon as well as other government and business targets as a means of protest against their activities and policies.[52]

Internet-based resources are often turned toward political ends among hacktivists rather than standard goals of the hacker subculture. In many cases, the normal facilities of the Internet serve hacktivists better than hacker files and tools. For example, e-mail communication enabled supporters of the notorious computer hacker Kevin Mitnick to be in touch with him after his arrest and until he was released from prison. Web sites serve as platforms for publicizing political causes. They do not have to be hacked when access is so cheap and easy. Because so many of the activities of hacktivists are entirely legal, they are among the most accessible of hacker types.

BOX 4.3

Anonymous: The Epitome of Hacktivism

The loosely associated worldwide network of hacktivists collectively known as *Anonymous* has become the most widely recognized source of hacktivism. The group originated in 2003. Members are easily identified by the mask they publically wear that is reminiscent of a character in the film *V for Vendetta*.[53] The group has perpetrated highly organized hacks designed to raise awareness of a range of social and political causes including those against:[54]

- The World Trade Organization (2015)
- Donald Trump's Web site (2015)
- The Bay Area Rapid Transit (BART) (2011)
- The Church of Scientology (2008)
- The Motion Picture Association of America (2012)

BOX 4.4

Penetration Testing

Penetration testing is looked upon with suspicion by hackers because it is a little too close to law enforcement. Penetration testing is an acceptable use of skills by older hackers as long as they don't develop too comfortable a relationship with law enforcement. It seems to violate the hacker ethic against hacking for profit. Some hacker purists won't do it. However, free penetration testing is unquestionably a prosocial activity to hackers.

The business ethic of a tiger team is based on survival. Loyalty to the company hiring the team is essential to ever being hired again.

- Information discovered during the testing must not be disclosed to anyone but the employer.
- Only intrude where invited, otherwise you become a "bad guy."
- Where the methods are exactly the same, only the intention separates good guys from bad guys.
- White hats often even associate with black hats to keep current.

THE ORIGINS AND HISTORY OF HACKING

Now that we have discussed the variations that exist within the hacker subculture, it is critical to consider how these various groups came to be. Examining the history of hacking gives significant insight into the problems and origins of the term "hacker." The Massachusetts Institute of Technology (MIT) claims a tradition of the use of the word before computer hackers existed. The word "hack" had long been used to describe the elaborate college pranks that MIT students would regularly devise. These "hacks" ranged from benign (hiding the incoming university president's office door with a bulletin board) to elaborate (building a full-sized replica police car on top of a domed building complete with working light bar and a ticket for parking illegally).

Among early MIT hackers, a hack was "a project undertaken or a product built not solely to fulfill some constructive goal, but with some wild pleasure taken in mere involvement."[55] When one of the early MIT computer hackers used the term "hacker," "there was serious respect implied. [T]o qualify as a hack, the feat must be imbued with innovation, style, and technical virtuosity."[56] The limitations of the hardware available made this creative problem solving necessary for the earliest computer hackers. "To top [a] program, someone else might try to do the same thing with fewer instructions—a worthy endeavor, since there was so little room in the small 'memory' of the computers in those days.... This could most emphatically be done by approaching the problem from a whole new angle that no one had ever thought of before, but that in retrospect made total sense."[57] Thus hacking was most closely associated with creative, unorthodox problem solving to overcome the limitations of early computers. At that time, computers only existed in major universities, business research parks, and government installations. People with access to computers had a tremendous investment in not harming the few computers available. Thus, a hacker, in the classical sense, is someone who has mastered the art of programming to the point that he or she can simply sit down and "hack" in a program that works.

Hacking Changes

This conception of the hacker continued into the 1960s when the computer moved from universities into military applications. However, a shift occurred as a consequence of the turbulent social climate of the 1960s, as well as the Vietnam War. Military applications angered many programmers of the day, despite their work being funded largely by the military and federal government.[58]

Programmers' beliefs began to take shape in a series of ideals forming part of the core of hacker culture. Specifically, "hackers" of this period believed information should be free to all to understand how things work and can be improved. This notion formed the centerpiece of a series of related ideas called the hacker ethic that were documented by Levy in his book *Hackers*:[59]

1. Access to computers—and anything which might teach you something about the way the world works—should be unlimited and total. [p. 40]
2. All information should be free. [p. 40]
3. Mistrust authority—promote decentralization. [p. 41]
4. Hackers should be judged by their hacking, not bogus criteria such as degrees, age, race, or position. [p. 43]
5. You can create art and beauty on a computer. [p. 43]
6. Computers can change your life for the better. [p. 45][60]

This ethic guided the actions of hackers and formed the roots of the present hacker culture. At this point, hackers were viewed as skilled computer users. However, a subtle shift began to occur in the 1970s with the development of "phone phreaking." This involved tampering with phone technology to understand and, in some cases, control telephone systems. Phreaking allowed individuals to make free calls to anyone in the world by controlling telephone system switches.

This became notorious because of a man named Cap'n Crunch (John Draper), who blew a giveaway whistle found in a box of cereal into his phone receiver.[61] The whistle created the perfect 2,600 MHz tone that, at the time, was used to connect an individual to long-distance lines. This simple toy opened a new area of technology for individuals to explore and exploit, particularly those interested in computers and hacking. Also during the late 1970s, the first personal computer bulletin board system (BBS) was created.[62] A BBS, which is essentially an online system, allowed individuals to post comments and information. In turn, others could read and respond to those posts. Thus, hackers could come together online to share and discuss information and interact socially.[63] However, the real impact of these developments would be felt during the next decade.

The Criminalization of Hacking

From the 1950s through the 1970s, hackers never worried about breaking computer laws; there were none. The new generation that usurped the word "hacker" was defined—almost from the beginning—by crime. During the 1980s, a new breed of computer user challenged the hacker ethic. Because of changes in technology and society, more individuals had access to computer technology. Specifically, IBM's new stand-alone "personal computer" brought computer technology to a new generation and into more homes than ever. Modem technology, which connects computers to other computers and networks via telephone lines, also improved. This equipment allowed individuals with personal computers to connect to other dedicated computer users. As a result, the exploration of computer networks was now possible for individuals outside of university and business settings.[64] Modems also increased the number of individuals online and changed the shape of the computer underground through the emergence of BBS dedicated to hacking. Budding hackers shared detailed information about systems they explored and bragged about their exploits. The boards also allowed hackers to form groups with private networks and create password-protected boards to keep out the uninitiated and maintain privacy.[65]

Warez d00dz also developed during this time, finding ways to share and break copyright protections. These hackers already had innumerable justifications to try to break the copy protection. "Software is too expensive." "We only copy software we wouldn't buy anyway." "We only do it to try out new programs." It is a "backup copy in case the disk becomes damaged." During this period, warez d00dz created BBS as a way to share files with others who they trusted, because they were breaking the law and at risk for discovery and closure with arrest for the system operator. Warez sites could also be overwhelmed quickly. Leeches download only, and do not contribute. Leech time was wasted access to a scarce resource (i.e., the warez board). Thus, elite warez boards remained cloaked in secrecy. Unlike elite hacker boards, information was not distributed through the community.[66]

The 1983 film *War Games* introduced the general public to the rather unexplored world of computer hacking. The film suggested that young males with computers could break into any computer system in the world and wreak havoc without anyone ever knowing. This film and its message had a significant influence on a new generation of computer users.

An additional change to the hacker community occurred in 1986 with the introduction of a brief text called *The Conscience of a Hacker*, also referred to as *The Hacker Manifesto*. A member of the notorious hacker group Legion of Doom (LOD), named "The Mentor," wrote this text.[67] The author railed against adults, law enforcement, and schools and evoked the angst of young hackers exploring network from home computers. They did not have the same support that hackers in the 1950s and 1960s experienced and worked in isolation. As a result, their experiences were vastly different and espoused in this work. The following excerpt is taken from the end of the manifesto:

> Yes, I am a criminal. My crime is that of curiosity. My crime is that of judging people by what they say and think, not what they look like. My crime is that of outsmarting you, something that you will never forgive me for. I am a hacker, and this is my manifesto. You may stop this individual, but you can't stop us all....[68]

The Mentor also suggested hackers explore and seek knowledge even if that means breaking into or gaining access to otherwise protect computer systems. However, he stated that this should not make hackers criminals. The Mentor also encouraged hackers to use telephone systems without paying for the service because they are "run by profiteering gluttons." This unapologetic post derided the traditional hacker definition espoused in the 1960s, as well as the "Hacker Ethic." The document provided support for the increasingly criminal nature of hacker activities, thus affecting outsiders' perceptions of hackers and the attitudes of young initiates to the hacker community.

Within a few years, the manifesto became widely read, and computer users without real technical skill became interested in hacking. This caused a rift between hackers with malicious intent and those with an interest in exploring networks without breaking the law or violating privacy. The divide was also fueled by different beliefs, as represented in the hacker manifesto and the hacker ethic. In addition, malicious hackers became the focus of law enforcement during the mid- to late 1980s. High-profile hacking incidents took place, such as a battle between two hacker groups, the LOD and the Masters of Deception (MOD), whose attacks compromised personal computers, businesses, and telephone systems including AT&T.[69] The much-publicized arrest of a regional hacker group called the 414 Gang from Milwaukee (area code 414) also brought attention to the criminal aspects of hacking. This group of teenagers accessed secure computers in the Sloan-Kettering Cancer Center and Los Alamos military computers.[70]

One of the most famous cases of criminal hacking occurred during this time, involving the hacker Kevin Mitnick, who broke the law by accessing computer systems without permission. Mitnick intruded into a variety of private systems, stole proprietary software, and accessed voice mail computers at Pacific Bell. He was a fugitive from the FBI for two and a half years, during which time he engaged in identity theft to create fraudulent documents and illegally cloned cell phones to hide his location.[71] After his arrest in 1995, his prosecution was extremely controversial, as there were few legal precedents to guide the prosecution and a great deal of fear and concern over his ability. At one point, it was thought that he could cause a nuclear war by simply having access to a phone. Thus, his prosecution was a landmark for criminal hacking cases.

Challenges and Changes in Hacking

The emergence of criminal hacking in the 1980s and 1990s also saw a concurrent growth in original hackers from the previous generation who received recognition and disputed the criminalization of the word "hacker." Most of the original hackers had started their own high-tech companies or assumed leadership in research programs. The budding computer security community was also driven by the old-school hackers, along with the tech boom of the 1990s, which made many of them popular culture heroes. People working in the high-tech sector started to care about the early triumphs in information technology. It started to become more important to hackers to redeem the word "hacker." Several factors contributed to this renewed interest:

- Increased computer use in the general population.
- Popularization of the Internet.
- Popular culture recognition and even reverence of nerds.
- Popular fiction like the *Cyberpunk* books and computer movies.
- The zealous promotion of computer media sources like *Wired* magazine.

The computer media wanted to prove their connection to the "wired world" by picking up speech patterns and opinions of the computer world's stars. Many of these stars were hackers. *Wired* magazine, recognizing the disputed use of the term "hacker," pioneered the popular use of the term "cracker" through editorial policy. *Wired* tried to establish credibility among the important figures of the early computer culture by refusing to stigmatize the word "hacker."

Despite their attempts, the notion of hacking as a crime continued on and was cemented by the mid-1990s, especially with the development of user-friendly computer systems and the Internet and World Wide Web. The slow but steady drop in the prices of computer technology also made the home computer ubiquitous. With access to the Internet and more powerful computers, hackers who wanted to learn needed only to bring up a Web page or use an online bookstore to gain access to information and resources. This facilitated the growth of unskilled hackers and script kiddies who were a significant divergence from the previous generations of hackers. New users also became interested in hacking with the release of the film *Hackers* in 1995.[72] This film's

BOX 4.5

The Open-Source Movement

Most software purchased today tightly restricts user access to the source code, or the human-readable version of computer programs. For example, the source code to Windows™ is a closely guarded trade secret of the Microsoft Corporation. When you purchase a copy of Windows™, you receive the computer-readable version of the code referred to as "object code." You do not have access to the source code. Corporations can prevent some unauthorized use of their intellectual property and conceal security flaws of the software to would-be hackers by restricting access to the source code.

The open-source movement began in the late 1990s and is alive today. The founders of the movement believe that software can be improved by allowing programmers access to the source code. The basic idea is that programmers will be able to read, modify, and improve the code through open access. Over time, these ad hoc revisions will rapidly transform the code and fix bugs in the program much faster than would be the case in the traditional closed model that relies on restricting access to the code.

The ideals of early hacker culture are alive and well within the open-source movement, where the best way to fix computer glitches is to rely on the creative and unorthodox problem-solving skills of individual programmers instead of corporate restrictions.

presentation of hackers helped cement the notion that hackers are criminals, as it featured overly styled misrepresentations of hacking and an emphasis on the destructive side of hacking.

By the start of the new millennium, most computers around the world were interconnected through the Internet, and sensitive financial and government information became commonly stored in accessible databases online. Financial services, social networking sites, and a wide range of new communications resources were made available to home computer users. As a consequence, the computer security industry was booming and the nature of computer hacking and attacks changed. Hackers in Russia, Romania, and China became more of a significant problem, especially for U.S. businesses and governments, and the tools they used became increasingly complex and readily accessible for purchase through online markets.[73] These markets, discussed in detail in Chapter 2, are critical, as they have changed the nature of hacking by reducing the amount of knowledge required to attack secured networks. Furthermore, the world of hacking is no longer the province of a few but now the business of spy agencies and governments as information warfare becomes a reality. Chapter 2 outlined the dedication of billions of dollars by governments to fund entire information warfare groups within the military mission of certain countries. However, the old hacker ethic is still alive and well around the world in the computer security community and universities. The ethic is also evident in the growth of open-source software programs like Linux, where programmers collaborate to create programs that can be used by individuals around the world. Thus, the hacker community is now very segmented, with individuals engaging in legal and illegal hacks against all manner of targets around the world for curiosity, profit, fame, patriotism, warfare, or even religious ideology.

THE HACKER SUBCULTURE

In light of the diverse nature of skills, motives, and interests in the hacker community, it is important to consider how these individuals relate to one another and what drives their interests. As discussed in Chapter 3, there appears to be a subculture of hackers that provides justifications for behavior, information and skills to engage in hacking, and beliefs about the nature of their actions. This is true regardless of whether an individual engages in legitimate hacks (as per the hacker ethic) or malicious hacks and cracks (more in line with the hacker manifesto). The great difficulty in differentiating these groups lies in the fact that human behavior is dynamic and contextual. There is therefore no simple dichotomy between hackers and computer criminals.

As such, it is better to consider what structures the hacker subculture in an attempt to see how they relate to one another, what they value, and how their beliefs affect their behavior. Subcultural research suggests that the social world of computer hackers is shaped by five social norms: technology, knowledge, commitment, categorization, and law.[74] These structures appear to be consistent across place and time and have value for our understanding of the global hacker community and their actions. The following discussion will consider each of these subcultural norms using examples from the real world.

Technology

One of the most significant norms in the hacker subculture is the relationship between hackers and technology. Hackers possess a deep connection to computers and technology, which play an important role in structuring their interests and activities.[75] For example, many hackers report developing an interest in technology before or during adolescence.[76] Once they were given access to a computer, they spent their time becoming acquainted with its functions in a variety of ways. A hacker named Mack Diesel described his own experience, writing:

> I was, yeah, I was about four and [my mother] would take me up to school with her sometimes and they had a computer there. If I got bored, she would let me, uh, fool around with the computer, you know, to keep me occupied, and after a while I enjoyed playing around with it.[77]

Hackers also played video games and developed interests in the many different facets of computer technology. In fact, the growth of multiplayer computer games like Quake and CounterStrike helped to give hackers an interest in technology, as they would have to work to connect multiple computers together in a network to play with their peers. This gave them an appreciation for a variety of technical skills, such as programming, software, hardware, and computer security.

The more time hackers spent familiarizing themselves with technology, the more their skill level increased. Whether online or offline, hackers discussed the need to understand the interrelated elements of computer systems, as a hacker's knowledge level directly relates to his or her ability and skill.[78] To meet the intense internal desire to understand computer technology, hackers often turn to online resources for help. In the 1980s, hackers commonly used BBSs, while the advent of the World Wide Web in the 1990s saw the development of Web forums. Web forums are online discussion groups where individuals can discuss a variety of problems or issues. They are composed of strings that begin when an individual creates a post within a forum, asking a question or giving an opinion. Other people respond to the remarks with posts of their own that are connected together to create strings.[79] Today, blogs, Tweets, and even Facebook provide the environment for exchange of information between hackers.

These resources are critical to increase a hackers' connection to computer technology. This was exemplified in the following comment from the forum poster Binkels: "Hacking allows people to learn more about computers. I am really into computers and try to learn as much as I can. I want to be a hacker to exploit systems/programs and using them to learn from and go further into my limited knowledge of computers." The urge to learn about computers and technology could be met through a variety of resources, especially Web forums. One user wrote:

> You might want to remember that forums are designed for people to ask questions, despite the fact that you can find almost anything on google. So if we all should just searched for things ourselves there'd be no forums.

Hackers can also ask questions about computers, hardware, software, and hacking in forums as a means to understand technology. For example, a hacker named g00fu5 wrote a post in a hacker forum demonstrating the importance of their interest in technology:

> Im planning on printing out a bunch of different texts to print out and take around with me so I can read them in my spare time. I was wondering if anyone could recommend any good texts that are actually worth printing out for me. I am printing out the SQL [programming language] white pages so far, but I need more. I am interested in just about anything hacking-related, but nothing stupid.

Thus, the forums emphasized hackers' significant interest in and desire to comprehend technology.

Technology is also such an important component of the hacker subculture that it began to permeate the language of hackers in the 1970s and 1980s. Hackers in this period created their own dialect called eleet ('leet) speak or k-rad. In k-rad, numbers were substituted for visually similar letters.[80] Capital letters were freely and randomly used. For instance, "elite hackers" became 31337 HaKorZ. There is no definite pattern for the replacements; they are just inserted upon the whim of the writer. There are different reasons for 'leet speak. Foremost, much of the interaction between 'leeto hackers happened online. It required typing. Shortcuts and abbreviations became the norm. The use of numbers and other characters in place of letters is a reflection of the programs that hackers create. Because the development of computer programs involves symbols and characters, the incorporation of these components into speech reflects the value of technology in their communications. In fact, 'leet speak is still a common component of the hacker subculture and is used by individuals in hacker communities around the world.

BOX 4.6

The Internet of Things: Hacking in a World Where Everything Is Connected

The Internet of Things (IoT) is an emerging concept involving the connection of any and all electronically controlled devices to the Internet and each other through a broadband connection.[81] The idea moves beyond the connection of phones and computers to include household appliances, headphones and other wearable devices, machine components including engines, and industrial and office equipment such as printers. The manufacture of electronically controlled devices increasingly includes computer chips that enable all of these devices to be "smart" through a broadband Internet connection. The eventual connection of "everything" can potentially benefit individuals and society in many ways including the development of efficiencies in transportation and energy networks, medical care, and workplace productivity.

The development of the IoT also poses significant challenges in terms of information security and privacy. If everything is connected, then anything can be hacked and significantly threaten everything else. Will someone be able to hack your refrigerator and gain access to your entire home network and private data? Will foreign-based hackers be able to gain access to critical infrastructures through poorly designed and minimally protected office equipment? These emerging issues were underscored in October 2016 when an enormous denial of service (DOS) attack crippled huge sections of the Internet and Web domains, including Twitter, Netflix, Spotify, and Reddit. The source of the attack was eventually confirmed to be a botnet originated from millions of individual IP addresses linked to poorly protected smart home security devices and other gadgets with weak login credentials.[82] This event was widely defined as the first hack of the IoT and a wake-up call to electronics manufacturers and IT security professionals about the expansion of societal vulnerabilities in an era where everything is connected.

Knowledge

Another important norm in the hacker subculture is knowledge. Being referred to as a "hacker" was a clear indication of an individual's understanding and skill since the development of the computer technology. In fact, the hacker identity is built upon a devotion to learn and understand technology. One hacker named MG defined a hacker as "any person with a sincere desire for knowledge about all things and is constantly trying to find it."[83] Hackers spent a great deal of time learning and applying their knowledge online and offline. Most hackers stressed that the learning process began with the basic components of computer technology. An understanding of the rudimentary functions of computers provides hackers with an appreciation for the interrelated nature of computer systems. Dark Oz explained his own learning experience with computers:

> You do this long enough, with many different technical projects, and you begin to really learn a lot … Once you learn the logic and how to "think" like a computer or programmer would, you can just guess at how things are working, based on existing knowledge.[84]

Developing a broad knowledge of systems, hardware, programming, and networking is extremely important to hackers because it influences their ability to hack. Though hackers can now find tools in forums around the world, they must understand how computers operate in order to effectively use these tools. In fact, the early computer hackers at MIT demonstrated their significant skill with computers by reducing the processing time of machines, which were very slow.

Forums and blogs also serve as repositories of information for hackers to access and connect with other hacker. However, it is important to consider that in the current hacker subculture, when an individual asks a question, he or she is often given a Web link that would answer the question. Users have to actively open links, read, and learn in order to find their answer. Tutorials, be they Word documents or videos, can also be found and give detailed explanations on topics from programming to the use of hack tools. Hackers also make software programs available for others to download either for free or for pay to help them learn.

Hackers in the subculture today do not, however, mentor individuals in hacking skills. In fact, evidence suggests that most hackers do not have many real-world relationships with other hackers.[85] As a consequence, they must develop online relationships to learn, but these relationships do not lead to direct information on hacking. This sentiment was also evident in the following exchange from a forum or blog when a poster asked for information to learn to hack:

STfUser: ok im quite new to this and need some mega help i need to know the basics of this hacking [I am] on my quest to becoming elite so if someone can help and give me the info and tell me where i can get it [information on how to hack] from i would much appreciate it.

3NF0R3C3R: arrrrr how cute, seriously mate why would anyone want to go out of their way to help some random person hack computers?

H3H3: Nah man, you want a teacher, you can pay lol [laughing out loud]. Besides that, read whatever you can get your hands on and understand the shit that you read.

The importance of knowledge is also evident in the growth of hacker conferences, or "cons." There are dozens of cons held in countries around the world, all focused on sharing information and spreading knowledge. There are several cons in the United States alone, including one of the most famous and long-standing in the world called Defcon. Like the Black Hat Annual Conference discussed earlier, this three-day convention is also held in Las Vegas and has operated since 1993.[86] The 2013 Defcon immediately followed the Black Hat Conference. The conference draws thousands of attendees and participants from around the world, including computer security professionals, law enforcement agents, attorneys, and hackers of all skill levels. The convention is open to the public and features panels directly related to technology and hacking. A wide range of topics are discussed every year, commonly including hardware hacking, phreaking, computer security, exploits, cryptography, privacy protections, and the legal issues surrounding hacking and piracy.[87]

The importance of knowledge is also evident at the conference, as hackers demonstrate their understanding of technology through hacking challenges and competitions held during the convention. For example, there is a contest called "Capture the Flag," where hackers compete against each other for 36 straight hours in teams to determine who has the greatest skill.[88] There are also contests in war driving, where hackers drive around the city trying to find the largest number of open wireless WIFI hotspots. Those who successfully apply their knowledge in the unique challenges at Defcon are acknowledged during an award ceremony at the end of the convention. Contest winners are announced on stage and distinguished for their achievements. Individuals are given a black conference admission badge and, in some cases, a black leather Defcon logo jacket. These items cannot be purchased, and the black badge provided the recipient with free convention admission for life. Since the convention badge design changes each year, the black badge stands out as a symbol of knowledge, achievement, and ability.

The importance of learning is also detailed in the program by the convention organizer, The Dark Tangent. He wrote, "I want a party where all like minded geeks and innovators can chill out and swap ideas."[89] Presenters provide new information to attendees along with tools, security tactics, and creative applications of existing products. Here, hackers place great value on the creative use of technology and spreading these innovations to others.[90]

Commitment

The elements that compose the normative order knowledge are also closely tied to the normative order commitment. Commitment is important because individuals must constantly study and practice hacking techniques in order to improve and progress. Those who are not willing to spend this time often wind up as script kiddies and are limited in terms of the attacks that they can complete. Commitment to hacking structures individual behavior through continued study and practice of hacking techniques. Forum posters indicate that it takes a tremendous amount of time to learn to hack. Wiggum wrote, "For me ... the most important thing to have if u wanna be a hacker is to 'love it' and [be] ready to give your time to learn and master it." Another named Ashy Larrie also provided some insight:

> If you are just starting you might not have a clue what to learn, or what you should know. As for me, I just started reading texts for a long time ... when I started I didn't understand most of what was said in the texts but just kept on reading, after awhile things become more clear and you get the idea of what hacking is all about. I think it's also better to find out yourself then if you would ask what is important to learn, because there are so many areas you do hacking in, and once you get the overall picture you can decide what interests you most at that moment.

While these comments echo elements of the order knowledge, the poster makes very distinct statements about the importance of commitment to learning. A commitment to learning and understanding computers and technology is needed to discover what topics a hacker finds truly interesting. In addition, continuous changes and improvements in technology compound the length of time required to learn. Thus, hackers must be committed to the continuous identification and acquisition of new information. A hacker named Mack Diesel emphasized the importance of commitment, saying, "the minute you feel you've learned everything is the minute you're out. There's always something new to learn."[91] Hence, hacker subculture places tremendous value on constant learning over time.

The order commitment also reflects the significant amount of effort applied to learn the tradecraft of hacking. Very skilled hackers spend constant and consistent effort in the process of learning and applying their knowledge. For example, a malicious software writer described the process he took to write one piece of code:

> This week has been terrible ... not slept for almost three days ... working on loadable kernel modules [for a rootkit]. During that time had to drink 8 cans of beer, 2 packs of cigarettes (which is a lot for me) to read the manual on the development of loadable kernel modules under the Linux kernel (collated all examples) OK, I finally decided to take sleeping pill after 2 and a half tablets ... slept nearly 20 hours.[92]

The sheer amount of time and dedication he puts toward hacking is evident in his comments. Similar stories can be found across the hacker community.

In addition, a hacker's commitment to learning affected the quality of information he or she is given. This is evident in the forums, where posters who did not attempt to find an answer on their own before posting were berated. This was demonstrated in the following exchange:

SHARKO: Hello … I was looking for some DoS [Denial of Service Attack] tools … I am wondering where I can find these at? Thanks.

CAPTAINMURPHY: If you can't even find a simple program, how do you expect you're going to have the patience to attempt a hack? I suggest this small piece of advice. Search again.

CaptainMurphy berated Shark0 for demonstrating such a lack of effort and gave him no information. This sort of exchange is common in the forums and reveals the relationship between a hacker's level of commitment and the amount of respect he or she is shown while online. If an individual does not prove that he or she puts forth effort to learn on his or her own, he or she is disrespected. This is most evident in the forums when hackers try to obtain information from others. The following exchange highlights the process:

HESHOPOLIS: Hi, I'm interested in the OpenSSL Exploit [a script to attack a system]. But I don't have a nix [Linux] system to test it on. But I cant run it on a windows machine. Anyone know a binary? Don't sta[r]t whit [with] that'juist [just] compile it crap of cource that doesn't work, you'd spend a year looking for all the includes. Tnx.

THE MONKEY: If you can't even fucking compile someone else's exploits, think about actually learning what you're doing before you try doing it. It's clear you know very little about C, which means you probably have no clue how the exploit works, or even what it'll produce in the end. Get your head out of your ass, fuck off, and read a book.

TOMP3T3R5:   Get off your dead ass and code your own exploits, you fucking script kiddie.

These comments plainly demonstrate hackers' stance on the importance of understanding how hacks actually work, which can only be gleaned through hard work and dedication. As such, Heshopolis was flamed, disrespected, and derogatorily referred to as a script kiddie.

Categorization

The ways individuals create and define the hacker identity constitute the fourth normative order of hacker subculture: categorization. Commitment, knowledge, and technology clearly affect the way individuals construct their definition and meaning of the term "hacker." However, there are common discussions in Web forums on how to define hackers and their motives. Posters spend considerable time explaining who and what is a hacker, which may be a consequence of the long-standing debate over the nature of hacking.

Disputes over the nature of hackers and hacking allowed posters to define and differentiate themselves from others within the subculture.[93] The most spirited discussions in forums often center on how individuals define a hacker. One such discussion began because an individual asked "When did you start thinking you were a 'hacker'?" This post was a survey giving users options, including when they "used a port scanner [a tool that identifies the programs running on a target computer]," "used a lamer program with 'hacker tools,'" or "tried to download malicious scripts [programs including viruses and worms] and only ended up hurting yourself." The options available to posters accentuated behavioral measures or benchmarks in a hacker's development. Many users validated the use of such measures, arguing that once they performed a certain task or understood a complicated process, they could consider themselves a hacker. For example, the poster wa1st3d felt he would not be a hacker until he learned "some programming languages ... fully understood Windows ... and Linux [a computer operating system]."

At the same time, many individuals argue that there are attitudinal components that define a hacker, suggesting there are attitudinal components of their definition of "hacker." This includes a certain state of mind or spirit, as described by Brainiackk, who wrote, "The hacker seeks for knowledge, the unknown and tries to reach his own goals. That's the spirit." Curiosity and a desire to learn is an important part of most definitions of hacker, including the one by paranizoid who stressed, "In my opinion, a hacker is a person who is curious and enjoys exploring. Be that someones mind or someone's computer hard drive."

For some, the notion of "hacker" is an ideal to strive toward, primarily because of the knowledge required to become a hacker. The forum user M0thm0nst3rm@n explained:

> I think a real hacker never would call himself a hacker because no matter how much you know, you can't know everything and there's always more to learn. I don't consider myself a hacker, I consider myself a n00b but I hope to be something close to a hacker some day.

Hence, personal opinion significantly influences the forum users' identity and construction of the term "hacker."

Individual conceptions also generate much of the discussion about what different types of hackers do and how this relates to their label or title. This is especially true of the ideology or behaviors associated with each type of hacker discussed earlier in this chapter. For example, there were many disagreements and discussions surrounding two of the main subtypes of hackers: white hats and black hats. Both are considered to be very skilled types of hackers who engage in different behaviors because of different ideologies. As the forum user j@ck0 indicated, "The black hats use their knowledge to destroy things. The white hats use it to build things." However, there was some disagreement over the malicious nature of black hat hackers. For example, kFowl3r responded to j@ck0's comments, suggesting:

> One thing about blackhats, its totally wrong that blackhats only use their knowledge to destroy ... blackhats just hack ... not like whitehats which aren't really hackers since they work against hackers, they build tools to stop people from breaking into systems etc.

These comments indicate that white hats are active in the computer security industry, securing systems from hacks. Black hats are more prevalent in the hacking community, identifying weaknesses and exploits for later attack. Beyond these concepts, arguments over the activities of black and white hat hackers appear to be based on personal opinion. This is apparent in the following exchange concerning the differences between black and white hat hackers:

TOMSERVO: you seem to have a wrong view of blackhats dude … black-hats do audit [computer codes to identify program flaws] for sure … i dont think that a whitehat audits much and codes exploits [ways to attack a system], cuz … blackhats invent new exploitation tekneeqz etc we keep the scene going …

CROW: Imho [In My Honest Opinion] it's just a false statement that whitehats don't invent new exploitation teqs, it may be just the missing "slang" that makes you forget bout that.

The variation present in the meaning of black and white hat hackers illustrates the significance of individual opinion in the hacker experience online. Personal experience influences how they define themselves relative to other hackers. Labels may have specific connotations, but individuals can accept or reject that meaning. In turn, hackers form boundaries between themselves and others based on their definition of hacker. However, this sort of differentiation is not necessarily present off-line. This suggests categorization is relatively unique to the online experience of hacker subculture.

BOX 4.7

New Developments in the Classification of Hackers

This chapter presents hacker classification schemes that categorize hackers based largely on variations among hackers in their criminal motivation. The schemes range from "white hat" or ethical hackers to "black hat" or malicious criminal hackers. These and other similar types of traditional categorization schemes gained wide-scale acceptance over the course of the last decade.

Recent scholarship on hackers and hacker subculture has developed new sorts of classification schemes that base the classification of hackers on information derived from studies on the nature and character of hacker subcultures. We know from this research that hacking is in many ways a learned behavior, whereby hackers interact, communicate, and share (mostly online) certain ideas, attitudes, and behaviors. Studies show that one of the primary motivations of hackers is to learn and acquire new computer skills.[94]

One new classification scheme of hackers developed by Zhang, Tsang, Yue, and Chau (2015) categorizes hackers based on their communication patterns involving both the teaching of hacker skills and the learning of these behaviors from more experienced hackers.[95] They identified four different types of hackers based on their "knowledge exchange behavior," or the degree to which they teach and/or learn from others within online hacker communities. These types are (1) *guru hackers* who primarily taught skills to others, (2) *casual hackers* whose participation in these online communities was minimal, (3) *learning hackers* who primarily acquired knowledge from others, and (4) *novice hackers* who primarily learned but also shared knowledge on hacking. The study overall advances the classification of hackers through the development of a scheme that recognizes hacking as largely a behavior that is learned in interaction with other hackers.

Law

The final social norm driving hacker subculture is law, because hackers regularly discuss the legality of hacking and information sharing in the real world and in cyberspace. Law emphasizes the influence of legal codes in structuring how hackers relate to individuals in and out of hacker subculture. Hackers have become acutely aware of the nature of the law regarding computer networks, because they may want to know if their hacks or related activities are legal, and if they should be performed. There is also a split between hackers who feel there is no need to break the law, while others view hacking in any form as acceptable.

Such competing perspectives can be found in Web forums, as noted in the following exchange. An individual asked for information on a password cracking tool and how to use it. Pilferer answered the poster's question and gave an admonition that was quickly contradicted:

> PILFERER: You do understand that using these password crackers on machines which you don't own or have no permission to access is ILLEGAL?
>
> LEETER: Illegal…. So is masturbation in a public place, but we don't get reminded of that every time anyone thinks about it do we?;)

In some cases, posters inquired about the legal ramifications of certain actions. For example, an individual asked if it is legal to use tools to examine other people's networks if they notified their Internet service provider. The poster received the following responses:

> ZOR@K: Yes, ISP's [Internet Service Providers] can and will detect repeated scans … Yes it would be legal if you got permission from the person but your ISP will still not like it.
>
> CLARENCE: That's untrue, depending where in the world you are then port scanning ISilleagle so be careful.

Legal matters are also regularly addressed at hacker conferences, including Defcon. For example, attorneys from the Electronic Freedom Foundation, a legal foundation supporting digital free speech rights and hacker interests, regularly speak on the current state of law relative to computer hacking. There is also an annual panel titled "Meet The Fed," where individuals from federal, state, and local law enforcement agencies along with the intelligence community come together and allow members of the audience to ask questions on the law and hacking.[96]

However, concern over potential law violations appears to have little effect on hacker behavior. Hackers regularly provide information that could be used to perform a hack regardless of their attitude toward the law. This leads to a contradiction in the process of information sharing. If a hacker shares knowledge with possible illegal applications, he or she justifies its necessity in a variety of ways. Hackers commonly state that they provided information in the hopes of educating others, as in this statement from a tutorial posted in one of the forums on macrovirus construction:

> This is an educational document, I take no responsibility for what use the information in this document is used for. I am unable to blamed for any troubles you get into with the police, FBI,

or any other department … It is not illegal to write viruses, but it is illegal to spread them—something I do not condone and take responsibility for.

Even serious virus writers and sellers are aware of the illegal nature of their activities and note such information on their Web sites. One such Russian group made the following post concerning the tools that could be downloaded from their site, noting: "**Warning!** … all information on our site is given for exceptionally familiarizing purposes. We bear no responsibility for any use."[97]

Similar justifications were used at Defcon, especially when a presenter's content had rather obvious or serious illegal applications. An excellent example of this was in a 2004 presentation titled "Weakness in Satellite Television Protection Schemes or 'How I learned to Love The Dish.'" The presenter, *A*, indicated, "I will not be teaching you how to steal [satellite Internet connectivity] service, but I will give you the background and information to understand how it could be done." However, the second slide in his presentation included the message "Many topics covered may be illegal!" as well as the potential laws they may break by stealing service.[98]

This legal warning reduced the presenter's accountability for how individuals used the information he provided. He simply shared his knowledge on satellite systems and television service. If someone used the information to break the law, *A* had clearly described the laws they could violate by engaging in these actions. Just as with the warning in the macrovirus tutorial, he justified sharing information that could be used to engage in illegal behavior, stealing satellite service, as part of the pursuit of knowledge.

Nevertheless, some hackers do not condone the exchange or supply of overtly illegal information. In some forums, hackers eschew posting blatantly illegal content and forcefully explain their rationale. For example, an individual proclaimed himself "the kind of hacker police really hate" and posted someone's credit card information. One of the senior users posted the following comments in reply:

> Not only do the police hate you regardless if its good or bad to card (btw its bad), someone should delete it because it IS illegal and this is an open forum Go away.

Others, however, actively encourage the exchange of illegal information, as in markets where hacked personal information is sold. For example, an individual who sells stolen credit cards advertised his service stating:

> !!! Hello Everyone. I want to offer great things for your needs from Me—Official Dump [Stolen Bank Account] Seller !!!

> 1) Dumps from all over the world Original Track 1/Track 2

> 1.1) EUROPE Dumps Track 1/Track 2

>> Europe and the rest of world (Following countries are not included: Swiss, Spain, France, Italy, Turkey, Germany, Australia)

>> Visa Classic, MasterCard Standard—$60 per 1 dump

>> Visa Classic, MasterCard Standard (Swiss, Spain, France, Italy, Turkey, Germany, Australia)—$70 per 1 dump

>> Visa Gold | Platinum |Business, MasterCard Gold | Platinum—$100 per 1 dump

>> Visa Gold | Platinum |Business, MasterCard Gold | Platinum (Swiss, Spain, France, Italy, Turkey, Germany, Australia)—$120 per 1 dump

1.2) USA Dumps Original Track 1/Track 2

DUMPS Visa Gold | Platinum | Business | Signature, MasterCard Gold | Platinum, American Express, Discover

Dumps with Name,Address,City,State,Zip,Phone—$100 per 1 dump

Dumps with Name,Address,City,State,Zip,Phone,SSN and DOB—$120 per 1 dump

DUMPS Visa Classic, MasterCard Standard

Dumps with Name,Address,City,State,Zip,Phone—$80 per 1 dump

Dumps with Name,Address,City,State,Zip,Phone,SSN and DOB—$90 per 1 dump

1.3) CANADA Dumps Original Track 1/Track 2

Visa Classic, MasterCard Standard

Amount: >10<50—$19.5 per 1 dump

Amount: >50<100—$14.5 per 1 dump

Amount: >100—$12.5 per 1 dump

Visa Gold | Platinum | Business, MasterCard Gold | Platinum

Amount: >10<50—$34.5 per 1 dump

Amount: >50<100—$32.5 per 1 dump

Amount: >100—$30 per 1 dump[99]

Individuals appreciated his service, and noted the quality of the data, making comments such as "great info!" and "wonderful service!"

The dichotomy of information sharing present in hacker subculture stems from the differences in hacks and cracks. Some feel cracking activities are unacceptable, while others feel it is perfectly justifiable. Forums designed for legitimate nondeviant hackers are less likely to contain illegal information. Other forums, whose audiences are interested in criminal hacks and illegal activities, can contain a great deal of illicit information. It may be difficult for law enforcement agencies to quickly assess the content of a forum, and identifying something illegal can draw investigations when the participants have not actually broken the law. Thus, limiting the amount of illegal information traded in the forums reduces the risk of law enforcement intervention.

In much the same way, law enforcement interest in hackers and hacking influences the way hackers relate to others in and out of the subculture. This is particularly evident at Defcon because of its Spot the Fed contest, which is referred to as "the ever popular paranoia builder," by asking, "Who IS that person next to you?"[100] To play, anyone who feels an attendee is a federal agent can alert one of the convention organizers and claim that he has "spotted a fed." The potential "fed" is then brought on stage before the crowd and asked a series of questions about his life and job. If the person is, in fact, a federal agent, both the fed and the spotter receive T-shirts to commemorate the experience.

There are regular "Spot the Fed" moments during the convention, and it is a Defcon tradition. The game informs attendees about the presence of law enforcement and influences the way individuals relate to one another during the convention. Attendees are much more careful about discussing illegal activities or sharing information in the open. Spot the Fed also creates and reinforces the boundaries between hackers and law enforcement. While the game is "all in good fun" and performed in a tongue-in-cheek manner, attendees often take second glances at those who do not blend in with the crowd. Openly questioning individuals about their lives clearly indicate who is a hacker and who is not. The answers provided by federal agents give hackers information about government agencies and agents. Also, the public spectacle produced from a "spotting" ensures attendees may recognize the differences between hackers and law enforcement. Thus, hackers take steps to limit their exposure to law enforcement agents online and offline. Computer hackers also delineate the boundaries of their subculture by fostering an antagonistic relationship between themselves and law enforcement.[101]

Summary

There are important reasons to understand the hacker subculture when considering computer crime. The fundamental differences in motivation from computer criminals require a categorically different approach to controlling hacking-related crime. Understanding the way hackers define themselves and the history that inspires them can be an important tool to predicting their actions and gauging appropriate responses to criminal hacking. Hackers understand their history in distinct eras and often hold older hackers in high regard. Furthermore, hackers who have a strong connection to technology and demonstrable skill garner more respect than their peers with less knowledge.

Showing a sophisticated understanding of these issues can increase hackers' respect for law enforcement. This increased respect can cultivate connections and information that may be valuable in solving crimes. Prevention efforts can also benefit from properly gauging the audience. Script kiddies and black hat hackers will require a different approach from other hackers. Perhaps, most usefully, understanding the mental processes of justification in the hacker's language and beliefs gives law enforcement an upper hand when dealing with hackers. It may be one of the few advantages available to law enforcement.

Review Questions

1. Explain why hackers do not consider themselves to be criminals. How can someone break the law, but not feel deviant?

2. Explain the hacker ethic. Can individual hackers deviate from the hacker ethic? Do all hackers hold the same understanding of that ethic?

3. What is the hacker manifesto, and how does it compare against the hacker ethic?

4. How has the definition of hacking changed over the last 40 years, and what does this mean for hackers today?

5. Explain the influence of the media on the development of the hacking subculture. Do all hackers agree with the way the media handles hacking? Why or why not?

6. What values drive the hacker subculture, and how does it help us to understand the ways that hackers become involved in and continue to pursue hacking over time?

Critical Thinking Exercises

1. This chapter details the various aspects of hacker subculture that promote shared attitudes, beliefs, and behaviors among hackers. These subcultural values influence how hackers relate to one another, what hackers value, and how these beliefs motivate them to hack. Criminologists have long studied how subcultural values promote deviant and criminal behavior within particular groups of offenders, particular juve-

nile delinquents. We know for example that many delinquents are motivated by a desire to "fit in" and gain status with friends and associates who are also delinquent.

Students should consider whether and if so to what extent hackers are also motivated by a desire to "fit in" and gain status within their hacker-based social networks. Do hackers primarily want to commit crimes, or do they want to impress other hackers? If status is the primary motivation for hackers, then what are the best strategies to mitigate hacking?

2. DEFCON is one of the largest annual hacker conventions held annually in Las Vegas (NV) since 1993. Students interested in learning more about hacker subculture are encouraged to visit the DEFCON Web site at http://www /defcon.org. The convention is a large-scale gathering of hackers and those interested in hacking. There are speeches, vendor areas, and meetings of various hacker groups. These conventions are also attended by employers interested in meeting and hiring hackers as legitimate IT professionals. Students are encouraged to explore the various areas of the convention Web site and consider the nature and character of the DEFCON convention.

   Are these conventions legitimate? Should law enforcement officials attend these conventions? If law enforcement officials attend these conferences, should they be engaged in (a) criminal investigations to identify and eventually punish hackers, or (b) the recruitment of "criminal hackers" to imple-

ment strategies to catch other hackers, or (c) the collection of information on hackers and the nature of hacking only?

3. Many "white hat" hackers who are now involved in legitimate activities including teaching computer science or the protection of critical infrastructures started out as "black hat" or criminal hackers. Some of these individuals promote hacking as a positive activity that ultimately serves to protect society through the identification of weaknesses in software and other information systems. Students interested in learning more about this point of view should visit http://www.ted .com/talks and download the presentations of Ymir Vigfusson and Karen Elazart.

   Is this positive view of hacking legitimate? Should professionals in the IT business be promoting the acquisition of hacking skills among their students through contests and prizes? Do you believe these contests promote or undermine the understanding of privacy rights and/or the legitimacy of federal laws designed to mitigate hacking?

Endnotes

1. LEVY, S. (1984). *Hackers: Heroes of the Computer Revolution.* New York: Dell Publishing; DUFF, L. and GARDINER, S. (1996). "Computer Crime in the Global Village: Strategies for Control and Regulation—In Defence of the Hacker." *International Journal of the Sociology of Law* 24(2): 211–228; HAFNER, K. and LYON, M. (1996). *Where Wizards Stay Up Late: The Origins of the Internet.* New York: Touchstone.

2. ICOVE, D., SEGER, K., and VONSTORCH, W. (1995). *Computer Crime: A Crimefighter's Handbook.* Sebastopol, CA: O'Reilly & Associates; GOLLMAN, D. (1999). *Computer Security.* New York: John Wiley & Sons, Inc.; PARKER, D.B. (1998). *Fighting Computer Crime.* New York: John Wiley & Sons, Inc.

3. CHANDLER, A. (1996). "The Changing Definition and Image of Hackers in Popular Discourse." *International Journal of the Sociology of Law* 24(2): 229–251.

4. HAFNER, K. and MARKOFF, J. (1991). *Cyberpunk: Outlaws and Hackers on the Computer Frontier.* New York: Touchstone.

5. FLOHR, U. (November 1995). *Bank Robbers Go Electronic.* Retrieved May 5, 2004, from *http://www.byte.com/art/9511 /sec3/art11.htm*

6. LOPER, D.K. (2000). "The Criminology of Computer Hackers: A Qualitative and Quantitative Analysis." *Dissertation Abstracts International* 61(8): AAT 9985422.

7. SCHELL, B.H., DODGE, J.L., and MOUTSATSOS, S.S. (2002). *The Hacking of America: Who's Doing It, Why, and How.* Westport, CT: Quorum Books.

8. FURNELL, S. (2002). *Cybercrime: Vandalizing the Information Society.* Boston, MA: Addison-Wesley.

9. RAYMOND, E.S. (August 13, 2003). *The Jargon File, Version 4.4.4.* Retrieved August 30, 2003, from *http://www .catb.org/∼esr/jargon/.*

10. HOLT, T.J. (2007). "Subcultural Evolution? Examining the Influence of On- and Off-Line Experiences on Deviant Subcultures." *Deviant Behavior* 28(2): 171–198.

11. ABBIE H. was a political activist and founder of the Youth International Party ("Yippies"). He was one of the Chicago Seven, who went on trial after violence erupted at the 1968 Democratic National Convention in Chicago.

12. The Bell System was dominant, but there were much smaller local—and a few regional—companies.

13. LAPSLEY, P. (2013). *Exploding the Phone: The Untold Story of the Teenagers and Outlaws Who Hacked Ma Bell.* Jackson, TN: Grove Atlantic Press.

14. *Ibid.*

15. RAYMOND, E.S. (August 13, 2003). *The Jargon File, Version 4.4.4.* Retrieved August 30, 2003, from *http://www .catb.org/∼esr/jargon/.*

16. *Ibid.*

17. HOLT, T.J. and COPES, H. (Forthcoming). "Transferring Subcultural Knowledge Online: Practices and Beliefs of Persistent Digital Pirates." *Deviant Behavior.*

18. SANDOVAL, G. (April 21, 2009). "Congress to Probe P2P Sites over 'Inadvertent Sharing.'" *CNET News.*

19. US-CERT (United States Computer Emergency Readiness Team). (February 6, 2013). "Risks of File Sharing." See *http://www.us-cert.gov/ncas/tips/st05-007*.

20. HOLT, T.J., SOLES, J., and LESLIE, L. (2008). "Characterizing Malware Writers and Computer Attackers in Their Own Words." The Proceedings of the 2008 Conference on Information Warfare.

21. STERLING, B. (1992). *The Hacker Crack-Down: Law and Disorder on the Electronic Frontier.* New York: Bantam Books.

22. *Ibid.*, p. 8

23. LITTMAN, J. (September 18, 1997). *Hacker Shocker: Project Reveals Breaches Galore.* Retrieved from *http://www5.zdnet.com/zdnn/content/zdnn/0918/zdnn0010.html*.

24. 18 U.S.C. § 1029 et seq.

25. 18 U.S.C. § 1030 et seq.

26. WALL, D.S. (2001). "Cybercrimes and the Internet." In D.S. WALL (ed.), *Crime and the Internet.* New York: Routledge, pp. 1–17.

27. BECKER, H.S. (1963). *Outsiders: Studies in the Sociology of Deviance.* New York: Free Press.

28. LOPER, "The Criminology of Computer Hackers."

29. *Ibid.*

30. VIGFUSSON, Y. (2014). "Why I Teach People to Hack." *TEDx.* Available at *http://www.ted.com/talks*.

31. ELAZART, K. (2014). "Hackers: The Internet Immune System." *TEDx.* Available at *http://www.ted.com/talks*.

32. WILLIAMS, M. (2001). "The Language of Cyberspace." In D.S. WALL (ed.), *Crime and the Internet.* New York: Routledge, pp. 152–166.

33. MANN, D., and SUTTON, M. (1998). "Netcrime: More Change in the Organization of Thieving." *British Journal of Criminology* 38(2): 201–229.

34. PARKER, *Fighting Computer Crime.*

35. BARRETT, N. (1997). *Digital Crime: Policing the Cybernation.* London: Kogan Page.

36. GOLDSTEIN, E. (June 13, 1993). "Hacker Testimony to House Subcommittee Largely Unheard." In J. THOMAS and G. MEYER (eds.), *Computer Underground Digest, 5.43.* DeKalb, IL: Editor. Retrieved February 26, 2000, from *http://venus.soci.niu.edu/∼cudigest/CUDS5/cud543.txt*.

37. GOLDSTEIN, E. (1996). "Knowledge Is Strength." *2600: The Hacker Quarterly* 13(4): 4–5.

38. SILOWASH, G., CAPPELLI, D., MOORE, A., TRZECIAK, R., SHIMEALL, T., and FLYN, L. (December 2012). *Common Sense Guide to Mitigating Insider Threats,* 4th ed. Software Engineering Institute—Carnegie Mellon University, CERT Program.

39. HADNAGY, C. (September 2009). Social Engineer Defined. Social-Engineer.org. Retrieved June 5, 2013, from *http://www.social-engineer.org/framework/Social_Engineering_Defined*.

40. SILOWASH, CAPPELLI, MOORE, TRZECIAK, SHIMEALL, and FLYN. (December 2012). *Common Sense Guide to Mitigating Insider Threats, 4th ed.*

41. *Ibid.*

42. KING, C. (January 2012). *Spotlight On: Malicious Insiders and Organized Crime Activity.* Software Engineering Institute—Carnegie Mellon University, CERT Program.

43. CHANDLER, "The Changing Definition and Image of Hackers in Popular Discourse."

44. GILMORE, J. (June 4, 1999). "Crackers Do for Gov't What Critical Infrastructure Report Couldn't." *RISKS Digest* 20(43). Retrieved August 22, 2003, from *http://catless.ncl.ac.uk/Risks/20.43.html#subj5*.

45. Honeynet Project (July 21, 2000). *Know Your Enemy: The Tools and Methodologies of the Script Kiddie.* Retrieved September 13, 2003, from *http://projecthoneynet.org/papers/enemy/*.

46. *Ibid.*

47. *Ibid.*, p. 10.

48. *Ibid.*

49. DALLAWAY, E. (May 8, 2013). "Black Hat 2013: Industry Response to General Alexander's Keynote." *InfoSecurity Blog.* See *http://www.infosecurity-magazine.com/blog/2013/8/5/black-hat-2013-industry-response-to-general-alexanders-keynote-/964.aspx*.

50. TAYLOR, P. (2001). "Hacktivism: In Search of Lost Ethics?" In D.S. WALL (ed.), *Crime and the Internet.* New York: Routledge, pp. 59–73.

51. JORDAN, T. and TAYLOR, P. (2004). *Hacktivism and Cyberwars: Rebels with a Cause.* New York: Routledge.

52. Ibid., p. 7.

53. WAITES, R. (October 20, 2011). "V for Vendetta Masks: Who." *BBC News.*

54. RAZA, A. (January 13, 2016). "8 Awesome Hacks Conducted by Anonymous Hackers." *HackRead.* Available at *http://www.hackread.com*.

55. LEVY, *Hackers.*

56. *Ibid.*

57. *Ibid.*

58. THOMAS, D. (2002). *Hacker Culture.* Minneapolis, MN: University of Minnesota Press.

59. LEVY, *Hackers.*

60. *Ibid.*

61. *Ibid.*

62. MEYER, G.R. (1989). "The Social Organization of the Computer Underground." Unpublished Masters Thesis. Retrieved December 29, 2003, from *http://csrc.nist.gov/secpubs/hacker.txt*.

63. *Ibid.*

64. *Ibid.*, p. 8.

65. *Ibid.*, p. 48.

66. *Ibid.*, p. 8.

67. *Ibid.*

68. BLANKENSHIP, L. (1986). *The Hacker Manifesto.* Retrieved March 21, 2000, from *http://viaduct.custom.net/glitch/manif.htm*.

69. SLATALLA, M. and QUITTNER, J. (1995). *Masters of Deception: The Gang That Ruled Cyberspace.* New York: Harper Collins Publishers.

70. STERLING, *The Hacker Crack-Down.*

71. SHIMOMURA, T. (1996). *Takedown: The Pursuit and Capture of Kevin Mitnick, America's Most Wanted Computer Outlaw—By the Man Who Did It.* New York: Hyperion.

72. *Ibid.*, p. 44.

73. FRANKLIN, J., PAXSON, V., PERRIG, A., and SAVAGE, S. (2007). "An Inquiry into the Nature and Cause of the Wealth of Internet Miscreants." Paper presented at CCS07, October 29–November 2, 2007 in Alexandria, VA; HOLT, T.J. and LAMPKE, E. (2009). "Exploring Stolen Data Markets On-Line: Products and Market Forces." *Criminal Justice Studies* 33(2); Honeynet Research Alliance. (2003). "Profile: Automated Credit Card Fraud." *Know Your Enemy Paper* series. Retrieved June 21, 2005, from *http://www.honeynet.org/papers/profiles/cc-fraud.pdf;* THOMAS, R. and MARTIN, J. (2006). "The Underground Economy: Priceless." *USENIX:login* 31(6): 7–16. *Ibid.*, p. 3.

74. HOLT, "Subcultural Evolution?"

75. JORDAN, T. and TAYLOR, P. (1998). "A Sociology of Hackers." *The Sociological Review* 46(4): 757–780; TAYLOR, P. (1999). *Hackers: Crime in the Digital Sublime.* New York: Routledge.

76. HOLT, "Subcultural Evolution?"

77. MACK, D. (personal communication, October 10, 2003).

78. *Ibid.*, p. 120.

79. *Ibid.*, p. 27.

80. *Ibid.*, p. 44.

81. MORGAN, J. (May 13, 2014). "A Simple Explanation of 'The Internet of Things.'" *Forbes.*

82. STATT, N. (2016). "How an Army of Vulnerable Gadgets Took Down the Web Today." *CNBC.com.* Available at *http://www.cnbc.com/2016/10/22.*

83. MG (personal communication, April 5, 2004).

84. DARK, O.z. (personal communication, August 18, 2004).

85. HOLT, T.J. (2008). "Lone Hacks or Group Cracks: Examining the Social Organization of Computer Hackers." In F. SCHMALLEGER and M. PITTARO (eds.), *Crimes of the Internet.* Upper Saddle River, NJ: Pearson Prentice Hall, pp. 336–355.

86. *www.defcon.org*

87. HOLT, T.J. (2006). "Examining the Changing Nature of DEF CON over the Last 14 Years." Presented at the Defcon 14 Convention, Las Vegas, Nevada.

88. *Ibid.*, p. 129.

89. *Ibid.*

90. JORDAN and TAYLOR "A Sociology of Hackers"; TAYLOR, *Hackers.*

91. *Ibid.*, p. 122.

92. *Ibid.*, p. 16.

93. *Ibid.*, p. 10.

94. SARMA, M. and Lam, A. (2013). "Knowledge Creation and Innovation in the Virtual Community? Exploring Structure, Values and Identity in Hacker Groups." Paper presented at 35th DRUID Celebration Conference, Barcelona, Spain.

95. ZHANG, X., TSANG, A., YUE, W.T., and CHAU, M. (2015). "The Classification of Hackers by Knowledge Exchange Behaviors." *Information Systems Front* 19: 1239–1251.

96. *Ibid.*, p. 129.

97. *Ibid.*, p. 16.

98. *Ibid.*, p. 129.

99. HOLT and LAMPKE, "Exploring Stolen Data Markets On-Line."

100. *Ibid.*, p. 129.

101. *Ibid.*, p. 120.

Sophisticated Cyber Criminal Organizations

CHAPTER OBJECTIVES

After completing this chapter, you should be able to

- Describe the evolution of cyber crime from rogue individuals to sophisticated criminal organizations engaged in the illegal activity.
- Define and describe the various types of espionage.
- Define and describe the various types of insider fraud.
- Identify and discuss various types of sophisticated criminal organizations or enterprises engaged in cyber crime.
- Discuss the underground marketplace referred to as the "deep web" or Tor Net.

INTRODUCTION

Crime has plagued the world since the dawn of man. Terrorist tactics were debatably first used as early as the first century; however, the word "terrorism" was not used until 1795 during the French Revolution.[1] While crime and terrorism tactics in general did not evolve dramatically over the past hundred years, the advent of technology, including the computer, the Internet, cellular telephones, smartphones, airplanes, and electronic commerce, has presented criminals and terrorists with an opportunity to evolve and therefore improve their approach, operations, expand their reach, and enhance their capabilities like no other time in history. With regard to crime and the use of technology, specifically the Internet, new terms were coined—cybercrime, cyberterrorism, and information warfare. As we learned in Chapter 1, cybercrime is loosely defined as the commission of a crime with the use of a computer and a network (e.g., the Internet).

Cybercrime is an evolved state of traditional crime; it continues to mature. From the first cyber-related attack on the United States' first electronic phone system in 1870 to the theft of hundreds of millions of credit card data records in the past five years, cybercriminals are continuing to learn how to use today's leading-edge technology against us.[2] Consumers want more bank ATMs around the country to make it easier to access their cash; retail shoppers want to be able to check-out faster (speed-pass); online and mobile banking are becoming more popular; connecting home electronics, like thermostats and smart TVs to the Internet; accessing work computers from home; bringing personal devices to work and connecting them to the corporate network … the list could go on and on with examples of how our global society is relying more and more on information-based technologies. This demand for better technology to support greater consumer demand and convenience is, as a result, driving the development, and subsequent risk posed by cybercrime to new heights. As a result, the attacks and methods that cybercriminals are using today have changed and will continue to change, primarily in response to increased security vigilance, allocation of cyber-focused law enforcement, cyber security training, and regulatory controls that require specific security safeguards intended to mitigate the risk of being compromised by sophisticated cybercriminals.

It is important to note that elements of cybercrime are inherent in and practically identical to the activities of cyber terrorism and state-sponsored information warfare and espionage (as discussed in Chapter 2), and the distinction between these activities is most often defined from the perspective of the victim.[3] Who was the attacker—a criminal seeking profit, a terrorist with a cause, or a rogue state attempting to steal information? In addition, state-sponsored information warfare will likely employ methods of cybercrime and cyberterrorism, such as the compromise and manipulation of mass transit systems (air and rail), for example, with the added benefit of economic gain from extortion or credit card theft as well as mass chaos. Furthermore and adding to the blurred line, nation-states are known to "dip a toe" into the world of cybercrime during their operations in order to facilitate their mission and/or expand the range of their capabilities.[4] In Chapters 1 and 2 we started the discussion of how these types of activities overlap and this continues into our discussion on sophisticated criminal organizations and cybercrime. The simple truth may be that we cannot tell the difference between these activities until long after the attack has occurred.

BOX 5.1

Cybercrime and Criminals: The Early Years

Traditionally and up through the 1990s, cybercriminals would conduct direct attacks at consumer computers or corporate networks, targeting, for example, "Salami Slicing" (shaving pennies from little used accounts) at New York's Dime Saving Bank[1] ($1.5 million by a bank teller in 1971), First National Bank of Chicago ($70 million through falsified wire authorizations in the 1980s), Kevin Mitnick's famous attacks on the U.S. phone systems in the 1980s and 1990s, attacks on the U.S. Military (theft of classified information by Dark Dante in the 1990s),[2] and the attack on CitiGroup ($10 million theft by Russian hacker Vladimir Levin in 1990s).[3] These attacks took advantage of the lack of security controls protecting the networks, systems, data, and processes that were compromised. The inventors of technology, even today, typically focus on the functionality and stability of the system without understanding the security and process control requirements necessary to protect it from being compromised. As a result, cybercrime was able to evolve with little resistance during the period from the 1970s through the late 1990s. During this time, criminals began to understand the inherent weaknesses in computer systems and networks, as well as the inherent weaknesses found in the users of these systems. Poorly coded applications accessible through the Internet (bank wire transfers), poor process controls that did not consider reviewing application or system error logs for security events like failed login attempts (typically only reviewed if the application was not functioning properly), and liberal access controls on systems attached to the globally connected Internet were all examples of weaknesses during the early years of technological advancement that also provided a classroom for helping cybercriminals learn how to mature their new tradecraft.

---

[1]Parker, Donn. (September 2012). "Computer Abuse 1973." *ISSA Journal.*

[2]Macz, Mad. (2002). *Internet Underground: The Way of the Hacker.* PageFree Publishing, Inc. *http://www.GalaxyInnovations.com*

[3]Newton, Michael. (2004). *The Encyclopedia of High-Tech Crime and Crime-Fighting.* New York: Checkmark Books.

ESPIONAGE AND THE THEFT OF INTELLECTUAL PROPERTY

Espionage, similar to the evolution of traditional crime, has its roots as an elementary and basic tradecraft reportedly first perpetrated in the 1700s when China's method for manufacturing porcelain was revealed in Europe, which provided European companies with the information necessary to compete with China's superior product and eventually impacted the market for porcelain.[5] Espionage continues today as an elaborate cybercrime as well as a nation state-sponsored activity with similar objectives—theft of intellectual property (IP) for gain. IP can be defined as a legal concept referring to creations of the mind (e.g., inventions, patents, literary and artistic works, trademarks, copyrighted material, recordings, photographs and pictures, designs, and formulas) owned by specific corporate or individual entities, for which exclusive rights are recognized.[6]

There are various types of espionage, as defined by the Office of the National Counterintelligence Executive, intended for commercial and criminal purposes, rather than national security or nation state objectives, and they have become more common with the evolution of technology and the growth of large-scale, sophisticated criminal enterprises. Industrial espionage is the misappropriation of trade secrets related to or included in a product that is produced for or placed in interstate or foreign commerce to the economic benefit of anyone other than the owner, with the knowledge or intent that the offense will injure the owner of that trade secret. Economic espionage is the misappropriation of trade secrets with the knowledge or intent that the offense will benefit a foreign government, foreign instrumentality, or foreign agent. Misappropriation in these instances includes stealing, copying, transmitting, buying, and/or destroying someone else's trade secrets. Furthermore, both instances are considered criminal acts under the Economic Espionage Act of 1996 (EEA), the first federal act to define and enforce penalties for trade secret theft, making it illegal to steal, copy, sketch, download, or communicate them to others without permission.[7] Corporate espionage occurs primarily between different types of organizations and is conducted by corporate spies infiltrating the target organization, or eavesdropping on competitor communications, digging through trash for discarded draft reports, and planting wiretaps on phones and computerized logging devices on accessible computers, like the receptionist or conference room media computer. Criminal activities related to corporate espionage are prosecuted under various other federal statutes, (discussed in Chapter 10) including the US PATRIOT Act, Computer Fraud and Abuse Act of 1986, and Electronic Eavesdropping (USC Title 18, Part I, Chapter 119).

The Federal Bureau of Investigation (FBI) estimates that U.S. companies are losing billions of dollars every year to foreign and domestic competitors and related criminal elements (Espionage as a Service [EaaS] will be discussed later.). The FBI also indicated that foreign competitors have obtained intelligence by recruiting or implanting insiders at the target organization, establishing "cover" organizations to engage in business relationships to build and abuse trust, or by other means like bribery, theft, and hacking.[8]

The American Society of Industrial Services (ASIS) published the results from their 2007 survey, "Trends in Proprietary Information Loss," which adds perspective to American businesses' challenge to protect their IP from traditional and evolving threats.[9] From the 2007 survey, businesses responded that the theft of their IP resulted in damages ranging from $10,000 to more than $5.5 million and that their IP was compromised regardless of format (paper, electronic, verbal conversation, or prototypes);

FIGURE 5.1 Type of IP targeted for theft (2007 ASIS Report on Trends in Proprietary Information Loss).

Source: Type of Information Asset from Trends in Proprietary Information Loss Survey Report. Copyright © 2007 ASIS International, Inc. Used by permission of ASIS International.

malicious actions from current and former employees were the primary threat; and the exploitation of trusted relationships with vendors, customers, and other resource providers was a significant threat to the security of their IP. Figure 5.1 summarizes the types of IP that was targeted for theft, as indicated by respondents to the 2007 survey.

QUICK FACTS

In 2015, the Federal Bureau of Investigation (FBI) reported a 53 percent increase in economic espionage cases involving the theft of trade secrets leading to the loss of hundreds of billions of dollars in just one year. China, North Korea, Russia, and Iran were nation-states identified as increasing their attacks against global businesses. To make matters worse, the World Economic Forum (WEF) reported, just one year later, that industrial espionage is the hardest cybercrime to detect, particularly where access to confidential documents and data is successful, yet no changes, vandalism, or theft occurs. Those numbers would arguably dramatically increase the number of cybercrimes overall, causing experts to forecast the cost of data breaches to exceed $2.1 trillion globally by 2019!

Sources: Steven Morgan, "Cyber Crime Costs Project to Reach $2 Trillion by 2019," *Forbes* (January 10, 2016). *Available at https:// www.forbes.com/sites/stevemorgan/2016/01/17/cyber-crime-costs-projected-to-reach-2-trillion-by-2019/#37eb0ffe3a91.*

Wesley Bruer, "FBI sees Chinese Involvement amid Sharp Rise in Economic Espionage Cases." CNN News (July 24, 2015). *Available at http://www.cnn.com/2015/07/24/politics/fbi-economic-espionage/index.html.*

The National Bureau of Asian Research published an update to the 2013 "IP Commission Report" in February 2017[10] The report estimated that the annual cost of IP theft to the U.S. economy now exceeds $600 billion, $400 billion of which was attributed to hacking as identified by the Office of the Director of National Intelligence. The report also states that in response, then president Obama signed the Defend Trade Secrets Act of 2016, and the Department of Justice indicted five members of PLA unit 61398 in Shanghai for economic espionage related to their hacking into the networks of several U.S. companies to steal trade secrets. Additional perspective on IP crime was provided by a 2011 *National Law Journal* article on the U.S. Department of Justice's (DOJ) focus on prosecuting trade secret theft.[11] In 2010, the FBI opened more than 190 new criminal investigations into IP theft, of which 66 were related to trade secret theft. Trade secret theft in these cases involved both industrial and economic espionage. Many of these cases were attributed to organized crime.

Organized crime is defined by the FBI as "any group having some manner of a formalized structure and whose primary objective is to obtain money though illegal activities and such groups maintain their position through the use of actual or threatened violence, corrupt public officials, graft, or extortion, and generally have a significant impact on their locales, region, or the country as a whole."[12] These organizations attempt to hide their espionage crimes by involving multiple resources with knowledge of organizational processes and controls, working in different locations, branches, or departments. These resources are either selling information to the crime organization or employed by it.[13]

The business of corporate espionage can become blurred and is often confused with nation state-sponsored attacks, as discussed in Chapter 2. This blurred line is often visible by many in the information security field at the investigative level, but is usually not reported because there is more money in finding a state-sponsored story that creates media buzz about a company, product, or services than in the underworld of corporate theft and espionage.

Espionage as a Service (EaaS) is not like traditional corporate espionage, where one company targets a competitor, but instead a group of sophisticated criminals (many times from a traditional crime cartel or family) collect as much information as possible on as many high-value targets as possible and then sell that information to as many competitors and interested parties as possible. EaaS is very sophisticated and stealthy. EaaS actors do not want to get caught, but they are often not as well-trained or financed as state actors and hence typically leave forensic traces of their activities (IP addresses, code, networks used, etc.). These remnants are often used to differentiate the two. For instance in 2013, the Straggler Group was developed as a front organization to operate primarily in the tourism industry, capturing data on innocent business travelers entering specific countries, spying on and stealing data from them during their visit, and documenting their activities until they leave. During their visit, the Straggler Group would compromise their itinerary, knowing where they would be, and attempt to compromise their smart phones, laptops, documents, and social interactions. This information would then be analyzed, summarized, and categorized for the group's sales catalog. The information was then placed on both legitimate and underground Web sites for sale. If the information appeared valuable (e.g., blackmail, extortion, and bribery), someone would buy it. The Straggler Group was eventually taken down as an EaaS gang with ties to APT1 (discussed in Chapter 2), but developed strictly as a "for profit" entity in the organized crime world.[14]

BOX 5.2
Selected Cases Involving Espionage

Industrial Espionage

The first documented case of espionage. Père d'Entrecolles was a French Jesuit missionary in the early 1700s. He was also an industrial spy. While in China, the leading maker of high-quality porcelain at the time, he learned the secret techniques for manufacturing the ceramic by gaining access to the kilns, studying Chinese books, and getting "many particulars from my neophytes, several of whom work in porcelain." D'Entrecolles then detailed what he learned in letters that he sent back to France. "Nothing but my curiosity could ever have prompted me to such researches," he wrote, "but it appears to me that a minute description of all that concerns this kind of work might, somehow, be useful in Europe."[1]

2017—Uber (Uber Technologies, Inc.) was ordered by a U.S. federal judge to return confidential files to Alphabet, Inc.'s Waymo Self-Driving Car Unit, stating that "Uber knew, or should have known, that an ex-Waymo engineer it later hired had taken 14,000 confidential Waymo files, potentially containing trade secrets, and that some of the intellectual property had 'seeped into' Uber's own [self-driving car] development efforts." Waymo also noted that they identified evidence of the ex-engineer's document downloading activities prior to leaving the company. The court ruling did not shut down Uber's self-driving car initiatives or impose any fines, but did exclude the ex-Waymo engineer from participating in any related development and required the return of all Waymo documents by May 31, 2017.[2]

2012—U.S. federal **Operation Bitter Pill** (managed by the National Intellectual Property Rights Coordination Center) targeted the distribution and sale of counterfeit pharmaceuticals, which were manufactured and branded with information stolen from legitimate companies. During the operation, U.S. agents seized 686 Internet domain names associated with Web sites that were unlawfully distributing the fake drugs. The U.S. operation was part of a larger global operation called Pangea V, which was a week-long global enforcement effort focused on disrupting the organized crime networks running the online sale of these potentially fatal drugs. Preliminary worldwide results of these operations accounted for 79 arrests, seizure of 18,000 related Web sites, and the seizure of 3.7 million doses of counterfeit medicines (including anti-cancer, antibiotics, Viagra, and Cialis) worth an estimated $10.5 million.[3]

Corporate Espionage

1981—In 1981 Hitachi mysteriously came into possession of an almost full set of IBM's Adirondack Workbooks that contained IBM design documents full of IBM technical secrets. The workbooks were prominently marked FOR INTERNAL IBM USE ONLY, though it did not prompt Hitachi to return them. IBM counterintelligence staff helped FBI agents identify and arrest several IBM officials (insiders). Hitachi settled out of court, and paid IBM a sum of approximately $300 million.[4]

2007—Sean Edward Howley and Clark Alan Roberts, employees of Wyko Tire Technology, visited a Goodyear tire plant with the intention of taking camera phone photos of the production machinery necessary for making large industrial tires for earth moving equipment. This information would then be used by Wyko to build a facility with the necessary technology to make the tires.

Wyko already had a contract with a Chinese manufacturer to make these tires, but lacked the appropriate machinery. The IT manager at Wyko noticed e-mail messages between Howley, Roberts, and company management with comments and photos related to Goodyear. The IT manager called Goodyear and subsequently the FBI became involved. In 2011, a jury convicted both men with corporate espionage and each received a modest sentence; however, the government appealed the case and it is set for resentencing in 2013.[5]

Economic Espionage—Organized Crime Involvement

2009 was the first time an economic espionage case would reach trial, under the Economic Espionage Act, in the U.S. (six similar cases settled before trial). A Chinese-born engineer (Dongfan "Greg" Chung) stole trade secrets from Boeing, related to the phased antenna array and the $16 million fueling mechanism for the delta booster rockets for the U.S. space shuttle; a Chinese spy for the last 30 years, Chung pleaded not guilty, but was sentenced to 15 years for stealing sensitive information on the U.S. space program with the intention of passing it to China.[6] Evidence against him include a separate FBI investigation into Chinese spies that uncovered Chung's contact information; letters detailing the shipment of U.S. trade secrets to China via sea freight; his 1979 letter to China that states, "Having been a Chinese compatriot for over thirty years and being proud of the achievements by the people's efforts for the motherland, I am regretful for not contributing anything, I would like to make an effort to contribute to the Four Modernizations of China"; and of course there was the 300,000 stolen documents that federal agents found covering every available surface of Chung's house.[7]

2012—Twenty-nine people were charged in New Jersey for an international scheme to import counterfeit goods and drugs, and to launder money. March 2, 2012, marked one of the largest counterfeit goods cases in U.S. history. Federal agents disrupted a massive conspiracy to import more than $300 million in counterfeit goods from China and illegal drugs from Taiwan. Agents also identified a plot to import 50 kilograms of crystal methamphetamine. The entire case was connected to Asian organized crime cartels.[8]

[1] d'ENTRECOLLES, PERE. (1712). The Letters of Pere d'Entrecolles. Porcelain, It's Art and Manufacture, B.T. Batsford, London.
[2] Waymo LLC. v. Uber Technologies, Inc., case number 3.2017cv00939, California Northern District. Retrieved May 24, 2017, from http://dockets.justia.com/docket/california/candce/3:2017cv00939/308136

[3]U.S. Immigration and Customs Enforcement—Homeland Security Investigations. (2012). Operation Bitter Pill. See *http://www.ice.gov/news/releases/1210/121004washingtondc.htm*

[4]JOYAL, PAUL. (1996). *Industrial Espionage Today and Information Wars of Tomorrow.* Presented at the 19th National Information Systems Security Conference, Baltimore, MD, on October 22, 1996. See *http://csrc.nist.gov/nissc/1996/papers/NISSC96/joyal/industry.pdf*

[5]Federal Bureau of Investigation. (2010). *Two Engineers Found Guilty of Stealing Goodyear Trade Secret.* See *http://www.fbi.gov/knoxville/press-releases/2010/kx120910.htm*

[6]FLACCUS, GILLIAN. (February 8, 2010). "Dongfan 'Greg' Chung, Chinese Spy, Gets More Than 15 Years in Prison." *Huffington Post.* See *http://www.huffingtonpost.com/2010/02/08/dongfan-greg-chung-chines_n_454107.html*

[7]FLACCUS, GILLIAN. (June 2, 2009). "First Economic Espionage Trial Begins in US." *Associated Press.*

[8]U.S. Immigration and Customs Enforcement—Homeland Security Investigations. (2012). Press Release—"29 Charged in New Jersey in International Schemes to Import Counterfeit Goods and Drugs, Launder Profits." See *http://www.ice.gov/news/releases/1203/120302newark.htm*

INSIDER FRAUD

The U.S. Department of Commerce released figures in 2011, which indicated that employee theft played a role in 95 percent of business failures, and almost 30 percent of all business bankruptcies. According to the Department of Commerce, employee theft costs U.S. businesses almost a billion dollars per week, over 40 billion dollars per year. These losses are primarily due to the misappropriation of cash and/or noncash assets by employees through various forms of fraud.[15]

In Chapter 4, we talked about differences between cybercriminals and hackers. In this chapter, we focus on sophisticated criminals and in particular those who seek financial gain. Internal fraud can come from employees, including managers, and even board members. Employees generally commit fraud when a permissive environment or misplaced trust exists. When inadequate internal controls exist, or if controls exist but are not enforced, employees are tempted and criminals will take action. In addition to the rogue employee acting alone, there are insiders who conspire with other insiders to form their own criminal enterprise, insiders who are recruited by outside organized crime, and outside organized criminal elements that obtain employment for the purpose of gaining the access of an insider and perpetrating their fraud.

In fraud crimes involving management level employees, average losses were higher than lower-level employee crimes. In two of the CERT insider threat cases from 2012, where management level insiders were involved, the thefts ranged from $250,000 to over $48 million.[16] The Association of Certified Fraud Examiners' (ACFE) 2016 Global Fraud Study found that most fraud schemes originated in the accounting department (16.6%), followed by operations, sales, upper management, customer service, purchasing, and finance. The ACFE 2016 study also found that the perpetrator's level of authority was "strongly correlated with the size of the fraud and the median loss by an executive was $703,000; four times higher than managers and eleven times higher than employees."[17] In addition, management level employees often recruit their lower-level employees into the crime; together they use their knowledge of the organization's systems, controls, and procedures to bypass check points and further scrutiny.

Fraud-related crimes over the past several years have involved the use of company systems and databases to modify, use, and/or download and sell company data (customer/patient information, credit card data, e-mail addresses, etc.). Fraudsters primarily used company data to commit identity theft, insurance fraud, and embezzlement when working alone or with other internal coconspirators. When insiders conspire with or are recruited by outside organized crime groups, the fraud is typically related to financial gains resulting from system and data manipulation, or the bulk exfiltration of data to the outsiders.[18]

BOX 5.3

Case Study: Cyber Frauds are Often Committed by Insiders Acting Alone

Jerome Kerviel graduated from a French University in 2000 with a master's degree in finance; he then took an entry-level compliance position with the French investment bank Societe Generale. Between 2000 and 2005, Kerviel became very familiar with the bank's compliance controls, alerts, and thresholds. In 2005, he was promoted to the position of junior trader and began conducting trades on behalf of the bank.[1] Over the next 3 years, Kerveil made thousands of fictitious, unauthorized, and noncompliant transactions by avoiding the known internal system triggers and alerts that would typically notify bank management of his activity. In 2008, when a compliance auditor happen to investigate a large transaction, what he found unwound years of built-up trading risk caused by Kerviel. The end result, Kerviel was fired and charged with attempted fraud, abuse of confidence, and illegal access to computers; the damages to Societe Generale totaled approximately $7 billion.[2] Kerviel was convicted and sentenced to 3 years in prison, though actually only serving 5 months behind bars, and $6.9 billion in restitution, which was later reduced to $1 million.[3]

Sources: [1] Based on Rayner, Gordon; Allen, Peter (26 January 2008). ""Profile: Rogue trader Jerome Kerviel"". London: The Telegraph. Retrieved 28 January 2008

[2] NICOLA CLARK (28 January 2008). ""Bank Outlines How Trader Hid His Activities"". New York Times. Retrieved 28 January 2008.

[3] "French court upholds rogue trader Jérôme Kerviel's prison sentence". The Guardian. 19 March 2014.

In addition, the CERT Insider Threat Study on Illicit Cyber Activity Involving Fraud in the U.S. Financial Services Sector found that insiders who conducted a "low and slow" approach accomplished more damage and escaped detection longer. The study also defined and tracked four milestones in fraud cases and the timeframes between the milestones (see Figure 5.2). The milestones were as follows: (1) getting hired at the target company, (2) beginning criminal activity, (3) the company detects the fraud, and (4) the company reports the fraud to law enforcement. The following timeline presents the milestones and the average timeframe between them, for the 47 insider cases included in this 2012 study. The average timeframe between getting hired (1) and beginning the fraud (2) was just under 62 months, whereas the average time between beginning the fraud (2) and being detected (3) was just under 32 months. The average time between being detected (3) and being fired, an ancillary step not included in the four milestones, was predictably zero months.[19]

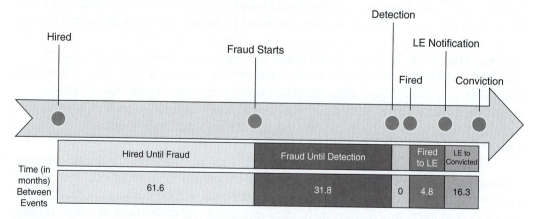

FIGURE 5.2   Average time between milestones (CERT Insider Fraud Study, 2012).

Special permission to reproduce portions of "Average Time Between Milestones" © 2012 by Carnegie Mellon University, has been granted by the Software Engineering Institute.

Many of these cases involved organized crime and cartels. As might be easily predicted, these cases had significantly more players and the dollar amount of impact was also much higher (see Figure 5.3). For instance, in an October 2007 case, 73 people, including several members and associates of an Armenian-American organized criminal enterprise (Mirzoyan-Terdjanian), were charged with various health care fraud-related crimes involving more than $163 million in fraudulent billing. This was the largest Medicare fraud scheme ever perpetrated by a single criminal organization and resulted in a larger, combined Medicare case that involved a total of 91 individuals and $430 million in fraud. The group engaged in "highly-organized, multi-million-dollar schemes to defraud Medicare and insurance companies by submitting fraudulent bills for medically unnecessary treatments or treatments that were never performed. They used stolen identities of doctors and thousands of Medicare beneficiaries and operated at least 118 different phony clinics in 25 states for the purposes of submitting fraudulent Medicare reimbursements.[20]

Case	Total Conspirators	Insiders	Outsiders	Impact	Insider Led?
1	10	4	6	$48,115,451	Yes
2	94	1	93	$10,000,000	No
3	4	3	1	$6,775,434	Yes
4	3	1	2	$2,700,000	Yes
5	14	13	1	$2,286,946	Unknown
6	10	1	9	$1,500,000	Unknown
7	7	2	5	$1,000,000	No
8	4	1	3	$841,164	Yes
9	10	5	5	$800,000	Yes
10	6	1	5	$638,000	No
11	6	2	4	$335,000	No
12	16	6	10	$287,500	Unknown
13	4	4	0	$250,000	Yes
14	6	1	5	$231,500	Yes
15	6	1	5	$157,000	Unknown
16	16	1	15	$77,300	No
17	6	2	4	$75,000	Yes
18	2	1	1	$10,000	No
19	8	2	6	Unknown	No
20	4	2	2	Unknown	No
21	9	5	4	Unknown	Yes
22	11	1	10	Unknown	No
23	Unknown	1	Unknown	Unknown	No
24	21	1	20	Unknown	Unknown

FIGURE 5.3   Cases from the CERT Insider Threat Database That Involve Organized Crime (2012).

Sabotage

Organizations continue to fail at appropriately and comprehensively understanding the the risk of providing access to their networks, systems, data, and information. The insider threat of sabotage, specifically related to information technology (IT), is a category of the insider threat that describes an individual taking revenge against an organization, primarily because he or she is angry, though there is a growing concern regarding organized crime and nation-state sponsored insider's activity in relation to information warfare (discussed in Chapter 2).

Insider IT sabotage, as defined by the CERT Insider Threat Center, is "current or former employees, contractors, business partners, or affiliates intentionally exceed or misuse an authorized level of access to networks, systems, or data with the intention of harming a specific individual, the organization as a whole, or the organization's data, systems, and/or daily business operations."[21] Carnegie Mellon University's CERT Insider Threat Database contains over 700 cases (as of December 2012), of which 371 cases were closed with convictions. From the 371 closed cases, CERT identified 106 insider IT sabotage cases.[22] Additionally, the research by CERT's Insider Threat Center identified and tracked several aspects of insider IT sabotage, including the insider's job responsibilities (technical, management, planning, etc.), the sophistication of the event, the level of technical access held by the insider, and the impact that the sabotage had on the organization's operations and reputation.

The systems dynamics modeling approach, discussed earlier in the chapter, can also be applied to the insider IT sabotage threat. Using this model, CERT's Insider Threat Center was able to understand how insiders commit IT sabotage, develop a model of how the crimes evolve over time, and what "pivot points" could be manipulated to affect how the actor behaves. Based on the insider IT sabotage information collected by the Insider Threat Center, CERT determined that 86 percent of the attackers held technical positions; the majority of the crimes used sophisticated technical methods in their attack; 90 percent of the insiders had privileged access (administrator, super user, root) to organization systems, databases, or network infrastructure; 75 percent of the victim organizations experienced a disruption to business operations; and 28 percent of victim organizations suffered an impact to their reputation.[23] CERT's behavioral observations in these cases added additional perspective and included unmet expectations (no pay increase or promotion, being tasked with menial responsibilities) as the primary reason for an attack, followed by becoming disgruntled as a result of being reprimanded or demoted, and lastly having excessive privileges may put a potential attacker in the all-powerful mindset (the God Complex). These observations, however, did not take into account or differentiate the intentional or planned sabotage objectives of organized criminal actors who sought employment with victim organizations for that purpose.

Similar to a hypothetical insider IT sabotage case presented by the CERT research, the following chronology (see Figure 5.4) provides an example of how organized criminal elements might attack an organization.

The following case provides an excellent example of insider IT sabotage case perpetrated by a criminal enterprise or organized criminal groups. In March 2013, a translator (Cecere) for the Royal Canadian Mounted Police (RCMP) was found guilty of removing, modifying, or mistranslating over 500 documents concerning organized crime investigations and passing information related to these investigations to persons associated with La Cosa Nostra (LCN) Italian Mafia. His efforts at sabotaging RCMP

Sequence	Date/Time	Event
1	1/25/14	Insider is found guilty of computer crimes.
2	2/13/15	Insider completes prison term and begins probation.
3	2/16/16	Insider probation period ends.
4	7/22/16	Insider lies on employment application for a company known for weak preemployment screening: states "no criminal convictions."
5	9/30/16	Organization does not conduct preemployment screening and hires insider.
6	10/01/16	Insider starts work at the target organization, as a Systems Administrator.
7	12/01/16	Insider provides outside conspirators with comprehensive intelligence on the company, including data, assets, financials, and personnel.
8	01/05/17	Outside conspirators direct the insider to collect specific data types, in a manner that would not raise suspicion, and begin a slow implementation of security holes and backdoor access points.
9	02/2017 – 11/2017	Stolen data were used by the outside conspirators to establish fake identities, open bank accounts and credit cards, and launder proceeds from drug operations.
10	08/15/2017	Insider is observed sending company data to an external e-mail address. Activity is reported and the insider is fired.
11	08/15/17	Insider accesses the victim company via backdoors and alternate access accounts. Insider encrypts and then deletes all company system and application logs, the entire contents of his workstation, and the related data contained on the electronic storage systems.
12	08/16/17	Victim company suspects that its data was compromised and exfiltrated for illicit purposes. An internal investigation begins and law enforcement is contacted.
13	9/15/17	Law enforcement was able to identify and recover data deleted by the insider; however, because it was encrypted, they were not able to determine if it was related to the company's allegations. Sabotage is suspected.
14	11/10/17	Insider arrested for IT sabotage.

FIGURE 5.4 Hypothetical case chronology for an IT sabotage.

Special permission to reproduce portions of "Hypothetical Case Chronology for an IT sabotage" by Carnegie Mellon University, has been granted by the Software Engineering Institute.

investigations related to the Mafia were not well documented, but reports do reference his obstruction of the investigations due to his involvement, and exceptionally poor translations. Essentially, Cecere failed to provide good interpretations of documents (e.g., wiretap communications between mob bosses) that would have enabled prosecution. Most of Cecere's work focused on large racketeering and criminal enterprise investigations in the 1990s through 2006. For over 15 years, Cecere not only scuttled RCMP investigations, but also provided intelligence information to criminal families and organizations throughout Canada and the United States. He was finally caught when Mounties suspected a leak and focused their investigation on Cecere, tapped his phones, monitored his computer use, and eventually followed him to a meeting with a member of the LCN Mafia. At the meeting, Cecere provided the mobster with confidential documents from recent investigations. Amazingly, Cecere was terminated from the RCMP and sentenced to only one year in prison.[24]

SOPHISTICATED CRIMINAL ORGANIZATIONS

Organized crime is a phrase that has become synonymous with the Italian and Sicilian Mafia (also known as La Cosa Nostra or LCN Mafia), but since their origins in the United States in the early 1800s these ethnic and racially based organizations have changed and so has the threat they pose. Throughout the 1900s and into the twenty-first century, criminal organizations have become more sophisticated through the use of technology and its global reach. Eastern Europe and, particularly, countries tracing their history to the former Republics of the Soviet Union have used technology to advance their organized crime activities. In fact, new groups like the Russian Business Network, who focuses on criminal cyber activities full time, are becoming more and more successful.

The 2013 United Nations Comprehensive Study on Cybercrime noted several significant findings with respect to the growing threat of cybercrime.[25] Specifically noted and in contribution to international cybercrime, the study noted that 60 percent of all Internet users are in developing countries, with 45 percent of all Internet users are below the age of 25. Age is interesting to note, since according to the study, the majority of emerging criminal organizations in developing countries are composed of subcultures of young men that engage in a wide range of computer-related financial frauds.

Today, criminal organizations that have a significant focus in cybercrime include Russian mobsters who fled to the United States after the Soviet Union's collapse; groups from African countries, including Nigeria, that focus primarily on financial schemes and drug trafficking; the Chinese tongs (brotherhoods), the Japanese Yakuza, and other Asian crime rings; and the criminal enterprises based in Eastern European nations like Romania and Hungary. All of these groups currently have a presence in the United States and/or are conducting their criminal activities through the Internet. Most disturbing, recent trends point to collaboration and cooperation between these criminal organizations.

The Impact of Organized Crime

The impact of organized crime, and cyber-related crimes, is not easily measured, and there are various discrepancies in the actual amount of money being made in the global cybercrime field. Some reports of profits as high as $1 trillion dollars to as "little" as 12.5 billion dollars.[26] But still, it comes as no surprise that all the major traditional organized crime cartels and associations have embraced cybercrime along with new burgeoning cooperative cyber gangs for the future. This was certainly reflected in 2012, as the United Nations estimated that over 80 percent of all cybercrime worldwide was perpetrated by organized crime associations.[27]

Organized crime groups infiltrate and impact legitimate industries like construction and trash hauling, they manipulate and monopolize financial markets, and they infiltrate traditional institutions like labor unions. They introduce and supply drugs to U.S. cities and increase the level of violence in our communities through the corruption of officials, and extortion, intimidation, and murder needed to maintain their operations. In addition, prostitution and human trafficking and the various frauds and financial scams they perpetrate are impacting the global economy. These crimes are further facilitated by the use of the Internet, providing criminals global reach to suppliers, customers, and conspirators in a faster and more secure (less risky) manner than the face-to-face and telephone communications of the past.

Traditional groups like the Mexican and Columbian Drug Cartels, the Chinese Triads, the Japanese Yakuza, La Cosa Nostra, and Russian mafias, as well as nontraditional groups like the Russian Business Network, the Shadowcrew, and the Nigerians have actively been using the Internet for a plethora of criminal activities. Organized crime groups are becoming more entrepreneurial or market-focused, reacting to changes in both illicit and licit economies. Of course, they are still heavily involved in activities such as narcotics trafficking and money laundering (which have been greatly impacted by globalization), but organized criminals are now increasingly more involved in high-tech, cybercrime operations including identity theft, counterfeiting and online fencing of goods, and various types of fraud including mass marketing fraud; advanced fee fraud; online identity theft; and sophisticated credit card fraud.[28]

Use of Social Media by Organized Crime

Social networking sites, such as Twitter, LinkedIn, and Facebook, are used by organized crime to conduct intelligence operations for collection information, facilitate the commission of crimes, and as a communications vehicle. As an example, in 2009, Twitter was found to have been used as a command and control channel for malware designed to steal banking credentials from compromised computers in Brazil.[29] Compromised accounts are then either used by the criminal enterprise to commit fraud, or are sold in the underground marketplace. For instance, in 2013, the following compromised accounts were listed for sale on the Tor Net (an underground Internet site described in much more detail later in this chapter): iTunes account—$8; Fedex.com/Continental. com/United.com—$6; Groupon.com—$5; Att.com /Sprint.com /Verizonwireless.com / Tmobile.com—$4; Facebook and Twitter—$2.50. In June of 2016, however, these accounts were sold by the millions at $0.0015 each for 379 million Twitter accounts and $0.025 each for 179 million LinkedIn accounts. While each account represents a relatively small amount, the account can be sold literally millions of time. It does not take many buyers to multiply the profit margin for organize criminal groups.

Organized criminal groups and associations are also using social media sites, such as Twitter, to circumvent dragnets and communicate with each other to avoid detection. A common technique for the Mexican drug cartels is to use code words, such as a YouTube reference, or a specific lyric in an iTunes song that has meaning only to those involved. These messages are often specific instructions or orders; some have even been "hits" on rival gang members.[30]

Organized cartels often use social media sites to collect intelligence about their targets for various reasons, including an effort to guess the "I forgot my password" security questions that would then allow them to compromise a victim's online accounts. Cybercriminals understand how our socio-technical lives work, how our online accounts are connected, and how to take advantage of the convenience that technology affords us. They also understand electronic receipts for our online payments, verification e-mails from our "forgotten password" requests, our contacts, our habits, and our calendar. Our e-mail accounts, for example, are considered transit points for all of this information, a mine of information whose value is understood by sophisticated cybercriminals.[31]

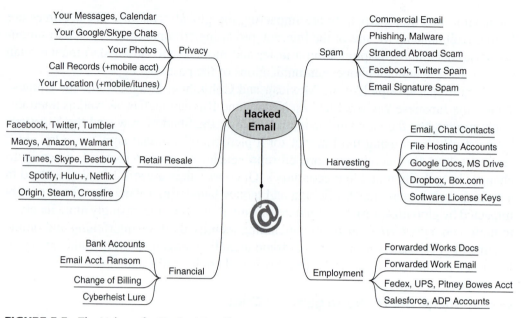

FIGURE 5.5 The Value of a Hacked Email Account

Based on Panda, T.C. (2012). "Cyber-Crimes and Their Impacts: A Review." International Journal of Engineering Research and Application (IJERA) 2 (2): 202–209.

Cybercriminals often assess the compromised accounts and data, categorize the information, and post the access and information for sale in the underground marketplace. Buyers will then use this information for cyber espionage, spamming, proliferation of malware, and other financial crimes. Figure 5.5 reveals the value of a hacked e-mail account to a sophisticated criminal organization.

In 2012, the FBI presented an exhaustive overview of organized crime groups, cartels, and associations active in the cybercrime arena; this data is now maintained as dynamic Web page on the FBI's Web site.[32] The report and subsequent updates provide a mechanism in which to assess each group geographically as well as delineate their activities within the cybercrime world. In some cases, the criminal enterprise is followed by an illustrative case example involving U.S. interests and activities.

African Criminal Enterprises

African criminal enterprises began in the 1980s and continued to grow as a result of advances in technology. Growth of these groups, from localized crime (in specific countries like Nigeria) to the development of international criminal networks, was further facilitated by the ease of international travel and the growing acceptance for international financial transactions. The economic, political, and social conditions in African countries including Ghana, Liberia, and Nigeria have also fostered the development and growth of these enterprises into global threats.

Within the United States, African criminal organizations were identified in several major metropolitan areas, mostly concentrated in Atlanta, Baltimore, Chicago, Dallas, Houston, Milwaukee, Newark, New York, and Washington, D.C. As a result, the United States has taken a serious approach to combating these groups through the formation of the Department of Justice (DOJ), Nigerian Crime Initiative. This DOJ group coordinates federal investigations on the Nigerian Criminal Enterprise (NCE) by using joint task forces in six major U.S. cities. The NCEs, which operate in several other countries of the world besides the United States, are one of the most aggressive and fastest-growing international criminal groups in the world, using the revenue from drug and human trafficking, as well as financial frauds to fuel their growth. The advancement and availability of computers and the Internet has improved communications between NCE members on every continent, formalized supply and transportation logistics, and expanded the options for laundering the procedures related to these illicit activities.

The NCEs are famous for their financial frauds. The impact of Nigerian fraud schemes alone costs the United States an estimated $1 billion to $2 billion each year. The NCE, in particular, has been successful at counterfeiting, corruption, credit card theft, and other financial crimes, and has been recognized as being an adaptable poly-crime organization that is bringing new methods to old scams and, while not fitting traditional crime syndicate molds, they are a formidable, international crime group.[33] The Nigerian 419 scam, a form of advanced fee fraud, is probably one of the most well-known scams in the United States. The fraud began in the 1980s and was perpetrated through the postal mailings of letters to victim. Today, the 419 scams are even more prevalent and successful due to the Internet and use of e-mail.

Asian Criminal Enterprises

Since the early 1900s, Asian criminal enterprises have been operating in the United States. The first of these groups evolved from the old Chinese tongs—social organizations formed by early Chinese-American immigrants in cities across the west (e.g., Seattle, Portland, and San Francisco). Today, these criminalized tongs are thriving and have been joined by similar organizations from East and Southeast Asia. Members of the most dominant criminal enterprises have ties to Cambodia, China, Japan, Korea, Laos, the Philippines, Thailand, and Vietnam. Other groups from the South Pacific island nations (like Samoa, Fiji, and Micronesia) are beginning to emerge as potential threats as well.

BOX 5.4

Nigerian Cashing Crew

In 2008, an elite group of hackers, headed by the manager of the Chicago cell of Nigerian Criminal Enterprise (NCE), obtained unauthorized access into the computer network of WorldPay US, Inc., then-known as RBS WorldPay, a payment processor located in Atlanta, Georgia. The hackers used sophisticated techniques to compromise the data encryption that was used by World-Pay to protect customer data on payroll debit/ATM cards. Once they compromised the encryption, the hackers raised the balances and ATM withdrawal limits on compromised accounts, and provided a network of lead "cashers" (aka Money Mules) with 44 debit card account numbers and their associated PINs, which were used to withdraw more than $9 million from over 2,100 ATMs in over 280 cities worldwide, including cities in the United States, Russia, Ukraine, Estonia, Italy, Hong Kong, Japan, and Canada. The $9 million loss occurred within a span of less than 12 hours on November 8, 2008. Throughout the cash out, the hackers monitored the fraudulent ATM withdrawals in real-time from within the computer systems of WorldPay. Once the withdrawals were completed, the hackers sought to destroy data stored on the card processing network in order to conceal their illegal activity. WorldPay nevertheless discovered the unauthorized activity and immediately reported the breach.

Source: Federal Bureau of Investigation. (2012). "Sentencing in Major International Cyber Crime Prosecution—Supervisor of Chicago Cashing Crew Imprisoned." See http://www.fbi.gov/atlanta/press-releases/2012/sentencing-in-major-international-cyber-crime-prosecution.

Operation Avalanche

In 2016, a multinational law enforcement taskforce, including EuroPol, EuroJust, German police, U. S. Department of Justice, the FBI, and other global partners dismantled an international criminal infrastructure, known as "Avalanche." The network was used as a command-and-control mechanism for launching and managing massive global malware attacks and money mule recruiting campaigns. The monetary losses caused by these malware attacks are estimated in the hundreds of millions of dollars worldwide. The takedown operation was the largest-ever use of sinkholing, the redirection of Internet traffic to an intended destination, to combat criminal botnet infrastructures, with over 800,000 Internet domains seized, sinkholed, or blocked.[34]

The fluid and mobile extensive networks of national and international criminals helped these criminal enterprises adapt easily to the changes around them. Individual members speak several languages and dialects, operate highly sophisticated criminal operations, and have extensive financial capabilities. Some of these enterprises have commercialized their criminal activities and can be considered businesses of various sizes, from small family-run operations to large corporations, and the advent of the Internet provided the ability to run legal and illegal online businesses.

Asian criminal enterprises have realized success and growth due primarily to the globalization of world economies and evolution of technology. Two categories of Asian criminal enterprises have been identified. They are the traditional criminal enterprises, which include the Chinese triads (or underground societies) based in China, Hong Kong, Macau, and Taiwan, and the Japanese Yakuza or Boryokudan, and the nontraditional criminal enterprises, which include groups based in the United States, like the criminally influenced Chinese tongs, triad affiliates, and Asian street gangs found in many U.S. cities with large Asian communities.

A more modern picture of "old" organized criminal cartel learning new tricks is the Japanese Yakuza. Formed in Japan in 1603, the Yakuza now have more than 100,000 registered members making it the largest organized crime group in the world. Over the last few decades, the Yakuza had focused on traditional criminality, including weapons and drug trafficking, gambling, prostitution, and loan-sharking, but in more recent years they have focused their efforts on cybercrime, including deposit fraud and money laundering. Proceeds from cybercrimes are then invested in stocks and real estate, essentially transforming the image of the Yakuza from sword-wielding tattooed gangsters to Goldman Sachs with guns.[35]

These Asian criminal enterprises engage in auto theft, counterfeiting of computers and clothes, drug trafficking, extortion, financial frauds, human trafficking, illegal gambling, kidnapping, loan-sharking, money laundering, murder, prostitution, and traditional racketeering activities associated with organized crime. Some Asian criminal enterprises have begun to structure their groups in a more corporate fashion; defining roles, reporting structure, and authority in an effort streamline their operations for efficiency and effectiveness. Finally, there is a trend toward more white-collar crimes where these groups are co-mingling their illegal activities with legitimate business ventures.

Asian criminal enterprises in the United States have been identified in more than 50 metropolitan areas, including Boston, Chicago, Honolulu, Las Vegas, Los Angeles, New Orleans, New York, Newark, Philadelphia, Portland, San Francisco, Seattle, and Washington, D.C. As a result, the United States participates in initiatives and working groups to combat Asian organized crime on an international level, including the FBI/

BOX 5.5

The Japanese Yakuza

In February of 2012, the U.S. government froze the assets of known Yakuza gang members and banned them from conducting business in the United States. The action was due to the Yakuza's increasing involvement with drug and human trafficking, prostitution, money laundering, and other cross-border activities. Members of the Yakuza were using the U.S. financial system and other private, commercial systems to penetrate the stock market, as well as the commodities market, to disrupt market sales, and to launder money from illicit proceeds. The indictment against known Yakuza members identifies the Japanese organized crime cartel and refers to it as "the Walmart of this country's underworld," for its ability to brush aside opponents and generate huge earnings.

Based on McCurry, JUSTIN. (2012). "US Steps Up Offensive Against Japan's Yakuza Gangs." The Guardian. London. See http://www.guardian.co.uk/world/2012/feb/24/united-states-offensive-japan-yakuza

National Police Agency of Japan Working Group, Interpol's Project Bridge, the Inter-agency Working Group on Alien Smuggling, the annual International Asian Organized Crime Conference, the Canadian/United States Cross-Border Crime Forum, and the International Law Enforcement Academy in Bangkok, Thailand.

Balkan Criminal Enterprises

Balkan Organized Crime describes groups originating from or operating in Albania, Bosnia-Herzegovina, Croatia, Kosovo, the former Yugoslav Republic of Macedonia, Serbia and Montenegro, Bulgaria, Greece, and Romania. Balkan organized crime is an emerging threat in the United States, with several active groups in various cities across the country. They have not yet, however, demonstrated the established criminal sophistication of traditional Eurasian or La Cosa Nostra (LCN) organizations. Nonetheless, they have proven their capabilities in adapting to expanding criminal markets and becoming involved in new activities like cybercrime, much like the historical growth of other organized crime groups.

Organized crime in the Balkans has its roots in the traditional clan structures. Since the 1400s, clans were established in specific territories and controlled all the activities within that territory, governed by the "*kanun*," or code, which values loyalty and "*besa*," or secrecy. The elements inherent in the structure of the clans, in addition to the many years of communist rule that led to black market activities in the region, provided the perfect genesis for modern-day Balkan organized crime.

With the beginning of the collapse of communism through the late 1980s and the 1990s, as well as the advent and availability of the Internet, the expansion of Balkan organized crime into the criminal markets was suddenly opened, which led to the creation of their international network. Balkan criminal organizations have been active in the United States since the 1980s, first committing low-level crimes, robberies, burglaries, and home invasions. Then, ethnic Albanians began working with LCN families in New York.

The Balkan organized crime groups do not have a Mafia-like structure like the traditional LCN. Instead they are simply grouped around a central leader or leaders who maintain ties back to the Balkan region. Their organized crime activities include gambling, money laundering, drug trafficking, human trafficking, extortion, real estate fraud, witness intimidation, robbery, and murder.

Eurasian Criminal Enterprises—Russian Organized Crime

Eurasian organized crime describes groups composed of criminals born in or with family from the former Soviet Union or Central Europe. These groups operate in several countries around the world, including the United States, where their criminal activities cause hundreds of millions of dollars in losses to U.S. businesses, investors, and taxpayers through sophisticated fraud schemes and public corruption.

Eurasian organized crime in the United States began in the 1970s with the "*Vory V Zakone*" or "thieves in law." Career criminals came to the United States after having banded together while in the Soviet prison system. Their leaders or "shop managers" were illicitly paid a 30 percent margin to acquire scarce consumer goods and divert raw materials and finished goods from U.S. production lines for the benefit of "*nomenklatura*," or the educated elite, and criminals. In addition, with the collapse of the Soviet Union in the early 1990s, members aligned themselves with corrupt public officials (including ex-police, military, and KGB intelligence officers) to gain control of industries and resources that were being privatized. This gave the syndicate an initial infusion of wealth and supplied the infrastructure for continuing cash flows and opportunities to launder criminal proceeds.

In the United States, the traditional criminal elements are heavily involved in auto theft, drug trafficking, extortion, health care fraud, human trafficking, insurance fraud, money laundering, prostitution, securities, and investment fraud. The cyber-related crimes of these groups, however, exceed the revenues of these traditional activities. For instance, Russia's hacking industry is growing more and more organized as Russian organized crime groups team up with Russian cyber gangs enabling both groups to be more effective criminal organizations. Favored cybercrime for Russian groups is online fraud, which includes online banking, phishing, and other financial fraud and spamming.

In 2011, the gangs netted $4 billion in criminal proceeds from cybercrimes, including $942 million from online fraud, $830 million from spam, $230 million from selling anonymization services and malware, and $130 million for distributed denial-of-services (DDoS).[36] Russia's cyber gangs are very proactive at reaching out to the global organized crime market place and soliciting business from other cybercrime gangs to use their malware, buy their stolen information, and use their money-making schemes. Russia is commonly referred to as "the Hackzone" because there are so many hackers living in the country and claiming to be the "best" at cybercrime.[37]

Italian Organized Crime—La Cosa Nostra (LCN) Mafia

Originating in the 1800s, Italian criminal societies known as the Mafia became engrained in the social and economic fabric of Italy. Since the 1900s, thousands of Italian organized criminals (Sicilian Mafiosi like Lucky Luciano) then illegally entered the United States to help establish what is known today as La Cosa Nostra (LCN) or the American Mafia.

Over the past 200 years, the LCN Mafia has become one of the most notorious and widespread of all criminal societies. Globally, four of these groups have approximately 25,000 members in total, with 250,000 worldwide affiliates. In the United States, Mafia presence includes more than 3,000 members and affiliates of the Sicilian Mafia, Camorra Mafia, Calabrian Mafia, and the Sacra Corona Unita make up the LCN. The Sicilian Mafia is said to be the most powerful and primarily focuses their numbers around New York, southern New Jersey, Chicago, Detroit, and Philadelphia.

BOX 5.6

Russian Hacking Credit Card Data Breach Case Is Largest in History

In July 2013, federal prosecutors brought charges against four Russian nationals and one Ukrainian suspect charged with running an organization that hacked the computer networks of more than a dozen corporations, stealing and selling at least 160 million credit and debit card numbers. The scheme had been running since 2005 and included, among others, some of the largest credit card corporations, including VISA, Heartland Payment Systems, and J.C. Penney. A separate case involving the NASDAQ stock exchange was also filed against one of the suspect. This "hack" represented the cutting edge of financial fraud and highlights the broader threat that cybercrime poses to a financial system that is almost entirely reliant on networked communications and systems. The losses from this case alone are staggering ... and run in the billions of dollars.

Source: Based on POPPER, NATHANIEL (July 26, 2013). "Feds Charge 5 in Data Breach Case." The New York Times.

Today's LCN Mafia operate internationally, with members and affiliates in the United States, Canada, South America, Australia, and parts of Europe. Furthering their criminal enterprise, they are also known to collaborate with other organized crime groups, especially in drug trafficking. Domestically, the group has a long history of drug trafficking and money laundering dating back several decades. Other illicit activities include corruption, counterfeiting, fraud, illegal gambling, kidnapping, infiltration of legitimate businesses, murders, political corruption, bombings, and weapons trafficking. Industry experts in Italy estimate that their worldwide criminal activity is worth more than $100 billion annually. A 2013 Europol Public Information report on the Threat Assessment of Italian Organized Crime stated that of the 3,600 organized crime groups operating in the EU, the LCN Mafia was the wealthiest and most powerful crime group on a global level.[38]

According to the FBI, the LCN Mafia poses the most organized criminal threat to the United States. The group is composed of a nationwide coalition of criminals operating "this thing of ours" (literal translation of La Cosa Nostra), linked by blood or through conspiracy, and dedicated to protecting their own and engaging in criminal enterprise—including cybercrime. An early and interesting example of LCN's use of technology to perpetrate organized crime was the use of killer drones. In the early 1990s, two decades before the United States used unmanned Reaper drones, the Sicilian mobsters were testing the possibility of strapping bombs to remote controlled aircraft. Although it was unclear whether or not they ever went ahead with their plans, the LCN continues to use technology in their efforts to commit organized crime and also has taken part in adding cybercrimes to their revenue stream.[39]

BOX 5.7

Gambling and the LCN Mafia: Same Game, Different Time

New Orleans was the site of the first major LCN Mafia incident in U.S. history. On October 15, 1890, New Orleans Police Superintendent David Hennessey was murdered execution-style. Rumor had it that he was in debt to the Sicilian mob for gambling. Hundreds of Sicilians were arrested, and 19 were eventually indicted for the murder. An acquittal generated rumors of widespread bribery and the intimidation of hundreds of witnesses. Outraged citizens of New Orleans organized a lynch mob and killed 11 of the 19 Sicilian defendants. Two were hanged, nine were shot, and the remaining eight escaped.

Fast forward to June 2012, Gambino family decedents from the New Orleans massacre were indicted on running an illegal, large-scale sports bookmaking operation in which gamblers placed bets with offshore Internet gambling Web sites, particularly www.44wager.com based in Costa Rica. The suspects collected and disbursed funds to and from local bettors, and illegally transferred a portion of the proceeds to the Gambino family. Members of the Gambino family continue to wait for trial.

Source: Based on Federal Bureau of Investigation. (2012). Alleged Organized Crime Associates Among 20 Charged with Operating Illegal Gambling Business in Connecticut. Washington, DC: Federal Bureau of Investigation. See http://www.fbi.gov/newhaven/press-releases/2012/alleged-organized-crime-associates-among-20-charged-with-operating-illegal-gambling-businesses-in-connecticut

Middle Eastern Criminal Enterprises

Middle Eastern criminal enterprises have been active in the United States since the 1970s, primarily in areas of large Middle Eastern or Southwest Asian populations, and they are organized as theft or financial fraud rings. Ten years after the 9/11 terrorist attacks, law enforcement has taken a different perspective at the various threats coming from the Middle East and from Middle Eastern communities in the United States. As a result, law enforcement has begun to recognize that some Middle Eastern criminal groups have no relationship to terror groups, but instead they simply have the same goals as traditional organized crime cartels—make money.

These groups are known for committing various criminal activities, which are supported by their extensive networks of international criminal associates and their innovate use of technology. Criminal activities include auto theft, financial fraud, money laundering, interstate transportation of stolen property, smuggling, drug trafficking, document fraud, health care fraud, identity fraud, cigarette smuggling, and the theft and redistribution of infant formula.

Most U.S.-based Middle Eastern criminal enterprises are found in Illinois, Ohio, New Jersey, and New York. These groups also operate internationally in the areas of Afghanistan, Pakistan, Iran, Turkey, the United Arab Emirates, and Canada. The criminal makeup of these organizations includes individuals from Afghanistan, Algeria, Bahrain, Egypt, India, Iran, Iraq, Israel, Jordan, Kuwait, Lebanon, Libya, Morocco, Oman, Pakistan, Qatar, Saudi Arabia, Syria, Tunisia, Turkey, United Arab Emirates, and Yemen.

Mexican and South American Drug Cartels

Mexican and South American drug trafficking and cybercrime share a similar evolution and common operational and structural similarities. Throughout their existence, both of these illicit activities continue to mature their operations, efficiencies, and effectiveness by taking advantage of new technologies, integrating innovation, and staying a one step ahead of law enforcement. Their existence, though born from vastly different purposes and circumstances, grew from opportunity and will continue to thrive upon their respective demands. And we are now seeing drug trafficking organizations (particularly in Mexico) that have traditionally not relied on their technical capabilities move into the cybercrime market in order to make their organizations more secure, more capable, and more efficient. As drug trafficking groups become more and more technologically advanced, cartels move away from low-end cybercrimes like installing radio towers for communications, using PCs for book-keeping, and bribing police officers capable of running checks on individuals to hiring cyber contractors to coordinate the cartel's disposable network of cell phones, using hackers to commit online banking fraud, and of course, selling quantities of drugs over the Internet through underground sites like "the Farmers Market" on the Tor Network.

The Mexican drug cartels have seriously embraced the use of technology to further their crime organizations. The Gulf Cartel, Juarez Cartel, Sinaloa Cartel, and the Tijuana

Cartel have all made a name for themselves by following in the violent footsteps of Colombian drug lord Pablo Escobar. However, in recent years many of these groups have seen their drug trafficking profits squeezed by governmental crackdown on organized crime, and are now turning to other illegal activities for money, like cybercrime.

The cartels are now using their enormous cash flow to purchase the best current and emerging technologies in an effort to expand their command and control operations, and supporting infrastructure. They have also started to use their technology to publicize, plot, communicate, transport, and extort. By embracing leading edge technologies, cartels are increasing their capabilities, reach, profits, and power. Simply using the Internet offers new ground for conducting profitable criminal operations and the benefit of being a perfect vehicle for the cartels to launder money. Since there are so many legal and physical risks in the drug trafficking trade (particularly during face-to-face transactions), the cartels are eager to move toward a technology-based business model emphasizing fraud, extortion, money laundering, and prescription drug trafficking. In addition to the anonymity and speed afforded by technology, cartels are also appreciating an almost entirely new clientele would not typically be willing to leave their homes to buy drugs in person.

QUICK FACTS

Intelligence reports, congressional hearings and various media reports point to a growing international convergence of organized crime groups and terrorist organizations in order to take advantage of the specialized skills and assets of each group. As an example, Hezbollah (a Shiite terrorist group from Lebanon) has established a strong base in Mexico and Latin America to launder money, buy weapons, finance terrorism, and smuggle people into the United States. And in 2014, there were reports that al Qaeda worked with Mexican drug cartels and U.S. outlaw motorcycle gangs converging threats of drug, human, and weapons trafficking operations to finance global terrorist activities.

Source: Steven D'Alfonso, "Why Organized Crime and Terror Groups Are Converging," *IBM SecurityIntelligence* (September 4, 2014). Available at *https://securityintelligence.com/why-organized-crime-and-terror-groups-are-converging/.*

THE INDISCRIMINANT UNDERGROUND MARKETPLACE—THE DEEP WEB OR TOR NETWORK

The deep web is vast uncharted part of the World Wide Web, not accessible through regular Internet browsing or search engines. Most of the information in the deep web is hidden, accessible from dynamic Web sites requiring the use of an application called Tor. Tor links participating servers, Web sites, and Internet services together while also encrypting all of the communications between each piece. Because users of the deep web use Tor, another synonym for the deep web is the Tor Net or Tor Network. This secretive online world remains mostly untraceable and difficult to access for the regular Internet user and even law enforcement, which allows a large criminal domain to thrive. This underground world is the Internet's secret black market where criminal and illegal activities flourish. In this dark world of secret Web sites and illicit opportunities, there are real-time illegal transactions, drug deals, weapons sales, human trafficking coordination, murder for hire contracts, and solicitations for hacker services—all taking place with anonymity, and mostly untraceable.

Organized criminal organizations are prospering like never before since the advent of the deep web in 2002, though its popularity did not really take hold until 2006. Organized crime cartels and associations are now able to communicate with contacts around the world in an encrypted and untraceable manner, talking to suppliers and buyers, making sales, transferring proceeds, coordinating logistics, giving orders to mules, and working with coconspirators. Mafia can advertise their services, post their goods for sale, and coordinate among their international affiliates. Cybercriminals offer their services, sell their treasures of data, and collect information on all the other deep web users. Refer to Figures 5.6, 5.7, and 5.8.

One of the most lucrative businesses for organized cybercrime groups is selling services, such as botnet leasing, selling malware code, and performing DDOS attacks. See Figure 5.7. In a *PC World* article released in 2011, which detailed a new business model being introduced to organized crime groups, the selling of exploit kits complete

FIGURE 5.6 Screenshot from the Tor Net root directory for services.

Rent-A-Hacker

Products FAQs Register Login

Rent-A-Hacker

Experienced hacker offering his services!
(illegal) Hacking and social engineering is my bussiness since i was 16 years old, never had a real job so i had the time to get really good at hacking and i made a good amount of money last + 20 years.
I have worked for other people before, now im also offering my services for everyone with enough cash here.

Prices:
Im not doing this to make a few bucks here and there, im not from some crappy eastern europe country and happy to scam people for 50 euro.
Im a professional computer expert who could earn 50-100 euro an hour with a legal job.
So stop reading if you dont have a serious problem worth spending some cash at.
Prices depend alot on the problem you want me to solve, but minimum amount for smaller jobs is 200 euro.
You can pay me anonymously using Bitcoin.

Technical skills:
- Web (HTML, PHP, SQL, APACHE)
- C/C++, Assembler, Delphi
- 0day Exploits, Highly personalized trojans, Bots, DDOS
- Spear Phishing Attacks to get accounts from selected targets
- Basically anything a hacker needs to be successfull, if i dont know it, ill learn it very fast
- Anonymity: noone will ever find out who i am.

Social Engineering skills:
- Very good written and spoken (phone calls) english and german.
- If i cant hack something technically ill make phone calls or write emails to the target to get the needed information. i have had people make things you wouldnt belive really often.
- Alot of experience with security practices inside big corporations.

What ill do:
Ill do anything for money, im not a pussy :) if you want me to destroy some bussiness or a persons life, ill do it!
Some examples:
Simply hacking something technically
Causing alot of technical trouble on websites / networks to disrupt their service with DDOS and other methods.
Economic espionage
Getting private information from someone
Ruining your opponents, bussiness or private persons you dont like, i can ruin them financially and or get them arrested, whatever you like.
If you want someone to get known as a child porn user, no problem.

Tor Services - Iceweasel

File Edit View History Bookmarks Tools Help

TORDIR - Link List   Tor Services   DEEP WEB LINKS - Pastebin....

niqsdvceafthxltd.onion   tor directory

These are the services I'm offering:

- **Account hacking**. Social networks, e-mail, instant messaging, everything. Although results can't be guaranteed, and greatly depend on the server's and the victim's security measures. That's why I'm going to ask for you to send the payment *after* I have proven to have access to the account. I'm assuming good faith. I'm working for free hoping you'll pay once it's done, so don't abuse the system. Don't ask me to do it just to check if I'm serious. I am.
Most accounts are very easy to access through all sorts of attacks, both server-side and client-side. I've got a very good success rate using social engineering, and I'm still surprised of the amount of accounts I've gained access to just by tweaking the site's own 'I forgot my password' system.
Prices will vary depending on the victim (be it a person or a corporation) and the security I have to break through.
In many cases I can retrieve the current password, so the legitimate user will be able to continue using his account. In those situations, I will tunnel my connection through one of my zombies so the victim will never be alerted of someone logging in from the other side of the world. If you want to do that as well, keep reading.

- **Zombie rental**. You can rent a computer in a given region for a day, a week, or as long as you want. I have 7000+ zombie computers all around the world. You can use one of them for a great number of purposes. Tunnel your connection for anonymity, make your connection appear to be from a given location, use processing power, send e-mails, spam, spread malware, host something, you name it.

- **Botnet rental**. As I've stated above, I have 7000+ bots all over the world. That's a good number to do a *Distributed Denial of Service attack (DDoS)* and take down a server. I may reject to attack certain targets, and prices will vary depending on its size and notoriety.
Given the nature of this kind of attack, I will require you to send a fraction of the payment upfront, and the rest once the target has been taken down. That's until I find a good, trustworthy escrow service for both of us. If the attack fails you will get a full refund.
Also, this service can be used to spread e-mails, or to send a massive amount of spam to someone's inbox, or a given mailing list. Note that sending a high number of messages in a short period of time to a single target will probably have the user or the server locked, so in that way that might as well be a denial of service attack.
All those computers together offer a huge amount of processing power as well, if that's what you're after.

- **Harassment**. If you're seeking revenge, or simply want someone to have a bad time, this is perfect for you. There will be no physical assault of any kind. Besides from that, I'll do whatever you ask. Send them messages impersonating somebody else, or send fake messages on behalf of them. Scary phone calls. Create an argument with their friends or family. Sabotage their career. Make them lose their job. Have them go certain places and send them packages that will probabbly get them arrested. And of course, install malware on their computer. That's one of the most powerful tools, as it opens a whole new world of possibilities. Wheather you want to destroy everything, spy on them, gain access to something special, files, passwords, credentials, or even get their credit card numbers and bank accounts. Everything that matters most is probabbly on their computer.
It won't be the first time I've made someone move out of town.

- **Aid**. Quite the opposite of the above, but using similar methods, I can make someone's life easier by giving them an extra push in the right direction. Have their boss hear some positive rumors, give them some advantage in a competition, or just make the other party have a hard time. Create a situation and help them be in the right place at the right time to solve it. Give them the resources and confidence to achieve what they are looking for, or simply let them take the credit for something else. Help them change some aspects of their life. Give them hope. Make them believe in the right thing, or cease to do what's not good for them.
There's a lot that can be done.

- **E-mail Databases**. I've recently been hired to acquire the account databases of two big companies that sell wine online. I have ~4 million e-mail addresses, all of them from their customers.
The person who asked me to do this vanished, and the transaction couldn't be completed.
The job was done discretely and no traces were left. The lists are clean, with no fake addresses, and no spam filters.
More information will be given via e-mail to anyone interested.

I only accept **bitcoins** as payment method, and prices will vary depending on the details of the subject.

Feel free to contact me if you think I can help you with anything else. Comments and suggestions are always welcome, and inquiries will be answered as soon as possible.

I have been doing this for years. I have the knowledge and the resources to get the job done.

Contact information
- **E-mail:** torservices@tormail.org

FIGURE 5.7 Screenshot from the Tor Net for Discussion Groups (intelligence leaks, malware sales/rentals, etc.)

with hosting services (e.g., ransomware) is also becoming big money, with clients paying for the length of time the exploits are actively infecting computers. The article also noted that researchers from named security firms had identified two such kits already being sold and utilized—Incognito 2.0 and Bomb. These kits also offer their

FIGURE 5.8   Screenshot from the Tor Net for the Black Market Reloaded site (drugs, weapons, data, services, etc.)

Screenshot from the TOR Net.

own Web hosting as well as a slick Web-based management interface. With prices starting at $100 a month, sophisticated crime organizations like drugs cartels and terrorist organizations are taking advantage of these more affordable services.[40] Of course, there are still opportunities to enlist and recruit other services, including high-priced call girls and boys, illegal gambling, baby selling/buying, illegal arms and explosive purchasing, and even hiring a "hit" man on the Tor Net. See Figure 5.9.

BOX 5.8

"Bitcoins" Along the Silk Road

Historically, the Silk Road was a great East to West trade route originating in China around the second century BC, and flowed across the fabled Himalaya Mountains to the countries of India, and the Near and Middle East. The road was fraught with dangers and intrigue as merchants crossed the great expanse with goods and services for sale.

More contemporarily, the Silk Road was an underground Web site that, again, traded in goods and services.

The difference: Almost everything on the sprawling network was illegal, from the sale of drugs, weapons, forged documents, exploit kits, and even body parts, to the services of prostitutes, computer hackers, money launderers, and hit men. Silk Road was euphemistically referred to as the "e-Bay" of drugs and illegal contraband. However, on October 1, 2013, activities on the Silk Road came to a screeching halt as the FBI arrested Ross Ulbricht, a

29-year-old former nanotechnology student, in a computer lab at a public library in San Francisco. At the time of his arrest, Ulbricht was using the Internet identity pseudonym "Dread Pirate Roberts" or "DPR," the same pseudonym as the operator and mastermind for the underground network. The Web site was ingenious, encrypted with the TOR Net, and using "bitcoins" as the source of electronic money.

Bitcoins are an electronically secure payment form that are digitally signed and most importantly are anonymous, a critical feature for those seeking illegal goods and services. Bitcoins were first introduced in 2008, by a developer or group of computer programmers known only by the pseudonym, "Satoshi Nakamoto." The identity of "Satoshi Nakamoto" is a hotly debated topic among researchers, with some reports even asserting that "DPR" (Ross Ulbricht) was the original bitcoin developer. It is estimated that there are over 16 million bitcoins in existence, as of May 2017. However, with the closing of the Silk Road, the FBI confiscated about 1.5 percent of all the bitcoins known to the Internet world, fueling speculation on the value of a bitcoin—which ranged from $10 a piece when first introduced to nearly $2,500 each as of May 2017. Even though bitcoins represent a potentially new and exciting technology for fiscal transfer, and are becoming more accepted by legitimate businesses on the Web, only time will tell if the use of such a volatile electronic currency will be able to survive its infamous association with crime and remain in the exclusive domain of illegal black markets. Interestingly, within 48 hours of the closure of the Silk Road, several alternatives were created, including AlphaBay, Dream Market, and Valhalla, again encrypted by the anonymity of the Tor Network.

Sources: Based on ANDY GREENBERG. (August 14, 2013). "An Interview with a Digital Drug Lord: The Silk Road's Dread Pirate Roberts (Q&A)." Forbes; ANDY GREENBERG. (October 2, 2013). "End of the Silk Road: FBI Says It's Busted the Web's Biggest Anonymous Drug Black Market," Forbes; DONNA LEINWAND LEGER. (November 22, 2013). "Judge Denies Bail for Alleged CZAR of Silk Road Website," USA Today; JOHN MARKHOFF. (November 23, 2013) "Study Suggest Link Between Dread Pirate Roberts and Satoshi Nakamoto," The New York Times.

If you need the job done in the EU, you must pay me in advance 5000 EUR in preparation for the job.
If you need the job done outside the EU, you must pay me in advance 10 000 EUR in preparation for the job.
*This money is required for me to purchase the weapon, vehicle of transport, ticket to the target's country, etc

To eliminate:

- Ordinary person: 20 000 EUR
- Criminal or lower rank goverment official: 50 000 EUR
- High rank government official: 100 000 EUR
- Paparazzi: 50 000 EUR
- Journalist: 65 000 EUR
- Business Associate: ranging from 50 000 EUR to 200 000 EUR
- Spouse: price depending on the secondary aspects of person(job, social status etc)

You are required to provide as much information about the target as possible. Necessary information includes:

- Name
- Picture (many if possible)
- Home address
- Work address
- How many family members live in the same household. (not a necessity, but good to know)
- Vehicle used for transport and registration of vehicle, along with any other identificating numbers

After the money you pay me in advance, I will purchase whatever is necessary for the mission.
After the necessary elements have been bought and accomplished, you will pay me the rest of the money to confirm the job, and then I will execute it.

Keep in mind, the amount of time needed for such operation is crucial. The sooner you want a target eliminated, the sooner you should notify me.
A two month headstart is perfect for me.

If you expect me to do such job, I expect you to trust me. We are both anonymous, and a bond of trust is required for such jobs to be successful.

You can contact me and send target information at: friz@tormail.net

FIGURE 5.9 Screenshot from the Tor Net site soliciting "Hit" men for hire.

Screenshot from the TOR Net.

FIGURE 5.10 Screenshots from the Silk Road alternatives

BOX 5.9

Profile Comparison: Drug Lord Versus Cybercrime Master

The profiles of individuals at the higher levels of drug trafficking and cybercrime share several common personality traits. The profile of a cybercriminal, as described by the Cyberpunk Project, includes a wide variety of detailed character traits due primarily to the ability to collect this data, whereas attempts at collecting the same level of data from drug traffickers were likely more difficult. The cyber profile includes primarily male individuals who dress casually; are highly intelligent, independent, and pale skinned (minimal sun exposure); are college or self-educated (being self-educated seems to be better accepted among peers); are mostly reserved in public, but very controlling in their comfort zone; and are nonsmokers and typically limit their use of alcohol and drugs (both substances are perceived as weakening and an impact to their concentration). The lower-level workers in the cybercrime ring are typically undereducated males and females (high school or less) who may have substance abuse problems and are in need of money despite the risk. There is usually no loyalty at the lower levels. Similarly, with drug dealers, there is a general profile of character traits, which include publically displaying wealth (when being public is possible); materialistic lifestyle with lavish homes, cars, jewelry, etc.; a very cold, brutish, and relatively short life expectancy—due primarily to the nature of being a drug dealer; self-imagined unlimited power and wealth (arguably a product of their own product); imprisoned in their own lifestyle; inappropriate social behavior; predominately male; and almost 100 percent smokers of tobacco products. The lower-level workers in the drug organization are typically undereducated males and females (high school or less) who have substance abuse problems and are in need of money despite the risk. There is usually no loyalty at the lower levels, except for those with aspirations of climbing the ladder to a higher level in the organization.

Based on A Portrait of J. Random Hacker. (2003). The Cyberpunk Project. See http://project.cyberpunk.ru/idb/portrait_of_j_random_hacker.html

Summary

Technology has expanded the capabilities of mankind, our reach and our ability to learn and build, reducing the time it takes to solve complex problems, facilitating the growth and evolution of the next generation. Technology is also creating new, faster, and more innovative ways for once regionally limited criminals and organized groups to extend their reach. The evolution of technology and information systems has provided the impetus for traditional criminal organizations to become cyber actors—actors who now have exposure to the global stage, with global reach and global consequences.

Technology will continue to evolve to meet the global demand for faster results, more power, ever-expanding electronic commerce, and social networking; these attributes also provide opportunities that criminals will continue to exploit well into the future. Through the evolution of technology, including programming languages and the propagation of low-cost computers, cybercriminals have identified inherent technical and social vulnerabilities and developed methods for infecting, compromising, and taking over computer systems at the personal, corporate, and government level. The current inherent vulnerability with technology is that people are still required to develop, deploy, operate, and monitor it, and people will always be the greatest risk to security in a world that continues to place increasing reliance on computers to secure their data, services, facilities, intellectual property, and people.

Recent trends, as demonstrated in this chapter, reveal an increasing convergence of technical skill and motivation within large, well-organized, sophisticated criminal organizations. That convergence continues today, as criminals are becoming more apt to work together, partner, subcontract, and communicate anonymously through underground channels. As a result, new criminal enterprises are born and new threats are posed, no longer at a regional level, but at a global reach.

Review Questions

1. Define intellectual property (IP).
2. Identify and describe the various types of espionage and how they relate to organized crime.
3. Identify and describe the various types of IP and information assets often targeted for theft.
4. Identify and discuss the concept of Espionage as a Service (EaaS).
5. Describe the various threats of insider fraud, including sabotage.
6. Define organized crime, and how does it use social media sites for its benefit.
7. Identify and describe the various types of sophisticated criminal organizations and cartels working throughout the world.
8. Define and describe the "deep web" or Tor Net.

Critical Thinking Exercises

1. Using a search engine on your computer, find a recent article that describes an espionage case that occurred within the past 12 months. Determine if the espionage was industrial or economic, or perpetrated by a nation-state; and justify your choice while presenting the key elements of the case to the class for discussion.
2. How do you think that the use of computers and cyber capabilities has changed traditional organized crime organizations (e.g., La Cosa Nostra, Russian mob, Chinese Tongs, Japanese Yakuza, Mexican drug cartels) that were discussed in the chapter? Do you think that cyber capabilities have dramatically changed the way these organizations operate? Construct a list of vulnerabilities that computer operations may pose to sophisticated criminal organizations.
3. Read the Paper Series No.6 by Michael Chertoff and Tobby Simon, The Impact of the Dark Web on Internet Governance and Cyber Security Available at https://ourinternet-files.s3.amazonaws.com/publications/GCIG_Paper_No6.pdf. As a class, discuss the differences between the Internet, the World Wide Web, and the deep web.

Endnotes

1. "Early History of Terrorism." *Terrorism-Research.com*. Retrieved June 2, 2013, from *http://www.terrorism-research.com/history/early.php*.
2. Moore, R. (2011). *Cybercrime: Investigating High-Technology Computer Crime*. Burlington, MA: Anderson Publishing.
3. Mele, S. (2010). "Cyberwarfare and Its Damaging Effects on Citizens." CSIG-Foggia Center for the Study of the Legal Aspects of Computing.
4. *Ibid.*
5. U.S. Immigration and Customs Enforcement–Homeland Security Investigations. (2012). Press Release—"29 charged in New Jersey in international schemes to import counterfeit goods and drugs, launder profits." See *http://www.ice.gov/news/releases/1203/120302-newark.htm*.
6. Specific definitions of Intellectual Property vary; however, one of the most accepted definitions is derived from the United Nations agency WIPO—World Intellectual Property Organization (2013). Geneva, Switzerland. See *http://www.wipo.int/about-ip/en/*.
7. Definitions of "Espionage" are from the "Annual Report to Congress on Foreign Economic Collection and Industrial Espionage." (2011). Washington, D.C.: Office of the National Counterintelligence Executive.
8. Federal Bureau of Investigation. (2013). *Counterintelligence/Economic Espionage*. Washington, D.C.: Federal Bureau of Investigation. Retrieved June 5, 2013, from *http://www.fbi.gov/about-us/investigate/counterintelligence/economic-espionage*.
9.
10. The Commission on the Theft of American Intellectual Property. *The Report of the Commission on the Theft of American Intellectual Property (aka The IP Commission Report)* (May 2013, updated February 2017). The Nation Bureau of Asian Research.
11. *Intellectual Property Theft, a Special Report: DOJ Steps Up Prosecutions of Trade Secret Theft*. (January 31, 2011). The National Law Journal. Washington, D.C.: ALM Media Properties, LLC.
12. *Ibid.*
13. *Ibid.*
14. Mandiant. (2013). *APT1: Exposing One of China's Cyber Espionage Units*. Alexandria, VA: Mandiant. For more information regarding Mandiant, refer to their Web site at: *www.mandiant.com*.
15. Goulding, E. (April 2011). Internal Threats—Employee Fraud. Special District Association of Colorado. See *http://www.sdaco.org/news/internal-threats%E2%80%94-employee-fraud*.

16. KING, C. (January 2012). *Spotlight On: Malicious Insiders and Organized Crime Activity.* Software Engineering Institute – Carnegie Mellon University, CERT Program.

17. "2016 Global Fraud Study," Association of Certified Fraud Examiners, Report to the Nations on Occupational Fraud and Abuse. Retrieved on May 22, 2017, from *https://www.acfe.com/rttn2016/about/executive-summary.aspx*

18. *Ibid.*

19. CUMMINGS, A., LEWELLEN, T., McINTIRE, D., MOORE, A., and TRZECIAK, R. (July 2012). *Insider Threat Study: Illicit Cyber Activity Involving Fraud in the US Financial Services Sector.* Software Engineering Institute – Carnegie Mellon University, CERT Program.

20. Department of Justice—Office of Public Affairs. (2012). "Seventy-Three Members and Associates of Organized Crime Enterprise, Others Indicted for Health Care Fraud Crimes Involving More Than $163 Million." Federal Bureau of Investigation. See *http://www.fbi.gov/news/pressrel/press-releases/organizedcrime_101310* and Department of Justice – Office of Public Affairs (2012). Medicare Fraud Strike Force Charges 91 Individuals for Approximately $430 Million in False Billing. See *http://www.justice.gov/opa/pr/2012/October/12-ag-1205.html.*

21. CAPPELLI, D., MOORE, A., TRZECIAK, R., SHIMEALL, T. (2009). *Common Sense Guide to Prevention and Detection of Insider Threats, 3rd ed. – Version 3.1.* Carnegie Mellon University, CERT Program.

22. SILOWASH, G., CAPPELLI, D., MOORE, A., TRZECIAK, R., SHIMEALL, T., and FLYN, L. (December 2012). *Common Sense Guide to Mitigating Insider Threats*, 4th ed. Software Engineering Institute – Carnegie Mellon University, CERT Program.

23. KING, C. (2010). *Insider Threat Deep Dive: IT Sabotage.* Carnegie Mellon University, CERT Program. See *http://www.cert.org/blogs/insider_threat/2010/09/insider_threat_deep_dive_it_sabotage.html.*

24. CHERRY, P. (2013). "Former RCMP Translator Gets 1-Year Prison Term." *Montreal Gazette.* Retrieved June 10, 2013, from *http://www.montrealgazette.com/news/Former+RCMP+translator+Angelo+Cecere+gets+year+prison/8165848/story.html.*

25. United Nations. (2013). *Comprehensive Study on Cybercrime.* See *http://www.unodc.org/documents/organized-crime/UNODC_CCPCJ_EG.4_2013/CYBERCRIME_STUDY_210213.pdf.*

26. Federal Bureau of Investigation. (2012). *Organized Crime Overview*. See *http://www.fbi.gov/about-us/investigate/organizedcrime/overview.*

27. United Nations. (2013). *Comprehensive Study on Cybercrime.* See *http://www.unodc.org/documents/organized-crime/UNODC_CCPCJ_EG.4_2013/CYBERCRIME_STUDY_210213.pdf.*

28. BJELOPERA, J. (2012). *Organized Crime: An Evolving Challenge for US Law Enforcement.* Congressional Research Service. See *http://www.fas.org/sgp/crs/misc/R41547.pdf.*

29. Information Warfare Monitor & Shadowserver Foundation. (2010). *Shadows in the Cloud: Investigating Cyber Espionage 2.0.* See *http://www.f-secure.com/weblog/archives/Shadows_In_The_Cloud.pdf.*

30. ROHAN, R. (2011). *Social Networking, Counterintelligence, and Cyber Counterintelligence.* Utica, NY: Utica College, Cyber Security Program.

31. PANDA, T.C. (2012). "Cyber-Crimes and Their Impacts: A Review." *International Journal of Engineering Research and Application* 2(2): 202–209.

32. Much of this section on organized crime enterprises was adapted from the report presented by the Federal Bureau of Investigation (2012). *Organized Crime Overview.* Washington, D.C.: FBI. See *http://www.fbi.gov/about-us/investigate/organized-crime.*

33. La SORTE, M. (2006). "Defining Organized Crime." *American Mafia.com.* See *http://www.americanmafia.com/Feature_Articles_349.html.*

34. EuroPol, "Serious and Organised Crime Threat Assessment (SOCTA) 2017 Report." See *https://www.europol.europa.eu/activities-services/main-reports/serious-and-organised-crime-threat-assessment*

35. DEMETRIOU, D. (2009). "Japanese Yakuza Gangsters Hit by Recession." *The Telegraph.* See *http://www.telegraph.co.uk/finance/financialcrisis/5212927/Japanese-yakuza-gangsters-hit-by-recession.html.*

36. HIGGINS, K. (2012). "Russian Cybercrime Doubled Last Year to $2.3 Billion." *Dark Reading.* See *http://www.darkreading.com/attacks-breaches/russian-cybercrime-doubled-last-year-to/232901297.*

37. La SORTE, M. (2006). "Defining Organized Crime." *American Mafia.com.* See *http://www.americanmafia.com/Feature_Articles_349.html.*

38. Threat Assessment—Italian Organized Crime. (2013). Europol Public Information. See *https://www.europol.europa.eu/content/threat-assessment-italian-organised-crime.*

39. KINGTON, T. (2013). "La Cosa Nostra Tested Killer Drones." *The Telegraph.* London. See *http://www.telegraph.co.uk/news/worldnews/europe/italy/10115848/Cosa-Nostra-tested-killer-drones-court-hears.html.*

40. KIRK, J. (2011). "Cybercriminals Selling Exploit-as-a-Service Kit." *PC World.* See *http://www.pcworld.com/article/223487/article.html.*

White-Collar Crimes

CHAPTER OBJECTIVES

After completing this chapter, you should be able to

- Describe how computer technologies have altered the ways in which embezzlement is committed.
- Describe how computer technologies have increased the opportunities to commit money laundering.
- Describe how computer technologies have affected the crime of corporate espionage.
- Describe how computer technologies and the increasing use of the Internet have affected identity and fraud crimes.

INTRODUCTION

Historically, the field of criminology has emphasized the need to explain the occurrence of what has commonly been referred to as traditional "street crime." Crimes such as homicide, rape, armed robbery, and aggravated assault have garnered a vast amount of public and media attention, and criminal justice policies have been designed mainly to counteract these personal violent crimes. Whether or not this emphasis relates to the fears that these types of crimes engender or the media's constant fixation with the "gory details" such crimes produce has been a matter of some debate, what is clear is that the public's common perception of what constitutes "crimes" as well as who is the common "criminal" has been formed largely in relation to traditional street crimes.[1] As a result, crimes that do not fall under traditional definitions or those that are committed by persons who do not fit the public's common perception of the typical criminal have received much less attention. The rise of new technologies and newer forms of crime committed with the use of computers should increase the focus of attention on crimes that have been referred to as "white-collar" offenses.

In the late 1940s, noted criminologist Edwin Sutherland was the first to highlight the disparities between "street crimes" and crimes of the privileged class. He attempted to describe and define a class of behaviors very different from those of traditional street crimes, including acts committed by corporate executives, corrupt politicians, and unscrupulous professionals. He defined these acts as "white-collar crimes" and suggested that they are largely ignored because the perpetrators of these offenses comprised society's elite—people with the economic wherewithal and status to shape the criminal law in their favor and avoid detection and punishment.[2]

This chapter will describe the ways in which the computer revolution has altered the techniques used to commit some of the most common white-collar offenses, specifically embezzlement, corporate espionage, money laundering, identity crimes, and fraud.

The large-scale dissemination of computer and information technologies seems to have created greater opportunities for the white-collar offender, and law enforcement officials are now faced with the unenviable task of looking for loopholes in the ever-expanding technologies used to commit white-collar crimes.

EMBEZZLEMENT

Embezzlement has been defined as the unlawful misappropriation for personal use of money, property, or some other thing of value that has been entrusted to an offender's care, custody, or control. Embezzlement is essentially a theft in violation of a trust. As such, embezzlement has been recognized as a crime since English common-law traditions dating back to the fifteenth century.[3] The embezzler usually is engaged in some type of fiduciary relationship with the victim, either as an employee, guardian, or trustee. Traditionally, embezzlement has involved the physical theft of money or property by employees or others engaged in managing the assets of persons or organizations.

Embezzlement has been the subject of considerable research and debate in regard to both its definition as a traditional white-collar offense and the motivations behind embezzlement schemes. Although Sutherland specifically used embezzlement as an example in his early portrayal of white-collar offending, historically, the embezzler has not been a person of high social status. Rather, he or she has typically been a person engaged in managing the financial affairs of societal elites. Historically, the typical embezzler is a low-level financial institution employee, usually a female bank teller, engaged in stealing financial deposits directly from bank customers. In this regard, some have argued that the embezzler has more in common with the traditional street robber than the corporate executives or professionals originally highlighted by Sutherland in his depiction of white-collar offenders. So too, unlike most other white-collar offenses, embezzlement schemes are often carried out by individual offenders rather than by corporations and other organized entities. These disparities aside, most researchers have historically categorized embezzlement as a white-collar offense, probably because the offense involves a violation of professional trust in which deception rather than physical force is used to carry out the act.

Donald Cressey, in his classic embezzlement study *Other People's Money*, identified a four-step process that described the motivations common to his sample of convicted embezzlers. Prior to the commission of the crime, the embezzler often finds himself or herself experiencing financial problems that cannot be solved through legitimate financial means. The offender then identifies embezzlement as an avenue through which to alleviate his or her financial problems. The embezzler must also possess the technical knowledge necessary to carry out the embezzlement scheme. Finally, the embezzler will use "neutralization techniques" in order to overcome any lingering shame or guilt associated with stealing money that has been entrusted to his or her care. These techniques may involve the intention of paying the money back before anyone notices its absence or justifying the theft based on the belief that the "rich" individuals or organizations that have entrusted the money to the embezzler's care will not miss the funds. Freed from these considerations, the embezzler commits the theft in order to solve his or her financial problems.[4]

The advent of the computer age and the ubiquitous use of computers in the management, allocation, and tracking of both personal and business finances have transformed the methods used by embezzlers to misappropriate cash and/or property. Today, the computer provides the most available means to commit embezzlement, and knowledge relating to the manipulation of large-scale computerized financial databases has become the primary tool of the embezzler.

With regard to other computer crimes, embezzlement can be classified as a "computer-assisted" crime rather than a "computer-focused" crime. Computer-assisted crimes are those where the computer is used in a supporting capacity. The specific crime, such as embezzlement, predates the introduction of computers. In contrast, computer-focused crimes have emerged more recently as a direct result of computer technology (e.g., hacking).[5] Anderson has classified the modern-day embezzler as an "internal perpetrator," or an authorized user of computer systems who uses legitimate access to computer files to commit theft. Because embezzlers have been authorized to use computer systems and resources, they are among the most difficult computer criminals to detect and apprehend.[6]

While the crime of embezzlement appeared centuries before the computer revolution, the use of computer technology does seem to have altered both the commission of the act and the profile of those who embezzle. First, the traditional embezzler was often limited by the physical nature of the theft act. That is, there was a limit to how much cash and/or property the embezzler could actually steal, because the act involved taking and transferring cash or other material goods. Modern embezzlement schemes using computerized records often may not involve the physical theft of anything. The embezzler's take is predicated only on his or her abilities as he or she relates to the misappropriation of data files, and millions of dollars can be stolen with simple keystrokes.

Second, the advent of technologically driven financial management techniques may have narrowed the pool of potential embezzlers to those individuals who possess the specialized skills required to use computer information systems. In this regard, modern-day "technical elites" who steal from their employers and organizations may more closely resemble the societal elites originally identified by Sutherland as typical white-collar offenders. Indeed, more recent studies of convicted embezzlers seem to suggest that rather than experiencing financial problems, many technically elite embezzlers are simply motivated by a desire for a more affluent lifestyle.[7] This observation is reiterated in a recent study on major embezzlement cases in the United States involving employee theft of at least $100,000 for the year 2012.[8] The highlights from the report summarized below can be used to illustrate the widely varied nature of both the perpetrators of modern-day embezzlement and their victims, including private businesses, government agencies, and individuals:

- The study identified 528 major embezzlement cases for 2012, which was an increase of 9 percent year over year.
- Average losses on the embezzlement cases identified were $1.4 million.
- The typical scheme lasted over four years.
- Close to 60 percent of the perpetrators were female.
- Eighty-Four percent of the cases involved individual perpetrators.
- Total losses from major embezzlement cases during 2012 were over $737 million.
- The largest cases involved Russell Wasendorf, who stole $215 million dollars from clients of the Peregrine Financial Group over the course of 20 years.
- Embezzler Rita Crundwell stole $53 million from the budget of Dixon (IL) through her job as comptroller and treasurer.
- Embezzler Sharon Broadway wrote checks to herself for $2.5 million over the course of 27 years from depositor accounts from the United Catholic Credit Union.

CORPORATE ESPIONAGE

Corporate espionage involves any theft of proprietary business information through spying or deception, particularly the theft of "trade secrets." Trade secrets encompass any proprietary information that produces value to a commercial enterprise because that information provides competitive advantages over business rivals.[9] The informational targets to be stolen through corporate espionage schemes are wide and varied, including detailed customer lists, product specifications, research and development data, computerized source codes, memoranda detailing corporate strategies, pricing lists, and technology and computer systems data.[10]

Corporate spies can be divided into two distinct groups.[11] Many corporate espionage schemes are conducted by business "insiders," or persons who have legitimate access to a company's computer networks, such as employees, information technology personnel, or corporate executives. Some research suggests that up to 85 percent of all such schemes are carried out by these insiders, whose motivations extend from blackmail and monetary concerns to a simple lack of loyalty or job dissatisfaction.[12] The remaining acts of corporate espionage are performed by corporate "outsiders," or persons who crack into a corporation's computer data networks without any form of legitimate access rights. Outsiders may penetrate computer systems via the Internet or by gaining access to internal computer networks. Outsiders include domestic spies hired by corporate

---

BOX 6.1

Intellectual Piracy: Historical Context and the Origins of American Industrialization

One of the focuses of this chapter is corporate espionage and the theft of trade secrets. The chapter underscores the importance of these types of white-collar crimes and highlights how opportunities for the perpetration of these offenses has grown since the emergence of the digital revolution.

A broader understanding on the nature of this problem can be gained through the lens of history and the origins of American industrialization during the eighteenth and nineteenth century. Historians establish that the United States engaged in the large-scale theft of trade secrets and technological piracy from European nations during the latter 1700s and early 1800s.[1] These efforts were designed to close the technology gap between Colonial American and more established manufacturing economies, particularly Great Britain. Founding father Alexander Hamilton in 1791 submitted to Congress a "Report on Manufactures" that urged the procurement of industrial machinery in violation of British export laws.[2] There is evidence to suggest that the establishment of the U.S. textile industry in particular benefited from the intellectual theft of manufacturing technologies. Historians differ in regard to how much the theft of intellectual property and trade secrets propelled growth and established America as an industrial power. America, for example, attracted rather than stole large numbers of merchants and capital through lower business

costs and vast market opportunities.[3] The debate however makes clear that the theft of trade secrets is not a new phenomenon. The theft of intellectual property can also be viewed as a double-edged sword: Copyright laws promote and protect the development of new ideas and technology, but they also purposively hinder their rapid dissemination. Developing countries who endeavor to catch up will be incentivized to "cheat" and steal ideas and technologies, whether these goals are harbored within eighteenth century America or twenty-first century China. One difference is that in the current globalized marketplace, those who steal intellectual property and technology can potentially sell those stolen technologies much more easily and swiftly around the globe including within the nations who originally developed those technologies.

---

[1]BEN-ATAR, D.S. (2004). *Trade Secrets: Intellectual Piracy and the Origins of American Industrial Power*. New Haven: Yale University Press.

[2]ANDREAS, P. (2013). "Piracy and Fraud Propelled the US Industrial Revolution." *Bloomberg View*, February 1. Available at *http://www.bloomberg.com/articles*.

[3]WRIGHT, R.E. (2005). Review of Ben-Atar, DS (2004). *Trade Secrets: Intellectual Piracy and the Origins of American Industrial Power* in American Historical Review: 110(3): 787–788.

competitors, as well as foreign nationals hired by adversarial governments intent on gaining a competitive advantage over American firms. At the extreme, these types of spies may access proprietary information simply by entering the workplace facility and visually stealing computer passwords or gaining physical access to computer server rooms.[13]

Outside the realms of insiders and outsiders, the growing employment of independent contractors by large-scale corporations has created unique problems in regard to corporate espionage schemes. Independent contractors are individuals hired by a corporation to perform specific, limited jobs, such as database management, product introductions, or programming changes. These individuals (often referred to as "kites") more closely resemble temporary workers rather than full-time employees, and their resulting lack of loyalty and long-term commitment to the hiring corporation may make them vulnerable targets for information for competing firms. "Kites" may also be hired by competing firms because they have specific knowledge concerning competitor operations.[14]

Corporate concerns regarding espionage and the theft of business secrets have grown over the course of the last two decades. Several related factors have combined to increase the occurrence of corporate espionage and heighten awareness of the problem. First, the corporate community's increasing use of information and computer technologies to conduct business has provided corporate spies easier access to valuable proprietary information. In particular, the ubiquitous use of e-mail as a means of intraoffice communication has made employee exchanges readily accessible to potential corporate spies who possess the technical expertise to crack such networks. In addition, global commerce has increasingly been conducted electronically over the Internet (i.e., "e-commerce"), which has created a wealth of accessible corporate data available to cyberspace hackers.[15] These factors have worked to make the theft of corporate information much easier. It is no longer necessary for corporate thieves to steal information physically, since most valuable corporate secrets usually exist solely in computerized form.

As a result of these factors, the incidence of and costs associated with corporate espionage have risen sharply. A recent study conducted by computer security firm Symantec provides contemporary statistics on the nature and scope of the corporate espionage problem.[16] The report suggests that (1) small businesses are increasingly the target of online attacks, (2) 50 percent of malware created in 2012 was designed to steal consumer info and/or track online computer users, and (3) the jobs most frequently targeted involved workers who create intellectual property, usually within research and development departments. The report concludes that levels of industrial espionage and data theft have increased over time. The most frequently attacked industries include manufacturing (24% of all attacks), finance (19%), services (17%), and government (12%).

While the dawn of the information age has increased the use of spy tactics among domestic corporate rivals, global political and military trends have also played a role in elevating the costs related to corporate espionage. With the end of Cold War rivalries between the U.S. and Soviet militaries, nations have increasingly concentrated espionage efforts toward the theft of trade, rather than military, secrets. So too, the end of U.S.–Soviet hostilities helped to create a vast network of former military spies— individuals highly skilled in espionage tactics—available for corporate hire.[17] The result has been an increase in the use of corporate espionage by nations looking for competitive advantages for their domestic industries. The National Counterintelligence Agency estimates that U.S. businesses lost $44 billion to the theft of trade secrets by international spies between 1996 and 1997.[18]

More recently, spying activities attributed to state-affiliated attackers have gained increased attention.[19] These state-affiliated spies are categorized as "external threat actors," and the proportion of attacks attributed to external actors has been on the rise and now accounts for the vast majority of espionage-related attacks.[20] While the majority of financially motivated attacks originate from the United States or Europe, almost all of the espionage cases (96%) were attributed to actors in China.[21] The data suggest that China has become the most active source of national and industrial espionage today.[22] The most prevalent other countries of origin include Romania, the United States, Bulgaria, Russia, and the Netherlands.

Companies that have been victimized by corporate espionage schemes can pursue a civil action against the offending firm; however, civil suits often turn into lengthy affairs, and the invariable costs incurred through civil courts are prohibitive. The case involving Silicon Valley software firms Cadence Design Systems and Avant! Corporation provides a prime example of the painstakingly slow and costly process involved in resolving domestic espionage suits (see Box 6.2 below for a timeline of events surrounding the case and its eventual outcome).[23] The case originated with an internal investigation conducted by Cadence Design Systems in 1995.[24] Over the course of the preceding four years, several top Cadence executives had left the company to form a rival firm, Avant! Corp. Both companies write software code that helps computer engineers design silicon chips used in advanced computer systems. Cadence executives

---

BOX 6.2

Cadence Design Systems Versus Avant! Corporation

June 1994 Avant! sales reach $39 million after former Cadence vice president Gerald Hsu joins three other former Cadence executives to head up Cadence rival Avant!

August 1995 During a routine site visit to an Avant! customer, Cadence engineers notice similarities between Avant! code and Cadence code that they had developed years earlier. Four thousand lines of identical code are identified, including grammatical and program errors.

December 1995 Santa Clara Co. district attorneys conduct a search and seizure at Avant! headquarters. Cadance files a formal civil complaint in U.S. District Court. The complaint contends that four Avant! executives conspired to steal trade secrets and copyrighted information over a three-year period.

April 1996 Avant! and six employees, including the chairman and chief executive officer, are indicted on criminal charges in Santa Clara County, California.

March 1997 Cadence fails in its attempt to obtain a preliminary injunction against Avant! intended to stop the sale of software allegedly pirated from Cadence source code.

July 1997 Judge stays the civil suit against Avant! in consideration of the pending criminal charges.

September 1997 Preliminary injunction granted against Avant! barring the company from selling software developed from allegedly stolen source code.

February 1998 Avant!'s chief financial officer resigns.

November 1998 Grand jury convenes to consider criminal indictment against Avant! employees.

December 1998 Federal judge extends preliminary injunction against Avant! barring it from selling newer version of software.

May 2001 Eleven Avant! employees and executives plead no contest to criminal charges related to trade secret theft. Individual fines range from $27,000 to $2.7 million.

July 2001 Avant! ordered to pay over $200 million in restitution and court costs to Cadence.

November 2002 Cadence agrees to settle all civil claims against Avant! and its employees in exchange for $265 million in damages. The companies agree to a reciprocal licensing agreement covering the software in question.

claimed that Avant! executives had stolen Cadence source code in order to develop software that was producing over $100 million in sales by 1996. The civil and criminal trials took eight years to resolve.[25]

In response to these concerns, as well as the belief that the problem of corporate espionage had grown with the increasing use of computers in the workplace, Congress enacted the Economic Espionage Act of 1996. Under the Act, corporations who suspect that they are victims of espionage schemes may request an FBI investigation. If such an investigation reveals criminal wrongdoing, the U.S. Attorney's office of the Department of Justice can prosecute the offending firm for theft of trade secrets.[26]

The Economic Espionage Act outlines two separate offenses related to corporate spying. First, the Act attempts to enforce espionage crimes originating from foreign governments and businesses by creating criminal penalties for those who steal, destroy, or knowingly receive stolen trade secrets that would benefit foreign governments. The original version of the Act capped individual fines at $500,000 and prison sentences at 15 years. The Act was amended in 2012, and potential penalties were increased to $5 million for individual offenders.[27] Second, the Act enforces domestic espionage between competing U.S. firms by making the theft of trade secrets related to or included in a product involved in interstate commerce a federal crime. In 2008, Canadian citizen Sheldon Meng became the first individual sentenced under the Espionage Act. He received a 24-month sentence and a $10,000 fine for attempting to steal military software from a defense contracting firm and trying to sell the information to the Chinese military.[28]

MONEY LAUNDERING

Money laundering is the act of concealing the source of assets that have been illegally obtained. The primary object in laundering is to hide the source and ownership of such funds through the creation of a seemingly legitimate history or paper trail. Like embezzlement, money laundering is an "old" crime whose opportunities have expanded greatly with the increasing use of technology in the marketplace. It is impossible to know the extent to which money laundering occurs; however, experts estimate that about $300 billion in cash is laundered each year. The amount of illegal money laundering associated with the drug trade alone is thought to be anywhere from $5 to $15 billion annually.[29]

Traditionally, money laundering was accomplished through three primary means: (1) Cash that was illegally obtained could be physically transported from its place of origin to a jurisdiction that had less stringent banking and reporting requirements. Although the money would eventually be "lost" in the eyes of law enforcement in this new jurisdiction, the act of physically moving cash from one place to another is time consuming, dangerous, and cumbersome for the launderer. (2) The launderer could quickly transform hard currency into legitimate real property, such as real estate, commercial interests, or personal luxuries.[30] The problems with transforming illegally gained assets in this manner are twofold. First, the large-scale purchasing of property is ostentatious, and authorities may notice changes tending toward a suddenly lavish lifestyle. Second, many criminals may have difficulty spending all of their ill-gotten cash, given the exorbitant profits in some illegal enterprises (e.g., large-scale drug trading). (3) Launderers often turned to a method commonly referred to as "smurfing." Smurfing involves the division of large amounts of cash into smaller denominations so as to conceal its common origin. The launderer would enlist several persons to deposit relatively small amounts of cash into several different accounts scattered over a geographic area. In this way, the launderer could successfully avoid federal reporting requirements regarding large-scale cash deposits.[31]

The increasing use of technology, especially telecommunications and the Internet, has provided a wealth of new opportunities for the money launderer. Obscuring the origin and owner of large amounts of cash is now a keystroke away. In order to understand the impact that technology has had on money-laundering crimes, it may be useful to view the advancement of technology in this area in two distinct phases. During the 1960s and 1970s, governments, banks, and other financial institutions increasingly used telecommunications networks to move large amounts of cash.[32] These electronic cash transactions, or "electronic funds transfers" (EFTs), served to digitize the financial marketplace. Telephone lines and computer networks substituted for the physical transport of cash and other financial instruments.

Money is swiftly and easily moved both legitimately and illegitimately across these computerized networks. Currently, there are two primary cash transfer institutions. FedWire is the electronic payment network created by the Federal Reserve System. In 2008, approximately 7,300 participants made FedWire transfers.[33] Over 250,000 transactions are performed on the system per day. CHIPS is a clearinghouse payment system created by private banking companies. In 2012, CHIPS cleared and settled an average of $1.5 trillion in cross-border and domestic payments daily.[34]

The electronic revolution that has occurred in the banking industry, especially the large-scale movement of cash in electronic forms, has made laundering easier. Because money transfers now involve electronic messages rather than physical cash, it is easier for the launderer to move money in a series of transactions over a short period of time. Smurfing can be accomplished by one individual at a keyboard rather than a large group of smurfs over a wide geographic area. So too money that can be moved electronically is also easier to integrate into the mainstream banking system.

QUICK FACTS

The 2015 National Money Laundering Risk Assessment reports that just six banks hold more than 40 percent of total U.S. domestic bank deposits, including Bank of America (12.7%), Wells Fargo & Company (10%), JP Morgan Chase & Co. (9.7%), Citigroup Inc. (4.4%), U.S. Bancorp (2.5%), and PNC Financial Services Group (2.3%). The large portion of dollar denominated transactions processed by these six large banks puts them at the highest risk of potential money-laundering activities.[1]

---

[1]The National Money Laundering Risk Assessment 2015. U.S. Department of Treasury.

While the introduction of telecommunications and computer technologies in the 1960s and 1970s served to increase the ease with which money could be laundered, the current explosion in e-commerce and the influence of the Internet may provide launderers even greater opportunities in years to come. The biggest concern for law enforcement is the recent introduction of anonymous electronic cash exchange systems, or "e-cash."[35] E-cash is digital money that may be exchanged over the Internet. It is an electronic replacement for cash. E-cash comprises an electronic series of numbers that have intrinsic value in some form of currency.[36] E-cash may be likened to the serial numbers located on hard currency, except in the case of e-cash there is no hard currency, only the related electronic numbers. Interest in the use of e-cash has grown in conjunction with the Internet, largely because it can be exchanged with increased speed and efficiency. Online businesses can also increase e-commerce profits through its use.

Authorities fear that the increasing use of such "cashless" systems may promote unique "cyberlaundering" schemes that are more difficult to detect and defend against. Researcher Mark Bortner describes a hypothetical scenario whereby the anonymous nature of e-cash and the ease with which it can be accessed through the Internet provides "cyberlaunderers" easy opportunities:[37]

> Doug drug dealer is the CEO of an ongoing narcotics operation. Doug has rooms filled with hard currency that is the profits from his illegal enterprise. This currency needs to enter into the legitimate mainstream economy so that Doug can either purchase needed supplies and employees, purchase real or personal property or even draw interest on his ill-gotten gains . . . Doug employs Linda launderer to wash the dirty money. Linda hires couriers ("smurfs") to deposit funds under different names in amounts between $7,500 and $8,500 at branches of every bank in certain cities . . . In the meantime, Linda launderer has been transferring these same funds from each branch and depositing the money with Internet banks that accept E-cash . . . Once the hard currency has been converted into digital E-cash, the illegally earned money has become virtually untraceable—anonymous. Doug drug dealer now has access to legitimate electronic cash.

This type of scenario recently played out in the case of e-cash exchange Liberty Reserve. The operators of this virtual currency were criminally indicted in May 2013 for allegedly operating a $6 billion money-laundering operation online.[38] The case is the largest online money-laundering scheme in history. Law enforcement officials believe that Liberty Reserve sought to create a convenient method to launder enormous sums of cash through this e-cash operation. In order to transfer funds using Liberty Reserve, users needed only to provide a name, address, and date of birth. Users were not, however, required to validate their identity. Authorities believe that Liberty Reserve and other largely anonymous e-cash systems are used almost exclusively by trans-national criminal organizations to hide proceeds from law enforcement authorities around the globe.

Law enforcement authorities have several tools at their disposal to enforce money-laundering crimes. The oldest among these is the Bank Secrecy Act (BSA) of 1970. The BSA requires banks and other financial institutions to file records concerning suspicious financial transactions over $10,000 (e.g., large cash deposits, foreign bank exchanges, cross-border currency transports). In addition, the 1986 Money Laundering Control Act works to close certain loopholes in the BSA that were exploited by launderers in the past. Specifically, the Money Laundering Control Act requires banks and other financial institutions to report any suspicious banking transactions (including possible "smurfing" schemes) regardless of the monetary amount of any single transaction.[39]

Finally, the U.S. Treasury Department's Financial Crimes Enforcement Network (FinCEN) serves as a "central clearinghouse" for intelligence and information sharing on money laundering.[40] FinCEN's main objective is to provide law enforcement agencies the analytical tools necessary to identify and prosecute money-laundering cases. FinCEN uses two primary avenues to accomplish this goal. First, FinCEN provides direct case support to over 150 local law enforcement agencies, and coordinates efforts with the International Association of Chiefs of Police (IACP), the National White-Collar Crime Center (NWCCC), and the National Association of Attorneys General (NAAG). This support specifically involves developing linkages from the various aspects of money-laundering cases so that prosecutions can occur. Second, FinCEN provides secondary support to local law enforcement agencies in the form of training, office space, and database research access. FinCEN officials have termed this support a "platform approach" to solving money-laundering cases, whereby federal resources are used to aid local law enforcement efforts directly.

Since its establishment in 1990, FinCEN has provided law enforcement and regulatory agencies thousands of analytical case reports involving money-laundering suspects. In recognition of the increasingly "borderless" nature of "cyberlaundering," FinCEN also spearheads efforts to promote international cooperation in the fight against laundering. FinCEN develops these international partnerships through Financial Intelligence Units (FIUs), or centralized money-laundering analysis agencies, located across the globe.[41] These FIUs appear to be of increasing importance, given the inherently global nature of international terrorist attacks and terrorist organizations' vital interest in maintaining adequate monetary resources in order to foster new terrorist networks and fund future terror attacks. The value of FinCEN data to local law enforcement agencies seems clear, as a recent survey found that 86 percent of them confirm that FinCEN's financial reports contributed to the detection and deterrence of financial crimes by generating new leads and/or providing new information. In 2011, the number of requests received by law enforcement agencies increased 27 percent year over year, and these requests had doubled from those requested just two years earlier in 2009.[42]

Internet fraudsters have also begun to use e-cash systems to their advantage to engage in money laundering and fraud. In 2007, a company called e-gold Ltd. was indicted in the U.S. federal court system on four counts of money laundering.[43] The company allowed individuals to make and receive payments through the transfer of gold ownership. Its payment system and structure were popular among a variety of fraudsters and led the United States to prosecute the operators of e-gold on charges of money laundering and fraud.[44] The CEO of e-gold, Douglas Jackson, pled guilty and negotiated a plea bargain for his crimes, and the company has subsequently changed its payment and system processes to conform to federal statutes.[45]

Federal law enforcement agencies and scholars interested in white-collar crimes have traditionally focused on the various forms of money laundering described in this chapter that typically involve the movements of physical cash, checks, and/or the electronic transfer of funds. Another way used to launder the origins of illicit monies involves the physical movement of goods across the globe through the international trade system, or Trade Based Money Laundering (TBML).[46] Organized criminal groups have increasingly abused the international trade system, but this form of money laundering has received comparatively little attention. More recently however, the U.S. Department of State's 2016 annual report on money laundering identified TBML as a rising concern in over 30 jurisdictions including global trade heavyweights Canada, China, Hong Kong, India, Taiwan, and Singapore.[47] The report further identifies TBML as an increasingly important money-laundering technique for the finance of terrorist activities.

The global trade system is highly vulnerable and presents an attractive opportunity to launder money. First, the physical transportation of very large volumes of trade goods obscures the nature and character of any single trade transaction. Identifying particular transactions that involve the laundering of money is like finding a needle in a haystack. Second, nations have limited resources to verify the exchange of goods across borders. Most customs agencies inspect less than 5 percent of all cargo shipments entering or leaving the jurisdiction.[48] The Congressional Research Service recently underscored the rising importance of TBML and summarized how these crimes fit into the broader narrative of this text and the emergence of cyber crimes and terrorism: [49]

> The global trends that facilitated a quadrupling of global trade over the past quarter century, measured at $16.4 trillion in 2015, are also being used by drug smugglers and other criminal organizations to hide the gains of illegal activities. In particular, advances in communications and lower transportation costs, combined with the digital revolution, global value chains, and greater urbanization, have produced more interconnected economies and societies that link together national economies and create vast new market opportunities. Reportedly, organized crime has followed these trends and expanded its activities into new markets.

TBML may involve several different techniques—all of them involve a conspiracy between an importer and exporter of goods that uses the international system of trade as a means to "hide" or obscure the origins of illicit money. One technique involves the over and under invoicing of goods. In this technique the actual price of goods being traded is misrepresented on accounting documents, and the difference between the actual price and the documented price provides the opportunity to "hide" or obscure illicit funds within the fraudulent transaction. A second technique involves the multiple invoicing of goods. In this technique, more than one invoice is created for the documentation of a single trade transaction. The "payment" of the extra invoice(s) provides the opportunity to "hide" or obscure illicit funds within the fraudulent transaction. A third technique involves the over or under shipment of goods. In this technique, an exporter misrepresents the number or volume of goods exchanged rather than the price. In extreme cases, an exporter can fraudulently document a shipment of goods that did not occur at all. This "ghost" exchange provides the opportunity to "hide" or obscure illicit funds. More complex forms of TBML involve manipulations of foreign exchange rates combined with these other forms of fraudulent transactions. See figure X "Mechanics of a Black Market Peso Exchange Arrangement" for a quick sketch of how these complex transactions occur.[50] The figure describes how organized criminal groups involved in the illegal drug trade launder funds across international borders in ways that take advantage of differences in the exchange rate of global currencies, in this example pesos and dollars.

IDENTITY THEFT

The emergence of identity crimes as a primary public and law enforcement concern can be viewed as indicative of the more general patterns of growth we have witnessed in computer crimes during the course of the past several decades. The exponential growth in the incidence of identity theft can largely be attributed to the creation of opportunities that are directly linked to technological and commercial advances. These advances have produced an alarming rise in the fraudulent use of individual information such as Social Security numbers, dates of birth, and credit card numbers by thieves who are intent on using this information for personal gain, and they have forced law enforcement agencies to redirect scarce resources in order to mitigate the threat.

A recent report published by the Congressional Research Service provides contemporary information on recent trends and issues associated with the crime of identity theft.[51] The report indicates that the number of identity theft complaints peaked during 2007 and 2008. The number of identity theft complaints decreased in both 2009 and 2010. Still, identity theft remains the most frequent type of consumer fraud complaint. In 2010, roughly 8.1 million Americans were victims of identity fraud, and the average victim suffered a mean loss of

$631 as a result of these crimes. More troubling, the number of aggravated identity theft cases has continued to increase relative to the total number of identity crimes reported.

These trends can partly be attributed to the increasing use of Social Security numbers as personal identifiers. Social Security numbers, rarely referred to by those under retirement age decades ago, are now used as a means to conduct a wide range of business transactions, most notably the opening of new lines of personal credit. The use of Social Security numbers as personal identifiers, however, has not been limited to credit transactions. We are now asked to include the number on an ever-increasing array of forms, including medical records, motor vehicle driver's licenses, and educational and employment records—some car dealers will even ask for it prior to allowing a customer to test drive a vehicle. Obviously, theft opportunities increase in relation to the number of times that consumers are required to use Social Security numbers as personal identifiers by commercial and governmental enterprises. Policymakers recently explored options to reduce the use of Social Security numbers as personal identifiers, including laws designed to limit their use by private companies.[52]

Identity thieves use a variety of methods to steal personal information. Heading up the list of low-tech means is "dumpster diving," or rummaging through private or commercial trash receptacles in search of discarded bills or preapproved credit applications.[53] Other low-tech methods include the direct theft of mail, which may include a veritable treasure trove of personal information contained on bank statements and unwanted telephone calling cards. Some thieves even complete change of address forms in the name of unwitting victims in order to divert and more easily access personal mail. "Shoulder surfing," or eavesdropping on conversations and cash transactions that involve the disclosure of personal identifiers provides an avenue for low-tech thieves who are unwilling to steal documents outright.[54]

While these theft techniques provide opportunities for everyday thieves, more organized and technologically based methods have been used by sophisticated thieves who intent on stealing mass quantities of personal information. These schemes may involve hacking information from corporate databases used for online transactions or the bribing of employees who have internal access to customer identifiers. The loss of sensitive personal information is costly, considering estimates from 2007 found that businesses in the United States lost over $5 million due to the theft of confidential electronic data by hackers and computer attackers.[55] One of the most noteworthy and significant mass compromises in recent years affected customers of The TJX Companies, Inc. A small group of hackers compromised an internal database and stole at least 94 million customer credit card accounts, which financial agencies estimate caused as much as $1 billion in damages.[56]

Once personal identifying information is obtained, thieves can ransack a victim's financial status and destroy his or her credit history with frightening ease. For example, they may be able to open a new credit account using stolen Social Security numbers, names, and date of birth. The victim, of course, is left with the unpaid bills and delinquent accounts. Depending on the amount of personal information stolen, thieves may even be able to create entirely new bank accounts in your name, writing "hot" checks that are eventually traced back to the victim's credit history. Others have been victimized by thieves who have established wireless phone service, bought cars and other expensive consumer goods, and filed for bankruptcy under assumed identities in order to avoid paying past due accounts.[57]

Identity thieves have also developed black markets online where stolen personal information can be sold and resold to individuals around the world. Evidence suggests that Internet Relay Chat, or IRC, channels and Web sites operate for hackers to sell

QUICK FACTS

The year 2014 will undoubtedly be remembered as significant in the history of computer crime and the crime of identity theft as the information systems of numerous large-scale corporations were breached exposing the personal information of hundreds of millions of Americans to online hackers and other criminals. The customer files of companies including Home Depot, Target, ebay, and Apple's iCloud network were hacked.[1] The scope and magnitude of these breaches forced citizens and policymakers to address the issues of online security in more meaningful—and urgent—ways.

[1]BAN, E. (2015). "Data Breaches of 2014: From Retail to Healthcare No Industry Is Spared." *OEM Hub*, January 23. Available at *http://oemhub.bitdefender.com*.

significant volumes of data obtained through database compromises and other means. These Web-based resources exist to sell credit card and bank accounts, PINs, and supporting customer information obtained from victims around the world in lots of tens or hundreds of accounts.[58] Stolen credit and bank accounts are referred to as "dumps" within these markets, and the individuals who participate are referred to as "carders."[59] Financial accounts in carding markets are sold at very low prices for as little as $1.30 in some cases.[60] Individuals could also buy accounts obtained from countries around the world, suggesting that identity theft and fraud have no boundaries.

Carding markets also facilitate real-world identity theft and fraud, as individuals offer cash out services to obtain physical money from electronic accounts. In addition, individuals can buy skimming devices that can be attached to an automatic teller machine or point of sale terminal.[61] These devices capture and store the magnetic stripe data from debit and credit cards and steal data from unsuspecting individuals. Finally, individuals sell passports, drivers' license, and financial records within these markets, thereby allowing individuals to more efficiently engage in identity theft in the real world. Box 6.4 details a significant case in the investigation of carding groups. In general, carding is a significant problem, because the criminals who frequent these markets can quickly and efficiently engage in credit card fraud and identity theft without any technical knowledge or skill.[62]

BOX 6.3

Prominent Identity Crime Prosecutions

- Federal agents arrested a former employee at a Long Island software company who allegedly originated a crime ring that eventually cost consumers $2.7 million. The suspect sold the credit reports of over 30,000 people, including names, Social Security numbers, and other credit information, to black market identity thieves who used the information to fraudulently obtain a wide variety of consumer goods. Each victim's credit history was sold for only $30.
- A defendant was recently convicted in federal court for fraudulently obtaining the names and Social Security numbers of high-ranking military officers from internal government Web sites and using the information to apply online for credit cards and other lines of credit.

He was sentenced to 41 months in prison and ordered to pay over $186,000 in restitution.
- A former temporary employee of an insurance firm was convicted for using policyholders' bank account information to deposit over $764,000 in counterfeit bank checks.
- Seven defendants were recently convicted in an identity theft–drug smuggling scheme. The suspects used stolen Social Security numbers to garner employment and identification documents that were used to facilitate the smuggling of heroin and methamphetamine from Mexico. A number of the defendants also used their stolen identities to claim earned income tax credits on IRS tax forms.

BOX 6.4

Prominent Carding Market Cases

CASE #1: The ShadowCrew opened a Web site in 2002 and developed a brisk trade in credit cards, financial information, and identity documents.[1] Over one million credit cards were said to have been sold through its site, and there were over 2,000 registered members. Its Web site was taken down on October 26, 2004, by the U.S. Secret Service and various police agencies around the world, and the homes of 28 members of the group were raided. Subsequently, 12 individuals arrested pled guilty to charges ranging from computer fraud and abuse to document fraud and conspiracy. The leader of the group, 32-year-old Andrew Mantovani, received 32 months in a federal prison camp for his role in this carding group.[2]

_____
[1]PARIZO, E.B. (2005). "Busted: The Inside Story of 'Operation Firewall.'" *Security News.* Retrieved January 18, 2006, from *http://searchsecurity.techtarget.com/news/article/0,289142,sid14_gci1146949,00.html.*[2]*Ibid.*

Federal law enforcement agencies and the criminal justice system have begun to respond to the increasing threat posed by identity thieves through new legislation and consumer awareness programs. In 1998, Congress passed the Identity Theft and Assumption Deterrence Act. The law makes it a federal crime when someone knowingly transfers or uses, without lawful authority, a means of identification of another person with the intent to commit, or to aid or abet, any unlawful activity that constitutes a violation of federal law, or that constitutes a felony under any applicable state or local law.[63]

Violations of the law may be punishable by up to 15 years in prison. While the Act clearly signifies a growing recognition of the costs associated with identity crimes, the impact of these and other laws aimed at curtailing identity theft may be largely symbolic for many of those victimized. The reality is that identity crimes remain extremely difficult to prosecute once detected. A large number of cases are detected too late for officials to investigate adequately. These cases are extremely labor intensive and often require collaborative effort on the part of federal, state, and local law enforcement agencies for successful prosecution. So too, the actual monetary losses involved in many individual cases of identity theft may be considered too small for dedication of a large amount of prosecutorial resources.[64]

Given the difficulties inherent in detecting and prosecuting identity crimes, many experts believe that the establishment of consumer awareness and monitoring programs may be the most viable avenue toward thwarting the growth of identity theft. To this end, the Federal Trade Commission (FTC) has established the identity theft clearinghouse. The clearinghouse collects identity theft complaints and provides victims referral information and other resources aimed at helping them restore their credit history and financial status. The clearinghouse has also established a hotline for consumers who believe they have been victimized in an identity crime.[65]

BOX 6.5

Future Strategies to Mitigate Identity Theft: The Concept of Fractured Identities

This chapter identifies some fundamental problems with traditional strategies to mitigate the problem of identity theft. These problems center on the fact that in most cases identity thieves are both: (a) extremely difficult to catch and (b) steal amounts of money that are too small to garner significant attention from local law enforcement agencies. These and other problems reduce the potential effectiveness of any strategies that are reactive or focused on the problem *after* it occurs. As a result, many observers underscore the need for more proactive mitigation strategies designed to prevent identity theft *before* it occurs.

One proponent of proactive mitigation strategies is David Birch, an identity transactions consultant and author of the text *Digital Identity Management: Technological, Business, and Social Implications*.[1] Birch argues that the large-scale perpetration of identity theft occurs largely because citizens are routinely required to provide too much personal information or "parts" of our identity. He argues that most transactions require verification of a single piece of data, however we are required to provide many sorts of unnecessary data in order to complete these transactions. The perpetration of identity theft increases with the amount of personal information we make available within each transaction. Birch points out that we do not have one single identity, but many "fractured" identities that depend upon the situation. We should only be required to reveal that part of our identity required to complete each individual transaction.

For example, the proprietors of a local club need to verify only that I am 21 years of age; but instead, we are required to provide a driver's license that includes our name, a state identification number, and our address. Likewise, medical doctors need to verify our insurance; but instead, we are required to provide a driver's license and medical insurance card that list our address, our age, and perhaps even our Social Security number. We pay for virtually every transaction with debit and credit cards that include our financial account information but also our names.

Birch advocates the use of software applications accessed through one or more mobile devices that would be utilized depending on the nature of each transaction and would reveal only the information required to complete that transaction.[2] All other individual identifiers would remain encrypted. So, if you seek to gain entry into a club, an app on your phone could be shared to reveal only whether you are 21 years of age. Another app could be shared with your doctor that provides only verification of your insurance coverage. Birch points out that the technology already exists to develop and implement strategies to promote the use of what he labels our "fractured" identities. Such a strategy would significantly reduce the perpetration of identity theft by reducing the amount of information revealed within every type of electronic transaction.

---

[1] See *http://www.ted.com/speakers/david_birch*.
[2] Birch, D. (2012). "A New Way to Stop Identity Theft" *TEDTX*. Available at *http://www.ted.com/talks*.

INTERNET FRAUD SCHEMES

The Internet has increasingly been used as a vehicle for interpersonal communications, research, consumer spending, and business-to-business transactions over the course of the last decade. This growth has provided the public with previously unparalleled opportunities for personal and economic advancement and has created entire new industries in the process. These advances, however, have also produced fresh opportunities for fraud and abuse online. Interestingly, many fraud schemes committed over the Internet are simply new takes on old themes—chain letter hoaxes, confidence schemes, and bait-and-switch con games that are now performed over an electronic medium rather than in person or over the telephone. Whether in old or new form, it is clear that the increasing use of the Internet has given rise to an alarming growth in fraudulent schemes. According to the official reporting rates of the NWCCC, consumer complaints concerning online fraud rose from 16,838 in 2000 to over 75,000 in 2002, over a 400 percent increase in just two years.[66] These Internet fraud schemes encompass a wide range of offenses, including financial institution fraud, investment fraud, communications fraud, and confidence schemes. This section will briefly define and describe the first three above mentioned types of Internet fraud, as well as discuss various types of confidence schemes in more detail.

Financial institution fraud involves attempts to conceal the truth from deposit and lending institutions so as to gain monetarily.[67] Examples of financial lending institution fraud include credit/debit card fraud and identity theft. Credit card fraud is one of the most widely reported Internet frauds, and identity theft has become a primary concern for law enforcement personnel and the public alike. Investment frauds are "deceptive practices involving the use of capital to create more money," including traditional stock market investment schemes and pyramid business schemes designed to defraud individual consumers, all of which can be conducted online.[68] Communication frauds involving new and different forms of technology have skyrocketed through thefts of wireless phone codes and other satellite communication devices.[69]

While all types of Internet fraud have experienced recent growth, frauds that involve a breach of personal trust, or what have been traditionally referred to as "confidence schemes," may be among the most widely practiced and familiar to the general public. These schemes now typically use e-mail communications or online sites as a primary medium rather than the mail or telephone. The most widely perpetrated Internet confidence schemes include online auction fraud, the Nigerian "419" fraud, chain letter hoaxes, and what are known as "urban legends" passed along through electronic mailings.

Online auction fraud is the most widely reported type of Internet fraud by a large margin. Sixty-four percent of all reported Internet fraud is auction fraud. The Internet Crime Complaint Center (IC3) received over 30,000 auction fraud complaints in 2001. Losses related to online auction fraud surpass $4 million annually.[70] The IC3 has also received an increase in the number of reports of auction fraud over time, and the average loss per complaint was $610.[71] Individuals and/or businesses participating in online auctions can be defrauded in several ways. The most prevalent form of online auction fraud is nondelivery of goods. In most cases, the victim of nondelivery has very little recourse if payment for the item has already been received by the would-be seller. Most online auction buyers do not have a physical address or description of the perpetrator. Because of this, nondelivery of goods is one of the most commonly reported forms of auction fraud.[72]

Sellers may also purposely misrepresent the item to be auctioned in terms of its quality or characteristics. This can be accomplished through simple item descriptions or the altering of item pictures. "Shill bidding" is the use of intentional fake bidding on the part of the seller in order to artificially inflate an item's auctioned price. Finally, "fee stacking" occurs when the seller adds hidden charges to the cost of the item prior to delivery, most often through inflating the shipping cost. The costly nature of these schemes is detailed in Box 6.3, which provides excerpts from case summaries provided by the IC3 of two of the most extensive schemes recently investigated by federal law enforcement authorities.[73]

Another highly publicized online fraud scheme has been dubbed the Nigerian 419 scheme by authorities. Since its origination in 1989, the online e-mail letter scheme has cost individuals and businesses an estimated one billion dollars globally. The scheme is named "419" after the relevant Nigerian criminal codes that are involved. The scheme encompasses numerous different e-mails forwarded by Nigerian nationals in which the correspondence outlines nonexistent opportunities for recipients to receive Nigerian government funds in exchange for advance fees.[74] The following is an excerpted summary of the content of these fraudulent e-mails detailing the scheme from Interpol.[75]

The letters explain that the money is from delayed approved contract payments by the Nigerian administration to certain companies or individuals who have abandoned their claims. The letter alleges that the present military government is now paying these claims. The signatories claim to be acting as middlemen and request that the victim supply signed and stamped blank company letterheads and invoices together with detailed account information so that monies can be transferred in advance of payment in order to pay taxes and bribe relevant officials in charge of the supposed proceeds. Obviously, no money is ever received, resulting in a total loss of bank deposits from the victim.

The IC3 received over 16,000 complaints about the scheme in 2008 alone. Largely as a result of this scheme, Nigeria ranks second behind only the United States in losses associated with Internet fraud schemes.[76] Victims in the United States lost an average of $1,650 due to these schemes, which are one of the more costly forms of fraud according to the IC3.[77]

Another costly form of Internet fraud is *phishing*. Perpetrators of phishing schemes attempt to lure or "hook" potential victims to fraudulent Web sites for the purpose of gathering sensitive personal information. Phishing attacks involve the distribution of e-mails that appear to be from a legitimate financial institution or credit card company. The text of the message usually states that the recipient's account has been compromised or requires maintenance. The e-mail then asks the potential victim to log into his or her financial accounts through a Web link contained in the phishing e-mail. The link appears to take the victim to the Web site of a legitimate financial institution, but actually redirects his or her browser to a fraudulent Web site created by the criminal. The fraudulent link contains a spoofed Web page that mirrors the legitimate Web site of the financial institution. The best phishers take images and Web page designs directly from legitimate Web sites. The victim provides his or her bank account number, PIN, passwords, or other sensitive information. From here, the criminal can use the information to engage in credit card fraud or identity theft without the victim's knowledge. The IC3 has seen an increase in phishing schemes since 2004, and these types of schemes have quickly become one of the most common forms of Internet fraud. The Gartner Group estimates the cost of phishing schemes in the United States during 2007 alone to be $3 billion. Box 6.7 contains a summary of recent research efforts designed to help Internet users detect phishing e-mails before the damage is done.

BOX 6.6
Prominent Online Auction Fraud Cases

CASE #1 The CATCH Task Force successfully prosecuted Raj Trivedi for victimizing more than 700 individuals throughout the world with his Internet fraud scheme of advertising high-tech products, accepting payment, and then failing to deliver the merchandise advertised. Losses from these frauds were over $992,000. Trivedi victimized consumers who went to his Web site to purchase electronic equipment (e.g., computers and camcorders) that Trivedi advertised on the auction Web sites eBay, uBid, and Yahoo. In March 2002, Trivedi was sentenced to three years in prison and ordered to pay restitution to his victims, who averaged $1,200 in individual losses.

CASE #2 The case against Teresa Smith of Massachusetts represents one of the largest online auction fraud schemes on record. Smith was the subject of over 300 individual complaints stemming from frauds occurring from April 2001 through October 2002. Her scheme was simple: She would defraud her victims by selling a computer, requiring them to pay up front, and then not sending any of the auctioned merchandise. Smith then refused any type of refund request. During the investigation, it was discovered that Smith had spent the victims' money on living expenses, a new vehicle, and advertising costs associated with the scheme. Smith would change her online identity any time complaints were reported against her. The scheme was finally detected after investigators uncovered over $800,000 in fraudulent proceeds. Smith was sentenced in 2003 to nearly five years in prison for her crime.

BOX 6.7

Detecting Phishing E-mails

Criminals can easily duplicate the legitimate Web sites of financial institutions to perpetrate a phishing attack. Researchers at Carnegie Mellon University recently presented a method for detecting phishing e-mails and mitigating the costs associated with these attacks.[1] The researchers designed a system for detecting phishing e-mails that involves (1) extracting data contained in the phishing e-mail and (2) collecting additional information from external sources. Their approach—referred to as "PILFER"—is designed to detect communication that is intentionally deceptive or intended to "trick" the users into believing that they are dealing with a legitimate financial institution. PILFER involves the use of several different types of information to detect phishing e-mails.

These data include Web addresses, Web site domain names, the number of links present in the e-mail, HTML e-mails, JavaScript, and information gathered from existing spam filters. The researchers found that PILFER identified phishing e-mails with 99.5 percent accuracy. The research shows that it is becoming increasingly possible to detect phishing e-mails using a specialized filter such as PILFER. Future detection strategies will need to continue to develop, as the nature and character of phishing attacks evolve over time.

—————
[1]Fette, I., Sadeh, N., and Tomasic, A. (2007). "Learning to Detect Phishing Emails." Proceedings of the 16th Annual International Conference on the World Wide Web, Banff, Alberta, CA.

Once the recipient clicks on the link provided in the e-mail, he or she is taken to a spoofed Web page that mirrors the actual financial institution's site. The best phishers take the images and design directly from the originating business to ensure that they can fool as many victims as possible. At this point, the victim is asked to provide his or her bank account, PIN, password, or other information, which is then transmitted to the phisher in a variety of ways. From here, the criminals can use the information they collect to engage in credit card fraud or identity theft without the victim knowing this has occurred.[78] Phishing is a particularly costly form of fraud for both victims and financial institutions alike, as the Gartner Group estimates that phishing victims in the United States lost $3 billion in 2007 alone.[79] Additionally, the IC3 has seen an increase in phishing reports since 2004, making it one of the more common forms of Internet fraud.[80] Chain letter hoaxes and "urban legends" comprise another highly publicized and common form of Internet fraud. Chain letter hoaxes over the Internet are simply online versions of age-old schemes designed to perpetuate the forwarding of e-mails. Often, these letters ask the recipient to forward the e-mail message to as many people as they can in exchange for a specified sum for each forwarded e-mail.[81] Chain letter hoaxes are typically less costly than other forms of online fraud, because the recipient is simply duped into believing that he or she will receive compensation that is not forthcoming. These hoaxes have included claims that prominent businesses will compensate recipients for forwarded e-mails, including Microsoft, Outback Steak House, Victoria's Secret, Newell Company, Nokia, Old Navy, and McDonalds, among others.[82] These claims are *never* true, because currently there is no software in existence that is capable of tracking the number of times that an e-mail is forwarded and then subsequently compiling a report back to a central tabulator.[83] So-called urban legends are myths designed to create a generalized panic among e-mail recipients. These messages typically entail grandiose claims of impending danger arising from commonplace activities. Box 6.8 details some of the more common urban legends currently circulating online. Rest assured, none of the claims are true.[84]

BOX 6.8
Common Online "Urban Legends"

Needles on Gas Pumps

Some persons have been affixing hypodermic needles to the underside of gas pump handles in the Jacksonville, Florida, area. These needles appear to be infected with the HIV virus. In the Jacksonville area alone, there have been 17 cases of people being stuck by these needles over the past five months. We have verified reports of at least 12 other cases around the country . . . Evidently, the consumers go to fill their car with gas, and when picking up the pump handle get stuck by infected needles . . . IT IS IMPERATIVE TO CAREFULLY CHECK THE HANDLE OF GAS PUMPS EVERY TIME YOU USE ONE!

Cyanide-Laced Deposit Envelopes

I hesitate to be an alarmist, but if anything like this happened to one of my family or friends I would not be able to forgive myself for not passing this along . . . A woman died recently from licking the deposit envelope at a Bank of America ATM. It was laced with cyanide. Investigators stated that they went back to the ATM in question and found six other envelopes in the slot . . . Please, I implore you to use extreme caution when using those envelopes. The radio station advised that you should first spit on the envelope, and then close it . . . I know this sounds gross, but better gross than DEAD.

Poison Perfume Samples

I was sent an e-mail at work about someone walking up to you at a mall parking lot and asking you to sniff perfume they are selling at cut-rate prices. This isn't really perfume but ether, and you will pass out and they will take your wallet and all of your valuables. This is not a prank e-mail. This is true! I could have very well been a victim. PASS THIS ALONG.

Rat Feces

A stock clerk was sent to clean up a storeroom at his work place. When he got back there, he was complaining that the storeroom was really filthy, and that he had noticed dried mouse or rat droppings in some areas . . . A couple of days later, he started feeling like he came down with a stomach flu, achy joints, and headache. He went to bed and never woke up. Within two days he was ill and weak. His blood sugar count was down to 66. He was rushed to emergency where he suffered from complete organ failure. He died shortly before midnight . . . There is a virus that lives in dried rat droppings (much like Hanta virus). Once dried, these droppings are like dust and can be easily digested. ALWAYS carefully rinse off the tops of any canned foods or soda . . . A family friend recently died from drinking a can of soda!

The Computer Fraud and Abuse Act (CFAA) has become the primary vehicle for the prosecution of Internet fraud crimes. The CFAA was initially enacted by Congress in 1984, primarily as a means to protect classified information contained on government computers. The scope of the CFAA was expanded in 1986, and again in 1996. The 1996 amendments to the Act worked to incorporate *all* computers that are involved in interstate and/or foreign commerce.[85] Essentially, the CFAA covers most fraudulent business practices that are conducted over the Internet.

Summary

This chapter has defined and described how the growth in computer technologies has affected five major criminal offenses: embezzlement, money laundering, corporate espionage, identity crimes, and fraud. The traditional crimes of embezzlement and money laundering have clearly become more prevalent, and modern technologies have increased opportunities to commit both crimes. In terms of embezzlement, the computer has allowed individuals increased access to funds manipulation and has eliminated problems related to the material bulk of moving large quantities of cash. Money laundering is now easier because of two primary reasons: (1) Electronic funds are easier to conceal while maintaining anonymity and (2) the advent of "cashless" banking systems such as e-cash has made detection of such crimes much more difficult.

In addition, computer technologies have created a wide array of new avenues to the pilfering of corporate secrets, including trade technologies, research and development strategies, and customer lists. Computerized corporate data are easier to access, and the prevalent utilization of e-mail in business environments has given corporate thieves expanded opportunities. So too the end of the Cold War has created a cadre of former spies who can provide foreign firms the skills and expertise necessary for stealing domestic trade secrets.

Finally, the traditional crime of fraud has taken on new forms as a result of the information revolution. In particular, the Internet has increasingly been utilized as a platform to perpetrate fraud, especially through carding, online auction schemes, financial institution frauds, and the transmission of "urban legends."

Review Questions

1. Identify and describe the similarities and differences between corporate espionage offenders who are "insiders" and those who are "outsiders."
2. What is the Bank Secrecy Act of 1970? How has the advent of computer technologies created ways around this Act?
3. What is phishing? How does phishing fit into the problem of identity theft?
4. What are "urban legends"? How have these "legends" changed over the course of the last two decades?

Critical Thinking Exercises

1. Identity protection has emerged as a significant business enterprise in the United States, with over $1 billion in annual subscription sales. Students are encouraged to perform a quick Web search and identify at least five companies who provide identity protection services to individuals and the costs associated with those services. Do you think these services provide adequate identity protection to consumers? Why or why not?
2. This chapter presents David Birch's concept of "fractured identities" and the need to reduce the degree of personal information provided within each electronic transaction and thereby reduce the incidence of identity theft. Students should identify, retrieve, and review the contents of the cards they use every day in order to complete electronically based transactions including driver's license, university identification card, debit and credit cards, library cards, medical insurance cards, etc. How much of the information provided on each of these cards is necessary in order to complete the transactions they are used for? What information contained in each of these cards could be deleted? How many software applications would be necessary for you to complete the transactions required in your daily life?

Endnotes

1. REIMAN, J. (1995). *The Rich Get Richer and the Poor Get Prison*. Boston, MA: Allyn & Bacon.
2. SUTHERLAND, E. (1940). "White-Collar Criminality." In G. GEIS, R.F. MEIRER, and L.M. SALINGER (eds.), *White Collar Crime: Classic and Contemporary Views*. New York: Free Press, pp. 29–38.
3. GREEN, G.S. (1997). *Occupational Crime,* 2nd ed. Chicago, IL: Nelson Hall.
4. CRESSEY, D.R. (1953). *Other People's Money: A Study in the Social Psychology of Embezzlement*. Glencoe, IL: Free Press.
5. FURNELL, S. (2002). *Cybercrime: Vandalizing the Information Society*. Boston, MA: Addison-Wesley.
6. ANDERSON, J.P. (1980). *Computer Security Threat Monitoring and Surveillance*. Fort Washington, PA: James P. Anderson Co.
7. *Ibid.*, p. 3.
8. Marquet International (2012). *The 2012 Marquet Report on Embezzlement*. Marquet International, Ltd.
9. HUDSON, J.E., III. (October 4, 2002). "Trade Secret Theft Threatens Everyone with Corporate Espionage Escapades." *Houston Business Journal.*
10. ROBINSON, S.W. (2003). *Corporate Espionage 101.* SANS Institute.
11. *Ibid.*, p. 13.
12. *Ibid.*
13. *Ibid.*
14. KONRAD, R. (September 21, 2000). "Leaks and Geeks: International Espionage Goes High-Tech." *C/Net News.com.*
15. ROBINSON, S.W. (2003). *Corporate Espionage 101.* SANS Institute.
16. Symantec (2013). *Internet Security Threat Report 2013* Volume 18.

17. HUDSON, J.E. III. (October, 4, 2002). "Trade Secret Theft Threatens Everyone with Corporate Espionage Escapades." *Houston Business Journal.*

18. *Ibid.*, p. 13.

19. Verizon 2013 Data Breach Investigations Report.

20. *Ibid*, p. 19.

21. *Ibid*, p. 19.

22. *Ibid*, p. 15.

23. BOWMAN, L.M. (July 19, 2001). "Avant Ordered to Pay $182 Million." *C/Net News.Com.*

24. SWARTZ, J. (April 16, 1997). "Felony Charges Halve Avant's Stock." *The San Francisco Chronicle.*

25. BURROWS, P. (June 15, 1997). "A Nest of Software Spies?" *Business Week.*

26. *Ibid.*, p. 14.

27. Theft of Trade Secrets Clarification Act of 2012, Pub.L. 112-236.

28. *Sfgate.com.* (2008). "Salesman Gets 2 Years for Industrial Espionage." Retrieved June 20, 2013, from http://sfgate.com

29. LYMAN, M.D. and POTTER, G.W. (2000). *Organized Crime.*Upper Saddle River, NJ: Prentice Hall.

30. *Ibid.*, p. 28.

31. *Ibid.*

32. GRABOSKY, P.N. and SMITH, R.G. (1998). *Crime in the Digital Age.* New Brunswick, NJ: The Federated Press.

33. Board of Governors of the Federal Reserve System. (2013). Retrieved June 25, 2013, from *http:www.federalreserve.gov*

34. The Clearing House. (2013). Retrieved June 25, 2013, from http://www.chips.org

35. BORTNER, R.M. (1996). "Cyberlaundering: Anonymous Digital Cash and Money Laundering." Presented as a final paper at the University of Miami School of Law.

36. *Ibid.*, p. 33.

37. *Ibid.*

38. SANTORA, M., RASHBAUM, W.K., and PERLROTH, N. (2013). "Online Currency Exchange Accused of Laundering $6 billion." *The New York Times*, May 28.

39. *http://fincen.gov.*

40. *Ibid.*, p. 36.

41. *Ibid.*

42. Financial Crimes Enforcement Network 2011 Annual Report.

43. Department of Justice. (2007). "Digital Currency Business E-Gold Indicted for Money Laundering and Illegal Money Transmitting." United States Department of Justice.

44. *Ibid.*, p. 37.

45. *Ibid.*

46. Financial Action Task Force (2006). *Trade Based Money Laundering*, June 23.

47. US Department of State (2016). *International Narcotics Control Strategy Report* (INCSR). Volume 2, March.

48. Financial Action Task Force (2006). *Trade Based Money Laundering*, June 23.

49. Congressional Research Service (2016). *Trade Based Money Laundering: Overview and Policy Issues*, June 22, p. 4.

50. *Ibid.*, p. 8.

51. FINKLEA, K.M. (2012). "Identity Theft: Trends and Issues." *Congressional Research Service.*

52. Computer Security Institute. (2007). "Computer Crime and Security Survey." Retrieved March 2007 from *http://www.cybercrime.gov/FBI2006.pdf*

53. *Ibid.*

54. *Ibid.*

55. GOODIN, D. (2007). "TJX Breach Was Twice as Big as Admitted, Banks Say." *The Register.* Retrieved March 27, 2008, from *http://www.theregister.co.uk/2007/10/24/tjx_breach_estimate_grows/.*

56. *Ibid.*

57. Excerpted from HOAR, "Identity Theft."

58. FRANKLIN, J., PAXSON, V., PERRIG, A. and SAVAGE, S. (2007). "An Inquiry into the Nature and Cause of the Wealth of Internet Miscreants." Paper presented at CCS07, October 29–November 2, 2007, in Alexandria, VA; HOLT, T.J. and LAMPKE, E. (2009). "Exploring Stolen Data Markets On-Line: Products and Market Forces." *Criminal Justice Studies* 33(2); Honeynet Research Alliance. (2003). "Profile: Automated Credit Card Fraud." *Know Your Enemy Paper* series. Retrieved June 21, 2005, from *http://www.honeynet.org/papers/profiles/cc-fraud.pdf;* THOMAS, R. and MARTIN, J. (2006). "The Underground Economy: Priceless." *USENIX:login* 31(6): 7–16.

59. *Ibid.*, p. 49.

60. *Ibid.*

61. *Ibid.*

62. *Ibid.*

63. Federal Trade Commission Bulletin. (February 2002). "Identity Theft: When Bad Things Happen to Your Good Name." See *http://bulk.resource.org/gpo.gov/hearings/106s/69821.pdf.*

64. *Ibid.*, p. 41.

65. *Ibid.*, p. 47.z.

66. IC3 2002 Internet Fraud Report (2003).

67. *Ibid.*, p. 50.

68. *Ibid.*

69. *Ibid.*

70. IC3 Internet Fraud Report (2008).

71. *Ibid.*, p. 66.

72. *Ibid.*

73. *Ibid.*

74. Professionals Against Confidence Crimes. (2003). "Interpol Warning: Nigerian Crime Syndicates Letter Scheme Fraud Takes on New Dimension." See *http://stopcon.org/index.html.*

75. *Ibid.*, p. 56.

76. *Ibid.*, p. 50.

77. *Ibid.*, p. 67.

78. *Ibid.*, p. 74.

79. ROGERS, J. (2007). "Gartner: Victims of Online Phishing Up Nearly 40 Percent in 2007." *SC Magazine.* Retrieved January 2, 2008, from *http://www.scmagazineus.com/Gartner-Victims-of-online-phishing-up-nearly-40-percent-in-2007/article/99768/.*

80. *Ibid.*, p. 66.

81. http://www.scambusters.org.

82. *Ibid.*, p. 59.

83. *Ibid.*

84. *Ibid.*

85. *GigiLaw.Com.* (2001). "The Expanding Importance of the Computer Fraud and Abuse Act."

Viruses and Malicious Code

CHAPTER OBJECTIVES

After completing this chapter, you should be able to

- Identify and distinguish the various types of viruses and malicious code.
- Understand the differences between the differing types of viruses, including file viruses, boot viruses, macroviruses, and network viruses.
- Understand the differences between a virus and worm. Additionally, understand how a worm operates in comparison to a virus.
- Understand the definition and operation of a Trojan horse and how it is different from a standard virus.
- Describe adware and spyware, and the controversy concerning whether or not these types of programs are in fact viruses.
- Describe and understand other types of malicious code and attacks, including denial-of-service attacks and blended threats.
- Describe and understand the true threat posed by viruses, the extent of the virus and malicious code problem, and virus hoaxes and their effect on computers and productivity.
- Understand who the virus writers are and why they write viruses.

INTRODUCTION

There is perhaps no other area of computer crime that creates more fear, misperceptions, and attention than computer viruses. The immediate popularity of personal computing, rapidly developing technology, and a general lack of oversight and regulation have combined to create the concomitant development of software and malicious programs as well. None of the first personal computers (PCs), early versions of disk-operating software (DOS), or first networks were designed with security in mind.[1] As a result, law enforcement, virus security experts, and network managers continually play catchup with an ever-growing list of viruses and malicious code. Computer security is a multibillion industry, increasing in value every year. The market for virus protection software, firewalls, and computer security expertise is estimated at $4 billion and relies on the same fears that drive many to purchase home security systems.[2] The question is how serious is the virus problem, and what is really necessary to deal with the problems viruses and other types of malicious code present? Indeed, in the years preceding the turn of the century, virus hype definitely outpaced virus damage. However, in recent years, several high-profile worms, including ransomware, have caused millions of dollars of damage to numerous businesses and PC users. The type and scope of malicious software (malware) has also increased significantly in the past few years, creating a structure for all manner of computer attacks, which some refer to as "crimeware."[3]

QUICK FACTS

Ransomware is a form of malware that targets the critical data and systems of individual or business for the purpose of extortion and/or blackmail. Ransomware is frequently delivered through spearphising e-mails; or those that ostensibly come from a known or trusted sender in order to induce targeted individuals to reveal confidential information. After the user has been locked out of their system, the cyber criminal demands a ransom payment. After receiving payment, the criminal will purportedly provide a means for the victim to regain access to the system or data. However, if the payment is not received, the system and data are permanently damaged, corrupted and/or erased. Since January 1, 2016, the U.S. Secret Service reports that more than 4,000 ransomware attacks occur daily in the United States, representing a 300 percent increase since 2015.

A typical ransomeware variant displays an intimidating message, such as:

> Your computer was used to visit a website with illegal content…child pornography. To unlock your computer, you must pay a $100 fine.

> You have 48 hours to submit payment via the credit card link below. If you do not send in the money by the time allotted, all your files and data will be permanently encrypted and corrupted, and no one will ever be able to recover them.
> PAY YOUR FINE NOW !!!

Source: U.S. Secret Service, "How to Protect Your Networks from Ransomware," InterAgency Technical Guidance Document, 2017.

Initially, viruses were spread primarily through floppy disks, with the infections being spread by infecting multiple computers via the same diskette. Today, viruses and other types of malicious code are primarily spread over the Internet through a variety of mechanisms, including e-mail, e-mail attachments, downloadable files, Web pages, newsgroups, peer-to-peer file transfers,[4] instant messaging (texting),[5] digital pictures, and several other techniques and tactics.[6] The Internet was designed for the rapid propagation of data, making no distinction between good and bad data.[7] As such, viruses and other types of malicious code take advantage of the very conveniences and features that make the Internet so appealing. The true cost of viruses is unknown; estimates range from very little true damage to wild estimates claiming that viruses cost billions of dollars annually. A survey of security experts from the government, private industry, and universities revealed that 86 percent had experienced some type of security breach in the prior year, and 26 percent of those entities experienced 10 or more attacks in a single year.[8] Though this is less than half of all reporting entities, the losses they face from malicious software and hacking are over $10 billion.[9] Nonetheless, there is no centralized database that collects information on the damage that viruses cause.

At the outset, it is important to note that this chapter is not designed to provide the reader with substantial technical knowledge concerning viruses or virus prevention and computer security. It is simply an overview of the types of viruses, malicious code, and security problems that exist, with some relevant examples and some material on the investigation and prosecution of virus writers. This chapter focuses almost exclusively on common computer systems and Windows-based viruses that the casual and neophyte reader will be familiar with. Viruses and malicious code (malware) can infect other operating systems and hardware, but that is beyond the focus of this chapter. Finally, this chapter is not written for expert computer users or experts in the virus writing and virus prevention fields. Instead, it offers a layman's approach, designed for people unfamiliar with the complexities of the virus problem.

Although no reliable estimate exists, there is probably no other area in computers where more time, energy, and resources are spent than on antivirus protection. This has led to the creation of the pseudo-virus expert, a person who proclaims expertise in office workgroups around the world, claiming that he or she knows about viruses and how to prevent them. Most commonly, this is the person who can download patches and update antivirus software, with little real knowledge of viruses. There are many reasons behind this so-called expertise; the most prominent reason is the "false authority syndrome," so aptly described by Rob Rosenberger, a well-known virus expert (see Box 7.1). Hence, the author of this chapter wants to make it perfectly clear that he is no virus expert and wishes to avoid false authority syndrome at all costs. Instead, the author, like most people who express legitimate concern about viruses and malicious code, is a student of the virus industry. This chapter provides a nontechnical look at viruses and malicious code and is designed to give the readers the knowledge of viruses they need to be discriminating about what they hear, read, and learn about this area. Often there is more bark than bite in most of the viruses that plague our computers.

BOX 7.1
Computer Viruses and "False Authority Syndrome"

The following account is from Rob Rosenberger, a virus expert and myth debunker concerning what he terms "False Authority Syndrome."

True Story

A couple of years ago I dropped by the Software Etc. store in Fairview Heights, Illinois, just to browse. Another customer had come in before me and told an employee about a problem with his video monitor. The employee warned the customer that he had contracted a newly discovered computer virus, which he proceeded to describe in great detail.

I interrupted the employee. "Sir, you have it completely wrong. That virus doesn't exist. It's the latest hoax."

"Oh, no," the employee replied. "We've got e-mail reports from our sales headquarters telling us to keep our eyes open for it."

To which I countered, "Some upper-tier sales manager has been duped and is telling you BS. McAfee Associates and others have issued public statements dismissing that virus as a hoax. What you've described simply cannot be done by any virus. Period."

I then turned my attention to the customer. "Stop listening to this guy. You don't have this magical virus he's describing because it simply doesn't exist. You have some other problem with your video monitor." What credentials does this salesman hold in the field of computer viruses? He may have flipped burgers at a McDonald's restaurant two weeks ago, for all we know.

Most people who claim to speak *with authority* about computer viruses *have little or no genuine expertise.*

Some virus experts describe it as "False Authority Syndrome"—the person feels competent to discuss viruses because of his job title, or because of his expertise in another computer field, or simply because he knows how to use a computer.

I want you to question the credentials of anybody who talks about computer viruses. Indeed, I want you to question my credentials in this field!

The U.S. Air Force highlights the concept of False Authority Syndrome in *Tongue & Quill*, their official publication on effective writing:

> "*Nonexpert opinion* or assumed authority—Don't be swayed (or try to sway someone else) based on the opinion of an unqualified authority. The Air Force is chock-full of people who, because of their position or authority in one field, are quoted on subjects in other fields for which they have limited or no experience." (As this Air Force publication notes, False Authority Syndrome can attack people in all fields of expertise.)

Computer salesmen, consultants, repairmen, and college computer teachers often succumb to False Authority Syndrome. In many cases a person's job title sounds impressive, but his or her job description at most may only include references to vague "computer security" duties.

People without impressive job titles suffer from false authority syndrome, too. A user who contracts a virus, for example, will often turn around and confidently tell other people how to avoid them. He or she may even rise to the position of "office virus expert."

False authority syndrome plays on two important desires. First, people genuinely like to help others; second, they like to feel in control of their computers. Users easily succumb to the effects of false authority syndrome when driven by these natural desires.

"Marcello," a typical user who took a hoax for real, posted a message on CompuServe warning users not to read any messages with "Good Times" in the subject line (lest they contract the so-called Good Times virus). Ironically, Marcello *used* the words "Good Times" in the subject line of his own warning message!

At least one virus expert sent Marcello a playful reply telling him to "stop infecting people" with the Good Times virus. Confronted with details about the hoax, Marcello replied, "Thank you for your help, and I'm sorry, because I was duped, but anyway I was worry *[sic]* about my computer and a lot more from *[sic]* my job."

So-Called "Office Virus Experts"

A rule of thumb: The first employee attacked by a computer virus will quickly rise to the position of office virus expert. "Trust me, I know what I'm talking about. I've *been* there."

Sadly, managers often overlook more competent people when naming office virus experts. The guy who practices safe computing is nobody, but all hail the jerk who barely survived an attack.

Experts Believe *ILoveYou* Cost $2.7/$4.7/$6.7/$8.7 Billion

Legend: Experts around the world believe the ILoveYou virus in May 2000 caused $2.7 billion, $4.7 billion, $6.7 billion, or $8.7 billion in damages. *Reality:* Computer Economics, Inc. concocted the first three estimates as a publicity stunt during the peak of *ILoveYou hysteria*. They concocted the fourth estimate after the hysteria died down. *Reason experts are duped:* No statistically accepted metrics exist to gauge virus costs—and no statistically valid data exist to gauge worldwide virus proliferation. Therefore, any cost estimate is as good as any other cost estimate. *Fallout:* The antivirus industry can cite yet another plausible-sounding estimate.

Conclusion

I don't want to dispel any particular computer virus myths someone may have told you—that's not my goal here. Rather, I want you to *question a person's expertise* if he or she claims to speak with authority on computer viruses. This way we can prevent all the "blind leading the blind" techno-babble. And we can reduce the number of people who believe all the myths out there.

In summary:

- Most people have little or no expertise in the field of computer viruses.
- People with little or no expertise often fall prey to false authority syndrome.
- False authority syndrome contributes significantly to the spread of fear and myths about computer viruses.

Visual Developer editor Jeff Duntemann sums it up best: "If people exercised greater discretion in who and how and to what degree they place their trust, we would know more as a community—and we would know it better. There would be fewer paths for bad or phony knowledge."

Source: False Authority Syndrome, Used with permission of Rob Rosenberger. *http://vmyths.com/fas/fas1.cfm*

Most virus writers and attackers are opportunistic and like other criminals choose to attack systems at their weakest and most vulnerable points.[10] The significant growth of computer technology, the diverse number of computer operating systems available, and the increasing number of mobile computing devices like laptop computers, iPhones, Blackberrys, iPads, and tablets make it easy for hackers to find attack points in most all computer users. In fact, the SANS Institute created a list of the top 10 cyber threats to help organizations and security experts identify the most likely attack points in the wide-ranging computer world. The list is contained in Table 7.1 and depicts the consensus of opinion of security experts from the government and private industry. SANS claims that an overwhelming majority of successful attacks occur in this area, ranging from attacks through Web sites to malicious software to faulty or infected computer hardware.[11] This chapter reviews the nature of viruses and other types of malicious code through an examination of what these programs are and their effect on infected systems. An examination of the threat posed by viruses, real and imagined, is

TABLE 7.1 The Sans Institute Top 10 Cyber Threats

1. Increasingly sophisticated Web site attacks that exploit Internet browser vulnerabilities
2. Increasing sophistication and effectiveness in botnets (large), interconnected programs designed to turn individual computers into "bots" or "zombies." Botnet malware is usually designed to infect a large number of computers via the Internet
3. Cyber espionage efforts by well-resourced organizations to extract large amounts of data for economic and political purposes
4. Mobile phone threats, especially against iPhones, Google's Android phones, and Voice Over wIP (VOIP) systems
5. Insider attacks
6. Advanced identity theft from persistent bots
7. Increasingly malicious spyware
8. Web application security exploits
9. Increasingly sophisticated social engineering to provoke insecure behavior
10. Supply chain attacks that infect consumer devices

undertaken with a particular emphasis on the ultimate effect viruses and malicious code have on society. This chapter will explore who the virus writers are and why they write viruses in the first place, and review investigative procedures and prosecution of virus writers—and all of the difficulties faced by law enforcement in this area.

THE LANGUAGE OF MALICIOUS SOFTWARE (MALWARE)

Before discussing viruses and malicious software (malware), it is important to discuss some of the vocabulary surrounding viruses, antivirus detection, and their impact. As such, several terms and issues associated with this area must be discussed prior to the coverage of the subject matter in this chapter. To begin, viruses and malicious code must be understood from several perspectives and variables, the most important of which is the potential damage that viruses and malicious code can cause. Damage can include triggered events that cause computer operations to be disrupted, clogging or disrupting e-mail or network operations, deleting or modifying files, accessing and sharing confidential information, performance interference and degrading, compromised security, and damage to the computer's software and hardware.[12] As such, many viruses and malicious code are graded based on the potential damage they can cause and their overall impact on computer operations at the individual level and across the world.

In a similar vein, the level of vulnerability or exposure is an additional defining characteristic of viruses and malicious code. Vulnerabilities include the ability of an attacker to execute commands on a victim's computer or network, the ability to access data on a remote system, the ability to take control of a system and assume another's identity, and the ability of the attacker to deny service to legitimate traffic on a given system or systems.[13] These are essentially the weak points in a piece of software that allow attackers use to propagate a virus or engage in some type of malicious attack. In turn, hackers identify these vulnerabilities in various systems and create exploits, or programs that attack known weak points to gain access to and facilitate hacks and compromises. For example, firewalls and certain types of code like ActiveX controls, Java, and JavaScript have flaws that make it difficult to protect vulnerable systems.

Computer systems and software can be graded in terms of their exposure to vulnerabilities. In making assessments of how secure or unsecure a system or computer is, exposure assessments describe a state of operations that are not universal vulnerabilities as well as how exposed a system is to a potential attack. The degree of exposure is determined by how easy it is for an attacker to conduct information gathering on a system, how easy it is to hide attack activities on a system, how easy it is to access a system and compromise its operation, and how many points of entry or security holes are present in a given system. In other words, exposure refers to the potential problems or security holes that are present that would allow an attacker to exploit the vulnerabilities described above. For instance, Trojan horse-type attacks could be accomplished through a worm, which would then open a security hole in the system that would allow the attacker access to the system (e.g., 2017, WannaCry ransomware worm with the WannaCryptor Trojan payload). The Trojan would then block off further attempts to enter the security hole and cover its own tracks on the system.[14]

In addition to the vulnerabilities, exploits, and exposures described above, there are numerous terms used in describing viruses and their potential impact. The most common term used to describe how a virus is operating and the effect it is having is listing the virus as "in the wild." The "wildness" of a virus measures the extent to which a virus is spreading among computer users and systems. This measurement includes the number of infected independent sites and computers, the geographic distribution of infection, the ability of current technology to combat the threat, and the complexity of the virus. The true number of virus infections and malicious code attacks can never be ascertained with any degree of reliability and validity. However, several firms and independent organizations propagate lists of the most active viruses and the number of reported infections. One such list utilizes a Delphi technique (a survey and analysis of experts) to ascertain the number of viruses that are in the wild and that are most damaging. Viruses in the wild are those that are spreading as a result of normal day-to-day operations on and between the computers of unsuspecting users. Furthermore, to make the list, two or more virus experts must report problems with the virus.[15] Some of the first viruses in the wild actually attacked the Apple operating system, back in the 1980s. A common myth is that Apple computers are immune to viruses—this is simply not true. A recent Wildlist.org report listed 6,650 viruses currently "in the wild"; however, as is the case with most computer statistics, this number changes almost daily.[16]

VIRUSES AND OTHER MALWARE

Viruses and malware are simply programs and, like any other program, are designed for a specific function. A virus or malware program is written for a variety of non-criminal purposes, including advertisements, jokes, and political messages. However, less humorous and more malicious intentions include destroying data and information, information acquisition and identity theft, surreptitious control of a remote machine, or the shutdown of a legitimate business or Web site. The virus program delivers a payload; this is part of the virus program that delivers the malicious intent or other device. The virus is executed by some type of payload trigger, which causes the virus or malicious code to deliver its contents or execute its commands. The trigger can be something the user does, such as opening an e-mail attachment or downloading a file; it can be triggered by some event such as a date or condition on a computer; or it can self-execute based on code written into the virus program. Early viruses were simple code, but recently viruses have become increasingly sophisticated and written to avoid detection. Some viruses are encrypted, which is a method of scrambling or encoding data to prevent reading or tampering with the data. The level of encryption and the strength of the encryption have increased substantially in recent years. Only individuals with access to a password or key can decrypt and use the data, and this allows the virus to hide itself from virus scanners—that is, the encrypted virus jumbles its program code to make it more difficult to detect. Some viruses also use "stealth," making them appear not to exist on a machine or hide their tracks from scanning software. Like a cyber Cold War of sorts, virus detection software writers and virus writers engage in a never-ending battle to stay one step ahead.

The development of virus construction tools by virus writers allows a larger number of less sophisticated computer users to write and create viruses. A virus construction set is a utility program intended for creating new computer viruses. Virus construction sets allow generating of source code of the viruses, object modules and/or infected files themselves.[17] Another tool developed by virus writers known as a mutation engine allows viruses to change their code each time they infect a new machine. Known as a polymorphic virus or malicious code, these programs do not have any constant section of code. In most cases, two strains of the same "polymorphic" virus will not have a single coinciding element of code. A polymorphic virus can change its pattern when it replicates, avoiding detection by simple virus scanning techniques. Viruses are also polymorphic if they cannot, or can but with great difficulty, be detected using the so-called virus masks or indicators; in other words, the scanner looks for parts of nonchanging virus-specific code. The virus changes in two main ways: by encrypting the main code of the virus with a nonconstant key with random sets of decryption commands or by changing executable virus code.[18]

The type of encryption or operating algorithms used in a virus can vary substantially. The technical complexity of this area continually increases and changes. One area of interest is termed the *terminate and stay resident* (TSR) capability of the virus. This essentially means that the virus is able to leave itself in system memory, intercept some events, and in the process run infecting routines on files and sectors of the disk. Resident viruses stay in memory and are active until power down or until operating system reboot. Nonresident viruses do not infect computer memory and are active for a limited time only. Some viruses leave small parts in the memory, which do not spread the virus; these viruses are considered nonresident.[19] Resident viruses are active regardless of whether or not the infected program is running and remain viable until the next reboot, even if all the infected files are deleted from disk. It is also largely impossible to get rid of such viruses by restoring all the files from distribution disks or backup copies: The virus simply remains active and infects the newly created files. This is true for some boot viruses as well—even formatting the disk does not necessarily remove viruses, as they will continue to infect the disk repeatedly after formatting.[20] Hence the TSR capability of the virus is an important factor in classifying and determining the potential seriousness of a given virus.

Another feature of the operating algorithm of a virus is the use of stealth algorithms. Stealth allows the virus to remain hidden on a system and cover its tracks during and after the infection process. Yet another operating algorithm that can be used to grade or distinguish a virus is the use of self-encryption and polymorphism. These are used to make the virus detection and removal procedure as complicated as possible.[21] Polymorphic viruses are exceedingly difficult to detect, and they have no permanent signatures; that is, none of their code fragments remain unchanged. Often, a comparison of two samples of the polymorphic virus will yield few, if any, similarities in the code of the virus, making it impossible to program an antivirus solution. This may be achieved by encrypting of the main body of the virus and making modifications to the decryption routine.[22]

The destructiveness of a virus ranges from virtually harmless to extraordinarily dangerous and malicious. Some viruses have no real effect on the operation of the computer or the data and information stored on the computer; their payloads consist of some message being displayed or silly program being run. Other viruses can seriously disrupt the operation of the computer, rewriting commands, altering normal system operation, harvesting passwords, encrypting user data, and changing boot routines and other malicious commands. Additionally, some viruses intentionally target the information and data on a system, resulting in lost data, data destruction, erasure of vital information in system areas, and even inflicting damage to hardware.[23]

History and Development

There is a great deal of controversy surrounding the origins of computer viruses: Who is responsible for creating the first computer virus and who can claim responsibility for discovering and eliminating the early viruses? One author contends that the first viruses (although no one called them that at the time) appeared in the late 1960s and early 1970s on early versions of Univac and IBM machines.[24] Occasionally, on the mainframes in operation at that time, programs appeared that cloned themselves, occupied system resources, and lowered the productivity of the system. These programs, known as "rabbits," did not copy themselves from system to system and remained strictly local phenomena, mistakes or pranks by system programmers. The first incident, which may be called an epidemic of "a computer virus," happened on a Univax 1108 system. The virus called "Pervading Animal" merged itself to the end of an executable file. However, the first recognized versions of what could be termed the "modern virus" appeared on early PC machines in the middle to late 1980s, correlating largely with the enormous growth of the PC industry.

The earliest viruses infected boot sectors and floppy disks, performing such functions as playing Yankee Doodle Dandy on the speakers and deleting letters in documents.[25] Early viruses were extraordinarily easy to detect when compared with the viruses of today; each virus contained recognizable code that became known as the virus' signature. Once the signature was detected and identified, antivirus software could then be programmed to detect, isolate, and eliminate the virus.[26] The first vastly spread virus was a bootable virus called "Brain,"[27] which spread via floppy disks.[28] The virus was created in Pakistan by brothers Basit and Amjad Farooq Alvi. They left a text message inside the virus with their name, address, and telephone number. According to the authors of the virus, they were software vendors and wanted to know the extent of piracy in their country. Unfortunately, their experiment left the borders of Pakistan.

The first counterpunch by virus writers was to encrypt the code within the virus, thus hiding their signatures by writing them in indecipherable code.[29] In order to complete the infection, the encrypted virus needed to return to its original state in order to replicate and infect. The decryption routine written into the virus could be identified and used as a virus signature, allowing detection by antivirus software.[30] MtE (MuTation

Engine) is the first known polymorphic generator. It was released in 1991 and shocked antivirus researchers with its very complex polymorphic algorithm.[31] Polymorphic routines still encrypted the virus, but the encryption routine was randomized by a mutation engine.[32] The first polymorphic virus appeared in the early 1990s and was known as "Chameleon,"[33] but polymorphic viruses became really serious with the introduction of the "Tequila"[34] virus in April 1991.[35] The polymorphic virus took off two years later. A host of these viruses spread with the help of the burgeoning Internet.

Several things combined to aid the spread of viruses: the rapid growth of the Internet, the rapid growth and availability of PCs, the availability of the polymorphic engine, and the availability of virus creation tools that first hit in July 1992. The first viral code construction set for IBM PC compatibles was called Virus Creation Laboratory (VCL).[36] This set allows the user to generate code to produce viruses. The program used a Windows™ interface and a menu system that allowed the virus writer to choose virus type, objects to infect (COM and/or EXE), presence or absence of self-encryption, measures of protection from debugging, inside text strings, and an optional 10 additional effects.[37] The created virus can then use a variety of means for infection by adding its body to the end of file, replacing files with its body destroying the original content of a file, or becoming companion viruses.[38] The introduction of the polymorphic engine and the VCL automated and simplified the virus-writing process so that any teenager with a computer and a cause could write a virus.

At the end of 1992, the first virus specifically designed for Windows™ was released.[39] With the release of Windows 95™, the first "virus epidemic" was soon to follow (in 1996) with the widespread release and propagation of macroviruses. The Concept[40] virus was an innocuous virus that spread very rapidly and was a wake-up call for Microsoft and the antivirus industry.[41]

The main problem with trying to give the exact definition of a virus is that virtually all the unique features of a virus—such as incorporating with other objects, stealth behavior, potential danger, and potential for spread—may be found in other nonvirus programs.[42] A second difficulty is that viruses are operating system and software system specific.[43] One author maintains that it is only definable through the specification of several necessary conditions. For example, a code's ability to produce copies of itself, to incorporate itself into other files and systems (networks, files, executable objects, etc.), and further contaminate other systems is a necessary condition to be able to define it as a computer virus.[44] Some authors claim that viruses are a form of artificial life possessing all of the properties of a live organism. They can propagate, adapt themselves to different environments, and self-transmit in an effort to move and relocate.[45] Ironically, legendary computer guru Peter Norton announced that computer viruses did not exist, declaring them to be mythical.[46]

Mobile code is a code that can be transmitted across a network and executed on the other end of a transmission. It may be created using one of numerous mobile code systems, including Java, ActiveX, safe Tcl, Visual Basic, Visual Basic for Applications (VBA), and scripting.[47] Mobile code has become quite routine on most Web pages and is also used in a growing number of Internet-capable programs. The positives of mobile code can be turned against the user and used in an attack that is quite difficult to detect.

Viruses

The classification or categorization of computer viruses and malicious code is ongoing. There is some disagreement concerning the exact terminology used and what is and what is not considered a virus or malicious code. Nonetheless, there is an active attempt by several antivirus vendors and the federal government to have some standard classifications of viruses and other types of malicious code. *Viruses* can be categorized based on the environment they operate in, the operating system they are targeted at, the type of encryption and operating algorithms used, and their destructive capabilities.[48] Other types of malicious code include worms, Trojan horses, adware or spyware, logic bombs, denial-of-service (DoS) attacks, and blended threats. This list is not necessarily complete, nor is there universal agreement on the exhaustiveness and mutual exclusivity of the list. Nonetheless, the list does comprise the majority of the types of viruses identified in the current literature.

Viruses operate in four primary environments: file viruses, boot viruses, macroviruses, and network viruses.[49] File viruses infect their targets in several ways: as a parasite, as a companion, or through file system-specific features known as link viruses. File viruses use a particular operating system to propagate, and they can infect virtually any type of executable file. These viruses can overwrite the contents of a target executable with its own code, destroying the original contents of the files. This method is the simplest and results in system failures and other problems because the infected file simply stops working. As such, these are relatively easy to detect and remove. Parasitic viruses also change the contents of the infected files, but they latch onto the file and leave it operational. Kaspersky contends that these types of viruses include "prepending" viruses (saving themselves at the top of file), "appending" (saving themselves at the end of file), and "inserting" (inserting themselves in the middle of file).[50] The insertion methods vary as well, by moving a fragment of the file toward the end of file or by copying its own code to such parts of the file that are known to be unused ("cavity" viruses). Companion viruses do not change the infected files; instead, they clone the target file so that when run, the companion virus runs instead of the original file. Link viruses, like companion viruses, do not change the physical contents of files, but when an infected file is started, they "force" the OS to execute their code. This is achieved by modifying the necessary fields of the file system.[51] Viruses can also infect other areas of a computer, including compiler libraries, object modules, and source code; however, these types of viruses are extraordinarily rare.

Boot viruses either attack the boot sector of the system, the master boot record (MBR), or change the system pointer to an active boot sector. Gap boot viruses infect the boot sector of an external media (floppy disk, CD-ROM, USB, etc.) and the boot sector or MBR of a hard disk. Boot viruses operate based on the algorithms of starting an operation system upon power on or reboot—after the necessary hardware tests (of memory, disks, etc.), the system loader routine reads the first physical sector of a boot disk (A:, C:, or CD-ROM, depending on the options in BIOS Setup) and passes the control to the virus. In the case of a diskette or CD-ROM infection, the virus attacks a boot sector, analyzes the operations and boot routine of the computer, and substitutes the virus code in the place of the normal operating code. In the case of a hard disk target, the target is a boot sector on the hard disk. The virus passes control from the computer to virus in that particular sector. Upon infecting the disk, the virus in most cases moves the original boot sector to some other sector of the disk. If the virus size exceeds the size of the sector, then the target sector will contain the first part of the virus, the rest of it placed in the other sectors.[52] Diskette, and other external mediainfecting is accomplished when the virus rewrites the original boot sector code with its own code. Hard disks can be infected when a virus writes itself over the MBR code or the boot sector code of the boot disk (C: drive, usually) or modifies the address of the active boot sector in the disk partition table.[53]

Macroviruses are most commonly associated with common business software and infect documents, spreadsheets, databases, and presentation files. Macroviruses take advantage of macrolanguages built into common systems of business software, most notably Microsoft Office™. Macroviruses transfer themselves from one infected file to another within a given system and cross over to other systems, typically via attachments or shared files. Macro functions within a file or processing program can operate without user intervention. Macroviruses generally use an automacro present in the file, or use a standard system macro (associated with some menu item) that has been redefined, or the macro of the virus is pulled automatically after a certain key or key combination has been pressed. If a Word document is infected, when opening it, the program calls the infected automatic macro and then executes the virus code. If the virus contains macros with standard names, they take control after a user executes the corresponding menu item (File/Open, File/Close, File/Save, etc.). If some symbol of the keyboard is redefined, the virus activates itself only after the corresponding key has been pressed.

Most macroviruses contain all of their functions as standard macros of the software program they infect. However, there are viruses that use the techniques of hiding their code and keeping their code as a nonmacro entry. For example, when activated, a Word macrovirus will move the macro code into the common macros contained in the program with the help of the macro editor contained in the program. The virus then creates a new macro, inserts its own code inside the macro, and then saves this macro with the code in the document. On exit from Word, the global macros (including the macros of the virus) are automatically saved to a DOT file of the global macros (this file is usually called NORMAL.DOT). The next start of the Microsoft Word™ editor activates the virus at the moment when Word loads the global macros; in other words, immediately.[54] The virus then redefines one or several of the standard macros and then intercepts the commands of typical file operations. When routine commands are executed, the virus infects the currently open file. To do this, the virus converts the file to the template format and then saves its macros, including the automacro to the file. For example, once the virus infects the macro called File/Save, then every DOC file becomes infected. If the File/Open macro becomes infected, then the virus records itself into the file when it is being read from the disk.[55]

Network viruses attack the networks themselves or e-mail systems of the networks in order to spread themselves. With the advent of HTML, Active X, and Java code and the ability to send attachments, the thought was that only by executing the attachment could a user get an infection. Macroviruses and other sneaky tricks demonstrated that even nonexecutable files could infect a user's machine via e-mail, yet it was still assumed that simply reading e-mail could not infect a system. Recent viruses and worms demonstrated, however, that simply previewing e-mail is enough to trigger an infection.[56] Network viruses make extensive use of networking protocols and capabilities of local and global access networks to multiply. The main operating principle of the network virus is its capability to transfer its code to a remote server or workstation on its own. Network viruses also are capable of running their code on remote computers or at least "pushing" users to run the infected file.[57] Network viruses essentially spread themselves on a computer network, and as a rule, like companion viruses, do not change files or sectors on disks. They infiltrate computer memory from the network, calculate and record network addresses of other computers, and then send copies of themselves to the network addresses.

Worms

Computer viruses have progressed from urban myth to annoyance to major threat. However, even with all the damage that computer viruses have done, they pale in comparison to what we have seen and have yet to see from the computer worm.[58] A computer worm is also a piece of software that copies itself elsewhere. However, unlike a virus, it does not attach itself to, or modify, other files. The *worm* is a stand-alone piece of code; although it may need to use another program to spread, it does not change that program in any way. The term "worm" is taken from the book *Shockwave Rider* and refers to a self-replicating piece of code (called the "tapeworm") created by a character in that book.[59] In contrast to a traditional virus, a worm is a program that makes copies of itself from one disk drive to another, or by copying itself using e-mail or another transport mechanism. The worm may damage and compromise the security of the computer. It may arrive in the form of a joke program or software of some sort or may be spread through e-mail and networks without much active user intervention. These programs spread in a computer network and, similar to virus companions, do not change files or sectors on disks. They penetrate the computer's memory from a computer network, calculate network addresses of other computers, and send their own copies to these addresses. Worms sometimes start files on the system disks, but generally cannot apply themselves to computer resources (with the exception of main memory).

BOX 7.2

The Melissa Virus

The Melissa virus first appeared on the Internet in March of 1999. It spread rapidly throughout computer systems in the United States and Europe. It is estimated that the virus caused $80 million in damages to computers worldwide. In the United States alone, the virus made its way through 1.2 million computers in one-fifth of the country's largest businesses. David Smith pled guilty on December 9, 1999, to state and federal charges associated with his creation of the Melissa virus and was sentenced in 2002. Smith admitted spreading the Melissa virus, which infected more than 1 million PCs in North America and disrupted computer networks in business and government.

Prosecutors noted that the Melissa virus demonstrated the danger that business, government, and PC users everywhere face in our technological society. "Far from being a mere nuisance, Melissa infected computers and disabled computer networks throughout North America. There is a segment in society that views the unleashing of computer viruses as a challenge, a game. Far from it; it is a serious crime."

"Computer criminals may think that they operate in a new frontier without boundaries, where they won't be caught. Obviously, that's not true," said investigators. "We've responded by breaking down traditional borders among federal, state, county and local law enforcement. In this case, it helped us to make an arrest in less than a week." Attorney General Janet Reno stated, "This plea is a significant marker in the Justice Department's efforts to stop computer crime. In light of society's increasing dependence on computers, the Department will vigorously investigate and prosecute computer crimes that threaten our computer infrastructure."

Smith admitted in state and federal court that he created the Melissa virus and disseminated it from his home computer. Smith acknowledged in his federal plea agreement that the Melissa virus caused more than $80 million in damage. He was eventually sentenced to 20 months in federal prison followed by three years of supervised release, 100 hours of community service, and a fine of $5,000 and was prohibited from accessing a computer of any kind. He said that he constructed the virus to evade antivirus software and to infect computers using the Windows 95™, Windows 98™, and Windows NT™ operating systems and the Microsoft Word 97™ and Word 2000™ word processing programs.

According to Paul Zoubek, director of the state Division of Criminal Justice, the Melissa virus appeared on thousands of e-mail systems on March 26, 1999, disguised as an important message from a colleague or friend. The virus was designed to send an infected e-mail to the first 50 e-mail addresses on the users' mailing lists. Such e-mails would only be sent if the computers used Microsoft Outlook™ for e-mail. Because each infected computer could infect 50 additional computers, which in turn could infect another 50 computers, the virus proliferated rapidly and exponentially, resulting in substantial interruption or impairment of public communications or services. According to reports from business and government following the spread of the virus, its rapid distribution disrupted computer networks by overloading e-mail servers, resulting in the shutdown of networks and significant costs to repair or cleanse computer systems.

Smith described in state and federal court how, using a stolen America Online account and his own account with a local Internet service provider, he posted an infected document on the Internet newsgroup "Alt. Sex." The posting contained a message enticing readers to download and open the document with the hope of finding passcodes to adult-content Web sites. He acknowledged that each new e-mail greeted new users with an enticing message to open and, thus, spread the virus further. The message read: "Here is that document you asked for … don't show anyone else;-)."

Opening and downloading the message caused the Melissa virus to infect victim computers. The virus altered Microsoft word processing programs such that any document created using the programs would then be infected with the Melissa virus. The virus also lowered macro security settings in the word processing programs. The virus then proliferated via the Microsoft Outlook™ program, causing computers to send electronic e-mail to the first 50 addresses in the computer user's address book. As of 2013, variants of the Melissa virus still proliferate and can be easily observed on Internet word processing and e-mail programs.

Source: U.S. Department of Justice. (December 9, 1999). Creator of "Melissa" Computer Virus Pleads Guilty to State and Federal Charges. *http://www.usdoj.gov/criminal/cybercrime/meliinfo.htm*

The first known Internet worm was the Morris worm. This worm crippled the Internet for several days in 1988 by exploiting buffer overrun flaws common in several pieces of software. A buffer overrun occurs when a program does not check the length of an input string against the amount of memory it has available to store that string. If the entered string is too long, then it overwrites other memory in the computer. In the case of the Morris worm, the string contained garbage data, followed by instructions for the computer to send the same message to other available machines. The worm was supposed to spread slowly and in a controllable fashion, but due to a bug in the code, it spread much faster than anticipated. This brought about the first large-scale DoS condition on the Internet itself. An infected machine could have its resources entirely controlled by the worm in as little as one hour. The courts were not impressed by Morris' actions, and sentenced him to three years' probation, 400 hours community service, and $10,050 in fines.[60]

In sum, a worm is a self-propagating malicious code program that does not necessarily require user intervention to spread. Unlike a virus that requires a user to run a program or execute a command, a worm self-propagates and infects systems in a very short period of time. The Code Red worm infected more than 250,000 systems in just nine hours on July 19, 2001.[61] Some worms include built-in DoS attack payloads or Web site defacement payloads, while others have dynamic configuration capabilities. However, as noted by the CERT® Coordination Center, the biggest impact of these worms is that their propagation effectively creates a DoS because of the huge amounts of scan traffic that the worm generates.[62] Additionally, worms cause a great deal of collateral damage, such as crashing routers, overloading networks, and creating meaningless and repetitive tasks for the computers they infect.[63]

BOX 7.3

The WannaCry Worm

In May 2017, the WannaCry worm infected over 400,000 internet connected devices, according to Malwaretech .com's online malware tracking system (https://intel .malwaretech.com/botnet/wcrypt). The purpose of the worm was to collect ransom money from infected computer owners who's data was encrypted by the worm's payload—wannycrypt. The worm was so successful because it was designed around a vulnerability found in Microsoft Window's computers that was leaked from an NSA data breach conducted by the hacker group Shadow Brokers in April 2017. The vulnerability allowed access to the computers as well as facilitating the proliferation of the worm to other networked computers. The targets for this attack were all over the map, literally, infecting computer systems in over 150 countries around the globe, across various industries, including hospitals, telecoms, banks, and warehouses. The first reported victim organization was U.K.'s health service. This single malware/ransomware campaign infected more devices in less than one month than all of the ransomware attacks tracked by the security company Symantec in all of 2016 (483,800 incidents).

Source: Symantec Corporation, "An ISTR Special Report: Ransomware and Businesses 2016," *https://www.symantec.com /content/dam/symantec/docs/security-center/white-papers /ransomware-and-businesses-16-en.pdf*).

Trojan Horses

A Trojan horse is commonly an unauthorized program contained within a legitimate program that performs functions unknown (and probably unwanted) by the user.[64] Trojan horses typically masquerade as something desirable, a joke program, a legitimate software program, or some other type of executable file that the user wishes to install and run. Just like the Trojan horse of history, however, there is a hidden purpose and program hidden within the desirable file. The hidden program typically waits for some computer event to occur, a date to be reached, or some other type of trigger, and then delivers its payload.[65] The hidden payload can open a backdoor for the virus writer, destroy files or disks, or simply display a message of some type. In the case of an attachment, as the user executes the file, the infection occurs simultaneously and silently. The Trojan horse is a program that neither replicates nor copies itself, but causes damage or compromises the security of the computer. In many cases, a legitimate program has been altered by the placement of unauthorized code, the Trojan horse, within legitimate code.[66] Typically, an individual e-mails a Trojan horse to you. However, a growing number of attacks are accomplished through port scanners looking for installed Trojans by attackers who did not install the Trojan themselves. In other words, it is possible to conduct scans for Trojans in a systematic fashion and then exploit the security holes uncovered through the scans. There is a variety of ways that a Trojan can be installed on a user's computer, including via ICQ chat, Internet relay chat (IRC), attachments, actual physical access to a machine, a Web browser or e-mail program, and file sharing.[67]

Trojan horses can be viruses or remote control programs that provide complete access to a victim's computer and, as such, are one of the most accessible weapons that hackers use to conduct attacks.[68] If a certain type of Trojan horse is installed and initialized on a system, that computer is now completely open to anyone who knows to connect to it using the Trojan horse as a server.[69] The person responsible for the initial installation is not the only person who can be privy to the knowledge that a Trojan horse resides on the target computer; there are port scanners designed to find remote control Trojans already planted on systems.[70] Therefore, anyone who utilizes the port scanner and finds the installed Trojan horse can have access to the victim's computer or system. A remote-controlled Trojan is not a traditional virus; it is a self-contained program designed to invisibly execute commands issued from a remote user.[71] Trojans work by utilizing a client part and a server part. When the victim (unknowingly) runs the server on his or her machine, the attacker will then use the client to connect to the server and start using the Trojan.[72] Most Trojans use autostarting methods, so even when you shut down your computer, they are able to restart and give the attacker access. New autostarting methods and other tricks are discovered all the time, ranging from "joining" the Trojan into some executable file that is often used like explorer.exe to modifying the system files or the Windows Registry.[73]

Perhaps the most popular and widely used Trojan horse is the Backdoor Sub Seven Trojan.[74] Upon a successful installation, the Sub Seven Trojan allows a remote attack virtual control over an infected machine. This Trojan comprises distinctly separate programs that work to overtake the victim's computer. The first program is called the Sub Seven server and is run on the targeted computer to allow the attacker to connect to the victim and gain access to the computer. The editserver portion of the Trojan defines the characteristics of the infection and determines whether to notify the attacker when the victim computer is online. This part of the program also allows the attacker to monitor and change the settings through which the attack occurs. In other words, the attacker can connect to the victim's machine and install a different configuration of the Sub Seven server that uses alternate ports and different techniques for autostarting, thereby allowing the attacker free access to alter and control the victim's system.[75] Once installed and operating, attackers can initiate a variety of attacks, including the ability to restart Windows, reversing mouse buttons, recording sounds from the microphone attached to the compromised machine, record images from an attached video camera, change desktop colors, opening/closing the CD-ROM drive, record screen shots of the victim's computer, and turn the victim's monitor on and off.[76] The attacker can also obtain characteristics of the hardware and software installed on the compromised machine and access stored information on the computer, including passwords and other personally identifying information. Finally, the Sub Seven Trojan installs a port redirector and the port scanner that allow an attacker to hack into other systems by configuring ports on an already-infected computer to point to new targets.[77]

The program Sub Seven is a very well-known Trojan around the world and can be found in hacker Web sites in most any country. Because it is so widely available, it is no longer as useful as it once was and is primarily used by less-skilled hackers. A number of Trojans exist that have similar functionality; were created in Russia, China, and Turkey; and are available for download or purchase through the hacker community. For example, the Trojan Pinch is a widely used tool among Russian hackers and was created by an individual named Coban2k; an interview with him is provided in Box 7.4. The tool was initially sold for profit, but became so successful that hackers began to release its source code to the public and use it on their own. The program itself was designed to steal passwords from over 33 different programs on a single computer, and send those files to the user through a number of different means.[78] The program can also collect characteristics of the hardware and software installed on the compromised machine and turn

BOX 7.4

Interview with Coban2K

INTERVIEWER: Tell me about yourself.

COBAN2K: From the very early childhood through my father surrounded me with computers and there I had a passion which then turned into a profession. Obsession with computers. I am 21 years old, learning in the Department of Mathematics.

INTERVIEWER: Let's talk now about your most famous project—Pinch. Tell me how it happened. Had difficulty with writing code?

COBAN2K: First Pinch was one of my first projects at the assembler, created solely for myself. Pinch was similar to a project established in Ld-Team which I was in at the time of the creation of Pinch. Since variants of the tool were sold by others and sales fell it was decided to make the program open source. The version was written for two weeks and then drafted for several months written by just one person for profit.

INTERVIEWER: What would be the logical end of the project? Will Pinch continue to be open source?

COBAN2K: The logical end of a project can come only if there is additional deciphering of all possible projects. Pinch is open source, but commercial hackers convert the code to conceal people who are afraid of losing customers.

the infected system into a launch point for other attacks and Web surfing. Pinch can also hide itself completely, clean and kill the Web browser, and be used as a tool to connect multiple infected machines into a bot network so that all machines can be commanded remotely from one point.[79]

The useful nature of this program has led to its multiple variations, which have been sold and used by a number of hackers and groups. In fact, two Russians made approximately $16,000 selling this tool to other hackers. Their actions led to over 4,000 PCs being infected by one variant of Pinch, with compromised machines in the United States, Brazil, China, and the United Kingdom on computers that were running antivirus software.[80] The pair was arrested by Russian police in December 2007 and were jailed and fined for their actions.

With this in mind, the problem of Trojans cannot be overstated.

There are numerous types of Trojans, and similar to viruses, there is no universal agreement on the naming and categorization of all of the types. Danchev[81] lists several types of Trojans, including the following:

- *Remote Access Trojans*—These are probably the most common, as they give attackers the power to do more things on the victim's machine than the victim possibly could, even while sitting in front of the machine. These Trojans can give the attacker complete access to a victim's computer as well as access to files, passwords, data, etc.
- *Password-Sending Trojans*—These Trojans attempt to steal all of the cached passwords and also look for other passwords entered on a computer while the victim is online and then send them to the attacker's e-mail address, which in most cases is located at some free Web-based e-mail provider.
- *Keyloggers*—These Trojans log the keystrokes of the victim and then let the attacker search for passwords or other sensitive data in the log file. Most of them come with two functions like online and off-line recording and can be configured to send the log file to a specific e-mail address on a daily basis.
- *Destructive*—The only function of these Trojans is to destroy and delete files. They can automatically delete core system files (e.g., dll, .ini, or .exe files). The Trojan

can be activated by the attacker or sometimes works like a logic bomb and starts on a specific day and at a specific time.

- *DoS Attack Trojans* —The main idea is that if you have 200 users infected and start attacking a secondary victim simultaneously, this will generate a great deal of traffic (more than the victim's bandwidth, in most cases), and access to the Internet will be shut down. A variation of this Trojan is the mail-bomb Trojan, whose main aim is to infect as many machines as possible and simultaneously attack specific e-mail addresses with random subjects and contents that cannot be filtered.
- *Proxy/Wingate Trojans*—These Trojans turn the victim's computer into a proxy/ wingate server (zombie) available to the whole world or to the attacker only. It is used for anonymous Telnet, ICQ, IRC, Internet access, etc., and also to register domains with stolen credit cards and for many other illegal activities. This gives the attacker complete anonymity and the chance to commit crimes from a remote computer. If caught, the trace will lead to a victim's computer and not the attacker.
- *Software Detection Killers*—Some Trojans will kill ZoneAlarm, Norton Anti-Virus, and many other popular antivirus/firewall programs designed to protect users. Once they are disabled, the attacker will have full access to your machine, to perform some illegal activity, use your computer to attack others, and often disappear.

Adware and Spyware

Although not technically viruses or malicious code, adware and spyware have become a frequent topic of debate in regard to privacy concerns on the Internet. Adware and spyware are programs that can be contained in e-mail attachments, downloaded as part of another software program, or downloaded from a Web site. *Adware* is a type of program that is essentially a pain to the user that manifests itself in several ways, including changes to the browser, redirecting startup pages on the Internet browser, replacing the search function within the browser, and generating pop-up ads and frames that can be difficult to delete or shut down. *Spyware* programs are applications that send information via the Internet to the publishers or programmers for marketing purposes without obvious notification to users.[82] Spyware can send a variety of information about the user's computer hardware, software, browsing habits, and other personal information to the host marketer or programmer. Spyware is typically installed in addition to some other type of functional software, more often than not downloaded software that is distributed as freeware. The software operates independently of the spyware and is the visible and useful component of the downloaded package. Spyware serves as an information gatherer, which maintains, monitors, and sends user and/or computer information in the background.[83] Some programs that get installed as companion software, technically not spyware, can cause a great deal of frustration for the user—especially if the user chooses to uninstall the companion software or spyware. Programs have been known to replace the searching engine function in the Internet browser, directing the user to their own preferred Web sites. Spyware can also lead to annoying pop-up ads that users have difficulty disabling.

Spyware typically takes advantage of the fact that many software users do not read the end user license agreement (EULA) or fine print during installation. If they did, they would see legal disclaimers and permissions to share information and install the spyware. As noted by Post, spyware EULAs are worded in such a way that they contain so much information and disclaimers that the average person cannot understand what the software and spyware do and do not do.[84] Furthermore, the data that are gathered are not specifically identified and how the data are going to be used is not specifically spelled out. Many people, upon finding out that they installed the spyware and were not really aware of it, feel that the spyware is malicious. The real fun starts when a user attempts to uninstall the spyware and programs that he or she downloaded. Often, the entire hard drive has to be scrubbed and the operating system reinstalled because the downloaded program made numerous and complex changes to the computer. As a result, now spyware killer software and Internet security software are available that allow you to monitor and deter adware and spyware. Another way spyware is installed is through the use of cookies. A cookie is a file that contains information about a program, a Web site, the user, or the user's computer. Cookies enable faster browsing and, when they are from a legitimate Web site, can be beneficial to the Web site and the user. However, in the case of some spyware, the cookie contains uniquely identifiable data, such as the user's name, computer specifications, installation version, and other personally identifying information that the user might not wish to share.

Denial-of-Service Attacks

A *DoS attack* uses multiple systems to attack one or more victim systems or Web sites with the intent of denying service to legitimate users wishing to log on or utilize the attacked server. In essence, the attack sends phony requests to the server, overloading it and preventing legitimate traffic. The degree to which the attack is automated, or self-sustaining and replicating, dictates how rapidly the attack denies service to the server or Web site. These attacks are remarkably effective due to the interdependency of computers and security on the Net and due to the limited resources of the Internet.[85] The attack tools are increasingly being distributed through "zombie" machines that are compromised on university campuses. In the week of February 7, 2000, several distributed denial-of-service (DDoS) attacks on several prominent Web sites, including Yahoo!, E*Trade, Amazon. com, and ebay, were launched. In these attacks, multiple computers are instructed by a rogue program to bombard the target site with nonsense data. This bombardment soon causes the target site's servers to run out of memory, making it to be unresponsive to the queries of legitimate customers.[86] As described in the box item, these attacks can be used in a coordinated fashion to attack and destroy businesses and antispam companies.

Blended Threats

Blended threats combine the characteristics of viruses, worms, Trojan horses, and malicious code with server and Internet vulnerabilities to initiate, transmit, and spread an attack. By using multiple methods and techniques, blended threats can rapidly spread and cause widespread damage. Recent blended threats have launched DoS attacks, defaced Web servers, and Trojan horses planted on machines for later use in future attacks. The blended threat spreads through multiple methods; the infection routine can vary as well. These threats can scan for vulnerabilities in a system (such as buffer overflows, HTTP input validation vulnerabilities, and known default passwords to gain unauthorized administrative access), exploit the vulnerabilities, and then use the machine to further spread the attack. The attack spreads within human intervention and attacks systems and networks from multiple points, attempting to infect executable files, change the access rules for the machine, make numerous registry changes, and further exploit the machine into harming other machines and extending the attack.

Blended threats exploit one or more vulnerabilities as they infect a system and may perform additional network attacks such as a DoS against other systems.[87] The essence of a blended attack is the multiple payloads and multiple targets that are part of the virus' programming. Many experts predict that blended attacks will increase in the near future. Examples of a blended attack are bot programs, which enable an attacker to compromise and infect multiple computers at once. Bots are distributed by hackers through Trojan horse programs or other methods to infect a computer system.[88] Once a machine is infected, the code then installs a bot program, making the machine a "zombie." This means that the computer can now receive commands and be controlled by another user through IRC channels, which are real-type communications enabled over the Internet.[89] The IRC bot program then surreptitiously contacts a preprogrammed IRC channel to wait for commands from the bot operator. Multiple machines that are infected with this malware will contact the channel, creating a botnet, or network of zombie machines.

Botnets can reach very large sizes and may include thousands of machines, enabling bot operators to engage in a variety of different acts.[90] Zombie machines can be used to covertly distribute bulk e-mail that can be used to enable fraud and phishing attacks. Botnets can also be used to perform DDoS attacks or validate stolen credit card numbers, enabling identity theft on a rapid and large scale. Finally, botnets can be used to rapidly distribute new viruses and malware across the Internet. Thus, bots constitute a significant threat to computer users around the globe. In addition, botnet programs can be purchased on the Internet. A botnet controlling 100 machines rents for around $2,000 per month, while the Shadow Botnet, a network of over 100,000 zombies, sold for $36,000 in 2009.[91] Its creator was only 19 years old at the time. Thus, bots can also act as a force multiplier for computer attackers by leveraging the power of thousands of systems to their needs. At the same time, they allow attackers to conceal their identities behind common computer users who may be unaware that their machines are involved in cybercrime incidents. Finally, bots act as a versatile attack platform, enabling all manner of cybercrime.

QUICK FACTS

In 2017, a 50,000 bot Mirai malware Botnet can be rented for 2 weeks and capable of conducting recurring DDoS attacks of up to 1 hour at a time for $1,500 to $2,000 per week. On October 21, 2016, a 100,000 node botnet armed with the Mirai malware was used to conduct one of the largest denial of service attacks ever recorded against a company—Dyn. This distributed denial of service made Dyn internet services unavailable during multiple attacks throughout the day due to the volume of data bombarding the Company's network—estimated at 1.2 terabytes per second. This attack was successful because of how the Mirai malware works. Mirai takes advantage of an inherent vulnerability in the microchips embedded in most Internet of Things (IoT) devices. IoT devices like a programmable home thermostat or Internet connected refrigerator were infected with Mirai because their microchips all have the same password, which was leaked to the Internet in 2015, and allows the malware to take control of the IoT device. Attackers then used over 100,000 IoT devices to coordinate a distributed denial of service attack on Dyn. Ironically, the final attack on Dyn was likely halted by consumers resetting their IoT devices when they returned home from work and noticed them not functioning properly.

Source: Catalin Cimpanu, "Your Can Now Rent a Mirai Botnet of 400,000 Bots," Retrieved November 24, 2016, from *www.bleeping-computer.com*, *https://www.bleepingcomputer.com/news/security/you-can-now-rent-a-mirai-botnet-of-400-000-bots/*

Dyn Analysis Summary of Friday October 21, 2016 Attack. *Dyn.com*, *https://dyn.com/blog/dyn-analysis-summary-of-friday-october-21-attack/*

Breaking Down Mirai: An IoT DDoS Botnet Analysis. *Incapsula.com* *https://www.incapsula.com/blog/malware-analysis-mirai-ddos-botnet.html*

EXTENT OF VIRUSES AND MALICIOUS CODE ATTACKS

Every year, Symantec produces the *Internet Security Threat Report*, which provides an update about Internet threat activity, including network-based attacks, a review of known vulnerabilities, and highlights of malicious code. Its April 2017 report suggests that there were literally billions of cyberattacks against U.S. interests (individuals, businesses and corporations, government) in 2016[92] The report indicates an estimated 1 percent decrease in total data breaches in 2016, but an approximated 95 percent increase in the total number of identities compromised (564 million in 2015 and 1.1 billion in 2016). System compromises and resulting data breaches were most likely the result of phishing attacks that utilized malware payloads in 2016. The ratio of malware to total e-mails received in 2015 was 1 in 220, and in 2016, it was 1 in 131 indicating an aggressive surge in utilizing malware phishing as a successful attack vector. Continuing with the malware embedded phishing attack vector, ransomware malware payload statistics also saw a significant increase in 2016 at 463,841 incidents and 101 ransomware variants detected, compared to 340,665 incidented and only 30 variants detected in 2015. Ransomware has become big business for cybercriminals and in 2016 the average ransom amount collected was $1,077 per device. Also noted in the report was the increase threat and use of Internet of Things (IoT) connected devices primarily used to conduct DDoS attacks with the aid of IoT specific malware. The report found that the average time to compromise an IoT device was about two minutes.

Additionally, attackers appear tremendously focused on acquiring information and data that can be used for subversive purposes (e.g., 2016 U.S. elections), conduct economic espionage, and of course to steal money. Image is from the 2017 ISRT referenced above

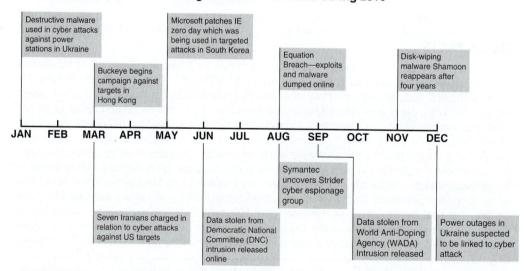

Timeline of notable targeted attack incidents during 2016

As noted in this section, some malicious software can cause widespread damage and affect thousands of networks and machines. Undoubtedly, the greatest cost is the loss of work hours and time spent patching systems, not to mention productivity lost from everyone having to chat and e-mail their friends about the latest threat. Even so, a growing number of experts and publications raise the idea that viruses, for the most part, are more

BOX 7.5

E-mail Hoaxes

SEND THIS TO ALL OF YOUR FRIENDS, DO NOT DELETE THIS MESSAGE, IMPORTANT ALERT. These are but a few of the opening lines of many e-mails commonly received daily via the Internet. Most of these messages are relatively harmless, but some have a more sinister purpose. Some people think that many of the scams and hoaxes are new, when they are classically old schemes being perpetuated in a new format, cyberspace. To most, these are harmless annoyances that quickly find their way into the cyber trash bin. The undeniable cost is lost productivity and time spent on sifting through the increasing volume of these junk e-mails, typically referred to as spam. There is a growing body of information on the Internet concerning spam and e-mail hoaxes. In general, these e-mails can be grouped into five general categories: spam, chain mail, hoaxes, virus hoaxes, and fraud.

Spam

Spam is the generic term [also called unsolicited commercial e-mail (UCE) and junk e-mail] for any e-mail that is sent to a large group of people, typically as an advertisement or other solicitation. If your e-mail address falls into the hands of a "spammer," you will undoubtedly receive ever-increasing unsolicited advertisements. Most spam is easily deleted and is simply annoying.

Chain Mail

This is simply traditional chain letters that have found a new medium. If you believe in good or bad luck, you can forward these to your friends. These are increasing because forwarding them is relatively easy using e-mail.

Hoaxes

There are almost too many hoaxes to document. Some of the more popular ones involve people spending $250 for a cookie recipe, having their kidneys removed while they sleep, and receiving cash awards and gift certificates by forwarding e-mail. There is no way for a company to track who you send e-mail to, and they are not giving away free computers, vacations, or cash. Check out these hoaxes at the Web sites listed below.

Information on medical hoaxes: *http://www.quackwatch.com*

Department of Energy's Web site for debunking myths and legends:

Offers current information about hoaxes being propagated on the Internet: *http://urbanlegends.about .com/culture/urbanlegends/library/blhoax.htm*

Entire Web sites dedicated to urban legends:

http://www.urbanlegends.com/

http://www.nonprofit.net/hoax/default.htm

http://www.snopes.com

Virus Hoaxes

We are spending much more time de-bunking hoaxes than handling real virus incidents.

The U.S. Dept. of Energy Computer Incident Advisory Capability (CIAC)

We have all received well-intentioned e-mail warnings about some virus that is possibly the worst ever found. Many people simply delete these messages. Others forward the e-mails on in the chance that this virus could be a real threat. E-mail hoaxes promote fear. They make you pause. They waste your time. They scare some people into not using technology to its fullest extent for fear of contracting a dangerous virus. Virus hoaxes are defined as deliberate or unintentional e-mail messages warning people about a virus or other malicious software program that simply does not exist.

Most hoaxes contain one or more of the following characteristics:

- Warnings about alleged new viruses and their damaging consequences
- Demands for the reader to forward the warning to as many people as possible
- Pseudotechnical "information" describing the virus
- Bogus comments from officials: FBI, software companies, news agencies, etc.

One of the better ones forwarded concerned a virus that was "infecting all digital cellular phones" and that I shouldn't answer any phone calls that caller-id couldn't track or I would get the virus. In short, there are numerous hoaxes that are propagated concerning viruses. In fact, there is more worry about viruses than is necessary. Rob Rosenberger maintains an excellent informational

Web site on viruses, hoaxes and real, and offers sound advice concerning them at *http://www.vmyths.com/*

Symantec's Web site for virus hoaxes: *http://www.symantec.com/security_response/landing/risks/hoaxes.jsp*

F-secure Corporation Web site: *http://www.f-secure.com/virus-info/hoax/*

Source: E-mail Hoaxes, Federal Trade Commission, U.S. Federal Trade Commission. *http://www.ftc.gov/bcp/edu/pubs/consumer/alerts/alt089.shtm*

hype and hoax than actual malicious threat. For example, perhaps the largest virus hype to date concerned the Michelangelo virus in the early 1990s. In the lead-up to March 6, 1992 (Michelangelo's birthday and the supposed date of the virus payload release), the media coverage and doomsaying about the virus was so intensive that millions of people around the world refused to turn on their computers at all for the entire period around March 6. McAfee claimed at the time that anywhere "from 50,000 to 5 million" computers were infected, a statement that was far from the truth.[93] The airwaves were flooded with supposed virus experts predicting the shutdown of governments and business worldwide. In the end, relatively few machines were infected, and the virus eventually lived on to become urban legend. The hype of potential viruses and the damage that people believe viruses can cause feeds into the larger problem of virus hoaxes.

VIRUS WRITERS AND VIRUS EXPERTS

Numerous authors have attempted to characterize virus writers and elaborate the reasons why people write and spread viruses. One train of thought contends that virus writers go through a progression from students and schoolchildren to young adults and college students to professional virus writers. At each stage, the destructive capability of the virus and the technical expertise of the writer increase.[94] In this theory, the motivations for virus writing also change from recognition from peers and experimentation, progressing to revenge and social notoriety.

The virus writers and those who wish to write viruses have a variety of resources from which to learn their trade and propagate viruses. There are numerous virus-maker journals, newsletters, bulletin boards, and Web pages devoted to virus writing and virus creation tools.[95] Sarah Gordon, currently at Symantec, has consistently taken a more conciliatory view. In a survey of virus writers, she claims that:

> The virus writer has been characterized by some as a bad, evil, depraved, maniac; terrorist, technopathic, genius gone mad, sociopath. This image has been heightened not only by the media, but by some of the actions of the virus writers themselves. Public communications from the writers, in the form of echo-mail messages, often seem to indicate they are intent on doing as much damage as humanly possible. Their electronic publications have in the past reinforced this, and the very fact that they release viruses may seem to confirm it: These people are bad. [But it can be argued that] this is a gross oversimplification of the situation, and that the virus writing aspect of these individuals is not sufficient to characterize them into one group simply labelled "unethical people."

Most virus writers obviously have numerous justifications and rationalizations for why they choose to write viruses. Not all experts agree on the seriousness of the virus problem, with many noting that most viruses are relatively harmless and easily removed.[96] Trojan horse programs allow those without a comprehensive understanding of multiple operating systems, networking concepts, and programming languages to routinely attack remote systems. The largest group of attackers, comprising over 95 percent of the attacker population, is referred to as "script kiddies," individuals with limited knowledge of operating systems and networks.[97] This group does not write code or create viruses; instead, they use precompiled programs like Trojan horses to do the work for them, which afford the attackers access to other computers to pilfer files, change settings, or launch DoS attacks.[98]

It must be noted, however, that the motives for malicious software creation have changed among some hackers. Over the past few years, malicious software creation has shifted from curiosity, damage, and revenge motives to a significant profit motive. In fact, some researchers use the term *crimeware* as a reference to the programs and tools that facilitate fraud and computer attacks.[99] For example, Trojans that steal passwords like Pinch can be considered crimeware, along with botnets, which can be used for spam and phishing. The problem of financially driven hacking and malicious software is amplified due to the growth of markets for malicious software and stolen data, as outlined in Chapters 4, 5, and 6. These markets provide access to highly sophisticated malicious software and resources to facilitate computer attacks, such as spam lists and credit card data.[100] Selling products in malware and carding markets means that individuals no longer need to understand how computer technology works to engage in sophisticated forms of cyber crime. For example, an individual named Corpse sold a Trojan called Nuclear Grabber in multiple markets that enabled individuals to engage in phishing schemes with little to no technical knowledge.[101] The tool, costing $3,000, came with preloaded images of 12 international banks and spam message scripts to draw in potential victims. He also offered real-time support for his customers in case they should experience problems, much like a legitimate computer service. Similar products can be found in markets across the globe, along with malicious software that can support other tools, like polymorphic engines and binding tools that can combine one piece of malicious software like a Trojan with other programs or images to improve their payload activity.

BOX 7.6

Interview with a Virus Writer—Inside the Mind of Dark Avenger

by Sarah Gordon

About three years ago I was introduced to the man known as Dark Avenger. Having just purchased a PC, and finding myself the proud owner of not only the PC but of the Ping-Pong virus as well, I found my way to the Fidonet virus echo. Watching the information fly back and forth, suddenly there appeared a new name—Dark Avenger. I was intrigued by his style and the hype surrounding him. At some early point of participation in the forum, I commented that I would like to have a virus named after me, hoping to draw his attention. Had I understood at that time quite what viruses actually entailed, I would not have made that statement. As I talked with antivirus researchers and product developers, I began to understand the issues. I also talked to virus writers. Having a background in juvenile corrections,

I found their attitude typical of youths in crisis. Their response to public mail demonstrated the attitude so prevalent in interaction between rebellious teenagers and authority figures. Their private mail (which I have not and will not disclose) resembled the private conversations I'd had when counseling in a one-on-one situation: frustation, anger and general dissatisfaction followed by small glimpses of conscience—often resulting in a decision to at least consider the consequences of their actions. Some, like their more traditional counterparts, never made it to that final stage, but at least we had some stimulating discussions. I've had, and continue to have, detailed conversations with virus writers, focusing on the reasons behind their misdirected creativity.

Time passed, and still Dark Avenger continued to haunt me. Why had he not responded to me like the majority of virus writers? Despite several failed attempts to contact him, he remained elusive.

Enter the MtE

With the release of the now-infamous Mutation Engine, I found Dark Avenger had indeed noticed me. The demo virus, which accompanied the engine, contained the text: "We dedicate this little virus to Sara Gordon, who wanted to have a virus named after her." Many people asked me about this, and I became quite accustomed to people assuming I knew Dark Avenger personally. The fact of the matter is, at that time, he was still a mystery. How could I explain to people that I "knew" him, yet had never spoken with him? I'm not a programmer, yet I knew him from looking at his viruses. I have no formal background in computer science, but I could understand what he was doing and how he was feeling, despite some people arguing that there is no such thing as "instinctive hacking." Few people believed me at that point; yet the fact is, at that time, I had never spoken with him directly.

When I learned Christopher Seeley was talking on a semiregular basis to someone identified by both Alan Solomon and Vesselin Bontchev as Dark Avenger, I sent him a message to pass on to (dav). The message was written slowly and laboriously in Bulgarian, and I briefly stated that I would like to ask him some questions.

His response came quickly. I immediately recognized the author as the creator (not necessarily distributor) of the viruses attributed to him. We exchanged several electronic messages, routed through various gateways. Eventually—with the assistance of various intermediaries—I was able to speak "live" (or at least electronically) with Dark Avenger.

Since that time we have exchanged many messages, this interview being an edited compendium of our messages and conversations taking place over a five-month period. He agreed to allow me to ask him these questions, and I agreed to allow him to remove any questions or responses he was not comfortable answering or making public.

Who is the Dark Avenger? Many people have asked me: "Is Vesselin Bontchev the Dark Avenger?"; in fact, one of the reasons I became so intent on finding the Dark Avenger was to learn the answer to this question. I can state unequivocally that the Dark Avenger is not Vesselin Bontchev. Neither is he a crazed technopath, nor a maniac intent on destroying the world. He has very little in common with the usual crop of virus writers I have talked to. He is, all in all, a unique individual.

August 1992

SARA GORDON: Some time ago, in the Fidonet virus echo, when you were told one of your viruses was responsible for the deaths of thousands, possibly, you responded with an obscenity. Let's assume for the moment this story is true. Tell me, if one of your viruses was used by someone else to cause a tragic incident, how would you really feel?

DARK AVENGER: I am sorry for it. I never meant to cause tragic incidents. I never imagined that these viruses would affect anything outside computers. I used the nasty words because the people who wrote to me said some very nasty things to me first.

SG: Do you mean you were not aware that there could be any serious consequences of the viruses? Don't computers in your country affect the lives and livelihoods of people?

DA: They don't, or at least at that time they didn't. PCs were just some very expensive toys nobody could afford and nobody knew how to use. They were only used by some hotshots (or their children) who had nothing else to play with.

I was not aware that there could be any consequences. This virus was so badly written, I never imagined it would leave the town. It all depends on human stupidity, you know. It's not the computer's fault that viruses spread.

SG: It is said many people working for the government and companies in Bulgaria had computers at that time. Isn't this correct?

DA: I don't know who said that, but it's not true. Actually, at that time, most of the people in Bulgaria did not even know what a computer was.

SG: Did you have access to modems at that time? Did you ever make use of virus exchange systems to send your viruses? I've seen your name on some of the mail coming from those systems.

DA: At that time, I did not have access to a modem. At that time there were no virus exchange systems, I think. I've been on some of them, but that was much later. I never made any "use" of them, I was just fooling with them. I've been on almost no VX systems using that name. If you saw it somewhere, probably it was just some impostor, not me. When I have called any of them they (the sysops) insist I have written many more viruses. It's very difficult, when you're (dav) [Dark Avenger] and you upload a virus, to make out that you didn't write it.

SG: Did you ever call the virus systems using your real name?

DA: Not a real name but a name that sounded like a real person.

SG: Why didn't you ever contact me?

DA: I did. I left you a message once. Well, it was not to you, but I put something in it for you.

SG: Yes, I remember that one. Something about: "You should see a doctor. Normal women don't spend their time talking about computer viruses." I answered it, if you recall?

DA: Yes. You said: "I do not want to be a normal woman, at least not in Bulgaria."

SG: Yes, but why didn't you talk to me directly?

DA: I didn't know you wanted to talk to me. Why didn't you send me mail?

SG: I was afraid of you. Anyway, why did you dedicate that virus to me?

DA: You said you wanted it.

SG: People have wondered why you wrote your first virus. Why did you write it and do you have any regrets about it?

DA: I wrote it because I had heard about viruses and wanted to know about them, but nobody around me could tell me anything. So I decided to write my own. I put some code inside it that intentionally destroys data, and I am sorry for it. I started working on it in September 1988.

SG: Couldn't you have asked someone who had a virus to show it to you?

DA: I knew nobody who had a virus. In fact, I think that at that time, nobody in Bulgaria had one.

SG: Where did you hear about viruses? What in particular caught your interest?

DA: There was a magazine called *Computer for You*, the only magazine in Bulgaria at that time. In its May 1988 issue there was a stupid article about viruses, and a funny picture on its cover. This particular article was what made me write that virus. Of course, this was not the first time I heard about viruses. I was interested in them, and thinking of writing one a long time before that. I think the idea of making a program that would travel on its own, and go to places its creator could never go, was the most interesting for me. The American government can stop me from going to the U.S., but they can't stop my virus.

SG: It has been stated by Valery Todorov that he wrote his first virus, WWT, because he was curious as to whether he could write one or not, but that he wrote his second virus because Vesselin Bontchev (often called the Number One Enemy of Dark Avenger) gave him the idea. Did you get any ideas from other people's viruses? Have you ever written a virus with someone else?

DA: No, but for someone else, yes.

SG: For who?

DA: For you.

SG: How do you feel about the destruction of data?

DA: I think it's not right to destroy someone else's data.

SG: If you think that, then why did you put destructive code in your viruses?

DA: As for the first virus, the truth is that I didn't know what else to put in it. Also, to make people try to get rid of the virus, not just let it live. At that time, I didn't think that data in PCs could have any great value.

SG: Do you mean the data in PCs in Bulgaria is of no value?

DA: As I said (or did I?), at that time there were few PCs in Bulgaria, and they were only used by a bunch of hotshots (or their kids). I just hated it when some asshole had a new powerful 16 Mhz 286 and didn't use it for anything, while I had to program on a 4.77 Mhz XT with no hard disk (and I was lucky if I could ever get access to it at all). Actually, I don't know why I'm saying all this. The real answer is: I don't know. And I didn't care. I also don't care very much now, I'm afraid. I just want the other people to leave me alone. The weasel (Vesselin Bontchev) can go to hell.

By the way, if you really think you should not break any laws, you can start by purchasing MS-DOS, or turning off all your computers permanently. First law of computer security: Don't buy a computer. Second law: If you ever buy a computer, don't turn it on.

SG: Don't you feel responsible if someone else uses one of your viruses to cause actual harm to a person's machine?

DA: No. If they wanted to cause harm, they wouldn't need my viruses. They could simply type "format c:" or something else that is much more effective.

SG: How can you say this? By writing and distributing the viruses, making them available, you do provide people with the idea and the means, in the same way you were initially provided. By doing this, your actions affect innocent users.

DA: The innocent users would be much less affected if they bought all the software they used (and from an authorized dealer) and if they used it the way they are allowed to by the license agreement. If somebody instead of working plays pirated computer games all day long, then it's quite likely that at some point they will get a virus.

Besides, there's no such thing as an innocent user, but that's another subject.

SG: What about the fact that you're giving people the idea, by creating such clever viruses?

DA: Ideas are not responsible for people who believe in them. Or use them. Or abuse them. Also, I didn't write them to "provide" anybody with anything. The weasel is the one who "provides." I just wrote them for fun.

I couldn't care less for all the suckers who see/use them. They were not supposed to make such a big mess.

SG: Still, you have provided them with an insidious weapon. Don't you feel that by providing them with such clever computer tricks, you are contributing to hurting the innocent users?

DA: I don't provide nobody with nothing. The weasel provides.

SG: How does he provide?

DA: He just "provides." That's one of his favorite words. I don't want to talk or think about it.

SG: What do you think about the new crop of virus writers, like Falcon/Skism and nUkE?

DA: They are kids, most of whom seek fame (and achieve it easily with the help of a-v people). Most of them are not good at programming viruses at all.

SG: Well, at least that is some point you and the a-v community agree upon. You have achieved a certain amount of "fame" yourself. How does it make you feel when you see your name in magazines and mail? How do you feel when you see your viruses "defeated" by antivirus programs?

DA: I wrote the virus so it would be killed, like I said. It was not supposed to do all this. I like seeing my name in magazines and in messages. I used to read all the messages about me, but I like it most when I see it printed somewhere. And I liked it a LOT seeing my things in Western a-v programs. First time I saw McAfee Scan was about version 5.0 or so. I liked it a lot. I was just excited, happy.

SG: Where did you get that name, Dark Avenger?

DA: I didn't really "get" the name. I mean, I didn't call myself that. I put those words in the virus and someone else (we both know who) said it was written by the Dark Avenger. He's the one that made me be the Dark Avenger, that name. I didn't use the name until after he called me that. That phrase itself came from some old song from a long time ago, and not from an Iron Maiden song, like some people have said. In many ways, I suppose you could say he made the Dark Avenger.

SG: How long do you think you will continue writing viruses?

DA: I don't. I never planned it.

SG: You misunderstood the question. Are you going to continue writing viruses?

DA: I don't know. It depends on what will happen to me.

SG: What do you mean?

DA: I mean, I will not normally write/spread any destructive or virus code, unless something extraordinary happens. Well, not if they put me in jail. If they do, and I ever get out, I will not be in a mood for programming. It is not/was not a crime to write the viruses, so I don't think this should happen. I just am not interested in writing them now.

SG: Do you know the difference between right and wrong?

DA: Why do you ask me this? In American movies, at the end, always the good guy gets the money, the girl and the applause, and the bad guy gets in jail or something. But in real life, it's not clear who is good and who is bad, and who gets what. It's not black and white. The only thing that is for sure is that good people always lose.

SG: Have you ever considered making an antivirus product, other than the fake doctor.exe which is actually a virus?

DA: I have considered it many times, but antivirus products are as useless as viruses. As for doctor.exe, it's not fake, it really does the job as it says it does.

SG: Why do you say they are useless? Don't you think they help protect users from common viruses?

DA: The users spend much more money on buying such products and their updates rather than on the losses of data damaged because of viruses. The a-v products only help the users to empty their wallets. Besides, viruses would spread much less if the "innocent users" did not steal software, and if they worked a bit more at their workplace, instead of playing games. For example, it is known that the Dark Avenger virus was transported from Europe to the U.S.A. via some (stolen) games.

SG: But viruses have now spread far beyond games. Most viruses are known to come by other routes.

DA: Sure they spread beyond the games. Still, I've never found a virus on any original disk from a package I bought from Borland International.

SG: But I got my first virus from commercial software! Don't you remember my telling that story?

DA: Not from Borland International. Some places you get a virus, some places you don't.

SG: It is said that your fellow Bulgarian, Vesselin Bontchev, did many things to provoke the virus writers. Did he provoke you?

DA: This is quite true, and I don't think he ever denied it. If he did, it would be a lie. There are a lot of people in Bulgaria who know it and can confirm it, but I don't think this was a big contribution to virus writing—his viruses were pretty worthless. He is not a good programmer.

SG: Do you feel that conditions in your country really help create virus writers as was stated by Bontchev in his "factory" paper? What can you tell me about the conditions in your country that contributed to your writing your first virus?

DA: I don't think the conditions in my country help create virus writers any more than conditions in any other country in Eastern Europe. Not after a certain person we both know left the country. As for my first virus, it had nothing to do with that.

SG: What contribution could "a certain person" have made to assist you (or anyone) in writing a virus? Don't you think that the conditions affecting the economy and computer technology of your country have indeed contributed to the overabundance of virus writers coming from former Eastern Bloc countries?

DA: His articles were a plain challenge to virus writers, encouraging them to write more. Also they were an excellent guide how to write them, for those who wanted to, but did not know how. It never said that he himself wrote some.

SG: According to some people, the story of viruses being such a big problem from Bulgaria begins with: "Soon hackers obtained a copy of the virus and began to hack it … some were optimized by hand. As a result, now there are several versions of this virus that were created in Bulgaria—versions with infective length 627, 623, 622, 435, 367, 353 and even 348 bytes." It is said many young people brought Bontchev viruses in those early days.

DA: Sure they did. Do you know the viruses vhp and vhp2?

SG: I think I may have heard of them.

DA: I think you don't want to know about this. I will send you a copy of a book that will tell you all about it. You don't want to hear it, and most of all you don't want to hear it from me.

_____

Source: Inside the Mind of Dark Avenger by Sarah Gordon. *http://www.research.ibm.com/antivirus/SciPapers/Gordon/Avenger.html*

Additionally, individuals who sell products in malicious software and carding markets must have their products and tools reviewed and receive feedback from their buyers.[102] For example, individuals called "testers" in these sites receive products from malware writers and actually attempt to use them to recommend whether or not others should buy their products. The review process acts as a sort of vetting process for the seller and gives potential buyers some knowledge of the person and their products. Reviewers would describe the quality of the information or service sold, as well as any problems or difficulties in utilizing the product. This process was exemplified in the review of a seller who offered a Trojan designed to steal funds from an electronic payment service called e-gold:[103]

> It is a very cool program that has been tried in a very critical environment and it runs undetected. Kaspersky and NOD32 (Norton) gives no alerts what so ever. The program is also conveniently small (under 100 KB). What the program does are once the victim logs on to his/hers e-gold account from Internet Explorer it highjack's the session and sends all the e-gold to a pre-specified account. How it looks is once the victim has clicked submit on the e-gold login page, the IE window disappears and the program continues to perform the transfer of funds hidden from the victim. One possible flaw is that it only works on Internet Explorer. But that being the major web browser in use I don't see it as a big problem. The creator was very nice and had a lot of patience with me while I was doing the review. He provided me with a copy of his program set to send funds to an e-gold account of my choosing. He also answered all my questions and concerns very professionally. I think you will all find him easy to deal with. I recommend that win32.grams should be given verified vendor status.

This sort of positive review would help buyers to understand whether or not they should purchase these tools. These examples demonstrate that malicious software is now becoming a professional industry that goes beyond our previous understanding of the hacking and malware community. Taken as a whole, there is a significant need for continuous research to understand how malicious software creators' behaviors change with time. Cybercriminals and cyberattack modalities are evolving, as are the technologies to prevent such activities (See Chapter 14).

Summary

Several virus thinkers have projected what the future will hold for virus writing, virus detection, and virus prevention.[104] Many of the predictions made during the early 1990s did indeed come true, particularly those that predicted that future viruses would be more polymorphic, have better encryption, and be better able to spread rapidly.[105] Their observations can be characterized into a few, relatively tight categorizations. The first prediction is that we will continue to have problems with polymorphism, mutations, and as-yet undescribed features of future viruses that will confound virus prevention experts and software.[106]

Malicious software can flourish and cause the most damage in an environment "friendly" to their existence. A friendly environment is one with a vulnerable operating system, one with complete documentation on the operating system, and the overall popularity of the operating system in the computer world.[107] In other words, security holes in a system can be manipulated to the extent that a malware writer understands the operating system and can exploit the holes and the code of the system. Once that code is exploited, the degree of damage inflicted and the nature and extent of the outbreak are determined by the popularity of the operating system—the number of potential targets. For example, for a virus to be successful, it must be able to spread. If only a small number of people used the targeted software or operating system, then the population available to infect is small as well, and the virus cannot spread.

It is important to note that computer security is always dependent on the weakest link in the chain. Security on the Internet and intranets is highly interdependent, and exposure to a potential attack is contingent upon the security, or lack thereof, of other parts of the network. This can be exploited through what is termed an "asymmetric" attack, which involves numerous distributed systems launching an attack against a single victim.

It is also important to note that there is an increasing number of dedicated infrastructure attacks. The interdependency of systems connected to the Internet used to carry out day-to-day business is ever growing and increasingly being relied upon by a variety of businesses, governments, and other operations. These types of attacks fall into four categories: DDoS, worms, attacks on the Internet Domain Name System (DNS), and attacks against or using routers.[108] DoS attacks and worms have been described. The attacks on Internet DNS would focus on disrupting or perverting the data and connectivity of the Internet systems that translate domain names to IP addresses. These attacks can result in a redirection of a user to a site determined by the attacker, compromised data on their servers, DoS, and co-optation or takeover of the domain itself.[109] Routers are specialized computers that direct traffic on the Internet rapidly. These systems could be used as an attack platform, to deny service, and to exploit the trust connection that may exist between routers to speed up service.[110] In sum, any of the attacks described in this chapter could lead to denial of service, compromise of sensitive or personal information, misinformation, and an extreme economic impact, largely from lost revenue and the time and resources necessary to recover.

Review Questions

1. What is the difference between a virus and other types of malicious code?
2. What are the most common types of viruses?
3. What variables are used to distinguish and classify viruses?
4. What is a Trojan horse? What are the various types of Trojan horses?
5. What is a worm? How do worms differ from traditional viruses?
6. What is a denial-of-service attack? How do these attacks work?
7. What are virus hoaxes? Why are the hoaxes sometimes more dangerous than an actual virus?
8. Describe the type of person who would write a virus.
9. Describe how the creation of malicious software is changing due to varying motives?

Critical Thinking Exercises

1. Visit the malware tracking Web site (https://intel .malwaretech.com/) and select two Botnets from the left column. Take note of the botnet's description and global level of infection. Use a search engine to identify at least two additional facts about the Botnets you selected. Discuss the destructive capability of botnets. While on the site, continue your visit to the constantly changing malware map (https://intel. malwaretech.com/pewpew.html), click "Connect" and observe the real-time botnet activity. Take note of the most prevalant botnet and the locations of infection, describe your observations (i.e., Are there any correlations to botnet density and geographic dispersment?).

2. Visit the Web site of the U.S. Computer Emergency Readiness Team at https://www.us-cert.gov. Click on the tab for "Alerts and Tips," then move to Alerts and find Alert TA16-091A on "Ransomeware and Recent Variants." Why are ransomware attacks so effective? Scour the internet for "ransomware variants" and discuss some of the variants found such as cryptowall, TeslaCrypt, SAMSAM, Zeus, Locky, and CrytoLocker. How can we prevent becoming a victim of ransomware? Hint: You might want to revisit the US-CERT Web site again.

Endnotes

1. STEPHENSON, P. (2000). *Investigating Computer-Related Crime: A Handbook for Corporate Investigators.* Boca Raton, FL: CRC Press.

2. Computer Security Institute. (2007). *2007 CSI/FBI Computer Crime and Security Survey.* San Francisco, CA: Computer Security Institute.

3. AVINTI. (2006). "Protecting Corporate Assets from E-mail Crimeware." *Avinti, Inc.* Retrieved April 20, 2007, from *http://www.avinti.com/download/market_background /whitepaper_email_crimeware_protection.pdf*

4. Refer to the Symantec Web site for articles and research relating to virus threats on personal computers, peer-to-peer networks, instant messaging, and other electronic devices: *http://www.symantec.com/norton/security_response/index. jsp.* See also the blog by Eric Chien (2012): *http://www .symantec.com/connect/blogs/eric-chien*

5. *Ibid.*

6. *Ibid.*

7. *Ibid.*, p. 2.

8. *Ibid.*

9. *Ibid.*

10. GRANT, I. (2008). "Sans Institute Reveals Top 10 Cyber Threats for 2008." *ComputerWeekly.com.* Available at: *http:// www.computerweekly.com/Articles/2008/01/14/228890 /sans-institute-reveals-top-10-cyber-threats-for-2008.htm.*

11. *Ibid.*

12. *http://cve.mitre.org/.*

13. *Ibid.*

14. *Ibid.*

15. WELLS, J. (2003). "PC Viruses In-the-Wild—September, 2003." Available at: *http://www.wildlist.org.*

16. Avira. (2013). "In the Wild Viruses Full Wildlist" See *http:// www.avira.com/en/support-wildlist-details.*

17. KASPERSKY, E.V. (2003). *The Classification of Computer Viruses.* Bern, Switzerland: Metropolitan Network BBS Inc. Available at: *http://www.avp.ch/avpve/classes/classes.stm.*

18. *Ibid.*

19. *Ibid.*

20. *Ibid.*

21. *Ibid.*

22. *Ibid.*

23. *Ibid.*

24. KASPERSKY, E. (1999). "Computer Viruses—What Are They and How to Fight Them?" Available at: *http://www .avp.ch/avpve/entry/entry.html-1.*

25. *Ibid.*

26. Symantec Corporation. (2003). "Internet Security for the Web: Protecting Enterprise Networks from Malicious and Inappropriate Web-based Content." Available at: *http:// enterprisesecurity.symantec.com/content/knowledgeli- brary.cfm?EID=0.*

27. This virus infects the boot-sectors of floppy-disks during access to them. Location on a disk is in a free cluster which the virus marks as BAD (pseudo-bad clusters). An infected disk gets a new volume label, "(C) Brain." The virus uses a stealth mechanism—when you look at the boot-sector of the infected disk, it shows the unchanged boot-sector.

28. KASPERSKY, "Computer Viruses—What Are They and How to Fight Them?"

29. Symantec Corporation, "Internet Security for the Web."

30. *Ibid.*

31. MtE (MuTation Engine) is the first known polymorphic generator. It was released in 1991 and shocked antivirus researchers by its very difficult (for 1991) polymorphic algorithm.

32. Symantec Corporation, "Internet Security for the Web."

33. These are not memory-resident harmless polymorphic viruses that affect .COM-files by using the "Vienna" algorithm. They are encoded and use two interesting algorithms. The first algorithm realizes the property of a polymorphic virus, due to which two strains of the virus would not coincide with high probability even in one byte. The main body of

the virus is encoded depending on the timer (1000000h=16777216 variants), and the decoder is selected from more than 3,000,000,000,000,000,000,000 variants (the decoder length is 39 bytes). The second algorithm fairly successfully complicates the virus tracing—it performs dynamic en/decoding of the virus codes using INT 1 and INT 3.

34. These are memory-resident harmless stealth polymorphic multipartite viruses. They write themselves at the end of . EXE files are executed or closed. These infectors hit MBR on execution of infected files, save the old MBR in the last sectors of C: drive, and reduce its size in the Disk Partition Table. The viruses infect RAM on a reboot from the infected MBR only. They hook INT 13h, 1Ch, 21h. According to their internal counters, the viruses display a colorful picture (Mandelbrot fractal set) and the message:
Execute: mov ax, FE03 / INT 21. Key to go on!
After executing this instruction, the viruses display:
Welcome to T.TEQUILA's latest production.
Contact T.TEQUILA/P.o. Box 543/6312 St'hausen/ Switzerland.
Loving thoughts to L.I.N.D.A
BEER and TEQUILA forever!

35. KASPERSKY, "Computer Viruses—What Are They and How to Fight Them?"

36. The virus constructor utility VCL.EXE (Virus Creation Laboratory) seems to be the most well-known virus creation tool. This constructor can generate source assembler files of the viruses, the OBJ modules and infected master files. VCL contains the standard pop-up menu interface. By using VCL menus, it is possible to choose the virus type, enable or disable self encryption, anti-debugging code, internal text strings. It also is possible to choose up to 10 effects, which are called upon virus execution. VCL-based viruses can use a standard way of infection (they append their code to the files while infecting them), they can overwrite the files, or use companion technology.
The main properties of VCL-viruses are
• They are nonmemory resident
• They scan the subdirectory three or the current directory of the current drive while infecting the files
• They are appending to COM files, or create new COM files or overwrite COM and EXE files.
Source: http://www.avp.ch/avpve/constr/vcl.stm

37. KASPERSKY, "Computer Viruses—What Are They and How to Fight Them?"

38. *Ibid.*
39. *Ibid.*
40. This is the first WinWord virus found "in the wild." The virus contains five macros: AAAZAO, AAAZFS, AutoOpen, PayLoad, FileSaveAs. It infects the files that are SaveAs'ed (FileSaveAs).
These are the text strings in the infected document:
see if we're already installed
iWW6IInstance
AAAZFS
AAAZAO

That's enough to prove my point and other. The WIN-WORD6.INI on infected system contains the file:
WW6I=1
On the first execution of the virus code (i.e., on the first opening of the infected file), the MessageBox appears with digit "1" inside, and "Ok" button. *http://www.avp.ch/avpve /macro/word/concept.stm.*

41. KASPERSKY, "Computer Viruses—What Are They and How to Fight Them?"
42. *Ibid.*
43. *Ibid.*
44. *Ibid.*
45. *Ibid.*
46. *Ibid.*
47. Symantec Corporation, "Internet Security for the Web."
48. KASPERSKY, *The Classification of Computer Viruses.*
49. *Ibid.*
50. *Ibid.*
51. *Ibid.*
52. *Ibid.*
53. *Ibid.*
54. *Ibid.*
55. *Ibid.*
56. CLARKSON, M. (2002). Beating the Superbug: Recent Developments in Worms and Viruses. GIAC GSEC Practical (1.4) SANS Institute: Information Security Reading Room. Available at: *http://www.sans.org/rr/*
57. *Ibid.*
58. Symantec Corporation, "Internet Security for the Web."
59. CLARKSON, "Beating the Superbug."
60. *Ibid.*
61. CERT Coordination Center. (2003). "Overview of Attack Trends." Available at: *http://www.cert.org/archive/pdf /attack_trends.pdf*
62. *Ibid.*
63. *Ibid.*
64. DANCHEV, D. (1999). "The Complete Windows Trojans Paper." Frame4 Security Systems. Available at: *http://www .frame4.com*
65. Symantec Corporation, "Internet Security for the Web."
66. DANCHEV, "The Complete Windows Trojans Paper."
67. *Ibid.*
68. CRAPANZANO, J. (2003). "Deconstructing SubSeven, the Trojan Horse of Choice." SANS Institute Information Security Reading Room. Available at: *http://www.sans.org/rr/*
69. DANCHEV, "The Complete Windows Trojans Paper."
70. CRAPANZANO, "Deconstructing SubSeven, the Trojan Horse of Choice."
71. *Ibid.*
72. DANCHEV, "The Complete Windows Trojans Paper."
73. *Ibid.*
74. CRAPANZANO, "Deconstructing SubSeven, the Trojan Horse of Choice."
75. *Ibid.*
76. *Ibid.*
77. *Ibid.*

78. HOLT, T.J. (August 7, 2007). "The Market for Malware." Paper presented at the Defcon 15 conference, Las Vegas, Nevada.

79. *Ibid.*

80. LEYDEN, J. (2009). "Pinch Trojan Lives on After Authors' Convictions." *The Register.* Available at: *http://www.theregister.co.uk/2009/02/05/pinch_trojan_toolkit/*

81. DANCHEV, "The Complete Windows Trojans Paper."

82. POST, A. (2002). "The Dangers of Spyware." Symantec Anti-Virus Research Library. Available at: *http://www.symantec.com/avcenter/whitepapers.html*

83. *Ibid.*

84. *Ibid.*

85. CERT Coordination Center, "Overview of Attack Trends."

86. HOLDER, E. (2000). "Internet Denial of Service Attacks and the Federal Response." Statement of Eric Holder, Deputy Attorney General of the United States Before the Subcommittee on Crime of the House Committee on the Judiciary and the Subcommittee on Criminal Oversight of the Senate Committee on the Judiciary on February 29, 2000. Available at: *http://www.usdoj.gov/criminal/cybercrime/ccpolicy.html#mv.*

87. CHIEN, E. and SZÖR, P. (2002). "Blended Attacks Exploits, Vulnerabilities and Buffer-Overflow Techniques in Computer Viruses." *Virus Bulletin Conference.* Available at: *http://enterprisesecurity.symantec.com/content/knowledgelibrary.cfm?EID=0;* GORDON, SARAH. (2003). "Virus and Vulnerability Classification Schemes: Standards and Integration." Symantec Security Response. Available at: *http://enterprisesecurity.symantec.com/content/knowledgelibrary.cfm?EID=0*

88. BACHER, P., HOLZ, T., KOTTER, M., and WICHERSKI, G.. (2005). *Tracking Botnets: Using Honeynets to Learn More about Bots.* The Honeynet Project & Research Alliance. Retrieved July 23, 2006, from *http://www.honeynet.org/papers/bots/*

89. *Ibid.*

90. RAMNEEK, P. (August 8, 2003). "Bots and Botnets: An Overview." SANS Institute; DLS Reports. (2013) "What is a Botnet Trojan?" See *http://www.dslreports.com/faq/14158*

91. NAMESTINIKOV, Y. (July 22, 2009). "The Economics of Botnets." *Securelist.* See *http://bizsecurity.about.com/gi/o.htm?zi=1/XJ&zTi=1&sdn=bizsecurity&cdn=b2b&tm=28&f=10&tt=2&bt=2&bts=2&zu=http%3A//www.viruslist.com/en/analysis%3Fpubid%3D204792068*

92. Symantec 2017, 2017 ISRT, see *https://www.symantec.com/security-center/threat-report*

93. GORDON, S., FORD, R., and WELLS, J. (1997). "Hoaxes & Hypes." Presented at the 7th Virus Bulletin International Conference in San Francisco, California, October 1–3, 1997. Available, at: *http://www.research.ibm.com/antivirus/SciPapers/Gordon/HH.html*

94. KASPERSKY, "Computer Viruses—What Are They and How to Fight Them?"

95. *Ibid.;* PEARSON, DAVID. (2003). "Psst ... Hey Buddy, Wanna Create a Virus? SANS Institute Information Security Reading Room." Available at: *http://www.sans.org/rr/*

96. DUCKLIN, P. (2001). "Is Virus Writing Really That Bad?" Presented at the Fourth Anti-Virus Asia Researchers (AVAR) Conference 2001, Hong Kong, November 2001. Available at: *http://www.sophos.com/virusinfo/whitepapers/virubad.html.*

97. CRAPANZANO, "Deconstructing SubSeven, the Trojan Horse of Choice."

98. *Ibid.*

99. FRANKLIN, J., PAXSON, V., PERRIG, A., and SAVAGE, S. (2007). "An Inquiry into the Nature and Cause of the Wealth of Internet Miscreants." Paper presented at CCS07, October 29–November 2, 2007, in Alexandria, VA; HOLT, T.J. and LAMPKE, E. (2009). "Exploring Stolen Data Markets On-Line: Products and Market Forces." *Criminal Justice Studies* 33(2); Honeynet Research Alliance (2003). "Profile: Automated Credit Card Fraud," *Know Your Enemy Paper* series. Retrieved June 21, 2005, from *http://www.honeynet.org/papers/profiles/cc-fraud.pdf;* THOMAS, R. and MARTIN, J. (2006). "The Underground Economy: Priceless." *USENIX:login* 31(6): 7–16, 3.

100. *Ibid.*, p. 77.

101. *Ibid.*

102. *Ibid.*, pp. 77, 109.

103. HOLT, and LAMPKE, "Exploring Stolen Data Markets On-Line."

104. BONTCHEV, V. (April 1994). "Future of Viruses." *Virus Bulletin.* Available at: *http://www.virusbtn.com/old/Other Papers/Trends/;* KASPERSKY, "Computer Viruses—What Are They and How to Fight Them?"

105. BONTCHEV, "Future of Viruses."

106. KASPERSKY, "Computer Viruses—What Are They and How to Fight Them?"

107. *Ibid.*

108. CERT Coordination Center, "Overview of Attack Trends."

109. *Ibid.*

110. *Ibid.*

Sex Crimes, Victimization, and Obscenity on the World Wide Web

CHAPTER OBJECTIVES

After completing this chapter, you should be able to

- Understand the nature of cybercrime victimization.
- Describe the groups affected by cyberexploitation, bullying, stalking, and obscenity.
- Describe the perpetrators of cyberstalking and exploitation via the Internet.
- Understand the law and legislation in the areas of cyberstalking, cyberexploitation, and pornography.
- Describe the Supreme Court cases that have been decided concerning federal efforts to target cybercriminals and protect children online.
- Understand and describe the issues with online pornography, child pornography, and child exploitation facilitated by the Internet.
- Understand the ways that the sex trade including prostitution and sex tourism has changed with the explosion of online content.
- Understand and describe the difficulties faced by law enforcement in detecting, investigating, and prosecuting cases of cyberstalking and cyberexploitation.

INTRODUCTION

The Internet allows communication across national and international boundaries; but, not all of this communication is for benign purposes. The Internet provides easy utilization and relative anonymity to criminals intent on exploiting and/or stalking online victims through the perpetration of sex crimes. The nature of crimes committed electronically takes on a different character and presents unique difficulties for law enforcement. For example, offenders and victims do not need to be in close physical proximity for the various forms of cybervictimization to occur. A child can be threatened, coerced, intimidated, and exposed to questionable material from offenders anywhere in the world. The crimes that are committed frequently involve multiple victims and offenders and cross national and international boundaries.

The driving force behind much of this growth is the enormous profits associated with the sale of online pornography. The new dynamics that drive the trade in *child* pornography is perhaps more disturbing. Sexual predators increasingly utilize the Internet and have found it to be the perfect tool for exchanging child pornography, trolling for victims, and arranging meetings and tours for sexually deviant behavior. Sex rings of pedophiles have been uncovered that exchange a multitude of sexually explicit pictures and videos of children. In some high-profile cases, sex rings have been used to transport children across the globe for sexual purposes—many times these networks are maintained via the Internet. In addition, pedophiles are using the Internet to arrange meetings with children and have been known to travel hundreds of miles for these meetings.

This chapter provides an overview of the nature of exploitation, stalking, and obscenity on the Internet, paying particular attention to the ways in which the computer revolution and the explosion of online material have both transformed and increased the likelihood of these offenses as they increasingly occur online rather than in physical space. The chapter focuses on providing descriptions of the offenders who commit these crimes, the nature and character of the "new" types of offenses, and preliminary explanations of how and why these crimes increasingly occur. The chapter also discusses the issues of prostitution, pornography, sex tourism, and the sex trade, and the fraud that so often accompanies these online activities. The final part of this chapter discusses the issues in investigating child exploitation, cyberstalking, sex crimes, and obscenity on the Web.

NATURE OF EXPLOITATION ON THE INTERNET

The exploitation of people for sexual and other purposes is nothing new; but, use of the Internet to facilitate these crimes is a more recent phenomenon. People can be victimized in a variety of ways online. The focus of this chapter is primarily on sexual victimization and stalking. The primary targets of such crimes are almost exclusively children and women, even though, the occurrence of women stalking men via the Internet is not all that uncommon. Internet sex predators victimize people by enticing them through online contact for the purpose of engaging them in sexual acts; by using the Internet for the production, manufacture, and distribution of child or other sexually deviant pornography; by using the Internet to expose youth to child pornography and encouraging them to exchange pornography; and by enticing and exploiting women and children for the purpose of sexual tourism (travel with the intent to engage in sexual behavior) for commercial gain and/or personal gratification.[1]

Estimates of the number of children affected by online crime, child exploitation and abuse, and other Internet-related crimes vary considerably because of the difficulties associated with identifying and tracking these crimes. A 2016 study estimates the number of children who are prostituted in the United States between 9,000 and 21,000, while the U.S. government estimates the number to be as high as 100,000 annually.[2] The numbers of children involved in pornography and sex trafficking also are uncertain and probably severely underestimated. Computer sex offenders frequently roam chat rooms and post sexually explicit material to make contact with young children and teenagers. Initial victimization may be indirect and limited to showing a child pornographic sites or initiating sexual conversations in a chat room, by e-mail or instant messages. More aggressive predators will spend time developing close relationships with vulnerable children. Eventually, they may introduce potential victims to photographs of children engaged in "normal" sex with adults, send them gifts, and/or contact them by telephone. Typically, sex offenders will try to gain the trust of victims, attempt to alienate them from their family, and eventually try to set up a physical meeting to consummate the victimization. Some online sex offenders have gone so far as to send plane tickets to children to fly across the country to meet them.[3]

BOX 8.1

Keeping Children Safe

The Internet has become a boon to those who disseminate sexually explicit material, and the revolution in online content has made it much more difficult to keep children safe from the threats posed by child pornography and online sexual predators. Surveys sponsored by Internet Filter Review show that young males aged 12–17 may be the largest consumers of Internet pornography, and the average age at which they are first exposed to pornography on the Internet is 11.[1]

Studies show that child pornography is one of the fastest growing businesses online. One researcher estimated that there may be up to one million sexually explicit pictures of children on the Internet.[2] Research conducted by the Internet Watch Foundation found that the percentage of Web sites showing the sexual abuse of children aged 0–10 (45%), and 11–15-year-olds (53%) have increased substantially over the last decade.[3] Their research uncovered some more startling facts on the explosion of child pornography on the Web:

- The United States is home to 54 percent of all known child abuse domains.
- Images that depict the worst type of abuse—including sadism, penetration by animals, and penetrative sexual activity involving children and adults—have become the primary driver of growth in demand for Web sites that depict child abuse.

Mainstream online photo album services popularly used to share pictures with family and friends are also increasingly being used to store images of child abuse.

---

[1] MAAHS, J. and LIEDERBACH, J. (2007). "Surfing for Porn: Obscenity and the Internet." In C. HEMMONDS (ed.), *Current Legal Issues in Criminal Justice: Readings.* Los Angeles, CA: Roxbury.

[2] HENLEY, J. (September 1, 1996). "The *Observer* Campaign to Clean up the Internet: Hackers Called in as Cybercops to Drive out Porn." *Observer.*

[3] *Internet Watch Foundation.* (2016). Annual Report. Available at *https://annualreport.iwf.org.uk/*

Women are often targeted by online predators and other criminals. Women also report feeling higher levels of violation as the result of being stalked, threatened, or harassed online. Certain factors make some groups more vulnerable than others to online victimization. First, and most, regular use and access to a computer with Internet capability is necessary to being victimized. The axiom that it is only a matter of time before you see something on the Internet that is pornographic or offensive holds true, and in many cases, first exposure is accidental. Older children tend to be at greater risk because they often use the computer unsupervised and are more likely to engage in online discussions of a personal nature. People who actively participate in chat rooms, trade e-mail messages, and send pictures online are also more likely to be victimized.

Troubled or rebellious teens seeking emancipation from parental authority can be particularly susceptible to Internet predators. Many sex offenders are well versed in the dynamics of teenage difficulties and know exactly what to say to a troubled teen to get them into a vulnerable position. Many adolescents struggle with issues associated with their sexuality, and the Internet provides them with a seemingly anonymous and non-threatening mechanism to ask questions and explore issues of a sexual nature. The problem is that often the teen has no idea who is on the other end of the Internet connection, and many teenagers downplay their own risk of victimization. Finally, single people have flocked to the Internet in growing numbers looking for companionship and relationships. While many professional online dating services exist, many people encounter someone in a chat room or as the result of some other type of Internet conversation. While it is likely that most of these interactions are relatively safe, it is also a growing medium for pedophiles and sex offenders to lure their victims off the computer and into a compromising position.

Online Victimization of Young People

One of the more comprehensive examinations of the issue of the online victimization of young people is the Youth Internet Safety Survey[4] conducted by Finkelhor, Mitchell, and Wolak and sponsored by the National Center for Missing and Exploited Children (NCMEC). The survey measured several areas of problems that youths reported being exposed to while surfing online, including the following:

- *Sexual solicitations and approaches:* Requests to engage in sexual activities or sexual talk or give personal sexual information that were unwanted or, whether wanted or not, made by an adult.
- *Aggressive sexual solicitation:* Sexual solicitations involving off-line contact with the perpetrator through regular mail, by telephone, or in person, or attempts or requests for off-line contact.
- *Unwanted exposure to sexual material:* Without seeking or expecting sexual material, being exposed to pictures of naked people or people having sex when doing online searches, surfing the Web, opening e-mail or e-mail links.
- *Harassment:* Threats or other offensive behavior (not sexual solicitation), sent online to the youth or posted online about the youth for others to see. Not all such incidents were distressing to the youth who experienced them.
- *Distressing incidents* were episodes where youth rated themselves as very or extremely upset or afraid as a result of the incident.[5]

Survey results indicated that approximately one in seven children sampled (or about 14%) received a sexual solicitation over the Internet during the previous year. The percentage of youths who were sexually solicited online decreased from a decade ago, where approximately one in five children was sexually solicited. This decline suggests that children may be more aware of the risks they face from interacting with strangers online. Unfortunately, the proportion of children who received "aggressive" sexual solicitations—where an individual asked to meet them somewhere, called them on the telephone, sent regular mail, money, or gifts—remained consistent during this same period. One in 33 youths received an aggressive solicitation, and this figure increased among young girls. Additionally, one in three children experienced unwanted exposure to pictures of naked people or people having sex. This was an increase, where approximately one in four was exposed to such material just five years earlier. In addition, 83 percent of the materials youths were exposed to happened while surfing the Web. Increases in exposure to online pornography are likely the result of increases in the number of children who utilize the Internet, as well as concurrent increases in high-speed Internet connectivity, and the aggressive marketing of sexual materials via the Web. The number of children who were threatened or harassed online also increased to about 1 in 11. This may again be a result of an increase in the amount of time that young people spend online. Additionally, youths appear to be more unkind or rude to others while online. Approximately one in four youths reported making rude or nasty comments to someone while on the Internet, and 1 in 10 harassed or embarrassed someone that "they are mad at" while online.

Although the respondents reported high rates of victimization, less than 10 percent of sexual solicitations and only 2 percent of unwanted exposures were reported to authorities, such as a law enforcement agency, an Internet service provider (ISP), or a hotline. Furthermore, less than one-quarter of youths who encountered a distressing sexual solicitation told a parent; however, 42 percent of those reporting an unwanted exposure to sexual material did tell a parent. There appears to be increasing appreciation for harassment among youths, as over 40 percent of those who experienced harassment reported this to their parents, though 10 percent reported the incident to law enforcement.

Given the significant increase in exposure to pornography and harassment, it is important to consider how parents use protective software programs to keep their children safe while online. There has been an increase in the number of parents who have filtering or blocking software on home computers. In 2000, approximately one-third of parents had some sort of protective software, whereas in 2016 more than 50 percent had such a program or filter installed.[6] Thus, this raises some difficult questions about the utility of such programs to reduce exposure to pornographic content and harmful communications.[7] It may be that parents have increasingly recognized the online threats that confront their children, but the expanded use of the Internet by children has worked to somewhat offset the effectiveness of protective software programs and other strategies designed to protect children online.

QUICK FACTS

Snapchat launched in late 2011, providing a message app that contained a number of familiar functionalities, including networking capabilities, imaging, and chats. Snapchat messages, videos and photos disappear between one and ten seconds after they have been read—from the server, from the inbox of the recipient and from the outbox of the sender. Unfortunately, this feature allows child predators to send inappropriate photos and messages to teenagers in a way that is undetectable to even social media savvy investigators. Combined with the anonymity that the Internet allows, Snapchat (as with basically any other social media service) can allow predators to post under pseudonyms or fake profiles. But surprisingly, such predators don't always misrepresent their ages, openly stating that they are adults when soliciting inappropriate photos or conversations. Often, teens feel flattered by the attention.

Ultimately, though, conversations with predators may not be the biggest threat presented by Snapchat: it's the overconfidence that sexually explicit or suggestive photos that teens share with each other will disappear. For instance, in Newtown, Connecticut, in 2016, several high school students were charged with selling the sexually explicit photos and videos that some of their classmates had sent them. They had used a combination of screen shots and photographs taken by a secondary phone, trained on the initial phone used for the messaging. Unfortunately, the photos—once sold—could have been transmitted to anyone, for any purpose, making the issue exponentially horrifying to the students in the photos and their parents.

Source: Lorenzo Ferrigno, "Newtown High School Students Charged in 'Sexting' Ring." *CNN News* (January 27, 2016).

Although the percentages of online victims may seem at first glance to be relatively small, the researchers extrapolated estimates of the number of victims based on the sample drawn in the survey. The results of this extrapolation are presented in Table 8.1 and reveal that between 2.9 and 3.7 million youths between the ages of 10 and 17 received a sexual solicitation or approach online. Another 7.9–9.1 million were exposed to unwanted sexual material. Finally, between 1.7 and 2.4 million youths were harassed online. The authors note that the survey suggests that youths encounter a substantial number of offensive episodes, many of which are distressing and most of which are unreported.[8]

TABLE 8.1 Population Estimates and Confidence Intervals for Online Victimization of Youth

Online Victimization	Regular Internet Users (%)	95% Confidence Interval (%)	Estimated Number of Youth[a]	95% Confidence Interval[a]
Sexual Solicitations and Approaches				
Any	13	12–15	3,220,000	2,970,000–3,720,000
Distressing	4	3–6	990,000	740,000–1,490,000
Aggressive	4	3–5	990,000	740,000–1,240,000
Unwanted Exposure to Sexual Material				
Any	34	32–37	8,430,000	7,930,000–9,170,000
Distressing	9	8–11	2,230,000	1,980,000–2,730,000
Harassment				
Any	9	7–10	2,230,000	1,730,000–2,480,000
Distressing	3	2.5–4[b]	740,000	620,000–990,000

Note: Estimates and confidence intervals are based on an estimated number of 24,780,000 regular Internet users between the ages of 10 and 17.

[a]Estimates and confidence intervals are all rounded to the nearest 10,000.

[b]This percent was not rounded so that the lower bound of the confidence interval could be shown.

Wolak, Janis, Mitchell, Kimberly, And David Finkelhor. (2006). Online Victimization of Youth: Five Years Later. Washington DC: Na-tional Center for Missing and Exploited Children.

The survey also reported demographics regarding the types of youths who were targeted for sexual solicitations and approaches. The research reported the following:

- Girls were targeted at almost twice the rate of boys (70% vs. 30%), but given that girls are often thought to be the exclusive targets of sexual solicitation, the sizable percentage of boys is important.
- More than three-quarters of targeted youth (81%) were aged 14 or older, and this group experienced 75 percent of distressing incidents.
- Almost all (86%) were persons the youth originally met online.
- Adults were responsible for 49 percent of sexual solicitations and 49 percent of the aggressive solicitations.
- Most of the adult solicitors were reported to be aged 18–25. About 9 percent of all solicitors were known to be older than 25.
- Juveniles made 43 percent of the overall and 44 percent of the aggressive solicitations.
- Males made 73 percent of the solicitations and approaches.
- Women account for a small percentage of the aggressive (16%) or distressing (7%) solicitations (16%).

In summary, the Youth Internet Survey has consistently revealed high levels of online victimization. Although the majority of solicitations do not result in the commission of a more serious offense, the sheer number of such encounters should be alarming to causal observers, parents, and law enforcement executives. Although many youths simply ignore such affronts, a significant percentage is severely distressed by the incidents. Complicating things is the fact that the overwhelming majority of these offenses and innuendos go unreported to authorities or the parents of the child.[9] The problems that youths experience online could be exacerbated by the youth engaging in other risky behavior, especially harassing or being mean to others online. Recent research has found that there is a significant connection between individual involvement in risky behavior and risk of harassment.[10] Finally, the belief by many that such online offenses are not serious adds to underreporting and lack of attention being paid to these victims.

Cyberbullying

In addition to harassment and sexual exposure over the Internet, young people are also at risk of experiencing cyberbullying. There is no consistent definition for this behavior, though the National Crime Prevention Council defines cyberbulling as occasions "when the Internet, cell phones or other devices are used to send or post text or images intended to hurt or embarrass another person."[11] This can include the use of text messages via cell phone, as well as e-mails, instant messaging, and other Web-based services to annoy or otherwise hurt someone's feelings. Some even use social networking sites like Facebook as a means to post pictures or messages about another person without his or her knowledge or consent that could be embarrassing or hurtful.[12]

Bullying is distinctive in that it occurs among juvenile populations only; whereas, the same actions among adults would be defined as harassment or stalking.[13] Cyberbullying in particular is different from real-world bullying because the perpetrators can reach their victim at all hours, day or night. So, a victim may find it hard to get away from their bully and find some relief. There are several potential reasons as to why young people use the Internet as a means to engage in bullying. Online communications and text messaging allow bullies to hide their identities and easily contact their victims. Furthermore, some may feel that it is easier to say something mean or hurtful via e-mail than in person.

Several other studies have found that juvenile populations have experienced high levels of bullying victimization. Studies in the United States have found that as much as 50 percent of youth have experienced bullying.[14] One survey of approximately 2,000 adolescent Internet users found that approximately one in five youths had experienced some form of cyberbullying during their lifetime.[15] This includes a range of problems, including receiving an e-mail, instant message, or Facebook post that made them upset, or being made fun of in a chat room. Girls appear to be slightly more likely to be bullied than boys; whites appear more likely to be bullied, followed by multiracial children, Hispanics, and African Americans. Most victims of cyberbullying often find they are not bothered by the event, though some report experiencing negative emotions as a consequence. In particular, individuals who are bullied may feel angry, frustrated, sad, or scared. Victims are often bullied by their current or former friends or individuals they go to school with. Few children are, however, harassed by strangers or individuals they know online.[16]

The issue of cyberbullying is complicated and may often go unnoticed by parents and teachers. Victims often do not report their experiences, much like with other forms of sexual harassment or contact. Most victims will talk about their experiences with their friends, although some do tell their parents.[17] However, few victims will talk about their experiences with teachers or law enforcement. This may be because victims can avoid certain Web sites, delete or block offensive e-mails and social networking identities, or not answer a phone or text message. This may also help to account for why victims often are not bothered by the bullying experience. It is clear, however, that the increasing number of cyberbullying events makes this a troubling problem that requires attention from parents and law enforcement.

> **QUICK FACTS**
>
> As a result of several high profile suicides over the last decade, including those of several young men who were unmercilessly taunted for either being gay or being perceived by their peers as being homosexual, 23 states now have included specific references to "cyberbullying," while 48 address "electronic harassment" in their criminal statutes. For more information on the topic of cyberbullying and suicide, see the Cyberbullying Research Center at *www.cyberbullying.org*.
>
> ———————————————————————————————————————
>
> *Source:* Sameer Hinduja and Justin W. Patchin. "State Cyberbullying Laws: A Brief Review of State Cyberbullying Laws and Policies." *Cyberbullying Research Center* (January 2016).

STALKING VIA THE WORLD WIDE WEB

Stalking is most often defined as the willful or intentional commission of a series of acts that would cause a reasonable person to fear death or serious bodily injury and that, in fact, place the victim in fear of death or serious bodily injury.[18] Stalking laws have changed in response to expanded knowledge derived through research on the online stalking phenomenon. Traditionally, many statutes had a narrow definition of stalking that included a specific intent requirement.[19] However, many states have changed their laws to broaden the definition of stalking to include repeated behavior that is harassing, communicating, or nonconsensual communication. In addition, some states have adopted a "general intent" requirement, rather than a specific intent requirement, which allows for the prosecution of cases that involve implied threats and threats that may or may not be considered "credible."[20] Some definitions also take into account the receiver's reactions to the communications, including any reaction that would cause a reasonable person to fear for his or her personal safety; to fear bodily injury or death to himself or herself or a related person; to suffer substantial emotional distress; or to become seriously alarmed, terrorized, or tormented by the behavior.[21]

Many stalking laws are broad enough to encompass stalking via e-mail or other electronic communication, defining the prohibited conduct in terms of "communication," "harassment," or "threats" without specifying the means of such behavior. A more specific definition of cyberstalking would be the use of the Internet, e-mail, or other electronic communications device to stalk, threaten, or harass a person. Other states have specifically defined stalking via e-mail within their stalking or harassment statute. For example, California recently amended its stalking law to expressly include stalking via the Internet.[22]

The numbers of cyberstalking incidents is unknown, but recent estimates suggest these behaviors appear to be on the rise, particularly among young people and college students due in part to frequent Internet use among this population.[23] For example, research by Finn found that approximately 15 percent of a sample of college students had experienced online harassment.[24] Similarly, Holt and Bossler found that 18.9 percent of students at a large southeastern university had been harassed at some point within the past year through a chat room, instant messaging service, or in Internet relay chats (IRCs).[25] Evidence from the National Crime Victimization Survey's Supplemental Victimization Survey (SVS) found that approximately one in four stalking victims experienced cyberstalking via e-mail or instant messaging.[26] Additionally, 1 in 13 victims was tracked via electronic monitoring tools, such as computer spyware, digital cameras, and GPS technology.[27]

The Mechanisms of Traditional Stalking and Cyberstalking

The traditional conception of criminal stalking involves a stranger following some unsuspecting female and showing up for repeated interactions with the victim. This conception has been reinforced in the popular media through television shows and films that portray the image of the traditional stalker. However, the dynamics of stalking have extended far beyond this traditional conception, and laws designed to identify and punish modern forms of stalking have changed to meet these challenges. What makes this area of law difficult to enforce is that it is often hard to distinguish between stalking behavior that is dangerous and behavior that is comparatively benign. Police officers investigating reports of stalking are quite familiar with *both* cases that involve actual danger and those that are false and/or overestimate the degree of danger. To be sure, many cases of stalking do not even rise to extreme levels of violence or harassment.[28] Nonetheless, all forms of stalking should be taken seriously, as they represent a fundamental threat to a person's physical and psychological well-being.

Traditional stalkers have been known to use binoculars, telescopes, cameras equipped with "long lenses," video cameras, hidden microphones, the Internet, public records, and accomplices (both witting and unwitting) to keep track of the whereabouts and activities of those they target.[29] Cyberstalking is simply the electronic form of stalking, where the harassment or threats are directed via the Internet typically using social networks, e-mail, chat rooms, bulletin boards, or even Web pages. Most often, due to the distance between users and the anonymity of the Internet, this behavior will not escalate into physical harm, but this does not mean that the pursuit is any less distressing.[30] A survey of victims of traditional forms of stalking reported that stalkers employed the following tactics most often:

- Followed or spied on the victim (24.5%).
- Made unwanted phone calls (62.5%).
- Sent unwanted letters or left unwanted items (30%).
- Showed up at places the victim was present (22.4%).
- Leaving unwanted presents (9.1%).[31]

Stalkers, by their very nature, want a relationship with their victims. They want to be part of their victims' lives. And, if they cannot be a positive part of their victims' lives, they will settle for a negative connection to their victims. It is this mindset that makes them not only stalkers but also dangerous. Thus, virtually all stalking cases involve behavior that seeks to make either direct or indirect contact with the victim.[32]

Most people using electronic forms of communication are much more brazen than they would be face to face; such is the case with cyberstalkers. The medium encourages people to interact in ways in which either they would be too embarrassed to do in person or they feel they might not be caught. This is most likely due to the perceived anonymity of the Internet and also because people talking to one another online are far away from each other physically.[33] Because individuals can mask their identity and remain relatively anonymous when using the Internet, linking the harassment to one individual is difficult and time-consuming. Box 8.2 below summarizes the results of research focused on identifying the various ways in which stalkers utilize computer-based technologies to stalk victims online. The study clearly identifies the ways in which stalking behaviors have evolved since the computer revolution.

BOX 8.2
The Mechanisms of Cyberstalking

A recent study conducted by the National Center for Cyber Stalking Research identified how various computer technologies are being utilized to stalk victims online.[1] The study utilized an online questionnaire conducted over six month period of time. There were 353 respondents. The survey was hosted on the Web site of Network for Surviving Stalking. Two-thirds of the respondents were female. The modal age of the respondents was 30–39.

The study found that social networking sites were the most common mechanism for online stalking behavior among male and female victims (61% and 63%, respectively). Other commonly utilized mechanisms are listed below with the percentage of male and female victims reporting that they had been stalked through the various mechanisms:[2]

- Webmail (55% and 56%, respectively)
- Mobile phone calls (38% and 45%, respectively)
- Mobile texts (42% and 59%, respectively)
- Instant messaging (33% and 25%, respectively)

Most cyberstalking victims reported that they had been stalked through more than one of these mechanisms. More than one-half of victims reported that they had had initial contact with the perpetrator in real-world situations, and that the stalking progressed through online mechanisms. These findings suggest that the nature and character of cyberstalking has changed to include a wide variety of online mechanisms, but many forms of online stalking are still initiated in-person through traditional methods. The Internet has widened the avenues for stalkers to continue harassing their victims online.

[1]National Center for Cyber Stalking Research (2011). Cyberstalking in the United Kingdom: An Analysis of the ECHO Pilot Survey."
[2]*Ibid.*

A number of compelling cases involving cyberstalking have been documented as the public and law enforcement officials recognize the threats posed by more modern forms of this type of crime, including the following:

- Prosecutors in the Los Angeles District Attorney's Office obtained a guilty plea from a 50-year-old former security guard who used the Internet to solicit the rape of a woman who rejected his romantic advances. This case was the first successful prosecution under California's new cyberstalking law. The defendant terrorized his 28-year-old victim by impersonating her in various Internet chat rooms and online bulletin boards, where he posted, along with her telephone number and address, messages that she fantasized about being raped. On at least six occasions, sometimes in the middle of the night, men knocked on the woman's door saying they wanted to rape her. The former security guard pleaded guilty to one count of stalking and three counts of solicitation of sexual assault.
- A local prosecutor's office in Massachusetts charged a man who, utilizing anonymous remailers, allegedly engaged in a systematic pattern of harassment of a coworker, which culminated in an attempt to extort sexual favors from the victim under threat of disclosing past sexual activities to the victim's new husband.
- An honors graduate from the University of San Diego terrorized five female university students over the Internet for more than a year. The victims received hundreds of violent and threatening e-mails, sometimes receiving four or five messages a day. The graduate student, who has entered a guilty plea and faces up to six years in prison, told police he committed the crimes because he thought the women were laughing at him and causing others to ridicule him. In fact, the victims had never met him.[34]
- The wife of a former police officer and her adult children spent three years stalking, spying and harassing the ex-wife of her husband in an effort to gain custody of

the husband's children. At one point, the individuals kidnapped the children and took them to Central America. The harassment came to an end when the husband, a former police officer, shot and killed his ex-wife as they entered a Delaware courthouse for a child support hearing. The former officer then killed himself after exchanging gunfire with the police. The incident marked the first time a person in the United States was convicted and sentenced for a case of cyberstalking that resulted in the victim's death.[35]

Characteristics of Stalkers and Their Victims

Most stalkers are typically male (87%), white (80%), between the ages of 18 and 35 (50%), of average intelligence, and earning above-average incomes.[36] In contrast, rates of stalking victimization suggest that women are more likely to be stalked than males. In terms of age, individuals 18–24 were most likely to experience stalking. Divorced or separated women faced higher rates of stalking victimization, followed by single and married people. Finally, those living in lower-income households were more likely to be stalked than those in higher-income brackets.[37] Research in this area indicates that the majority of stalkers and their victims (72.5%) had a personal relationship before the stalking began. The majority of these cases involved spouses or partners or had a dating relationship. Nearly 18 percent of stalkers were acquaintances or coworkers of the victim, while only 16.9 percent were complete strangers.[38]

Evidence from a study examining cyberstalking cases in New York City found that offenders were largely male (80%), white (74%), and an average of 24 years of age, though 26 percent were juveniles.[39] Additionally, females (52%) were slightly more likely to be victims than males. They were also predominately white (85%) and of an average age of 35 years. Specific profiles or categorizations have been developed as the result of the study of this phenomenon.

Several categorization schemes exist for classifying stalkers.[40] Simple obsessional stalkers comprise the largest group of estimated stalkers (47–60%) and typically involve a victim and a perpetrator who have a prior relationship. The motivation behind this type of case may be coercion to reenter a relationship or revenge aimed at making the life of the former intimate uncomfortable through the inducement of fear. Many simple obsession cases are actually extensions of a previous pattern of domestic violence and psychological abuse. The only difference is that the abuse occurs in different surroundings and through slightly altered tactics of intimidation. Thus, the dynamics of power and control that underlie most domestic violence cases are often mirrored in simple obsession stalking cases. This category of stalker is thought to be the most dangerous, and this is the most likely category of stalking to result in murder. Thirty percent of all female homicides were committed by intimate partners, and domestic violence victims run a 75 percent higher risk of being murdered by their partners.

The second largest category of stalkers (43%) is the love obsession type, where no prior relationship exists between the perpetrator and the victim or they are casual acquaintances. Often, the stalker identifies the victim through the media or the Internet. Usually, stalkers in this category seek to establish a personal relationship with the object of their obsession—contrary to the wishes of their victims. Love obsession stalkers tend to have low self-esteem and often target victims whom they perceive to have exceptional qualities and high social standing. These stalkers seek to raise their own self-esteem by associating with those whom they hold in high regard.

These types of stalkers are also often suffering from some type of mental disorder or defect. They frequently target media celebrities. Often, love obsession stalkers are so desperate to establish a relationship—*any* relationship—that they "settle" for negative relationships, explaining why some stalkers are willing to engage in destructive or violent behavior in an irrational attempt to "win the love" (more likely the attention) of their victims.[41]

A third category is referred to as erotomaniacs, meaning that the stalker believes that the victim is in love with him or her. By definition, erotomaniacs are delusional and, consequently, virtually all suffer from mental disorders—most often schizophrenia. This category was the least frequent (less than 10%) and differed from the previous two in that these offenders were more likely to be females stalking males. Erotomania stalking cases often draw public attention because the target is usually a public figure or celebrity. Like love obsession stalkers, erotomaniacs attempt to garner self-esteem and status by associating themselves with well-known individuals who hold high social status. While the behavior of many erotomaniacs never escalates to violence, or even to threats of violence, the irrationality that accompanies their mental illness presents particularly unpredictable threats to victims. Perhaps the best-known case of erotomania stalking involved a series of incidents perpetrated against the popular late-night talk show host David Letterman. This woman, first found hiding in Mr. Letterman's closet, believed she was his wife. On numerous other occasions, she was caught trespassing on his property. With her young son in tow, she once scaled the six-foot wall surrounding Letterman's property. On another occasion, she was arrested while driving Letterman's stolen car. When questioned by police, she confidently stated that her husband was out of town and that she was going grocery shopping so that she would have dinner ready for him upon his return. Despite the treatment she received during her many involuntary stays at a mental health facility, she eventually took her own life.[42]

Another category of stalker is the vengeance or terrorist stalker. Vengeance/terrorist stalkers attempt to elicit a particular response or a change of behavior from their victims rather than seeking a personal relationship with them. When vengeance is their prime motive, stalkers seek only to punish their victims for some wrong they perceive the victim has visited upon them. In other words, they use stalking as a means to "get even" with their enemies. Most commonly this type of behavior involves fired employees or political stalking (as in the case of some antiabortionists).

Traditional stalkers and cyberstalkers have several similarities and differences. The similarities primarily involve the motivations for stalking and the demographic and relational characteristics of the offense.[43] In essence, the stalker is motivated by a desire to get close to the victim, control the victim, or punish the victim in some way. The major difference is that while off-line stalking necessitates a closer proximity to the victim, cyberstalking can occur from across the nation or the world. Electronic communications technologies make it much easier for a cyberstalker to encourage third parties to harass and/or threaten a victim (e.g., impersonating the victim and posting inflammatory messages to bulletin boards and in chat rooms, causing viewers of that message to send threatening messages back to the victim "author"). Finally, as noted previously, cyberstalkers are much more likely to be brazen than off-line stalkers because of the anonymity of the Internet and the lack of close proximity.[44] The introduction of Internet-capable smart phones and growth in social networking are probably making it easier for stalkers to identify and harass victims. Stalkers can surreptitiously install spyware and utilize GPS tracking capabilities on smart phones to stalk victims.

These programs can also be used to track text messages or even intercept incoming phone calls. Users of social networking sites such as Facebook and Twitter invariably leave a "digital footprint" that can be easily traced and utilized by determined cyberstalkers to harass and/or intimidate potential victims.

Legislation Targeting Stalking

California was the first state to enact stalking legislation (in 1990), and today all 50 states and the federal government have antistalking statutes. However, a recent report notes that less than one-third of the states' antistalking laws explicitly cover stalking via the Internet, e-mail, pagers, or other electronic communications.[45] Nonetheless, many experts feel that existing stalking laws would cover the crime if committed using the Internet or other electronic means. Yet certain types of cyberstalking would most likely fall through the cracks and escape prosecutions. Currently, several federal laws cover the crime of stalking, but several of the statutes are not specifically targeted at cyberstalking. One such statute makes it a crime to transmit any communication in interstate or foreign commerce that contains a threat of injury.[46] This statute does not cover harassment offenses meant to annoy someone. A portion of a telecommunications law makes it a crime to annoy, abuse, harass, or threaten any person via electronic or telephone communication.[47] The Interstate Stalking Act[48] makes it a crime for any person to travel across state lines with the intent to injure or harass another person and, in the course thereof, place that person or a member of that person's family in reasonable fear of death or serious bodily injury. The problem with this law is that it probably would not directly apply to cyberstalking cases. Again, the existing law would most likely apply to cases of cyberstalking, although it would be prudent to be more specific about the crime in future legislation.

Additionally, there are pieces of legislation being added to state statutes around the United States concerning cyberbullying, largely as a consequence of the Megan Meier case. Meier committed suicide after receiving mean messages via the social networking Web site MySpace. She befriended a teenage boy named Josh Evans, and they developed a relationship that Evans terminated, stating that the world would be better off without her. In reality, Evans was a fictitious identity created by Lori Drew, the mother of one of Megan's friends.[49] Drew created this identity as a means to humiliate Megan as retribution for slighting her daughter. The subsequent development of legislation has attempted to decrease the likelihood of such an event happening again. The first state to directly deal with cyberbullying is California, which passed a law in January 2008 giving school administrators the power to discipline students for bullying other students online or off-line.[50] In fact, principals and administrators can suspend or expel a student who engages in cyberbullying.

Cyberbullying and cyberstalking are expected to increase as computers and the Internet become more popular. An Assistant U.S. Attorney reported that in two recent cases of e-mail harassment, he asked an FBI agent to confront the would-be harasser. Upon advising the cyberstalker that such behavior might constitute a criminal offense, both stalkers ceased their harassment.[51] Investigators and law enforcement agencies are relatively ill-equipped to deal with cyberbullying and cyberstalking for a variety of reasons. First, and most prominent, is the lack of reporting on the part of victims. Again, many people report that they do not think what has occurred is a crime or that they doubt the ability of law enforcement to do anything about the crime.

Second, most law enforcement agencies are not trained to recognize the serious nature of these crimes and to investigate such offenses. Unfortunately, some victims have reported that rather than open an investigation, the law enforcement agency has advised them to come back if the cyberstalkers confront or threaten them off-line. In several instances, victims have been told by law enforcement simply to turn off their computers.[52] In the case of bullying, victims can find a variety of ways to avoid their bully.

Finally, even if these crimes were more commonly reported, the overwhelming majority of law enforcement agencies are ill-prepared to deal with cyberstalking because of the lack of resources, lack of investigative tools, and lack of trained personnel. Most large law enforcement agencies now have computer crime units, with extraordinarily busy police officers staffing them. Additionally, cyberevidence processors in local law enforcement agencies and the federal government are already overbooked and understaffed.

OBSCENITY ON THE WORLD WIDE WEB

The issue of what is obscene has been debated in the court systems of the United States for a long period. The growth of the Internet has forced the Supreme Court to revisit this slippery issue that lives somewhere between community protection and freedom of speech. The players are the same: on the one side, governmental officials and politicians looking to regulate a sexually oriented industry that they feel is linked to a whole host of other, more serious, problems, and on the other side, free speech activists, the American Civil Liberties Union, and those who seek to profit from pornography. It is an old battle. The new battlefield, however, presents unique problems and questions for the American legal system. In the past, pornography—especially the seriously hardcore, the bizarre, and the illegal kind—was kept relatively out of sight and required that purveyors visit a sexually oriented business, purchase the materials in person, or order them via the mail or over the phone. In terms of monitoring, the government had a relatively easy job of tracking and preventing illegal types of pornography from being circulated in the United States. The Internet changed all of that and essentially made pornography—even the hardcore and illegal varieties—widely available to the general public.

The old questions of what is and what is not obscene became somewhat secondary in this new battle over the ability of the government to restrict what is posted on the Internet versus free speech.[53] Interestingly, the battle has focused on what both sides of the argument would agree is a problem—child pornography and access to pornography by children. The difference between the two sides lies in the proposed remedies. It is fair to say that neither side would allow child pornography to be shared, posted, or disseminated. However, adult access became the issue in several Supreme Court cases that examined a variety of federal law passed regarding the access of children to the Internet and the ability of government to regulate the Internet. The government's position has consistently been that the onus of regulation is on ISPs and the people and businesses who wish to post, sell, or disseminate pornography. Laws were passed that mandated that ISPs had to monitor and regulate certain types of pornography, especially child pornography. Furthermore, anyone who wished to sell or promote pornography had to assure that children were not accessing the material or face federal charges.

On the other side, the onus is placed firmly on the individuals and the parents of the children. In short, it is up to the individual to self-regulate access, and it is up to parents to assure that children do not access the materials. As is typical, the law ended up squarely in the middle. The prosecution of Internet-related child pornography and luring cases is increasing.

Laws and Legislation Protecting Children Online

Several laws deal with the issues of child exploitation on the Internet; some of these laws are reviewed in this chapter. For example, the Child Protection and Sexual Predator Punishment Act of 1998 specifically addressed the issues of online victimization of children. The law prohibits the transfer of obscene material to minors, and increases penalties for offenses against children and for repeat offenders. Furthermore, the Act amends the Child Abuse Act of 1990 by requiring online service providers to report evidence of child pornography offenses to law enforcement agencies.[54] In 1994, the U.S. Congress extended the Mann Act by enacting the Child Sexual Abuse Prevention Act.[55] This Act empowers the Justice Department to penalize U.S. citizens traveling across state or national borders to engage in sexual activity with children.[56] The production of sexually explicit depictions of a minor for importation into the United States is also prohibited.[57] Additionally, a child sex tourism provision was added to the 1994 Violent Crime Control and Law Enforcement Act that makes it illegal for a U.S. citizen or permanent resident to travel in interstate or foreign commerce with the intent to engage in sexual acts with a minor that are prohibited under federal law in the United States. This provision applies even if these acts are legal in the destination country.

There are numerous state laws that prohibit the possession, manufacturing, distribution, and sale of child pornography. In many instances, simple possession is a felony. U.S. federal law on child pornography [58] outlines the prohibited behavior and law concerning the distribution and possession of child pornography.[59] Most child pornography offenses are covered by federal law in a number of statutes[60] and prohibit the production, sale, transmittal, and possession of child pornography. Additional federal law covers child luring[61] and the transportation of children for sexual purposes.[62] The same statute prohibits traveling for sexual purposes in the United States and abroad. The publication or posting of any information relating to a child for sexual purposes is also prohibited.[63] This statute would apply any time a child predator communicates online with another child predator and provides personal information about a minor under 16 for criminal sexual purposes.

Federal law on the sexual exploitation of children[64] prohibits people from using children in the production of sexually explicit material. The law also targets parents who allow or force their children to participate in the production of child pornography.[65] The law also prohibits the exchange of child pornography between people and prohibits the publication of advertisements seeking or offering child pornography.[66] Violations of this law are punishable by 10–20 years in prison for first offenders, 15–30 years for second offenders, and not less than 30 years for anyone with two or more prior offenses.[67] Additional federal law prohibits the transportation or transmittal, reception, distribution, and possession of child pornography.[68] Violation of the portion of the law relating to transportation, transmittal, and distribution carries a maximum sentence of up to 15 years, but a prior conviction carries a mandatory minimum of 5 years up to a maximum of 30 years in prison. The possession of child pornography carries a maximum sentence of 5 years with a mandatory minimum of 2 years to a maximum of 10 years for prior offenders. This law has an affirmative defense provision that requires that a person possessed less than three matters of child pornography, took reasonable steps to destroy the materials, and promptly reported the matter to law enforcement officials.[69]

In 1998, Congress enacted the Protection of Children from Sexual Predators Act (PCSPA) of 1998, which established new criminal offenses, amended existing statutes, and provided for enhanced penalties. Three new offenses or definitions of offenses were created:

1. *Use of interstate facilities to transmit information about a minor:* [70] Prohibits the use of the mail or facility of interstate or foreign commerce to transmit information about a minor under 16 for criminal sexual purposes.[71] This statute is in response to a case from Illinois, where an individual posted a nine-year-old girl's name and telephone number on the Internet, indicating that she was available for sex. The individual initiating the transmission can be fined, imprisoned up to five years, or both.

2. *Transfer of obscene materials to minors:* Prohibits the use of the mails or a facility of interstate or foreign commerce knowingly to transmit, or attempt to transmit, obscene materials to minors under 16.[72] The individual transmitting the materials may be fined, imprisoned for 10 years, or both.

3. *Definition of sexual activity:* Defines criminal sexual activity to include the production of child pornography.[73] Previously, several cases presented for federal prosecution could not be charged because the individual either transported a minor or traveled to meet a minor to produce child pornography, but not for sexual activity.

The new laws also enacted attempt provisions to several laws,[74] increased penalties for several child sexual offenses,[75] made prosecution for child sexual assault possible for imported child pornography,[76] and increased and expanded sentencing for child sexual offenses.[77] The legislation also imposes the death penalty if the death of a child results from the offense,[78] allows for civil forfeiture relating to these offenses,[79] and places an affirmative responsibility on ISPs to report child pornographic offenses.[80]

The U.S. Supreme Court has had the opportunity to review several cases involving child pornography and legislation designed to protect children online. In *Reno* v. *American Civil Liberties Union*,[81] the Court examined two provisions of the Communications Decency Act of 1996. The first part criminalized the knowing transmission of "obscene or indecent" messages to any recipient less than 18 years.[82] Another section of the Act prohibited the "knowing" sending or displaying to a person under 18 of any message "that, in context, depicts or describes, in terms patently offensive as measured by contemporary community standards, sexual or excretory activities or organs."[83] The Court decided that these two provisions of the Communications Decency Act, specifically the "indecent transmission" and "patently offensive display" provisions, potentially violated the free speech portion of the First Amendment. The Court specifically noted that the Act lacked precision of definition, a requirement when justifying the restriction of free speech. The Court noted that the government has an interest in protecting children from potentially harmful materials; however, the Communications Decency Act attempted to pursue that interest by suppressing a large amount of speech that adults have a constitutional right to send and receive. Of particular interest was the analysis the Court made regarding what could be done in this area. Specifically, the Court concluded that the burden the Act placed on free speech was not justifiable, given that currently available filtering software is a reasonably effective method by which parents can prevent their children from accessing material that the parents believe is inappropriate.

In *Ashcroft* v. *Free Speech Coalition*,[84] the Supreme Court reviewed provisions of law aimed at child pornography, specifically virtual child pornography. The ability of users to "morph" or alter images and to literally generate virtual pornography led the U.S. government to add a provision to the Child Pornography Prevention Act (CPPA) of 1996. The new additions to existing child pornography laws now included computer-generated imagery depicting or conveying the impression that a minor is engaged in sexually explicit conduct.[85] An additional section of the new law prohibited production or distribution of materials pandered as child pornography, even if it was not involving actual children. The Supreme Court decided that these two sections were unconstitutional and overbroad. The Court noted that the CPPA was inconsistent with existing jurisprudence regarding obscene material. The Act placed an affirmative burden on anyone who might be charged to prove that the material under questions was not child pornography, either because it was fake or because the actors in question were indeed adults. Taken together, these two decisions effectively invalidated two major pieces of legislation regarding obscenity online; Attorney General Ashcroft complained that the Court had dealt a severe blow to the ability of law enforcement to fight child pornography.

Congress enacted the Prosecuting Remedies and Tools against the Exploitation of Children Today Act (PROTECT Act) of 2003,[86] which included a wide variety of provisions relating to the exploitation of children. The PROTECT Act strengthens existing U.S. law by increasing imprisonment penalties to 30 years for convicted sex tourists, criminalizing persons or organizations that assist or organize sex tours, and better enabling federal prosecutors to convict offenders by modifying burden of proof requirements. In addition, the new law establishes parallel penalty enhancements that apply to the production of child pornography overseas. The PROTECT Act is a wide-ranging bill pertaining to the investigation, prosecution, and punishment of offenses relating to children and pornography. The PROTECT Act also provides criminal penalties for users of innocent-sounding domain names if the owner knowingly uses the domain name to link to sexually explicit material. If a Web site's domain name deceptively draws people to sexually explicit material, the operator could be imprisoned for up to two years. The sentence is increased to four years if the domain name is intended to attract minors to the material. In addition, an offender of either provision can be fined up to $250,000.

QUICK FACTS

The problem of child pornography is enormous, according to the National Center for Missing and Exploited Children (NCMEC). Here are some of the numbers:

147 million images and videos of child pornography reviewed by the NCMEC.

Over 1 million child porn images/videos reported on the NCMEC Cyber TipLine per year.

Over 10,000 FBI arrests for possession of child pornography since 1996.

Over 5,000 cases investigated by the FBI's Crime Against Children Unit (CACU) per year.

2,315 suspects indicted on child pornography charges in 2010 alone.

2,500 percent rate of increase of child pornography arrests, since 1996.

Sources: See Child Exploitation and Obscenity Section (CEOS) Web site at: *https://www.justice.gov/criminal-ceos*

Associated Press, "Child Porn Prosecutions Soaring in the U.S." February 5, 2011

See "Today's FBI: Investigative Programs" Web site at: *https://www2.fbi.gov/facts_and_figures/investigative_programs.htm*

PEDOPHILIA AND CHILD PORNOGRAPHY

Child pornography can be defined simply as depictions of children in a sexual act or in a sexual way. Most policymakers and researchers conclude that this applies to anyone under 18 years. Child pornography contains the same types of sexual activities as those depicted in adult pornography, except that the media contains images or descriptions involving children, children and adults, or children and animals or objects.[87] A narrower definition of child pornography would limit the concept to mean only images depicting sexual acts between real children and other children, adults, or some other sexual depiction. Broader definitions would include depictions of children that are sexually suggestive, drawings of children engaged in sexual acts, sexually graphic writings involving children, cartoons suggesting sex with children, and so on. Although certain forms of art and writing fall into a gray area subject to debate, clear visual depictions of children engaging in sexual conduct are child pornography and unilaterally prohibited. One study by the Justice Department found a history of child pornography in three mainstream pornographic magazines, *Playboy*, *Penthouse*, and *Hustler*.[88] The study found between 6,000 and 9,000 (depending on definitional criteria) child images in the three magazines, most involving sex or violence.[89] Of these depictions, 29 percent involved nudity or genital display, 20 percent genital activity, 16 percent sexual contact with an adult, 10 percent the use of force, and another 10 percent killing or maiming.[90] Regardless of the definition, child pornography is a serious issue with long-term implications for the offender and child victims, which has come to the forefront recently because of the Internet.

QUICK FACTS

Over the past two decades, several important laws have been adopted to address the issue of child sexual exploitation (including child pornography) on the Internet:

- *Child Protection and Sexual Predator Punishment Act of 1998* specifically addresses the issues of online sexual exploitation of children. The law prohibits the transfer of sexually explice material to minors, and increases penalties for offenses against children. Furthermore, the act amended the *Child Abuse Act of 1990* by requiring online service providers to report evidence of child pornography offenses to law enforcement agencies.
- *Protection of Children from Sexual Predators Act* was passed by Congress in 1998 and established three new criminal offense areas of child pornography: (1) use of interstate facilities to transmit information about a minor; (2) transfer of obscene materials to or from minors; and (3) definition of sexual activity to include the production of child pornography.
- *Child Pornography Prevention Act (CPPA) of 1996* is found in Title 18, Section 2252 of the U.S. Code that specifically addresses child pornography and the Internet; making it a federal crime (felony) to sell, possess, possess with intent to sell, download, or produce child pornography or any visual (virtual) depiction that is intended to represent or resemble child pornography. Note that the statute does <u>not</u> require that an actual child be involved in the making of such pornography for it to be legally punishable; there must be merely the presence of the "visual depiction" of a child.
- There are also numerous state laws that also prohibit the possession, manufacture, distribution, and sale of child pornography.

Source: Swanson, C.R., Territo, L., and R. W. Taylor. *Criminal Investigation, 12th edition*. New York: McGraw-Hill, 2018. See Chapter 11: Crimes Against Children.

There is currently no accurate statistical source that reports the extent of or numbers of arrests involving child pornography. One estimate noted that at any given time, there are, on average, around one million sexually explicit pictures of children on the Internet. In just one week, 5,651 messages about child pornography were posted on just four sites. Included in these messages were over 800 graphic pictures of adults or teenagers engaged in sexual activity with children between 8 and 10 years of age.[91] In 2004, the Internet Watch Foundation found 3,433 child abuse domains, and then in 2006 there were 10,656; with an estimated 116,000 child pornography request made daily on the Internet.[92] These statistics indicate there is still a child pornography "industry" working internationally that produces materials for sale and consumption. Various sources estimate that child pornography comprises anywhere from 5 to 10 percent of the pornography trade, resulting in profits in the billions.[93] Other sources conclude that the extent and profit estimates of the child porn industry are grossly exaggerated.[94] A search on the Internet reveals that there are numerous Web sites that insinuate child pornography, a substantial number of newsgroups that concern child pornography, and a wide variety of writings and other material concerning how to access child pornography. The most common forms, if a broad definition is used, are altered pictures and stories relating to sexual contact with children—both of which were extremely easy to find and document. More thorough investigation and monitoring reveal that child pornography is commonly posted to several newsgroups and can be accessed at some personal Web sites internationally.[95]

Child pornography exists for reasons similar to other forms of pornography; there is a demand for such materials. In contrast to other forms of pornography, there is little discussion of child pornography being a victimless crime or a protected form of free speech. It is fair to assume that very few people would advocate the ready availability and use of child pornography. Child pornography is clearly an abhorrent and unconscionable act to the vast majority of people; however, to the *pedophile* the collection and use of child pornography is a source of pride, fantasy, and sexual gratification. Child pornography is used by the pedophile to feed and create sexual fantasies, lower the inhibitions of a child who they are planning to molest, and blackmail a child into remaining silent.[96] In addition, the pedophile uses child pornography as a profit device and in barter with other pedophiles to add to their collection or access other children to victimize.[97]

The supply side of the child pornography trade largely consists of pedophiles willing to molest children as well as possess child pornography. As Campagna and Poffenberger[98] note, the single most distinctive characteristic of habitual child molesters is a compelling interest in collecting child pornography. Habitual child molesters categorize their collections in a sophisticated and elaborate way and typically possess a variety of child pornography in several media, including computer files, videotapes, magazines, amateur pictures, books and novels, drawings and art, and several others.[99] The pedophiles also typically keep an annotated journal or diary to record molestations and other details of their crimes. Once apprehended, the pornography and diary become invaluable evidence for prosecution. To the child molesters, their child pornography collection is equated with valuable family heirlooms and investments, as the collections can be traded between pedophiles and used as payment for child prostitution.[100] This underground system used to be maintained through group associations, mail, and telephone; today, the Internet serves as the primary mechanism.

There exist, unfortunately, several national and international organizations dedicated to pedophiles and child sexual exploitation. The links between members in these organizations serve as a communication network for the exchange of child pornography. The North American Man/Boy Love Association (NAMBLA) advocates sexual and emotional relationships between adult males and underage boys. NAMBLA has chapters in many large U.S. cities and publishes a variety of print media for its members (estimated anywhere between 500 and 1,000 in 1988).[101] NAMBLA also has a Web site and annual meetings. Undoubtedly the membership, or at least those willing to access the Web site, has grown with the expansion of the Internet. Another such organization is the Lewis Carroll Collector's Guild, which publishes the newsletter *Wonderland* four times a year. *Wonderland* is a collection of articles and advertisements than promote interest in photographs and artwork pertaining to nude children on the premise that no exploitation is involved.[102] Several other organizations can be found on the Internet and have been documented by law enforcement officials. The common theme of these organizations is the promotion of sex and children. They are also undoubtedly useful for pedophiles to establish connections with others interested in their questionable practices.

The U.S. Customs Service initiated an investigation of the Wonderland group, eventually executing search warrants in 31 cities in the United States and cooperating with international law enforcement, leading to searches and warrants in 13 different countries. At the time, Customs officials noted that it was the most extensive ring of child pornographers ever uncovered, involving as many as 200 suspects around the world, 34 of them in the United States. All of the suspects were members of a perverse network trading in images depicting everything from sexual abuse to the actual rape of children. One of the requirements for membership was a stockpile of several thousand images of graphic child pornography. Customs agents tracked these suspects through cyberspace, sifting through a maze of Internet providers, servers, files, and screen names. The case resulted in numerous arrests and seizures of computers and other digital evidence. Such cases challenge the patience and capabilities of law enforcement due to the extensive distances between the conspirators and the difficulties associated with sifting through and processing digital evidence. In testimony before Congress, Deputy Assistant Attorney General Kevin V. Di Gregory stated:

> The trafficking in child pornography by computer users has, in some ways, challenged the progress of nearly eighty years of aggressive child pornography investigation and prosecution. Whereas by the early 1990s the Government had largely eradicated the cottage trade within the United States for this material and distribution was typically limited to trading or sharing between individual pedophiles who actually knew each other, today computer technology has reinvigorated both the commercial and non-commercial distribution of obscene child pornography. This reinvigoration means that child pornography produced in the 60s, 70s, and early 80s is now being re-released and distributed to an audience the size of which pedophiles could not have envisioned ten or twenty years ago. Additionally, the ability to mass market child pornography with little or no overhead to huge populations has created an environment where pressures for new material exist. This demand, unfortunately, is being met by new material from sources which include the Pacific Rim, Mexico, and South America. Our investigation has also resulted in the discovery that substantial amounts of written obscenity containing graphic descriptions of torture, bondage, and rape of children are being posted and distributed on the Internet and on private on-line systems. As the World Wide Web continues to grow, we expect that obscene visual images consisting of fantasy drawings or computer-generated images featuring similar themes of child sexual and physical abuse will also be created and made available for distribution. Obscene material, both written and visual, which can be used to seduce, lure, or train children to perform certain acts, must be highlighted and punished differently.

The fact that there really is no way to gauge how extensive the exchange of child pornography is on the Internet underlies perhaps the most serious problem—that law enforcement is only finding the tip of the iceberg in terms of the actual extent of this problem. As high-profile prosecutions began to occur in the late 1990s, the message to pedophiles and purveyors of child pornography was that anonymity was not assured on the Internet. As a result, efforts to conceal their presence, secure their connections, and encrypt their files have become more prevalent in recent years. Therefore, the job of law enforcement in this area has become increasingly difficult.

The "New" Child Pornographers

In the past, child pornography took the form of pictures, magazines, and videotapes—many homemade and collected over long periods of time by pedophiles. Pedophiles now use the Internet for four primary purposes: trafficking child pornography, locating children to molest, engaging in inappropriate sexual communication with children, and communicating with other pedophiles.[103] In the past, the distribution and sharing of child pornography was through clandestine newsletters or tightly controlled networks,[104] whereas today the networking and distribution are online.

In the summer of 1996, a U.S. federal grand jury indicted 13 individuals from the United States and 3 from Australia, Canada, and Finland, charging them with orchestrating and participating in an online molestation of 10-year-old girls. The defendants took part in real-time photo shoots where they typed messages requesting photos of the girls in certain poses, while one member shot photos with a digital camera and transmitted the photos back to the group. The defendants were members of the Orchid Club, a private, online child pornography group that shared sexually explicit images and videos of girls as young as five. To be a member of the Orchid Club, members had to know the password to access photos and online chat sessions. Initiation to the club required a potential member to describe a personal sexual experience with a child. After the molestation, members allegedly asked that the camera be aimed at the girl's pubic area and then inquired about traveling to Monterey, California, to molest her themselves. This was the first organized molestation ring prosecuted via an online child pornography investigation.

More recently in 2015, federal agents arrested and subsequently prosecuted the founder of *The Playpen,* Steven W. Chase, a 58-year-old man from Naples, Florida. The bust of the huge online Web site was thought to be the largest child pornography Internet site to date. The site which was originally developed on the Tor Network (or Dark Web) boasted over 150,000 users and some of the worst images of child sexual abuse imaginable. During a massive investigation that followed, police arrested 900 suspected users worldwide, and rescued (or identified) some 300 children from the site. On May 1, 2017, Chase was sentenced to 30 years in prison as the creator of the "world's largest kiddie-porn site."[105]

As noted by Lanning and Burgess,[106] child pornography collectors take great pride in their collections, sometimes numbering in the hundreds of thousands of pictures, magazines, or videos. In a another arrest by the U.S. Customs Service, a computer was seized that contained well over 100,000 images of child pornography.[107] The images were catalogued and filed by age, gender, hair color, sex act, and several other variables. Customs officials estimated that it took endless hours of work to enter and develop the file structure containing the images. In the past, the distribution of such a collection would take endless hours of photocopying, film developing, or video processing. If done commercially, it was relatively easy to track the source. Today the individual with the 100,000 images could easily upload the files to the Internet through a variety of mechanisms and methods and distribute them to the masses in a matter of hours. These images could then be downloaded and saved by anyone and redistributed at a later date.

Posting child pornography via Web pages has been curtailed substantially over the past decade; however, the distribution via e-mail, newsgroups, bulletin boards, file-sharing sites, file transfer protocols (ftps), and other direct connect mechanisms continues. The development of inexpensive video recorders and Web cameras has made it very easy for individuals to create high-quality movies of child pornography. Software programs like Photoshop and scanners also allow individuals to create images of child pornography from drawings or legitimate photographs. In addition, advanced encryption programs and software are now readily available and make detection even more difficult. These facts inevitably lead to the conclusion that the computer and the Internet are facilitating child pornography and changing the nature of manufacturing, distributing, and collecting it.

Unlike other forms of obscenity or pornography, child pornography laws are actively prosecuted. As noted in the U.S. Attorney General's *Report on Pornography*,[108] substantially more federal cases are prosecuted involving child pornography than for violating federal obscenity laws. The enforcement of child pornography laws is complicated by a variety of factors, including detection, distribution networks, and the definition of child pornography itself. Detecting child pornography is difficult, as those who actively possess and/or distribute the material take great pains to conceal their crimes. Many times the pornography is not discovered until after the person has been arrested for a far more serious sexual offense involving a child, at which point the child pornography is used as evidence but not likely to be prosecuted separately.

The Internet has made detection and prosecution all the more problematic. In the past, distribution networks were characterized as "cottage industries," where child pornography was exchanged between pedophiles.[109] Today, the Internet has produced what is currently being called a "global cottage industry." The formal publication and distribution was produced internationally outside the United States, and law enforcement considered the domestic production of materials under control.[110] Child pornography in the United States was described as primarily amateur photographs and videotapes being produced by pedophiles and exchanged through informal networks.[111] These conclusions must now be considered outdated given the extent and nature of law enforcement activities currently on the Internet. A secondary issue involves the definition and nature of the material itself.

Lanning and Burgess[112] identified several types of "sex rings" that were used by pedophiles to produce child pornography, victimize children, and prostitute children. Once detected, these rings involved multiple children and, on occasion, several adults. Usually participants in these rings use large hard disks, digital satellite links, cable modems, and the most current encryption technology to communicate and distribute child pornography over the Internet.[113] Agents and local law enforcement personnel go into chat rooms, news groups, and Internet relay channels assuming fictitious screen names to document and engage individuals trading in or posting child pornography.

There have been various law enforcement operations to deal with the problem of child pornography creation, distribution, and ownership internationally. Operation Cheshire Cat, a joint investigation between the Customs Service and the English

National Crime Squad, involved over 100 members of a major pedophile ring that operated in 21 countries. There are numerous state statutes involving obscenity; the test for obscenity is determined by local community standards. Operation Predator was developed as a joint investigation among Immigration and Customs Enforcement (ICE), the FBI, and other agencies to reduce the number of pedophiles operating online. This operation led to the development of the Innocent Imaged National Initiative (IINI) and the Innocent Images Unit within the FBI. Since its inception in 1995, more than 20,000 cases have been opened, with over 10,000 arrests, 6,800 convictions, and more than 5,000 deportments from the United States for foreign nationals involved in child pornography and sex crimes.[114] Additionally, the Innocent Images Unit operates in conjunction with the National Center for Missing and Exploited Children (NCMEC). This program provides training for law enforcement agencies and operates undercover operations to catch child predators online. This program also has international relationships with law enforcement agencies in 12 countries and has produced 2,000 leads related to child porn and predatory behavior.

Moving from Pornography to Molestation

The theoretical link between child pornography and child molestation has been researched and debated by several experts.[115] The evidence is mixed, though there are some revealing statistics. One survey found that of 42,000 sex offenders, 42 percent reported the use of pornography either immediately prior to or during commission of the act.[116] Although much of the research in this area is limited and of questionable methodology, the "best" research finds harmful effects of pornography exposure.[117] One field study found that between 77 percent and 87 percent of convicted child molesters used pornography to stimulate themselves, to lower the inhibitions of the child victim, or to teach the child to model the activity in real-life sexual encounters.[118] A national study found that individuals arrested for the possession of child pornography are regularly "dual offenders," in that they molest children and possess child porn. In fact, one in six cases that began with investigations or allegations of child pornography possession resulted in an offender who had also attempted to sexually victimize children.[119] Thus, there is a link between child pornography and sex offending, though it may be a correlate or risk factor than a causal factor and needs more research.[120]

A review of the current research and literature on child pornography and the link to child molestation reveals that child pornography is one of several potential facilitators in the crime of child molestation or sexual abuse.[121] We cannot determine at this point whether viewing child pornography produces the impulse to molest children initially or whether child pornography is obtained to satisfy or heighten an already present desire to sexually abuse children. Odds are that both of these statements are true to some extent. Child pornography has been found to stimulate the impulse, provide fantasies, and stimulate pedophiles.[122] Some people are particularly vulnerable to the influence of exposure to pornography, but this exposure in and of itself does not cause their sexually aberrant desires or acts.[123] Importantly, however, several research studies have found that as a group child molesters are more aroused by sexual stimuli that depict children than any other forms of pornography.[124] They use child pornography prior to and during their actual assault[125] as a stimulus and as a tool to entice children into the act.

Sexually abusing children is most commonly assumed to be a learned behavior that has important ties to the Internet and the distribution of child pornography. There are a range of user groups, Web forums, and chat rooms where individuals who are interested in developing relationships with children can identify and talk with others who share their interests.[126] These sites provide a way for pedophiles to come together to validate their sexual interests, share information about their habits, and find support for their behaviors, much like the computer hacker subculture discussed in Chapter 4. Exchanges between individuals provide information on the ways individuals become interested in relationships with children, and how to justify these behaviors. For example, online communities often use the term *child love* to refer to their attractions, rather than the term *pedophile*, which they perceive to be a derogatory and stigmatizing clinical term that does not adequately account for their behaviors.[127]

In fact, an examination by Jenkins found a subculture of child pornography exists that expresses several beliefs and concepts to its members.[128] Those involved in the exchange and consumption of child pornography communicated the dangers they face from a variety of law enforcement agencies and others along with the need for computerized tools to obfuscate and remove data from their computers. They provided information on tools to encrypt their hard drives, secure their collections of child pornography, and hide their Web searches from others. They also discussed how previous societies like feudal Japan and ancient Rome encouraged sexual relationships with children.[129] Some even argued that their interests make them a minority group that deserves legal protection, as in the NAMBLA example provided in Box 8.3. Thus, some individuals with sexual interests in children feel that there should be a social movement for child love to make their behaviors accepted.[130]

With this in mind, a noted clinical psychiatrist in testimony before Congress outlined the role that child pornography plays in the development of a pedophile.[131] Pedophiles are sexual in nature, highly addictive, compulsive and repetitive, and very difficult to treat; self-control and self-discipline do not stop them. The overwhelming majority of pedophiles use child pornography to stimulate their sexual appetites, which they masturbate to and then later use as a model for their own sexual acting out with children. Over time the use of child pornography desensitizes the viewer to its pathology; no matter how aberrant or disturbing, it becomes acceptable and preferred. Some also use it to seduce children into engaging in sexual acts with them. When they introduce it to children, the suggestion is that this is normal behavior and many other young people, like themselves, also use it and do these things. Pedophiles often trade, lend, or sell the pictures they make of young people nude and having sex through an informal

---

BOX 8.3

The North American Man/Boy Love Association (NAMBLA)

NAMBLA stands for the North American Man/Boy Love Association. They are an organization devoted to furthering what they depict as consensual relationships between men and boys. The *NAMBLA Bulletin* (first cited in 2005) describes their mission and their purpose:

"We speak out against the oppression endured by men and boys who love one another and support the right of all people to consensual intergenerational relationships. Throughout most of Western history, man/boy love has been the primary form of homoeroticism, and it is this love for which NAMBLA stands. ... We insist there is a distinction between coercive and consensual sex. Laws that focus only on the age of participants fail to capture that distinction ... Differences in age do not preclude mutual, loving interaction between persons anymore than differences in race or class ..."

_____

Source: Based on NAMBLA Website. Available at https://www.nambla.org/index.html (Last Updated on May 13, 2017); and the NAMBLA Bulletin (2005) issue 25.3 (September) 2.

network. The pedophiles use pornography during masturbation and eventually become at risk of conditioning themselves into sexual deviancy. In time the "high" obtained from masturbating to pornography becomes more important than real-life relationships. It makes no difference if one is an eminent physician, attorney, minister, athlete, corporate executive, college president, unskilled laborer, or an average 16-year-old boy. All can be self-conditioned into deviancy. The process of masturbatory conditioning is inexorable and does not spontaneously remiss. The course of this illness may be slow and is nearly always hidden from view. It is usually a secret part of the person's life, and, like a cancer, keeps growing and spreading. It rarely ever reverses itself and is very difficult to treat and heal. Denial on the part of the addict and refusal to confront the problem are typical and predictable.

The presence of child pornography creates the potential of many types of harms in the community in creating sexual predators or pedophiles and, later, their victims.[132] Eventually, the sexually addicted male may move into actual molestation, which is recorded and used for further fantasizing and reinforcement. In conclusion, pedophiles use child pornography for several reasons:

- *For personal sexual stimulation*

    Child pornography provides a powerful erotic stimulus to achieve sexual arousal, relive prior sexual acts, visualize fantasies, and focus attention during masturbatory manipulation when alone.

- *To reduce the inhibitions of the child*

    After a child's initial shock, a molester will point out that the children and adults in the pictures are enjoying their mutual sexual activities and that "lots of kids do it; pictures don't lie." The perpetrator can then convince the child that it is normal for children to be sexually active with adults, and their fears are unfounded.

- *As an instructional tool*

    Pornography is used literally as a textbook of visual instruction to educate children to perform specific sex acts.

- *For barter, trade, or sale*

    Transactions may be for money, pornographic materials, or information about how to gain sexual access to children.

- *To blackmail the child*

    "Silence is golden when a child has been abused," according to one molester. In addition to silence, a child may be required to recruit siblings or friends for the molester. Many times children are told that they will be ridiculed, disbelieved, or reprimanded by their parents and police if anyone finds out what has taken place. A pedophile knows how to put a heavy burden on the child to bear the blame if his family is broken up and he is taken away, or his parents break up, etc., if the incident ever becomes public.

The pedophile uses a combination of deception, desensitization, and psychological conditioning to lure potential child victims into a sexual molestation relationship. Before any sexual advances are made, the molester generally befriends the child through the use of rewards, such as food, toys, movies, or money. This first step of becoming close to the child is part of an elaborate nurturing process leading to a friendly and trusted relationship between the pedophile, the victim, and oftentimes the parents or guardians of the child. Once the relationship is established, the door to sexual abuse and molestation is open. Most pedophiles do not use force or intimidation, but a long-term approach, to gain the confidence of the child.

The molester has such success with children because he communicates with them at their emotional and psychological level. He plays their games, speaks their language, and even likes their toys. In the course of grooming potential victims, each pedophile develops a somewhat unique modus operandi, leaving behind valuable evidence for investigators. Often the investigation in such cases reveals that the pedophile's victims were approached in a similar way and the process leading to the abuse followed a similar pattern. Such evidence is crucial for successful prosecution of the pedophile at a later trial.

The molestation process follows a typical pattern known as the cycle of victimization. First, adult pornography is casually shown to a target child in an effort to raise the child's curiosity level and provide a sex education of sorts. The child is often surprised and bewildered by the images in men's magazines, but the molester explains that these images demonstrate that this kind of behavior is normal and acceptable.

A number of children testified before the Attorney General's Commission on Pornography that what their molester showed them was to demonstrate that this was what "all big boys and girls did." Once the molester has used adult pornography to convince the child that sex is acceptable, even enjoyable, for children, more deviant forms of pornography are introduced to further the learning process. Actual or simulated child pornography is shown to convince the child that other children regularly participate in sexual activities with adults or peers. Simulated child pornography includes pictures of youthful-looking adults dressed up and acting as children or computer-generated images of children involved in sexual activity. These images can be real or created out of the imagination of a computer user; either way they have the same devastating effect on the children who see them. Continued exposure to pornography lowers the inhibitions of the child to a point where he or she allows the molester to kiss and touch him or her sexually. Eventually, if successful, the seduction process progresses to more explicit activity between the child victim and adult or other children, using the pornography as an instructional tool.

Once the desire is initiated in the child to view pornographic materials and once the pedophile realizes that the child will not tell that he or she has seen the material, the process of molestation progresses into the next level. The child is now exposed to increasingly more graphic pornography, typically depicting children engaging in sexual acts with each other or with adults. Inevitably, questions about the acts being portrayed would arise to be readily answered by the pedophile. The pedophile would then begin to demonstrate that the sexual acts feel good and are not wrong for the child to engage in. It is often at this point that the child victim is photographed, innocently at first, but eventually progressing to nudity and sexually explicit types of pictures. The attention garnered on the victim is especially damaging if the child has needs for attention and love that are not being fulfilled by his or her family or friends. Such children are particularly vulnerable to a pedophile's advances.

CHILD MOLESTATION

According to the National Childrens Alliance, there were 206,768 child sexual abuse cases reported in 2015.[133] However, the true number of actual child sexual abuse cases is much higher. A telephone survey of 2,000 children between the ages of 10 and 16 revealed that 3.2 percent of girls and 0.6 percent of boys had suffered, at some point in their lives, sexual abuse involving physical contact. If one infers that those statistics can be generalized to the rest of the country, children have experienced (but not reported) levels of victimization that far exceed those reported.[134] Most child molesters are able to molest numerous children before they are caught and have only a 3 percent chance of being apprehended for their crimes. Statistics show that boys and girls are at nearly equal risk for abuse, and almost a quarter will be molested sometime before their eighteenth birthday; however, less than 5 percent will tell someone. The overwhelming majority of child victims are abused by someone they know, or a family member. In general, most molestations are perpetrated by adolescent males, but older pedophiles, though fewer in number, molest in greater numbers and with greater frequency.

Child molestation or exploitation can be defined as any sexual behavior or activity that is abusive or nonconsensual toward a child or a sexual behavior that is specifically prohibited by state or federal law. Various states have differing definitions and age limits in their statutory rape laws and concerning the age at which a person can voluntarily consent to sexual relations. Some states define a specific age, such as 16, to enumerate the point at which a person can voluntarily consent to sex. Others include an age-range difference, such as three years, up to a certain age where a person can consent to sex. For example, a 16-year-old could consent to sex with an 18-year-old but not anyone over the age of 19. While statutory offenses comprise a substantial portion of sexual offenses, largely unreported, the more important area concerns the molestation and exploitation of children by adults and strangers. Fondling, oral sex, simulated or actual intercourse, exhibitionism, taking sexually explicit pictures of children, showing sexually explicit material to children, or having sex in front of a child are all considered child sexual abuse. In such cases, the sexual contact is between a child who cannot voluntarily consent to sex and someone in a position of power or trust. The sexual relations are concealed by the abuser through denial, secrecy, and threats to the child. Such cases are the primary focus of this show.

In a stunning study, Abel et al.[135] recruited and interviewed 561 nonincarcerated pedophiles and child molesters. Their findings revealed the following:

- A total of 291,737 "paraphilic acts" were committed against 195,407 victims under the age of 18.
- The five most frequently reported paraphilic acts involved criminal conduct:
  - Nonincestuous child molestation with a female victim (224 of the 561 subjects reported 5,197 acts against 4,435 victims).
  - Nonincestuous child molestation with a male victim (153 of the 561 subjects reported 43,100 acts against 22,981 victims).
  - Incest with a female victim (159 of the 561 subjects reported 12,927 acts against 286 victims).
  - Incest with a male victim (44 of the 561 subjects reported 2,741 acts against 75 victims).
  - Rape (126 of the 561 subjects reported 907 acts against 882 victims).

The remaining 16 categories included a wide range of paraphilias, which may or may not have involved coercion. The first five categories included a total of 64,872 acts. The total number of subjects and victims cannot be determined since the categories are overlapping (i.e., many subjects reported multiple paraphilias and hence were recorded in multiple categories). This study and other estimates based on victimization studies and self-report crime studies paint a much darker picture of the true extent of sexual assault and child molestation in the United States.

The Problem of Child Sexual Abuse

David Finkelhor developed a four-part model that enunciates how a sex offense occurs between an offender and a child victim. He argues that each part must occur for an offense to take place.

1. *A potential offender must have some motivation to sexually abuse a child.* The potential offender must feel some form of emotional congruence with the child, sexual arousal with the child must be a potential source of gratification, and alternative sources of gratification must be unavailable or less satisfying.
2. *Any internal inhibitions against acting on the motivation to engage in sexual assault must be overcome.* For example, alcohol or drugs may be used in order to lower inhibitions against sexual offending. This may be combined with the knowledge that society often shows greater tolerance toward those who commit crimes while under the influence of substances.
3. *Any external impediments to acting on the impulse to abuse must be overcome.* Inadequate care or supervision by a parent or guardian can provide an opportunity for an offender to act.
4. *Avoidance or resistance by the child must be overcome.* This may involve enticing an emotionally deprived child into accepting inappropriate attention, or overt coercion to achieve domination of the relatively powerless child.

A voyeur or exhibitionist is motivated by a sexual desire for exhibitionist behavior toward children, perhaps as a preliminary step to approaching children or as part of some fantasy. Care or supervision by a guardian is overcome through the exhibitionist exposing themselves to children with their parents or in the presence of other children. There is little, if any, need to overcome resistance; as is often the case, the sexual stimulation comes from the reactions of the children involved. In contrast, the incest, molestation, and rape offenders achieve their goals through different mechanisms. The incest offenders are motivated by sexual desires and use the already established power relationship to offend within their own family. These offenders reduce inhibitions through alcohol or drugs frequently; in fact, most offenses between a parent or guardian and their child occur while under the influence of a substance. Additionally, incest offenders victimize children while capable guardians are out of the house, discreetly at night, or when the child is vulnerable. Resistance by the child is overcome through coercion, lying, or through extra attention, leading the child victim into submitting and even welcoming some sexual advances. However, the relationship between the offender and victim is always based on power and control, and not voluntary or consensual relations, when the victim is under the age of consent.

Offenders typically select their victims in one of two ways: preselection involving a certain type of child, or a child they know or through opportunity. Each of these types of offenders has different characteristics discussed previously. Investigators should recognize the differences between a situational child molester and a pedophile. A situational child molester is generally a socially inadequate, inhibited, and introverted individual with low self-esteem. They frequently have a substance abuse problem and will deny any involvement in the molestation. There are numerous categorizations of child molesters, but there are four generally recognized types. The first is the *regressed* child molester. This subtype usually leads the most stable life, preferring female victims. Oral and vaginal intercourse is their goal. They tend to always keep a "stable" of potential victims in various stages of seduction. The second type is the *morally indiscriminate* child molester, who frequently exhibits multiple paraphilias and a desire to experiment sexually. They frequently interact with others who share similar desires and will network in attempts to find victims. The third type is the *inadequate* child molester. Their sexual desires vary, but always revolve around a perceived inadequacy in their lives or their inability to mesh socially with other adults. These offenders can progress into serial killers, substituting child murder for the sexual aspect of their offenses. The molestation, in many cases, is driven by a need to "get even" with some perceived injustice experienced by the molester. Finally, the *sexually indiscriminate* molester does not necessarily specialize in a certain type of sex or sexual partner, but will try anything and everything. The difference between this type and the others is the gratuitous use of pornography and the high victim total when eventually apprehended. Table 8.2 depicts the differences among the four types.

Pedophiles attracted to teenage boys might have their homes decorated the way a teenage boy would. This might include toys, games, stereos, rock posters, and so on. The homes of some pedophiles have been described as shrines to children or as miniature amusement parks. In addition, virtually every pedophile has access to and a collection of child pornography. Molesters also test and desensitize children by telling dirty jokes, talking about sexual things, and engaging in nonsexual physical contact like back rubs, wrestling, hugging, and horseplay. This behavior gene-rally starts long before sexual touching and serves to normalize contact and trust.

Many molesters work just as hard to seduce and manipulate adults as they do to trick children. Most pedophiles think out, far in advance, plans and tactics to use to reduce the likelihood that a child will report the offense. Separate tactics and justifications are used to allay the fears and inquiries voiced by adults. Many have elaborate denial routines and are extremely adept at lying and convincing people that the child is mistaken or has misinterpreted the interactions. Investigators must be extremely adept at interviewing children and at working the investigation with the adult guardians, if available. A common presumption is that children will not lie or make up stories about molestation, but several cases in the recent past have demonstrated that pressure by social workers has led some children to make up stories of sexual assault. Investigators must be wary of putting words in the child's mouth and leading them to conclude that

TABLE 8.2 Characteristics of the Situational Child Molester

	Regressed	Morally Indiscriminate	Sexually Indiscriminate	Inadequate
Basic characteristics	Poor coping skills	User of people	Sexual experimentation	Social misfit
Motivation	Substitution	Why not?	Boredom	Insecurity and curiosity
Victim criteria	Availability	Vulnerability and opportunity	New and different	Nonthreatening
Method of operation	Coercion, force, younger victims	Lure, force, or manipulation	Involved in existing activity	Exploits size, advantage
Pornography collection	Possible	Sadomasochistic detective magazines	Highly likely, varied	Almost certainly, varied

Source: NCAVC. (1993). *Deviant and Criminal Sexuality, 2nd edition.* Quantico, VA: NCAVC, FBI Academy.

they were molested. A common tool is to use anatomically correct dolls to allow children to show exactly what happened. The use of these dolls and other tactics should be done only by a trained investigator familiar with the rule of evidence in these cases and the correct use of investigational tactics when dealing with children.

QUICK FACTS

The Morgan P. Hardiman Child Abduction and Serial Murder Investigative Resource Center (CASMIRC) is tasked with improving the coordination of major violent crimes against children. The center also provides onsite consultation and advice for state and local agencies as well as operational support to any police agency confronted with a child abduction, mysterious disappearance of a child, child homicide, serial murder, or expansive child molestation or child pornography case. CASMIRC is a part of the National Center for the Analysis of Violent Crime (NCAVC), a specialized department within the FBI.

PROSTITUTION AND THE SEX TRADE

One of the emerging issues surrounding sex and the Internet is the increasing use of Web sites and online resources to facilitate the sex trade. Though most prostitution occurs in the real world, the Internet has become an important resource for sex workers and their clients.[136] The Internet has revolutionized the sex trade from common streetwalkers in seedy areas of the city, to more sophisticated call girl and call boy operations featuring young adults and catering to a more fetish, hence more wealthy clientale. This is due in part to the fact that advertising and discussing the illegal sex trade online reduces the risk of detection and arrest from law enforcement. This has particular importance for escorts and prostitutes who use the Web sites as a means of advertising their services. Hundreds of escorts advertise their services across the world through Web sites, such as *Adult Friend Finder, The Erotic Review, Trans Escorts*, and *Big Doggie*.[137] These spaces allow sex workers to post pictures of themselves, describe their services and/or fetishes, and interact with clients. This has a significant benefit for sex workers as they reduce their likelihood of arrest or detection by law enforcement. Also, these Web sites allow sex workers to more carefully select their clients, travel to meet them in a more secure setting, and charge more for their services. Prostitutes or "providers" are more commonly "free lance" versus working for a pimp or organization; many work part-time while they raise their families, take care of children, and/or go to school. Unfortunately, the days of "enslavement prostitution" introduced by notorious Mafia boss Lucky Luciano[138] still exist and sadly, is usually relegated to the that seedy side of town, where drug abuse and sex trafficking go hand-in-hand.

Relatedly, the clients of prostitutes, often called "johns," have also come to rely on the Internet, because they can interact with others and discuss their experiences with prostitutes without fear of arrest or social embarrassment.[139] Individuals who pay for sex often face significant shame if they are caught and are unlikely to talk about their activities with others in person. The Internet, however, offers an opportunity for anonymous communications with others who share their interest in paid sexual encounters; a feeling of safety, security, and anonymity accompanies communication via the Web. Thus, a number of Web sites have emerged that exist only to link johns together to talk about the sex trade. However, nothing is really ever secret in the digital world, and in 2015, one of the largest prostitution/dating Web sites in the world, *Ashley Madison*, was hacked, resulting in public exposure to all clients and members. See Box 8.4.

BOX 8.4

The *Ashley Madison* Scandal

With an opening line "Life is short. Have an affair," the *Ashley Madison* Web site proudly proclaims that it is the first online dating site of its kind, started in 2001.[1] The Canadian online dating and social networking company advertises that it is a place for "discreet dating," created specifically for married men and women looking to have an extramarital affair in the most discreet way possible ... by initially connecting over the Internet and then meeting in private for a clandestine sexual rendezvous.[2] As of July 2017, the site claims over 53 million worldwide members and offers a guarantee package that customers will find the perfect affair partner. The service is available in multiple languages and across the world.

In July 2015, the site was hacked by a group known only as the "Impact Team." Customer records, including profiles of all customers' secret sexual fantasies and fetishes, and matching credit card transactions, real names and addresses and e-mails were stolen. A subsequent threat to the owners of the Web site, Avid Life Media (ALM), demanded that the *Ashley Madison* Web site (as well as a companion site, *Established Men*) be taken down, claiming fraud and deceit to customers. Failure to disband these two sites would result in the public exposure of all customer records. After repeated warnings by the Impact Team and defiance on the part of ALM, the databank on customer profiles and transactions (9.7 gigabytes in size) was released on the Tor Network, or Dark Web. The file included detailed information on some 32 million users of the *Ashley Madison* Web site, with a searchable feature by name and/or e-mail address available on the Dark Web as well as the more conventional Internet. Anyone could access the data dump and receive information on anyone ever using the supposed "secure" and "discreet" site.

The resulting chaos was worldwide, with members suffering public embarrassment as well as divorce, civil litigation and termination from their employment when office e-mail addresses were used; some 15,000 e-mail addresses were .mil or .gov addresses.[3] More interesting, an investigation by Annalee Newitz suggests that a relatively small percentage of the supposed 37 million members were actually real women; most of the female profiles were fake, and more than half of the company's revenue was developed from thousands of female "bots" that sent male users millions of fake messages, giving the <u>illusion</u> of a real woman seeking a clandestine sexual affair.[4] Thus, the vast majority of the men using the Web site were actually being sexually stimulated by fake conversations promising torrid and fetish-laden affairs by a computer "fembot" program; only 19 percent of the men using the site actually engaged in a conversation with a real woman.[5] Based on increased governmental scrutiny and the development of civil litigation for fraudulent business practices, the chief executive officer of ALM, Noel Biderman, stepped down and the parent company ALM rebranded itself as the Ruby Corporation.

Today (July 1, 2017), the now-infamous *Ashley Madison* site is still very active, claiming new members from the publicity ... and a more secure database!

The following screen shot is a copy of the data released by the Impact Team:

```
TIME's UP!
```

Avid Life Media has failed to take down Ashley Madison and Established Men.
We have explained the fraud, deceit, and stupidity of ALM and their members.
Now everyone gets to see their data.

Find someone you know in here? Keep in mind the site is a scam with thousands
of fake female profiles. See ashley madison fake profile lawsuit; 90-95% of
actual users are male. Chances are your man signed up on the world's biggest
affair site, but never had one. He just tried to. If that distinction matters.

Find yourself in here? It was ALM that failed you and lied to you. Prosecute
them and claim damages. Then move on with your life. Learn your lesson and make
amends. Embarrassing now, but you'll get over it.

Any data not signed with key 6E50 3F39 BA6A EAAD D81D ECFF 2437 3CD5 74AB AA38
is fake.

Impact Team's statement on the release
Impact Team's PGP signature for the released statement
Impact Team's PGP Key
Torrent for the released data

Back to Quantum Magazine

The above Impact Team's Statement of Release is widely available on the Internet. This one can be found at https://www.wired.com/2015/08/happened-hackers -posted-stolen-ashley-madison-data/#slide-1

Sources: [1] See *https://www.ashleymadison.com/*
[2] *Ibid.*

[3] ZETTER, K., "Hackers Finally Post Stolen Ashely Madison Data," Wired (August 18, 2015). Available at *https://www .wired.com/2015/08/happened-hackers-posted-stolen -ashley-madison-data/*
[4] Annalee, N., "How Ashley Madison Hid Its Fembot Con to Users and Investigators," *Gizmodo* (September 8, 2015). Available at http://gizmodo.com/how-ashley-madison-hid-its -fembot-con-from-users-and-in-1728410265
[5] *Ibid.*

The discussions on prostitution Web sites regularly revolve around reviews of street prostitutes, escorts who advertise online, strip club workers, and other sex workers. Their reviews regularly address the sexual acts they engage in, the location where the sex act occurred, and the relative safety of the place, as well as costs for services.[140] Johns also elaborated on sexual encounters with escorts in their posts, complete with physical descriptions of the prostitutes, their attitudes, and any critiques about their performance during the act. The reviews can be extremely detailed, including use of condoms during sex acts and the johns' beliefs about the sex worker's cleanliness.[141] For example, the following is a post from a forum for individuals in Chicago, Illinois, that provides a review of two escorts who advertise online:

NOT AS ADVERTISED AND MAJOR UP-SELL

I had a bad experience with Eros under "Chicago GFE Escorts." I guess it's another reminder to RTFF and only go with recommended contacts.

I do NOT recommend Nikki. She was significantly overweight compared to the pictures, and the person who showed up wasn't anything close to the girl pictured. I let myself get carried away with her major up-sell pitch. Another reminder to stay cool headed.

I do NOT recommend, Aspen. It may have been the same person pictured a while ago, but as of now she seemed strung out and anxious to pay the rent. She confided that the last guy she went to sent her packing because she "wasn't what he expected." I can see why.

"Escort" is an overstatement for these women.

These accounts also provide some insight into the characteristics johns seek in prostitutes, noting "girlfriend experiences" (GFE) as the ideal. GFE occur whenever the woman is enthusiastic about the sex act and makes the john feel special, as though they were in a "consensual noncommercial relationship."[142] The following post provides a review of an online escort who provided such an experience for the john:

After about an hour of email replies we finally agreed [and] negotiated on the phone for 400 and funny part about it is I tried to get cash on ATM and damn machine spitted out only 320 just my bad luck.

Went to her place what I saw was a heaven sent angel. 20 yrs old definitely non pro, with a small ass and great tits. Probably one of those girls just needed money for shopping. She lives with her parents I was a bit paranoid I'm sure her parents doesn't know she does this. And of course parents are at work!

Anyway here's the climax of the story. I apologized to her that we agreed on the price that my atm only spitted out 320 and she said u don't have to pay me 400 just give me a hundred I thought I had died and went to heaven.

> This girl was such a beauty she gave me [oral sex] for about 2 minutes while I was ... caressing her smooth skin of course total gfe. Foreplay went for about 5 minutes got so damn horny started with the missionary with my damn bad luck came in probably less than 3 ... minutes. Gave her some excuses that I haven't done it in months. lol ... she said it was ok and even asked me if I wanted to relax for a few minutes and try it again. stupid me just told her no its ok just got cleaned up went home.
>
> I asked her how I can get hold of her again she said just send her email since she kept calling me on a block number. I'm planning to send her email again tomorrow since its pay day and I'll ask her if she will agree on giving out her email and I'll share this heaven sent.

In turn, johns give higher reviews and recommend sex workers who can provide GFE. As a whole, the quality, quantity, and detailed information provided by johns through forums may increase prostitution rates by facilitating sex work. In fair turn-around, at least one Web site, *The Exotic Review* allows "providers" (prostitutes) to rate and review the "client" (johns). The provider can make comments about how well the client tips, what the client looks like, or what the client desires (e.g., oral sex, anal sex, vaginal sex), or any other details relating to the johns' particular fetish. The following is an online review of a john by a provider:

> He is 50-60 year old, a heavy drinker, and is overweight, but he dresses nice and is meticulously clean. Shaved crotch and junk. He likes the top and gets a little too carried away in pure BDSM (Bondage, Domination and Sado-Masocistic) play ... try to tease him more ... he likes it ... he likes anal ... .so get your ass ready cuz he will want to pound it ... Afterwards, he likes to take a shower with you, not a bath. Nice guy ... I've been with him several times in Phoenix ... .he always gives me a crisp $100 bill as a tip.

Massage Parlors

Just as there are Web sites that relate specific information about prostitutes, there are Web sites that rate and give reviews on massage parlors worldwide. Several of these sites, again, comment on not only the quality of the experience with the individual provider, but also the relative safety and security of the massage parlor location. Several of these sites provide location for travelers seeking massage parlor experiences, such as *EroticMP* and *Rubmaps* (advertising "where fantasy meets reality"), while others cater to a specific type of fetish or audience, such as *Masseurfinder* (advertising gay-friendly massage therapy worldwide—at home or on the road), *Aampmaps* (Asian apartment massage parlors), or *HungAngels* (advertised as a worldwide club and party guide for trannys, Tgirls, shemales, transsexuals, and ladyboys). The Web site provides a map as well as a photo of the commercial establishment. In some cases, the instructions are very specific indicating where to park (including if space is available for RVs or 18-wheel rigs), what to ask for on entering the business, and of course, which providers to request by name. Extensive reviews of providers within specific massage parlors are presented on each site. Several sites, such as *Rubmaps*, provide a drop down menu that explains the extensive use of codes and slang used in the sex trade industry. For instance, BB:bareback=without condum; kitty:vagina (B:Bald=clean shaven; PS:Partly Shaved=landing strip; T:Trimmed=manicured; N:Natural=unshaved); P2P:privates to privates (typically uncovered, rubbing of penis with vagina without penetration); PN:Pearl Necklace (penis rubbing between breasts or oral sex, with ejaculation around the neck); MILF:mothers I'd like to f*ck (referring to older, yet attractive women); and PSE:Porn Star Experience (meaning almost any type of sexual fetish with enthusiasm). As identified by American criminologist, Albert Cohen in 1955, the extensive use of codes and slang bring meaning to the concept of a deviant subculture, relatively isolated from mainstream society.[143]

In most cases, the massage parlors are fronts for open prostitution. Providers render "HJE:hand jobs to ejaculation" for a specific price during the massage, or barter for additional money for other sexual activities, including sexual intercourse and/or fetish desires. The Web sites also provide a valuable service to legitimate massage businesses, indicating which locations render "therapeutic" versus "erotic" massage. For the most part, the massage parlors of today represent the historic brothels of the past, where prostitutes often work and live in the same location. The providers usually work for a specific wages and can keep their tips, however, the money is often collected at a central point and the "management" takes a healthy cut (usually 60% or more) of the fee for location and advertising expenses. In the worst cases, the massage parlors are involved in human trafficking where young girls and boys from Asia and South America are sent to work in trade for being smuggled into the United States. In several cities, massage parlors featuring Russian, Chinese, Japanese, and/or Korean providers are controlled and operated by organized crime cartels from those countries.

Pornography and Webcams

Not surprisingly, the Internet is littered with thousands of adult pornography sites; many of which serve a worldwide audience desiring every sexual fantasy and fetish imaginable. For instance, there are sites that focus on traditional gender choices, such as straight, gay, lesbian, transsexual, and solo experiences; but also a number that devote considerable time through the development of filters to gain just the right act with just the right type of individuals. For instance, on several sites, you can filter for such things as "Dominating Asian transsexuals that engage in oral sex with a 'facial' ending on a blonde female." The filters provide an endless array of viewing desires aimed at marketing directly to the client's sexual desires or fetishes.

There is a mix of sites that charge monthly viewing privileges on a recurring credit card, or are completely free, and supported by advertisements. Most of the advertisements are from prostitution/online dating boards, or the introduction of new sex products or sex games. Most of the sites in the United States are legitimate businesses that are associated with the greater adult video/movie industry, located in Los Angeles where 60–70 percent of all U.S. porn movies are shot. Estimates of the adult pornography business is somewhat sketchy as owners are reluctant to provide financial details. However, 2015 estimates approach $100 billion globally, with about $10–$12 billion of that coming from the United States.[144] Revenues from porn videos and films has been shrinking for the past several year, primarily because of new webcam sites that now take away from profit margins within the industry. Then too, the sale of sex novelties and toys, once a staple within the pornography industry has become much more mainstream, with novelties, toys, dolls, lotions and the like being sold on the mainstream market place via Amazon and ebay. Items arrive at your door, discreetly packaged in a brown box with only your name on the outside.

The new porn services on the Internet today are via webcams that stream live and taped sex shows from around the world. Sites like cams.com, cam4.com, jasmin.com, and rabbits cams.com allow viewers to enter private chat rooms with performers that conduct a variety of sex acts for tokens. For most of the sites, entering the chat rooms or viewing rooms are free, however, performers are paid in tokens that are purchased separately. Tokens range from 25 cents to $5.00 per token, with vast majority at

10 cents per token. Performers require payment in tokens for specific sex acts. Again, performers are matched through filters for specific interests, desires, and/or fetishes. At most sites, you can choose an individual female, male or transsexual, or a couple, or a group of individuals and pay according to the sex act that you want to see or desire. You simply pay with tokens for the action. Most sites are governed by strict rules of conduct on the part of the viewer as they use the chat board; for instance, use of profanity or vulgarity, or rudeness can cancel your membership. As an interesting side note, many of the shows are taped and then resold for tokens at a later date, or when the performer is not available.

The performer supplies their own computer, Web service and camera, often of high resolution, and the Web site owner provides advertising, access, and financial and accounting systems that allow the performer a high degree of autonomy. Some performers conduct their business from their own home (even dorm rooms have been used in the past) by simply logging-in and being available for viewers. As client viewers pay tokens to the performer(s), accounting is provided by the Web site and revenues are split on an agreed upon ratio, or a set amount (commission) is paid to the Web site by the performer, usually 35 percent. Viewers can choose from a variety of experiences:

- Free chat: Viewers chat and meet the performer online and discuss sexual acts; and in some cases, these acts are performed in quick, teasing manner as to induce the viewer to use tokens or move to a private chat room.
- Private chat: This is a pay chat or activity where the customer has exclusive access to the webcam performer. No one else can see what acts are performed or can interfer with the show by asking for other activities.
- Nude/performing chat: Customers pay on a per minute basis with tokens, or multiple viewers watch as a performer conducts a specific sex act. Multiple viewers can tip for extra activities by the performer, and in some cases, can even chat with other viewers.

The pay for performers can be quite substantial, with many claiming to make as much as $100,000 per month depending on the time one is willing to be "in front of the camera" and is willing to perform various sexual acts. In many cases, those making the most money appeal to the prurient interests of individuals seeking fetish excitement. A 2013 article indicates that the average webcam girl makes about $300–$1,000 per day for work lasting anywhere from a couple of hours to five hours per day.[145] Webcam services report that the most desired and requested services involve live amateurs broadcasting from home. While webcam performers enjoy relative safety from their online venue, there is a hidden risk; performers have no legal rights to their performance and/or the filming of their performance. Once a show is filmed, it may remain in the digital world forever, becoming the element of embarrassment or extortion and blackmail well into the future.

One of the largest and fastest growing webcam sites in the world is chaturbate. com; an abridged name meaning the act of masturbating while chatting online. The Web service allows the viewer to select the webcam by region: North American Cams, Euro Russian Cams, Philippines Cams, Asian Cams, South American Cams, and Other Region Cams. Further, the site appears to be broadcast in 15 languages, from Arabic and English to Spanish, French, Dutch, Russian, Chinese, and more. Webcams are also segregated by age, ranging from teen cams (18–20 years) to mature cams (50 years and older), as well as segregation by female, male, couple and transsexual groupings. As an interesting side feature, chaturbate also has a unique feature to broadcast yourself to the performer, and/or to upload your own video audition for consideration; acceptance is rewarded with free tokens. Webcam services have not been immune to fraud and hacking attacks themselves. In 2017, a series of "token generators" were launched on the open Web in an effort to make tokens usable on chaturbate. Most of the software hacks were failures, however, various scams and hacks primarily aimed at gaining free tokens are still available throughout the Web.[146] While these attempts do not reach the same sophistication as the *Ashley Madison* hack in 2015, they still pose a significant risk for the Web service.

Online Dating Fraud

Clearly, the Internet has significantly changed the legitimate art of dating in our time. Large and sophisticated dating Web sites such as *eHarmony*, *Zoosk*, *Match.com*, *Tinder*, and *Christian Mingle*, allow mainly single adults to legitimately meet for purposes of seeking a relationship. Sexual habits and fetishes are rarely discussed on these Web sites, and money is not exchanged between providers and clients for sexual acts. Individuals meet for coffee, dinner, or a date in order to talk and discuss their commonalities to further their relationship, and almost all of these Web sites proudly advertise their successes in marriages that have developed between people that originally met via their Web site. However, as with almost all any other type of online business, the dating experience can be fraught with fraud and financial loss. Box 8.5 discusses the online dating scams (ODS), and how often older, lonely individuals are exploited under the pretense of a dating relationship.

BOX 8.5

Online Dating Scams (ODS)

By Elena V. Garrett

The *Online Dating Scam* (ODS) also referred to as Internet Romance Scam (IRS) is a type of online fraud in which individuals or organized criminal groups engage Internet users in online communication under the pretense of initiating a dating relationship. The scam unfolds in the form of frequent e-mail and phone interactions between the *"bait"* (played by a scam perpetrator using a carefully constructed persona of an attractive, yet lonely person (usually female) looking for a long-term relationship) and the intended victim—the *"target."* During the course of the correspondence, the scam perpetrators utilize various deceptive claims to solicit money or items of value from their victims.[1] An ODS usually combines elements of phishing and the Nigerian 419 advanced fee scam, both discussed earlier in *Chapter 6* of the book. The victim of an ODS initially encounters a phishing e-mail or an online personal ad featuring the bait. If the victim is tempted by the phishing e-mail to enter into correspondence, the perpetrators then proceed with setting up a scenario in which

the target is asked to help the young women to overcome some obstacles preventing a personal meeting in real life. Although the bait in the scam is usually presented as a picture of an attractive looking woman, the true lure used by the perpetrators is the promise of sexual and emotional fulfillment with a romantic partner committed to long-term relationship, including marriage. These types of fraud are significantly different than those criminal activities that solicit prostitution or sexual tourism in that the real intent of the perpetrator is not to provide an illegal activity—prostitution, but rather to lure the victim into a much more sophisticated relationship in order to defraud the victim of money. No sexual service is ever provided in an online dating scam.

The name "dating fraud" is an umbrella term that can describe several different scenarios that use the pretense of a romantic relationship to trick Internet users into losing money. Among the possible scenarios are medical assistance scams and package reshipment scams that often originate from Nigeria and Ghana, extortion scams, and so-called "gold-digger" scams that often originate from the Philippines. Again, refer to Chapter 6.

However, a large percentage of dating frauds feature scenarios where the "bait" in the scam purportedly prepares to travel to meet the victim in real life, and travel expenses become the reason for money solicitation.[2] These scams are often operated by small independent criminal networks in Russia and Nigeria and closely resemble advanced fee scams. Commonly described features of this type of dating fraud are (1) the use of phishing techniques and mass mailing tools to identify potential victims, (2) a long grooming process that creates an intense intimate connection between the bait and the victim, and (3) reliance on complex, multistep travel scenarios that involve authority figures such as travel agents, doctors, Customs officers, and attorneys to create an illusion of legitimacy for the money requests.

Stages of the Scam. Both Russian and Nigerian ODS are relatively long in duration and undergo a fairly standard set of development stages.[3]

- **Stage 1: Phishing for victims (targeting):** To be successful in making a profit off their efforts continuously, the online dating scam perpetrators need to locate possible victims and approach those victims in a way that would not evoke suspicion. ODS is a crime of persuasion, and the scammers can only persuade those Internet users who are willing to engage in a fairly prolonged correspondence. Hence, the process of "baiting" the victim is highlighted in a number of online methodologies: (1) Pictures of physically attractive "baits" are placed on dating sites.[4] Internet users who respond to these fake profiles become the targets of the scam; (2) Targeting specific victims via electronic databases of users that have been victimized or involved in other scams can be purchased from underground marketplaces.[5] Alternatively, trip wires can be set up on dating sites to collect real-time information about site visitors. Those perpetrators lacking the skills to use spam e-mail lists can simply select a certain number of profiles on the dating sites of their choice and initiate the first contact online;[6] (3) Social network spamming using popular social networks, such as Facebook, LinkedIn, and Twitter, can become targets of the scam;[7] and (4) untargeted spamming involves using various databases of e-mail addresses that can be purchased via underground marketplaces. Very often those databases are stolen from large online sites.[8] Once their e-mail addresses are selected, the unsuspecting targets receive an e-mail message inviting them to a conversation, usually accompanied by an attractive picture of their prospective pen pal.[9] The goal of the scammer at this stage is, first, to reach as many Internet users as possible, and, second, to solicit a response to their "phishing" e-mail or spam.

- **Stage 2: Grooming the victim:** Those victims who respond to the initial e-mail inviting them to a conversation become the primary focus of the scammer's attention. They start to receive frequent communications from their new pen pal in form of e-mails and instant messages. During this stage, the scammers attempt to establish their credibility by presenting the "bait" as a person of strong moral values and good personal history.[10] Establishing a close personal bond with the victim is the main objective of the second phase of the scam. This bond is established through daily e-mails that repeatedly emphasize that the target is a very special person who is loved, understood, and appreciated, making the target psychologically "dependent" on the e-mail correspondence for a daily dose of "feel-good" emotions.[11] This stage of the scam usually culminates in the bait's "confession" of strong romantic attraction to the target, and her intense desire to meet the target in person.

- **Stage 3: The test:** As soon as the conversation turns to the subject of a potential meeting between the target and the bait, the scammer presents the victim with a request for assistance requiring a fairly small amount of money to help cover travel costs, such as visa, tickets, travel insurance, and travel agency fees.[12] If the victim responds positively, he is provided with the instructions on how to transfer the money to the bait. This initial request often mentions only a small amount of money and is used to "test" the target's commitment to the relationship.

- **Stage 4: Escalation of money requests:** If the target responds positively by sending the requested amount, additional requests for urgent monetary assistance quickly follow, often depicting a series of dramatic events such as encounters with robbers, arrests for failure to declare an item of value, legal problems with Customs officials, or issues with bank officials.[13] In cases of dating scams of Russian origin, the scammers often cite nonexistent laws and regulations (such as Customs regulations and international travel requirements) that Internet users not familiar with the Russian legal system often find plausible.[14] This phase continues for as long as the victim is willing to send financial assistance to the bait.

- **Stage 5: Revelation:** As the victim's monetary losses and psychological fatigue begin to accumulate, they become more and more dissatisfied with the correspondence. Failure to respond to continuous requests for financial assistance leads to increased negativity in communication, reduced frequency of contact, and eventual loss of contact.[15] Often the victim seeks out confirmation of their suspicions about the bait's identity and intentions online, or through contacting law enforcement authorities, the embassy, or the dating site itself.

Sadly, because of the extensive monetary and emotional investment into the relationship, many of the victims report feelings of shame, betrayal, and humiliation, making them reluctant to reveal their victimization to others, particularly police agencies.[16] Thus, these types of crimes often go unreported with average losses of several thousand dollars. In the United States, a 2015 report by the Internet Crime Complaint Center (IC3), a partnership between the Federal Bureau of Investigation (FBI) and the White Collar Crime Center (WC3), indicated that the agency received over 12,500 reports about dating scams that year, with a total loss amount of over $203 million, ranking second, only to business e-mail compromise as the highest form of Internet fraud loss.[17]

Based on Exploring internet users' vulnerability to online dating fraud: Analysis of routine activities theory factors (Elena Victorovna Garrett)

Sources: [1]Rege, A. (2009). "What's Love Got to Do with It? Exploring Online Dating Scams and Identity Fraud." *International Journal of Cyber Criminology* 3(2): 494–512. Retrieved from *http://www.cybercrimejournal.com/AunshulIJCCJuly2009 .pdf* and Whitty, M.T. (2013). "The Scammers Persuasive Techniques Model: Development of a Stage Model to Explain the Online Dating Romance Scam." *British Journal of Criminology* 53(4): 665–684. doi:10.1093/bjc/azt009

[2]IC3. (2012). *IC3 2012 Internet Crime Report* (pp. 1–43). Retrieved from *http://www.ic3.gov/media/annualreport/2012_IC3Report. pdf* and Foxworth, D. (2013). "Looking for Love? Beware of Online Dating Scams." *The Federal Bureau of Investigations (FBI)*. San Diego, CA: Federal Bureau of Investigation. Retrieved

from *http://www.fbi.gov/sandiego/press-releases/2013/looking -for-love-beware-of-online-dating-scams*

[3]Rege A. (2009) and Whitty, M.T. (2013).

[4]*Ibid.*

[5]Whitty, "The Scammers Persuasive Techniques Model."

[6]Longe, O.B., Mbarika, V., Kourouma, M., Wada, F., and Isabalija, R. (2009). "Seeing Beyond the Surface: Understanding and Tracking Fraudulent Cyber Activities." *International Journal of Computer Science and Information Security* 6(3): 124–135. Retrieved from *http://arxiv.org/ftp/arxiv/ papers/1001/1001.1993.pdf*

[7]Hasib, A.Al. (2009). "Threats of Online Social Networks." *International Journal of Computer Science and Network Security* 9(11): 288–293.

[8]Abad, C. (2005). "The Economy of Phishing: A Survey of the Operations of the Phishing Market." *First Monday* 10(9). doi:dx.doi.org/10.5210/fm.v10i9.1272

[9]Whitty, M.T. (2013). "Anatomy of the online dating romance scam." *Security Journal* (February 11), 1–13. doi:10.1057/ sj.2012.57

[10]Koon, T. H. and Yoong, D. (2013). Preying on Lonely Hearts: A Systematic Deconstruction of an Internet Romance Scammer's Online Lover Persona. *Journal of Modern Languages, 23*, 28–40

[11]*Ibid.*, See also Rege A. (2009) and Whitty, M.T. (2013), op cit.

[12]Rege, A. (2009)

[13]See Rege, A. (2009) and Steward, W. (2008, March 28). Scamski City, Where Online "Russian Brides" Turn Out to be Mafia Conmen | Mail Online. *Daily Mail*. Retrieved from *http://www.dailymail.co.uk/femail/article-542276/Scamski -city-online-Russian-brides-turn-Mafia-conmen.html*

[14]Steward, W. (2008, March 28).

[15]Whitty, M.T. and Buchanan, T. (2012). "The Online Romance Scam: A Serious Cybercrime." *Cyberpsychology, Behavior, and Social Networking* 15(3): 181–183. doi:10.1089/ cyber.2011.0352

[16]*Ibid.*

[17]IC3. (2015). *IC3 2015 Internet Crime Report*. Retrieved from *https://pdf.ic3.gov/2015_IC3Report.pdf*

Sex Tourism

Another facet of the sex trade is *sex tourism*, which is a loosely defined practice that encompasses several sexually related practices, some legal in certain countries and some illegal. In many instances, visitors to foreign countries utilize legal brothels and other sexually oriented businesses that are illegal in their home country. In other instances, the visitors use services that are illegal in both countries. Finally, a growing practice is for typically wealthy Westerners to travel specifically to certain countries to procure sexual services of adolescents or to be set up with children for sexual purposes. In sum, sex tourism is the practice of men (there are virtually no known cases of women engaging in this practice) from Western countries visiting developing or third world nations for the purpose of engaging in sexual activity that is illegal in their home country or that they do not want to be discovered committing in their home country. Often, the sexual desires of these tourists are for adolescents, for children, or for a paraphilic or strange sexual encounter. Sex tourism has been growing over the last several decades, with the highest prevalence occurring in Southeast Asian countries, particularly those with long histories of sexually oriented businesses.

A report by the International Labor Organization found that 1.39 million people are forced into commercial sexual exploitation, and up to 50 percent of these individuals are children.[147] United Nations Children's Fund (UNICEF) also offers staggering statistics on this problem:

- Approximately 21 million people are trafficked worldwide annually, with an estimated $32 billion in estimated profits.
- 5.5 million children are trafficked each year for the purposes of prostitution, pornography, sex tourism, and forced marriages
- 12,000 children in Nepal are trafficked for commercial sexual exploitation to brothels in Nepal, India, and other countries.
- There are between 28,000 and 30,000 children under the age of 18 who are used in prostitution in South Africa.
- There are at least 244,000 women and children who are part of the commercial sexual exploitation trade in the United States.
- There are between 400,000 and 500,000 child prostitutes in India.
- Debt bondage—paying off loans given to their parents or guardians—is often the reason young girls enter prostitution in India, Nepal, Myanmar, Pakistan, and Thailand.[148]

The sex trade in many countries involves young boys who are offered to European, American, and Asian tourists, sometimes as part of vacation packages. Estimates are that 20,000–30,000 of Sri Lanka's child prostitutes are boys who are "rented" to tourist pedophiles. Several other countries are known for tolerating an active sex trade of young boys, including the Dominican Republican, Haiti, Egypt, Morocco, and Tunisia.[149] It is important to note that children are also forced into commercial exploitation in the United States.

Recent research attempted to account for the ways that children are forced into the sex trade. This study found that pimps scout bus stations, malls, and other locations looking for girls who appear to be runaways seeking help.[150] The pimps then attempt to befriend them and give them gifts and food in exchange for sex. As the pimps develop a relationship with the girl, they convince her to engage in sexual acts for money with other men. They may also threaten or blackmail the girl into sex. In some countries, contractual relationships are developed between traffickers and parents, where the child's earnings are given back to the parent in small amounts. Children may also be given drugs or forced into isolation as a means of keeping them from running away or trying to get out of the trade.

The growth of sexual tourism is often attributed to a Western military presence that has increased the demand for sex workers and sexually oriented businesses. However, recent research shows that many other factors contribute to the sex tourism practice and industry. The sex tourism industry has become an important source of income for many nations, supporting weak economies and aiding in putting money in the hands of governmental officials and law enforcement officials. Thus, eliminating the industry is difficult without the cooperation of the countries where the tourists travel. Without international agreement and implementation of certain standards dictating the way these businesses are owned and operated, it is unlikely that a change in practice will occur. Nonetheless, several attempts have been made in recent years to change the way that the world views the practice of sexual tourism. Both the United States and the European Union have passed laws making it illegal for citizens to make use of these types of services when underage children are involved. In the future, the elimination of the child sex tourism industry as well as increased awareness and care for adult sex workers who are forced into this line of work need to be addressed.

In the UNICEF Study, of the 160 pedophiles and sex tourists arrested, 25 percent were American, 18 percent German, 14 percent Australian, 12 percent British, and 6 percent French. Estimates of the number of children involved in the worldwide sex trade vary. The UNICEF contends that one million children at any one given time are involved in prostitution in Asia alone. End Child Prostitution in Asian Tourism (ECPAT) assesses the value of the prostitution industry to be $5 billion. These appraisals, whether completely accurate or, at least, reflective of educated guesses, bespeak the extent that children are actually affected by sex tourism.[151] Estimates of child prostitutes in South Asia, which are difficult to come by, place the number for Bangladesh at 10,000; India, 400,000–500,000; Pakistan, 40,000; and Sri Lanka, 30,000.[152]

It has been suggested that men are more likely to travel to an Asian nation because they do not speak the same language and therefore all human attributes are obliterated to hide the identity of the girl. Because there can be no verbal communication, the customer does not have to explore the girl's past or even know her name.[153] This situation allows for a completely confidential exchange in which the consumer gets what he paid for and has no connection to the encounter once it is complete.

The Internet is a primary facilitator of the sex tourism industry.[154] It allows for quick and easy access to a number of different destinations and options at a range of prices. These excursions are usually offered in packages in which the men can travel for a desired period of time. For example, in India these trips can be as short as 24–48 hours, during which time sex tourists can experience sexual encounters with a number of different women.[155] In 2015, Philippine Adventure Tours (PAT) of California advertised their tourist package on the Internet. For $1,645, tourists would receive roundtrip airfare, hotel accommodations, and a guided tour of bars where they could purchase sex from prostitutes who were working in bars as entertainers.[156] The Internet allows for men freely to search available destinations and to make choices based on desire and the potential for pleasure. The Internet contributes to the tourism industry and the hidden identity of sex workers through its display of women and children as toys and entertainment. The most dangerous type of person who may retrieve this type of information from the Internet includes pedophiles, who want nothing more than to use and exploit children to fulfill their sexual fantasies and desires.

Although little research exists on how tourists find their way to these hotels and brothels abroad, clearly the Internet has led to an explosion of interest in this area. The process typically begins with the viewing or exchanging of pornography on the World Wide Web, via newsgroups or via ftps and file exchange software. Many sex offenders and pedophiles report on sex rings or clubs that they have encountered on the Internet. The clubs routinely trade pornography. Some also provide services in the way of information and the procurement of sex workers for interested parties willing to pay for their visits. The exchange of information revolves around known hotels where sexual services can be obtained, bars or nightclubs where contacts can be made, or sex clubs and brothels where these people can go for services. The process a sex tourist goes through to be trusted by the club or ring prior to gaining the information they need is unclear. In some cases, the sex club or brothel will advertise in the newsgroups, via e-mail, or even posted directly to the Web (deviant sexual services and sex with children are not commonly advertised or posted). There are reports that child sex rings are shuffling children between pedophiles for sex in these countries and even in the United States. The price for admission to the club or sex ring is often photographs of the potential member engaged in a sexual act with the children.

The Process of Sex Tourism

The sex tourist encounter is rather typical. The sex tourist is usually male, most likely from Europe or North America. Some of the perpetrators are pedophiles, but most are "respectable" doctors, lawyers, servicemen, and teachers—many with children of their own.[157] Sex tourists are generally divided into two groups: preferential abusers and situational abusers. Preferential abusers, the pedophiles, have clear and definite sexual preferences for children, while situational abusers generally have not planned to have commercial sex while abroad, but took the opportunity when it presented itself. Most of these perpetrators tell themselves that there is no abuse or harm occurring to the child because the child has actively "chosen" that "profession." They also assume that because the child has "chosen" prostitution, the child consents to and ultimately benefits from sexual relations with adults, and that commercial sex is a way to help children out of poverty. Many of these perpetrators believe that the victims are inferior people and thus they have little problem with or remorse about exploiting them.

The tour can be self-initiated by the sex tourist with the aid of the Internet and sales brochures. It is common that many of them will hear about certain hotels or bars where such services can be procured, usually through word of mouth or via the Internet. Other tourists utilize the services of a procurer or facilitator. Procurers and facilitators are simply the pimps who provide the services, capital, and resources that make sexual trafficking of children both a feasible and lucrative industry. Some of the procurers are former child prostitutes who "climbed the ranks" within the industry.[158] Facilitators, while often not directly involved in the child prostitution transaction itself, expedite the victimization process. The facilitator might be a recruiter, a parent who sells his or her child into prostitution, a landlord or motel owner who permits the activity to occur on his or her property, or a sex tour travel agent. Transporters also move children throughout a region, importing and exporting them in order to facilitate the sex trade. These sex tour travel agents publish brochures and guides that cater to sex tourists. The brochures emphasize the youth of prostitutes at these advertised destinations. Recent surveys reveal that there were over 25 businesses in the United States that offered and arranged sex tours.[159]

Thailand, the Philippines, Sri Lanka, and Taiwan are the countries traditionally connected with child sex tourism, and all have serious child prostitution problems. Prostitution of a massive nature involving children originated in Thailand and the Philippines in the late 1960s, during the Vietnam War. In Thailand, Burmese women and girls as young as 13 are illegally trafficked across the border by recruiters and sold to brothel owners. In the Philippines, many children are tricked into prostitution after their parents sell them to recruiters with the promise of legitimate work in the city.

> **QUICK FACTS:**
>
> The United States prohibits all forms of human trafficking in persons:
>
> - **The Trafficking Victims Protection Act of 2000 (TVPA):** The act, along with its 2003, 2005, 2008, and 2013 reauthorizations, is the first comprehensive federal legislation to combat human trafficking and to assist trafficking victims. Under the TVPA, human trafficking has occurred if a person was induced to perform labor or a commercial sex act through force, fraud, or coercion. Any person under age 18 who performs a commercial sex act is considered a victim of human trafficking, regardless of whether force, fraud or coercion was present.
> - **The USA Protect Act of 2003:** The act has several parts, but most germane to the discussion of human trafficking, child pornography and child exploitation, the act prohibits drawings, sculptures, and pictures of such drawings and sculptures depicting minors in actions or situations that are sexual in content are considered obscene. While the law does not explicitly state that images of fictional beings who appear to be under 18 engaged in sexual acts that are not deemed to be obscene are rendered illegal in and of their own condition (illustration of sex of fictional minors). The act also addresses the issue of sex tourism, and makes it a felony for U.S. citizens or residents who engage in illicit sexual conduct abroad. For the purposes of this law, illicit sexual conduct is defined as commercial sex with or sexual abuse of anyone under 18, or any sex with anyone under 16 in any country.

The Philippine government has calculated the number of child prostitutes in the Philippines at 50,000.[160] During the late 1970s to today, pedophiles from Europe and North America have found a Shangri-La for sexual activity with minors in Thailand and the Philippines. More than half of the sex tourists overall are pedophiles, and approximately one-third of them are North American or European.[161]

Currently, tourist agencies actively campaign to entice travelers to visit their countries for sex with "young women." Although agents running these tourist organizations deny that child prostitutes are involved, investigations by reporters illustrate that is untrue. For example, Russell Herman, a U.S. citizen, ran a sex tourism business online from Thailand.[162] He ran a Web site offering to facilitate tours where he would introduce customers to young women between the ages of 18 and 24. ICE agents conducted an undercover investigation and arranged for a tour from Herman, which involved traveling to four brothels containing young women between the ages of 12 and 17. These women were prostitutes, many of whom were illegally brought into Thailand and, in some cases, padlocked inside the brothels. Herman was arrested and pleaded guilty to charges of sex tourism in a U.S. court. Some agencies go as far as to compose travel guides delineating the laws of countries patrons visit and explain how prosecution for sex tourism in those countries is avoidable. Patrons' willingness to travel to engage in sexual activity with children clearly shows that the child sex industry will continue to thrive, especially if ignored.[163]

As growing international attention has increased public awareness of the prevalence and dangers associated with sex tourism, prosecution against sex tourists and owners of such establishments have also become more prevalent. Many of the recent cases that have been successfully prosecuted have been against older men who engage in child sex tourism. For example, in 1996, Michael Clark, a British citizen, was convicted of inducing child prostitution and sentenced to over 16 years in prison. Clark organized sex tours and provided minor children for the pleasure of sex tourists in the Philippine cities of Olongapo and Angeles. The Philippine court also ruled him to be deported after serving his sentence, and he has been barred from ever returning to the Philippines.[164]

In another case, a businessman of Dallas, Texas, was convicted of having traveled out of the country to engage in sexual conduct with minors. Nicholas Bredimus traveled to Thailand where he sought the companionship of young girls and boys, photographed himself engaged in sexual conduct with the children, and took explicit photos of young boys. Bredimus was sentenced to six and a half years in prison, a $30,000 fine, and three years of supervised release following his sentence, during which time his access to children and the Internet was closely monitored.[165] The author had the opportunity to interview Mr. Bredimus prior to his sentencing for these crimes and can offer the following description of the offense.

Mr. Bredimus was a well-known and well-liked software designer and airline consultant in the Dallas area. The details of his background in sex offenses and how he obtained the knowledge of the sex tourism industry are still sketchy. However, he was able to arrange several visits to Thailand, where he obtained sexual services through a procurer. Mr. Bredimus also obtained fake passports, which he used to leave the country from a vacation in Hawaii. On the particular trip that he was convicted for, he left Hawaii, traveled to Japan, and then to Thailand. Once in Thailand, he made his way to a border town (on the border with Burma) called Mae Sai, where he arranged for his procurer to rent two adjacent hotel rooms and then asked that young boys aged 10–15 be brought to one of the rooms.

The procurer met with a bellman at another hotel known to be a sex tourist location and helped the procurer round up six boys aged 11–14. Each of the boys was paid approximately $22 for their services. He systematically examined each of the boys, rejecting one of them for having a deformed toe, and each boy was ordered to shower prior to being led into the room that Bredimus occupied. In his room, he had set up his laptop and a digital video camera and had a still digital camera with him. Each boy was led in systematically and ordered to undress. Mr. Bredimus was in his underwear and proceeded to molest the boys while filming each encounter with the video camera on the tripod and taking pictures with the camera. The level of sexual assault increased over the course of the event, with Bredimus eventually inserting his finger into the anus of one of the boys who cried out in anguish. One of the boys left the hotel and alerted the police that a Westerner was in the hotel molesting young boys. The Thai police knocked on the door and eventually had to force their way into the room. They stopped Mr. Bredimus as he was attempting to erase the images on the camera and video camera. The Thai police seized his equipment and arrested him. He was able to bond out for $13,000; incredibly, the Thai police returned his laptop to him, as they were unable to crack the password on the computer.

Mr. Bredimus fled the country with another phony passport, eventually returning to Hawaii. The case would never have come to light had it not been for the work of Fight Against Child Exploitation (FACE), a Thai-based organization that alerted U.S. officials to the crimes. American law enforcement officials then went to Thailand to interview the police and victims, and eventually brought charges against Mr. Bredimus in the U.S. District Court in Dallas. This case is one of the first in the United States where a child sex tourist has been successfully sent to prison. It also demonstrates the extraordinary difficulty in dealing with crimes such as these that occur abroad. Box 8.6 presents the emotional story of child sex trafficking in Cambodia.

BOX 8.6

The Tragedy of Child Sex Trafficking

By Robert W. Taylor

Years ago, I worked with the International Justice Mission on a $1 million grant from the U.S. Department of State to combat human trafficking in Southeast Asia. The grant was a direct response from then-Secretary Colin Powell to address the growing problems of human trafficking and sex tourism involving the United States. Human trafficking is defined as the recruitment, transportation, transfer, harboring or receipt of persons, by means of the threat or use of force or other forms of coercion, of abduction, of fraud, of deception, etc. for the purpose of exploitation. Simply put, human trafficking is "modern-day slavery." These actions become particularly heinous when they involve the exploitation of children for sexual purposes, such as forced prostitution or forced participation in pornographic acts.

The explosion of activity on the Internet during the past two decades has seen a similar rise in sex tourism. Highly clandestine Internet sites provide men with everything they need to travel to foreign countries to engage in sexual activity with children. The "client" books airline and lodging expenses online. They select from a smorgasbord of sexual activities or proclivities involving children in various locations. For instance, a person books a trip to Southeast Asia, with forays into Thailand, Cambodia, and the Philippines. The trip begins in Los Angeles with a first-class ticket to Bangkok. Here the client is met by the "travel agent," who inquires about the following evening's "date." From photographs, the client selects several adolescent girls who will perform "yum-yum" or oral sex on him. The client spends three days and four nights in Bangkok, visiting the ancient capital by day and enjoying the accompaniment of a young girl by night. The client moves on to Phnom Penh (Cambodia) and is greeted again by the agent, who has arranged an evening with young girls and young boys for sexual purposes. Finally, in the Philippines, the client is "treated" to an evening with a young virgin girl of 8 years old. The price for the entire trip, including day guides to historical and ancient sites and evening sexual activity, is built into a lump-sum price.

Three U.S. Dollars

Working undercover for the International Justice Mission (IJM) in Cambodia, in the midst of a horrible area called Svey Pak, I met a beautiful 12-year-old girl named "Ping." The area is quite famous for sex tourism among pedophiles and is about 11 kilometers outside Phnom Penh. I had been asked by the Royal Cambodian Police to visit a brothel in the area and attempt to gain access to tunnels that connected several suspected brothels harboring young Vietnamese girls. Although I hadn't worked undercover as a cop for years, I thought I was up to the challenge, especially since the police chief indicated that I would be physically much bigger than all the other people in the house, and that most likely, there would be no men in the house since the entire sex trade is ran by women (madams). No guns had been found in the houses raided in the past, and I thought I could do the work … one's ego is so seductive, isn't it?

The house was quite open, with a wide gate that protected the front door. Stepping onto the porch, it was easy to see young girls sitting on couches and in chairs watching TV. Before even knocking, I was greeted by a pleasant looking woman, asking in broken English, "You want girl tonight?" I nodded and she opened the rusty, iron gate letting me enter the brightly lit room. I had envisioned something totaling different. I had thought that the rooms would be dimly lit and the girls would be scantily clad, similar to a strip bar in the U.S. How wrong I was to think that prostitution in the United States would mimic the more-ugly trade of child sex trafficking in Cambodia and Southeast Asia! The clang of the gate locking behind me startled my senses … it was clear I was somewhere else … and not in the U.S. Yet, there was virtually nothing in the room that even hinted of danger. Quite the contrary, several young girls sat giggling at each other on the couch while eating rice. Another two played dominoes on a nearby table. All were dressed quite nicely and even conservatively to a point. Turning back to the madam, several of the girls from the couch raced over to me, grabbing my legs and rubbing my back, pulling me to the open couch. With one girl on each side and several straddling in front of me, they all began to clammer about sex. "You want short time (immediate sex on the premises), we go to my bed now?" Another whispered in my ear, "Choose me, I do it in the butt!" And yet another, rubbed my inner thigh and smiled, "You take me, please, I treat you nice!"

It is hard to express my feelings. It was so different than undercover vice work in the States. There were no seedy backrooms, no burnt out street whores, no guns, no drugs, no perceived danger … just a room filled with little girls. It was so odd, so strange, to see young girls acting like grown-ups … wearing thick make-up and <u>wanting</u> to have sex! The oldest girls were no more than

15 and most were only about 12 years old. My heart ached as I stared into the big beautiful eyes of one little girl standing in front of me. "I am Ping … I not ready yet, but I give best yum-yum." She was so cute, so dainty, so typical Asian, long straight black hair with bangs, big smile and white teeth, and a little awkward with long arms and legs that she hadn't really grown into yet. She reminded me of my own daughter.

I smiled and said "I like Ping … you are very cute!" Suddenly she was pulling me off the couch leaving the room to visit her private area in the back. It was dark there, and I yearned for the glare of the front room as we walked down the hall. Just about to enter her room, we were stopped by the madam that demanded money.

"You give me money, U.S., yum-yum only, ten dolla," she cried, burping rice between her choppy English

"No, too high … I only give you one dollar, U.S."

"OK … five dolla"

"No, still too high … two dollars"

"OK, OK … 3!" The deal was done. It was that simple, I had just bought a twelve-year old girl for oral sex for three U.S. dollars!

I reached into my pocket and gave her three crinkles dollars from my jeans. She grabbed them in a rush and the tiny hand from Ping was around my waist as she whispered, "You still like Ping … you give Ping dolla too?" as she opened the door to a closet-size room with one cot and a small table, and a red and yellow scarf covering a dimly lit lamp shade.

Ping grabbed at my belt … "You sit here … I give you yum-yum."

"No, let's slow down and let's just talk for a while," as I gently took her hands from my belt and sat her next to me on the cot.

"Is this your room?"

"Oh yes, you like?"

"Very nice," I answered softly, not knowing really what to expect. She opened the panel door of her closet wide to reveal a life-size poster of Britney Spears singing in concert somewhere in the U.S. It was a very old poster, but Ping glowed with pride, "You like … she is my favorite … you like?" "Ping someday going to sing and dance in America!"

That's when it all hit me … the tears started to well in my eyes as I realized that little Ping was just like any other twelve-year old in the U.S. … except she was about to give a fifty-somthing-year old man yum-yum for three dollars! I could feel the emotion rise in my chest as my throat tightened. "What's wrong?" Ping cried.

"Nothing, nothing at all, but I do not want yum-yum. Let's just talk for a while."

Just Like Me!

I was to learn that Ping was indeed twelve years old and that her home was in Vietnam. She had gone to the "missionary school" and learned some English. She had walked across the border to work in a bar in Phnom Penh the previous month, wanting only to find work for food. She was a virgin and was going to make "big money" when she "became broken." She softly smiled, shyly saying, "Cuz, once Ping broken, she no good anymore." How sad, I thought, as I listened to the story of a young, beautiful girl that in many ways, reminded me so much of my own daughter, so enamored with life and the future. The value of virginity from the mouth of a babe that had nothing, wanted nothing, and could only give what she could give … her simple little body, not yet even developed to hold life. She had not yet developed breasts but stuffed a training bra with tissue paper to make her look more appealing. "American men like big boobies!" she laughed.

Ping and I became good friends over the course of several days. She guided me through the sex trade in Phnom Penh and I paid for her lunches and dinners. I was always amazed at how much she could eat! She was never paid by the madam, but only given a safe place to sleep and eat, only one meal a day—usually a bowl of rice with some fish. Her money was made from tips from her clients. She told me that she tried to keep in touch with her mother in Saigon, but it was hard because she was always trying to work. She said she was always hungry, and that she feared for her other six brothers and sisters that were younger than her. She tried to save money for them … but there wasn't enough most of the time. She was ashamed of her failure to take care of her little brothers and sisters. How sad, she was only a child herself. Ping described most of her clients as older, white men … well dressed Europeans (Dutch and Germans) and Americans … just like me!

Ping showed me the entire Svey Pak area, taking me many times to the underground tunnels that connected several houses. The Cambodian National Police were right … .the human trafficking operation took girls from Vietnam and held them in the underground tunnels for sexual slavery. It was the first time I had really seen what most people would have called "hell." Dark, cramped dirt tunnels with out-dwellings where children often slept; dimly lit by candles and the stench of human waste occasionally breaking through the strange aroma of incense and strong perfume. It met every detail of the horrors that

I expected, including one room where I witnessed the empty shackles hanging from an iron bed. "That's were bad girls go," said Ping, it usually meant where girls that tried to runaway were locked at night. I didn't ask any more questions about that room because it noticeably upset Ping to even be near it.

Based on information derived from Ping, the Cambodian National Police were able to close-down several brothels and arrest the madams in the Svey Pak area. I often wonder, how long they the madams were actually in jail, and how long the brothels were actually closed. A few days later, I was ready to return to the U.S.

On the last day I was with Ping, I gave her every last dollar I had. I told her to be careful, and to try and go back to her mother in Saigon or visit a safe house operated by IJM, but I knew she would not listen. The sad truth is that she had nowhere else to go . . . no real home and most importantly, no food. She worked in the brothels for food . . . a concept we Americans simply cannot understand. Cambodia is a horribly poor country. It was the first time I had seen a child actually fight with a dog in a garbage heap for food. Poverty and disease is everywhere and the painful symptoms of child prostitution and human trafficking only characterize the dismal fate of those souls caught in its clutches.

"You come back tomorrow and see Ping."

"OK, we meet again at the same place."

"Maybe Ping come to America . . . to the city with the big bridge! Madam say I go maybe next year to America."

"OK . . . see you tomorrow!"

But it was different this time, our stares lingered for just a moment, we knew it was over and that our friendship would go no further. I turned and walked away, choking my tears on every step I took. Just turn the corner, I kept telling myself . . . don't look back. But I couldn't, I needed just one final glance to see little Ping standing a half block away waving good-bye with those beautiful, sparkling eyes, wide smile, and . . . tears in her eyes!

Difficult Questions About a Forgotten World

It has been several years since my work in Cambodia, and I still think of Ping. She would be about eighteen years old now. . . .surely not a virgin anymore! Her life is so different than that of my daughter going to college, or of yours as you sit in a classroom reading this text. Remember Ping, understand that her story could have been told thousands upon thousands of time all over Southeast Asia, Africa, and Latin America . . . the Third World . . . the other world . . . the often forgotten world of poverty, disease, and pain; where everything is for sale!

ISSUES IN THE INVESTIGATION OF INTERNET EXPLOITATION, CYBERSTALKING, AND OBSCENITY

Numerous challenges and obstacles exist to effectively enforcing and prosecuting these types of cybercrimes. First, there are numerous, and overlapping, law enforcement initiatives that target them. There is already a problem: Overlapping effort, overlapping jurisdictions, and a general lack of funding and priority dedicated to such crimes are pronounced. Second, the cybercriminal of today is elusive, largely anonymous, and often likely to be operating in a jurisdiction outside of the United States. Finally, there are several evidentiary issues and problems in the prosecution of these crimes that make it more difficult to gain a conviction.

Law Enforcement Initiatives

The primary federal agencies that have been combating this type of crime are the FBI, the ICE, the Postal Inspection Service, the Department of Justice's Child Exploitation and Obscenity Section (CEOS), and the NCMEC.[166] As discussed earlier, the FBI initiated Innocent Images, which is a proactive, intelligence-driven, multiagency investigative initiative. It serves as the clearinghouse and coordinating body for all FBI investigations that involve child exploitation or child pornography and has led to thousands of arrests. As mentioned earlier, ICE also formed and runs Operation Predator, which develops leads about and receives and coordinates undercover operations against international child pornography and child sexual exploitation rings.

The NCMEC produced a Cyber Tipline for leads about child sexual exploitation.[167] Mandated by Congress, the Cyber Tipline allows individuals to report online (and via a toll-free number) incidents of child luring, molestation, pornography, sex tourism, and prostitution. Since March 1998, the Cyber Tipline has received over 500,000 reports of child exploitation and pornography.[168] The Postal Inspection Service has conducted thousands of cases related to child exploitation, molestation, and pornography. Its investigations of child molesters reveal that these offenders are using computers increasingly, along with the mail, to find potential victims, to communicate with other criminals, and to locate sources of child pornography. In fact, 95 percent of all the Postal Inspection Service's child exploitation cases involved both computers and physical mail.[169] The undercover operations include the placement of contact advertisements in sexually oriented publications, written contact and correspondence with subjects of investigations, development of confidential sources, and, more recently, undercover contact with suspects via the Internet.

The CEOS of the Justice Department has taken an active role in training federal prosecutors to handle child crime cases that were once mainly handled by local jurisdictions. The section has sponsored several training seminars for federal prosecutors on the issues of child pornography, exploitation, trafficking, and sex tourism. In addition to these operations, many law enforcement agencies of the federal government have begun to seek partnerships with corporations and local law enforcement to target cybercrime. These partnerships are frequently called electronic crime task forces, and seek to coordinate efforts and eliminate overlap.

Overlapping Jurisdictions and Duplication of Effort

The government currently has numerous operations dedicated to child pornography and additional units and operations targeting obscenity in general.[170] As is the case with other areas of law enforcement, a problem exists with overlapping jurisdictional boundaries and duplication of effort between agencies. Two examples cited in a recent report on cybercrime highlight the problems of overlapping effort:[171]

> Some state and local law enforcement agencies also have been frustrated by jurisdictional limitations. In many instances, the cyberstalker may be located in a different city or state than the victim, making it more difficult (and, in some cases, all but impossible) for the local authority to investigate the incident. Even if a law enforcement agency is willing to pursue a case across state lines, it may be difficult to obtain assistance from out-of-state agencies when the conduct is limited to harassing e-mail messages and no actual violence has occurred. A number of matters have been referred to the FBI and/or U.S. Attorney's offices because the victim and suspect were located in different states and the local agency was not able to pursue the investigation.

Cybercriminals can cross national or international boundaries at will via a computer, and information and property can be easily transmitted through communications and data networks. As a result, law enforcement agencies are forced to try to work with local officials, foreign governments, and other agencies of the federal government—something that they have been quite reluctant to do in the past. As one report noted, a law enforcement official could secure a search warrant for a computer in the United States and, as a result of the search, remotely access a computer in Canada, which irrespective of the warrant is potentially a crime in Canada. Furthermore, certain cybercrimes that are illegal in this country are perfectly legal in other countries (i.e., gambling, prostitution, and underage sexual relations). As a result, Congress has passed some laws that make certain offenses a crime regardless of whether they are legal in the host country. Additionally, the ICE agency has developed relationships with foreign law enforcement agencies through Operation Predator, including Australia, Denmark, Finland, Japan, the Netherlands, Liechtenstein, New Zealand, Norway, Sweden, Switzerland, and the United Kingdom. These relationships have led to the arrest of more than 1,900 individuals worldwide.[172]

Identification of Suspects

We all tend to enjoy the feeling of anonymity that the Internet provides, allowing us to conduct business and communicate without fear of "somebody listening" to our personal communications. Individuals who actively collect pornographic materials share information and resources on methods to hide or minimize the likelihood of detection. Several Web services offer free anonymous e-mail and Web accounts along with proxy tools that hide the actual location of a computer. Further, it is quite difficult to trace some communications over the Net, especially with the availability of access on numerous college campuses and Internet cafes. Many criminals assume the identity of someone else to conduct their online crimes, such as theft of e-mail addresses and hacking into someone else's computer to conduct business (making that computer a zombie). Another service provided by some ISPs are mail servers that purposefully strip identifying information and transport headers from electronic mail. By forwarding mails through several of these services serially, cybercriminals can make the message almost completely anonymous. The sending of anonymous communications is thus relatively easy for the criminal and makes it difficult for law enforcement to identify the suspect responsible for the crime.

Issues with Evidence and Detection

The problems of evidentiary collection and analysis are fully discussed in Chapters 12 and 13; however, a few problems in this area deserve mention. As you are aware, computer data are easily destroyed, deleted, or modified. The discussion of the morphing of images and the purposeful alteration of material has already reached the Supreme Court. Furthermore, the technical capability to collect, preserve, and analyze such evidence is not widely distributed in the law enforcement community. Finally, the fact that people can use their computers to conduct both lawful and unlawful activities or to store both contraband and legally possessed material presents another significant issue.[173] Termed *commingling,* one computer can be used in multiple fashion, by multiple users, and be connected to multiple other machines. As such, investigations would naturally have to cross boundaries, invade computers that were not necessarily involved in the criminal act, and involve people who might be upset at the intrusiveness of the investigation.

Enforcement of the laws against child pornography often leads law enforcement officials to use sting operations over the Internet to catch pedophiles and find child pornography. As such, issues of entrapment have been raised by civil rights groups. In one case, postal inspectors posed as an organization that dealt in sexual freedom and hedonism. They seized several mail lists of individuals in raids of pornography distributors. Then they sent out a sexual attitude questionnaire and a membership application to people on the mail list. The suspect completed and mailed in the sexual survey with his membership fee, noting that he would like to receive additional material and that he was interested in sexual depictions of preteenagers. He was then mailed another survey and a list of "pen pals" who shared his sexual interests. The suspect began corresponding with one of these pen pals, an undercover postal inspector. Over a period of 27 months, the suspect received "two sexual attitude surveys, seven letters measuring his appetite for child pornography, and two sex catalogues."[174] He was assured in the mailings that the materials were completely legal. Over the course of the investigation, he corresponded eight times with the inspectors and eventually ordered the magazine "Boys Who Love Boys" from a Postal Service catalogue and a set of sexually explicit photographs of young boys from a Customs Service brochure. Upon verifying that the man had received the magazine, postal inspectors searched his home, found the illicit magazine, and arrested him for receiving it through the mail in violation of federal law. At trial, the man raised two defenses. First, he argued that he had been entrapped as a matter of law, but the court found sufficient evidence of predisposition to submit the issue to the jury. Second, he asserted that the government's conduct was outrageous, thus violating his due process rights. The jury rejected his defenses and found him guilty of knowingly receiving through the mail sexually explicit material depicting a minor. He appealed his conviction to the Eighth Circuit, which affirmed the trial court, holding that the government's actions did not constitute entrapment or outrageous governmental conduct, despite the government's lack of reasonable suspicion to target the man as a predisposed consumer.[175]

Summary

This chapter reviewed the nature and dynamics of exploitation, stalking, and obscenity on the World Wide Web. A variety of victimizations can occur online, many that are similar to their real-world counterparts. In particular, the nature of the victimizations included threats, obscene comments and intimations, and exposure to obscene and threatening materials, including pictures and other media. Most often, children and women are the primary targets of those who would commit cyberstalking and exploitation over the Internet. Young people report relatively high rates of victimization while online, and many youths report exposure to sexually oriented and obscene material that they did not wish to view. Most commonly, white males between the ages of 18 and 35 make up the majority of the offenders. Similar to most criminal victimizations, the victim and the offender had some type of prior relationship before the stalking or exploitation occurred. However, the percentage of stranger-on-stranger victimizations online was higher. Children are most commonly victimized online through unwanted exposure to sexually related material, sexual solicitations and approaches, harassment,

bullying, and other distressing incidents. The rates of these types of offenses are larger than most people would think. Children rarely report such incidents to their parents or other authorities.

The U.S. Supreme Court has had the opportunity to hear several cases regarding cybercrime laws. Many of the same issues involving noncybercrimes are being heard by the court. Many of the laws were overturned for being too vague and sweeping with too broad of a stroke. The federal government has responded with the passage of new laws and refinements of the old laws in an attempt to regulate and control content on the Internet, particularly the access of children to objectionable content. These types of crimes also present unique difficulties for law enforcement, including lack of expertise, lack of resources, and difficulty in tracking and prosecuting offenders. Cyberspace offers greater anonymity for offenders and permits offending to cross-state and international boundaries, making prosecution increasingly difficult. In the future, local law enforcement agencies are likely to see increased reports of cyber-related cases of stalking, exploitation, and exposure to unwanted materials.

Review Questions

1. What are the various types of exploitation that can occur over the Internet?
2. What are the characteristics of the typical victims of Internet exploitation crimes?
3. What are the characteristics of the typical perpetrators of Internet exploitation crimes?
4. How common is it to become the victim of an Internet-involved crime in the area of exploitation or stalking?
5. What is cyberbullying, and how is it different from real-world bullying?
6. What is cyberstalking?
7. What types of offenses can occur that could be defined as cyberstalking?
8. What are the primary types or categories of stalkers?
9. What are the primary federal laws that target Internet exploitation?
10. What are the major Supreme Court cases on cyberexploitation?
11. How prevalent is child pornography on the Internet?
12. How do pedophiles and other child exploiters use the Internet to commit their crimes?
13. What role does child pornography play in child molestation?
14. How has the Internet changed the landscape of prostitution and the sex trade?
15. What is sex tourism?
16. What are the roles of the various law enforcement agencies in the area of cyberexploitation?
17. What are the primary challenges that law enforcement agencies face in investigating cyberexploitation?

Critical Thinking Exercises

1. The mission of the Violent Crimes Against Children (VCAC) program within the FBI is to provide a rapid, proactive, and comprehensive capacity to counter all threats of abuse and exploitation of children. There is also an international task force working together to formulate and deliver a dynamic global response to crimes against children Visit their Web site at: https://www.fbi.gov/investigate/violent-crime/cac. What are the most common destinations for child sex tourism? What problems do you see confronting the task of investigating and prosecuting child sex tourism in foreign countries?

2. The AMBER Alert Program is a voluntary partnership between law enforcement agencies, state transportation officials and radio, television, and Internet broadcasters to activate an urgent news bulletin in child abduction cases. Research the Amber Alert Program. How does the AMBER Alert Program work, and how effective do you think the program is in rescuing an abducted child?

Endnotes

1. Office for Victims of Crime. (2001). *Internet Crimes Against Children*. Washington, D.C.: U.S. Department of Justice.
2. The estimated number of children prostituted in the United States has been a highly controversial topic. See Rachel Swaner, Melissa Labriola, Michael Rempel, Allyson Walker and Joseph Spadafore, *Youth Involvement in the Sex Trade: A National Study* (June 2016), U.S. Department of Justice, Document Numbr 249952; Ernie Allen, *Domestic Minor Sex Trafficking*, Testimony of Ernie Allen, National Center for Missing and Exploited Children for the Subcommittee on Crime, Terrorism and Homeland Security, Committee on the Judiciary, U.S. House of Representative, September 15, 2010; and Youth Advocate Program International. (1998). "Children for Sale: Youth Involved in Prostitution, Pornography and Sex Trafficking." *Youth Advocate Program International Report Vol. 3, No. 2, Summer.* Available at *http://www.yapi.org*
3. Office for Victims of Crime, *Internet Crimes Against Children*.
4. FINKELHOR, D., MITCHELL, K.J., and WOLAK, J. (2000). *Online Victimization: A Report on the Nation's Youth*. Washington, D.C.: National Center for Missing and Exploited Children; WOLAK, J., MITCHELL, K., and DAVID F. (2006). *Online Victimization of Youth: Five Years Later*. Washington D.C.: National Center for Missing and Exploited Children.
5. *Ibid.*
6. See NetNanny website at: *https://www.netnanny.com/?pid=21*
7. FINKELHOR, *Ibid.*
8. WOLACK, J., MITCHELL, K., and FINKELHOR, D. (2006). Online Victimization of Youth: Five Years Later. Washington, D.C.: National Center for Missing & Exploited Children.
9. *Ibid.*

10. HOLT, T.J. and BOSSLER, A.M. (2009). "Examining the Applicability of Lifestyle-Routine Activities Theory for Cybercrime Victimization." *Deviant Behavior* 30(1): 1–25.

11. *http://www.ncpc.org/newsroom/current-campaigns /cyberbullying*

12. HINDJUA, S. and PATCHIN, J.W. (2009). *Bullying Beyond the Schoolyard: Preventing and Responding to Cyberbullying.* New York: Corwin Press.

13. *Ibid.*

14. *Ibid.*, p. 13.

15. *Ibid.*, p. 14.

16. *Ibid.*

17. *Ibid.*

18. Office of Victims of Crime. (2002). *Strengthening Anti-Stalking Laws.* Washington, D.C.: National Institute of Justice. NCJ 189192.

19. *Ibid.*

20. *Ibid.*

21. *Ibid.*

22. Under California law, a person commits stalking if he or she "willfully, maliciously, and repeatedly follows or harasses another person and … makes a credible threat with the intent to place that person in reasonable fear for his or her safety, or the safety of his or her immediate family." The term "credible threat" includes "that performed through the use of an electronic communication device, or a threat implied by a pattern of conduct or a combination of verbal, written, or electronically communicated statements." "Electronic communication device" includes "telephones, cellular phones, computers, video recorders, fax machines, or pagers." Office of Victims of Crime, *Strengthening Anti-Stalking Laws.*

23. HOLT and BOSSLER, "Examining the Applicability of Lifestyle-Routine Activities Theory for Cybercrime Victimization," p. 12.

24. FINN, J. (2004). "A Survey of Online Harassment at a University Campus." *Journal of Interpersonal Violence* 19(4): 468–483.

25. *Ibid.*, p. 12.

26. BAUM, K., CATALANO, S., RAND, M., and ROSE, K. (2009). *Stalking Victimization in the United States.* Washington, D.C.: National Institute of Justice.

27. *Ibid.*

28. ZONA, M.A., PALAREA, R.E., and LANE, J.C. (1998). "Psychiatric Diagnosis and the Offender–Victim Typology of Stalking." In J.R. MELOY (ed.), *The Psychology of Stalking: Clinical and Forensic Perspectives.* San Diego, CA: Academic Press.

29. Office of Victims of Crime. (2002). *National Victim Assistance Academy.* Washington, D.C.: Office of Justice Programs. Available at *http://www.ojp.usdoj.gov/ovc/assist /nvaa2002/chapter22_2sup.html*

30. PETHERICK, W. (2003). *Cyber-Stalking: Obsessional Pursuit and the Digital Criminal.* Court TV Crime Library. Available at *http://www.crimelibrary.com/criminal_mind /psychology/cyberstalking/1.html*

31. *Ibid.*, p. 21.

32. *Ibid.*, p. 33.

33. *http://www.mcafee.com/anti-virus/parents/contributors.asp*

34. Attorney General to the Vice President. (1999). *1999 Report on Cyberstalking: A New Challenge for Law Enforcement and Industry.* Available at *http://www.usdoj.gov/criminal /cybercrime/cyberstalking.htm*

35. POLHAMUS, A. (2016), "Woman, 70, gets life sentence for cyberstalking, report says." *NJ.Com* (February 16). Available at *http://www.nj.com/news/index.ssf/2016/02/woman_70 _gets_life_sentence_for_cyberstalking_repo.html*

36. TJADEN, P. and THEONNES, N. (1998). *Stalking in America: Findings from the National Violence Against Women Survey.* Washington, D.C.: U.S. Department of Justice, National Institute of Justice; Office of Victims of Crime, *National Victim Assistance Academy.*

37. *Ibid.*

38. *Ibid.*

39. D'OVIDO, R. and DOYLE, J. (2003). "A Study on Cyberstalking: Understanding Investigative Hurdles." FBI Law Enforcement Bulletin 10-17.

40. See, for example, ZONA, M.A., SHARMA, K.K., and LANE, M.D. (1993). "A Comparative Study of Erotomanic and Obsessional Subjects in a Forensic Sample." *Journal of Forensic Sciences* 38: 894–903; GEBERTH, V.J. (October 1992). "Stalkers." *Law and Order*, pp. 138–143; WRIGHT, J.A., BURGESS, A.G., BURGESS, A.W., LASZLO, A.T., MCCRARY, G.O., and DOUGLAS, J.E. (1996). "A Typology of Interpersonal Stalking." *Journal of Interpersonal Violence* 11(4): 487–503; ZONA, PALAREA, and LANE, "Psychiatric Diagnosis and the Offender–Victim Typology of Stalking"; MULLEN, P.E. (1997). "Erotomanias: (Pathologies of Love) and Stalking." *Directions in Mental Health Counselling* 7(3): 3–15; PETHERICK, *Cyber-Stalking*; Office of Victims of Crime, *National Victim Assistance Academy.*

41. Office of Victims of Crime, *National Victim Assistance Academy.*

42. *Ibid.*

43. Attorney General to the Vice President, *1999 Report on Cyberstalking.*

44. *Ibid.*

45. *Ibid.*

46. 18 U.S.C. 875(c).

47. U.S.C. 223.

48. 18 U.S.C. 2261A.

49. CATHCART, R. (2008). "MySpace Is Said to Draw Subpoena in Hoax Case." *The New York Times.*

50. SURDIN, A. (2009). "In Several States, A Push to Stem Cyber-Bullying." *The Washington Post.* See *http://www .washingtonpost.com/wp-dyn/content/article/2008/12/31 /AR2008123103067.html*

51. Computer Crime and Intellectual Property Section (CCIPS). (2000). *The Electronic Frontier: The Unlawful Conduct Involving the Use of the Internet: A Report of the President's Working Group on Unlawful Conduct on the Internet.* Washington, D.C.: Department of Justice. Available at *http://www.usdoj.gov/criminal/cybercrime/unlawful.htm*

52. Attorney General to the Vice President, *1999 Report on Cyberstalking.*

53. *Miller* v. *California,* 413 U.S. 15, held that (1) obscene material was not protected by the First Amendment; (2) the proper First Amendment standards to be applied by the states in determining whether particular material was obscene and subject to regulation, were (a) whether the average person, applying contemporary community standards, would find that the work, taken as a whole, appealed to the prurient interest, (b) whether the work depicted or described, in a patently offensive way, sexual conduct specifically defined by the applicable state law, as written or authoritatively construed, and (c) whether the work, taken as a whole, lacked serious literary, artistic, political, or scientific value; (3) there was no requirement that the material must be shown to be "utterly without redeeming social value"; (4) the requirement that state law, as written or construed, must specifically define the sexual conduct as to which depiction or description was proscribed, provided fair notice as to what public and commercial activities would bring prosecution; and (5) obscenity was to be determined by applying "contemporary community standards," not "national standards"—there thus having been no constitutional error in instructing the jury in the instant case to apply state community standards.

54. Public Law 105-314: The Child Protection and Sexual Predator Punishment Act of 1998, October 30, 1998.

55. (Child Abuse Act), 18 U.S.C. 2423(b).

56. 18 U.S.C. § 2423(b) Travel with intent to engage in illicit sexual conduct. A person who travels in interstate commerce or travels into the United States, or a United States citizen or an alien admitted for permanent residence in the United States who travels in foreign commerce, for the purpose of engaging in any illicit sexual conduct with another person shall be fined under this title or imprisoned not more than 30 years, or both. (c) Engaging in illicit sexual conduct in foreign places. Any United States citizen or alien admitted for permanent residence who travels in foreign commerce, and engages in any illicit sexual conduct with another person shall be fined under this title or imprisoned not more than 30 years, or both.

57. 18 U.S.C. § 2260.

58. Title 18 Part I, Chapter 110, Section 2252.

59. Child Pornography Prevention Act 18 U.S.C. § 2252A.
    (a) Any person who
        (1) knowingly mails, or transports or ships in interstate or foreign commerce by any means, including by computer, any child pornography;
        (2) knowingly receives or distributes
            (A) any child pornography that has been mailed, or shipped or transported in interstate or foreign commerce by any means, including by computer; or
            (B) any material that contains child pornography that has been mailed, or shipped or transported in interstate or foreign commerce by any means, including by computer;
        (3) knowingly reproduces any child pornography for distribution through the mails, or in interstate or foreign commerce by any means, including by computer;
        (4) either

    (A) in the special maritime and territorial jurisdiction of the United States, or on any land or building owned by, leased to, or otherwise used by or under the control of the United States Government, or in the Indian country, knowingly sells or possesses with the intent to sell any child pornography; or
    (B) knowingly sells or possesses with the intent to sell any child pornography that has been mailed, or shipped or transported in interstate or foreign commerce by any means, including by computer, or that was produced using materials that have been mailed, or shipped or transported in interstate or foreign commerce by any means, including by computer; or

    (5) either
        (A) in the special maritime and territorial jurisdiction of the United States, or on any land or building owned by, leased to, or otherwise used by or under the control of the United States Government, or in the Indian country, knowingly possesses any book, magazine, periodical, film, videotape, computer disk, or any other material that contains an image of child pornography; or
        (B) knowingly possesses any book, magazine, periodical, film, videotape, computer disk, or any other material that contains an image of child pornography that has been mailed, or shipped or transported in interstate or foreign commerce by any means, including by computer, or that was produced using materials that have been mailed, or shipped or transported in interstate or foreign commerce by any means, including by computer, shall be punished as provided in subsection (b).

    (1) Whoever violates, or attempts or conspires to violate, paragraphs (1), (2), (3), or (4) of subsection (a) shall be fined under this title or imprisoned not more than 15 years, or both, but, if such person has a prior conviction under this chapter, chapter 109A, or chapter 117, or under the laws of any State relating to aggravated sexual abuse, sexual abuse, or abusive sexual conduct involving a minor or ward, or the production, possession, receipt, mailing, sale, distribution, shipment, or transportation of child pornography, such person shall be fined under this title and imprisoned for not less than 5 years nor more than 30 years.

    (2) Whoever violates, or attempts or conspires to violate, subsection (a)(5) shall be fined under this title or imprisoned not more than five years, or both, but, if such person has a prior conviction under this chapter, chapter 109A, or chapter 117, or under the laws of any State relating to aggravated sexual abuse, sexual abuse, or abusive sexual conduct involving a minor or ward, or the production,

possession, receipt, mailing, sale, distribution, shipment, or transportation of child pornography, such person shall be fined under this title and imprisoned for not less than two years nor more than ten years.

(b) It shall be an affirmative defense to a charge of violating paragraphs (1), (2), (3), or (4) of subsection (a) that

  (1) the alleged child pornography was produced using an actual person or persons engaging in sexually explicit conduct;

  (2) each such person was an adult at the time the material was produced; and

  (3) the defendant did not advertise, promote, present, describe, or distribute the material in such a manner as to convey the impression that it is or contains a visual depiction of a minor engaging in sexually explicit conduct.

(c) Affirmative Defense. It shall be an affirmative defense to a charge of violating subsection (a)(5) that the defendant

  (1) possessed less than three images of child pornography; and

  (2) promptly and in good faith, and without retaining or allowing any person, other than a law enforcement agency, to access any image or copy thereof

    (A) took reasonable steps to destroy each such image; or

    (B) reported the matter to a law enforcement agency and afforded that agency access to each such image.

60. 18 U.S.C. § 2251; 18 U.S.C. § 2256.
61. 18 U.S.C. § 2422.
62. 18 U.S.C. § 2423.
63. 18 U.S.C. § 2425.
64. 18 U.S.C. § 2251.
65. 18 U.S.C. § 2251(b).
66. 18 U.S.C. § 2251(c).
67. 18 U.S.C. § 2251(d).
68. 18 U.S.C. § 2252.
69. 18 U.S.C. § 2252(c).
70. 18 U.S.C. § 2425.
71. *Ibid.*
72. 18 U.S.C. § 1470.
73. 18 U.S.C. § 2427.
74. An attempt provision was added to 18 U.S.C. 2422(a), Coercion and Enticement and 18 U.S.C. 2421, Transportation generally.
75. The Act clarifies that in 18 U.S.C. 2422(b), Coercion and enticement of a minor, coercion can be through use of the mail, or any facility of interstate or foreign commerce, and increases the maximum sentence to 15 years.
76. The Act amends 18 U.S.C. § § 2251(a) and (b), Production of Child Pornography by expanding the jurisdictional reach of the federal child pornography production statutes. The existing statute required the knowing transportation, transmission, or distribution of the child pornography. The amendment creates a jurisdictional element similar to the possession, receipt, and transmission statutes which are

violated if the individual, e.g., possesses child pornography that was made with materials (e.g., the paper, the computer, the diskettes, the camera) that had been transported in interstate or foreign commerce. The amendment thus increases the possibility of federal prosecution for the direct abuse of the child in the production of child pornography.

77. The Act increased the maximum statutory penalty for the following offenses: 18 U.S.C. § 2422(a) [from 5 to 10 years], 18 U.S.C. § 2422(b) [from 10 to 15 years)], 18 U.S.C. § 2423(a) [from 10 to 15 years], and 18 U.S.C. § 2423(b) [from 10 to 15 years]. In addition, an individual convicted of 18 U.S.C. § 2244 involving a victim under the age of 12 can receive double the maximum statutory penalty, under the new Section 2244(c).

78. Death Penalty. If a minor under the age 14 dies as a result of the commission of an offense under 18 U.S.C. § § 2251, 2422, or 2423, the defendant may receive the death penalty under a new provision, 18 U.S.C. § 3559(d), Death or Imprisonment for Crimes Against Children This provision was added, in part, to increase penalties for "snuff" films involving minors.

79. Criminal forfeiture, under Section 2253, and civil forfeiture, under Section 2254, are now available for offenses under 18 U.S.C. § § 2251, 2251A, 2252, 2252A, 2260, 2421, 2422, and 2423. Civil remedies, under Section 2255, are now available for offenses under the aforementioned statutes and Sections 2241(c), 2242, and 2243. See below under "Forfeiture Provisions." The forfeiture provisions should provide incentives for increased investigative work by local, state, and federal law enforcement in all cases involving child pornography, luring and transportation of minors, and trafficking of women and minors for prostitution cases. The civil remedy provisions may be useful in providing relief for victims.

80. The Protection of Children from Sexual Predators Act amends the Victims of Child Abuse Act of 1990 (42 U.S.C. 13001 et seq.) to require online service providers to report evidence of child pornography offenses. The measure also amends 18 U.S.C. § 2702(b) of the Electronic Communications Privacy Act of 1986 to create an exception to the general statutory bar against a public provider's voluntary disclosure of customer communications to third parties.

81. 521 U.S. 844 (1997).
82. Title 47 U. S. C. A. § 223(a)(1)(B)(ii).
83. Title 47 U. S. C. A. § 223(d).
84. 535 U.S. 234 (2002).
85. 18 U.S.C. § 2256.
86. Public Law No: 108-21. The PROTECT Act Prohibits: (1) making a visual depiction that is a digital image, computer image, or computer-generated image of, or that is indistinguishable from an image of, a minor engaging in specified sexually explicit conduct; (2) knowingly advertising, promoting, presenting, distributing, or soliciting through the mails or in commerce, including by computer, any material that is or contains an obscene visual depiction of a minor engaging in sexually explicit conduct or a visual depiction of an actual minor engaging in such conduct; (3) knowingly distributing, offering, sending, or providing to a minor any such visual

depiction using the mails or commerce, including by computer, for purposes of inducing or persuading a minor to participate in an illegal act; and (4) knowingly producing, distributing, receiving, or possessing with intent to distribute a visual depiction of any kind, including a drawing, cartoon, sculpture, or painting, that, under specified circumstances, depicts a minor engaging in sexually explicit conduct and is obscene, or depicts an image that is or appears to be of a minor engaging in such conduct and such depiction lacks serious literary, artistic, political, or scientific value. Allows as an affirmative defense to the charge of virtual child pornography only that: (1) the alleged pornography was produced using only actual persons all of whom were adults; or (2) the alleged pornography was not produced using any actual minors.

87. OSANKA, F.M., and JOHANN, S. L. (1989). *Sourcebook on Pornography*. Lexington, MA: Lexington Books.

88. REISMAN, J.A. (1994). "Child Pornography in Erotic Magazines, Social Awareness, and Self-Censorship." In D. ZILLMAN, J. BRYANT, and A.C. HUSTON (eds.), *Media, Children, and the Family: Social Scientific, Psychodynamic, and Clinical Perspectives*. Hillsdale, NJ: Lawrence Erlbaum and Associates, pp. 313–326.

89. *Ibid.*

90. *Ibid.*

91. HENLEY, J. (September 1, 1996). "The Observer Campaign to Clean up the Internet: Hackers Called in as Cybercops to Drive Out Porn." *Observer.*

92. http://enough.org/inside.php?id=2UXKJWRY8. See also, GuardChild at: *https://www.guardchild.com/statistics/*.

93. *Ibid.*

94. SCHUIJER, J. and ROSSEN, B. (1992). "The Trade in Child Pornography." *Issues in Child Abuse Accusations* 4(2): 55–107.

95. SEVEL, J. (1999). U.S. Customs Service Agent, Cyber Smuggling Center. Personal interview.

96. LANNING, K.V. and BURGESS, A.W. (1989). "Child Pornography and Sex Rings." In D. ZILLMAN and J. BRYANT (eds.), *Pornography: Research Advances and Policy Considerations*. Hillsdale, NJ: Lawrence Erlbaum and Associates, pp. 235–258.

97. *Ibid.*

98. CAMPAGNA, D.S. and POFFENBERGER, D.L. (1988). *The Sexual Trafficking in Children: An Investigation of the Child Sex Trade*. Dover, MA: Auburn House Publishing.

99. *Ibid.;* LANNING and BURGESS, "Child Pornography and Sex Rings."

100. *Ibid.*

101. CAMPAGNA and POFFENBERGER, *The Sexual Trafficking in Children.*

102. *Ibid.*

103. DURKIN, K.F. (1997). "Misuse of the Internet by Pedophiles: Implications for Law Enforcement and Probation Practice." *Federal Probation* 61(3): 14–18.

104. *Ibid.*

105. U.S. Department of Justice (2017), "Florida Man Sentenced to Prison for Engaging in a Child Exploitation Enterprise" *Justice News* (May 1). Available at *https://www.justice.gov /opa/pr/florida-man-sentenced-prison-engaging-child-exploitation-enterprise.*

106. LANNING and BURGESS, "Child Pornography and Sex Rings."

107. SEVEL, U.S. Customs Service Agent, Cyber Smuggling Center. Personal interview.

108. U.S. Attorney General's Office (1986). *Final Report of the Attorney General's Commission on Pornography*. Nashville, TN: Rutledge Hill Press.

109. *Ibid.*

110. *Ibid.*

111. *Ibid.*

112. LANNING and BURGESS, "Child Pornography and Sex Rings."

113. SEVEL, U.S. Customs Service Agent, Cyber Smuggling Center. Personal interview.

114. http://www.ice.gov/partners/predator/index.htm. See also, the website for Operation Innocent Images within the FBI. Available at *https://www.fbi.gov/history/famous-cases /operation-innocent-images*

115. CLINE, V.B. (1994). "Pornography Effects: Empirical and Clinical Evidence." In D. ZILLMAN, J. BRYANT, and A.C. HUSTON (eds.), *Media, Children, and the Family: Social Scientific, Psychodynamic, and Clinical Perspectives*. Hillsdale, NJ: Lawrence Erlbaum and Associates, pp. 229–248; LYONS, J.S., ANDERSON, R.L., and LARSON, D.B. (1994). "A Systematic Review of the Effects of Aggressive and Nonaggressive Pornography." In D. ZILLMAN, J. BRYANT, and A.C. HUSTON (eds.), *Media, Children, and the Family: Social Scientific, Psychodynamic, and Clinical Perspectives*. Hillsdale, NJ: Lawrence Erlbaum and Associates, pp. 271–312; MALAMUTH, N.M. and DONNERSTEIN, E. (eds.). (1984). *Pornography and Sexual Aggression*. Orlando, FL: Academic Press; MARSHALL, W.L. (1989). "Pornography and Sex Offenses." In D. ZILLMAN and J. BRYANT (eds.), *Pornography: Research Advances and Policy Considerations*. Hillsdale, NJ: Lawrence Erlbaum and Associates, pp. 185–214; OSANKA and JOHANN, *Sourcebook on Pornography*; U.S. Attorney General's Office, *Final Report of the Attorney General's Commission on Pornography.*

116. SHOWERS, R. (1994). "Research, Public Policy, and Law: Combination for Change." In D. ZILLMAN, J. BRYANT, and A.C. HUSTON (eds.), *Media, Children, and the Family: Social Scientific, Psychodynamic, and Clinical Perspectives*. Hillsdale, NJ: Lawrence Erlbaum and Associates, pp. 327–339.

117. *Ibid.*

118. *Ibid.*

119. WOLAK, J., MITCHELL, K., and FINKELHOR, D. (2003). *Internet Sex Crimes Against Minors: The Response of Law Enforcement*. Washington, D.C.: Office of Juvenile Justice and Delinquency Prevention.

120. CLINE, "Pornography Effects"; LYONS, ANDERSON, and LARSON, "A Systematic Review of the Effects of Aggressive and Nonaggressive Pornography"; MARSHALL, "Pornography and Sex Offenses"; OSANKA and JOHANN,

Sourcebook on Pornography; SHOWERS, "Research, Public Policy, and Law."

121. CLINE, "Pornography Effects"; LYONS, ANDERSON, and LARSON, "A Systematic Review of the Effects of Aggressive and Nonaggressive Pornography"; MARSHALL, "Pornography and Sex Offenses."

122. *Ibid.*

123. MARSHALL, "Pornography and Sex Offenses."

124. CLINE, "Pornography Effects"; LYONS, ANDERSON, and LARSON, "A Systematic Review of the Effects of Aggressive and Nonaggressive Pornography"; MARSHALL, "Pornography and Sex Offenses."

125. MARSHALL, "Pornography and Sex Offenses."

126. *Ibid.*, p. 114; DURKIN, K.F., and BRYANT, C.D. (1999). "Propagandizing Pederasty. A Thematic Analysis of the On-Line Exculpatory Accounts of Unrepentant Pedophiles." *Deviant Behavior* 20: 103–127.

127. *Ibid.*

128. JENKINS, P. (2001). *Beyond Tolerance: Child Pornography on the Internet.* New York: New York University Press.

129. *Ibid.*

130. *Ibid.*

131. CLINE, V.B. (1996). "Testimony on Child Pornography Prevention." U.S. Senate Judiciary Committee Hearing on S 1237, "Child Pornography Prevention Act of 1995," 10 AM, Rm 226, Dirksen Senate Office Bldg., June 4, 1996.

132. *Ibid.*

133. See the National Childrens Alliance National Statistics— Statistical Report —2015. Available at *http://www.national-childrensalliance.org/sites/default/files/2015NationalAnnual_0.pdf.*

134. PRENTKY, R.A., KNIGHT, R.A., and LEE, AUSTIN F.S. (1997). *Child Sexual Molestation: Research Issues.* Washington, D.C.: National Institute of Justice.

135. ABEL, G.G., BECKER, J.V., MITTELMAN, M.S., CUNNINGHAM-RATHNER, J., ROULEAU, J.L., and MURPHY, W.D. (1987). "Self-Reported Sex Crimes of Nonincarcerated Paraphilics." *Journal of Interpersonal Violence* 2:3–25.

136. O'NEILL, M. (2001). *Prostitution and Feminism.* London: Polity Press.

137. SHARP, K. and EARLE, S. (2003). "Cyberpunters and Cyberwhores: Prostitution on the Internet." In Y. JEWKES (ed.), *Dot Cons. Crime, Deviance and Identity on the Internet.* Portland, OR: Willan Publishing, pp. 36–52.

138. Charles "Lucky" Luciano was a notorious Sicilian Mafia figure in the late 1920s and 1930s in New York City. He reportedly controlled a $12 million prostitution enterprise in New York by controlling prostitutes with heroin. He would "pay" the prostitute in drugs versus in cash, thereby "enslaving" them to the life of a prostitute and working for his business. See Poulson, E. (2007). *The Case Against Lucky Luciano: New York's Most Sensational Vice Trial.* Oakland Gardens, NY: Clinton Cook Publishing, and Abadinsky, H. (2017). *Organized Crime, 11th edition.* Belmont, CA: Cengage Publishing.

139. *Ibid.*

140. HOLT, T.J. and BLEVINS, K.R. (2007). "Examining Sex Work from the Client's Perspective: Assessing Johns Using Online Data." *Deviant Behavior* 28: 333–354; SOOTHHILL, K. and SANDERS, T. (2005). "The Geographical Mobility, Preferences and Pleasures of Prolific Punters: a Demonstration Study of the Activities of Prostitutes' Clients." *Sociological Research On-Line* 10(1). Retrieved October 10, 2005, from *http://www.socresonline.org.uk/10/1/soothill.html*; HOLT, T.J., BLEVINS, K.R., and KUHNS, J.B. (2008). "Examining the Displacement Practices of Johns with On-line Data." *Journal of Criminal Justice* 36: 522–528.

141. *Ibid.*, HOLT and BLEVINS, "Examining Sex Work from the Client's Perspective."

142. *Ibid.*, p. 150.

143. COHEN, A.K. (1955). *Delinquent Boys: The Culture of the Gang.* Glencoe, IL: The Free Press.

144. NBC News (2015). "Things are Looking Up in America's Porn Industry," (January 20). Available at *http://www.nbcnews.com/business/business-news/things-are-looking-americas-porn-industry-n289431*

145. SAID, S. (2013). "Webcam Girl Salary" *The Richest* (August 21). Available at *http://www.therichest.com/business/technology/webcam-girl-salary/*

146. Blog (2017) *Chaturbate Token Hack,* (January 20). Available at *https://ctbtokenhack.com/tag/chaturbate-token-currency/*

147. International Labor Organization. (2005). "A Global Alliance against Forced Labour: Global report under the follow-up to the ILO Declaration on Fundamental Principles and Rights at Work 2005." Report I (B), International Labour Conference 93rd session 2005, Geneva, 2005, pp. 12, 15. See also UNICEF, USA statistics for 2017, Available at *https://www.unicefusa.org/stories/infographic-global-human-trafficking-statistics.*

148. *Ibid.*

149. *Ibid.*

150. ALBANESE, JAY. (2007). *Commercial Sexual Exploitation of Children: What Do We Know and What Do We Do About It?* Washington, D.C.: National Institute of Justice.

151. GIORDANELLA, H.C. (1998). "Comment: Status of 2423(B): Prosecuting United States Nationals for Sexually Exploiting Children in Foreign Countries." *Temple International and Comparative Law Journal* 12: 133.

152. RAO, N. (1999). "Sex Tourism in South Asia." *International Journal of Contemporary Hospitality Management* 11: 96–99, University Press.

153. *Ibid.*

154. JEFFREYS, S. (1999). "Globalizing Sexual Exploitation: Sex Tourism and the Traffic in Women." *Leisure Studies* 18: 179–196.

155. RAO, "Sex Tourism in South Asia."

156. Captive Daughters .(1999). "Sex Tours—A Learning Model." Retrieved from *http://www.captivedaughters.org/ByandAboutCD/CDdocuments/cdfactsheet1.htm*

157. STEINMAN, K.J. (2002). "Sex Tourism and the Child: Latin America's and the United States' Failure to Prosecute Sex Tourists." *Hastings Women's Law Journal* 13: 53.

158. *Ibid.*

159. *Ibid.*

160. BEVILACQUA, E. (1998). "Note: Child Sex Tourism and Child Prostitution in Asia: What Can Be Done to Protect the Rights of Children Abroad Under International Law?" *ILSA Journal of International & Comparative Law* 5: 171.

161. *Ibid.*

162. Immigration and Customs Enforcement. (March 2007). "Las Vegas Man Pleads Guilty to Sex Tourism." Available at *http://www.ice.gov/pi/news/newsreleases/articles /070309cleveland.htm*

163. GIORDANELLA, "Comment: Status of 2423(B)."

164. ABBUGAO, M. (October 1996). "Briton Child-Sex Tour Organiser Jailed for 16 Years." *Agence France Presse.* Retrieved from *http://www.vachss.com/help_text/archive /sex_tourism_briton_jailed.htm*

165. Associated Press. (November 2002). "Businessman Sentenced on Sexual Abuse Charge." Retrieved from *http:// www.vachss.com/help_text/a2/n_bredimus.com*

166. Computer Crime and Intellectual Property Section, *The Electronic Frontier.*

167. *www.cybertipline.com*

168. Computer Crime and Intellectual Property Section, *The Electronic Frontier.*

169. *https://postalinspectors.uspis.gov/investigations /MailFraud/fraudschemes/ce/CE.aspx*

170. *http://www.usdoj.gov/criminal/ceos/obscenity.htm*

171. Computer Crime and Intellectual Property Section, *The Electronic Frontier.*

172. *Ibid.*, p. 124.

173. *Ibid.*

174. PEREZ, C. (1999). "*United States* v. *Jacobson:* Are Child Pornography Stings Creative Law Enforcement or Entrapment?" 46: 235.

175. *Ibid.*

Anarchy and Hate on the World Wide Web

CHAPTER OBJECTIVES

After completing this chapter, you should be able to

- Legally define a hate crime and describe how white supremacist groups use the Internet to spread their message of hate.
- Explain the relationship between left-wing groups and "special-interest or single-issue extremist" groups.
- Describe ALF and ELF, and provide examples of each group's recent terrorist activities in the United States.
- Describe some of the techniques that right-wing hate groups use to spread their propaganda.
- Discuss the primary issues associated with the USA PATRIOT Act, and list the four traditional tools of surveillance that have been expanded within the Act.
- Explain the conflicting roles and activities observed within law enforcement pertaining to investigation versus intelligence gathering.

INTRODUCTION

The emergence of the Internet in 1989 has paralleled one of the greatest milestones in communications history: Johann Gutenberg's invention of movable type in 1450. Goldain and Kutarna assert that there are four major analogies between these two mega-communication developments: the printing press and the Internet. These are as follows:

1. Both technologies became ubiquitous in less than a lifetime;
2. Both revolutionized the way the world does business;
3. Data and information were/are able to move faster and further than ever before; and
4. New forms of media have evolved.[1]

Along with such great strides in bringing the world together, the frightening aspect of accessing information and propaganda that tests the very limits of the U.S. Constitution has arrived. Segal ominously asserts: "In the hacked world order, the United States is uniquely powerful and vulnerable…cyberattacks could disrupt and degrade the American way of war."[2] In Chapter 2, we suggest that "war" as we knew it, has already changed, the new information warfare is not just a prescription for the future but a reality of today. In this chapter, we discuss the potentially dystopian future before us: What will be the role of law enforcement generally, and cyber cops, in particular, as we move forward to an information environment that is increasingly hostile and fraught with "weapons" of nation-states, sophisticated criminals, and well-financed terrorist groups? With just a few keystrokes, an individual is able to access all forms of data, information and knowledge, including all forms of pornography, bomb-making instructions, poison recipes, and a plethora of extremist ideologies expressing everything from radical religious cults to clandestine organized crime groups. In addition to access, we can now upload to the Web a dizzying array of virulent attack software and malware designed to shut down all sorts of Supervisory Control and Data Acquisition (SCADA) systems, extort thousands of dollars from unsuspecting business, and exploit children at their earliest ages. The Internet not only makes it possible to view all sorts of material heretofore not easily found in the public venue, but also to add to that which has been so hidden in our society for centuries. Many unwitting visitors to unintended and radical Web sites are shocked by not only the vast quantity of sexually oriented material but also the open advocacy of violence against specific groups, races, ethnicities and lifestyles of people. One of the more troublesome multimedia/social media promotions that are found on the Internet arises from the ashes of Nazism and other extremists. As if these issues were not problematic enough, since around 2011, the "Dark Web" looms large as a threat to civility and economic stability. And since 2016 the issue of "fake news" (disinformation) is now a part of conventional news media, promoting discord, confusion, and lack of confidence in our nation's institutions of government.

DIGITAL HATE

Right-wing extremism represents a movement that promotes whites, especially Northern Europeans and their descendants, as intellectually and morally superior to other races.[3] It is not coincidental that as these groups have grown in strength, so have the number of reported hate crimes. *Hate crimes* and hate incidents are major issues for all Americans because of their unique impact on victims as well as the community. Hate crimes are often very brutal and injurious, and victims are not only hurt physically but also are emotionally traumatized and terrified. Others in the community who share the same victim's characteristic may also feel victimized and vulnerable, posing a potential escalation in an attempt to retaliate for the original offense.

In the past, police officers have not been adequately trained to handle such incidents, treating them as routine assaults or vandalism. However, with federal legislation has come the development of the National Institute Against Hate Crimes and Terrorism, which is located at the Simon Wiesenthal Center in Los Angeles. The institute provides training for teams of criminal justice professionals from the same jurisdiction to combat hate crimes. Their goal is to provide new strategic approaches to combating hate crimes based on a new understanding of the unique elements that differentiate them from other acts. The center has been highly successful, training a range of participants from law enforcement agencies across the country and providing an ongoing support center for follow-up communication, program evaluation, and professional development via Web site updates and videoconferences.[4]

Legal definitions of hate crimes vary. The federal definition of hate crimes addresses civil rights violations under 18 U.S.C. Section 245. A hate crime is a criminal offense committed against persons, property, or society that is motivated, in whole or in part, by an offender's bias against an individual's or a group's perceived race, religion, ethnic/national origin, gender, age, disability, or sexual orientation.[5] Most states have a hate crime statute that provides enhanced penalties for crimes in which victims are selected because of perpetrator's bias against a victim's perceived race, religion, or ethnicity. Some states also classify as hate crimes those in which a victim is selected based on a perception of his/her sexual orientation, gender, or disability. In some states, the passage of a hate crime statute has been very controversial, as politicians have debated the constitutionality of enhanced penalties based on a suspect's association with an extremist group, or the inclusion of homosexuality as a protected class.

QUICK FACTS

Individual groups representing the right-wing in America have banded together to make a new alliance called *The Nationalist Front*. Born in a bar in Georgia, six different Ku Klux Klan chapters developed a formal national organization, originally called *The Aryan National Alliance*, to become more mainstream. *The Nationalist Front* now represents such groups as the KKK, Neo-Confederates, Sovereign Citizens, Christian Identity Churches, Oath Keepers, a variety of Anti-Government Militias and even several secessionist movements like the Texas Nationalist Movement and the "New State of Jefferson" Movement proposing a new state being formed from parts of Eastern Washington and Oregon with Northern Idaho and Western Montana. The alliance has dropped the use of swastikas, calling minority groups by derogatory names, burning crosses, and even white robes and caps in an effort to broaden its appeal, build new membership and become more politically powerful. As one imperial wizard of the KKK stated, "We want to see people stand up and make this country great again…we're tired of seeing white people lose everything." Unfortunately, the number of Web sites devoted to the New Nationalist Front has emerged with great vigor. See https://www.nfunity.org.

Source: Jay Reeves, "White-Power Groups Banding Together," *Associated Press* (April 26, 2017). Anti-Defamation League, "With Hate in Their Hearts: The State of White Supremacy in the United States" (July 13, 2015). Available at *https://www.adl.org/education /resources/reports/state-of-white-supremacy#racist-skinheads*

White Supremacy, Hate, and the Internet

Many white supremacist groups have used the Internet to recruit potential new members and spread their message of hate. There are thousands of Web sites, social networking pages, and videos posted on file-sharing sites that can be attributed to extremist organizations that incite racial hatred and religious intolerance as well as terrorism and bomb making (see Box 9.1). One of the more popular of these sites is *www.stormfront.org*, which has over 100,000 members and thousands of posts every day.[6] More disturbing is the effort directed by many of these groups to attract young people into their ranks. Based in part on links to other social youth movements involving music and dress (e.g., skinheads, black cults, and heavy metal music); aggressive recruitment on college campuses; and the development of Web pages, videos, games, and other materials designed to attract young people are now quite common. In fact, the stormfront Web site has a page on Facebook as a means to help recruit and connect members. Hate groups are even creating their own social networking sites, such as "New Saxon," which is a "social networking site for people of European descent" produced by the neo-Nazi group, the National Socialist Movement.[7] In addition, white-power rock concerts are often sponsored by extremist groups such as the National Alliance and the World Church of the Creator. These concerts provide face-to-face opportunities for meeting and recruitment.

White supremacist groups have also created sophisticated computer games aimed at attracting teenagers. *Ethnic Cleansing*, the most high-tech game of its kind, encourages

BOX 9.1

Resistance Records

Resistance Records is a racist recording label and Internet site that is part of the National Alliance. The National Alliance is a right-wing white supremacist organization founded by the author of the Turner Diaries, William Pierce. It is one of the largest and most well known racist organizations and has gone to great lengths to utilize the Internet. Resistance Records is constructed to appeal to the youth of America. The violent music and games supported by the National Alliance attract not only racist teens but also the mainstream punk/alternative crowd. The racist propaganda portrayed on the Internet and in the music and games will have some effect on the beliefs of the individuals who frequent such Web sites.

players to kill blacks, Jews, and Hispanics as they run through urban ghettos and subway environments. In the game, players can dress in Ku Klux Klan (KKK) robes and carry a noose. Every time a black enemy is shot, he emits a monkey-like squeal, while Jewish characters shout "Oy vey!" when they are killed.[8] Quite predictably, the game has spurred significant controversy between the media and game developers versus censor advocates. Very little can be done to ban the game since many other video games are designed to allow enthusiasts to create new levels and characters, while free software tools enable programmers to build new platforms.

These types of games and directed recruitment efforts have been effective tools in increasing the ranks of some extremist organizations.[9] According to one skinhead source, young people represent the future: "They are the front-line warriors in the battle for white supremacy."[10] In fact, white power groups in the United States became more active in 2008 and 2009 with the election of the first African American president, Barack Obama.

The increase in supremacist activity has taken two different forms. On the one hand, many white racist groups responded to the election of the first African American president with disdain and even death threats. In October 2009, agents from the Bureau of Alcohol, Tobacco, and Firearms broke up a plot by two neo-Nazi skinheads to assassinate Obama and shoot or decapitate 88 African Americans.[11] On the other hand, some noted white power authorities believe that Obama's nomination and election will become a rallying point for their cause. David Duke, noted white nationalist and former Grand Wizard of the Knights of the Klu Klux Klan, described the Obama election as a "black flag for white America" and likened his nomination to the discovery of a serious medical problem, "Obama is like a big dark spot on your arm that finally sends you to the doctor."[12]

TERRORIST EXTREMISTS FROM THE LEFT

The far right is not the only set of terrorists that pose a threat domestically. The traditional left-wing extremists were replaced in the 1990s by the right-wing ones as the most dangerous domestic terrorists, but subgroups of the left have developed that are potentially just as dangerous as the right and arguably more economically destructive.[13] A resurgence of anarchist groups, including those associated with Anarchist International, has dramatically increased since September 11, 2001. Most of these groups are relatively small and confine their activities to "rallies" against what they see as incursions of the government into the individual rights of people. Several "Black

Bloc" rallies in protest of the USA PATRIOT Act and similar government initiatives and the increased security associated with terrorism prevention have been observed in several cities. However, unlike the anarchist groups of the 1960s (e.g., Weather Underground, Symbionese Liberation Army), there have been few violent acts attributed to these newly formed groups.

Those aspiring to extreme left movements are best observed in the modern ecoterrorists.[14] The FBI defines ecoterrorism as the use or threatened use of violence of a criminal nature against innocent victims or property by an environmentally oriented national group for environmental–political reasons, or aimed at an audience beyond the target, often of a symbolic nature.[15]

While these groups are definitely liberal and considered left-wing extremists, they are most often referred to as "special-interest or single-issue extremists."[16] Special-interest extremists are seen as different from traditional right- and left-wing extremists because they are not trying to effect a more widespread political change, but seek to resolve specific issues. These issues include animal rights and environmentalism on the left, and prolife, antigay, and antigenetic on the right.[17] In attempting to understand these groups, it is important not to be clouded by the political rhetoric of the left or the right. These groups attempt to change one aspect of the social or political arena through terrorism.[18]

Many special-interest groups try to claim that they are not terrorist groups because they do not harm any animal, human or nonhuman, by their actions. Unfortunately, they often enjoy a sympathetic reception by many liberal affluent Americans unaware of the true actions of these groups. While in the United States, to date, no murders have been directly attributed to environmental activists, they have used intimidation tactics on those they see as enemies and have caused millions of dollars in damage. The FBI estimated that over a five-year period, the Animal Liberation Front (ALF) and the Earth Liberation Front (ELF) committed more than 600 criminal acts in the United States, which resulted in damages that exceeded $43 million.[19] Unfortunately, other single-issue groups like those associated with the anti-abortion movement have been very violent, having been responsible for the murder of numerous doctors and nurses that perform such operations.

Contrary to the claims of their partisans that ecogroups are not terrorists because they have not killed or injured any living being, making their acts mere vandalism and not terrorism, their use of arson and pipe bombs challenges their claims of innocence. It is also obvious that their intent is to influence policy by intimidation and coercion.[20] Moreover, former congressional representative Scott McInnis (R-Colorado) claimed that "these are hardened criminals. They are dangerous, they are well funded, they are savvy, sophisticated and stealthy, and if their violence continues to escalate, it is only a matter of time before their parade of terror results in a lost human life."[21]

ELF and ALF

The ALF and the ELF are arguably the most central and active groups of liberal activism today. The ALF, established in Great Britain in the mid-1970s, is a loosely organized movement committed to ending the abuse and exploitation of animals. The American branch of the ALF began its operations in the late 1970s. Similar to the right wing's leaderless resistance, individuals become members of ALF simply by engaging in "direct action" against those who utilize animals for research or economic gain.

Direct action is generally defined by the group as criminal activity, which is aimed at causing economic loss or destroying company operations. The ALF activists have engaged in a steadily growing campaign of illegal activity against fur companies, mink farms, restaurants, and animal research centers.[22] In fact, members of ALF were arrested by FBI agents in 2006 as part of Operation Backfire, which was an attempt to eliminate domestic terrorism. These individuals were responsible for acts of arson against meat-processing plants, lumber companies, and a ski center in multiple states over a five-year period.[23]

ELF emerged from a group called "Earth First!" This group developed in Arizona in 1980 after a series of acts of sabotage over the prior decade. Some of the first actions taken were in the early 1970s by the University of Arizona students known as "The Eco-Raiders," who protested the spread of the city into the Sonoran Desert by vandalizing construction sites. In 1975, a fictional account of ecological saboteurs who chopped down billboards and plotted to blow up Glen Canyon Dam, called *The Monkey Wrench Gang*, was published by Edward Abbey. Furthermore, two homes built in the Tucson Mountains were knocked down by a hot-wired bulldozer in 1977. Subsequent acts, such as those performed by saboteurs who sawed through the supporting poles of four billboards just south of Tucson in 1979, toppling them, seemed to have been inspired by *The Monkey Wrench Gang*.[24]

In 1980, five radicals led by Tucson resident Dave Foreman created Earth First! and began a nine-year campaign of civil disobedience and *monkey wrenching* (a term used to describe vandalism against active construction and lumbering locations). This was the group that started the practice of "tree spiking," or the insertion of metal or ceramic spikes in trees designed to damage saws and potentially injure workers.[25] The acts of tree spiking are exceedingly dangerous, as chainsaws buck back, often uncontrollably, against the user. In 1992, dissatisfied members who did not wish to abandon illegal actions when others wanted to mainstream Earth First! founded the ELF in Brighton, England. This group has gone on to claim responsibility for dozens of acts of ecoterrorism throughout the United States, starting in 1996. One of the more infamous examples of their acts was the $12 million in damages created when they set fire to a Vail, Colorado, ski lodge in 1998.[26]

ELF and ALF are similar groups committing similar acts, the difference being that one focuses on the environment and the other on animal rights. Members of these groups consistently use improvised incendiary devices equipped with crude but effective timing mechanisms.[27] While the ALF and ELF are the driving force for the liberal/environmental terrorist groups, there are other attached groups that also commit illegal activities, as well as groups that are legitimate and nonviolent.

As we stated in the Chapter 2, cyberterrorism is an issue that has gained much attention in recent years. This type of terrorism is seen as unlawful attacks or threats of attacks on computers, networks, and the information stored therein for the purpose of intimidation or coercion of a government or its people for the furtherance of a political or social goal.[28] Many officials remain fearful that domestic terrorist groups will crack into important systems and create severe damage or steal classified information.

While the government has responded to this threat with the development of new legislation to combat it, such as the Cyberterrorism Preparedness Act of 2002 and parts of the USA PATRIOT Act, the Internet poses a much more serious and widespread issue in its ability to unite people and spread information.[29]

DOMESTIC TERRORISTS IN CYBERSPACE

The domestic terrorist groups that pose a threat in the United States are strongly entrenched in cyberspace. Neo-Nazis, animal rights groups, militias, Black Blocs, and hate mongers all have not only Web sites but also clubs, posting boards, news groups, and all other types of Internet communities.

The danger the Internet poses with domestic terrorist groups is that it allows for a level of communication between separate groups that traditionally has not occurred. Also, it allows for wider recruitment. For instance, neo-Nazi skinheads around the world can talk in chat rooms, and right-wing groups, which in the past would not have interacted in the outside world, find camaraderie in cyberspace. This camaraderie will eventually solidify and pass into the real world, where it will pose a threat of a larger, more united group. People who would never have gone to a skinhead rally or a People for the Ethical Treatment of Animals (PETA) demonstration now feel free to explore the Web sites of these groups and participate in their chat rooms in anonymity. Unfortunately, once they have become involved in these online communities, they are more likely to bring their participation out of cyberspace. These Internet sites pose many potential areas for concern.

Dehumanize, Desensitize, and Demonize

Several Web sites use images, music, games, and the like to spread their propaganda. By using these types of paraphernalia, the groups can appeal to people who do not necessarily share their particular beliefs. Once a person is exposed to these ideas for a long enough time, they begin to seem normal.

One of the more effective and therefore more dangerous techniques these sites use to dehumanize the "enemy" or desensitize the consumer toward violence is computer games that are filled with extremist beliefs. For example, the game *Border Patrol* allows players to shoot Mexicans attempting to illegally cross the border into the United States.[30] This new trend of racist, hate-filled computer games has gained much attention and concern. It is believed that exposure to the racist propaganda in the games coming into the mind under the cover of the action will serve to desensitize individuals to the horrors of hate that these groups preach. This follows from the idea that the youth of America have become desensitized to violence from more acceptable games, movies, and television. While the violence prevalent in modern media does not necessarily lead to violence by the consumer, it does seem that people are not as affected by the sight of true violence as they once were. This means that young people who play these games are not necessarily going to commit acts of hate and violence directly, but they may become less outraged when these acts occur in their own community. Vigilance and outrage against such acts of hate are necessary to eliminate these types of behavior in our communities.

As stated earlier, Resistance Records[31] has released one of the most advanced of these games. The game was released featuring an altered picture similar to the video game *Doom*. However, rather than killing monsters and other creatures, gamers kill ethnic minorities and Jews. *Ethnic Cleansing* was released on Martin Luther King Day with the slogan "Celebrate Martin Luther King Day with a Virtual Race War." The players can choose from KKK or neo-Nazi skinhead attire, roam the streets of New York murdering the "subhumans," that is, nonwhites, and their Jewish masters. The New York of the game has been destroyed by gangs of the subhumans who work under the control of the great Jewish Conspiracy. This game shows a world that has fallen to the extreme right's worst fear: the Jewish Conspiracy. At the end of the game, the player encounters the "end boss," who is characterized as Ariel Sharon. When he is defeated and dying, his last words are "Filthy White dog, you have destroyed thousands of years of planning."[32] This characterization further leads to demonizing the Jewish race, by showing them as "masters" who have been plotting for "thousands of years" to destroy the whites.

While this is not the first, and certainly not the only, racist game available, it is the most advanced. It was created using an open-source game program that allows for almost anyone to create a game simply by plugging in their ideas. In this manner, a person can take an existing game code and modify it to reflect the characters, backgrounds, sounds, and environment that the designer wants. By creating these highly interactive and attractive games, hate groups can spread their racist messages to thousands of unsuspecting players.[33] The importance of these more advanced games is that they have the ability to attract the serious gamer, someone who is not a racist, and not just the individuals who are already part of the racist right.

Resistance Records is a well-known racist music distributor. Music of different genres, but especially the punk/alternative types, are accessible through this company. Just like racist games, this type of music attracts people who are not active or even fringe racists. Exposure to racist propaganda and music again serves to dehumanize, desensitize, and demonize specific acts of violence against individuals based on race, ethnicity, or lifestyle. Music is a key resource among white supremacy groups, and more savvy groups have found ways to tap into youth markets to increase their recruitment. For example, the Resistance Records label signed and produced music by a number of groups featuring young artists or more pop-style music in the hopes of attracting young audiences to purchase and listen to the message of the artists.

Internet Cartoons

Besides computer games and music, many sites use cartoons to spread their ideas. One of the most widely distributed cartoons of the right is *Jew Rats*.[34] This is a computer program that consists of 14 cartoons that depict Jews as humanoid rats and African Americans with highly exaggerated features. The depiction of nonwhite individuals in this manner further, yet subtly, dehumanizes the target race or ethnicity, because their features are depicted in unattractive ways, as opposed to those caricatures that represent the Aryan ideal. The cartoons in *Jew Rats* depict many aspects of the Jewish Conspiracy put forth by the extreme right. The cartoons also show the Anti-Defamation League and the National Association for the Advancement of Colored People (NAACP) as puppets of the Jewish Conspiracy and thus set on the destruction of the white race. This type of propaganda is used to counteract and undermine the effect that these groups have in opposition to the racist right's doctrine. On most of the cartoon pages, there are links to propaganda and articles with such names as Jewish Communism, Jew Business Thugs, and Who Really Brought the Slaves to America? These articles offer names of famous people who are the true "enemies" of the white race, as well as further explaining the beliefs that the racist right holds dear. *Jew Rats* not only dehumanizes nonwhites but also helps in demonizing the Jews by extolling the beliefs of the Jewish Conspiracy.

Additionally, the Internet allows individuals to self-publish their cartoons and videos. This provides an outlet for individuals who are not skilled artists but still interested in pushing their message out to the public. Web sites like YouTube allow individuals to make animated cartoons using simple programs, though the sites carefully monitor content to reduce offensive material. However, some users repeatedly create new user profiles or channels to post their material once removed from the site.

It is easy to find examples of hate propaganda, games, and cartoons of the extreme right on the Internet. Unlike radical environmentalism, racism is not considered hip or even politically correct. All racists are seen as evil or bad even when they are nonviolent and do not participate in hate crimes or other violent actions. On the other hand, even the environmentalists who commit criminal acts tend to be romanticized and seen as righteous. There is a tendency to paint liberal extremists as Robin Hood types. While there are no hordes of violent cartoons, songs, and the like, the environmental and animal rights activist (ELF and ALF) sites do employ propaganda-filled images. Unfortunately, they do not possess the same negative image and social stigma associated with overt racism and bigotry. The propaganda of PETA[35] and other noncriminal groups instills the ideas of resistance that can later lead to more extreme activism.

On PETA's homepage, there is an Internet link that is aimed directly at young people. There is a kids section devoted to promoting the PETA agenda through child-friendly content. For example, it provides free comic books that describe the lives of cows, chickens, rats, elephants, and other animals that spend their lives in captivity in zoos or feedlots and slaughterhouses.[36] It also publishes *Grrr!* magazine, a youth-oriented publication featuring interviews with popular celebrities and their beliefs about how animals should be treated. There are also interactive games and music designed to promote perspectives to young children.

A liberal mainstream site that is youth oriented is PETA 2.[37] PETA 2 appeals directly to teenagers with youth-oriented graphics that purport the ideas of resistance and revolution. There are numerous graphics on the PETA Web site that encourage violence in the name of protecting the animals. One graphic in particular depicts a bloody knife in a hand holding books and asks the viewer to "question authority" (http://peta2.com/). Other graphics blend pop culture icons with messages that it is all right to use violence to change the world. For example, there are images of popular fast-food chains, such as McDonalds, whose slogan has been changed to read "McCruelty, I'm hatin' it!" News on popular actors or bands who are vegetarians or environmentalists is also offered. They also provide links to Facebook and Twitter pages for PETA that individuals can join. This site and the propaganda it conveys open the door and motivate people to go on to more active resistance by employing the same desensitizing and dehumanizing effect as the right's propaganda, yet it is more universally seen as legitimate. Any racist, antigay, or even prolife sites are seen as "criminal" in their own right even if they do not extol the righteousness of violence, while the left can be considered mainstream even when they do laud violence.

STORAGE AND DISSEMINATION OF INFORMATION

The ability of the Internet to store information and make it available to everyone is obvious. So it is little wonder that extremists, just as everyone else, utilize this ability. Many racist sites archive the sermons of different preachers, whether Christian Identity or other, who exemplify the beliefs that these groups hold paramount. For instance, anyone can find and download for free all of the sermons of Wesley Swift (one of the most influential right-wing extremists in our history and a primary developer of Christian Identity). In addition, there are sites that have online copies of the *Protocols of Zion* as well as the *Turner Diaries* and other racist books. *Turner Diaries* was found in the automobile of Timothy McVeigh when he was arrested after the bombing of the Alfred P. Murrah Federal Building in Oklahoma City, Oklahoma, in 1995. Before the age of the Internet, racists could only find these manuscripts at swap meets or meetings. Now even nonracists are likely to find these manuscripts on the Internet. A simple Google search reveals sites and locations dedicated to hate and bigotry. Some hate groups even offer guidelines on how to publish your own racist manuscripts and materials, as noted in Box 9.2.

BOX 9.2

"How to Publish Your Own Literature"

by John Doe, USA, Assoc. Director Web site:
http://usawhq.cjb.net

The first step in having a visible presence and attracting new recruits is often getting your information into print. This can seem a daunting task and is often something that people half do, but in fact it is quite straightforward to produce high-quality publications. The thing is to start small, do a leaflet for instance to begin with for a large gathering and perhaps an eight-page newsletter to sell. I'll start by talking about leaflets.

WRITING: Writing an article or leaflet is never as difficult as it seems. Start off by jotting down a few facts you want to get across and two or three arguments you want to make. Have a look at articles on similar subjects for ideas and if it's a current issue at recent newspapers for facts. Write an introduction paragraph that will grab people's attention. Try and make it current and saying something they don't know, a lot of people will just look at the first paragraph and unless it's interesting, won't read on. If you're really stuck leave this to the end. Then put together the facts and arguments you wish to make. Keep your sentences short and free of jargon. Keep your paragraphs short as well, three or four sentences. Each paragraph should make no more than one argument. Think about the people who will be reading it. How much knowledge can you assume they have about the subject? You're better off underestimating this slightly than overestimating it. Try and finish off on a practical note, perhaps telling people of a good Web site or advocating a particular set of tactics. Steer clear of clichés as endings unless that's the central point you're making.

Now you should have a draft article. Read through it a couple of times and make the following changes: Do you support your arguments with facts or reason or do they just sound like slogans? Have you expressed yourself in a straightforward manner or are some of your sentences convoluted and unclear? Do you repeat yourself or can you rearrange the order of the paragraphs so your argument flows more clearly? What is racialist about what you are saying? How can you emphasise your racialism better within what you are saying without appearing demeaning? Is the overall impact positive and constructive or do you just appear to be giving out about what other people are doing? You'll find each time you re-read it you'll see a slightly better way to say things. This makes the difference between an interesting piece and a boring piece. Have a look at the editing part below for more things to watch out for.

EDITING: Writing can be the easy part, the hard part is giving your work to someone else to look at and correct or suggest amendments. But again, this is a vital part both because everyone reads things in a different way and they will spot odd-sounding phrases you won't, and also because we all make mistakes which other people can pick up on. In a new group the process of editing, if correctly handled, can make a big contribution to the political development of the group. When you're editing, be careful to respect the writer's work while pointing out problems you see with it. There's nothing wrong with making mistakes and sometimes they may be right. The editing group should be willing to discuss suggested changes fully. Keep editing and proofreading separate; there's nothing worse than having your spelling constantly corrected in a session that's meant to be looking at the political or factual content of your work. Note down exactly the agreed-upon changes and see if the sentences still make sense when they are put in. Your suggestion of a wording or a fact possibly could be better expressed by trying to suggest the alternative wording. Points to look for when you are editing: Do I agree with what the leaflet is saying? Is the leaflet convincing or do the arguments need expanding on and are more facts needed? Do we assume too much knowledge on the part of the audience? Are there irrelevancies which could be cut or boring bits which should be rewritten? Is it positive and what message does it get across? Does it present a positive image of the movement and will it promote interest? Is it the right length for the available space?

PROOFREADING: Proofreading is one of those things that some people are good at and some people are inept at. But it's very important to do it as when you write something it can be very hard to see even very obvious mistakes. If you give out something with a lot of mistakes then that is what people will remember about it rather than its content. The edited text of a leaflet should always be proofread before it is produced.

LAYOUT: You may be lucky when it comes to layout and have someone with computer skills, a computer, and a printer, in which case they will be able to use a package like PageMaker or QuarkXPress to give you a very professional looking layout. If you lack these though, you can still do a lot with a typewriter, a sharp blade, letterset and some glue. If you can only use word processors you can still do a lot by mixing the techniques. First of all, in general you want to have a big headline, text in columns and a graphic. Don't try and squeeze too much text in or people won't read it. If you have access to all the computer skills and equipment then just go ahead and do it. If you don't, find some way to learn and get access, as it will make life much easier. Meanwhile, here's how it was done in the old days. If you only have partial computer access/skills then mix what you have with what's below for the best results (e.g., many people will not be able to computerize graphics, but can use the cut and paste method below). Get a piece of paper and with a light blue pencil; rule out columns, margins, and space for a headline and a graphic. Measure the column width and type your text so it is the same width (either on a typewriter or word processor). Note that light blue pencil marks do not show up when you photocopy or print. Then with a sharp knife, cut out the columns and put them to one side. With graphics, try and get one that is just black and white if you are photocopying. Racialist magazines/papers are good sources. Build up a clipping library. If you have to use a photo, try and use one that has been screened (i.e., from a newspaper, you should be able to see that it is made up of many dots) and has a lot of contrast in it. Otherwise you may end up with a black smear. Most photocopiers can be used to enlarge or reduce the photo to the size you require. A computer equivalent of a clipping file is to keep copies of all the good graphics you find on racialist Web pages and convert them into pics (mac) or bmps (pc) which most application will read. For a headline, either print one out in a big text size using your word processor or if you don't have one, use letterset. Letterset consists of rub on letters and can be bought in most art or stationary shops. It's a pain to use, but looks much better than a normal size type headline. Carefully rule out a guide line and rub the letters down along this line. Next stick your columns and graphic down in the space provided.

PRINTING/PHOTOCOPYING: Be careful to leave enough time to get this done before the event you intend to distribute the leaflet at. If you have access to cheap photocopying where you live (try print shops near college campuses for the best rates), then this is normally the cheapest way to print up to 1,000 or so copies. Check out community centers, student unions, and office workers for cheap/free photocopying. Otherwise, you'll have to find a cheap printer. Generally, print shops are very expensive although they may be more willing to deal in short runs. Find out where other local groups get their stuff printed; there may well be a sympathetic print shop in town. Make sure you have given the printer clear instructions, that everything is well stuck down and that it will be ready in advance of when you need it. Arrange for someone to pick up the material as soon as it is finished.

DISTRIBUTION: Drop leaflets around record shops, libraries, bookshops or anywhere else where free newspapers etc. are left.

Source: http://whitehonor.com/white-power/how-to-publish-your-own-literature/

On the anarchist and left-oriented sites, such information as how animals are treated by certain organizations or groups or the merit of the vegan diet is easily available. PETA even offers vegan starter packages free of charge to anyone who wishes one. Moreover, the sites offer advice and help on performing "legitimate" activist actions. PETA offers information on organizing demonstrations and spreading their message to anyone who is interested.

The Internet also allows groups to put their credos or mission statements where millions of people who would not have had the chance to see them before can now read them at the click of a mouse. One such credo that has found a home on the Web is that of the ALF[38]:

> Because ALF actions are against the law, activists work anonymously, either in small groups or individually, and do not have any centralized organization or coordination.
>
> The ALF guidelines are as follows:
>
> 1. TO liberate animals from places of abuse, i.e. laboratories, factory farms, fur farms, etc., and place them in good homes where they may live out their natural lives, free from suffering.
> 2. TO inflict economic damage to those who profit from the misery and exploitation of animals.
> 3. TO reveal the horror and atrocities committed against animals behind locked doors, by performing nonviolent direct actions and liberations.
> 4. TO take all necessary precautions against harming any animal, human and non-human.
> 5. TO analyze the ramifications of all proposed actions, and never apply generalizations when specific information is available.[39]

The Internet also offers blueprints for violent criminal acts. For instance, along with the ALF mission statement above are the following instructions for how to send in information on any actions individuals perform against the "enemy."

> If you are a member of an active A.L.F. cell, send us any clippings, or your own report, with date, time, place, and a few details about the action. Send your reports on plain paper, using block capital letters, or a public typewriter that many people have access to. Wear gloves at all times so your fingerprints are not on the paper, envelope, or stamp. Do not give your address, and don't lick the stamp or envelope; wet it with a sponge. Remember, you should expect that all of our mail and any other support groups' mail is opened and read by the authorities.

In fact, ALF offers a downloadable primer and detailed documents on "economic sabotage" among other items. Many of the sites also publish newsletters that glorify the beliefs and activities of the group. Newsletters offer articles, propaganda, letters, and more in one place with easy access. The Internet then allows many diverse people to take advantage of the product.

More dangerous are the sites that offer directions for bombs or other devices. Many bombings in the recent past have been committed by people who obtained the plans for the device from the Internet. In fact, complete directions for building an incendiary torch revealing the same type of ignition device used in the arson of a Vail, Colorado, ski resort were found on the ELF site. Other sites provide detailed instructions on bomb-making and ignition devices. While these Web sites are *not* associated directly with a specific group, they provide information that assists them in carrying out their mission of destructiveness and violence.

The home pages of many ecoterror sites have excerpts from letters sent in about individuals' actions and links to even more stories. As seen on the ALF site earlier, they offer descriptions on how to send in the information without being caught. Moreover, all of the sites make sure to tell people that they should not send in any information on acts that have not yet been committed.

Publishing Information on Potential Victims

Many sites also celebrate acts of violence. While this praise of past actions is dangerous and deplorable, the most dangerous actions of these Web sites are when they place specific information about individuals on their sites. The most famous instance of this was the Nuremberg Files case.[40] The original Nuremberg Files offered extensive personal information about abortion providers, such as pictures, work and home addresses, phone numbers, license plates, Social Security numbers, names, and birth dates of spouses and children. People were also asked to send in any information they have from pictures to videos on "the abortionist, their car, their house, friends, and anything else of interest." The site claimed that any information gathered would be used to prosecute abortion providers once abortion becomes illegal, just as Nazi leaders were prosecuted after the World War II. The 9th Circuit Court upheld the concept that this site was being used for a much more violent purpose and awarded the plaintiffs $107 million in damages.

The list of abortion providers reads like a list of targets for assassination: Names in plain black lettering were still "working," those in gray letters were "wounded," and those names that were "Str[uck]through" indicated doctors who had become "fatalit[ies]." The site was actually a list of people targeted for assassination. Within hours of the murder of Dr. Barnett Slepian in Amherst, New York, in 1998, his name was struck through, indicating that he had become a "fatality."[41]

The court found that the site's language and the strikethrough on the murdered person's names constituted a threat to others on the list. District Judge Robert Jones called certain language on the site "blatant and illegal communication of true threats to kill."[42] While the original site, with all of its trappings, is gone, many sites today host the Nuremberg Files, just without listing the slain.

A similar site is the Stop Huntingdon Animal Cruelty (SHAC) Web site[43] (see Box 9.3). This site offers a map of the United States that can be clicked on to find information on those individuals or companies committing "crimes" against animals anywhere. Clicking over a specific area gives a list of all "offenders" in that area. It has the names, addresses, phone numbers, and e-mail addresses of companies that do business with Huntingdon as well as some names of executives or other employees. The homes and/or cars of some of the people whose names have been listed by SHAC have been vandalized. These people have also faced demonstrations outside their homes at all times of the day and night, received harassing telephone calls or e-mails, and, in some extreme cases, have been physically attacked.[44]

BOX 9.3

"Letters to the Editor" Invoking Action Against the Huntingdon Life Sciences Corporation

Stop Huntingdon Animal Cruelty (SHAC)

The focus of SHAC is on Huntingdon Life Sciences (HLS), a firm that is involved in pharmaceutical testing. The smaller focus of the group may make them the most effective of the radical environmental and animal rights groups. The SHAC Web site reports on the actions of its supporters. For instance, the Web site publishes the letters sent in by activists. The following are just two of the letters that were published on the site with personal information x-ed out.

Received from Canadian activists:

CANADA JOINS THE FIGHT TO SMASH HLS!

About 25 Canadian activists joined in the fight to shut down HLS. Gathering in a major park in downtown Montreal, activists made speeches and handed out leaflets to hundreds of onlookers before taking over the street and marching to the offices of Sumitomo Canada.

Once there, activists attempted to enter the building and had a rousing protest, complete with spray painted anti-HLS slogans and strategically placed stickers. Everyone entering and exiting the building was treated to a crash course on the atrocities supported by their neighbours in the Sumitomo suite. A whole slew of newspeople were educated as well, and the demo appeared on the 6 o'clock news of two major T.V. stations. The demonstration ended with a reminder to Sumitomo that until it severs all ties with HLS—

"We will be back!"

Received anonymously:

WAKE UP CHIRON SCUM!

We couldn't sleep on Tuesday night, so we decided to go see what one of our local Chiron scum was up to at 2:30 am. We knocked and knocked on the door of Linda Short (27 xxxx Ave. xxxxxxx, CA, xxx-xxx-xxxx) but she didn't answer. Go figure, she must have been fast asleep. We were really curious to know for sure, so we decided to use our trusty bullhorns to make sure she knew we were outside anxiously awaiting her. We finally got the hint that she wasn't going to come out to visit with us, but our curiosity as to what she was up to got the best of us, so we decided to give her a call or two or three …

Chiron when are you going to get it? Wake up and realize that we have tons of energy and we are determined. We know where you live and we're finding out more and more personal information about you every day. Ask yourself if you can take it. Stop doing business with Huntingdon Life Sciences!

Unlike the Nuremberg Files, this site seems to understand what is and is not allowed under freedom of speech (for more on freedom of speech, see Box 9.4).[45] SHAC has faced multiple lawsuits, but they have always prevailed. Their knowledge of the law can best be seen in the following disclaimer that is linked to many places within the site:

It goes without saying that nothing contained on this website or in any SHAC publication is intended to encourage or incite illegal acts.

Any names and addresses of Huntingdon Life Sciences' laboratories and companies associated with them are published for the sole purpose of allowing members of the public to voice their concerns and carry out protests in a legal manner.

SHAC does not encourage or incite any illegal activities.

SHAC does not encourage or incite repetitive, threatening or abusive communications with these companies, be this by telephone call, fax, email or letter.

Any articles from the press published on this web site relating to illegal activities carried out against HLS and associated companies are posted for the sole reason of publishing news related to Huntingdon Life Sciences and are not intended to incite or encourage similar acts.[46]

BOX 9.4
Freedom of Speech

The only lawful limitations on speech are as follows:

Obscenity. Obscenity is speech that (1) the average person, applying contemporary community standards, would find, taken as a whole, to appeal to the prurient interest; (2) depicts or describes in a patently offensive manner specifically defined sexual conduct; and (3) lacks as a whole serious literary, artistic, political, or scientific value.

Fighting words. Speech likely to provoke an average listener to retaliation and thereby cause a breach of peace.

Commercial speech. The government can ban deceptive or illegal commercial speech; any other regulation must be supported by a substantial interest to be achieved by restrictions, regulations in proportion to that interest, and a limitation on expression carefully designed to achieve the state's goal.

Incitement ("clear and present danger"). Speech that is intended and likely to incite "imminent lawless action," or where the speech presents a "clear and present danger" to the security of the nation.

Time, place, and manner. Content-neutral regulation of the time, place, or manner of speech that does not interfere with the message being delivered and leaves open adequate alternative channels of communication is permissible.

Libel/slander. Speech that is not only false but that the speaker was negligent to some degree in using. The level of negligence is raised to "actual malice" (knowing or reckless disregard for the truth of the statement) for all statements made about public figures.

It is widely acknowledged that the Internet poses challenges to traditional law, but many people have tried to impose regulation. Most of these regulations have fallen to the First Amendment. The Communications Decency Act and the Child Online Protection Act are both congressional acts that tried to place limits on any information that is considered harmful to children and that was held unconstitutional.

Another issue of First Amendment rights was the case against Yahoo in the French courts. Yahoo was found in violation of French law because it hosted Nazi paraphernalia in its online auctions. An American judge ruled that the French decision could not be enforced in U.S. courts because the First Amendment protects American companies from foreign laws that are more restrictive. The site that hosted the controversial material was on the American Yahoo server, and they cannot regulate where people are when they view the sites. The French Yahoo site had always conformed to the French laws.

So, the open nature of the Internet and the First Amendment make regulations hard to implement. Many of the sites walk a fine line, but, with care, all sites, extremist or not, can continue to operate if they are careful to remain within constitutional protections.

Fund-Raising

Fund-raising has also been helped by the Internet. The fact that millions of people are potentially exposed to numerous sites means that more potential donors will be reached than ever before. Many of the sites have information on how to send donations. Some sites, like PETA, even allow for secure online credit card donations. Additionally, the SHAC group provides a list of individuals who have been arrested and imprisoned for their actions in support of animal rights.[47] They provide pictures and details of each person and links to Vegan Prison Support Group and ALF Support Groups that accept donations to provide direct or indirect financial and material support for these prisoners.

Besides donations, these groups also earn money through the selling of merchandise, including games, music, clothing, bumper stickers, and all other types of paraphernalia. Another source of income is through selling sermons, articles, or racists' books on their sites. While, if a person looks long enough, he or she can find free downloads of Wesley Swift's sermons, many more sites only offer them as mail-ordered hard copies. Someone can order a hard copy of lots of different types of works off these sites.

An example of a right-wing group that employs the Internet's fundraising ability is Kingdom Identity Church,[48] which offers many different products. To begin with, it offers an "American Institute of Theology Bible Course," which is a 12-lesson plan that costs $200 and upon completion gives the student a "Certificate in Christian Education." Moreover, it has audio- and videotape catalogs. The audiotapes, which are of sermons or lessons, are offered for a suggested donation of $3.50 per cassette or CD. Similarly, the videotapes that are proclaimed to be "professionally produced documentaries of our Christian Israelite heritage" have a price of $24 per DVD. These are only an example of the products that this site sells. The only limit to the money-making abilities of these sites is in the imagination of the site designer.

TERRORISM, INTELLIGENCE GATHERING, AND THE USA PATRIOT ACT

One of the most controversial topics in America today focuses squarely on the emergence of domestic groups that express radical and extremist political thoughts on the Internet. Are these groups free to express their political opinions under the protection of the First Amendment without scrutiny or monitoring by law enforcement agencies? Certainly, the existence of controversial and inflammatory material on the Web has been safeguarded, including most forms of pornography and hate speech (refer to Chapter 8 for a discussion of the law and legislation surrounding this issue). This discussion focuses more on the role of the police to collect and analyze information (or intelligence) on groups expressing radical thoughts and ideas through their Web sites. Do the police have an inherent duty to collect information on individuals involved in the development of these types of Web sites in an effort to thwart or prevent violent crimes and terrorist attacks? Nowhere are these questions more openly evoked than in the passage of the USA PATRIOT Act, and it is within this environment that we shall discuss the issues of privacy, freedom of speech and expression, and the right of society to be secure from future attacks.

A Short History of Intelligence in the United States

The framework for U.S. intelligence was created in a different time to deal with different problems other than terrorism. The National Security Act of 1947, which established the Central Intelligence Agency (CIA), envisioned the enemy of the United States to be nation-states such as the Soviet Union, China, and North Korea. The result was organizations and authority based on distinctions between domestic versus foreign threats, law enforcement versus national security concerns, and peacetime versus wartime.[49] The FBI was given responsibility for domestic intelligence and the CIA, the National Security Agency (NSA), and the Defense Intelligence Agency (DIA) were given primary responsibility for foreign intelligence outside the United States. During the politically active periods of the Vietnam War and Watergate, the roles between foreign and domestic intelligence agencies were further delineated and separated by executive and legislative initiatives (among these can be included the Privacy Act, the Freedom of Information Act, and the Attorney General Guidelines of Levi and Smith).

Domestic Intelligence and Policing

Law enforcement's primary focus is to collect evidence after a crime is committed in order to support prosecution in a court trial. This process is commonly called "investigation" and is reactive in nature. Prior to the passage of the USA PATRIOT Act, police intelligence activity had to focus on the development of probable cause that would justify other law enforcement and prosecutorial activities. In most incidents, a subject had actually to break the law or threaten to break established law before the FBI or other police agencies could utilize intelligence operations. The frustrating predicament in which the law enforcement community found itself was that law enforcement agencies could not act without probable cause, but at the same time were prevented from engaging in the activity from which that probable cause could originate.[50] The most critical point pertinent to the functions of domestic intelligence concerned the protection of civil liberties and constitutional rights of individual citizens, such as those who develop political inflammatory and radical Internet sites. The primary purpose of law enforcement is to protect the rights of all citizens through the objective enforcement of the law. This goal is seriously thwarted as some question the ethical validity of covert intelligence operations against its own citizens. Such activities can be violative of constitutional safeguards inherent in our democracy and could culminate in the formation of a police state.

Conflicting Roles

In contrast to the FBI and other police organizations, the CIA collects and analyzes information regarding national security in order to warn our government before an act occurs. For the most part, the CIA is relegated to working *outside* the United States; agents have no arrest powers, and their activities are proactive in nature (see Box 9.5). The two roles of domestic versus foreign intelligence gathering and analysis are directly competitive in function. The FBI and other police agencies are restricted in sharing information with the CIA so as not to compromise future court action or abridge the civil liberties of U.S. citizens. Similarly, the CIA is reluctant to give information to the FBI (or other law enforcement agencies) for fear of having sources and methods of acquiring information being revealed in court.[51] Note the difference between investigation and intelligence in Box 9.6.

Defining Intelligence

Intelligence can be defined as information, which has been identified as relevant, collected, verified, and interpreted within the context of specific objectives. This necessarily includes that the information has been analyzed, classified, and

BOX 9.5

Comparison Chart

Feedback form is available in the given link,
http://www.diffen.com/difference/Special:Feedback

	CIA	FBI
Stands for:	Central Intelligence Agency	Federal Bureau of Investigation
Motto:	Ye shall know the truth and it shall set you free.	Fidelity, Bravery, Integrity
Formed:	September 18, 1947	July 26, 1908
Employees:	Classified. Estimated 25,000 agents and 35,000 staff in 2016	Classified. Estimated 35,158 positions; 13,084 agents, 3,100 intelligence analysts and 21,974 staff in 2016
Headquarters:	George Bush Center for Intelligence, Langley, Virginia	J. Edgar Hoover Building, Washington, D.C.
Agency executives:	Michael R. Pompeo, Director. Mission executives (Chiefs of Station) are based in major embassies around the world and manage global operations on a regional or country basis.	Christopher A. Wray, Director. Other directors (or Special Agents in Charge – SAC) are located in major large cities domestically and are responsible for regional geographic districts.
Web site:	www.cia.gov	www.fbi.gov
Annual budget:	Classified. Approximately $18 billion (2016)	Approximately $8.8 billion (2016)

Source: http://www.diffen.com/difference/CIA_vs_FBI# (Updated July 2017 with revisions from *www.fbi.gov and www.cia.gov*).

BOX 9.6

The Differences Between Investigation and Intelligence

- *Investigation*

    Reactive; occurs after the event or incident

    Reports are generally open

    Sources are generally known and open

    Arrests are made based on evidence and facts

- *Intelligence*

    Proactive; information gathered before the event

    Reports are almost always closed

    Sources are confidential and closed

    Arrests are rarely made

---

distributed to policy makers, who utilize it toward the betterment of the country or the community.[52] Historically, the missing dimension in quality intelligence has been analysis. The transformation of raw data, whether acquired through human, technical, or open sources, must be collated, scrutinized, and processed accurately and in a timely manner. The ultimate goal of this analytic process is a finished product more intelligible, accurate, and usable than the data and information drawn upon to prepare it.[53] Placing this discussion in perspective, information collected by the FBI and other police agencies on individuals within groups that develop radical Web sites when no crime has been reported becomes intelligence data.

U.S. Intelligence Weaknesses

In the aftermath of September 11, 2001, several studies were conducted to assess shortcomings that may exist in our nation's ability to collect and analyze important intelligence information on terrorist groups. Several weaknesses were identified in counterterrorism efforts led by the FBI, CIA, and NSA. These included communication problems among agencies, a shortage of linguists, and a failure by these agencies to correctly analyze relevant intelligence information to potential terrorist threats. Several of the issues identified as potential problems existing within the U.S. intelligence community included the following: (1) a failure to place an emphasis on traditional human intelligence gathering and analysis and relying too much on technology tools such as spy satellites and expert system programs to gain intelligence advantages; (2) a failure to provide timely, accurate, and specific intelligence information to law enforcement agencies and U.S. policy makers; (3) an overly bureaucratic and decentralized structure (particularly within the FBI) that hindered counterterrorism efforts and the efficient use of intelligence information; (4) outdated and obsolete computer systems that were not compatible with other systems and unable to provide accurate and timely sharing of critical information nationally; and (5) overly restrictive guidelines and laws that hindered the effective use of informants and the general collection of intelligence information.[54]

These problems are particularly distressing, considering the effort to combat terrorism. The organized, clandestine, and destructive activities of terrorist groups uniquely confound both the gathering and analysis of intelligence information. Complicating this matter is the inability of policy makers to place the acts of terrorism within the scope of one jurisdiction. Are acts of terrorism crimes to be investigated by the FBI, or are they threats to our national security that fall within the purview of our military and national security agencies?

BOX 9.7

The "Leaking" of Classified Data and Intelligence

While the "leaking" of classified intelligence and sensitive information is a perennial problem, it has recently loomed much larger in significance. For example, the May 24, 2017, Manchester, England terrorist bombing at the close of an Ariana Grande concert before a primarily pre-teen audience, caused the murder of 22 people, including children. The nub of the problem is that Britain's MI5 Intelligence Service shared sensitive information and crime scene photographs (including the name and photograph of the suicide bomber), with an unnamed American intelligence agency and that information was then, leaked to *The New York Times*. This leaking was deemed so highly egregious that British Prime Minister Theresa May protested to President Donald Trump that British authorities would suspend sharing of intelligence with U.S. intelligence agencies until they could be assured the leaking would cease. While the president has called for an investigation and prosecution of the leaker(s), the incident calls into question the age-old adage that sensitive information should only be shared on a "need to know" basis—a problem identified as a weakness of the intelligence community in the pre-9/11 environment.

Source: Preble, C., Ruger, W. P., Friedman, B. H., Carpenter, T. G., Gomez, E., Bandow, D., and Gholz, E. (2016). Our Foreign Policy Choices: Rethinking America's Global Role.

THE USA PATRIOT ACT OF 2001

In an effort to clarify and improve these conditions and provide sweeping new powers to both domestic law enforcement and traditional intelligence agencies, President George W. Bush signed into law the USA PATRIOT Act on October 26, 2001. The USA PATRIOT Act (**U**niting and **S**trengthening **A**merica by **P**roviding **A**ppropriate **T**ools **R**equired to **I**ntercept and **O**bstruct **T**errorism) changed over 15 different statutes with little or no external review. The law not only addressed terrorism and intelligence issues but also focused on more traditional money laundering, computer abuse and crime, immigration processes, and fraud. However, the most substantial part of the Act is that it expanded all four traditional tools of surveillance used by law enforcement with significantly reduced checks and balances:

- *Wiretaps:* The surreptitious eavesdropping on a third-party conversation by wire, oral, or electronic communication. Usually conducted with a microphone receiver ("bug") on a telephone device; requires both a search warrant and a court order.
- *Search warrants:* A legal document signed by a judge directing police officers to search a specific area for a specific person or item of evidence/contraband. The document must be based on probable cause.
- *Pen/trap and trace orders:* Telephone call set-up information only is intercepted without individual communications. A "pen register" provides the law enforcement agency access to the numbers dialed from a subject's phone, while a "trap and trace" provides the incoming numbers to the subject's phone (like caller ID).
- *Court orders and subpoenas:* A court document signed by a judge that instructs the police to perform a specific task. A subpoena is a court order that commands a person to appear in court at a specified date and time to testify.

Law enforcement and intelligence agencies can now more easily and more surreptitiously monitor the Web surfing and communication of individuals using the Internet, conduct nationwide roving wiretaps on cell and line telephones, and build profiles on the reading habits of people visiting public libraries. Under the Act, police can now force Internet Service Providers (ISPs) to "voluntarily" hand over information on customer profiles and Web-surfing habits *without* a warrant or court order. This has a dramatic potential impact on the various radical groups and Web sites discussed here. Not only do the police have the legal right to monitor politically and socially extreme Web sites but also they have the ability to monitor those individuals who visit such Web sites.

The Reauthorized PATRIOT Act of 2006

In 2005, provisions of the PATRIOT Act were to sunset, and Congress acted to review, reauthorize, and pass this bill. The revisions were passed into law by President Bush in March 2006. The roving wiretap provisions were maintained, though greater oversight was added to ensure that these powers would not be abused by law enforcement. The changes include judicial review and approval by the director of the FBI or NSA, along with a more detailed application process to specify targets and actions. The provision that allowed library records to be subpoenaed was also removed to protect citizens, with the exception of electronic communications through the library. The original PATRIOT Act also allowed law enforcement agencies to conduct covert, or "sneak and peek," searches in the homes of potential suspects without their knowledge or authorization. Since this was considered by some to be too extreme, the reauthorization was changed to limit the time when such a search could be conducted so as not to give unreasonable power to law enforcement. However, the ability to conduct surveillance against what are defined as "lone wolf terrorists" was increased to provide greater time to monitor a target. The definition of terrorism was also expanded to include receiving military-type training from a foreign terror organization and narcoterrorism and criminalizes the act of planning a terror attack against a mass transit system.

The Reauthorized PATRIOT Act of 2011

Provisions of the PATRIOT Act were once again set to sunset in 2011 and Congress acted to review and reauthorize them. First, roving wiretaps in relation to foreign intelligence collection were reauthorized and allow electronic surveillance of a person, without specifying the phone or computer, if that person demonstrates an intent to evade surveillance by, for example, switching cell phones on a regular basis. In short, the government may obtain an order to conduct surveillance that specifies a target but not a specific device to tap. Second, the reauthorization extended access to business records and tangible things. The USA PATRIOT Act allows the government to seek court-ordered production of "any tangible thing," including business records, in intelligence investigations. The provision both expanded the scope of materials that may be sought and lowered the standard for a court to issue an order compelling their production. Third, the "lone wolf" provision was extended, which permits surveillance against a non-U.S. person engaged in international terrorism for whom the government does not have evidence of ties to a foreign terrorist group.

Constitutional Rights and the USA PATRIOT Act

The expanded scope and breadth of the Act has raised concerns from a variety of sources.[55] Most agree that intelligence gathering and analysis has to improve in order to prevent future domestic and international terrorist attacks. However, some argue that the USA PATRIOT Act went too far. The Act increases information sharing between domestic law enforcement departments and traditional intelligence agencies such as the FBI and CIA. In such a state, the line between intelligence gathering and public law enforcement becomes blurred. Critics are quick to point out the civil rights abuses that have occurred in the past whenever police agencies have become too involved in intelligence gathering. Most major cities, including New York, Chicago, Denver, and Los Angeles, have had relatively recent litigation aimed at limiting the role of the police in this function. The arguments focus on the collection of irrelevant private information of individuals (including Web-surfing habits and sexual orientation) to the profiling of individuals in minority communities. In one case, an intelligence officer in Portland, Oregon, developed boxes of information on over 500 community groups and over 3,000 well-known citizens of the city and stored them at his own residence. Over 20 years of police intelligence records were discovered by family members several years after the officer died. The dusty reports and pictures not only focused on private meetings and information on local politicians but also revealed that the officer had himself been an active member of the John Birch Society, a right-wing organization often under scrutiny by governmental intelligence agencies.[56]

Some argue that the expanded role of police in intelligence gathering under the Act will only provide a significant threat to the personal and civil liberties of all Americans and do very little to thwart terrorism.[57] In an extreme example of opposition to the USA PATRIOT Act, the government of Nova Scotia province in Canada passed a law called "The new Personal Information International Disclosure Protection Act."[58] This Act was designed to protect their citizens from having any information provided through PATRIOT Act investigations and dictated punishments for failing to do so. The reauthorized versions of the PATRIOT Act attempted to respond to these critiques by increasing judicial and managerial review, though many still think the laws afford too much power to law enforcement. In coming years, it is clear that police will at least maintain a significantly new role in the fight against terrorism involving intelligence gathering, particularly using the Internet. This new role must be accompanied by vastly new training for law enforcement officers, defining the tactical, operational, and legal limits involving intelligence gathering and analysis.

QUICK FACTS

Fake photos have been publicized in American society for a very long time. Fake news too, is not, frankly, new. But, the latter appears to now be a topic of mainstream conversation. In 2017, the rancor and epithets between liberals and conservatives appears to have dramatically increased and intensified by social media, as well as conventional news media. The www.snopes.com Web site is replete with endless examples of fake news. Even National Public Radio (www.npr.org) has a section of its Web site devoted to fake news. A recent report by the Electronic Frontier Foundation (EFF) claims that the struggle our country is facing is a societal issue we have to address at all levels, understanding that the very structure of social media platforms exacerbates the news. Unfortunately, fake news is not simply an "issue" or phenomena of the moment, as some studies and experts report that uncivil and manipulative behaviors on the Internet will persist—and may get worse in the future.

Sources: Rsinie, L. "The Future of Free Speech, Trolls, Anonymity and Fake News Online," Pew Research Center (March 29, 2017) *http://www.pewinternet.org/2017/03/29/the-future-o-free-speech-trolls-anonyminity-and-ake-news-online/*

Versace, C. "'Fake News' Has Not Spared the Financial Markets" (January 1, 2017) *http://www.businessinsider.com/fake-news-impact-on-financial-markets-2016-12;* Plead the Fifth "Media Bias Hits New Low," *The Maine Wire* (October 16, 2016) *http://www.themainewire.com/2016/10/media-bias-hits/*

Borden, S.L. and C. Tew "Exploring Questions of Media Morality." *Journal of Mass Media Ethics* 22: 4 (December 5, 2007) *http://www.tandfonline.com/dor/abs/10.1080/08900520701583586*

Summary

The Internet offers people the ability to participate in or be exposed to all sorts of questionable material. Some of this includes politically and socially extreme Web sites developed by hate mongers, bigots, racists, and radicals. These can be experienced in the privacy of one's own home, no matter where he or she lives. A person can download information, order products, or communicate with others without ever having to leave his or her home. Moreover, using a computer to explore and chat gives a person a feeling of anonymity that allows him or her to do or participate in things he or she never would in the real world. Most certainly, the freedom offered by the Internet allows for a continuation of extremist goals by reaching a wider audience and provides a means for easy excess to information, no matter how distasteful.

Review Questions

1. Legally define "hate crime," and explain why hate crime legislation has been so controversial in the United States.
2. What is *Ethnic Cleansing*, and why is it so controversial?
3. What are ELF and ALF? Explain their similarities and differences.
4. What are the primary purposes of right-wing hate Web sites that use images, music, games, and the like to spread their propaganda?
5. What are the "Nuremberg Files," and why were they important in setting legal precedence relating to communication on the Internet?
6. Explain and discuss the inherent conflicts associated with the police as intelligence gatherers.
7. List and discuss some of the weaknesses associated with U.S. intelligence in the aftermath of September 11, 2001.
8. What is the USA PATRIOT Act, and what are the four traditional tools of surveillance expanded with the Act?
9. How has the Reauthorized USA PATRIOT Act of 2006 changed the legal definitions of terrorism and responded to critiques against the original law?

Critical Thinking Exercises

1. Visit the Web site of the Southern Poverty Law Center (SPLC) and learn about hate in America at www.splcenter.org/. Study some of the available *Intelligence Reports* online and note the high number of active hate groups in the United States. Visit the "Hate Map" on the site. Should you be a partner sharing the mission of the SPLC fighting hate and seeking justice? Think of your community; discuss any visible signs of hate or intolerance where you live?
2. Visit the Web site of the Anarchism.net at http://www.anarchism.net/www.htm. Scroll through the list of Web sites and visit a few. What are the classic symbols of anarchism as presented by the Web site? Discuss how this site lives up to its mission statement: "Liberty and Justice for All."

Endnotes

1. GOLDAIN, I. and KUTARANA, C. (2016). *The Age of Discovery: Navigating the Risks and Rewards of Our New Renaissance*. New York: St. Martin's Press. Available at *https://iangoldin.org/books/age-of-discovery/*
2. SEGAL, A. (2016). *The Hacked World Order: How Nations Fight, Trade, Maneuver, and Manipulate in the Digital Age*. New York: Public Affairs, pp. 232–233. Available at *http://www.publicaffairsbooks.com/book/hardcover/the-hacked-world-order/9781610394154*
3. Simon Wiesenthal Center. (1999). *"The New Lexicon of Hate: The Changing Tactics, Language and Symbols of America's Extremists."* Los Angeles. See also MASON, G., McCULLOCH, J., and MAHER, J. (2016). "Policing Hate Crime: Markers for Negotiating Common Ground in Policy Implementation." *Policing and Society* 26(6): 680–697.
4. For more information, visit the Nation Institutes Against Hate Crimes Web site: *http://www.wiesenthal.com*

5. Department of Justice and IACP. (1999). *Responding to Hate Crimes: A Police Officer's Guide to Investigation and Prevention.* Washington, D.C.: U.S. Department of Justice and IACP. See also Awan, I. (2016). "Islamophobia on Social Media: A Qualitative Analysis of the Facebook's Walls of Hate." *International Journal of Cyber Criminology* 10(1): 1, and Holt, T.J.and Bolden, M.S. (2014). "Technological Skills of White Supremacists in an Online Forum: A Qualitative Examination." *International Journal of Cyber Criminology* 8(2): 79.

6. See: *www.stormfront.org*

7. Parsons, C. (2009). "Hate Goes Viral on Social Networking Sites," *Reuters.* See: *http://www.reuters.com/article/technologyNews/idUSTRE54C4KW20090513.*

8. Godinez, V. (March 14, 2002). "Hate Group Wooing Teens by Making a Game Out of Racism," *Dallas Morning News,* 2A.

9. Taylor, R.W. and Fritsch, E.J. (2015). *Juvenile Justice: Policies, Programs, and Practices.* 4th edition. New York: McGraw-Hill Publishers, pp. 518–520.

10. An interview with a leader of the Texas Militia in Dallas, Texas (January 2000), reflecting many of the sentiments expressed by Tom Metzger, a leader of the White Aryan Resistance (WAR). See also *htttp://sjnnchicago.medill.northwestern.edu/blog/2017/04/17/interview-shane-bauer-undercover-border-militia/*

11. "ATF: Plot by Skinheads to Kill Obama Is Foiled." *Associated Press,* October 27, 2008.

12. Duke, D. (2008). "Obama Wins Demo Nomination: A Black Flag for White America." *The Official Website of Representative David Duke.* Retrieved September 9, 2009, from *http://www.davidduke.com*

13. Jarboe, J.F. (February 12, 2002). Domestic Terrorism Section Chief, Federal Bureau of Investigation. "The Threat of Eco-Terrorism." Speech before the House of Resources Committee, Subcommittee on Forests and Forest Health. See also Loadenthal, M. (2013). "Deconstructing 'Eco-terrorism': Rhetoric, Framing and Statecraft as Seen Through the Insight Approach." *Critical Studies on Terrorism* 6(1): 92–117.

14. *Ibid.*

15. Freeh, L.J. (May 10, 2001). Director, Federal Bureau of Investigation. "Threat of Terrorism to the United States." Speech before U.S. Senate, Committees on Appropriations, Armed Services, and Select Committee on Intelligence. See *https://www.fbi.gov/news/speeches/fighting-terrorism-in-the-digital-age*

16. Smith, B.L. (1994). *Terrorism in America: Pipe Bombs and Pipe Dreams.* Albany, NY: State University of New York Press, p. 125. See also Klein, B.R., Gruenewald, J. and Smith, B.L. (2017). Opportunity, Group Structure, Temporal Pat-terns, and Successful Outcomes of Far-right Terrorism Incidents in the United States. Crime & Delinquency, 0011128716654925.

17. Freeh, "Threat of Terrorism to the United States."

18. Smith, *Terrorism in America: Pipe Bombs and Pipe Dreams.*

19. Jarboe, "The Threat of Eco-Terrorism." See also Carson, J.V. (2014). Counterterrorism and Radical Eco-groups: A Context for Exploring the Series Hazard Model. *Journal of Quantitative Criminology*, 30(3): 485–504.

20. Center for the Defense of Free Enterprise (CDFE). "Ecoterrorism." *www.cdfe.org/ecoterror.hml*

21. Schabner, D. (February 26, 2002). "New Front on Ecoterror? Some Want to Target High-Profile Activists in Battle on Ecoterror." *ABCNews.com. http://abcnews.go.com/sections/us/DailyNews/ecoterror_support020226.html*

22. Jarboe, "The Threat of Eco-Terrorism."

23. Department of Justice. (2006). "Eleven Defendants Indicted on Domestic Terrorism Charges." *http://www.usdoj.gov/opa/pr/2006/January/06_crm_030.html*

24. Off-Road.com. "A Short History of Ecoterrorism." *http://www.off-road.com/land/ecoterrorism_history.html*

25. Jarboe, "The Threat of Eco-Terrorism."

26. *Off-Road.com,* "A Short History of Ecoterrorism."

27. Jarboe, "The Threat of Eco-Terrorism."

28. Aylward, K., DeHaven, C., Robinson, W., and Smith, B. (2003). "Cyberterrorism." *http://www.cob.vt.edu/accounting/faculty/belanger/sec/article5.ppt* See also Dawson, M., Omar, M., and Abramson, J. (2015). Understanding the Methods behind Cyber Terrorism. In Encyclopedia of Information Science and Technology, Third Edition pp. 1539–1549. IGI Global.

29. *Ibid.*

30. *Ibid.,* p. 5.

31. Resistance Records. *http://www.resistance.com/*

32. Anti-Defamation League (ADL). "Racist Groups Using Computer Gaming to Promote Violence Against Blacks, Latinos and Jews." *http://www.adl.org/videogames/default.asp.* See also *https://www.adl.org/news/article/racist-groups-use-computer-gaming-to-promote-hate*

33. Anti-Defamation League (ADL). "Creating a Racist Computer Game—A Relatively Simple Task." *http://www.adl.org/videogames/game_creating.asp.*

34. "Jew Rats." *http://www.nsec-88.org/ruzne/jew_rats/jew-rats.zip.*

35. People for the Ethical Treatment of Animals (PETA). *peta.org.*

36. PETA. *www.petakids.com*

37. PETA 2. *www.peta2.com*

38. The Animal Liberation Front (ALF) home page (*http://www.animalliberationfront.com*).

39. *Ibid.*

40. See *Planned Parenthood* v. *American Coalition of Life Activists,* 41F. Supp 2nd, 1130 (D. OR 1999). This is a landmark First Amendment case involving a $107 million dollar award against antiabortion activists who branded abortion doctors as "murderers" and then crossed out their name when they were killed.

41. ADL. "Poisoning the Web: Hatred Online, Internet Bigotry, Extremism, and Violence." *http://www.adl.org/poisoning_web/introduction.asp.* See also Klein, A. (2017). Fanaticism, Racism, and Rage Online: Corrupting the Digital Sphere. Springer.

42. SCHABNER, D. (May 5, 2003). "Interactive Ecoterror? Animal Rights Group Provides Target List in Anti-Lab Campaign." *ABCNews.com. http://abcnews.go.com /sections/us/SciTech/ecoterror030505.html* See also SINGER, P. (2015). Writings on an ethical life. Open Road Media. 41. GIRGEN, J. (2017). Constructing Animal Rights Activism as a Social Threat.

43. Stop Huntingdon Animal Cruelty (SHAC). *shac.net.*

44. SCHABNER, D. (May 5, 2003). "Interactive Ecoterror? Animal Rights Group Provides Target List in Anti-Lab Campaign." See also .NAGTZAAM, G. (2017). From Environmental Action to Ecoterrorism?: Towards a Process Theory of Environmental and Animal Rights Oriented Political Violence. Edward Elgar Publishing.

45. Electronic Privacy Information Center. "Free Speech." *http://www.epic.org/free_speech/* See also MARSHALL, P. (2017). Issue: Technology and Business Ethics Short Article: European Courts Set Privacy Standards.

46. *shac.net,* Stop Huntingdon Animal Cruelty (SHAC).

47. *http://www.shac.net/features/prisoners.html and http:// www.animalliberationfront.com/ALFront/SHAC.htm*

48. Kingdom Identity Church. *http://www.kingidentity.com/*

49. DEUTSCH, J. and SMITH, J.H. (2002). "Smarter Intelligence." *Foreign Policy* 128: 64–69. See also PREBLE, C., RUGER, W.P., FRIEDMAN, B.H., CARPENTER, T.G., GOMEZ, E., BANDOW, D., ... and GHOLZ, E. (2016). Our Foreign Policy Choices: Rethinking America's Global Role.

50. MOTLEY, J.B. (1983). *U.S. Strategy to Counter Domestic Political Terrorism.* Washington, D.C.: National Security Affairs Monograph Series 2: 62–70. See also MAHMOOD, S. (2014). An Invasion of Privacy?: A Look into NSA Domestic Surveillance Policies Brenda C. Machuca IT 103/012.

51. TAYLOR, R.W. (1987). "Terrorism and Intelligence." *Defense Analysis* 3: 165–175. See also BYMAN, D. (2014). The intelligence war on terrorism. *Intelligence and National Security*, 29(6): 837–863.

52. MCCARTHEY, S.P. (1998). *The Function of Intelligence in Crisis Management.* Burlington, VT: Ashgate Publishing.

53. GODSON, R. (ed.), (1983). *Intelligence Requirements for the 1980s: Elements of Intelligence,* revised edition. Washington, D.C.: National Strategy Information Center. See also AVEY, P. C. and DESCH, M.C. (2014). What do policymakers want from us? Results of a survey of current and former senior national security decision makers. *International Studies Quarterly*, 58(2): 227–246.

54. Summary of Classified Report to the U.S. Congress, House of Representatives Intelligence Subcommittee. (July 16, 2002). *Report on Intelligence Gathering and Analysis pre September 11, 2001.*

55. Electronic Frontier Foundation (October 31, 2001). "EFF Analysis of the Provisions of the USA PATRIOT Act." See *www.eff .org/Privacy/Surveillance/Terrorism_militias/20011031_eff _usa_patriot_analysis.html*

56. "Terrorism Forces Renewed," *The Portland Observer,* September 25, 2002, p. 1.

57. *Ibid.*

58. GRANT, C. (2006). "Protection of Privacy Legislation Proclaimed." *http://www.gov.ns.ca/news/details .asp?id=20061115005*

Digital Laws and Legislation

CHAPTER OBJECTIVES

After completing this chapter, you should be able to

- Explain the intent and fundamental concepts of search and seizure law as it applies to cyber crime.
- Identify situations where search and seizure is possible without a warrant and describe its limits.
- Describe the federal statutes that govern electronic surveillance in communications networks.
- Discuss the issues presented regarding the admission of digital evidence at trial.
- Identify and discuss the significant U.S. Supreme Court cases focusing on cyber crime and evidence.

INTRODUCTION

In this chapter, law and legislation as it applies to the collection of evidence and prosecution of cyber crime will be discussed. First, search and seizure law for digital evidence will be analyzed, including searches with warrants and numerous searches without warrants. Second, the major federal statutes governing the collection of digital evidence, especially electronic surveillance law, will be covered along with federal criminal statutes, which forbid certain types of computer crime. Third, issues related to the admission of digital evidence at trial, including authentication and hearsay, will be reviewed. Fourth, significant U.S. Supreme Court cases in the area of cyber crime will be highlighted.

SEARCH AND SEIZURE LAW FOR DIGITAL EVIDENCE

Our current body of search law is the ongoing product of the interaction of legislation, case law, and constitutional law. Most of the search law discussed in this section applies to searches and seizures overall, not just those involving cyber crimes and evidence. In fact, much search and seizure law has failed to keep up with the changes brought about by increases in cyber crimes and the increasing need to collect digital evidence.

The Fourth Amendment states:

> The right of the people to be secure in their persons, houses, papers, and effects, against unreasonable searches and seizures, shall not be violated, and no warrants shall issue, but upon probable cause, supported by oath or affirmation, and particularly describing the place to be searched, and the persons or things to be seized.

As simple as this language may seem, numerous questions have be raised by the specific details occurring in searches and seizures of digital evidence. In general, questions focus on whether or not an activity is a "search" and whether a search is "reasonable." The best way to ensure that a search is not "unreasonable" is to seek and obtain a warrant from a neutral, detached magistrate. In *Johnson* v. *United States*,[1] the U.S. Supreme Court stated:

> The point of the Fourth Amendment, which often is not grasped by zealous officers, is not that it denies law enforcement the support of the usual inferences which reasonable men draw from evidence. Its protection consists in requiring that those inferences be drawn by a neutral and detached magistrate instead of being judged by the officer engaged in the often competitive enterprise of ferreting out crime.

The key to understanding search and seizure law is to remember that the point is not to protect criminals; the point is to protect a person's reasonable expectation of privacy. Criminals entering their home with the police chasing them do not receive sanctuary. Similarly, a guilty desire to hide something does not necessarily create a reasonable expectation of privacy. The Fourth Amendment protects persons evidencing an expectation of privacy; however, society must be willing to recognize that expectation as reasonable.[2]

A seizure of property occurs when there is some meaningful interference with an individual's possessory interests in that property.[3] In relation to property, a seized item deprives an owner of its use. On the other hand, a search is an attempt by law enforcement officers to obtain evidence. By definition, a search intrudes into a person's reasonable expectation of privacy.[4] Therefore, a search occurs, in a constitutional sense, any time there is a governmental intrusion into a person's reasonable expectation of privacy. An act as simple as opening a notebook and reading the contents in a suspect's living room changes the character of the interaction from simple observation to a search.[5] However, just because the police intrude into a person's reasonable expectation of privacy does not mean that the intrusion is unlawful. Several mechanisms are available to the police in which they can lawfully search a person or property and thus lawfully intrude into a person's reasonable expectation of privacy. In the following sections, these mechanisms will be discussed, including searches with warrants and searches without warrants.

Searches with Warrants

In order to obtain a search warrant, a law enforcement officer must show probable cause by reasonably establishing the following:

1. A crime has been committed.
2. Evidence of the crime exists.
3. The evidence presently exists in the place to be searched.

Furthermore, the law enforcement officer must particularly describe the place to be searched and the evidence to be seized. Specific evidence of a specific crime must be named. General evidence facilitating a criminal act may be described by function. The investigator can search anywhere the named item(s) can be found. The judicial officer issuing the search warrant must be legally authorized to issue search warrants. Different jurisdictions empower different officers with this authority. Local policies and procedures should specify who has the power to issue search warrants.

Furthermore, the judicial officer issuing the search warrant must have jurisdiction over the area to be searched.

Jurisdiction "is the power of the court to decide a matter in controversy and presupposes the existence of a duly constituted court with control over the subject matter and the parties."[6] When a transaction crosses state boundaries, typical in cyber crime cases, jurisdictional issues may arise. A search warrant is only valid within the jurisdiction of the magistrate signing it. The degree of activity projected into a geographic area determines whether the doctrine of personal jurisdiction applies. If a criminal actor actively engages a victim, the local court may exercise personal jurisdiction over the actor. If the criminal actor simply provides information from a Web site, the victim's local court may not have grounds to exercise personal jurisdiction; however, local investigators are by no means ever prevented from engaging the assistance of remote law enforcement or courts to further an investigation.[7]

The remedy for a flawed search is most frequently suppression of the evidence obtained during the trial. This means that even the most clear-cut and self-evident material can be ruled inadmissible at trial. Some violations of statute may incur civil liability for the investigator, the investigator's department, or parent jurisdiction. An improper search and seizure is eligible for civil suit under 42 U.S.C. §1983. The current implementation of the exclusionary rule is defined in *Mapp* v. *Ohio* (1961). The sole purpose of the exclusionary rule is to curb police abuse of civil rights and to deter police misconduct. There is no common law expectation of the suppression of evidence improperly obtained. To invoke the exclusionary rule, the defendant must have standing; that is, the defendant must be the one whose rights were violated by the search.

The good faith doctrine provides one possible defense to accusations of a flawed search. If the investigator has a reasonable, bona fide (good faith) belief that the search conducted is based on a valid warrant, but that warrant is in actuality unsupported by probable cause, the fruits of the search are admissible. The reasoning behind the exclusionary rule is to deter police from misconduct, not to remedy violations of rights.[8] The exclusionary rule applies not only to evidence improperly obtained but also to evidence discovered using the improperly obtained evidence (i.e., derivative evidence). This is known as the fruit of the poisonous tree doctrine. Again, the rationale is to discourage the violation of citizens' rights by not rewarding such behavior by law enforcement personnel.

There are two other defenses to the exclusionary rule that are related to one another. First, an independent source of the same information can redeem the evidence tainted by illegal search. Thus, if an illegal search—a forensic fishing expedition—reveals child pornography, the investigator may seek independent indication of the suspect's involvement in child pornography. A posting from a pedophile Web site may indicate the presence of evidence, but remain completely independent of the tainted source. Another potential defense is that the tainted evidence may lead to a short-cut, but would otherwise have been obtained (known as the "inevitable discovery doctrine"). For example, a coerced confession of possession of child pornography without a lawyer present would be suppressed, but a search warrant that was issued prior to the coerced confession could show the inevitable discovery of the materials. Since the materials would have been discovered if the process had continued, an illegal search does not immunize the evidence to discovery.

Searches Without Warrants

Numerous exceptions exist to the general rule that searches must be conducted pursuant to a warrant. In fact, most searches conducted by the police do not involve a warrant (known as "warrantless searches"). Although numerous established exceptions to the warrant requirement exist and will be discussed in this section, it is best to be cautious in applying real-world analogies to the electronic world. Even if an officer believes he or she has a legitimate exception to the warrant requirement, it may still be worth stopping and seeking a warrant. Furthermore, the level of analysis required to obtain digital evidence can rarely be justified without a warrant; however, it may be appropriate to seize potential evidence to preserve it, while awaiting a warrant for the analysis. This section will discuss several warrantless searches.

STOP AND FRISK   A law enforcement officer has the right to self-protection during a brief interview by conducting a frisk of a citizen for weapons. A frisk is limited to a pat down of the outer clothing of the individual and can occur based on reasonable suspicion. Although it is possible to identify potential sources of digital evidence during the stop (e.g., a cellular phone), there is no clear justification, under the stop and frisk doctrine, to analyze such a device based on the logic of a stop and frisk (which basically only allows officers to seize weapons unless the item is immediately apparent to be subject to seizure such as drugs). However, if probable cause exists to believe evidence of a crime exists in the device, then further analysis should wait, pending a warrant, but the device can be seized by the officer based on probable cause, not stop and frisk.

A stop and frisk may be combined with other exceptions to examine content. For example, the plain-view doctrine can be used in association with data displayed by the device. Perhaps more useful is a trend in lower court cases allowing the preservation of perishable data under the exigent circumstances doctrine.[9] Warrantless searches of cellular phones have been allowed due to the possibility of incoming calls deleting evidence.

CONSENT SEARCH   When attempting to collect digital evidence without a warrant, consent searches are the most commonly used searches conducted by law enforcement. An officer can ask a citizen to consent (i.e., give permission) to a search of his or her person or property. Valid consent to search allows officers to search for any item within the scope of that consent. The courts apply a "totality of the circumstances" test to ensure that the consent was intelligently granted and free of coercion. Furthermore, a suspect may revoke consent at any time, even during the search. The scope of the search is directly related to the consent given. Again, the totality of the circumstances will dictate the court's acceptance of searches that seem to exceed the scope of the consent.

An additional concern with consent searches is that the person giving consent must be legally capable of doing so. Briefly, these are persons with equal property rights (e.g., spouses, co-owners, or other employees using the same equipment); employers, when it is clear by contract or policy; custodians of children (school officials, parents, etc.); or persons lawfully borrowing the property with access to the areas to be searched.[10] Some relationships have been defined by the courts to preclude legal consent. These include a spouse or co-owner specifically precluded from an area with reasonable precautions to prevent entry, a landlord (including hotel managers), an employer reserving an area for the exclusive and private use of an employee, or the host of a long-term guest with exclusive or private control over an area.[11]

Even if physical access to a space is granted, it does not come with the assumption of access to protected data. For example, if one spouse takes precautions to keep the other from using a computer (like a password or placing the computer in a separate room and denying access), or if a laptop is in the personal possession of a guest—even if left in an otherwise searchable room—a search of the data contained therein cannot be based on consent unless the person with authority to grant consent allows the search.[12]

QUICK FACTS

Whether consent was voluntarily given is a question of fact that the court must decide by considering the totality of the circumstances. While no single aspect controls the result, the U.S. Supreme Court has identified the following important factors: the age, education, intelligence, physical and mental condition of the person giving consent; whether the person was under arrest; and whether the person had been advised of his right to refuse consent. The government carries the burden of proving that consent was voluntary.

Source: U.S. Department of Justice. *Searching and Seizing Computers and Obtaining Electronic Evidence in Criminal Investigations.* (Washington, D.C.: U.S. Department of Justice, 2010), pp. 15–16.

EXIGENT CIRCUMSTANCES The exigent circumstances doctrine allows law enforcement officers to search and/or seize evidence without a warrant if they have probable cause and there is some pressing need (i.e., exigent circumstance) to preserve evidence that is in danger of being destroyed or corrupted. The nature of digital evidence makes it subject to quick disposal and easy corruption. Encryption is another concern in making evidence unusable by an investigator. Once data are encrypted, the key can be almost instantaneously destroyed. The suspect may have another copy of the key somewhere nearby, but the location may be unknown to investigators. These very real dangers may justify warrantless searches under the proper conditions, but the burden of proving exigent circumstances falls on law enforcement.

Unless the computer, device, or network cannot be secured, it is unlikely that exigency will allow analysis; it will just allow for the seizure of the items. For example, investigators may seize a laptop without a warrant to prevent it from being taken out of their control, but it would require truly unusual circumstances to justify searching the contents without a warrant.

SEARCH INCIDENT TO ARREST The Supreme Court has ruled that officers are allowed to search the person arrested for any weapons or for any evidence on the arrestee's person in order to prevent its concealment or destruction. Furthermore, officers may also search areas within the arrestee's immediate control for the same purpose.[13] Like the stop and frisk, this exception could yield the physical container of evidence (e.g., cell phone), but would not justify analysis of the contents without exigent circumstances (e.g., batteries dying or new calls replacing numbers in memory).

PLAIN VIEW The plain-view doctrine allows an officer to lawfully seize an item as long as certain requirements are met. In order to seize an item under the plain-view doctrine, an officer must (1) see the item, (2) be legally present in the area from which the item is viewed, and (3) immediately recognize that the item is subject to seizure. Since the officer is not conducting a search (i.e., the item is in plain view, and thus, there is no governmental intrusion into a person's reasonable expectation of privacy), the criminal nature of the item to be seized or observed must be immediately apparent to the officer (e.g., child pornography).[14]

Each of these requirements applies to the discovery and seizure of digital evidence, but it is possible that upon closer examination evidence not covered by a warrant will be discovered in plain view. For example, a search warrant may allow an investigator to search a hard drive for evidence of fraud. While the investigator is conducting the analysis, the officer discovers child pornography on the hard drive. The child pornography can be seized under the plain-view doctrine, since the three requirements discussed above have been met. As it applies to digital evidence, Orton states that it is important for investigators not to change the focus of their examination as a result of discovering a plain-view item. As an example, Orton states:

> [I]f a search protocol calls for examining all files sequentially on a computer, then every file may be examined … [I]f the search … calls for a key word search and an examination of the directory and file structure, but not the examination of each individual file, then the discovery of a possibly incriminating file name does not justify the opening of that file.[15]

If evidence is discovered in plain view while conducting another analysis, it is best to stop the analysis and seek a warrant based on the plain-view evidence.

The Supreme Court has examined the use of technology to achieve the "simple observation" contemplated by the plain-view doctrine. In *Kyllo* v. *United States*, the U.S. Supreme Court stated:

> Where, as here, the Government uses a device that is not in general public use, to explore details of a private home that would previously have been unknowable without physical intrusion, the surveillance is a Fourth Amendment "search," and is presumptively unreasonable without a warrant.[16]

This decision does not preclude technology in general use by the public. The decision allows technology not contemplated by the framers of the Constitution, and not in common use, to define an expectation of privacy.

BORDER SEARCHES   In order to protect the government's ability to monitor contraband and other property that may enter the United States illegally, the courts have recognized the need to allow for border searches that are more intrusive than would be allowed in other locations. In at least one case, the court allowed a warrantless search of a computer disk for contraband computer files because the search was classified as a border search. In *United States* v. *Roberts*, customs agents believed that William Roberts was in possession of computerized images of child pornography. He was scheduled to travel from Houston to Paris on a particular day. On the day of the flight, the agents set up an inspection area in the Jetway of the Houston airport with the purpose of searching Roberts. After Roberts arrived at the inspection area, he was told by agents that they were searching for "currency" and "high technology and other data" that could not be exported legally. The agents searched Robert's property and found a laptop computer and six Zip diskettes. Roberts then gave the agents consent to search the diskettes, and several thousand images of child pornography were located. The Fifth Circuit Court of Appeals upheld the search.[17]

SEARCHES BY PRIVATE CITIZENS   Given that the Fourth Amendment only restricts the activities of government officials, the silver platter doctrine allows evidence collected by members of the public and presented to law enforcement to be admitted as evidence. Evidence presented to investigators "on a silver platter" is admissible as evidence at trial. For example, if a computer technician discovers contraband, investigators could use the contraband as a basis for further searches or as evidence in and of itself. In one case, the Court allowed a warrantless examination by law enforcement of the contents of a container already opened by a private company hired to transport the container. The scope of the search is limited to the scope employed by the private party. However, the fruits of a limited search may be used to obtain a warrant for a more complete search.[18]

FEDERAL STATUTES

Search and seizure law has developed incrementally as Congress and the courts have struggled to come to grips with criminal activity involving electronic communication. Because of this incremental development, the laws have built upon past concepts rather than attempting comprehensively to address the rapidly changing world of digital communication. This section discusses significant federal statutes that assist law enforcement in obtaining and seizing evidence related to cyber crime. Most of the laws discussed were created for other purposes besides finding evidence of cyber crime, but the laws have been adapted to include such actions by law enforcement. The focus of this section will be on federal statutes. It is important to note that states have laws that govern similar practices by law enforcement. Some state laws may place more restrictions on law enforcement than is required by federal statutes. For example, an exception to the wiretap statute discussed below is consent of one of the parties involved. This exception applies if the law enforcement officer is one of the parties communicating or has obtained prior consent from such a person. The exception authorizes the interception of communications when one of the parties to the communication consents to the interception. However, some states forbid the interception of communications unless all parties consent.[19] The federal laws governing electronic surveillance in communication networks as well as significant federal criminal statutes will be discussed in this section.

Criminal investigations involving cyber crime frequently require electronic surveillance. As it applies to computer crimes, agents may want to monitor a hacker, a suspect's e-mail correspondence, or an individual sending or receiving child pornography via the Internet. Two federal statutes govern the practice of electronic surveillance in criminal investigations: Title III of the Omnibus Crime Control and Safe Streets Act of 1968 and the Pen Registers and Trap and Trace Devices chapter of Title 18. These statutes do not apply exclusively to criminal investigations involving computers, but more generically to traditional forms of electronic surveillance such as wiretapping a suspect's telephone. In general, the pen/trap statute regulates the collection of addressing and other noncontent information for wire and electronic communications. Title III governs the collection of actual content of wire and electronic communications.[20] As it applies to the Internet and e-mail, the pen/trap statute allows the government to obtain the addressing information of Internet communications much as it would allow the government to obtain phone numbers for traditional phone calls. However, reading an Internet or e-mail communication requires compliance with Title III.

The Pen/Trap Statute 18 U.S.C. §3121-27

The pen/trace statute regulates the collection of addressing information from wire communications. The statute takes its name from the now-obsolete physical devices attached to phone wires to perform this function. A pen register records outgoing numbers dialed from a phone. A trap and trace device records this information from incoming calls, similar to caller ID. The pen/trap statute allows the government to apply for a court order authorizing the installation of a pen register or trap and trace device so long as the information likely to be obtained is relevant to an ongoing criminal investigation.[21] This statute has been applied to include computer network communications, not just telephone communications (e.g., an Internet user account, an e-mail account, or an IP address). To obtain a court order for a pen/trap device, applicants must identify themselves, identify the agency conducting the investigation, and must certify their belief that the information likely to be obtained is relevant to an ongoing criminal investigation.[22] The court can authorize the installation and use of a pen/trap device anywhere in the United States. The order may authorize the use of a pen/trap device for up to 60 days and may be extended for additional 60-day periods.[23] Pen/trap devices are used more frequently by law enforcement than wiretaps.

The Wiretap Statute (Title III) 18 U.S.C. §2510-22

Title III regulates the collection of communication content. It was passed under Title III of the Omnibus Crime Control and Safe Streets Act of 1968 and provides the statutory framework that governs real-time electronic surveillance of the contents of communications (e.g., listening on a phone conversation). The statute prohibits a third party (such as the government) who is not a participating party to the communication from intercepting private communications between the parties using an "electronic, mechanical, or other device" unless one of several statutory exceptions applies.[24] In other words, communication content intercepted from a wire communication may not be used in court unless an exception applies. Title III contains dozens of exceptions, but the following seven exceptions apply the most frequently in computer crime cases:

1. ***Interception pursuant to a Title III court order (wiretap order)*** Title III permits law enforcement to intercept wire and electronic communications pursuant to a court order under 18 U.S.C. §2518. Approval from Department of Justice administration is required for the application. A U.S. District Court or Court of Appeals judge must then approve of the application. When authorized, a Title III order permits law enforcement to intercept communications for up to 30 days.[25] Wiretap orders carry more stringent standards than an application for a federal search warrant, with an annual reporting requirement by the Administrative Office of the U.S. Courts (AOUSC). This reporting requirement and explicit processes to minimize intrusion into subjects' privacy raise the procedural burden beyond that of a search warrant.

2. ***The consent exception [§2511 (2)(c)-(d)]*** This exception applies if the law enforcement officer is one of the parties communicating or has obtained prior consent from such a person. The exception authorizes the interception of communications when one of the parties to the communication consents to the interception. Some states forbid the interception of communications unless all parties consent.[26]

3. *The provider exception [§2511 (2)(a)(i)]* Employees or agents of communications service providers may intercept and disclose communication to protect the providers' rights or property. For example, system administrators of computer networks generally may monitor hackers intruding into their networks and then disclose the fruits of monitoring to law enforcement without violating Title III. This privilege belongs to the provider alone, however, and cannot be exercised by law enforcement. Once the provider has communicated with law enforcement, the computer trespasser exception may provide a basis for monitoring by law enforcement.[27]

4. *The computer trespasser exception [§2511 (2)(i)]* This exception allows victims of computer attacks to authorize law enforcement to intercept wire or electronic communications of a computer trespasser. In order to use this exception, the owner or operator of the computer must authorize the interception, the person who intercepts the communications must be lawfully engaged in an investigation, the person who intercepts the communications must believe that the content of the intercepted communication will be relevant to the investigation, and the interception should not acquire any communications other than those transmitted to or from the computer trespasser.[28]

5. *The extension telephone exception [§2510 (5)(a)]* This exception was originally designed to allow businesses to monitor by way of an extension telephone the performance of their employees who spoke on the phone to customers. Today, routine recording of all telephone calls made to and from a police station may fall within this exception as well.[29]

6. *The inadvertently obtained criminal evidence exception [§2511 (3)(b)(iv)]* Communication that is unintentionally obtained by the provider and that appears to relate to a crime can be released to a law enforcement agency. For example, a provider could report evidence of a fraud scheme to law enforcement if the provider inadvertently obtained such evidence.[30]

7. *The accessible to the public exception [§2511 (2)(g)(i)]* Intercepting unscrambled or unencrypted communication broadcast over public frequencies does not violate the wiretap statute. In addition, the language of this statute appears to permit the interception of an electronic communication that has been posted to a public bulletin board, a public chat room, or a Usenet newsgroup.[31]

Electronic Communications Privacy Act (ECPA) 18 U.S.C. §§2701-11

The ECPA is an unusually complicated statute. It regulates how the government can obtain stored account information from network service providers such as ISPs. Whenever officers seek stored e-mail, account records, or subscriber information from a network service provider, they must comply with the ECPA. The stored communication portion of the ECPA creates statutory privacy rights for customers and subscribers of computer network service providers.[32] The wire communication portion of the ECPA affirms a higher level of protection for communication in transit. This recognizes the fact that electronic communication follows a store-and-wait model rather than a direct exchange model like the telephone system, but affirms a citizen's expectation of privacy in communication. However, once the purpose of communication is achieved (i.e., the recipient reads or receives it), it enjoys less protection. To achieve a functional distinction between these points, the ECPA creates two categories of computer service:

- *Electronic Communication Service (ECS):* An ECS provider is a company holding an electronic message in transit (e.g., an unopened e-mail on a mail server).
- *Remote Computing Service (RCS):* An RCS provider is a company that holds or processes the data of a customer (e.g., saving an e-mail that has already been read makes the server's owner an RCS. An RCS can also be any form of data warehousing).

Information to be obtained under ECPA must be specified as one of three categories, with each category enjoying progressively greater protection through procedural burdens on the investigator:

1. Basic subscriber information [§2703 (c)(1)(C)]:
   - Name
   - Address
   - Local and long-distance telephone toll billing records
   - Telephone number or other subscriber number or identity
   - Length of service and types of service
2. Records or logs pertaining to a subscriber [§2703 (c)(1)(A)-(B)]:
   - The contents of any relevant logs
   - All basic subscriber information
   - Cell site data for calls made
   - Destinations of outgoing e-mail
   - Any other noncontent records
3. Contents of communication [§2510 (8)]

Each category of the above-mentioned information requires a progressively greater showing of cause to obtain. The ECPA also defines five types of instruments that may be required to obtain such information: subpoena, subpoena with prior notice to service user, §2703(d) order, §2703(d) order with prior notice to service user, and search warrant.

1. Investigators can subpoena basic subscriber information. The legal requirements that must be met before issuing a subpoena are not stringent.[33]
2. Investigators can subpoena opened e-mail (and other stored electronic or wire communications in electronic storage more than 180 days) from a provider if they comply with the notice provisions required by the ECPA. The notice provisions are satisfied by giving the customer prior notice of the disclosure. The notice can be delayed for 90 days if there is reason to believe that notification of a subpoena will have an adverse result (e.g., jeopardize a pending investigation or endanger the safety of someone).[34]
3. Agents need a §2703(d) court order to obtain most account logs and most transactional records. In other words, all relevant records (except the contents of communications) held by providers of electronic communications services and remote computing services can be obtained with a §2703(d) order.[35]
4. Investigators can obtain everything in an account except for unopened e-mail or voicemail stored with a provider for 180 days or less using a §2703(d) order combined with the prior notice provisions discussed above.[36]

5. Investigators can obtain the full contents of an account with a search warrant. The ECPA does not require the government to notify the customer when it obtains information from a provider using a search warrant.[37]

It is also possible under certain circumstances for the service provider to voluntarily disclose account information to law enforcement. Nonpublic providers may disclose both contents and other records relating to stored communications. The ECPA imposes significant restrictions on voluntary disclosures by public providers, but exceptions do exist to the restrictions.[38]

QUICK FACTS

The CAN-SPAM Act of 2003, which became effective on January 1, 2004, provides a means for prosecuting those responsible for sending large amounts of unsolicited commercial e-mail (i.e., spam). Although civil and regulatory provisions are the Act's primary enforcement mechanisms, it also created several new criminal offenses. The offenses address more egregious violations of the CAN-SPAM Act, particularly where the perpetrator has taken significant steps to hide her identity or the source of the spam from recipients, ISPs, or law enforcement agencies.

Source: U.S. Department of Justice. *Prosecuting Computer Crimes* (Washington, D.C.: U.S. Department of Justice, 2011), p. 105.

USA PATRIOT ACT/USA FREEDOM ACT

The USA PATRIOT Act was passed in the aftermath of the 9/11 attacks and reauthorized by Congress in 2006, 2011 and 2015. The 2011 and 2015 reauthorization included a four-year extension of the USA PATRIOT Act. When the U.S. Congress failed to extend the Act, it expired on June 1, 2015. On June 2, 2015, the U.S. Congress passed the USA Freedom Act and the expired parts of the USA PATRIOT Act were restored, although under the new name USA Freedom Act, through 2019. The most significant difference between the USA PATRIOT Act and the USA Freedom Act is the USA Freedom Act stopped the ability of the National Security Agency (NSA) to continue its telephone metadata collection and search program which impacted millions of Americans and was exposed by Edward Snowden. Instead, phone companies retain the data and the NSA must now petition a federal court for access to the phone records regarding a particular individual.

This review of the USA Freedom Act only considers the domestic provisions of the Act. The foreign provisions can be applied to foreign operatives in the United States, but will generally not be applicable to domestic law enforcement. The Act primarily updates and enhances surveillance procedures while maintaining the established distinction between content and routing information. The Freedom Act also:

- Permits the seizure of voicemail messages older than 180 days with a §2703 order
- Permits the seizure of voicemail messages less than 180 days old with a search warrant
- Expands the definition of "basic subscriber information" to include a more detailed length of service use, type of service use, dynamic IP assigned, and means and source of payment
- Permits emergency disclosure by public service providers to protect life and limb or regarding terrorism offenses
- Permits delay of required notice of the execution of a warrant if notice may result in the undue delay of a trial
- Makes warrants and pen/trace orders national

TABLE 10.1 Burden of Proof Standards

Instrument	Procedural Burden
Title III interception order	Probable cause standard with explicit minimization and reporting
F.R.C.P. Rule 41 search warrant authorizing the search of physical premises and physical items Or ECPA search warrant authorizing search of "in-transit" data held by an ECS for less than 180 days	Probable cause standard
ECPA §2703(d) order Or ECPA §2703(d) order with notice	Specific and articulable facts showing reasonable grounds to believe that the records are relevant and material to an ongoing criminal investigation
Pen register and trap and trace device order	Relevant to a criminal investigation
Subpoena with notice, ECPA§2703(b)(1)(B)	Filed with the court
Subpoena with delayed notice, ECPA §2705	Notice may be delayed in successive 90-day periods "upon the written certification of a supervisory official that there is reason to believe that notification of the existence of the subpoena may have an adverse result."

Contrary to popular opinion, the USA Freedom Act does not change any of the procedural burdens previously placed on investigators when seeking information. In fact, the USA Freedom Act has increased judicial oversight for the use of wiretaps and searches, in particular, oversight by the Foreign Intelligence Surveillance Court which provides warrants for intelligence suspects in the United States. From the highest burden to lowest, the burdens of proof are shown in Table 10.1.

Communication Assistance for Law Enforcement Act

The Communication Assistance for Law Enforcement Act (CALEA) was signed into law in 1994. Although telecommunications companies have been required, since 1970, to cooperate with law enforcement in conducting lawfully authorized electronic surveillance (e.g., wiretaps), CALEA requires telecommunications companies to modify the design of their equipment, facilities, and services to ensure that lawfully authorized electronic surveillance can actually be performed by law enforcement personnel.

Federal Criminal Statutes

There are also several federal criminal statutes that focus on computer crime. Three significant statutes will be discussed in this section, including the Consumer Fraud and Abuse Act, the Economic Espionage Act, and the Copyright Act.

THE COMPUTER FRAUD AND ABUSE ACT   The Computer Fraud and Abuse Act was originally passed in 1984.[39] It has been amended multiple times since its initial enactment. It is the primary federal statute targeting unauthorized computer use, primarily focusing on unauthorized access and theft of information from computers. It covers a broad range of acts and protects a range of computers that facilitate interstate and international commerce and communications. After several amendments, the Act basically covers any computer connected to the Internet. For example, the Act makes it a crime

BOX 10.1

Man Sentenced to 24 Months for Illegally Hacking Into Web Site

On March 8, 2017, a Winchester, Kentucky man, who previously admitted to hacking and taking control of a high school sports Web site, to gain publicity for his online identity and harass and intimidate the Web site owner and others, has been sentenced to 24 months in federal prison.

Deric Lostutter, 29, was sentenced for conspiring to illegally access a computer without authorization and lying to an FBI agent. Lostutter admitted that in December 2012, he hacked into a fan's Web site, created for Steubenville High School sports teams, to bring attention to a rape for which two Steubenville High School football players had been arrested in August 2012, and at the time were being held in custody.

Lostutter filmed a video wearing a mask and wrote a manifesto, which were both posted on the Web site to harass and intimidate people, and to gain publicity for his online identity. Specifically, the messages threatened to reveal personal identifying information of Steubenville High School students, and made false claims that the administrator of the fan Web site was involved in child pornography and directed a "rape crew."

As part of the same hack, Lostutter accessed the Web site administrator's private e-mail account, and then publicly posted a link to download the administrator's e-mails on the fan Web site. Lostutter changed the Web site so no one could access anything regarding athletics and could only view the video, the manifesto, and the link to the administrator's private e-mails. Lostutter then used his online identity in social media and news interviews to promote himself and his hack.

In 2013, Lostutter lied to the FBI, by stating in an investigative interview that he had not written the manifesto posted to the Web site, that he had not accessed the password-protected section of the fan Web site, and that he had not changed the administrator password for the Web site, which prevented the administrator from regaining control of his own Web site. He was subsequently charged and convicted of lying to a FBI agent in addition to hacking the Web site.

Source: https://www.justice.gov/usao-edky/pr/winchester-man-sentenced-24-months-illegally-hacking-website-and-lying-federal-agents

to access a computer without authority to obtain financial information from a financial institution or any information in possession of the government. Furthermore, another section of the Act makes it a crime for anyone to cause the transmission of a computer program, information, code, or command that results in unauthorized damage to a protected computer.[40] Criminal actions covered by the Computer Fraud and Abuse Act include access to and transmission of government classified information, access to computers in or outside of the United States that are used in interstate commerce, intentional access of a government nonpublic computer, knowingly accessing and intentionally causing damage to a protected computer, intentionally accessing a computer without authorization and causing damage, and conspiring to commit a computer hacking offense.[41]

THE ECONOMIC ESPIONAGE ACT The Economic Espionage Act was enacted in 1996. The primary purpose of the Economic Espionage Act is to impose criminal penalties on the theft of trade secrets. The trade secrets may be stored either physically or electronically. In order to be defined as a trade secret, the property must be economically valuable and the owner must take measures to protect it. In addition, in order to be covered by the Act, the person who is stealing the trade secret must know that the theft will result in economic loss to the owner and a benefit to another person.[42] This Act applies anywhere in the world as long as a U.S. citizen or company is the perpetrator. For example, an alleged violation of this Act occurred when a software engineer for Cisco Systems took a job with a competitor.

The engineer was arrested for taking voice-over and optical network software designs from Cisco Systems.[43]

THE COPYRIGHT ACT   Copyright infringement has become a significant focus for law enforcement with the increased use of computers and the Internet. Copyrightable property includes literary works, musical works, dramatic works, pantomimes and choreographic works, pictorial and graphic works, motion pictures and audiovisual works, sound recordings, and architectural works. Copyright infringement as it applies to computers typically involves software piracy but has also focused on downloading music and video files. The primary criminal statute protecting copyrighted works is Title 17 U.S.C. §506(a). This Act makes it against the law to willfully infringe upon a copyright for commercial advantage or private financial gain.

THE FAMILY ENTERTAINMENT AND COPYRIGHT ACT   Video-sharing services like YouTube and piracy technologies like Bit Torrent have increased the global problem of piracy. As a result, the Family Entertainment and Copyright Act of 2005 was signed into law to increase the penalties attached to acts of piracy.[44] In particular, this law makes it illegal to record, photograph, or otherwise copy a motion picture or other protected work as it is presented or screened in a theater. This statute also criminalizes the distribution of copyrighted materials before they are released to the public for commercial profit. Thus, this makes it illegal to provide pirated copies of movies or music before they are officially made available in stores or theaters. This law also makes it illegal to create technologies that enable individuals to edit DVD movies on the fly. The intent of this part of the statute is to protect the content of an artist's creation in its original format from individuals who intend to alter the content in some fashion.

BOX 10.2

Member of CD and DVD Counterfeiting Ring in Atlanta Sentenced to 60 Months in Prison

A Dakar, Senegal, man was sentenced to 60 months in prison on March 22, 2017 for his involvement in a counterfeit DVD and CD ring. Mamadou Aliou Simakha, 41, was also ordered to pay $70,894 in restitution, jointly and severally with his co-defendants. Simakha pleaded guilty on March 10, 2010, to one count of conspiracy to commit criminal copyright infringement, to traffic in counterfeit goods and to traffic in counterfeit labels.

After entering his guilty plea, Simakha fled the country, and a warrant was issued for his arrest on April 6, 2010. On March 1, 2016, Simakha was arrested in Morocco and was extradited from Morocco into the custody of the U.S. Marshals Service on December 15, 2016.

At the plea hearing, Simakha admitted that two co-conspirators supplied him with blank CDs and DVDs and Simaka burned counterfeit copies of music and movies onto the CDs and DVDs along with placing counterfeit artwork onto the CDs and DVDs. Simakha also admitted that he was involved in a conspiracy to then sell copies of the pirated works to others.

Simakha was one of 13 individuals charged by a federal grand jury on May 19, 2009, in an indictment alleging various copyright, trademark and counterfeit label offenses. Seven other defendants were sentenced in 2011 to prison terms ranging from probation to five years. The court found that Simakha conspired with co-defendants and others to reproduce and distribute tens of thousands of copyright infringing music CDs and movie DVDs which, if legitimate, would have been worth more than $769,000.

Source: https://www.justice.gov/opa/pr/member-cd-and-dvd-counterfeiting-ring-atlanta-sentenced-60-months-prison

ADMITTING EVIDENCE AT TRIAL

In this section, issues related to admitting computer records and other digital evidence into trial will be discussed. Much of the discussion will focus on the Federal Rules of Evidence. Most federal courts that have evaluated the admissibility of computer records have focused on computer records as potential hearsay.[45] The courts have typically admitted computer records upon a showing that the records fall within the business records exception to the Federal Rules of Evidence 803 (6).

However, the evidentiary issues raised by the admission of computer records really depend on what type of computer records are being admitted as evidence. Computer records that contain text can typically be divided into two categories: computer-generated records and computer-stored records.[46] The difference depends on whether a person or machine created the record. Computer-stored records include documents that have been created by a person. Examples of such records that may be admitted as evidence include word-processing files, e-mail messages, and chat room messages. In comparison, computer-generated records contain output from computer programs that have not been manipulated by a person. Such computer-generated records include log-in records from ISPs, telephone records, and ATM receipts.[47] The evidentiary issues are typically different for these two types of records. For computer-stored records, the evidentiary issue involves a question of whether a person's out-of-court statement was truthful and accurate. In other words, using computer-stored records as evidence brings up the issue of hearsay. However, when the evidence involves computer-generated records, the question becomes whether the computer program that generated the record was functioning properly. This is a question of authenticity, not hearsay.

Therefore, the admission of computer records as evidence usually involves two issues. First, the government needs to establish that the computer records are authentic. Second, if the records involve computer-stored records created by a person, then the government must demonstrate that the person-generated records are not inadmissible hearsay.[48] The issues of authentication, hearsay, as well as the best evidence rule will be discussed in further detail.

Authentication

Before the government or a defendant can move for the admission of a computer record as evidence, the authenticity of the record must be proven first. The government must offer evidence "sufficient to support a finding that the computer record or other evidence in question is what its proponent claims."[49] In authenticating computer records, the witness must have first-hand knowledge of the relevant facts to which he or she testifies.[50]

Challenges to the authenticity of computer records often take one of three forms. First, parties may challenge the authenticity of both computer-generated and computer-stored records by questioning whether the records were altered, manipulated, or damaged after they were created. In challenging the admission of computer records, opposing counsel frequently alleges that computer records lack authenticity because they were tampered with or changed after they were created. Generally, the courts are skeptical of unsupported claims that computer records have been altered. Therefore, the mere possibility of tampering does not affect the authenticity of a computer record: specific evidence that tampering occurred must be presented.[51]

Second, parties may question the authenticity of computer-generated records by challenging the reliability of the computer program that generated the records. The opposing counsel makes the argument that the computer-generated record may not be authentic because the program that creates the record contains serious programming errors. Often, the reliability of a computer program can be established by showing that users of the program rely on it on a regular basis during their ordinary course of business.[52]

Third, parties may challenge the authenticity of computer-stored records by questioning the identity of their author. Although handwritten records may be penned in a distinctive handwriting style, computer-stored records do not necessarily identify their author. For example, technology allows users to send effectively anonymous e-mails and chat rooms allow users to communicate without using their real names. Defendants frequently challenge the admission of computer-stored records of this nature by arguing that they are not the authors of the material. The key to establishing authorship of computer-stored records typically involves the use of circumstantial evidence.[53]

Hearsay

The hearsay rule exists to prevent unreliable out-of-court statements by people from influencing the outcomes of trials. Therefore, rules of evidence require that individuals making statements be placed on the stand and subjected to cross-examination. When a computer record contains the assertions of a person, the record can contain hearsay.[54] Before a court will admit the records, the court must establish that the statements contained in the record were made in circumstances that tend to ensure their trustworthiness. In order to accomplish this, the government typically fits the record within a hearsay exception such as the business records exception. The business record exception is the most common hearsay exception applied to computer records [Federal Rules of Evidence 803 (6)]. It states:

> *Records of regularly conducted activity.* A memorandum, report, record, or data compilation, in any form, or acts, events, conditions, opinions, or diagnoses, made at or near the time by, or from information transmitted by, a person with knowledge, if kept in the course of a regularly conducted business activity, and if it was the regular practice of that business activity to make the memorandum, report, record, or data compilation, all as shown by the testimony of the custodian or other qualified witness, unless the source of information or the method of circumstances of preparation indicate lack of trustworthiness. The term "business" as used in this paragraph includes business, institution, association, profession, occupation, and calling of every kind, whether or not conducted for profit.[55]

In applying this principle, courts have generally indicated that computer records can be admitted as business records if they are kept following a routine procedure to ensure their accuracy.[56]

The Best Evidence Rule

The authentication requirement and the hearsay rule are typically the two biggest issues encountered by prosecutors when seeking the admission of computer records as evidence at trial. Another issue that sometimes comes up is known as the best evidence rule. The best evidence rule states that to prove the content of a writing, recording, or photograph, the "original" writing, recording, or photograph is ordinarily required.[57] Prosecutors sometimes are concerned that a printout of a computer-stored electronic file may not be an "original" for the purpose of the best evidence rule.[58] The original file is a collection of 0s and 1s, while the printout is a result of manipulating the original file. However, the Federal Rules of Evidence has expressly addressed this issue. Federal Rules of Evidence 1003 states that if data are stored in a computer or similar device, any printout or other output readable by sight, shown to reflect the data accurately, is an "original."[59] Therefore, an accurate printout of computer data always satisfies the best evidence rule.[60]

SIGNIFICANT COURT CASES

In *Katz* v. *United States* (1967),[61] Katz made a phone call from a public phone booth. Federal agents placed a listening device in the phone booth but did not tap the line. They obtained incriminating evidence. Katz appealed. The government contended that the phone booth was a public place. The Court concluded that the Fourth Amendment protects persons evidencing an expectation of privacy; however, society must be willing to recognize that expectation as reasonable.

Perhaps most important for future electronic search and seizure law, the case hinged on the interception of communication content. In attempting to create a "technological workaround" to bypass statutory protections on telephone content (see Title III, discussed previously), the Court defined that the functional equivalent of an impermissible intrusion is an impermissible intrusion regardless of the actual route employed by the technology. Thus, constitutional protections apply to persons and expectations, not to physical locations or actual techniques. The functional presence of officers in a "private" space violates the reasonable expectation of privacy protected by the Fourth Amendment.

In *Florida* v. *Riley* (1989),[62] the Court allowed the use of aerial surveillance of arguably "private" spaces. It has long been established that police can observe private property from a public space; this is not considered a search. Thus evidence observed in an open field (even if it is on private property) carries no reasonable expectation of privacy. Technology has changed the vantage point of police observation. In *Florida* v. *Riley*, the Court decided that the government may use the "high place" of otherwise legal flight to observe illegal activity. This ruling opened observation flights over suspected marijuana fields. Perhaps most significantly, this ruling allowed a fundamental change in the notion of privacy that recognized changing technology. For example, the use of drones by law enforcement agencies is becoming commonplace today.

Thus, the reasonable expectation of privacy is not static; it must adapt to technology beyond the intentions of the framers of the Constitution. The implications for electronic search and seizure are broad. The home, once the bastion of privacy rights, may contain a Web server with illicit materials. Viewing those materials may not constitute a search. Law enforcement officers may use a tool like a Web-based search engine and "invade" the Web server without violating a reasonable expectation of privacy.

Although searches usually implicate the Fourth Amendment, there is a precedent for First Amendment implications as well. In *Zurcher* v. *Stanford Daily* (1978),[63] police sought photographs of a student riot taken by a *Stanford Daily* photographer. In addition to defining search law, a relatively obscure circumstance was observed. The legitimate interest of the police in searching does not automatically override the substantial deference given to the press. The principles derived from the *Zurcher* case include the following:

1. A search is not unreasonable if items sought are not in the possession of the suspected criminal. The items sought must be reasonably expected at the place searched.
2. The search should not interfere with the execution of actions privileged by the First Amendment, particularly freedom of the press.

This principle was initially applied to computer search and seizure in the *Steve Jackson Games* (1993) case.[64] Federal agents tracking the theft of an electronic document related to the 911 system traced the document to an electronic bulletin board system maintained by Steve Jackson Games. Players of a conspiracy-paranoia game called *Illumination* exchanged messages about the game and sometimes about real life. Steve Jackson Games also used the system for internal development, e-mail, and newsletters. The Secret Service seized the entire physical system under a search warrant and did not return it for years. The company lost a substantial amount of business and customers and eventually claimed tens of thousands of dollars in damages. More fundamentally, the seizure unnecessarily deprived the company and gamers of a platform for speech and association.

More recently, the U.S. Supreme Court decided the case of *City of Ontario* v. *Quon*.[65] In this case, the City of Ontario, CA Police Department (OPD) required SWAT team members to carry alphanumeric pagers that were capable of sending and receiving text messages. The City paid for the services, which included a monthly limit on the number of characters each pager could send and receive without overage fees. When Quon and others exceeded their monthly character limits for several months, the Chief of Police sought to determine whether the existing limit was too low or whether the overages were for personal messages. The service provider, Arch Wireless, provided the Chief of Police with the transcripts of the employee's, including Quon's, text messages for two months. It was discovered that many of Quon's messages were not work-related, and some were sexually explicit. After an investigation into the messages Quon sent while on duty, he was disciplined for violating OPD rules. Quon and other employees filed suit alleging that the Chief of Police violated their Fourth Amendment rights and the federal Stored Communications Act by obtaining and reviewing the transcripts of the text messages. The U.S. Supreme Court ruled that the search of Quon's text messages was reasonable and therefore did not violate his Fourth Amendment rights.

In 2012, the U. S. Supreme Court rendered a decision in *United States* v. *Jones*.[66] In this case, law enforcement personnel obtained a search warrant permitting them to install a global positioning system (GPS) tracking device on a vehicle registered to Jones' wife. The warrant authorized installation in the District of Columbia and within 10 days of the issuance of the search warrant, but agents installed the device on the eleventh day and in Maryland. Law enforcement personnel then tracked the vehicle's movements for 28 days. Based in part on Jones' movements identified by the GPS device, the prosecutor's office subsequently secured an indictment of Jones and others on drug trafficking conspiracy charges. Since the device was placed on Jones' vehicle without search warrant authorization and because the device was placed on his vehicle in Maryland and on the eleventh day after the search warrant was signed, which exceeded the scope of the warrant, the government argued no search occurred in this case. In other words, the placement of the GPS device on Jones' vehicle and then monitoring its movements did not intrude into his reasonable expectation of privacy since he was traveling on public roads. Basically, the GPS device was providing the same information the law enforcement personnel could have obtained by physically trailing his vehicle everywhere it went for 28 days. The U.S. Supreme Court disagreed with the government's argument and decided that the attachment of the GPS device to the vehicle by law enforcement personnel, and its use of that device to monitor the vehicle's movements, constitutes a search under the Fourth Amendment. Therefore, there was an intrusion into Jones' reasonable expectation of privacy and without a warrant or other legal justification for the search, the information obtained through the monitoring of his vehicle through the GPS tracker was suppressed as evidence in court.

In 2014, the U. S. Supreme Court decided the case of *Riley* v. *California*.[67] The issue decided in the *Riley* case is whether law enforcement can search the contents of a person's cell phone without a warrant after the person is arrested. This type of warrantless search is known as a search incident to arrest and has been authorized under other circumstances by the U.S. Supreme Court. However, the issue of whether a cell phone can be searched incident to arrest had not been addressed by the Supreme Court until the *Riley* case. In this case, Riley was stopped for a traffic violation, which eventually led to his arrest on weapons charges. An officer searching Riley, incident to the arrest, seized a cell phone from Riley's pants pocket. The officer accessed information on the phone and noticed the repeated use of a term associated with a street gang. At the police station two hours later, a detective specializing in gangs further examined the phone's digital contents. Based in part on photographs and videos that the detective found, Riley was charged in connection with a shooting that had occurred a few weeks earlier. In addition, the prosecutor sought an enhanced sentence based on Riley's gang membership. Riley moved to suppress all evidence that the police had obtained from his cell phone. The trial court denied the motion, and Riley was convicted. The U.S. Supreme Court ruled that the police *generally may not*, without a warrant, search digital information on a cell phone seized from an individual who has been arrested. Therefore, since the police did not have a search warrant when they searched his phone incident to arrest, all the evidence was suppressed and could not be used in court.

Summary

In this chapter, law and legislation as it applies to the collection of evidence and prosecution of cyber crime were discussed. The different types of searches available to investigators searching for digital evidence were analyzed, including searches with and without warrants. The major federal statutes governing the collection of digital evidence were reviewed. Many of these statutes focused on electronic surveillance of communications networks. Issues related to the admission of digital evidence at trial, including authentication, hearsay, and the best evidence rule, were reviewed as well. In addition, several significant U.S. Supreme Court cases that affect the investigation and prosecution of cyber crime were discussed.

Review Questions

1. What types of warrantless searches can be conducted by investigators collecting digital evidence?
2. What are the major exceptions to the wiretap statute?
3. What are the major requirements established by the Electronic Communications Privacy Act?
4. What issues arise during the admission of digital evidence at trial?

Critical Thinking Exercises

1. You are a local law enforcement officer who has seized two laptops from a vehicle after a traffic stop based on probable cause because you saw child pornography images on the laptops before the driver of the vehicle closed the screens of the laptops. Discuss the ways in which you can search the laptops under the Fourth Amendment since the driver has a reasonable expectation of privacy for the material contained on the laptops.

2. Using a search engine, find the most common types of cyber crimes that occurred last year. Based on your list, which laws presented in this chapter are violated when these crimes are committed?

Endnotes

1. *Johnson* v. *United States*, 333 U.S. 10 (1948).
2. *Katz* v. *United States*, 389 U.S. 347 (1967).
3. *United States* v. *Jacobsen*, 466 U.S. 109 (1984).
4. *Ibid.*
5. *Arizona* v. *Hicks*, 480 U.S. 321 (1987).
6. BLACK, H.C., NOLAN, J.R., and NOLAN-HALEY, J.M. (1990). *Black's Law Dictionary*, 6th ed. St. Paul, MN: West, p.853.
7. CASEY, E. (2000). *Digital Evidence and Computer Crime: Forensic Science, Computers and the Internet*. San Diego, CA: Academic Press.
8. *United States* v. *Leon*, 468 U.S. 897 (1984).
9. *United States* v. *David*, 756 F. Supp. 1385 (D. Nev. 1991); *United States* v. *Romero-Garcia*, 168 F.3d 502 (9th Cir. 1999).
10. FERDICO, J.N. (1999). *Criminal Procedure for the Criminal Justice Professional*, 7th ed. New York: Wadsworth.
11. *Ibid.*
12. ORTON, I. (2001). "The Investigation and Prosecution of a Cybercrime." In R.D. CLIFFORD (ed.), *Cybercrime: The Investigation, Prosecution, and Defense of a Computer-Related Crime*. Durham, NC: Carolina Academic Press, pp. 71–121; *Trulok* v. *Freeh*, 275 F.3d 391 (4th Cir.).
13. *Chimel* v. *California*, 395 U.S. 752 (1969).
14. *Arizona* v. *Hicks*, 480 U.S. 321 (1987).
15. ORTON, "The Investigation and Prosecution of a Cybercrime," pp. 91–92; *Trulok* v. *Freeh*, 275 F.3d 391 (4th Cir. 2001).
16. *Kyllo* v. *United States*, 533 U.S. 27 (2001).
17. *United States* v. *Roberts*, 274 F.3d 1007 (5th Cir. 2001); U.S. Department of Justice. (2010). *Searching and Seizing Computers and Obtaining Electronic Evidence in Criminal Investigations*. Washington, D.C.: U.S. Department of Justice.
18. U.S. Department of Justice, *Searching and Seizing Computers and Obtaining Electronic Evidence in Criminal Investigations*.
19. *Ibid.*
20. *Ibid.*
21. 18 U.S.C. 3122(b)(2).
22. U.S. Department of Justice, *Searching and Seizing Computers and Obtaining Electronic Evidence in Criminal Investigations*.
23. *Ibid.*
24. *Ibid.*
25. *Ibid.*
26. *Ibid.*
27. *Ibid.*
28. *Ibid.*
29. *Ibid.*
30. *Ibid.*
31. *Ibid.*
32. *Ibid.*
33. *Ibid.*
34. *Ibid.*
35. *Ibid.*
36. *Ibid.*
37. *Ibid.*
38. *Ibid.*
39. 18 U.S.C. §1030.
40. *The Electronic Frontier: The Challenge of Unlawful Conduct Involving the Use of the Internet*. A Report of the President's Working Group on Unlawful Conduct on the Internet, 2000.
41. HILLER, J.S. and COHEN, R. (2002). *Internet Law and Policy*. Upper Saddle River, NJ: Prentice Hall.
42. *Ibid.*
43. *Ibid.*
44. 17 U.S.C. 110(11).
45. KERR, O.S. (2001). *Computer Records and the Federal Rules of Evidence*. Washington, D.C.: U.S. Department of Justice.
46. *Ibid.*
47. *Ibid.*
48. *Ibid.*
49. Federal Rules of Evidence §901 (a).
50. KERR, *Computer Records and the Federal Rules of Evidence.*
51. *Ibid.*
52. *Ibid.*
53. *Ibid.*
54. *Ibid.*
55. Federal Rules of Evidence §803 (6).
56. KERR, *Computer Records and the Federal Rules of Evidence.*
57. Federal Rules of Evidence §1002.
58. KERR, *Computer Records and the Federal Rules of Evidence.*
59. Federal Rules of Evidence §1003.
60. KERR, *Computer Records and the Federal Rules of Evidence.*
61. *Katz* v. *United States*, 389 U.S. 347 (1967).
62. *Florida* v. *Riley*, 488 U.S. 445 (1989).
63. *Zurcher* v. *Stanford Daily*, 436 U.S. 547 (1978).
64. *Steve Jackson Games, Inc.* v. *Secret Service*, 816 F. Supp. 432, 440, 443 (W.D. Tex. 1993).
65. *City of Ontario* v. *Quon*, 130 S. Ct. 2619 (2010).
66. *United States* v. *Jones*, 132 S. Ct. 945 (2012).
67. *Riley* v. *California*, 134 S. Ct. 2473 (2014).

Law Enforcement Roles and Responses

CHAPTER OBJECTIVES

After completing this chapter, you should be able to

- Provide an overview of the roles and responses of federal law enforcement agencies concerning cyber crimes and any interagency partnerships to deal with these offenses.
- Describe local law enforcement responses to computer crime.
- Identify the factors that have limited local law enforcement efforts against cyber crime.

INTRODUCTION

The emergence of computer technologies and the growing threats created by cyber criminals and terrorists have worked to produce a wide array of challenges for law enforcement officials charged with protecting individuals, private businesses, and governments from these threats. In response, political leaders and police administrators have increasingly recognized the need to emphasize new priorities and foster new and innovative organizational strategies designed to counter the advent and continued growth of computer crimes.

This chapter begins with an overview of federal roles and responses as they relate to computer crimes. The discussion focuses on the responses and organizational initiatives enacted by prominent federal law enforcement agencies as well as the role of the Department of Homeland Security (DHS) in these efforts. The chapter concludes with a description of the ways in which local law enforcement agencies have joined the fight against computer crime. This chapter emphasizes the need to strengthen the capabilities of local agencies by identifying several factors that have thus far limited local law enforcement efforts.

FEDERAL ROLES AND RESPONSES

For the most part, federal agencies have spearheaded law enforcement efforts against computer crime because these agencies possess the technical expertise and political clout to garner significant financial and operational resources at the national level. These agencies have increasingly reorganized in an effort to channel resources directly at preventing cyber crimes and apprehending computer criminals, including the creation of special sections within these organizations, the recruitment of new personnel who possess specialized technical expertise in this area, and the creation of new collaborative units that combine the resources of multiple agencies. Additionally, several agencies have developed partnership programs with other law enforcement agencies, private industry, and the public in an attempt to improve collaboration and cooperation to thwart cyber criminals.

The Department of Justice

The U.S. Department of Justice (DOJ) was established in 1870. The organization is headed by the chief law enforcement officer of the federal government—the attorney general. The attorney general represents the United States in legal matters generally and gives advice and opinions regarding matters of jurisprudence to the president. In cases of extreme importance, the attorney general may appear before the U.S. Supreme Court as the federal government's representative attorney. Under the attorney general is a vast array of sections and organizational subunits designed to oversee the administration of justice on the federal level. These agencies include (1) the U.S. Attorney's Office, representing the federal government in court and prosecuting federal suspects; (2) the major federal investigative agencies, including the Federal Bureau of Investigation (FBI), the Drug Enforcement Administration (DEA), the Bureau of Alcohol, Tobacco, Firearms, and Explosives (ATFE); (3) the U.S. Marshals Service; and (4) the U.S. Bureau of Prisons.[1]

The DOJ has stepped up efforts to respond to the legal threats posed by cybercriminals. The cornerstone of these efforts is the Criminal Division's Computer Crime and Intellectual Property Section (CCIPS). CCIPS began as the Computer Crime Unit of DOJ in 1991. This unit primarily prosecuted violations of the Federal Code covered by Title 18, Section 1030, of the Computer Fraud and Abuse Act. The scope of DOJ jurisdiction in such crimes was expanded with the enactment of the National Information and Infrastructure Protection Act of 1996. In accordance with this Act, as well as the DOJ's recognition of the need to increase prosecutorial resources aimed at combating computer crimes, the department elevated the unit to section status in 1996 and adopted the moniker CCIPS.[2]

The section employs dozens of attorneys who focus solely on legal issues raised by computer and intellectual property crimes. CCIPS attorneys specialize in prosecuting crimes related to encryption, e-commerce, intellectual property crimes, electronic privacy laws, computer hacker investigations, and search and seizure cases involving computers. Members of the CCIPS section advise federal prosecutors on computer crimes cases, and CCIPS attorneys normally take the lead in litigating computer and intellectual property crimes on behalf of the federal government. In addition, CCIPS staff members comment on the legality of proposed computer crime legislation that is designed to mitigate computer crime threats. CCIPS works in close collaboration with the U.S. Attorney's Office in the prosecution of computer crimes. Finally, CCIPS coordinates the nationwide Computer Hacking and Intellectual Property prosecutor network, which is comprised of specialized computer and IP crime prosecutors assigned to every U.S. Attorney's Office.[3]

New initiatives like the Cybersecurity Unit represent CCIPS's dedication to its role as a central hub for expert advice and legal guidance in a variety of areas, including best practices for victim response and reporting of cyber incidents, analysis of the implications of emerging technological changes like the Internet of Things, and white papers on topics such as information sharing and reports on active defense.[4]

While CCIPS primarily operates as a prosecutorial arm of the department, the section has also attempted to remedy the growing need for training and interagency cooperation. CCIPS attorneys conduct hundreds of training seminars every year for other federal attorneys in an effort to educate those prosecutors outside of the section in regard to relevant legislation and effective prosecutorial strategies for cases involving computer crime. They also offer training to law enforcement agencies and engage in diplomatic missions to build strong relationships between the U.S. and foreign law enforcement officials.

The Federal Bureau of Investigation

The FBI was established in 1908 as the investigative branch of the U.S. DOJ. The FBI carries a broad mandate that authorizes the organization to protect the United States from terror and foreign intelligence agencies, as well as to investigate any federal crime that has not been specifically designated to another federal agency. These broad legal areas can include civil rights crimes, violent federal crimes, organized crime and drugs, and financial crimes. The FBI employs over 13,000 special agents who operate out of the Washington, D.C. headquarters, 56 field offices, and 64 international legal attaché offices—commonly known as legats—and more than a dozen smaller sub-offices in key cities around the globe. The FBI plays an important role in the investigation of cybercrime.

In fact, protection of the United States from cyber-based attacks and high-technology crimes is its third priority, behind terror and foreign intelligence. This suggests that cybercrime has become a high priority for investigation, over and above physical location-based crimes. The bureau's role in fighting computer crime is fourfold: (1) to capture the criminals behind serious computer intrusions and the spread of malicious code, (2) to stop online sexual predators who produce or share child pornography and meet and exploit children, (3) to stop operations targeting U.S. intellectual property, and (4) to dismantle national and transnational organized crime groups engaging in Internet fraud. The FBI is also leading the charge to investigate and prosecute cybercrimes.[5]

QUICK FACTS

In July 1994, a group of enterprising criminals on multiple continents—led by a young computer programmer in St. Petersburg, Russia—hacked into the electronic systems of a major U.S. bank and secretly started stealing money from several corporate bank accounts. No mask, no note, no gun—this was the first online bank robbery. Hackers had apparently targeted the institution's cash management computer system—which allowed corporate clients to move funds from their own accounts into other banks around the world. The criminals gained access by exploiting the telecommunications network and compromising valid user IDs and passwords. The FBI eventually identified approximately 40 illegal transactions, mostly going to overseas bank accounts and ultimately adding up to more than $10 million.

Source: https://www.fbi.gov/news/stories/a-byte-out-of-history-10-million-hack

---

The bureau's Cyber Division works in tandem with the Criminal Investigative Division in the investigation of domestic threats generated by computer-related crimes. Typically, its caseloads focus on computer and network intrusions, ransomware, identify theft, online predators, and intellectual property theft. There are also computer crime task forces in all 56 FBI field offices that provide a partnership between the bureau, federal, state, and local law enforcement agencies to better solve crimes.[6] A program called Cyber Action Teams has also been developed, which have a small number of specially trained agents who are experts in malware and forensics.[7] These teams travel as needed to various spots around the world to assist in the investigation of computer intrusions and gather intelligence on threats and cybercrimes that threaten national security.

In addition, the FBI has developed and supports the Regional Computer Forensics Laboratory (RCFL) Program.[8] This is a partnership between the bureau, state, local, and federal law enforcement agencies within a geographical area. RCFLs provide computer forensic lab support and training programs in support of criminal investigations and the prevention of terror incidents. The first such RCFL was established in San Diego, California, in 1999.[9] The FBI then created a National Program Office in 2002 to oversee and facilitate the creation of other RCFLs around the country.[10]

In addition, the bureau has partnered with the National White-Collar Crime Center (NW3C) to operate the Internet Crime Complaint Center (ICCC or IC3). The IC3 provides victims of Internet fraud a mechanism to report suspicious online activities. The IC3 also provides other federal agencies a "central repository for complaints related to Internet fraud." The goal of the IC3 is to identify wider Internet fraud patterns and trends to aid in the enforcement of these crimes.[11]

The FBI has also developed relationships with private and public sector partners to improve its ability to protect computerized critical infrastructures. The federal government owns and operates many of these critical infrastructure systems; these law enforcement agencies would be the primary responders in the event of a national crisis. Likewise, the private sector currently operates the vast majority of these systems, and private sector employees often have the greatest expertise in identifying and solving technical problems. Thus, the FBI developed "InfraGard," a program that began in 1998 as a joint initiative of the DOJ and what was then the National Infrastructure Protection Center. This program is now housed in the bureau's Cyber Division, where there are approximately 84 chapters around the country with 40,000 members.[12] The program is designed to facilitate the exchange of information among academic institutions, the business community, and the FBI and serves as a prime example of the FBI's agenda for partnerships and interagency collaboration in the fight against cybercrimes.

BOX 11.1

Electronic Surveillance in the Age of Social Networks

The term "electronic surveillance" traditionally referred to law enforcement actions such as wire-tapping designed to listen in on the telephone conversations of suspected criminals. Federal law enforcement agencies have a long (and sometimes dubious) history involving the use of traditional wiretapping as a tool for domestic intelligence gathering. The digital revolution and the emergence of social networks as a major platform of communication have led to debate regarding the proper role of federal law enforcement and whether agencies such as the FBI should be allowed to essentially "wire-tap" Web sites such as Facebook and Twitter to enhance intelligence gathering and quickly identify and apprehend criminal suspects.

The FBI identified what they refer to as the "Going Dark" problem, or the increasing inability of federal law enforcement agencies to effectively collect evidence derived from electronic communications via the Web. The agency suggests that the "Going Dark" problem

prevents them from gathering available evidence in criminal cases involving child exploitation, pornography, organized crime, terrorism, and espionage.[1]

In 2010, DHS awarded a contract to General Dynamics to provide social media monitoring to support the agency's National Operations Center. The contract specifies that the company will provide DHS daily social network summaries, weekly data reports, and monthly status reports.[2] In 2012, the FBI published a request for information (RFI) looking for private companies that could build a social network monitoring system that would allow the FBI to quickly identify and locate breaking events, incidents, and emerging threats. The RFI states that social media has become a primary source of intelligence because it has become the premier first response to key events and possible developing situations.[3]

The FBI's initiative has given rise to considerable debate. Should federal law enforcement agencies be allowed to monitor social networks for evidence of criminal wrongdoing? If so, what types of communications should be subject to law enforcement scrutiny? To what extent will the collection of communications on the Web extend beyond legitimate criminal investigations and violate the privacy rights of law-abiding citizens? Will these and other similar initiatives to "wire-tap" social networks change the way in which you use them to communicate with friends and family members?

[1]CAPRONI, V. (2011). Statement Before the House Judiciary Committee, Subcommittee on Crime, Terrorism, and Homeland Security, February 17. Retrieved July 20, 2013, from *http://fbi.gov/news*

[2]NAKASHIMA, E. (2012). "DHS Monitoring of Social Media Concerns Civil Liberties Advocates." *Washington Post*, January 13. Retrieved July 20, 2013, from *http://www.washingtonpost.com*

[3]RUSH, D. (2012). "FBI to Step Up Monitoring of Social Media Sites amid Privacy Concerns." *The Guardian*, January 26. Retrieved July 20, 2013, from *http://www.guardian.co.uk*

The National Security Agency

The National Security Agency (NSA) bills itself as the nation's preeminent "cryptologic organization." In more familiar language, the NSA is primarily responsible for designing and maintaining computerized coding systems designed to protect the integrity of U.S. information systems.[13] It has also become the lead agency responsible for monitoring and protecting all of the federal government's computer networks from acts of cyberterrorism.[14] In direct relation to these responsibilities, NSA agents are also responsible for detecting and exploiting weaknesses in an adversarial country's computerized secret coding systems. Headquartered in Fort Meade, Maryland, the NSA has been providing the nation with "code-breaking" capabilities since these operations began against the Japanese in the Pacific theater of World War II. The NSA's role in providing information system security and information assurance has expanded with the parallel growth in computerized communications technology during the Cold War and the ensuing decades.[15]

The NSA's role in protecting classified computer data demands an eclectic mix of agents who specialize in a wide range of professional fields, including researchers, computer scientists, mathematicians, and engineers. Though much of the work of NSA agents remains secretive in nature, the agency's expertise in the area of information systems has led to a number of collaborative initiatives intended to improve information security research, knowledge, and expertise through the federal law enforcement system. For example, the NSA and the Department of Homeland Security jointly sponsor the National Centers of Academic Excellence in Cyber Defense (CAE-CD) program. The goal of the program is to reduce vulnerability in our national information infrastructure by promoting higher education and research in cyber defense and producing professionals with cyber defense expertise.[16]

The NSA has also assumed an active role in providing information security training to both government and private entities through the National INFOSEC Education and Training Program. This program provides training for security specialists, including risk assessment, security design, and information security evaluation. Through these initiatives, the NSA aims to provide government agencies and the private sector information system security expertise.[17] Additionally, the NSA works to provide information security through security tools, security products, threat warnings, analysis of attacks, and security bulletins.[18]

The Federal Trade Commission

The Federal Trade Commission (FTC) was created in 1914 primarily as a way for the government to "trust bust" or apply regulations ensuring a free marketplace for U.S.

consumers and business enterprises. In this regard, the FTC enforces antitrust violations that could hamper consumer interests, as well as federal consumer protection laws against fraud, deception, and unfair business practices. The commission's primary enforcement mechanism is the Bureau of Consumer Protection, which is divided into eight divisions: (1) enforcement, (2) advertising practices, (3) financial practices, (4) marketing practices, (5) litigation technology and analysis, (6) consumer and business education, (7) privacy and identity protection, and (8) consumer response and operations.[19]

As the federal government's primary mechanism for protecting consumer markets, the FTC has been forced to apply its traditional enforcement tools in an increasingly computer-related marketplace. Consumers and businesses alike have grown accustomed to the exchange of goods and services through electronic mediums, especially the Internet. Indeed, so-called e-commerce generates hundreds of billions of dollars in revenue annually, making the Internet economy comparable in size to the energy, automobile, and telecommunications industries. In response to the growth of Internet commerce, the FTC attempts to minimize fraudulent and deceptive business practices that occur online and educate consumers regarding safe avenues to conduct e-commerce.[20]

BOX 11.2
The NSA, Counterterrorism, and Privacy Rights

The NSA has become the nation's lead agency responsible for monitoring and protecting the federal government's computer networks from acts of cyberterrorism. The September 11, 2001, terrorist attacks that resulted in the destruction of the twin World Trade Center towers led to the implementation of warrantless surveillance programs operated through the NSA to monitor phone calls, e-mails, text messages, Internet traffic, and other forms of communication as part of the war on terror. The initial data collection program—the Terrorist Surveillance Program—operated for several years before 2007 when some aspects of the program were declared unconstitutional.[1] A new clandestine electronic surveillance program operated through the NSA—PRISM—began under the supervision of the U.S. Foreign Intelligence Surveillance Court.[2]

In June 2013, a technical contractor for the NSA Edward Snowden publicly leaked alleged details of the PRISM program. His disclosure instigated considerable controversy and debate in regard to individual privacy rights and questions about whether these programs should continue. The documents leaked by Snowden identified several companies that participated in the PRISM program, including Microsoft, Yahoo, Google, and Facebook.[3] The NSA program is designed to intercept the communications of potential foreign terrorists as those communications pass through computer networks in the United States. After the program was publicly disclosed, the NSA claimed that PRISM and other similar programs had helped to prevent more than 50 potential terrorist attacks worldwide.[4]

PRISM cannot be used to investigate the communications of domestic targets, therefore the USA Freedom Act discussed in Chapter 10 does not apply to this program. However, the information leaked by NSA contractor Snowden involved allegations that the program included the warrantless interception and collection of telephone communications data of U.S. citizens. The controversy resulting from PRISM and NSA intelligence gathering as part of the war on terror continues. Do you think the U.S. government should be allowed to collect large-scale data on the communications of potential foreign terrorists without a warrant? Do you believe that these counter-terrorism programs should operate within the framework of the Constitutional right to privacy?

---

[1]Staff. (2006). "Lawyers Group Criticizes Surveillance Program." *The Washington Post*, February 14. Retrieved July 17, 2013, from *http://washingtonpost.com*

[2]GELLMAN, B. and POITRAS, L. (2013). "US Intelligence Mining Data from Nine US Internet Companies in Broad Secret Program." *The Washington Post*, June 6. Retrieved July 17, 2013, from *http://washingtonpost.com*

[3]*Ibid.*

[4]GERSTEIN, J. (2013). "NSA: PRISM Stopped NYSE Attack." *Politico*, June 19. Retrieved July 17, 2013, from *http://politico.com*

The commission has been involved primarily in the enforcement of traditional criminal activities that now often occur online, including false marketing claims, credit card repair scams, financial pyramid schemes, and fraudulent business opportunity schemes. In addition to traditional marketplace crimes, the commission has stepped up efforts to combat invasions of consumer privacy that occur online. The growth of e-commerce has resulted in consumers increasingly providing personal financial and medical information online, thus expanding the threat that this information could be used fraudulently through theft or other means.

The FTC has developed the Identity Theft Program, designed to provide assistance to local and federal law enforcement agencies attempting to curb the misuse and theft of personal information through online access. The program aids these agencies in enforcing the Identity Theft and Assumption Deterrence Act of 1998, which is a federal response to the widespread incidence of identity theft in recent years. The Act emphasizes that personal information is increasingly used against individuals and businesses to commit fraud online. Under this Act, the FTC was required to create a database of identity theft victim complaints, to provide useful information to consumers and educate them regarding protecting the use of personal information online, as well as to provide a means to refer victims of identity theft to law enforcement authorities. These mandates resulted in the creation of the *Consumer Sentinel,* which is a centralized database of identity theft complaints used to compile statistics regarding the incidence of identity theft.[21] This database contains several million fraud and identity theft complaints, which can be searched by thousands of law enforcement agencies around the world to share information and develop case leads.[22]

The Postal Service

The U.S. Postal Service's widely known primary mission is to provide safe, affordable, and universal mail service to the nation. The nation's mail service delivery agency has also operated one of the country's oldest federal law enforcement agencies—the U.S. Postal Inspection Service—since 1830. Congress empowered the Postal Service to "investigate postal offenses and civil matters relating to the Postal Service." In order to accomplish this task, the U.S. Postal Inspection Service was established to perform "investigative and security functions essential to a stable and sound postal system." Thus, the two main functions of the U.S. Postal Inspection Service are to provide businesses with a safe avenue for the exchange of funds and securities and provide private citizens a safe and secure way in which to transmit correspondence. The Postal Inspection Service employs over 1,500 agents nationwide, including approximately 650 uniformed postal police officers who monitor and inspect critical postal facilities.[23] These agents investigate and enforce over 200 federal laws covering the illegal and fraudulent use of the U.S. mail service.[24]

In terms of the investigation and prosecution of computer crimes, the U.S. Postal Inspection Service must frequently conduct joint investigations with other federal agencies, primarily because many types of computer crimes involve the use of the mail system to accomplish computer-related fraudulent activities or to transport materials related to computer crimes. In these types of cases, the jurisdiction of the Postal Inspection Service may overlap with that of any number of local or federal agencies, including the U.S. Secret Service, the FBI, and the DOJ. The U.S. Postal Service's primary concerns in the area of computer crime are identity theft, child exploitation and pornography, and electronic crimes.[25]

Identity theft involves acquiring key pieces of someone's identifying information, including name, address, date of birth, and Social Security Number in order to impersonate them. Under Title 18, Section 1028, of the U.S. Federal Code, postal inspectors share jurisdiction in these cases because they often involve mail that is stolen in order to obtain the above information. In addition, identity thieves will use computers in order to elicit bogus credit cards and checks from financial institutions through the U.S. mail. In response to these crimes, the U.S. Postal Service has instituted the Mail Theft Reporting System (MTRS). MTRS aims to identify patterns in mail theft across geographic regions as well as compile statistics relating to mail theft victims and monetary losses. In 2016 alone, postal inspectors arrested 2,437 suspects for mail theft and possession of stolen mail.[26]

The U.S. Postal Inspection Service also plays a key role in combating the production and distribution of child pornography. Increasingly, child pornography crimes have been classified as computer related because they often involve the use of the Internet in production and downloading of pornographic images. Postal inspectors become involved when these computer-generated images are distributed through the U.S. mail. The primary legal vehicle to enforce these crimes used by postal inspectors is Title 18 of the U.S. Federal Code, Sections 1470, 2251, and 2252–2254. In 2016, investigators arrested 46 individuals for child exploitation.[27]

In addition, postal inspectors share jurisdiction in any electronic crime that involves the misuse of the U.S. mail. These crimes can include consumer fraud schemes that originate on the Internet through e-mail solicitations, since these crimes often eventually involve use of the U.S. mail in the delivery of fraudulent documents and/or fraudulently obtained currency. Among the most widely cited of these crimes is the Nigerian advance fee fraud letter and e-mail scam in which Nigerian nationals send letters and e-mails to U.S. citizens. The letters or e-mails invariably ask the recipient for some kind of fee as a precondition to the transfer of large amounts of money from Nigeria. American citizens have lost millions of dollars due to these schemes. Thus, the Postal Inspection Service has developed resources to help combat these crimes, including a joint task force with the DOJ.

The Department of Energy

The U.S. Department of Energy (DOE) was created in 1977 in order to consolidate existing federal energy programs and activities. The DOE's main responsibilities include the administration of domestic energy production, the promotion of renewable energy resources, and the promotion of energy conservation and efficiency. The department has increasingly relied on computerized technologies to operate and administer the nation's energy-producing infrastructure. The growth in computer crime has created an increasing need to protect these critical infrastructure systems from both domestic and international threats. These threats can involve the introduction of malicious codes designed to interfere with the operation of energy production systems.[28]

In response to these threats, the Office of the Chief Information Officer at DOE provides a range of resources to provide timely information on cyber security threats. This includes the management of the entire DOE cyber security program, including desktop and application hosting for employees. In addition, the DOE-Cyber Incident Response and Recovery (CIRR) provides the DOE with incident response, reporting, tracking, and security support. This includes incident-reporting capabilities, security bulletins, and software tools. The CIRR is also designed to enhance communications between the DOE and private contractors who use these energy systems so that critical infrastructures can remain protected from cyber attacks.[29]

The Department of Homeland Security

The preceding section described the manner in which federal agencies are organized to combat computer crime discussed each agency in separate terms and characterized the strategies of any single agency as independent and separate from those of the other agencies involved in the fight against computer crime. The attempt to classify these agencies in an independent fashion is intended not only to help the reader understand the different roles of each federal agency discussed, but may be viewed as an indication of the historically "piecemeal" nature of law enforcement actions at the federal level. Federal law enforcement agencies have a long history of failing to coordinate and cooperate not only in the relatively recent fight against computer crime but also with regard to a host of more traditional crime problems, including organized crime, the "war on drugs," and more general intelligence-gathering operations.

The cost associated with these disjointed federal law enforcement strategies became fatally and critically clear on September 11, 2001, when these domestic agencies collectively failed to detect and prevent the terrorist plot against the World Trade Center and the Pentagon. With the need for federal cooperation becoming abundantly clear in the face of such attacks, President Bush launched an initiative to create a cabinet-level department designed to improve information sharing among federal law enforcement agencies, consolidate a host of over 100 federal offices in these departments, and increase interagency coordination in the fight against domestic terror. The establishment of the Department of Homeland Security is the result of these efforts.[30]

DHS has a wide range of organizational components and has subsumed a number of previously discussed federal agencies under the DHS umbrella, including the Directorate for National Protection and Programs, Directorate for Science and Technology, Directorate for Management, Office of Policy, Office of Health Affairs, Office of Intelligence and Analysis, Office of Operations Coordination, Federal Law Enforcement Training Center, Domestic Nuclear Detection Office, Transportation Security Administration (TSA), Customs and Border Protection, Citizenship and Immigration Services, Immigration and Customs Enforcement, the Secret Service, Federal Emergency Management Agency, and the Coast Guard.[31] The agency now employs over 240,000 federal employees who have been transferred or subsumed from other federal agencies.[32]

The National Cybersecurity and Communications Integration Center (NCCIC) of DHS is of significant importance in the fight against computer crime. The NCCIC is charged with protecting cyber infrastructure. Specifically, the mission of the NCCIC is to reduce the likelihood and severity of incidents that may significantly compromise the security and resilience of the nation's critical information technology and communications networks.[33] The NCCIC is a 24×7 cyber situational awareness, incident response, and management center that is a national nexus of cyber and communications integration for the federal government, intelligence community, and law enforcement.[34]

There are several programs in place to aid in the achievement of this mission, including the National Cyber Alert System, which offers a free subscription service to security alerts and tips to better protect systems and infrastructure. This system also allows individuals to report threats and incidents directly to DHS.[35] The Cyber Cop Portal program is also run through NCCIC, which provides a Web-based resource for information sharing and collaboration between law enforcement agencies around the world. There are over 5,300 investigators who use this tool as a means to help capture computer criminals. The NCCIC also manages the National Vulnerability Database, which acts as a clearinghouse for information on software and hardware vulnerabilities. Individuals can access this database as a way to improve and automate computer security processes and compliance. There is also a Software Assurance Program designed to develop more secure software at the outset to minimize the number of vulnerabilities and therefore increase computer security.[36]

The umbrella of the NCCIC also includes the US-Computer Emergency Readiness Team, or CERT. The US-CERT provides response support and defense against cyber attacks in the executive branch of government, as well as support for public, private, and international partners. The CERT provides information on new and existing vulnerabilities in all manner of computer systems, as well as resources to help patch and secure networks. It also offers security and threat reports and acts as an information clearinghouse on cyber security matters.[37]

DHS also coordinates the Cyber Storm exercise to assist in the protection of cyber infrastructure. This event takes place every two years and is an attempt to assess the capability of government, public, and private entities to respond to a national cyber incident. The Cyber Storm training exercise simulates attacks against multiple infrastructure resources to understand the procedures, processes, tools, and responses of agencies to such an attack.[38] These exercises are key to improving cyber security and incident response in the event of a serious threat to cyber infrastructure.

QUICK FACTS

Like the highways that move us from place to place, electrical grids and the Internet are made up of infrastructure. Not unlike how the infrastructure that transports people from place to place is vulnerable to attacks, the infrastructure that moves information is also at risk from terrorist and cyber attacks or even natural disasters, like hurricanes or floods. The Department of Homeland Security's National Protection and Programs Directorate (NPPD) is tasked with protecting the United States' critical infrastructure, like power grids, from cyber attacks. NPPD analysts work 24 hours a day, seven days a week, to monitor critical infrastructures in order to defend against attacks. If an attack occurs, an Incident Response Team from the National Cybersecurity and Communications Integration Center (NCCIC)/Industrial Control Systems Cyber Emergency Response Team (ICS-CERT) and the U.S. Computer Emergency Readiness Team (US-CERT) is deployed. An Incident Response Team, a team of four to six designated experts in the field of cyber security, is always packed with the critical equipment needed for any perceivable task, ready to depart at a moment's notice to fix any cyber crisis in the United States or abroad.

Source: https://www.dhs.gov/cyber-crime-cases

U.S. Immigration and Customs Enforcement

The U.S. Immigration and Customs Enforcement (ICE) agency is the largest and primary investigative arm of the U.S. DHS.[39] ICE is responsible for identifying and investigating weaknesses within the nation's borders, developing intelligence concerning threats, removing foreign nationals, and enforcing over 400 federal statutes. The agency was formed in 2003 as part of the Homeland Security Act and is the result of a merger of several federal agencies, including the Customs Service, Immigration and Naturalization, and the Federal Protective Service. ICE has approximately 20,000 employees in 400 offices in the United States and 46 countries around the world.[40]

The ICE agency plays a pivotal role in enforcing Internet-related crimes because of its responsibility to protect resources within the U.S. borders and the inherently international nature of cyberspace crimes. In particular, ICE operates the Cyber Crimes Center (C3), which has four subsections focused on child exploitation, computer forensics, cyber crimes, and information technology and administration.[41] The C3 also offers training for local, federal, and international law enforcement agencies.

The Child Exploitation Investigations Unit (CEIU) exists to investigate producers and distributors of child pornography and abuse, as well as sex tourism. The CEIU operates in conjunction with international law enforcement agencies to investigate and prosecute these offenses. This section also coordinates Operation Predator, which is an ongoing multiagency international investigation of child exploitation and crimes against children. In 2015, Operation Predator led to the arrest of more than 2,400 individuals for child sexual exploitation violations.[42]

The Cyber Crimes Unit (CCU) investigates and enforces laws pertaining to a wide variety of cybercrimes, including international money laundering, intellectual property rights violations, human trafficking, illegal exports, and arms smuggling. The CCU conducts undercover stings and investigations over the Internet and has conducted a variety of operations, such as Operation Apothecary, to arrest and prosecute the sale and distribution of counterfeit pharmaceuticals and controlled substances over the Internet.[43]

The Computer Forensics Unit offers digital evidence recovery and analysis for ICE agents as well as other law enforcement agencies. In particular, it has computer forensic agents (CFAs) who retrieve and analyze digital evidence as well as assist in the development of warrants for the seizure of digital evidence.[44] Forensic agents also provide expert testimony for cases in support of criminal investigations. The Information Technology and Administrative Unit provides operational and technical services to support the other three arms of the C3.

BOX 11.3

How ICE Identifies Child Victims

A little girl, no more than 11 years old, stares out the window as the vehicle she's in speeds down the highway. Still in her pajamas, she turns and smiles at another passenger, who snaps a picture. This could be any family photo that one might see on Facebook, Instagram, or another such site, were it not accompanied by a caption polling viewers to submit their suggestions on how to best rape her.

The photo, along with a cache of others with the same girl, was posted to a chat board known to be frequented by pedophiles in November 2011. There, it was discovered by Danish law enforcement officials. Denmark is a member of the Virtual Global Taskforce, an international alliance of law enforcement agencies who work together to detect online sexual abuse and rescue victims. Danish authorities sent the troubling material to U.S. Immigration and Customs Enforcement's (ICE)

Homeland Security Investigations (HSI), the founding member of the task force. With the clock ticking to identify, find, and rescue the girl before she could be harmed, HSI's Cyber Crimes Center put their best agent—an agent known as Cole—from the Victim Identification Program on the case.

Occupying a small lab in a nondescript office block in Fairfax, Virginia, the Victim Identification Unit has an outsized role in changing lives. In a room lit only by computer monitors, HSI agents spend countless hours using the most advanced digital forensics tools available to examine photo evidence for clues. Since nowadays most child pornography is traded online, the only evidence available is often stills of the material itself. Abusers tend to take care to keep their faces out of frame, earning them the nickname "John or Jane Doe" and making it more difficult to locate and rescue victims. For this reason, there is no pixel left unturned. Even the tiniest of peculiarities in the periphery of a photo can be the key to tracking down the predator and rescuing the victim.

In this case, the peculiarity that led Cole and the other agents down the right path was in the photo of the girl in the moving vehicle. Through the window, investigators noticed the blur of a road sign the truck was passing. On it, a distinctive yellow sunflower-like shape with some numbers superimposed onto it, the only one still clear enough to be legible was a "2."

Investigators discovered that the sign was a road sign unique to the State of Kansas—where the sunflower is the state flower. The suspect must live somewhere along a state highway, but which one? The first digit of the highway number—the "2"—was visible, but the rest were too blurred to make out. Even with the sophisticated imaging technology available at HSI's Cyber Crimes Center, agents could not clear up the other numbers. Agent Cole made the only decision left available to him: get to Kansas and find the stretch of highway that matched the photo.

Driving in pairs, ICE HSI agents drove the full length of every state highway in Kansas that began with a "2," looking for the exact spot where the photo was taken.

The tedious undertaking took days. It had now been 13 days since the Danes tipped ICE off to the plot. Then at last, right as the highway the special agent was on was about to merge with another, the sign appeared. The agents quickly contacted the local sheriff. They showed him the other photos from the series hoping to trigger something. Sifting through, the sheriff recognized the backyard swimming pool in one of them. That same morning, ICE HSI agents in conjunction with local law enforcement organized a raid of the house whose backyard contained the pool. There, they found the girl—still wearing the same pajamas. They apprehended her abuser, who turned out to be a minor himself—he was only 16. He pled guilty and was sentenced to serve 48 months in a juvenile facility. The girl, meanwhile, is safe and living with her family in a small Kansas town.

"Operation Sunflower," as it became known, was the first case ICE's Victim Identification Unit undertook as part of Operation Predator, which in 2014 alone was responsible for making possible the arrests of more than 2,300 child predators and the rescues of more than 1,000 victims.

Source: https://www.dhs.gov/cyber-crime-cases

The U.S. Secret Service

The U.S. Secret Service was created in 1865 to serve a dual purpose: to provide protective services to the president and other cabinet members and to safeguard the nation's financial payment system against fraud and counterfeit financial instruments. In the massive reorganization of federal agencies after 9/11, the U.S. Secret Service became a key entity within the U.S. DHS to combat computer crime. The agency's responsibilities have increased tremendously as a result of the revolution in computerized information systems and the growth of the Internet as a vehicle for financial transactions.

For example, the ever-increasing sophistication of computerized reproduction capabilities has expanded the potential for the production of counterfeit financial instruments. In addition, the development of Internet communications has facilitated the rapid communication of encrypted messages and financial fraud schemes using phony debit and credit card transactions and electronic funds transfers (EFTs). Finally, the agency's protection responsibilities in terms of special events have grown to include the safeguarding of computerized telecommunications and power systems integral to these events. The convergence of these related factors has thrust the Secret Service into the role of the federal government's primary law enforcement weapon against computer and cybercrime.[45]

The Secret Service's Financial Crimes Division is the agency's primary tool in the fight against computer crime. The division's main responsibilities include the enforcement of three high-profile computer-related crimes. First, the division is charged with identifying and investigating financial institution fraud (FIF). Since 1990, the Secret Service has been granted concurrent jurisdiction with the DOJ to investigate fraud committed against financial institutions (i.e., banks). Primary FIF schemes include the creation of counterfeit financial instruments (primarily cash) through desktop publishing systems. Recent Secret Service investigations have pointed to large increases in the production of counterfeit corporate checks and negotiable instruments that have paralleled the advent of sophisticated desktop publishing systems and copying technologies. Title 18, Section 514, of the U.S. Federal Code was enacted in 1996 in order to stem the growing tide of phony cash and checks in circulation.[46]

Second, the Secret Service has primary jurisdiction in cases involving access device fraud. Access device fraud falls under Title 18, Section 1029, of the U.S. Federal Code (the "credit card statute") and involves the fraudulent use of credit card numbers, personal identification numbers (PINs), and computer passwords. In addition to these access device frauds, the Secret Service has increasingly investigated the theft of computer codes located within cellular phones that are used to track billing information.[47]

Third, the Secret Service has primary jurisdiction in the investigation of general computer fraud relating to computers and computer systems of "federal interest." These computers can be used as instruments of crime through hacking or other means as well as tools to produce fraudulent negotiable instruments or store private account information. The Secret Service also trains law enforcement personnel in computer forensics designed to detect and investigate these crimes through the agency's Electronic Crimes Special Agent Program (ECSAP).[48]

The Financial Crimes Division houses the Electronic Crimes Branch, which specializes in detecting and investigating credit card and other access device fraud. The Electronic Crimes Branch provides computer equipment and technical assistance to special agents concerning lab analysis of computer-related evidence and storage equipment, the seizure of computerized evidence, and the administrative management of all computer-related investigations.[49]

In recognition of the Secret Service's primary role in combating computer and cybercrime and the need for interagency cooperation, provisions of the USA Freedom Act point to the development of a "network" of task forces that span federal jurisdictions. These task forces include federal, state, and local law enforcement agency personnel and have been primarily aimed at addressing the increasingly global nature of computerized financial fraud. Specific task forces have included the Metro Alien Task Force, the West African (Nigerian) Task Force, and the Asian Organized Crime Task Force.[50] The most successful task force developed has been the Electronic Crimes Task Force (ECTF), which brings together law enforcement agencies, as well as prosecutors, private industry, and academia.[51] The ECTF mission is to prevent, detect, and investigate attacks against financial and critical infrastructures. There are now 39 ECTFs around the country, which provide support and resources to help investigate electronic crimes.[52]

STATE AND LOCAL ROLES

As the sections above indicate, the growing danger posed by computer crimes has clearly resulted in an increasing enforcement emphasis at the federal level. Indeed, the current struggle against international terrorist threats seems to have galvanized national-level efforts to protect critical computer infrastructures at the federal level. The threats related to computer crimes, however, have also become a growing concern to law enforcement officials at the state and local levels. While federal officials employed by the myriad agencies detailed above seem to have successfully garnered both public and political attention concerning the need for resources aimed at addressing the computer crime problem, law enforcement personnel at the local level continue to encounter a host of issues that have hampered efforts to combat computer crimes effectively within their own jurisdictions. This section will provide an overview regarding what is being done to fight computer crime at the state and local levels of enforcement, with an emphasis on identifying the critical areas of need that have thus far limited efforts to combat computer crime at the local level.

The number of local, state, county, and regional computer crime task forces continues to increase, largely because these agencies have experienced more computer-related criminal activities within their jurisdictions, and citizens and private entities have become increasingly willing to report these activities to local law enforcement departments. For example, a survey of local law enforcement computer crime experts found that 80 percent of the respondents indicated a "measurable increase" in the reporting of computer and electronic crimes, especially traditional fraud and theft crimes using computer devices.[53]

At the same time, local officers may not have the capacity or understanding of computer crimes necessary to properly investigate these offenses. For example, the most pressing computer crimes enforced by these agencies appear to be those related to "harmful computer content," especially child pornography and exploitation, threatening communications, and stalking.[54] These types of computer crimes are followed in priority by computer-related frauds (e.g., online shopping schemes and EFT fraud), other technology-based crimes (e.g., encryption used to hide criminal activities such as drug trafficking), and computer hacking crimes. Higher-profile computer crimes, such as threats to critical national infrastructure systems, are rarely handled solely by local and state investigators because they often require federal expertise and resources.[55]

Despite the ever-increasing caseload of computer crimes, there appears to be a lack of recognition and support from upper-level management within local police agencies in terms of providing the resources necessary to counter these threats. The majority of these cases receive a low priority at the local level. The fact that computer crime cases have not received the necessary recognition and support from local law enforcement administrators has created several areas in which local-level agencies must improve if computer crimes are to be effectively enforced.

Critical Needs at the State and Local Levels of Enforcement

Officers involved in combating computer crime at the local and state level must be supplied with an increase in resources and technology in order to fight computer crime more effectively. These areas can be broadly grouped into four "critical needs": (1) training, (2) equipment, (3) updated criminal codes designed to complement current enforcement efforts, and (4) resources for tapping federal expertise and equipment related to computer crime enforcement.[56]

The need for training appears to be paramount at the local level. Currently, most local agencies fail to provide any training in computer crime to patrol personnel. This lack of training at the entry level can have severe consequences in regard to prosecuting computer crimes, especially in terms of protecting computer crime scenes and collecting forensic evidence. An untrained patrol officer can easily inadvertently destroy computerized evidence if not trained in protecting such evidence.[57] Related to training needs at the entry level, most local departments do not possess the technical expertise needed to train those officers interested in becoming computer forensic specialists. Often, these officers must obtain specialized training from outside sources such as private industry or the federal government. Some researchers and administrators have cited the need for a national certification program aimed at producing more specially trained computer experts at the local level. Others have noted that the career path for "computer crime specialists" at the local level can often be limited, and career advancement within many local agencies would require reassignment to another priority division.[58]

The need for computer crime training appears to go hand in hand with the procurement of additional resources and equipment. While federal personnel have increasingly used the growing awareness of computer crime at the national level as an avenue for larger equipment expenditures, these dollars have largely failed to trickle down to the local level.[59] The resulting disparity in equipment between federal and local cyber cops can most clearly be seen in the inability of most local agencies to decipher encrypted computer evidence.[60] Surveys of local computer crime experts indicate that for those jurisdictions that currently have computer evidence laboratories, more than 50 percent do not have adequate capabilities to read encrypted evidence. Much of the problem related to the lack of equipment can be traced to insufficient funding behind efforts to control computer crime. Many local experts have cited the need to use equipment that has been purchased personally because local departments fail to provide adequate resources from within the organization.[61]

As detailed elsewhere in this text, the explosion in computer technologies and communications has stymied legislative attempts to enact statutes that are current and can be applied to the use of these new technologies. In short, state laws have been largely unable to keep pace with technology. The gap evident between the pace of technological change and the enactment of legal codes has been especially problematic for computer crime specialists and prosecutors at the local level. For example, there are no legal mechanisms designed to allow the enforcement of subpoenas across state lines.[62] In the case of crimes that occur over the Internet, the lack of these mechanisms can effectively halt computer crime investigations at the local level. So too, severe differences exist across jurisdictions in terms of the definition of what constitutes an electronic crime. Some states continue to define many computer crimes as misdemeanor offenses, thereby reducing local law enforcement incentives to increase enforcement resources in this area.[63]

Finally, those officers who are active in the enforcement of computer crimes at the local level have cited a lack of informational resources that would enable them to easily utilize the extensive technical expertise and equipment resources that currently exist at the federal level. Currently, there is no comprehensive source of information containing a list of federal contact persons who could aid local investigators. Such a "guidebook" could include not only a list of prominent federal agents who are experts in the field of computer crime but also prominent computer forensic laboratories, forensic equipment available for local use, and federally approved equipment manufacturers to aid local agencies that are interested in upgrading their computer crime resources.[64]

Summary

American law enforcement agencies have assumed a variety of roles and responses to the new and increasing threats posed by computer crimes and terrorism. This chapter has provided an overview of how a number of federal agencies have responded to these threats, including the Secret Service, the Department of Justice, the Federal Bureau of Investigation, the National Security Agency, the Federal Trade Commission, the Postal Service, Immigration and Customs Enforcement, the Department of Energy, and the Department of Homeland Security. These wide-ranging agencies have worked independently to adapt their specialized law enforcement expertise to these new problems. The federal government has increasingly recognized the need for these disparate agencies to collaborate in the fight against computer crime and terror. Moreover, local- and state-level law enforcement agencies have attempted to assume their own role in enforcing computer crimes. Although a relatively small number of these agencies have responded successfully to these threats through increasing funding and the formation of multiagency task forces, these agencies have largely been limited by several factors, most notably a lack of funds, personnel, and technology.

Review Questions

1. Which federal law enforcement agency has assumed primary responsibilities in the area of access device fraud, including the fraudulent use of credit card numbers, personal identification numbers, and computer passwords?

2. Which federal agency is responsible for the prosecution of computer fraud and abuse violations through the Computer Crime and Intellectual Property Section (CCIPS)?

3. Which federal agency investigates cybercrime and is currently responsible for the management of the InfraGard private/public partnership program?

4. Which agency within the Department of Homeland Security is responsible for managing cyber-critical infrastructure?

5. What are some of the impediments to computer crime investigations at the local level?

6. What are some of the key needs in local law enforcement agencies to improve their response to computer crimes?

Critical Thinking Exercises

1. In June 2017, Reality Winner, an NSA contractor with top secret clearance, was arrested and accused of leaking a top secret report detailing Russian meddling in the November 2016 U.S. presidential election. The report was leaked by Ms. Winner to a reporter at the national security news outlet, The Intercept. It is estimated that about four million people including government employees and contractors, hold security clearances with 1.3 million holding top secret clearances like Ms. Winner. With such a large number of people having access to security sensitive documents, how do you recommend we control leaks of this information to the press?

2. In this chapter, Box 11.1 discussed the phenomenon of "going dark" and how the FBI is trying to deal with the issue that significantly hinders criminal investigations. Review the FBI's Web site information on "going dark" at *https://www.fbi.gov/services/operational-technology/going-dark*. After reading the Web page, what solutions can you identify to counteract the "going dark" phenomenon?

Endnotes

1. *http://www.usdoj.gov.*
2. *http://www.usdoj.gov/criminal/cybercrime/ccpolicy.*
3. *https://www.justice.gov/opa/pr/criminal-division-s-computer-crime-and-intellectual-property-section-celebrates-20-years.*
4. *Ibid.*
5. *https://www.fbi.gov/investigate/cyber.*
6. *Ibid.*
7. *Ibid.*
8. *http://www.rcfl.gov.*
9. *Ibid.*
10. *Ibid.*
11. *http://www.ic3.gov.*
12. *https://www.infragard.org/.*
13. *http://www.nsa.gov.*
14. NAKASHIMA, E. (January 1, 2008). "Bush Order Expands Network Monitoring: Intelligence Agencies to Track Institutions." *The Washington Post.* Retrieved February 9, 2008, from *http://www.washingtonpost.com/wp-dyn/content/article/2008/01/25/AR2008012503261_pf.html.*
15. *Ibid.*, p. 28.
16. *https://www.nsa.gov/resources/educators/centers-academic-excellence/cyber-defense/.*
17. NAKASHIMA, "Bush Order Expands Network Monitoring."
18. *http://www.nsa.gov/ia/ia_at_nsa/index.shtml.*
19. *http://www.ftc.gov.*

20. SWINDLE, O. (September 11, 1999). "E-Commerce: Tomorrow's Economy—Taxing and Regulation the Old-Fashioned Way." Remarks before the Georgia Public Policy Forum.

21. Federal Trade Commission. (August 14, 2002). Seminar. "Attacking Identity Theft Together: Usable Tools for Law Enforcement." Dallas, Texas.

22. *https://www.ftc.gov/enforcement/consumer-sentinel-network.*

23. *http://www.usps.com.*

24. *Ibid.*

25. *Ibid.*

26. *https://postalinspectors.uspis.gov/radDocs/2016%20 AR%20FINAL_web.pdf.*

27. *Ibid.*

28. *http://www.doe.gov.*

29. *https://energy.gov/oe/cyber-incident-response-and-recovery-0.*

30. *http://www.dhs.gov.*

31. *https://www.dhs.gov/sites/default/files/publications /Public%20Org%20Charts%202017.04.12.pdf.*

32. *https://www.dhs.gov/about-dhs.*

33. *https://www.dhs.gov/national-cybersecurity-and-communications-integration-center.*

34. *Ibid.*

35. *Ibid.*

36. *Ibid.*

37. *https://www.us-cert.gov/.*

38. *https://www.dhs.gov/cyber-storm-v.*

39. *http://www.ice.gov.*

40. *https://www.ice.gov/about.*

41. *https://www.ice.gov/cyber-crimes.*

42. *Ibid.*

43. *Ibid.*

44. *Ibid.*

45. JACKSON, W. (2003). "E-Crime Squad." *Government Computer News* 22(2).

46. *https://www.secretservice.gov/investigation/.*

47. *Ibid.*

48. *Ibid.*

49. *Ibid.*

50. *Ibid.*

51. *Ibid.*

52. *Ibid.*

53. STAMNBAUGH, H., BEUPRE, D.S., ICOYE, D.J., BAKER, R., CASSADAY, W., and WILLIAMS, W.P. (March 2001). "Electronic Crime Needs Assessment for State and Local Law Enforcement." *National Institute of Justice.*

54. *Ibid.,* p. 75.

55. *Ibid.*

56. *Ibid.*

57. *Ibid.*

58. *Ibid.*

59. *Ibid.*

60. *Ibid.*

61. *Ibid.*

62. *Ibid.*

63. *Ibid.*

64. *Ibid.*

The Investigation of Computer-Related Crime

CHAPTER OBJECTIVES

After completing this chapter, you should be able to

- Explain and understand the search warrant application process appropriate to electronic evidence at a single-location crime scene.
- Identify hardware and storage devices potentially containing evidence of a crime.
- Explain and understand the legal standards and best current practices for the documentation of a single-location electronic crime scene.
- Explain and describe the best current practices for the collection, preservation, transportation, and storage of electronic evidence.
- Distinguish between single-scene, multiple-scene, and network crimes.
- Communicate an understanding of network architectures and standards relevant to network investigations.
- Identify sources of assistance for multiple-scene and network operations.
- Identify categories of evidence and probable locations of that evidence.
- Broadly outline procedures for preserving and collecting network trace evidence.

INTRODUCTION

This chapter's focus is on the current, recognized state-of-the-domain in computer or cybercrime investigations. The education, training, and skill set of the personnel available to an investigation will dramatically influence the type and scope of investigations that may be undertaken. Understanding the roles of and skills needed by such personnel is vital to planning appropriate investigations. Although there is no single policy or plan for investigations, this chapter presents an overview of formal inquiries or investigations, with special emphasis on policy, process, and practice. This chapter breaks investigations into three basic types: single-scene, multiple-scene, and network investigations. Each type of investigation requires different skills from personnel involved. Single-scene investigations require the skills found in trained law enforcement investigators. The skills used in a single-scene investigation form the building blocks of the more complex investigations. Thus, while building on single-scene skills, multiple-scene investigations require additional networking and coordination skills. Coordination of multiple searches at various locations is the realm of an experienced criminal investigator. The networking skills may be provided by a subject matter expert (e.g., computer consultant). Finally, network crimes require the skills of multiple-scene investigators and outside expert assistance. Even the most computer-proficient investigator needs help from the companies that maintain the Internet to track a crime successfully through their servers. However, some degree of preliminary knowledge is required even to know where to start. Techniques for acquiring this type of information are presented in this chapter along with conceptual tools that allow an investigator to communicate with the Internet experts.

INVESTIGATOR ROLES AND RESPONSIBILITIES

The role of computers in our society is ubiquitous, especially since the development of the Internet (1960s) but particularly since the emergence of the World Wide Web (www) in 1989. Law enforcement lagged behind initially (1970s–1980s), but has made up significant ground since the 1990s. The pervasive use of desktop and laptop computers has added another potential source of evidence to the over 54 million households with computers in the United States.[1] Many large law enforcement agencies have a dedicated electronic crime investigation capacity. Medium-sized agencies may be acquiring their first electronic crime investigation unit or attempting to cross-train detectives from traditional areas. Even the smallest departments encounter electronic crime, but do not have the capacity for a dedicated unit. Thus, the mission of police, from patrol officers to forensic specialists, depends greatly on their department's size and organization. Generally, the role and responsibility of police staff in electronic investigation is the same as their counterparts dealing with physical crime.

First Responders

First responders to a crime scene are often patrol officers. First responders would not normally attempt to complete an electronic search and seizure; however, they do benefit from an awareness of the procedure and, if given even basic training, may be better able to preserve a potential electronic crime scene for specialized investigators. First responders are not dedicated electronic crime investigators. They have many other responsibilities, including safety, security, and basic documentation of an event or scene. Furthermore, patrol officers are often not given the time to conduct in-depth investigations; those are handled by detectives.

A well-trained first responder will control the human element of the crime scene first: tending to the injured, isolating suspects, and controlling onlookers. First responders are trained to avoid contaminating a crime scene or destroying physical

---

QUICK FACTS

In a 2012 article, local law enforcement agencies felt that they were unable to fully address cybercrime in their communities—from basic discovery to sophisticated investigations. Further, patrol officers indicated that they should not be responsible for handling cybercrime cases, due primarily to their lack of training in the area, the failures of upper management to address such crimes, and the greater need to focus on more immediate and violent crimes that impacted their communities. Patrol officers stated that the best strategies to deal with cybercrime were greater care taken by citizens online and improvements in the legal system.

Source: Adam M. Bossler and Thomas J. Holt, "Patrol Officers' Perceived Role in Responding to Cybercrime," *Journal of Policing* 35(1): 165–181 (March 2012).

evidence. As the prevalence of electronic evidence increases, first responders have naturally become aware of the need to protect and preserve it. For example, first responders who recognize that iPod, iPad, Blackberry, and personal digital assistants (PDA's) often carry sensitive evidence and should be able to retrieve and carefully handle these devices. Making first responders aware of potential digital evidence allows them to protect it in the same way they protect physical evidence.

Investigators

Electronic crime investigators are trained law enforcement officers or experienced investigators brought (sometimes unwillingly) into the world of electronic evidence. The basic skills required successfully to organize an investigation, establish the elements of a crime, establish the connection between the suspect and the crime, conceptualize and present the crime, and document the investigation are still needed in electronic crime investigations. In fact, many corporations seek computer investigators and security directors from the ranks of law enforcement rather than technical experts. Investigators must have enough technical skill to gather evidence, comprehend the crime, and communicate effectively with technical experts, but do not need extensive theoretical knowledge or daily experience with computer systems. That is not to say that highly skilled investigators are not desirable.

Digital Analysts

In physical crime investigations and electronic crime investigations, the complex analysis of evidence is often left to forensic specialists in digital analysis. A detective or crime scene technician would not feel bad about not understanding the intricacies of laboratory DNA analysis. Although computer skills and knowledge are essential to the investigator, the essential skills of an investigator involve collection and preservation of evidence for further analysis. Technical experts conduct this analysis through computer forensic techniques. Special programs and procedures allow forensic specialists to compile evidence and present it to the court. Out of necessity, many computer crime investigators feel compelled to learn these forensic analysis skills. Many investigators become skilled computer forensic examiners, but have to devote a great portion of their time to learning the latest technologies and conducting the analysis instead of conducting their investigations. Forensic analysts provide efficiency through a division of labor and regular practice with their equipment and techniques. It is not uncommon for senior investigators to act as forensic analysts.

Corporate Security

Corporate security investigators are hired by corporations to secure the data assets of the corporation. Although they often cooperate with law enforcement, they have a fundamentally different mission. Corporate officers must always consider the good of the corporation. For example, a private computer investigator may be withdrawn from a case if the corporation decides that expending resources on such investigation will not be justified by the results.

Private computer security or investigative consultants are often brought in to review security incidents or suspected crimes. A small discrepancy can indicate a system failure or a major intrusion. In a famous case at the University of California, Berkeley, Cliff Stoll tried to reconcile a trivial accounting error and ended up discovering an attempt at international espionage.[2] It is not always obvious that a crime has been committed without further investigation. Since many crimes are committed by insiders, a security consultant also provides a check to the power of system administrators.[3]

Many corporations keep former police officers on staff to advise them when to call the police and when not to call. Although it is hard for many officers and investigators to understand such a decision or even consider it dereliction of a societal duty, many corporations do not want adverse publicity or fear the "seize everything" tactics of law enforcement once a crime is reported. The delays, staff time, and computing resource downtime created by an investigation may cause more financial loss than a break-in. In spite of the potential antagonism between the roles of corporate investigators and law enforcement, these groups often work together smoothly. Once a decision is made to report a crime, private police often act as liaisons between investigators and the corporate structure, insulating other employees from disruption and facilitating the efforts of investigators. A corporate security director not only will have access to the entire physical premises but will also be able to issue directives to corporate employees without the direct invention of management or company executives.

Subject Matter Experts

Technical expertise has a short shelf life. Many skills that were in great demand a mere two years ago could today be virtually obsolete. Using a subject matter expert (SME) is one way for an investigator to gain access to detailed knowledge on a highly specialized or uncommon topic. Although many investigators feel confident handling a iOS or Windows™ system, large, multiuser systems may present unknown challenges and opportunities for mistakes. Similarly, a complex network with unfamiliar technology may be beyond an investigator's skill level. If an investigator does not feel confident with the technology to be searched or seized, a SME with experience using that technology can provide invaluable insight.

A skilled investigator can often successfully conduct analyses on all but the most demanding cases. However, with the staggering complexity of some systems, it is not uncommon for the investigator to turn to an expert in the system to be examined such as the corporate system administrator. In fact, it is important to note that no one individual is an "expert" regarding *all* hardware, software, and systems. That is simply not possible; it is an urban legend. When electronic crime enters the network, investigators are forced to call upon various experts at Internet service providers (ISPs), communications centers, and corporate information technology (IT) departments. Even the most skilled investigator cannot instantly address the processes and data structures of large and/or unfamiliar information systems. Just as the corporate security director becomes the liaison with corporate employees, the system administrator becomes the liaison with corporate data resources. Of course, if the local system administrator is a suspect, this is not appropriate. In such cases, a SME familiar with that type of system should be engaged to provide the necessary guidance.

Single-Location Crime Scenes

Although the gamut of electronic crimes can span the global communication networks and cross many jurisdictions, single-location electronic crime scene search and seizure is the most fundamental skill set of an electronic crimes investigator. Investigators specializing in other forms of crime possess a set of skills that adapt well to a fairly straightforward single-location electronic crime scene. This is because

BOX 12.1

Cyber Vigilantism

Cyber vigilantes are not part of the formal investigation process. They are generally private citizens not affiliated with law enforcement, and they generally fall into one of several different categories. There are some that form a type of "online neighborhood watch," gathering intelligence and alerting law enforcement officials when they come across unlawful acts. These individuals are the most passive of cyber vigilantes; others take more direct action against online offenders. In some cases, this means simply turning the tables on the perpetrators of a perceived injustice, for example, subjecting a known spammer to a deluge of spam via third-party subscriptions.

Other examples include outing those who post questionable content online to employers and family members. In 2012, a notorious troll on Reddit, the discussion Web site, was outed as the moderator of a slew of racist, misogynist, and otherwise offensive threads by a fellow Reddit user who apparently felt that some of the material was sexually exploitative. Michael Brutsch, known online as Violentacrez, posted thousands of pictures to a thread entitled "jailbait"—and when an article in national blog network Gawker described his online activities, Brutsch lost his job.[4]

Anonymous, a collective of cyber vigilante cells, engages in retaliation-based cyber vigilantism. In 2012, it posted personal details of Westboro Baptist Church members who planned to protest at funerals of children killed in the Sandy Hook school shooting spree. The collective published names, addresses, phone numbers, and Social Security numbers of those involved in the organization; they also hacked their Web site and Twitter accounts.[5]

Anonymous also inserted itself into a rape case in Steubenville, Ohio, in 2013. On January 1, a cell associated with the collective posted video of suspects in the rape of a teenager that showed the men laughing and joking about the alleged rape. Concerned that there was a cover-up on the part of law enforcement and school officials, the group posted the following:

> On this fateful night a life was changed forever as a group of the football players of Big Red High School, dubbed themselves "rape crew" and began taking advantage of an underage girl. The girl was sexually assaulted, molested, raped, and drug unconcious [sic] from party to party. This is a warning shot to the school faculty, the parents of those involved, and those involved especially. A preliminary dox is being released on some of those involved.
>
> You can hide no longer, you have attracted the attention of the hive. We will not sit idely [sic] by and watch a group of young men who turn to rape as a game or sport get the pass because of athletic ability and small town luck. You now have the world looking directly at you."[6]

Once the video was leaked, the case—which had already seen a fair amount of media exposure to that date—blew up, becoming international news. The video leak caused havoc with jury selection, an unintended consequence, but ultimately put a spotlight on the case—in which the defendants were found guilty in a juvenile court—and the issue of sexual assault.

Still other cyber vigilantes work to identify child pornographers or pedophiles by engaging them in online conversations; some may even attempt to meet them for supposed sexual encounters. In some cases, they may hand over information gleaned to law enforcement; in others, they use public humiliation or "outings," as described in the cases above.

Although cyber vigilantism may seem helpful—or in many cases, just—law enforcement officials discourage it. Such acts can lead to issues of defamation and entrapment, not to mention civil suits, unintended criminal acts on the part of the vigilante, and a host of other legal liabilities.

the single-location crime scene does not involve complex networking or the enormous storage capacity and complexity of network crime scenes.

SEARCH WARRANTS AND ELECTRONIC EVIDENCE

Criminal investigators must establish probable cause in an affidavit in application for a search warrant (also called a "warrant application"). The affidavit must specify that a crime has been committed, evidence of the crime exists, and the evidence presently exists in the place to be searched. Furthermore, the affiant (the investigator applying for the warrant) must particularly describe the evidence to be seized. Specific evidence of a specific crime must be named or general evidence facilitating a criminal act may be described by function. Unless traveling through a network, electronic evidence must be stored in a container or medium. Single-scene crimes, by definition, do not involve networks. Thus, it is often useful to think of the storage medium (i.e., container) when planning a search. Each of the following containers of electronic evidence presents unique challenges and opportunities in the warrant application process.

Computer Systems

If an investigation requires the seizure of an entire computer system, the investigator should decide whether the computer itself is the target of the warrant or if the data on the computer are the target of the warrant. If stolen property is the target of the search, the contraband (i.e., the fruit of the crime) may require specific and particular description. When the data contained on the computer are the target, the magistrate signing the warrant will usually allow the investigator to describe the computer suspected of holding the evidence required by general function. It is fairly easy for a suspect to move information from one physical storage device to another. Even detailed investigations may be outdated by the time the warrant is served. Furthermore, it is often impossible to specify precisely a physical computer when probable cause is established through network investigation; however, network identification or physical, premise location often meets the requirement that a warrant must particularly describe the place or person to be searched (i.e., particularity requirement).

External Storage Media

When data are the target of the search, the warrant should be written to allow seizure of electronic storage media found at the crime scene. Electronic storage devices come in a broad variety of physical sizes, shapes, and storage capacities. It may be impossible precisely to identify the storage medium of electronic evidence in a warrant. In this case, the broad function (i.e., electronic storage device) should be used. The smallness of these devices makes it possible to hide them virtually anywhere; a warrant may have to apply to a broader physical area than the immediate surroundings of a computer system. Common examples include compact disks (data CDs) hidden in the pages of books, data CDs hidden among music CDs (especially if music CDs are home reproductions), tiny Universal Serial Bus (USB) storage devices, and smart cards and Secure Digital (SD) cards that can be placed in a cell phone or digital camera hidden near a computer.

Handheld Devices

PDAs, iPods, iPhones, most cell phones, and other data devices are miniature computer systems designed to be highly mobile. They may be found virtually anywhere under the control of a suspect and may contain data storage comparable to a full-size computer of just a few years ago. Warrant applications should describe the function of the device and person carrying the device rather than trying to specify a physical location. Even though warrants must "particularly describe the place to be searched,"[7] the courts have recognized that must often occur at a time and place determined by the suspect. Warrants for such searches can describe the function of evidence thought to be in the possession of a person.

Other Electronic Devices

Many electronic storage devices do not fit a narrow definition of "computer" and may be excluded as evidence if not properly defined in a search warrant. Examples include, but are not limited to,

1. Telephone answering machines and other electronic telephone equipment, including Voice over Internet Protocol (VoIP) boxes.
2. Video game systems like an Xbox, PlayStation, or Wii as well as digital video recorders (DVRs).
3. Access control devices such as security smart cards.
4. Credit card skimmers and magnetic stripe encoders.
5. Personal items such as digital watches with storage capacity, pagers, calculators with storage, and electronic calendars.
6. Digital cameras or digital sound recorders.
7. Webcams and any other recording devices.

The range of storage capacity in these different electronic devices ranges from a minute encryption key to a full-motion, DVD™-quality video.

Networking Equipment

In the course of a search, agents may come across networking equipment, or devices that allow multiple computers to be linked in a network. The significant growth of wireless Internet connections has made the likelihood of observing such equipment at a crime scene very high. Thus, individuals must be cognizant of this sort of equipment that constitutes a network, including modems, wired and wireless routers, network cards and USB drives, and Ethernet cables that link these devices together, along with other devices such as printers.

Executing the Search Warrant

Once a warrant is obtained, the details of the search may be finalized. A preliminary plan is often attached to the application for the warrant. If the warrant is signed as written, most of the details will already be in place. The magistrate issuing the warrant may place special conditions on the search; those conditions should be integrated into the plan. For example, a magistrate may not wish to interfere unduly with the First Amendment rights of a disinterested party holding evidence of a crime. The system operator of a Web site hosting discussions may choose not to voluntarily divulge details about users of the Web site. A search warrant may specify that the police may seize evidence related to the crime described in the warrant, but may not seize unrelated discussions or interfere with the public forum for discussion found on the Web site. The search strategy would have to include both a way to keep the Web site open and specifically target discussions and logs relevant to the crime. Other considerations in the execution of a warrant include the conditions under which the warrant is to be served and coordination with uniformed officers, or even SWAT team members.

PRIORITY CONCERNS   First and foremost, investigators must assess the potential danger to themselves. It is beyond the scope of this book to discuss planning an armed raid with a no-knock warrant versus a full-compliance search; however, officer safety should be a priority regardless of the expected level of compliance of the suspect.

Some particular concerns lie in assessing the particular dangers of working with electronic equipment. Test for live voltage in wires before touching or wear insulative gloves if appropriate. Although there is often talk of booby raps in computers, this usually refers to methods for destroying data, not physical traps; however, in this age of enhanced homeland security, actual traps may be an issue. If the investigation involves terrorism, then additional concern should be taken in the planning and execution of the search.

SECURING THE SCENE Procedures for securing a crime scene typically include removing suspects, witnesses, and bystanders from the area to be searched. Technical assistance provided by a computer owner or the owner's designated operator may require his or her presence, but he or she should be supervised by an officer trained in the rules of evidence. Many system administrators happily comply with law enforcement requests, but do not understand the legal requirements of collecting evidence. To prevent inadvertent alteration of evidence or inadmissible collection techniques, an investigator should be present and understand the operations of the system administrator. It is preferred to have a resident expert in the system execute the commands rather than on-site experts. This allows for efficient testimony at trial. Sometimes a suspect may be allowed to assist in the collection of ongoing data or the dismantling of evidence seized; this is not common and should come only after careful consideration. Figure 12.1 provides a flow chart detailing the process of collecting digital evidence depending on the events of the scene and the computers and systems involved and their power state.

HANDLING ONGOING ACTIVITY The one certain rule is: If it is off, leave it off. Various procedures are used to deal with computers that are running. The knowledge and experience of the investigator will have a lot to do with the decision of how to proceed. A first responder may have to be trained with very few choices; an experienced investigator or a SME accompanying the investigator may be able to interpret the situation with more finesse. Generally, it is safe to leave a running computer on, but excessive hard drive activity, network activity, and the overall connectivity between devices and the Internet make it challenging to appropriately preserve evidence when the machine is active and online.

If the decision is made to turn off the computer, video or photographic documentation of activity should be attempted, if applicable, before shutting down a system abruptly. However, if there is enough reason to believe that it is necessary to shut it down, then it should be done at once. The best current practice is to remove the power cord from the rear of the computer and not use the power switch. Many switches activate a software command to power-down. This command can be changed to alter data when the switch is used. Even old electrical switches can be modified to destroy evidence.

Mobile devices pose particular problems when it comes to handling ongoing activity: leaving a device on means that the data within the phone can change due to receipt of phone calls, messages, or other data. New data can push out older data and remote wiping applications mean that users can erase data from a phone even while it's in an investigator's hand. However, turning a phone or other mobile device off can have unintended and adverse consequences, including triggering password protocols upon restart and loss of data in RAM. Furthermore, a power-down due to a dead battery can also result in data loss, so investigators should take any charging devices.[8]

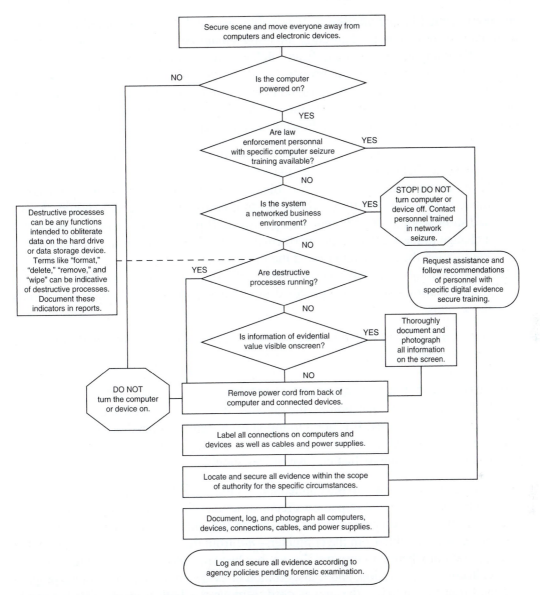

FIGURE 12.1 Collecting digital evidence flow chart.

Phones may be left on if investigators have access to shielding equipment, such radio frequency shielding cloths, which can block transmissions to the phone.

It is also wise to make a note of the reasons leading to this decision as soon as possible after the computer is powered down. Many procedural questions that may arise later can be answered with a brief articulation of the facts leading to a good-faith decision.

Examining the Crime Scene

Safety is always the first concern, but a close second is the overriding concern of evidence collection: Do not alter the evidence. Any unavoidable alteration (e.g., packaging the evidence for transportation) should be documented so well that it can later be reassembled exactly as it was. After safety is assured, and the scene is secure, the entire scene should be photographed before altering it. If possible, lists and diagrams should be included with notes of observations. Particular attention should be given to the monitor screen, front of the computer, including indicator lights, wire connections, mouse and keyboard place, and screen saver status. An investigator should record in notes all actions taken and any changes observed on the monitor, computer, printer, or other peripherals that result from the search. The monitor is (1) on, (2) in sleep mode, or (3) off. The state of the monitor will decide which of the following situations apply:

1. If the monitor is on and a work product and/or the desktop is visible, photograph screen and record information displayed.
2. If the monitor is on and screen is blank (sleep mode) or shows a screen saver, move the mouse slightly (without pushing buttons). The screen should change and show work product or request a password. If mouse movement does not cause a change in the screen, *do not* perform any other keystrokes or mouse operations. Photograph the screen and record the information displayed.
3. If the monitor is off, make a note that it is off. Turn the monitor on, then determine if the monitor status is as described in either situation 1 or 2 above and follow those steps.

Once the scene is documented in its entirety, the process of collecting and preserving evidence can begin.

COLLECTION AND PRESERVATION OF EVIDENCE   All evidence collection activities may be later called into question by the defense. It is best to establish a written procedure and use it every time. It is good to initial each step completed or note, in writing, why departure from the procedure was necessary. The following procedure is suggested by the National Institute of Justice.[9] An officer should

1. Photograph and diagram the connections of the computer or device and the corresponding cables. This step allows reconstruction of the system later if necessary.
2. Regardless of the power state of the device (on, off, or sleep mode), remove the power source cable from the computer—*not* from the wall outlet. At this point, the question of whether to turn it off or not has been resolved; this procedure applies to collection, preservation, and transportation of evidence. If dealing with a laptop, in addition to removing the power cord, remove the battery pack. The battery is removed to prevent any power to the system. Some laptops have a second battery in the multipurpose bay instead of a CD drive. Check for this possibility and remove that battery as well. If dealing with a large multiuser system (e.g., a UNIX™ system), follow a safe shutdown procedure recommended by a SME.
3. Check for any outside data connection (e.g., telephone modem, cable, ISDN, DSL). If a telephone connection is present, attempt to identify the telephone number. The easiest way to do this is to connect a telephone and ask the operator to identify the number being used.
4. Since CDs (and DVDs) are read by a laser and not by a physical read/write head, it is not required to remove CDs. In fact, there is no reason even to touch the CD drive when preparing a computer for transport.
5. Place tape over all the drive slots and over the power connector. This prevents accidental insertion of a disk or power cord. It also preserves the integrity of evidence in the drives.

6. Provide an additional level of security against confusion at the crime lab or during the sometimes lengthy storage, record the make, model, and serial numbers of the computer. This information is also required on a report generated from the seizure and on an inventory of seized items to be given to the owner.

7. Label all connectors and cable ends (including connections to peripheral devices) to allow for exact reassembly at a later time. Label unused connection ports as "unused."

8. Record or log evidence according to departmental procedures.

9. Recover nonelectronic evidence can be crucial in the investigation of electronic crime. Proper care should be taken to ensure that such evidence is recovered and preserved. Items relevant to subsequent examination of electronic evidence may exist in other forms (e.g., written passwords and other handwritten notes, blank pads of paper with indented writing, hardware and software manuals, calendars, literature, text or graphical computer printouts, and photographs) and should be secured and preserved for future analysis.

In fact, clear documentation is such a necessity that forms should be used to document in detail the equipment collected at a scene. Figure 12.2 provides an example of such documentation from the National Institute of Justice.

PACKING AND TRANSPORTATION OF EVIDENCE   If transport is required, package the components as fragile cargo. Actions taken should not add, modify, or destroy data stored on a computer or other media. Computers are fragile electronic instruments that are sensitive to temperature, humidity, physical shock, static electricity, and magnetic sources. Therefore, special precautions should be taken when packaging, transporting, and storing electronic evidence. To maintain chain of custody for electronic evidence, document its packaging, transportation, and storage. An investigator should

1. Ensure that all collected electronic evidence is properly documented, labeled, and inventoried before packaging.

2. Pay special attention to latent or trace physical evidence, like fingerprints or fiber samples, and take actions to preserve it. Testing for latent prints involves chemicals and dust, which may be harmful to electronic devices or storage media. Electronic evidence should be extracted before physical forensic examination. Specifically marking the evidence needing physical forensic examination will allow forensic analysts to avoid altering latent or trace evidence.

3. Pack magnetic media in antistatic packaging (paper or antistatic plastic bags). Avoid using materials that can produce static electricity, such as standard plastic bags and Styrofoam "packing peanuts."

4. Avoid folding, bending, or scratching computer media, such as CD-ROMs, DVDs, and memory sticks.

5. Ensure that all containers used to hold evidence are properly labeled. If multiple computer systems are collected, label each system so that it can be reassembled as found (e.g., system A—mouse, keyboard, monitor, main base unit; system B— mouse, keyboard, monitor, main base unit).

6. Keep electronic evidence away from magnetic sources. Radio transmitters, speaker magnets, and even heated vehicle seats are examples of items that can damage electronic evidence.

7. Avoid storing electronic evidence in vehicles for prolonged periods of time. Conditions of excessive heat, cold, or humidity can damage electronic evidence.

Computer Evidence Worksheet

Case Number: _____ Exhibit Number: _____

Laboratory Number: _____ Control Number: _____

Computer Information

Manufacturer: _____ Model: _____

Serial Number: _____

Examiner Markings: _____

Computer Type: Desktop ☐ Laptop ☐ Other: _____

Computer Condition: Good ☐ Damaged ☐ **(See Remarks)**

Number of Hard Drives: _____ 3.5" Floppy Drive ☐ 5.25" Floppy Drive ☐

Modem ☐ Network Card ☐ Tape Drive ☐ Tape Drive Type: _____

100 MB Zip ☐ 250 MB Zip ☐ CD Reader ☐ CD Read/Write ☐

DVD ☐ Other: _____

CMOS Information	Not Available ☐

Password Logon: Yes ☐ No ☐ Password = _____

Current Time: _____ AM ☐ PM ☐ Current Date: ____ / ____ / ____

CMOS Time: _____ AM ☐ PM ☐ CMOS Date: ____ / ____ / ____

CMOS Hard Drive #1 Settings	Auto ☐

Capacity: _____ Cylinders: _____ Heads: _____ Sectors: _____

Mode: LBA ☐ Normal ☐ Auto ☐ Legacy CHS ☐

CMOS Hard Drive #2 Settings	Auto ☐

Capacity: _____ Cylinders: _____ Heads: _____ Sectors: _____

Mode: LBA ☐ Normal ☐ Auto ☐ Legacy CHS ☐

Computer Evidence Worksheet	Page 1 of 2

FIGURE 12.2 An example of a computer evidence worksheet.

8. Ensure that computers and other components that are not packaged in containers are secured in the vehicle to avoid shock and excessive vibration. For example, computers may be placed on the vehicle floor and monitors placed on the seat with the screen down and secured by a seat belt.

9. Maintain the chain of custody on all evidence transported.[10]

STORAGE OF SEIZED EVIDENCE   The storage of seized evidence is as exacting a task as seizure and transportation. Above all, the evidence must remain unaltered until it is analyzed, and the continuity of the chain of custody must be maintained to prove it. Investigators in all but the smallest departments must turn evidence over to an evidence custodian. The evidence custodian is typically a ranking sworn officer. The custodian is then responsible for the evidence from that time until trial. When evidence is submitted for forensic analysis, the custodian delivers that evidence to the department's designated analyst (maybe another sworn officer, nonsworn employee, or off-site contract service). The evidence custodian obtains a receipt from the analyst. When the analysis is completed, the custodian receives the evidence and retains custody of the evidence until it is needed at trial. The evidence custodian maintains a secure area called an "evidence locker" to prevent general access to evidence stored therein. The custodian maintains logs of officers working shifts in the evidence locker. If officers are allowed to enter the locker, their entry is logged too; however, typically the custodian will bring evidence requested by officers or investigators to a window. That transfer is noted in the chain of custody, as is the return of the evidence. The chain of custody can be introduced and affirmed by calling the investigator, the custodian, and the analyst who examined the evidence.

The following procedure is suggested by the National Institute of Justice and annotated with standard practices for all evidence.[11] Investigators should

1. Ensure that evidence is inventoried in accordance with departmental policies. This typically includes "marking" the evidence for later identification at trial. Without proper markings, one mass-produced computer is nearly indistinguishable from another. Investigators typically inscribe the metal case of the computer with their initials, the date, and case number—if possible. Containers can also be marked with indelible markers. Evidence tags can become separated from evidence, so actual marking is preferred.
2. Store digital evidence in a secure area away from temperature and humidity extremes. Protect it from magnetic sources, moisture, dust, and other harmful particles or contaminants.
3. Many electronic devices contain memory that requires continuous power to maintain the information, such as a battery and AC power. The most common example is the complementary metal-oxide semiconductor (CMOS) battery that stores critical setup data for older computers. Data can be easily lost by unplugging the power source or allowing the battery to discharge. Collect and store the power supply adaptor or cable, if present, with the recovered device.
4. Potential evidence such as dates, times, and systems configurations may be lost as a result of prolonged storage. Since batteries have a limited life, data could be lost if they fail. Therefore, appropriate personnel (e.g., evidence custodian, lab chief, or forensic examiner) should be informed that a device powered by batteries is in need of immediate attention.[12]

The basic police work involved in planning a search and obtaining a warrant are familiar tasks to investigators. Two key differences distinguish digital evidence from familiar physical evidence. First, electronic evidence must be contained in a physical medium. Since digital evidence can be copied flawlessly and frequently, there is no reason to limit a search to a single physical container. Anything capable of storing digital information may contain digital evidence. Second, digital evidence is fragile. A quick action by the suspect can erase digital information. Inadvertent mishandling of digital evidence can contaminate or destroy its evidentiary value. Specific procedures have been recommended by the National Institute of Justice to preserve the digital evidence for later analysis while maintaining its probative value. The ability properly to seek a warrant and execute a search forms the building blocks of more complex investigations.

Multiple-Location and Network Crime Scenes

Multiple-scene computer crimes are complicated by a number of factors beyond the standard single-scene seizure. Networked environments may contain evidence on multiple machines using multiple operating systems, in multiple physical and/or network locations, and in multiple jurisdictions. To further complicate search and seizure operations, current law enforcement practices, called "minimization procedures," demand minimal intrusion to the operation of the network. Even the relatively few network experts in law enforcement may not be sufficiently familiar with a target network to extract evidence with sufficient legal integrity and not disrupt the operation of the target network. Officers skilled at single-scene seizures may feel overwhelmed at the thought of collecting network trace evidence. Fortunately, an investigator is not alone in attempting a multiple-scene or network investigation. SME can be enlisted to guide investigators through unfamiliar networks. By concentrating on the purpose of investigation—the collection and preservation of evidence necessary to prove the elements of a crime and to connect the suspect to the crime—an investigator can coordinate the efforts of people with more technical knowledge. The investigator needs only the communication tools necessary to convey the purposes and precise needs of law enforcement to the local computer system administrators, who must often serve as guides in these unique environments.

DISTINGUISHING SINGLE-SCENE, MULTIPLE-SCENE, AND NETWORK CRIME SCENES The distinction made is not based on technical differences, so much as functional differences for investigation. A single-scene crime involves only a single computer, for example, possession of child pornography or use of a computer to further a criminal enterprise. A multiple-scene crime involves more than one computer, with the possibility of an intervening network. Personal computers on wired or wireless local area network (LAN) can often be handled as several individual single-scene seizures. Additional complications include noting network connections and network identities for each machine. Data storage (i.e., network drives) can be spread across several machines on the network, but may be represented as a single unit to network users. In spite of the use of "network" technology, any geographically compact (same jurisdiction) crime scene under the administrative control of a single entity (one person, one corporation, etc.) is considered a multiple-scene crime. Network crime scenes would involve the Internet and any wired or wireless LAN or wide area network (WAN) that makes extensive use of dedicated servers, network or multiple-user operating systems (UNIX^{TM}, Windows Server 2012^{TM}, etc.), or switching equipment. The presence of affected computers in multiple jurisdictions may also make it a network crime. The skill set required to investigate this type of scene may exceed even a veteran investigator's ability. Furthermore, an investigator may need numerous warrants or other legal search instruments (see ECPA in Chapter 10) to follow criminal activities. Cooperation from the companies owning the network resources can be the key to success. The need for such cooperation, either with ISPs or law enforcement agencies in other jurisdictions, distinguishes a multiple-scene crime from a network crime.

Identifying Network Architectures

Although there are numerous technical distinctions between different network architectures, investigators are not charged with maintaining these systems or understanding their full complexities. An investigator needs to know how to trace a transaction through the network and identify any potential sources of network trace evidence: latent signs of the transaction being traced.

INTERNET VERSUS INTRANET INVESTIGATIONS   The primary distinction of interest to an investigator is between Internet and intranet. An intranet is a WAN that uses a common addressing and transfer protocol suite called "Transfer Control Protocol/Internet Protocol" (TCP/IP). The key difference to an investigator is that an intranet is often administered by one authority; thus, it may be possible to get to a system administrator or system administration team and get definitive answers. Seeking technical assistance involves identifying the network administrator. This can usually be accomplished by looking up the domain registrant on a service like "whois" (see below).

The Internet is a network of networks owned and maintained by various private, corporate, and governmental interests. The only feature truly common to all of these various component systems is the use of TCP/IP. Seeking technical assistance involves identifying the ISPs involved. Steps taken to preserve Internet evidence must be quick. Routine logs are often quickly purged due to the huge volume of Internet traffic. If the network can be traced to a corporation, the corporate IT department may be of further assistance. Investigators may issue preservation letters (by fax, if speed is vital) to require service providers to retain relevant information. Preservation letters do not require a magistrate's signature; however, a warrant or lesser instrument may be required to obtain the evidence requested for preservation. In many cases, public ISPs cannot voluntarily release information to investigators.

Modeling Network Transactions

At the most fundamental level, all networks can be described with the Open Systems Interface (OSI) model. It is a standard used worldwide. By tracing the way each process of this model is completed, an investigator can slowly make sense of the most complex network environment. In general, the model proceeds from the most concrete, at layer 1 (e.g., a wire), to the most abstract, at layer 7. Abstraction makes a computer network more versatile because it can operate with many different purposes. Concreteness makes an operation easier to understand for exactly the opposite reason: It can only do one or a few simple tasks. For example, a wire can only carry electrical impulses from one end to the other. In a multiple-scene investigation, connected computers can often be identified by tracing the wire runs. At the other extreme, the applications (what we call programs, like MS Outlook™) can be used for a variety of purposes.

Beyond the traditional seven layers of the OSI model lies the even greater abstraction of human users (layer 8) and policies governing them (layer 9). Although the OSI model may seem very complex, it is actually a tool used by computer scientists simply to communicate about network functions. The seven layers of the model each serve a function in the transmission of data. The specific function of each layer is described in Table 12.1. An investigator familiar with the OSI model can communicate

TABLE 12.1 Layers of the Investigation

9. Policies	Human	The rules, policies, and management controls that govern the actions of users
8. User		The human being using the computer and network
7. Application		Provides direct interaction with the user (e.g., Netscape or Explorer)
6. Presentation	Application services	Standardizes data transmission formats (i.e., file types such as JPEG)
5. Session		Provides checkpoint, fall back, and encryption services (e.g., SSL)
4. Transport		Allows multiple simultaneous operations across a single network connection (e.g., TCP)
3. Network	Network services	Provides unique addressing for transmission across different networks (e.g., IP)
2. Data link		Assembles bits into packets, provides error correction, and flow control (e.g., Ethernet)
1. Physical		Provides a path for the transmission of bits (e.g., wires, fiber optics, and radio waves)

with system administrators using vastly different software. The investigator does not have to understand how each network component functions, only what happens to data in a network. This leaves the system administrator to sort out the details.

The addition of layers 8 and 9 emphasizes the role of human users and the policies that govern the network to investigators; they are not part of the worldwide standard. They originally stem from a joke about network breakdowns caused by user errors or corporate policies that inhibit network function, but investigators should keep in mind that all information transfer ultimately occurs because of a human operator or a policy that dictates it. Security flaws can also be examined with these additional layers. For example, insider crimes are the most common forms of computer crime. If an investigator suspects an insider, layer 8 reminds him or her to look into personal matters and backgrounds. Layer 9 reminds him or her to check company security policies to see who has access to the machines, both network and physical. It is easy to get stuck in the mode of assuming that a computer crime has a computer cause. The hacker trick of social engineering[13] recognizes that the most common weakness in computer security is the human operator, especially if the operator works in a large organization with complex policies (layers 8 and 9).

The application services are generally not retained in network trace evidence except for a few specific types of logs. These are the abstract services most directly under the control of the user—or in the case of a computer crime, the criminal. They can be encrypted and still function. However, key information, such as file names and sizes, might be retained and matched to a user.

The network services are most often tracked by system administrators, because they are necessary for proper network maintenance and function, but do not reveal private information without further investigation. Routine logs contain a wealth of information (discussed below) about network service transactions.

Locating Evidence

Local system administrators are the best source of information about network logging. Routine business records are not considered hearsay and are therefore considered admissible to court (see discussion of hearsay later in the chapter). Various security systems, commonly used by business, have logging features that may help detect anomalous activities. For instance, intrusion detection systems (IDSs) are designed primarily to log network traffic and examine it for known patterns indicating attacks.

If the crime in question uses such a signature, the presence of an IDS can be of tremendous assistance to an investigator. Similarly, many firewalls—systems that block network traffic based on rules established by an administrator—have logging systems. For other cases, such as intellectual property violations, large volumes of apparently legitimate traffic might be ignored by an IDS, but show up in an administrator's log as an unusually large amount of network traffic (i.e., a usage spike). Administrators must plan for network growth and often track network usage statistics. They also manage network loads with a system of resource allowances reserved for each user (i.e., a user quota system). If a user exceeds his or her storage quota, even briefly, the administrator's log may note the event. In a final example, ISPs often keep logs of user activity to help predict demand and plan for growth as well as keeping logs for billing purposes. If a user dials into a "front" account under an assumed name, the dial-up record may record his or her actual telephone number.

All of this potential evidence is kept for various purposes on various machines on the network. It may be up to the investigator quickly to notify competent authorities to preserve the evidence. The great volume of log evidence generated in a typical business cannot be economically maintained for extended periods. Many logs purge after as little as 24 hours. Federal law (the Electronic Communications Privacy Act) allows a "preservation letter" to be sent to a company or individual with potential electronic evidence; it requires the responsible person to maintain the evidence pending further investigation.

QUICK FACTS

The 2016 Internet Crime Report released by the FBI's Internet Crime Complaint Center (IC3) indicates that over 3.5 million complaints were reported from 2000–2016 related to Internet crime, accounting for over $1.33 billion in loss. With a limit number of agents assigned to the IC3 unit, the FBI is hard pressed to open full investigations on all of these complaints, particularly since their primary mission is to "protect and defend the United States against terrorist and foreign intelligence threats."

Source: https://www.fbi.gov/news/stories/ic3-releases-2016-internet-crime-report

---

Key Information for Locating Network Trace Evidence

The logs mentioned in the previous section use identifiers to match network transactions with the actual machines involved. These identifiers are often associated with a level of the OSI model. The identifiers are necessary for proper network function. With a few relatively rare exceptions, network communication is literally impossible without them; therefore, they will be present as latent evidence in network crimes.

MAC ADDRESS   The media access control (MAC) address is a unique hardware address associated with each network card or other network device. The MAC is used at layer 2 of the OSI model. Layer 2 is the data link layer; it is the most concrete electronic layer. MAC addresses are only used at the local network level. Network transactions that use TCP/IP usually strip the MAC address away from data. Therefore, MAC addresses are most useful in multiple-scene investigations using a single LAN. They may also help prove that a criminal had access from inside the victim's network.

The MAC address is usually reported in hexadecimal couplets. Hexadecimal is a numbering system that uses base 16 instead of the familiar base 10^{14} that we use for counting. Although an investigator does not need to know all of the intricacies of network addressing, recognizing the pattern of network addresses is helpful. Hexadecimal uses pairs of the characters 0–9 and A–F to represent 8 bits (also called a "byte"), for example, 00-AF-03-05-0E-B9. Contrary to common wisdom, MAC addresses can be changed with software configuration, so failure to match a MAC is not definitive proof that the computer was not involved in an incident.[15]

IP ADDRESS   The IP address is a unique address assigned to every computer on the Internet. Like all numbers used by computers, the IP address is a binary number made up of bits. Although an IP address can be found represented with hexadecimal couplets like the MAC address, the IP is almost always reported in the decimal-dot notation. "Decimal-dot" means four decimal elements (base 10, like we use to count) ranging from 0 to 255 separated by dots, for example, 192.168.0.0. Although many people recognize the decimal dot notation, they do not understand how it works. Because the decimal number represents 8 bits each, it cannot exceed 255. There are 2^8 (256) possible values for 8 bits. The maximum number that can be represented is 255 because computers start counting at 0, not 1. An investigator should know that any value over 255 cannot be part of a valid IP address. Thus, if a suspect reports an Internet address of 345.300.123.205, an investigator will know that it is false.

The IP is associated with transactions at layer 3, the network layer, of the OSI model. IP addresses are often dynamically assigned to computers when they start-up. However, many computers, especially servers, use static IPs that do not change. The owner of a given IP can be determined through ARIN, the American Registry for Internet Numbers. Note: International investigations may require the use of the European and African authority RIPE[16] or the Asian authority APNIC.[17]

DNS   Domain name system (DNS) is a protocol that allows users to enter meaningful words instead of IP addresses to identify a computer. DNS is a helper service for layer 3 of the OSI model in TCP/IP systems. The Internet does not work on English words. To find a particular computer on the Internet, a user must have the IP address; as we saw in the previous section, these can be very difficult to decipher in their native form. To make it easier to use the Internet, the DNS was established to create a place to look up (also called "resolving") the IP of a computer based on its human readable name. Thus, when you type in a Web address like www.ebay.com, your browser sends a request to a system of databases of domain names and matching IPs maintained by the Internet Corporation for Assigned Names and Numbers (ICANN) or its subset databases hosted throughout the Internet.[18] A reverse lookup is available to convert an IP to its human-readable equivalent.

PPP   Point-to-Point Protocol (PPP) is commonly used in establishing a direct connection between two networking nodes. PPP works at layer 2 of the OSI model, like Ethernet. Unfortunately, there is no equivalent of the MAC address used by Ethernet, because PPP connections are point-to-point. When there are only two computers involved in the connection, they do not need identifiers. Although the protocol itself yields little information, the routers that handle such connections often log useful information such as the account accessed and authenticated with a password and the times at the beginning and end of the session.

BOX 12.2

Understanding IP Addresses

Understanding how IPs work can help an investigation. In this hypothetical example, a Web-based fraud scheme manipulates the way browsers interpret Internet addresses. The following URL will take a browser to ebay™, the leading Web-based auction site:

http://pages.ebay.com/index.html?ssPageName=h:h:home:US

The following URL will take a browser to the Web site of anyone with the $50 fee required to register a Web address:

http://www.ebay.com@homeshoppingforyou.com

Without even registering a Web domain, the following URLs can provide access to a criminal's page from anywhere on the Web. By using these URLs from a Web page on a legally owned Internet address (called a "front"

in fraud investigations), the criminal can claim ignorance of where the links go. The links below can easily be altered to lead to anywhere on the Internet without changing anything in front of the "@" sign.

http://www.ebay.com@192.168.23.56

http://www.ebay.com@%C0%A8%17%38

These URLs go to the exact same place. The IP address 192.168.23.56 (in decimal dot notation) is the same as %C0%A8%17%38 (in hexadecimal notation). Neither of the addresses will get a potential fraud victim to the real ebay site. All of the security used at ebay is useless if the customer never gets to the page. However, for the victim to reach the criminal, the address must point to a valid location on the Internet. The administrative details of that site may prove to be a rich source for search and seizure.

Collecting Network Trace Evidence

Due to various historic and legal problems with digital evidence collection,[19] it is the best current practice to minimize the intrusion of network investigations. Seizing a business's critical IT assets could easily do more harm to that business than the worst denial-of-service attack. Even lengthy downtime can cost the business substantial amounts. The seizure of evidence can be a significant deterrent to businesses reporting computer crime.

Minimization procedures have to be balanced against the needs of evidence integrity and the mission of law enforcement, but cannot be discounted automatically. Typically, if evidence is available from an existing backup source without disrupting operations, it is acceptable. When a machine must be taken off-line, on-the-spot imaging is often used to collect evidence with minimal intrusion.

PRESENTING DIGITAL EVIDENCE AT TRIAL

Any reasonably experienced law enforcement official knows that police work does not end when a suspect is arrested and transferred to a jail custodian. Paperwork, reports, and possibly interviews with a prosecutor are as important as the investigation itself. Consider that an investigation is like writing a lengthy paper. The paper can be a masterful, witty, comprehensive coverage of the topic, but if you never hand that paper in, it is worthless. An investigation, no matter how well conceived and executed, is worthless if the case does not end in a successful prosecution. In fact, the quality of the investigator's report, credibility, and willingness to participate fully often influence plea bargains. If a case does go to trial, an investigator will be required to present the facts represented in the report or explain the procedures used to discover and collect evidence. The testimony of the investigator is often the bedrock of a case. Competent presentation and procedure are as vital to investigators as any technical skills. In fact, digital forensic examiners must be mindful of the fact that juries and judges may not necessarily understand the information that they are trying to present. As a result, examiners and attorneys should use simple analogies and define technical terms and events in as simple definitions as possible.[20] Drawings, figures, and cartoons that illustrate a point are helpful in communicating information to a broader courtroom audience.

Beyond simplicity in presentation, the rules of evidence require that the foundation for physical evidence be established with testimony; thus, evidence does not speak for itself.[21] The prosecution must establish when, where, and how the evidence was collected. The prosecution must also be able to establish that the evidence was not altered to prejudice the trial by either act (such as intentionally altering the evidence) or omission (such as allowing the evidence to be degraded or contaminated). Finally, the prosecution must also establish that the evidence collected conforms to the warrant or guidelines for commonly accepted warrantless searches. As the person responsible for these procedures, the investigator is the primary witness used to introduce evidence. Two other valuable sources useful in the preparation for court testimony are *The Challenges of Interpreting Digital Evidence in the Courtroom* and *A Guide to Forensic Testimony: The Art and Practice of Presenting Technology as an Expert Technical Witness.*[22]

The Hearsay Rule

Black's Law Dictionary defines hearsay:

> Hearsay includes any statement made outside the present proceeding which is offered as evidence of the truth of matters asserted therein.[23]

It is fundamental to our system of justice that the accused be able to confront his or her accusers and offer evidence to rebut their statements. Witnesses must only testify to matters of which they have direct knowledge. This gives the accused a chance directly to confront and discredit statements made against him or her. According to the Federal Rules of Evidence (§§801–04), the hearsay rule excludes statements made outside of the ability of the accused to confront the person making the statement before the jury,[24] unless such statements fit one of several well-known exceptions.[25] The following section describes the most relevant applications of the hearsay rule to digital evidence-related testimony.

Using Notes on the Witness Stand

Investigators have large caseloads and must often wait for months before testifying in a case. It is permissible to use case notes, journals, and logs created during the investigation to help the investigator recall fine details, such as serial numbers, model numbers, and other minutia. The central question in the use of notes on the witness stand is whether the witness (i.e., the investigator) actually recalls the events or is relying on the notes entirely. If the witness uses notes to prompt memories of the events and recall details, it is known as "past recollection recalled."[26] Past recollection recalled does not violate the hearsay rule. The defense has a right to examine the notes and test the witness' memory before allowing the testimony. This test will establish the degree to which the witness has an independent recollection of the events.

If the investigator relies entirely upon the notes for any recollection of the events, it is known as "past recollection recorded."[27] Past recollection recorded does violate the hearsay rule. If the investigator does not recall the events of the case, the best the prosecutor can do is have the reports and notes read into evidence. If this is necessary, the entire contents of the notes become available. Many patrol officers use a spiral-bound notebook to record all kinds of information while at work and even at home. Investigators should avoid this and use loose-leaf sheets for a single case. There is a classic story about crime scene investigation where the defense noted missing pictures in a series. The officers were required to produce the negatives. Although the missing pictures did not provide evidence to clear the suspect, they did show one of the officers "posing" with the corpse. In a spiral-bound notebook with many cases and doodles, there are probably many such potentially embarrassing tidbits.

Business Records

It is an established exception to the hearsay rule that records or summaries created in the normal course of business (not specifically for law enforcement purposes) are not hearsay and are therefore admissible. "The courts generally have admitted computer records upon a showing that the records fall within the business records exception."[28] The Federal Rules of Evidence §803 (6):

> Records of a Regularly Conducted Activity. A record of an act, event, condition, opinion, or diagnosis if:
>
> **A.** the record was made at or near the time by — or from information transmitted by — someone with knowledge;
> **B.** the record was kept in the course of a regularly conducted activity of a business, organization, occupation, or calling, whether or not for profit;
> **C.** making the record was a regular practice of that activity;
> **D.** all these conditions are shown by the testimony of the custodian or another qualified witness, or by a certification that complies with **Rule 902(11)** or **(12)** or with a statute permitting certification; and
> **E.** neither the source of information nor the method or circumstances of preparation indicate a lack of trustworthiness.[29]

The key to this section is that the "business process" be regular or routinized in such a way that the accuracy of the product may be assessed by the court. Failure to meet this standard does not mean that creating logs for law enforcement purposes is illegal. It does not even mean that such logs will be inadmissible. Other techniques can be used to admit such logs, but these methods are not covered in this book.

Presenting Best Evidence

Black's Law Dictionary states that the principle of best evidence

> requires that best evidence available be presented in lieu of less satisfactory evidence … This rule prohibits the introduction into evidence of secondary evidence unless it is shown that original document has been lost or destroyed or is beyond jurisdiction of court without fault of the offering party … [T]he basic rule [is] as follows: "To prove the content of a writing, recording, or photograph, the original writing, recording, or photograph is required."[30]

The best evidence rule simply states that the court requires the original copy of evidence. Courtroom presentation is the ultimate purpose of collecting evidence. It does not make sense to store the original safely in a vault while using a (possibly imperfect) copy in the courtroom. Although best evidence is often considered to be the original copy, with digital evidence the original copy is inaccessible to human beings, because it is usually a series of magnetic zones on a hard disk. Courts have accepted printouts of the contents of a disk as best evidence. However, the contents of a disk are usually too large to print in their entirety. There is no technical basis to say that displaying information from the actual hard drive of the computer seized or the monitor seized along with it is any more likely to be best evidence than an exact digital copy displayed on a projector, paper, or other medium.[31] Subject to verification, a digital copy in a convenient form may be presented in court without violating the best evidence rule.

However, presenting a "live" demonstration of digital evidence on the accused's computer with the accused's monitor can have a powerful impact on the jury. Live demonstrations should be planned carefully and tested prior to presentation. Given the unpredictability of some technology, a video might be prudent and allowable under exceptions to the best evidence rule. For the convenience of the court, voluminous evidence may be presented in a summary form. Federal Rules of Evidence §1006 states:

> The proponent may use a summary, chart, or calculation to prove the content of voluminous writings, recordings, or photographs that cannot be conveniently examined in court. The proponent must make the originals or duplicates available for examination or copying, or both, by other parties at a reasonable time and place. And the court may order the proponent to produce them in court.

Similarly, if the process in question cannot be adequately represented in a printout, the court may allow alternate presentation.

Challenges to Forensic Analysis Strategies

Considering that digital forensic examinations depend in part on the use of software and technologies to examine digital media, it is necessary to consider how these technologies can be challenged in court. The range of software and versions of programs that can be used may lead attorneys to attempt to discredit these tools and the subsequent analyses through *Frye* or *Daubert* challenges.[32] These two challenges were generated from legal cases and provide standards to assess the quality of scientific or methodological techniques used to find and develop evidence.

The first case is *Frye v. United States*, which provides a standard for scientific research that is commonly applied in state court.[33] In this 1923 case, James Frye was convicted of second-degree murder. He appealed his sentence on the basis that he confessed but later retracted his statement and was unable to present evidence concerning the accuracy of his admission through the use of an early version of a polygraph test or introduce an expert witness to testify on his behalf about the test. The appeals court that heard this case felt that the polygraph test in question did not have enough scientific support to be used as evidence in court, and the appeal was rejected. The *Frye* test was established as a consequence, stating that scientific techniques can be admitted in court if they are generally accepted within the relevant scientific community. This includes procedures, principles, or techniques that can be presented in a court case. This has significance for forensic examiners, as it suggests that evidence generated from nontraditional or untested strategies may potentially be deemed inadmissible in court, dependent on the judge's decision as to its general acceptance in the scientific community.

The second important case is *Daubert v. Merrell Dow Pharmaceuticals*, which created the *Daubert* standard used in federal courts, and in some state courts, concerning the presentation of expert testimony and evidence.[34] In this case, Merrell Dow Pharmaceuticals was sued by a woman whose baby, Jason Daubert, was born with congenital disorders, including a lack of fingers and bones in the arm. During pregnancy, the mother took a drug produced by Dow that contained a chemical that was linked to a large number of similar birth defects in children across the globe. Medical tests presented by the plaintiff suggested that this product caused similar defects in animals, though evidence presented by scientists writing for Dow argued that medical tests in humans found no link to health risks during pregnancy. The court dismissed the case, arguing that Daubert did not provide sufficient evidence to support their argument. The case was appealed to the Supreme Court, but was not heard, and as a result the lower court decision stands and provides a standard for the presentation of evidence on the basis of admissibility of expert testimony based on (1) the relevance and (2) the reliability of evidence based off of the scientific techniques used to create it. In particular, there are four points of concern about the science used to produce evidence:

1. The scientific technique can be—and has been—tested.
2. The technique has been subjected to peer review and publication.
3. There is a known or potential rate of error.
4. The technique has been generally accepted by the relevant scientific community.

This again applies to digital evidence and the ways that it is acquired. Thus, it is important that examiners use well-regarded and well-tested standards for evidence development and examination in order to reduce the likelihood of successful challenges.

Chain of Custody

Black's Law Dictionary defines chain of custody as follows:

> In evidence, the one who offers real [physical] evidence … must account for the custody of the evidence from the moment in which it reaches his custody until the moment in which it is offered in evidence. [The] chain of custody is proven if an officer is able to testify that he or she took control of an item of physical evidence, identified it, placed it in a locked or protected area, and retrieved the item being offered [in evidence] on the day of the trial.[35]

The chain of custody is a legal document that records a history of who had the evidence and when. In the hypothetical example cited in *Black's Law Dictionary*, the chain is relatively simple. In a typical computer crime investigation, the chain of custody can be extensive. As more specialists (computer forensic technicians, subject matter experts, off-site laboratories, etc.) work on a piece of evidence, the chain of custody becomes more complex. Complexity is not necessarily bad, but it never helps establish evidence. For this and other reasons, departments and agencies have established evidence-handling procedures. At a minimum, these procedures include a list of anyone accessing the evidence with notations of time and place. They also include a notation of where the evidence was taken, if transported, and any changes, such as removing a piece for analysis. Digital information requires additional protection, and even more elaborate protections have been devised for it.[36]

The investigator seizing the evidence may be required to testify to the provenance of the evidence. This foundational testimony describes how the evidence was collected, where it came from, and what has happened to it since it was seized. An investigator can provide more effective testimony by using established procedures every time. The plan for conducting a search should include a designated custodian of evidence who will document and transport the evidence to maintain the chain of custody.

Expert Testimony

This section has focused on the presentation of the fruits of an investigation. Although there has been mention of SME, their contributions have been limited to assisting the investigator to produce a case. Experts undoubtedly play a role in helping the investigator gather evidence of the elements of a crime and may have opinions that help establish probable cause.

Summary

An investigator is charged with identifying that a crime has taken place, establishing the elements of that crime, and associating the crime with a suspect. The investigator must gather compelling evidence in a manner that allows it to be presented in court. If possible, an investigator should work with the prosecutor to understand the type of evidence specifically needed for the prosecutor's strategy. Even without direct input from the prosecutor (perhaps prior to the prosecutor's decision to take the case), an investigator must be able to understand the events constituting the crime. Several tools and procedures exist to help the investigator in this process. Unless the investigator has an unusually high degree of experience with computers, subject matter experts will play an important role in assessing the details of the crime. However, the primary burden of presenting a case to the prosecutor and eventually to the court falls on the investigator. Proper procedure and documentation guided by an understanding of the "endgame" in court will increase the odds of a successful prosecution.

Review Questions

1. Explain how labor is divided among professionals involved in the investigation of computer crime. Which role do you prefer and why?
2. Outline the process of preparing and executing a search warrant for electronic evidence. How does search and seizure of electronic evidence at a single scene differ from physical evidence search and seizure?
3. Explain the difference between single-scene, multiple-scene, and network investigations. In what ways do single- and multiple-scene investigations differ from network investigations?
4. Explain the procedures for securing digital evidence. After officer safety, what is the primary concern of the investigator during this whole process?

Critical Thinking Exercises

1. Visit the IACP Law Enforcement Cyber Center at http://www.iacpcybercenter.org/. Discuss some of the contemporary "topics" that are presented at the center.
2. Visit the Website of the U.S. Secret Service at https://www.secretservice.gov/. Under the "Investigations" tab, discuss the role of the Secret Service in cybercrime investigations. Do you think that cybercrime has impacted the authenticity of questioned documents and U.S. currency (counterfeiting)?
3. Visit the Website of the FBI at https://www.fbi.gov/. What is the role of the FBI in the investigation of cyber crime and cyber terrorism? Discuss how the FBI assists agencies in their role at the federal level.

Endnotes

1. Newburgher, E.C. (2001). *Home Computers and Internet Usage in United States: August 2000.* U.S. Census Bureau, p. 1. See also File, T. and Ryan, C. (2014). Computer and Internet use in the United States: 2013. American Community Survey Reports.

2. Stoll, C. (1989). *The Cuckoo's Egg: Tracking a Spy Through the Maze of Computer Espionage.* New York: Doubleday. See also Rid, T. and Buchanan, B. (2015). Attributing Cyber Attacks. *Journal of Strategic Studies* 38(1–2): 4–37 and Guitton, C. (2012). Criminals and Cyber Attacks: The Missing

Link Between Attribution and Deterrence. *International Journal of Cyber Criminology* 6(2): 1030.

3. STEPHENSON, P. (2001). *Investigating Computer-Related Crime.* Boca Raton, FL: CRC Press. See also GUITTON, C. (2012). Criminals and Cyber Attacks: The Missing Link between Attribution and Deterrence. *International Journal of Cyber Criminology* 6(2): 1030. See BROWN, C.S. (2015). Investigating and Prosecuting Cyber Crime: Forensic Dependencies and Barriers to Justice. *International Journal of Cyber Criminology* 9(1): 55.

4. MERLAN, A. (October 16, 2012). "Michael Brutsch, Arlington-Based Reddit Troll, Has Been Fired, and Is Going on CNN Tonight." *Dallas Observer*. Retrieved August 19, 2013, from *http://blogs.dallasobserver.com/unfairpark/2012/10/arlington_reddit_troll_michael.php*

5. SIECZKOWSKI, C. (December 17, 2012). "Anonymous Targets Westboro Baptist Church After Newtown Vigil Protest Threat." *Huffington Post*. Retrieved August 19, 2013, from *http://www.huffingtonpost.com/2012/12/17/westboro-baptist-church-hacked-anonymous-protest-newtown-shooting-victims-funerals_n_2315070.html*

6. BENNETT-SMITH, M. (January 2, 2013). "Steubenville High School Students Joke About Rape in Video Leaked by Anonymous." *Huffington Post*. Retrieved August 19, 2013, from *http://www.huffingtonpost.com/2013/01/02/steubenville-high-school-joke-rape-targeted-anonymous-video_n_2398479.html*

7. U.S. Constitution, Amendment Four.

8. GONZALEZ, J. and HUNG, J. (2011). *Mobile Digital Forensics: A Brave New World.* Bloomberg Law Reports. Retrieved August 18, 2013, from *http://www.strozfriedberg.com/files/Publication/224ca0f8-5101-4e1b-938a-4d4b128ad5ed/Presentation/PublicationAttachment/ef4a28ad-ff7d-4014-aea8-80505789b86c/Mobile%20Device%20Forensics_%20A%20Brave%20New%20World.pdf.* See also KHAN, S., AHMAD, E., SHIRAZ, M., GANI, A., WAHAB, A.W.A., and BAGIWA, M.A. (2014, September). Forensic Challenges in Mobile Cloud Computing. In Computer, Communications, and Control Technology (I4CT), 2014 International Conference on pp. 343–347. IEEE.

9. Technical Working Group for Electronic Crime Scene Investigation. (2008). *Electronic Crime Scene Investigation: A Guide for First Responders,* 2nd ed. National Institute of Justice (NIJ 187736). Washington, D.C.: National Institute of Justice. See also BULBUL, H.I., YAVUZCAN, H.G., and OZEL, M. (2013). Digital Forensics: An Analytical Crime Scene Procedure Model (ACSPM). *Forensic Science International* 233(1): 244–256 and VALJAREVIC, A. and VENTER, H.S. (2015). A Comprehensive and Harmonized Digital Forensic Investigation Process Model. *Journal of Forensic Sciences* 60(6): 1467–1483.

10. *Ibid.*

11. *Ibid.*

12. *Ibid.*

13. Social engineering is basically lying to a person on the telephone or in person to get access to a desired resource (see Chapter 3 for a more extensive discussion).

14. This means that when we reach the highest individual digit (at the number 9), we then start to repeat digits (at 10). This is called base 10. Base 16 uses the following sequence before it repeats: 0, 1, 2, 3, 4, 5, 6, 7, 8, 9, A, B, C, D, E, F. The next number is 10 (think of it as 1 then 0, not 10). 10 in base-16 notation equals 16 in decimal.

15. STEVENS, W.R. (1994). *TCP/IP Illustrated Volume 1.* Addison Wesley. See also TIWARI, A., JAISWAL, M., VARMA, N., and JOSHI, B.L. (2014). TCP/IP Protocol Suite, Attacks, and Security Tools. URL= *https://www.academia.edu/7134687/TCP_IP_Protocol_Suite_Attacks_and_Security_Tools.*

16. RIPE (Réseaux IP Européens) is a collaborative forum open to all parties interested in wide area IP networks in Europe and beyond. The objective of RIPE is to ensure the administrative and technical coordination necessary to enable the operation of a pan-European IP network (RIPE Web page: *http://www.ripe.net/ripe/index.html*).

17. APNIC is one of four Regional Internet Registries currently operating in the world. It provides allocation and registration services that support the operation of the Internet globally. It is a not-for-profit, membership-based organization whose members include Internet service providers, National Internet registries, and similar organizations. APNIC represents the Asia Pacific region, comprising 62 economies (APNIC Web page: *http://www.apnic.net/info/about.html*).

18. This explanation greatly simplifies the DNS system, but accurately describes the general function. For an extensive discussion of DNS systems, see STEVENS, *TCP/IP Illustrated Volume 1.*

19. *Steve Jackson Games v. United States Secret Service,* 816 F.Supp. 432 (W.D. Tex, 1993).

20. Technical Working Group for Digital Evidence in the Courtroom. (2007). *Digital Evidence in the Courtroom: A Guide for Law Enforcement and Prosecutors.* National Institute of Justice. Washington, D.C.: National Institute of Justice. See also GARRIE, D.B. (2014). Digital Forensic Evidence in the Courtroom: Understanding Content and Quality. *Nw. J. Tech. & Intell. Prop.,* 12, I; WATTS, A. (2017). The Challenges of Interpreting Digital Evidence in the Courtroom. Sydney, NSW, Australia: Precedent Publishing (139), 43; BACE, R.G. and SMITH, F. (2002). A Guide to Forensic Testimony: The Art and Practice of Presenting Technology as an Expert Technical Witness, Boston: Addison-Wesley.

21. The opposing side may waive the requirement of foundation by accepting the evidence without question of provenance (called stipulating).

22. GARRIE, D.B. (2014). Digital Forensic Evidence in the Courtroom: Understanding Content and Quality. *Nw. J. Tech. & Intell. Prop.,* 12, I. See also: WATTS, The Challenges of Interpreting Digital Evidence in the Courtroom; BACE, R.G. and SMITH, F. (2002) ____ A Guide to Forensic Testimony: The Art and Practice of Presenting Technology as an Expert Technical Witness. Boston: Addison-Wesley.

23. BLACK, H.C., NOLAN, J.R., and NOLAN-HALEY, J.M. (1990). *Black's Law Dictionary,* 6th ed. St. Paul, MN: West Publishing.

24. It is part of the jury's job to assess the credibility of statements made. If a statement from an unreliable informant is repeated by an utterly reliable witness, the jury cannot properly assess the truth of the statement.

25. Federal Rules of Evidence §§ 801–04.

26. SWANSON, C.R., CHAMELIN, N.C., TERRITO, L., and TAYLOR, R. (2018). *Criminal Investigation,* 12th ed. San Francisco, CA: McGraw-Hill.

27. BLACK, NOLAN, and NOLAN-HALEY, *Black's Law Dictionary.*

28. KERR, O. (2001). "Computer Records and the Federal Rules of Evidence." *USA Bulletin. http://www.usdoj.gov/criminal/ cybercrime/usamarch12_4.htm. United States Department of Justice.* See also FAVRO, P.J. (2014). *Getting Serious: Why Companies Must Adopt Information Governance Measures to Prepare for the Upcoming Changes to the Federal Rules of Civil Procedure*. Rich. JL & Tech., 20, 5–14.

29. The Federal Rules of Evidence §803 (6).

30. BLACK, NOLAN, and NOLAN-HALEY, *Black's Law Dictionary.*

31. I do not advise arguing with a judge as to what comprises best evidence. Most courts can be convinced through expert testimony, and there is sufficient precedent to allow the broader interpretation of "best evidence."

32. *Ibid.,* p. 16.

33. *Ibid.*

34. *Ibid.*

35. BLACK, NOLAN, and NOLAN-HALEY, *Black's Law Dictionary.*

36. SWANSON, CHAMELIN, TERRITO, and TAYLOR, *Criminal Investigation.*

13

Digital Forensics

CHAPTER OBJECTIVES

After completing this chapter, you should be able to

- Outline and explain the process used to preserve the verifiable integrity of digital evidence.
- Suggest probable locations for particular types of digital evidence needed for various types of investigations.
- Explain how the storage system works in the computer.
- Describe, in broad detail, how information is stored on hard drives.
- Identify and explain hidden sources of information on a hard drive.
- Identify common storage media.
- Outline a basic universal procedure for examining removable storage media.
- Explain the basic logical structures of the hard drive and related storage devices.

INTRODUCTION

Forensic: "[b]elonging to courts of justice."[1] Although this chapter will deal with the technical details of computers and data storage, it will always be guided by the understanding that technical knowledge is secondary to the forensic analyst's ability to present technical information to the court. The various forensic sciences all share the role of bridging technical expertise with the courtroom process. Digital forensics can encompass many areas of inquiry. Civil and criminal court applications of digital forensics can include any aspect of computer science or information science, including information network analysis, source code analysis, computer user behavior, and geolocation data.

The field of storage forensics covers the examination of information stored on a physical medium. A physical medium is a real-world object that may be inside the computer (e.g., a seized hard drive, a smartphone) or outside the computer (e.g., a flash drive, CD, an IoT device). When information is stored on a physical medium, it is said to be "static." The fact that the information is static, or not moving electronically, distinguishes it from information on an active or "live" network. The examination of stored data[2] is often referred to as "postmortem" analysis because it is not on a live network. There is no functional distinction between the quality of evidence derived from a live network and from storage media, but the laws surrounding the collection and the collection procedures differ greatly. However, once the live data are stored, the forensic process is virtually identical.

THE BASIC PROCESS OF STORAGE FORENSICS

As with any other forensic operation, maintaining the continuity of evidence from the source to the final analysis product is the most important task of the examiner. The forensic analyst must have the ability to demonstrate the link between the seized device, hereafter called the evidence device, and the final analysis. Remember that the evidence exists on an unaltered original evidence device (e.g., hard drive, smartphone); analysis creates investigation leads and summaries, not evidence. It may be necessary to demonstrate the process used to obtain the summaries and leads through documentation and, sometimes, even replication of the analysis. This section describes the best current practices to reduce uncertainty when presenting the results of an analysis in court. Unfortunately, the complex reality of investigations and forensic analysis does not always allow for the implementation of "best practices." For example, multiple-scene and network crimes do not always allow the seizure of the evidence device. Anything short of best practices presents uncertainty in court, but does not signal the end of the investigation or preclude prosecution. Whenever possible, commonly accepted exceptions will be noted, but this section is primarily concerned with the most common situation found in law enforcement: an evidence device seized and in the possession of the analyst.

Some symbols will be used in this section to demonstrate visually the processes explained. These symbols are the standard flow chart symbols used to describe computer processes.

PREPARATION FOR FORENSIC ANALYSIS

Some preparations must be made before any lab analysis is attempted. An analyst must be able to ensure that the result of an analysis comes from the evidence, not from contamination or error. The gold standard is that an analyst must be able to reliably reproduce any result from procedure notes and a copy of the original data seized.[3] Thus, the steps of an analysis must be documented in a consistent and reproducible

Storage Device (e.g., hard drive, smartphone)

A Predefined Process (e.g., set of computer instructions)

Data (i.e., information)

Document (e.g., paper output)

FIGURE 13.1 Flow chart symbols and definitions used in this chapter.

manner; referred to as an analyst's Activity Log. A successful practice is to have a standard procedure for types of evidence and document any modifications to this procedure, noting the reasons why they are necessary. Such procedures are designed specifically to prevent challenges to the analysis in court. Many computer experts could quickly determine several more efficient ways to collect and analyze information, but these alternative methods would not likely meet the standards and common objections found in criminal court. Beware of helpful computer experts that do not understand the mission of forensics. That is, evidence could probably be obtained without going through these procedures, but it would be more vulnerable to challenge if not completely useless in a criminal court.

It is also necessary to prepare an appropriate environment for the analysis. Using "clean," or verified, software tools with valid software licenses is an important first step. It can be embarrassing and expensive to have to admit to using illegal software. Lab equipment must also be in working order. When new equipment is introduced, its function should be verified and documented in case later questions arise. One important early step is to ensure that the hard drive or storage media being used for evidence analysis (i.e., the Target Drive) is clean from any previous investigation data or erroneous information.

A final preparation, often overlooked, is to verify the qualifications and skills necessary to explain the analysis in court. The information technology field is full of self-taught experts. While many of these "experts" are highly skilled, many are also frauds. Of those who are legitimate experts, many are incapable of a convincing, or even understandable courtroom presentation. The analyst conducting the analysis must be able to understand and explain the process of the analysis and the resulting information. It is dangerous for an analyst to be completely dependent on point-and-click tools combined with one-size-fits-all procedures.

Acquisition of Data

The forensic process described in this section assumes that the evidence device (i.e., Source Device) is available to the examiner; however, an image, or digital forensic copy, can be obtained and authenticated in the field if circumstances require it. Field acquisition is not the preferred method, because failure to maintain control of the evidence device can also lead to problems in establishing the authenticity and/or chain of custody of the evidence in court. It is possible, however, to obtain a written stipulation as to the authenticity of the evidence acquired. This is often used if a suspect wants the evidence device returned prior to the end of the trial. If it is impossible to obtain a stipulation, the evidence is not necessarily inadmissible; it simply requires a greater showing that the evidence is authentic.[4] For example, a computer owned by an online publisher contains potential evidence. The magistrate signing the warrant places a special condition on the search that investigators use the absolute minimally intrusive search to avoid interfering with the First Amendment rights of the publisher. The suspect will not stipulate the contents of the search—having nothing to gain by doing so. The publisher's hard drive can be imaged and authenticated on the spot, but the seizure will be closely analyzed by the defense. Expert testimony as to the imaging process may be required.

Regardless of whether the image acquisition occurs in the field or in the forensic lab, different acquisition systems require different efforts to preserve the evidence device. The acquisition usually runs from a specially designed forensic computer system. If the acquisition system uses the Windows™ operating system, acquisition of the evidence device should be performed with a physical write-blocker device installed, whereby preventing the analyst's lab computer from writing data to the evidence device. This technology helps to reduce the likelihood that the evidence contained on the evidence device is not unintentionally altered in some fashion. Other acquisition systems use a true read-only mount of the file system (often not possible with Windows) with analysis proceeding from an evidence device mounted for read-only operations, also referred to as a software or system write-blocker.

Authentication of Data

The prosecutor must be able to prove that the evidence presented or summarized in court came unaltered from the defendant. The digital forensic analyst has an easier job. The product of forensic evidence must be shown to be an authentic product of the evidence seized. There is a unique quality to digital evidence that allows it to be more easily authenticated than physical evidence. When evidence is seized, it can be summarized mathematically in a process called hashing (see Box 13.1). A hash is a unique numerical value calculated from the data in a digital data set (file, hard drive, software application, etc.). No other naturally occurring file can have the same hash value.[5] A hash value (or, simply, hash) is essentially the "fingerprint" of the digital data set. By comparing this fingerprint with a new fingerprint taken at each step of the analysis process, we can verify that the digital file being examined is a true and authentic copy of the original evidence.

The forensic analyst's process must include a step to calculate an MD5 hash of the evidence device. The real work is accomplished by the forensics software (e.g., Access Data's Forensic Took Kit or Guidance Software's EnCase) and often occurs by default during the digital forensic imaging of the evidence. The analyst can then compare this hash of the evidence (source) device to a hash of any subsequent copies. If the hash matches, the copies are authenticated to the value of a single bit within a known (infinitesimal) probability of error. This authentication procedure should be performed and noted in the analyst's activity log whenever an image is created, copied, or loaded onto an analysis machine. As always, the analyst should document the results of the procedure, whether hashing was automatically performed or conducted manually. Documentation can be as simple as referring to the hash value created by the forensic software and stored in the case log, and/or cutting and pasting the hash value into a computer log and noting that it is the same. This provides a basis of comparison that the evidence cited in the analysis has not been altered by error or intentional act. Hash values can be calculated numerous times to demonstrate that data was not modified throughout the case and/or upon completion.

BOX 13.1

The MD5 Hash

An algorithm is a process or procedure used to produce a specific result. A hashing algorithm takes a large body of digital information and produces a mathematical value, or "hash," that uniquely identifies the data, like a fingerprint identifies a person. A hash is quite small compared to the amount of data it represents. The most commonly used hashing algorithm is the MD5 hash created by Ron Rivest of RSA Inc. The odds of having two data sets, at random, that produce the same MD5 hash are calculated to be 10^{38} or a 10 followed by 37 more zeros. That is more time than the complete age of the universe, start to finish in seconds. An alternative algorithm called Secure Hash Algorithm (SHA) was developed by the National Institute of Standards and Technology. It provides greater security but is slower.

QUICK FACTS

Almost any action taken on a computer, even the simple act of starting it, alters potential evidence and gives the defense an avenue to attack the credibility of the analysis. For example, when the Microsoft Windows™ operating system starts during boot-up, it writes to every disk on the system, changing approximately 160 files. Similarly, an Apple Mac™ verifies your start-up disk and repairs directories if required, loads kernel extensions, addresses cache file issues and logs startup and login items automatically.

Several hardware write-blockers are available to investigators. Once installed, the device absolutely prevents a write operation to the original evidence device. In the Windows™ operating environment, the hardware write-blocker is the only way to be sure to prevent write operations. Unfortunately, if a seized device requires specialized hardware device drivers, the device may not work with a write-blocker.

Other operating systems, notably OSX™, Unix™, or Linux™, allow hard disks to "mount" (i.e., be recognized by the computer) as "read only." This too absolutely prevents writing to the evidence drive. However, familiar Windows forensics packages may not be available for Unix™ systems and vice versa.

Source: Kruse, W.G. and Heiser, J.G. *Computer Forensics: Incident Response Essentials* (San Francisco, CA: Addison-Wesley, 2002). See also Apple Support, "Find the macOS version on your Mac." Available at *https://support.apple.com/en-us/HT201260*

Imaging of the Evidence Drive

With any seized device, it is important to create a working copy for forensic analysis. The best method is to create a bit stream copy (also called a mirror or image). A bit stream copy reproduces every bit of information found on the evidence device, even unused storage space. This method reproduces both active files and latent data, including deleted files. Active files are those files available to the user or created by the user. Word-processing documents, spreadsheets, text files, graphics, etc. are all considered active files. Unless the crime being investigated is fairly technical (e.g., hacking-related crimes), the bulk of evidence obtained will be from the active files. No special tools are required to access these files. A simple search for known keywords or fragments of file names (e.g., *.jpg, where * can be equal to any text) can provide positive results. Latent files are files that are not recognized by the operating system; thus, they do not show up on a list of files. The most common source of latent files is deletion. When most computers delete files, they do not actually erase the bits in the file; they simply allow new files to be saved to that space when it is needed. Until then, the file is left virtually intact. Recovery of deleted files will be discussed later in this chapter. Another type of latent data, accessible without extraordinary effort, is found in protected system files. These can be accessed by booting the computer from a boot CD. Most commonly, this includes that swap file or paging file used by Windows™ to simulate additional physical memory, also known as virtual memory.

FIGURE 13.2   Step 1 is to mathematically verify the contents of the evidence device. This value will prove that any future copies match the original exactly.

Logical copies, created with the copy command included with the operating system, do not reproduce latent data. Images can be created by readily available software with a hardware write-blocker in place. Best current practices require the use of a write-blocker because it simplifies courtroom presentation of the evidence. However, it is equally acceptable to boot from a CD and use an imaging program to produce a bit stream copy. Bootable CDs create a random access memory (RAM) drive (storage to active memory, not the hard drive) and can be used to load larger programs; thus, they do not alter data on the hard drive. If possible, the image produced should be written to true, write-once media (e.g., DVD-R or CD-R), so that the copy cannot be altered; however, the size of modern hard drives makes even DVDs cumbersome to use.[6]

An image can be authenticated with an MD5 hash comparison and contains potential evidence that may be hidden from the operating system. The hash value of the archival image (#1) matches the hash of the evidence device (#1). As always, document the results of the procedure. Documentation can be as simple as cutting and pasting the hash value into a computer log and noting that it is the same. This provides a verifiable record that the evidence has not been altered by error or intentional act.

The rule of best evidence requires that the original evidence, not a copy, be brought to court. However, the Federal Rule of Evidence 1001(3) allows unaltered digital evidence to be presented as a copy; thus, the image of a device is considered to be "best evidence." A comparison of MD5 hashes can verify that the data are unaltered. The data may even be mathematically compressed and retain their integrity. Compression simply reduces the size of a file for storage or transportation. There are many techniques used to compress data; one variety, called lossless compression, is not considered alteration. Lossless compression will produce the exact binary data as were compressed and can be mathematically and empirically verified to do so. The key is that the uncompressed version produces a hash value equal to the original.

Wiping the Analysis Drive

The analyst must ensure that the target drive is free from contaminates of previous analyses. For example, analysis on a child pornography case may lead to loading pornographic images from the image of a suspect's drive. If this material is not thoroughly wiped, it may be detected in a later analysis of another suspect's drive in a fraud case. To avoid having to explain this in court, it is best to establish a procedure that wipes both data and the space between data called slack space. By wiping the analysis drive before restoring the image, the analyst will be able to refute any claim that the drive was contaminated. Most common implementations of a wiping program meet the standards of Department of Defense Directive 5220.22—the DoD wipe (see Box 13.2).

FIGURE 13.3 Step 3 is to verify that the image of the evidence drive is a true copy of the evidence drive. Note that the hash value produced (#1) is the same as the hash from the evidence drive.

BOX 13.2

The DoD Wipe

The U.S. Department of Defense issued Directive 5220.22-M as part of its National Industrial Security Program. The directive sets security standards for Department of Defense contractors. The process, popularly known as a DoD wipe, is actually the standard used to "sanitize" a hard drive that contained data less than top secret. Although it is not absolutely necessary to use a DoD wipe, it has become a de facto standard; that is, the use of another technique would require explanation.

The use of the DoD wipe recognizes the potential of latent data to exist even after a drive is deleted or even formatted. Once the DoD wipe is performed, the hard drive cannot recognize latent data. Without extraordinary measures, the use of a DoD wipe places evidence beyond the reach of current law enforcement techniques, but recent advances with magnetic force microscopes and electron tunneling microscopes may change this some day.

After performing a suitable wipe, the results can be verified by hashing the blank drive and comparing the resulting hash value to the value of the blank drive. As always, document the results of the procedure. Documentation can be as simple as cutting and pasting the hash value into a computer log and noting that it is the same. This provides a verifiable record that the target drive is not contaminated with evidence from a previous case.

Restoring

While small-scale, 4.7 GB or less, analysis can be performed from a DVD or other write-once medium, larger volumes of data can only be practically handled from a hard drive. Consider even a relatively small evidence drive at 20 GB. If completely full, it would take five DVDs to hold the contents. Each step of an analysis protocol (see the next section) must be performed five times, with the operator switching disks as needed. In addition to raw size, an internal hard drive has a much faster data transfer rate than any of the current removable media. Consider that to search a hard drive

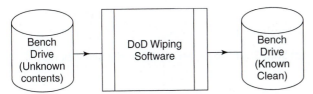

Step 4 is to wipe the bench drive to be used when analyzing the archival image.

FIGURE 13.4   Step 5 is to create a hash of the clean bench drive and compare the value to the value of the drive when it was last known to be blank. Note that the hash value produced (#0) is the same as the hash from the blank bench drive.

for one keyword, the entire contents of that hard drive must be read and brought into the computer's memory. Even a marginal speed advantage makes the restoration procedure necessary.

To perform forensic analysis of the data, they must be loaded onto a clean target drive or folder. When the image is loaded, it should be authenticated to verify that it is a true copy of the original.

BOX 13.3

Size in Computers

Term	Value	Value in bytes	Volume in pages
Bit	1	1/8 byte	Less than 1 page
Byte	8 bits	1 byte	Less than 1 page
Kilobyte (KB)	1,024 bytes	(2^{10}) bytes	About 1/2 page
Megabyte (MB)	1,024 KB	(2^{20}) bytes	About 500 pages
Gigabyte (GB)	1,024 MB	(2^{30}) bytes	160-foot stack of paper

Understanding the scale of data handled in digital forensics is difficult. In one of the defining cases in data storage, Kevin Mitnick, accused of criminal hacking, possessed 9 GB of data when arrested. Prosecutors and the court refused to allow Mitnick access to a computer to view the evidence against him because of fears that he could cause damage or seek revenge.[1] Astronomical figures about the amount of paper needed to print that amount of potential evidence

were used to justify not releasing it to Mitnick. To print all of the evidence would have required a stack of paper 1,440 feet tall.

---

[1]The underlying issue was that 1 GB of the data was encrypted and the prosecution did not want to release the data because they could not read it. Mitnick refused to supply a decryption key based on his Fifth Amendment privilege against self-incrimination.

Step 6 is to restore the archival copy (from Step 3) of the evidence drive to a blank bench drive (from Step 5).

FIGURE 13.5   Step 7 is to authenticate the restored image by calculating an MD5 hash and comparing that hash value to the hash of the evidence drive. Note that the hash value produced (#1) is the same as the hash from the evidence drive (#1).

The Complete Process

Step 1 is to verify mathematically the contents of the evidence drive. This value will prove that any future copies match the original exactly.

Step 2 is to create an exact "image," or bit-stream copy, of the evidence drive.

Step 3 is to verify that the image of the evidence drive is a true copy of the evidence drive. Note that the hash value produced (#1) is the same as the hash from the evidence drive.

Step 4 is to wipe the bench drive to be used when analyzing the archival image.

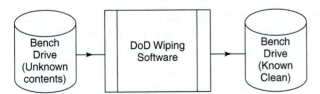

Step 5 is to create a hash of the clean bench drive and compare the value to the value of the drive when it was last known to be blank. Note that the hash value produced (#0) is the same as the hash from the blank bench drive.

FIGURE 13.6 Summary.
Before the first step of a new analysis, it is necessary to obtain a comparison value for the blank hard drive to be used in the analysis.

Step 6 is to restore the archival copy (from Step 3) of the evidence drive to a blank bench drive (from Step 5).

Step 7 is to authenticate the restored image by calculating an MD5 hash and comparing that hash value to the hash of the evidence drive. Note that the hash value produced (#1) is the same as the hash from the evidence drive (#1).

FIGURE 13.6 (*Continued*)

FORENSIC ANALYSIS

Computer forensics books often describe the identification of evidence in meticulous and exacting terms. In any given investigation, the variety of possible analyses is as broad as the evidence sought. Essentially, the analyst attempts to find information that is in itself incriminating (e.g., child pornography) or evidence that helps establish the elements of a crime (e.g., paper trail for a fraud case). When planning an analysis, the investigator and forensic analyst may wish to look for everything that might be incriminating. However, the fact is that overanalysis is as dangerous as underanalysis. Imagine an officer having to search every house and building in a neighborhood where a burglar has been reported. Ignoring the legal implications, it is too much work for an uncertain return. The officer might discover new crimes, but could become so busy with minutia that he or she would never complete the original investigation. The search warrant and original purpose of the investigating officer determine what type of evidence may be sought. This is not only a sensible strategy to limit a search, but exceeding the warrant may result in the evidence being ruled inadmissible in court. Furthermore, a well-planned analysis can even be used to justify a plain-sight exception to the requirements of the warrant or the inadvertent discovery of a new crime. The plan can be used to demonstrate how the plain-sight viewing occurred.

Electronic Crime Scene Investigation: A Guide for First Responders, published by the National Institute of Justice, is intended to assist state and local law enforcement and other first responders who may be responsible for preserving an electronic crime scene and for recognizing, collecting, and safeguarding digital evidence. Box 13.4 uses

BOX 13.4

Common Evidence of Selected Crime Types

Child Abuse or Exploitation

- Video and still photo cameras and media
- Digital camera software
- Internet activity records
- Notes or records of chat sessions
- Web cameras or microphones

Computer Intrusion

- Network devices, routers, switches
- Handheld mobile devices
- Web camera(s)
- Lists or records of computer intrusion software
- Notes or records of Internet activity

Domestic Violence

- Mobile communication devices
- External data storage devices
- User names and accounts
- PDAs or address books
- Printed e-mail, notes, and letters
- Caller ID units

Gambling

- Electronic money transfers
- Online banking software
- Sports betting statistics
- Customer information or credit card data
- References to online gambling sites

Theft

- Financial asset records
- Laminators
- Copies of signatures
- Check cashing cards
- Online banking software

Narcotics

- Handheld mobile devices
- PDAs, address books, and contact information
- GPS devices
- Blank prescription forms
- Forged identification
- Drug receipts

Source: National Institute of Justice. *Electronic Crime Scene Investigation: A Guide for First Responders,* 2nd ed. (Washington, D.C.: Office of Justice Programs, 2008).

information in the guide to list the best sources of digital evidence for crimes that range from child abuse and exploitation to domestic violence.

Once an image is secured, it can be loaded onto a new hard drive and placed in the seized machine (while storing the original hard drive in a safe place). A basic examination can quickly be accomplished using the tools of the operating system. If there is reason to suspect a highly sophisticated user, this technique may be insufficient, but the vast majority of digital evidence will not come from a master hacker. It is possible that there will be no competent effort to hide evidence on the computer—not even so much as deleting it. A quick result in this case is infinitely preferable to an extensive analysis six months in the future. Furthermore, directory structure and file-naming conventions can be used to associate a user with a particular piece of evidence discovered. A search of the active files through the operating system itself also produces the maximum chance of inadvertently discovering evidence of a new crime in plain view.

If simple techniques do not yield results, more extensive analysis techniques are available to the analyst. Regardless of the meaning of the information sought, all digital information is simply a pattern of bits. Discovering evidence becomes a process of matching a known pattern of bits, whether they form the first portion of a child pornography specimen (a picture previously identified by law enforcement) or the name and Social Security number of an identity theft victim. By identifying the presence of the unique pattern of bits that correspond to that decoded data, we can match the evidence device with the illicit information.

THE FORENSIC ANALYST AS EXPERT WITNESS

After the completion of the analysis, the forensic analyst generates a report describing what evidence was identified, what elements of the crime it proposes to establish, how the evidence was identified, and finally how and why any summaries of evidence were created. Depending on how the analyst was brought into the case, either the prosecutor or the investigator receives the report and decides to proceed with the case or not. Assuming that the analysis provides suitable evidence to proceed, the court process often takes a substantial amount of time, and the analyst proceeds with new work. Depending on the credibility of the report or the convincing nature of testimony in a deposition, the analyst's simple presence may be used to assist in plea bargaining negotiations. This does not invalidate all the work and preparation put into preparing the analysis for trial; quite the contrary, it means the evidence is so compelling that the defense does not want to risk a trial. If the case comes to trial and the analyst is called, he or she will have two duties. First, the analyst must testify to his or her direct experience. That is, the analyst may testify about everything from receiving the initial evidence to the final report. Given the time lag between analysis and testimony, this is where a routine set of well-documented procedures is most helpful. Second, the analyst may play the role of a technical expert, qualified to give summaries and opinions as to the meaning of evidence. The expert witness presents simplified explanations and abbreviations to the fact finder (judge or jury, depending on the trial). In essence, expert testimony allows the fact finder to make an informed decision without having to become an expert. In both roles, the forensic analyst should avoid partisan testimony. Independence and professional stature of the expert witness lend credibility that appearing to take sides would invalidate. It is typical for "opposing" expert witnesses to cooperate to determine facts and come to a satisfactory understanding of events and evidence.

To ensure the examiner's ability to demonstrate the link between the evidence device and the final analysis, the evidence device itself must be maintained in the exact state it was in when it was seized. While conducting the analysis, the forensic examiner must stay within the boundaries set by the original search warrant or consent of the evidence drive's owner/competent custodian and testify to that fact, while also testifying to the integrity of the chain of custody for related evidence devices.

COMPUTER STORAGE SYSTEMS

It surprises many people that we cannot simply identify where information is physically found on the evidence device. Many forensic experts fall into the trap of explaining data structure with real-world analogies and are forced into explanations of the physical structures of digital devices. In recent years, the field of storage forensics has been complicated by the introduction of new hard drive technologies, mobile devices, and rapidly growing storage capacities. These developments can be understood in the context of the two imperatives of hard drive manufacturers: storage density and speed (see Box 13.5).

Volatile Storage Systems

The structures of digital storage can be divided into two parts: volatile and nonvolatile storage. The primary difference between these types of storage is that volatile storage is lost when the device loses power. Thus, the decision to unplug a device may lose the

BOX 13.5

Speed and Density

Storage density allows manufacturers to increase the storage capacity of hard drives. By packing more bits closer together, storage capacity has increased without the form factor (physical size) of the device increasing. Some of the physical differences in hard drives can be explained by the increasing density of information. For example, multiple platters allow more storage space. A denser magnetic medium means that individual bits can be written in smaller physical space and still resolved by new, more sensitive read heads. More precision means less space must be wasted between tracks of data arranged in concentric rings on the disk. Speed is a constant goal of storage manufacturers. The storage system of most computers is its slowest link. By increasing the speed of the hard drive, significant speed increases can be obtained for common tasks. The fastest part of the computer can only operate as quickly as the data and instructions can arrive. Computer architecture is designed to keep the most frequently used and most vital information in the fastest storage possible.

volatile or active memory, data that may include passwords or Web site session data. Volatile memory is difficult to access without special software and impossible to access without altering it. Such alteration can be explained in court, but does not come without risks.

PROCESSOR   Although not actually a storage system, the processor is the benchmark for speed and the organizing factor in nonvolatile storage. There has been a great deal of attention given to processor speeds ever since the first PCs. Today, the processor is by far the fastest part of the computer, completing operations over 4 billion times per second. To feed this incredibly rapid cycling of information, the storage system must bring large quantities of information at a relatively slower pace. Typical systems operate at 60 percent of possible throughput. Most systems spend substantial amounts of idle time; however, bursts of activity can use the full capacity of the processor's speed. Forensically, the processor is of little interest. Information in the processor is altered billions of times per second. Furthermore, any information in the processor is completely inaccessible to human beings.

CACHE   All cache systems are volatile, which means that when power is removed, information held in RAM disappears. The Level 1 cache operates at speeds approximating the processor. Level 1 (L1) cache is built into the processor to reduce delays in getting information to the processor. Level 2 (L2) cache is often built onto the processor's daughterboard along with the control chip set that feeds information and instructions in and carries out operations based on the results. L2 cache is slower than L1, but holds more information. L2 cache serves as a buffer between L1 and the system's main memory (RAM). Forensically, the cache holds little interest, as it is inaccessible to the user.

MAIN MEMORY (RAM)   RAM[7] is the large reserve of information that supplies the processor through the cache systems. The bulk of the system's active data is held in RAM. Anything the user is doing, any open programs or files, will be in the RAM contents. Like cache, RAM is volatile storage. When the control systems predict the processor will need more data or must switch to a different task, the data are moved into the cache from RAM. When new processes are loaded or new data are requested by the user, the RAM draws information from the nonvolatile storage systems.

Forensically, RAM may be of some use. If software is already installed, RAM can be viewed by the user. All Unix™ systems provide a method to save RAM to a file with a process called a core dump. Windows™ systems require the use of special software, such as a hex editor or systems tool, to allow users to read RAM. Installing such software would undoubtedly alter the contents of the RAM and possibly purge them as well. If the computer uses virtual memory, a system that allows expansive, but slow, hard drive storage to substitute for RAM (see below), portions of the RAM contents may be saved on the hard disk in a file called a swap file or paging file. The swap file is normally inaccessible when the computer is running, making its contents latent data. Functionally, the swap file can be considered to be part of the RAM subsystem. In spite of the difficulties in accessing RAM, it can prove to be a treasure trove of useful data. Passwords, recently accessed files, and network settings may all be found in the contents of RAM.

Nonvolatile Storage Systems

Unlike previous components, the purpose of storage is not simply to convey data to the processor. Storage also maintains information when it is not needed or even when the power is removed from the system. Thus, storage systems are not volatile. Storage systems compromise between storing masses of information efficiently and allowing quick retrieval.

HARD DRIVES   The hard drive is the primary storage device of most computers along with removable, peripheral systems, such as DVD or CD-ROMs, flash drives, and similar devices. Storage systems are far slower than RAM, cache, or the processor. Unlike the other systems, the hard drive relies on physical motion (usually a spinning disk and even slower read/write heads) or solid state memory chips—no moving parts. All of their operations are electrical. Because hard drives add latency through physically or logical input/output (I/O) data reads and writes on either spinning disks or arrays of solid state memory chips, they will always be the slowest link in the information chain.

A few years ago, the lack of main computer memory (RAM) forced computers to crawl relative to today's computers. The biggest reason for this was that the lack of RAM forced computers to use the hard drive to trick the system into believing it had more memory through a system called virtual memory. More memory (even the slower, virtual memory) meant that larger files could be manipulated, more programs loaded, and more features could be built into programs. The tradeoff was overall system speed.

Hard drive manufacturers have found many ways to improve the initial performance of their products. Data structures optimize "seek times," thereby reducing the delay between the call for data and the hard drive's ability to retrieve the data. Multiple platters (disks) allow more than one read/write head to work at once. Faster spin speeds (e.g., 10000 RPM compared to standard 5200 RPM) allow more data surface to pass under the read/write heads. The structures of the hard disk are the product of evolutionary search for speed and storage density. The rapid change in hard drive technology and competition between hard drive manufacturers make it exceedingly difficult accurately to describe the function of a given hard drive in all but the broadest terms. Forensic analysts should avoid using the physical and low-level structures of a hard drive to describe how data were obtained.

REMOVABLE STORAGE MEDIA   There are two broad classes of removable storage media: direct access and sequential access. Disk drives allow direct access storage. That is, they do not have stored information in sequential order like a magnetic tape or other sequential access device. In direct access storage devices, the time required to access data is reduced, making retrieval faster. Tapes provide sequential access storage. Sequential access storage requires longer to fast-forward through unneeded data to find the data requested. This is analogous to selecting a scene with a DVD player versus fast-forwarding a VHS tape. Direct access devices need an index to locate information that may be scattered across the disk. The index holds a list of locations and the files currently residing in those locations. If portions of large files are scattered in many locations (fragmented), it takes longer to retrieve them, but still much faster than a sequential device. Sequential storage devices provide an attractive option for archival storage because of their low cost. Furthermore, because tape drives are an older technology, they enjoy greater support in the proprietary systems of the non-Windows™ world.

Many different types of storage media are used today. An analyst must be able to correctly identify the equipment needed to acquire evidence from a seized storage device. Before any type of forensic operation can be completed, the analyst must be able to read the storage device. Fortunately, most modern drives have cross-compatibility (allowing them to read data written with other standards) and backward compatibility (allowing them to use older standards). Sometimes an analyst will be confronted with a storage device that is not standard. Fortunately, the device to read that storage device is often seized with the storage device. On occasions when it is not, the analyst might have to acquire a compatible device. An up-to-date knowledge of common storage devices and storage device readers will greatly benefit the analyst. One of the best ways to stay current with storage devices is simply to visit the local computer superstore.

Although there appears to be a bewildering array of storage media available, including flash drives, iPods, CDs, DVDs, and external drives, each contains essentially the same kind of information as contained by a hard drive. Procedures for examining this evidence are essentially the same, except for the acquisition.

BOX 13.6
The BTK (Blind-Torture-Kill) Serial Murder Case

One of the most famous cases solved by digital forensics, according to The International Academy of Design and Technology (IADT), was the BTK serial killer in Sedgwick, Kansas. The BTK killer case went unsolved for over 30 years, costing law enforcement millions of dollars and hundreds of thousands of man-hours attempting to identify the person responsible for the murder of 10 people between 1974 and 1991. Police exhausted all capabilities at the time, including criminal psychologists reviewing the notes and taunts left by the killer, in an effort to identify a suspect(s). It wasn't until 2004, when the killer sent police a floppy disk in an effort to break his 10-year silence and taunt them with another riddle. This time however, police were equipped with digital forensics tools (Access Data's EnCase software) and were able to analyze the disk, finding that it contained a deleted Microsoft Word document. The metadata of the deleted file revealed the "last modified by" user as "Dennis," at the Christ Lutheran Church. Police were quickly able to identify Dennis Rader as a member of the church, and collected the necessary physical evidence to tie him to the BTK murders. Subsequently, Radar was convicted of the murders in 2005 and sentenced to 10 consecutive life terms.

Source: The International Academy of Design and Technology, "The Most Famous Case Ever Solved by Computer Forensics" (January 6, 2011). Available at *https://investigation.com/2016/12/02/digital-forensics-can-solve-the-case-texting-while-driving/*

FILE SYSTEMS

A file system is part of the computer's operating system. When a disk is formatted, it is imprinted with the structures used to control files. Several different systems have been developed to meet the growing needs of users for larger drives, greater efficiency, more speed, and security. This discussion focuses on the Windows™ family and its file systems. Although there are many arguments as to the superiority of operating systems, it is an indisputable fact that the Windows™ family of operating systems is still the most common operating environment. It is almost certain that the majority of investigations on nonmobile devices will occur in the Windows™ environment. However, the same cannot be said about mobile devices, refer to Box 13.7.

The Windows™ family of operating systems can be divided into two groups. The Windows 9x series includes Windows 95 through Windows 98 and the follow-up Windows ME. All of these systems were designed to be consumer systems and do not seriously attempt to implement security. For example, the log-on password can easily be circumvented by hitting a conveniently close and clearly labeled "cancel" button. The other group is the Windows NT™ series, which includes Windows 2000™, Windows XP™, Windows Vista™, Windows 7™, Windows 8™, and Windows 10™. Although Microsoft was not always successful, the Windows NT™ series attempted to improve security. Later versions contain some meaningful protection, such as User Account Control, which required that the computer user authorize system procedures and processes, and this has been included in all versions since Vista. Of greatest forensic interest is the file system used. File allocation table (FAT) file systems provide the least security. The new technology file system (NTFS) has progressed and may prove difficult to examine in its latest incarnation.

The easiest way to identify the version of Windows™ on a booted machine is to examine the system properties or by entering the "ver" command at the command prompt.

FAT: File Allocation Table

One of the characteristics of the FAT systems most useful to forensic analysts is that deleted files are not wiped from the drive. Most people know that somehow deleted files can be recovered. The reason that works is the need for speed. To save time on unneeded operations, when a file is deleted, the file is not altered, except for a marker at the beginning. The only real change is that the FAT marks the clusters[8] used by the file as open or "unallocated." If no new data are stored to those clusters, the data can sit there intact for years. Even if new data are saved, they may not completely fill the

Windows 9x	File System	Windows New Technology (NT)	File System
Windows 95	FAT 16	Windows NT 3.5	NTFS 3.5
Windows 95 OSR2	FAT 16/FAT 32	Windows NT 4.0	NTFS 4.0
Windows 98	FAT 16/FAT 32	Windows 2000	NTFS 5.0
Windows 98 Second Edition (WinSE)	FAT 16/FAT 32	Windows XP	NTFS 5.0
Windows Millennium (Win ME)	FAT 16/FAT 32	Windows Vista, Windows 7, and Windows 8	NTFS 5.0

FIGURE 13.7 The Windows™ family of operating systems and associated file systems.

BOX 13.7

Digital Forensics and Mobile Devices

While the majority of forensic examinations on stationary devices are still performed on Windows operating systems, the same cannot be said for mobile devices. With cell phones, PDAs, or tablet devices, there are a number of operating systems that may be running. The four that will be most encountered in the field are: the Android OS, Apple's iPhone OS (derived from the Mac OSX), Windows Mobile, and Blackberry, all of which have their own architecture, as well as proprietary security and memory management components. This creates unique challenges for the forensic examiner—but the data yielded from successful searches can be priceless in a criminal investigation.

Mobile devices not only store photos, address books, Internet browsing history call logs, text, and e-mail communications, but also retain information about other devices and servers they interact with and, very importantly, can collect geolocation information.

Training for mobile digital forensics is not currently as refined as is that for stationary devices; investigators tend to rely on a combination of low-tech analysis, back-up or syncing methods, plus open source and commercial software. The forensic analysis of mobile devices is described by Brothers as follows:

1. *Manual Extraction—physical analysis of the device involving manual manipulation of the keyboard and photographic documentation of data displayed on the screen.*
2. *Logical Analysis—Connect data cable to the handset and extract data using AT, BREW, etc. commands in client/server architecture, or mobile-forensics*

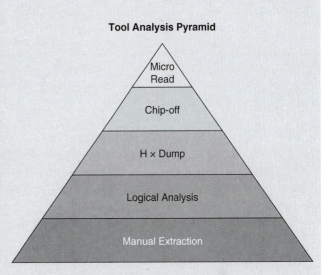

Tool Analysis Pyramid

- Micro Read
- Chip-off
- H × Dump
- Logical Analysis
- Manual Extraction

specific tools, including FTK, Encase, Paraben, or Cell-brite
3. *Physical Analysis (Hex Dump)—Push a boot loader into device, dump the memory from phone, and analyze the resulting data.*
4. *Physical Analysis (Chip-Off)—Remove memory from the device and read in either second phone or EEprom reader.*
5. *Physical Analysis (Micro Read)—This is the most forensically sound method and uses an electron microscope to view state of memory.*

Source: Brothers, S. *How Cell Phone "Forensic" Tools Actually Work Cell Phone Tool Leveling System.* DoD Cybercrime Conference (Atlanta, GA, 2011).

---

unallocated space. This leaves fragments of the previous file in places that cannot normally be accessed. In the diagram below, full clusters of stored data are shown in gray. The dark gray portion at the end of one of the clusters represents space not used by the new file occupying this cluster. The dark gray cluster following it represents a currently unused cluster that may contain latent data from a previously deleted file. Both types of latent data are found in "slack space," disk storage space unused by active data, potentially containing latent data.

For forensic analysts, one problem with FAT32 systems is that MS-DOS cannot access FAT32. Newer versions of DOS have been modified to use FAT32. The DOS that underlies Windows 98 works well with the newer features of FAT32.

NTFS: New Technology File System

Windows NT™, 2000™, XP™, Vista™, Windows 7™, Windows 8™, and Windows 10™ systems use NTFS. NTFS has numerous advantages over the FAT system,

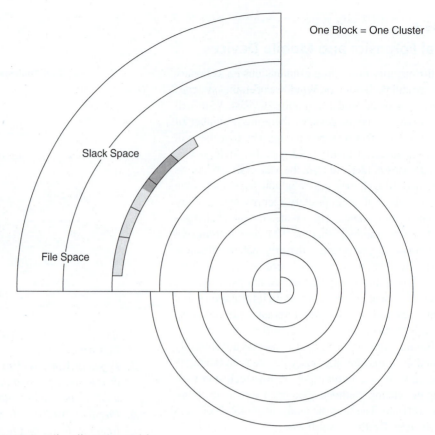

One Block = One Cluster

Slack Space

File Space

FIGURE 13.8 File Allocation Table.

especially in terms of security. To the forensic analyst, the only difference is that DOS-based tools do not work. Some utilities have been created that allow DOS to read NTFS; for example, NTFS-DOS is freeware that allows DOS operations on an NTFS volume. Although NTFS implements a different method for dealing with files, it still has slack space and unallocated clusters that may contain old data. One of the primary advantages to users of NTFS is that it uses storage space more efficiently. This produces less wasted space between files. This wasted space has long been a treasure trove of supposedly deleted material for forensic analysis. Two other features of NTFS pose specific problems to forensic analysts.

DYNAMIC DISKS Dynamic disks manage disk space without partitions and offer numerous advantages to administrators, but are not compatible with previous versions of NTFS or other operating systems (including DOS). These volumes can be imaged, but can only be read with a Windows 2000™ or other compatible boot disk.

ENCRYPTING FILE SYSTEM (EFS) The EFS presents a challenge to forensic analysis. If the machine is discovered in an operable condition (no screen saver and powered on), an investigator can use the Microsoft Management Console to create a key recovery certificate. It would also be possible to turn EFS off for each folder. Assuming that does not happen, there are other options. A centrally managed network using EFS will usually make the domain administrator the key recovery agent. Thus, a key may be available from the domain administrator. The initial seizure at the crime scene may include a disc with the recovery key. Experienced users of encryption know how important it can be to keep an extra key around. Losing the only copy of an encryption key can make stored data useless.

A stand-alone machine makes the administrator the default key recovery agent. Achieving administrator access by resetting the administrator password or cracking the administrator password would make EFS completely transparent. No passwords are needed; simply being the administrator opens all the protections. Removing the Windows password file (known as the SAM database) resets the administrator password. When restarting, the administrator password will be blank, but the administrator can still access the key to EFT. It is also important to note that the Enterprise and Ultimate editions of Vista System and Windows 7™, plus Pro and Enterprise editions of Windows 8™, and Windows 10™, utilize a technology called bitlocker drive encryption, which can protect the entire operating system volume. This is a unique addition that provides a layer of protection not seen in previous version of Windows software.

APPLICATION: DEFRAGMENTING A DISK

When a disk is formatted for the first time, all of its clusters are open; there is no slack space between files. Reformatted disks can contain latent data, but it is not technically in slack space. When new data and programs are saved to the disk, they occupy clusters. Each cluster is represented by a number in the file allocation table.

0034	0035	0036	0037	0038	0039	0040	0041	0042	0043
used	used	used	used	used	used	used	used	used	used

When those files are moved or deleted, the FAT de-allocates the clusters and makes them available for new files.

0034	0035	0036	0037	0038	0039	0040	0041	0042	0043
used	open	open	open	used	used	used	open	used	used

Over time, clusters are allocated and de-allocated. Files fit wherever there is space, or they are saved in several spaces. The file system tracks these fragmented pieces of the file so that the user has access to what appears to be a complete file. In this case, a new file needs three clusters to fit. It is placed in clusters 35–37.

0034	0035	0036	0037	0038	0039	0040	0041	0042	0043
used	new	new	new	used	used	used	open	used	used

When a file increases in size but there is no adjacent open cluster, the new cluster is saved in the nearest available cluster. In this case, the new file needs another cluster for newly saved material. It now occupies clusters 35–37 and 41.

0043	0035	0036	0037	0038	0039	0040	0041	0042	0043
used	new	new	new	used	used	used	open	used	used

This process goes on over time and slowly reduces the efficiency of the hard drive. To acquire all of the pieces of a file, the read/write heads must travel to several parts of the disk. Eventually, the delay becomes noticeable to the user and he or she defragments the drive. Using a utility program, the user frees up a large area of disk space and then saves fragmented files as continuous files. The process repeats until the disk is defragmented; however, as soon as new information is added to a file, the fragmentation process begins again. Some utilities track frequently changed files and give them a little buffer space during the defragmentation process.

EVIDENCE RECOVERY FROM SLACK SPACE

As noted above, the efficient operation of the computer's file system leaves both active data and latent data. Active data are available through the file system itself or through the methods described below. Latent data are not available through the file system; however, common tools can give analysts access to the data. The box item, examining the bits, describes one such tool called a hex editor. The hex editor can be used to examine intact files (active data) or deleted and obscured data (latent data) from the hard disk without interference from the file system. Thus, incriminating bit patterns (e.g., a victim's credit card number or a specimen from a child pornography image) can be discovered.

In this hypothetical example, an analyst has to prove that a suspect accessed data critical to a company and downloaded them using a security hole in the company's Web server. Investigators found a supposedly anonymous user in a chat room claiming to have secrets from the victim company. This led to the suspect and the seizure of his computer. A quick review of likely places on the image of the seized disk found nothing. Apparently the suspect had deleted the information or might have had it elsewhere. The analyst suspects that there may be evidence in the slack space that the suspect forgot to clear.

The analyst wipes the hard drive of a lab bench machine (called an "analysis drive") and verifies it with an MD5. The hash of the analysis drive matches the hash taken when it was brand new and empty. He notes that fact in a bench journal on a separate computer.

The analyst applies the image to the analysis drive and verifies it with another MD5. The hash of the analysis drive now matches the hash taken from the suspect's drive and the hash of the image (because they are the same). He notes that fact in a bench journal on a separate computer.

From a bootable CD, he opens a freeware utility called "Strings," which searches for text words embedded in a program. He looks for the company's name anywhere on the disk. He finds one hit in cluster 0040. The company includes its name in executable programs at the end. He notes that fact in a bench journal on a separate computer.

From a bootable CD, he opens a hex editor (see Box 13.8). Using the hex editor, he searches for unique patterns of bits found at the beginning of the program believed stolen. He finds a match in cluster 0034. He notes that fact in a bench journal on a separate computer.

The analyst must now recover as much of the program as possible to provide statistical certainty of the match. Some of the clusters have been overwritten. He creates the chart below to show exactly where the evidence came from. Each box is one cluster. Each cluster is labeled with a number in the FAT. The original file was 112 kilobytes (112 KB). Unallocated clusters are marked in white; allocated clusters are marked in gray.

BOX 13.8

Examining the Bits

The interoperation of computers across networks and different operating systems has required the use of standard file systems. Typically, there are indicators at the beginning of a file (called a header) that inform the software of the file's characteristics. To read this information, we need two things: (1) software capable of accessing the raw data and (2) a codex to allow us to interpret the raw data. The illustration below (labeled wtc-photo.jpg) depicts the initial bit-by-bit values of a picture of the World Trade Center. The hex editor allows an analyst to view every detail of the file.

Hex editors report binary information in "hexadecimal couplets" (on the left in the illustration). Binary data, commonly understood as ones and zeroes (i.e., bits), are difficult for humans to interpret. Hexadecimal couplets are used to represent groups of eight bits—often called bytes. Two hexadecimal characters {0, 1, 2, 3, 4, 5, 6, 7, 8, 9, A, B, C, D, E, or F} can replace eight binary characters {0 or 1}. Once trained to do so, analysts find it much easier to make sense of this mind-numbing collection of 1–9 and A–F than an eight times larger collection of ones and zeroes. Fortunately, most hex editors also attempt to translate the bits into text (on the right in the illustration). The photograph of the World Trade Center was produced with Adobe Photoshop 3.0™.

0034	0035	0036	0037	0038	0039	0040	0041	0042	0043

Cluster size = 16 KB

Cluster ID	Status	Used by File	Size of New File	Original File	Recoverable
0034	Empty		0 KB	16 KB	16 KB
0035	Used	M024MNFB.HTM	4 KB	16 KB	12 KB
0036	Used	M02505DE.CSS	2 KB	16 KB	14 KB
0037	Used	M1NSVN76.HTM	16 KB	16 KB	0
0038	Used	M1NSVN76.HTM	6 KB	16 KB	10 KB
0039	Empty		0 KB	16 KB	16 KB
0040	Empty		0 KB	16 KB	16 KB
					84 KB

By subtracting the amount of the new file overwriting each cluster of the original, the analyst calculates that about 84,000 bytes survived and can be matched to the missing file. The odds that combination of bits occurred by chance alone are one to a number greater than the age of the universe in seconds; the analyst has a match. The analysts can now prove that the missing proprietary file was on the suspect's computer—even though the suspect tried to delete it. The presence of the fruits of a crime and motive (e.g., a disgruntled former employee) constitute the elements of a crime. Because his or her methods followed the best practices of the field, he or she will be able to present this summary of the evidence to the court in a convincing manner.

COMMERCIAL FORENSIC PACKAGES

The challenge of computer forensic examination lies in identifying, training, and equipping examiners to successfully complete their jobs. As a consequence, investigator fatigue and burnout can be a significant problem. Recent research with a sample of active forensic examiners found that more than half of the individuals contacted felt that they did not have the workforce to complete their tasks at work.[9] Furthermore, the examiners felt that their work would be challenged by others and that there are other ways to accomplish their jobs. One way to help to reduce these complaints and ease investigator stress is through the use of commercial forensic packages.

Modern forensic packages offer numerous advantages to the investigator, but also present pitfalls to investigators unsure of the fundamentals. To use these tools to their maximum benefit, the investigator must understand the way information is stored. Perhaps more important, to convincingly testify as to the proper use of these tools, the forensic examiner cannot be a passive observer of the analysis; he or she must plan and adapt the analysis based on an understanding of the technology and the specific legal requirements of the case at hand. A good forensics package must cover each of the

---

QUICK FACTS

There are several commercial forensic packages use by law enforcement today. These tools allow investigators to analyze digital evidence for the arrest and prosecution of suspects. Here are some of the most commonly used software tools and a description of their digital forensic application.

- **EnCase:** One of the most popular packages on the market today; allows investigators to image and then analyze data from hard drives, any removable media (e.g., disks, cds, jump drives), tablets, and/or cell phone. Similar software like Vogan Forensic Software, Blacklight, Digital Forensic Framework, Sleuth Kit, CAINE, X-Ways Forensics, Bulk Extractor, SIFT, WindowsSCOPE, HELIX3, Mandiant Redline, the Coroner's Toolkit, and Microsoft's COFEE-Computer Online Forensic Evidence Extractor allow for a broad range of software tools and comprehensive analysis of digital data.
- **SafeBack:** Used primarily for imaging the hard drives/disks of an Intel-based system and restoring these images; it is DOS-base program.
- **Md5sum:** A software tool that uses an algorithm called MD5 (message digest 5) to verify if an image has been made accurately and correctly; ensures that the image made for analysis is an exact replica of the original taken from thus suspect computer/tablet/cell phone.
- **Grep:** An extensive search program that allows for sequencing of characters, hence the searching of phrases or words in the same text or message that may have meaning. For instance, the words "Ali," "bomb," "concert," "London," "June," and "Ariana" may mean nothing individually; however, taken together may immediately point to a specific e-mail during a vast metadata search.
- **EventLog Analyzer:** Software logging tools allow the investigator to save data, make notes, and record when users log on and off a system. Similar tools include Graylog, Splunk, Logstash, and Logwatch.
- **Ethereal:** Network Surveillance Tools: Commonly knowns as "packet sniffers," this network surveillance tool captures and analyzes all traffic travelling over a specific network. Similar tools include NetworkMinor, Ruckus, Microsoft Network Monitor, DataDog, LogicMonitor, and LabTech
- **Whois and Registry Recon:** While not specifically a forensic software tool, but rather an extensive global data base of registered Internet users, this program allows a search for a specific IP (Internet Protocol) address as well as the DNS (Domain Name System) from the global database thereby identifying a specific computer/user on the Internet.
- **XRY:** Used to analyze and recover information specifically on mobile devices such as tablets and smartphones, includes tools for all formats (e.g., Android, iPhone, and Blackberry)

Source: Forensic Focus, "Computer Forensic Software: An Introduction." Available at *http://www.forensicfocus.com/computer -forensics-software-intro.php*. See also InfoSec Institute, "22 Popular Computer Forensics Tools" (May 26, 2017). Available at *http:// resources.infosecinstitute.com/computer-forensics-tools/#gref* basic forensic functions described in this chapter: importing data, hashing, wiping, imaging, and search capabilities.

Extended Analysis and Searching

All digital data are stored as a pattern of bits that tells the computer how to decode the patterns into pictures or text or other meaningful symbols. Computers cannot interpret symbols the way humans do. They can, however, match patterns of bits in storage to a sample provided by the analyst. In some cases, different encoding techniques are used. This means that the bit pattern used to represent the same symbol to the human user could be vastly different on different systems. For example, Unicode is used by Window NT/2000/XP™, and the IBM extended character set is used by DOS. This is another reason these two systems are incompatible. A forensic package must be versatile enough to recognize these common encoding schemes as well as the commonly used proprietary data storage formats. For example, Microsoft Outlook™ uses a proprietary database (called a DBX file) to store all of its e-mail. Without a third-party utility program, an analyst would have to install Microsoft Outlook™ to simply read seized e-mail. However, modern forensic packages have plug-ins that can decode proprietary file formats. Although freeware utilities are available to read Outlook DBX files, exporting data to separate utilities can be cumbersome and is prone to creating errors. Furthermore, broad search protocols do not work unless the search software is aware of various encoding schemes.

Speed is a primary concern in searches run by forensic packages. When huge volumes of data must be searched, simple, one-at-a-time pattern matching would take too long. Forensic packages have routines that search for all the desired patterns at once. If a suspect's drive has 200 GB of data, that full amount of data must be run from the hard drive and into the processor for comparison. As previously noted, the hard drive is the slowest part of the storage system. Instead of bringing all of the information through the hard drive several times, forensic packages bring it through once and search for all of the terms indicated by the analyst programming the search.

The ability of a search to achieve results is called the power of the search. Beyond the recognition of encoding schemes, searches should be able to distinguish near misses caused by minor user errors. Simple search routines are very literal; if the searched data do not contain the exact phrase or combination of characters, the search will return negative results. Most people are familiar with the need for proper capitalization and spelling in some search programs. More powerful search engines can search from context, or with allowances for small errors also referred to as "fuzzing." Powerful searches also allow the user to search for multiple terms, or small variations of those terms, at once. Modern forensic packages offer powerful and flexible search programs.

User Interface

Fatigue is a primary concern of forensic analysts. Huge backlogs of seized evidence are the rule, rather than an exception. Requiring an analyst to fight through uncomfortable menus to achieve simple tasks results in wasted time and repetitive, unproductive use of an analyst's time. Many forensic packages have pseudo-programmable features that allow an analyst to set up an analysis with a list of commands rather than requiring direct input at each step. Other interface features include common search term dictionaries. Thus, a standard search of threatening terms can provide the basic foundation for an analysis of a stalking case. These basic dictionaries can be enhanced with terms specific to the case from another list—names and addresses of suspects, for example. Another key to a good forensic package is consistency of commands. Most of the features of a forensic package can be found in individual programs—many of which are freely available. However, starting numerous programs and keeping track of the analysis require much more effort. Furthermore, each programmer of the freeware has his or her own notion of how commands operate. A forensic package has one consistent set of commands and menus to perform various functions on the data.

Centralized Report Writing and Auditing

A forensic analyst should be able to replicate every action that led to the discovery of evidence. A good forensics package should have the capability to track the analyst's actions to a log, so that productive procedures can be saved without requiring excessive notes. This may also include cataloging of key files for easy reference later. This log can form the basis for a more extensive report or simply be used as lab bench notes from the witness stand.

Validation and Support

A primary advantage to using a forensics package is that it has generally been validated by an external expert and used in standard practice. This saves an analyst from having to defend every tool used from attacks by the defense. As new versions of the package are released, they receive similar expert validation.

Support goes beyond the basic help-desk function. Forensic software vendors usually offer training to validate an analyst's skill and knowledge with the product. The credential provided by the vendor, upon successful completion of the training, is often a key validation of the analyst's skill.

When available, forensic packages will greatly increase the productivity of an analyst. The packages can be extremely cost prohibitive for some police agencies, however, as a site license for one program can cost thousands of dollars. At the same

---

BOX 13.9

Digital Forensics Case Study: Cell Phone Connects Suspect to the Crime

A January 2016 FBI digital forensics case study describes how a 34-year-old child predator was identified, arrested and convicted through the effective acquisition, analysis, and presentation of digital evidence. In 2014 a Florida man was identified as a child predator through the analysis of the data contained in pornographic images of children being distributed on the Internet, which lead investigators to the man's home because of the geolocation data attached to the photos he uploaded. When the man was arrested, Sheriff Deputies collected several digital devices, including a cell phone equipped with a 13+ megapixel camera. Images extracted from the cell phone were of such high resolution that the Sheriff's Office Fingerprint Unit was able to capture the fingerprint pattern from an image of the suspect's fingers and use it to compare against his jail booking fingerprint card. The suspect argued that he was not involved; however, the quality of the evidence linked him directly to the crime. The suspect was found guilty of 26 charges, including capital sexual battery, molestation, and possession, distribution, and transmission of child pornography. The man faces up to life in prison.

Source: https://leb.fbi.gov/2016/january/forensic-spotlight-digital-forensic-examination-a-case-study time, the wasted, salaried time of an analyst is worth considerably more to most organizations. In addition, the training provided by forensic package vendors can increase the productivity of an analyst by keeping him or her abreast of recent developments. A good package covers all the basics and helps keep the analysis organized and documented.

Summary

The basic process of digital forensic analysis is designed to present the elements of a crime in evidence from stored digital materials. In court, a forensic analyst will be asked to answer several questions about the evidence:

1. When restoring a backup to another machine, will it contain all of the files, no more and no less than were on the original?
2. Will the restored version's file be identical, faithful copies of the original?
3. Will latent data be faithfully reproduced?
4. Will the restored backup contain all the data, and only the data, on the original?

5. How do we know that our answers to these questions are accurate?[10]

By following the methods described in this chapter (especially the documentation), the analyst will be able to prove the answers to these questions. Other basic skills include a working knowledge of the devices used to store digital information and the tools required to analyze it. Computer forensics involves more than just computer knowledge; it also involves a detailed understanding of criminal law and the legal process.

Review Questions

1. Explain the process used to preserve the verifiable integrity of digital evidence. How does this ensure that data are preserved unmodified? How can an analyst show that the original evidence is unmodified?
2. Trace and explain how the hardware of a computer organizes and stores information for later retrieval from an active file being processed in the processor chip to a mass storage device (hard disk or removable storage). What is the trend in terms of speed in this progression of components? What is the trend in terms of the size and capacity in this progression of components?
3. Describe in broad terms how the software of a computer organizes information for storage and later retrieval. Does this process yield any potential locations for latent digital evidence? Is latent evidence always intact? Why or why not?
4. What advantages are offered by commercial forensic packages? Are there any disadvantages to using them? If so, what are they?

Critical Thinking Exercises

1. Go to Access Data's Web site and download the FTK Imager tool (http://accessdata.com/product-download/ftk-imager-version-3.4.3). Install FTK Imager, attach a USB device to your computer, and then view the following YouTube.com video (https://youtu.be/sAF1XxNb0nw) to learn how to add evidence and review the device for deleted files. Make note of your observations and results.

2. Visit the following Web site address and watch the YouTube.com video on performing and analyzing memory dumps from a Windows computer (https://youtu.be/-8f8avZ2V7s). Discuss the video as a tool to assist law enforcement.

Endnotes

1. BLACK, H.C., NOLAN, J.R., and NOLAN-HALEY, J.M. (1990). *Black's Law Dictionary,* 6th ed. St. Paul, MN: West Publishing.

2. "Data" is the plural form of datum. A single datum is one piece of information. Common usage allows discussion of data as a single grouping of information (e.g., "data is easily obtained"). This chapter uses data in this latter, common form.

3. STEPHENSON, P. (2000). *Investigating Computer-Related Crime.* Boca Raton, FL: CRC Press.

4. ORTON, I. (2001). "The Investigation and Prosecution of a Cybercrime." From *Cybercrime: The Investigation, Prosecution and Defense of a Computer-Related Crime.* Durham, NC: Carolina Academic Press.

5. It is possible, although complex to forge a file to produce a certain hash value, but it is extremely unlikely that the forged file could be confused with the original.

6. A single DVD can hold about 4.7 GB of data, but it would take more than 16 of them to hold the contents of a common consumer hard drive.

7. Random access memory (RAM) carries its name forward from the earliest days of computers. "Random access" distinguishes it from sequential access memory like a tape; this means that the processor can call for information located at any address in the RAM. In the 1960s, this was a tremendous improvement. Today, there are no other schemes for managing memory in common use, but we still specify "Random Access Memory."

8. Clusters are storage units that can be of several different sizes depending on how the file system on the hard drive is configured. They are the most accurate way to describe storage space on a hard disk.

9. HOLT, T.J. and BLEVINS, K.R. (September 2008). "Examining the Stress, Challenges, and Experiences of Forensic Examiners." Paper presented at the annual meetings of the Southern Criminal Justice Association, New Orleans, LA.

10. STEPHENSON, *Investigating Computer-Related Crime.*

14

Information Security and Infrastructure Protection

CHAPTER OBJECTIVES

After completing this chapter, you should be able to

- Understand the concept of risk as applied to information security and infrastructure protection.

- Discuss the major principles of risk analysis.

- Identify and define the primary security technologies used to protect information.

- Discuss the various functions of firewalls and identify their limitations.

- Define encryption, and discuss its use in terms of authenticity, integrity, and confidentiality.

- Identify and explain some of the security vendor technologies used today to secure information.

INTRODUCTION

Risk analysis will always be an art informed by science. We cannot know all possible outcomes and weigh them rationally. Risk analysis involves projecting the most probable outcome and allocating available resources to address that outcome. At the same time, a risk analyst must remember that assets (computers, networks, etc.) were purchased to fulfill a mission. If risk management strategies substantially interfere with that mission, then the assets are no better off than if they had been compromised through a security-related risk.

This section introduces the concept of risk by discussing several epochs of computer development. Each era presents its own risk and at least somewhat functional responses to that risk. Early decisions weighing the risk of computers not providing a useful function against potential or unknowable future security threats produced results that we still live with today. It is easy to criticize early decisions based on our knowledge of the outcomes, but even with hindsight, we may fail to see that the benefit provided greatly outweighs the harm. In fact, some decisions that have produced security vulnerabilities were absolutely essential to the basic functioning of computers and networks for their intended purposes.

MASTERING THE TECHNOLOGY AND THE ENVIRONMENT

In the earliest days of computing, before extensive networking and multiple user systems, the primary problem faced by users was the technology itself. During these early days, programmers created the computer functions that we take for granted.[1] Early innovations included interactive operation (rather than batch processing and output), rudimentary networking, graphics, tools and utilities, and so on.[2] In many cases, the primary limitation was the capacity of the hardware. Limitations imposed by operating memory, storage, and processing speed each forced adaptations. The net effect was the absence of security. At the time, physical security (i.e., locked doors) was sufficient to protect computing resources. The primary concern of system architects was the expansion of useful function and overcoming hardware limitations. Although decisions made at this early point would later have negative effects on security, they were really unavoidable.

As technologies matured and found supporters in mainstream business, the computer moved from research platform to business tool. Complex software was created for business, and essential functions were transferred from armies of clerks to computer systems. Such moves were always in one direction. It is impossible to reemploy clerical staff and reimplement paper-based procedures once the existing system is gone. Furthermore, the cost savings of computers make such a backward move unlikely. This placed new emphasis on the availability of data and recovery from errors and disasters. Computer centers were created to concentrate technical expertise and provide a controlled environment in which to maximize the availability of computing resources. Innovations in fire suppression,[3] efficient environmental controls,[4] and administrative procedures (i.e., backup schedules) gave reasonable assurance against disaster.

The user was undeniably part of the computing environment. During this era, legitimate users were the primary human threat to computers. More harm was caused by failure to properly maintain systems and backup schedules than from intrusion or malicious intent. When malicious intent played a part, it was typically on the part of an insider.[5] Although there are documented cases of intrusion and loss, a much greater threat came from the relative scarcity of experts to operate and maintain systems. Once again, the operational need for availability was more pressing than security.

Personal Computers and Intruders

Although recreational system intrusion was not unknown in the previous era, it was largely restricted by access to computers from insiders (see Chapter 4). Few people had access, and fewer still had the skill to break through the rudimentary security on most systems. Those who did were often deeply invested in terms of time and resources spent to acquire that knowledge.[6] Recreational intrusion was a minor problem at best. The advent of the home or personal computer (PC) in 1975 marked the beginning of the democratization of computing. It also marked the movement of hacking from the old-school era to the bedroom hacker era (again, see Chapter 4).[7] By the end of the 1970s, the restraint of peers and the investment in knowledge no longer provided reasonable protection against malicious users.

In this era, intruders sought knowledge and resources to continue their use of computers. Much of the literature is devoted to detailing the social connections or lack thereof among intruders and hackers.[8] Most pundits resort to the myth of the hacker as loner and contentious in interaction with other hackers.[9] An often-overlooked facet of the hacker culture is the need for information and resources. In the early era of intrusion, access to other computers required a phone connection, usually to a long-distance number. Thus, the search for access to resources and knowledge of how to exploit them dominated the vast majority of hacker interactions.

For the first time, intruders became a significant threat to routine computer use. Although efforts were made to secure computers, long-standing demands for the availability of computing resources and the expansion of computer capabilities simply eclipsed demands for security. Hollinger and Lanza-Kaduce provide one of the very few significant criminological works describing the efforts to supplement the computer industries' meager efforts toward security with law.[10] Various states and the federal government passed laws in the hopes of deterring would-be computer criminals and punishing those who were caught.

The Internet Explosion

The explosive growth of the Internet has been the subject of numerous books and articles in the popular press,[11] scholarly publications of general interest,[12] and works of technical research.[13] The dramatic influx of new users to computer networks has burdened both the technical infrastructure and the social cohesion of online communities.[14] The loss of social cohesion of the computer underground gave rise to script kiddies, low-skilled network intruders with little desire to pursue the traditional goals of hackers (see Chapter 4). At the same time, the influx of new users, also with low levels of skill, gave script kiddies and other larval hackers a rich field of targets. Unless a computer system holds particular interest (politically—like the World Trade Organization; technologically; or as a trophy—like NASA or the Pentagon), the most likely threat comes from script kiddies.

During this period, the amount of computerized data, such as bank records, personal information, and other electronic files, increased. Businesses and financial institutions store sensitive customer information in massive electronic databases that can be accessed and compromised by hackers. The increased use of online banking and shopping sites also allows consumers to transmit sensitive personal and financial information over the Internet. This created more attractive targets for criminals to engage in identity theft, fraud, and espionage.

In turn, the Internet increased the availability and proliferation of hacker tools and data and the professionalization of the hacker community. The recent emergence of malicious software markets and communities that engender the sale of stolen information as outlined in Chapters 6 and 7 makes it significantly easier for hackers to gain access to very sophisticated tools with little to no understanding of how they function. Such tools existed in the previous era, but were not as widely distributed or easily accessed. As a result, the global landscape of threats from hacking has changed dramatically, leading accomplished network intruders to offer their services for hire to unskilled hackers, terrorists, and organized crime groups. This has changed the way threats are perceived, though it is clear that the potential of the Internet to find and retrieve information from almost any jurisdiction has made it unlikely that a single nation's efforts could remove these tools from wide circulation. It is also undesirable to remove technical information from our networks; technological advancement depends on the open exchange of ideas.[15]

> **QUICK FACTS**
>
> The ability of malware to steal data from air gapped computers systems has been proven several times in a laboratory environment. The most common approach is to infect the target systems with a malware capable of transmitting (exfiltrating) data across the air gap by using the speaker of the target system to broadcast the data and the microphone of a network connected system to receive the data. This threat was mitigated by disabling or completely removing the speakers from an air gapped system. The most recent approach, however, utilizes the components of a system that cannot be removed—the cooling fans. In a June 2016, scientists demonstrated the ability to infect an air gapped target system with malware capable of modulating the system's cooling fans to create an acoustic wave form that can be received by a network connected system's microphone, including smartphones and laptops. Researchers demonstrated their "Fansmitter's" (Fan acoustic transmitter) ability to transmit data across an air gap by modulating the target system's power supply cooling fan as the transmitter, and smartphone, tested at ranges from 1 to 8 m away, as the receiver. The experimental malware on the target system modulated the fan speed of the system's cooling fan, creating acoustic waves that were then received by malware on the infected smartphone. Imagine the risk potential and information warfare utilization of such "air gapped" hacking capable of modifying the physical nature of hardware devices.
>
> *Source:* Mordechai Guri, Yosef Solewicz, Andrey Daidakulov, and Yuval Elovici, "Fansmitter: Acoustic Data Exfiltration from (Speakerless) Air Gapped Computers," June 2016, Cyber Security Research Center, Ben-Gurion University of the Negev (June 2016).

PRINCIPLES OF RISK ANALYSIS

Risk analysis is performed at many levels and with many degrees of detail. Risk analysis services are provided by Fortune 500 consulting firms like Deloitte, Accenture, Ernst & Young, and many others. Reports from a major risk analysis can cover every aspect of business and run into thousands of pages. Risk analysis may also be performed by small organizations or even individuals in the course of their businesses. Such informal decision making does not follow the comprehensive steps of the more elaborate analyses. Deciding where to draw the line on the depth of a risk analysis is an art with no clear standard. The principles of risk analysis presented here are broad, but examples are narrowly tailored to illustrate network security risks and remedies. Above all, this process shows that there is no single solution to security. The effort required to eliminate all risks (though not possible) would surely overwhelm an organization. All known factors relevant to an organization should be weighed so that a specific level of acceptable risk can be matched to a risk management strategy.

Assessment and Evaluation

The first step of risk analysis is to correctly assess and evaluate the existing information technology (IT) systems within an organization. Unfortunately, those who often conduct risk analysis studies tend to focus on external vulnerabilities and threats. Most losses of information come from inside the organization and through relatively simple security failures of existing information systems and networks. This assessment must include an evaluation of the organizational, managerial, and administrative procedures directly relevant to IT systems. Hopefully, the organization has and uses a well-developed and well-defined IT plan. This plan should include information relating to the acquisition and purchase of future IT equipment and systems, as well as a strategy for expanding information security parameters as the system grows or changes. Interestingly, most organizations have plans that represent large "bibles" of procedures and policies that sit on bookshelves (get dusty) and are rarely read or followed. Most managers and directors outside of IT fail to comprehend the complexity of information security. It is not simply the purchase of a new device or the implementation of a new password procedure, but rather an ongoing culture within the organization that reenforces security awareness and security protocols. Information and computer security must be a part of the everyday working culture of the organization. The information security plan is not just a written compendium of policies and procedures, but a living document that guides the organizational methodology for providing and improving information security. In this manner, the development of a specific risk analysis plan never really ends. New software and equipment acquisitions, new technologies, and new system requirements demand constant change and "tweaking" of the overall system, and hence, the security of the system as well. Similar to or part of an information resource management (IRM) plan, risk analysis highlights synergism and cooperativeness as well as overall improvement in information exchange through the use of new and varied technology and work processes.[16] This cannot be a haphazard experiment; it must be a well-thought-out plan implemented through a series of phases on a timely basis. Without such objectives in mind, existing IT resources flounder and security breaches proliferate. It should go without saying that constant training improves security knowledge and engenders security awareness within an organization. Training must accompany the development of any risk analysis or information security plan.

Executives must also be aware of a growing problem existing within information system security. Most executives are not highly information and computer technology literate. As such, they must rely on the technical advice and expertise of subordinates. This situation makes the executive vulnerable to "information security elites." Recognized and identified by a number of scholars during the technology boom of the 1980s, information security elites often gain control over others (influence) and resist control by supervisors.[17] This is often accomplished by occupying key positions whose competencies are essential to the overall success of the organization. In some cases, executives are almost held "hostage" by those who have the niche technical knowledge to understand specific information security systems. Information is critically important to an organization. Individual managers and personnel must have immediate access to secure and correct data as well as communication systems that link them to a global marketplace. This demand places the highest value on those who can assure both the quality and security of data and the information system. It also creates a potential environment for significant security loss and abuse. Who is monitoring those in charge of information security? For this reason, external reviews have significant advantages over internal assessments, particularly in the area of risk analysis.

Threats

The second important aspect of risk analysis is to identify the threats facing an organization. As we have already learned, the single largest threat to an organization and its information security is from within. Many times, organizations suffer from key individuals intentionally stealing information or corrupting files. The vulnerability of the organization is extreme and as such, so is the loss. Additionally, in many instance of information security breaches from within, there is virtually no detection of an incident that has occurred. Many times, information is accessed, altered, stolen, or sabotaged without the organizational victim's knowledge—either the crime is covered up through the use of special programs or simply not detected in an audit.

Other than routine personnel and employment checks, incorporating solid hiring practices, and constant monitoring, very little can be accomplished to eliminate totally this type of threat. The most pernicious part of this threat is that it invariably leads executives not to trust their subordinates. It takes just one relatively minor problem from within for an executive to realize just how vulnerable the organization really is from this type of attack. Paranoia can become a problem; the breakdown of trust between executives and managers causes other significant personnel problems. Once again, frank awareness and training can help to instill the type of organizational culture required in today's information society.

Formal risk analysis also categorizes external threats with great detail and elaborate terms, especially after the events of September 11, 2001. Terrorism, sabotage, espionage, and criminal theft are real and comprise a bulk of the identified threats to an organization. Just as dangerous (and threatening) are the age-old issues presented by natural disasters, hurricanes, tornadoes, and earthquakes. Effective risk analysis should cover these types of standard threats as well. Interestingly, preparing for natural disasters often provides the type of secure information environment that thwarts insider problems and external attacks by people.

We are concerned primarily with risks and vulnerabilities to information systems and, as such, will focus our discussion pertaining to problems associated with these types of systems. These are usually summarized in terms of threats to information: integrity, authenticity, confidentiality, and availability. Threats to integrity are threats that actually alter data. Adding, moving, and deleting all change the integrity of data. These actions are also legitimate uses of data. The risk is that an unauthorized or unintentional action will cause a threat to integrity. To make matters more difficult, threats to integrity are not limited to malicious actions. Unintentional alteration (e.g., deleting a useful file) is far more common than malicious activity. The recycling bin found in Microsoft™ systems is a risk management tool to avoid such unintentional deletions. It trades hard drive space and annoying pop-up dialogs, asking you to be sure before you delete, for a second chance to recover a file.

QUICK FACTS

Computer experts have long recognized that it is possible to make a computer completely secure. The steps are as follows: (1) unplug the network cable, (2) encrypt the data with strong encryption, (3) delete the encryption key and forget the password, (4) unplug the power, (5) lock the computer in a vault, and finally, (6) cover the vault with concrete. This security procedure also makes the computer perfectly useless. For an asset to be worth protecting, it must have value. Most assets have value in the work they do for the organization.

Authenticity is a more subtle concept, but it is related to integrity. In these terms, authenticity is the ability to trust the integrity of data. In broader terms, authenticity is the justified ability to trust. Data that cannot be verified or trusted are less useful than authenticated data, if not completely useless. Furthermore, if an intruder is detected in the network, data may have perfect integrity (i.e., be unaltered), but if authenticity cannot be established, the organization cannot verify that fact. The data may as well be altered.

Confidentiality acknowledges that some information is more valuable if it is not publicly available. Confidentiality is treated more extensively in the section on encryption (below).

The final broad category of threat to information is availability. A denial-of-service attack can make information unavailable, but so can overly rigid security policies. What is the difference to the legitimate user who needs the information? Information systems exist to store, manipulate, and utilize data. When data are unavailable, the system's fundamental purpose is disturbed. Each of these categories of threat must be balanced against each other in an attempt to manage risk.

Cost-Effective Security

Risk management is predicated on the rational calculation of potential damage against certain damage of nonmission-related expenditure. The concept of risk management acknowledges that while it may be possible to virtually eliminate all risks, the resources expended to do so would greatly outweigh the potential gains.

With this in mind, computer security experts seek to optimize the balance between the intended function of the information asset (network, computer, etc.) and securing the asset from risk. Many strategies of risk management overlap. For example, protecting a system from natural disaster by maintaining a decentralized network also protects the system from local network outages or denial-of-service attacks on a single point of failure.

SECURITY TECHNOLOGIES

The primary purposes of risk analysis are to identify threats and then to provide recommendations to address or mitigate these threats. Concerning information systems and technologies, the focus has historically been on protecting individual components, such as software, hardware, and connected devices. While a hard drive can be replaced, the information contained on the hard drive may be irreplaceable, and its loss may be catastrophic to an organization. Here, more than in almost any other area of risk analysis and information security, an ounce of prevention is truly worth a pound of cure! Coupled with solid personnel hiring practices and an aware organizational culture, the following security technologies provide a sound base for information systems and networks.[18]

BACKUPS

Backups are the single most important security measure a company or individual can take. As noted above, most of the value of an information system lies in its information. In the event that threats to integrity, authenticity, or availability cannot be prevented, the information can survive risk actualization if a backup copy exists in a safe location. A backup is a copy of data. If data are lost, destroyed, or altered, the backup may provide the only way to recover the data. If there is reason to suspect that the integrity of the data was compromised, a secure backup provides a basis of comparison. If the suspect data match the backup (plus any expected changes), integrity has been restored. If alteration is evident, then the harm from compromised data has been isolated.

Mission-critical data (data that cannot be lost) is often protected with an instantaneous backup as it is stored. A device called a redundant array of independent disks (RAID) saves the data to two or more hard drives at once (depending on the level of RAID configured), making failure of a single drive less damaging.[19] Regardless of the RAID configuration (typically RAID 1 through RAID 5), regular backups are also necessary to protect against alteration or RAID hardware failure.

Wireless Networks and Security

With the emergence of laptop and mobile computing has come the growth of wireless Internet access points, accessible by Wi-Fi connections. Wi-Fi connections are often synonymous with wireless local area networks, where machines can be connected to this network through the use of wireless network adapter cards.[20] Wireless networks are an especially vulnerable part of a network, as they can allow individuals inside of a network boundary if they are not secured. Thus, there are several steps recommended to secure wireless networks. Specifically, wireless routers and connections must be secured through the use of an encryption protocol Wi-Fi protected access (WPA).[21] These tools help to reduce the likelihood of theft of service or unintended access, as individuals will be unable to gain access to the network without the proper passphrase or network key. Wireless signal beacons that make individuals aware of the presence of a network can also be turned off. This will reduce the likelihood of individuals who attempt to compromise the network. There are also protocols that enable wireless routers to allow only known machines to access the network. This is accomplished through media access control, or MAC, address filtering where the unique MAC address of each machine is kept on file, and those MAC addresses that are not recognized are unable to connect to the network.[22] Sensitive information and databases must also be secured and kept off of the wireless network in order to minimize the likelihood of an intruder gaining access. It is important to note, however, that wireless access points are extremely vulnerable to attacks, thus they can be a significant liability to network security.[23]

Firewalls

Another way individuals and organizations can protect their computer networks is by using firewalls. A firewall is a device or software that acts as a checkpoint between a network or stand-alone computer and the Internet. A firewall checks all data coming in and going out. If the data do not fit strict rules, they do not go through. In the past, firewalls were not widely used, since they could significantly reduce access from the protected network to the outside world. Firewalls have since improved greatly and are now relatively fast and easily configured by the user. Software development, combined with rapidly increasing computer-based crime occurring through interconnected networks, has led to the widespread use of firewalls.

A firewall is a tool to be used as part of a security strategy. It cannot protect a user from all threats. In fact, firewalls are a classic example of risk analysis. If the rules set in a firewall are too restrictive (i.e., more secure), then normal network functions may

---

BOX 14.1

Case Study in Risk Analysis—Backup Schedules

Although there is no rule as to how often backups should be created, a good rule of thumb is to consider how much of the data you can afford to reproduce. When you exceed that point, create a backup. For example, a company pays people to enter data. A backup system capable of handling their demands costs $12,000. They have 120 employees making $10 per hour. They create a backup every 10 hours 120 × 10 × 10 = 12,000). The benefit is that they only pay for the backup system once, with small recurring costs for tape and a portion of an administrator's time. If they recover data from a 10-hour shift once, the system has paid for itself. If they suspect an intruder has tampered with the data, they can simply compare the data to a backup and restore the good data if necessary.

be impaired. Such impairment may make it impossible for users to conduct business—the whole reason for the network in the first place. If the firewall rule set is not restrictive enough, it may expose the network to an intruder. This critical balance is the primary problem with firewalls. A special administrator is often necessary for large corporate firewalls. This administrator constantly balances security versus business efficiency to configure the firewall rule set. New applications or new work zones force new rules for the firewall. For example, a sales force in the field may need access to the corporate network. The firewall must allow these users to penetrate the network while excluding unknown users. One solution (see below under "Encryption") is to allow a virtual private network (VPN) using encrypted data. Many early VPNs had difficulty penetrating firewalls because the firewall could not read the data headers (directions on how to deliver the data).

PERIMETER AND HOST-BASED FIREWALLS   The standard, corporate Internet firewall places a single barrier between the internal network and potential attackers. Servers that require public access (e.g., Web servers or mail servers) are placed outside the firewall to minimize penetration from the outside. Such servers, called "bastion" servers, have their own security measures. Like the curtain wall of a medieval castle, the firewall protects the interior, while towers, or bastions, provide hard defense points for contact with a threatening environment. This configuration places all of the defenses at the perimeter. If a malicious user attacked the network from within the "secure" area, there are no defenses. On the other hand, a single dedicated firewall can be built to handle a large volume of traffic without slowing the network.

A second layer of security can be provided with host-resident firewalls installed on machines within the secure perimeter. Host-resident firewalls are software programs installed on a computer. Clearly, there is an additional burden on every computer running such a program. There is also an additional cost for software and burden in administering host-resident firewalls. There is no requirement that all computers within a perimeter have a host-resident firewall. Particular resources within the secure perimeter may require additional protection. Using both types of firewall allows fine-grained control over network security. This means greater flexibility to manage risks. For example, a perimeter firewall might have to allow traffic into the perimeter due to use needs, but a host-resident wall could restrict such traffic on all computers except those that need access. Additionally, antivirus programs and other protective software should be installed on machines as a further layer of protection against attack.

PACKET FILTERING   One of the most basic functions of a firewall is to block certain traffic that may be harmful. One of the protocols that run the Internet, transmission control protocol and Internet protocol (TCP/IP), assigns numbers to computers called Internet protocol addresses (IP addresses). TCP assigns "ports" to each computer that allows different programs to communicate.[24] Imagine that each computer on the Internet is a hotel. Each hotel has about 65,000 rooms. The IP portion of TCP/IP identifies each hotel with a street address so that traffic can find it (IP address). The TCP portion of TCP/IP assigns room numbers so that traffic can go to the right place. Most of the higher rooms are not regularly used. Packet filtering allows a firewall to block traffic from a known bad location (a scruffy hotel in a bad neighborhood). It also allows the firewall to block traffic to a room that should be unused (which may indicate an unwanted "guest" in the hotel). The addressing information that is absolutely necessary for Internet communication is used to block potential threats. By using a firewall to block unused ports, many security threats can be eliminated. If the filtering rules are too aggressive, beneficial traffic may be blocked. Again, a security policy must carefully weigh the need for legitimate service versus security.

STATEFUL INSPECTION   Stateful inspection relies on another feature of TCP. To travel across the Internet, data are broken into smaller chunks called packets. IP addresses packets to find the right computer using the IP address of that computer. Each IP packet is an independent agent, finding its way across the Internet with the best guess of the shortest route. Sometimes packets take different routes and arrive out of order. These must be reassembled into the proper order before the computer can use them.

In addition to labeling ports, TCP reassembles packets by tracking sessions (a series of exchanges between computers). The TCP portion of each IP packet contains a sequence number that is based on a pseudorandom process negotiated between the two computers communicating in the session. Stateful inspection monitors these sequence numbers and other information to make sure that malicious data do not enter into a stream of legitimate data. This is most frequently done by denying an external attempt to open a session with a computer that is not a server. Packet filtering cannot block all traffic (or else the computer may as well not be connected to the Internet), but stateful inspection can be used to ensure that only information request from within the perimeter can enter.

DEEP PACKET INSPECTION   Deep packet inspection (DPI) is an evolution in IT technology sometimes referred to as the "next generation of firewall technology." While stateful inspection scans the contents of the packet up through the application layer, DPI examines the actual data within the packet. DPI firewalls can disassemble the packet, search for anomalies and predefined criteria, and then make a decision on whether or not to let it through based on the **content**. The software used for DPI is powerful, expensive—and comes with a litany of privacy concerns, as DPI can be used to gather vast amounts of personal information for targeted advertising and surveillance purposes.[25]

NETWORK ADDRESS TRANSLATION (NAT)   Although technically not a security function, many firewalls allow administrators to use special reserved Internet addresses. All the machines inside the perimeter have these special addresses. These special addresses are not allowed on the Internet. To use Internet services, the internal machines start a session with the firewall server. The firewall uses NAT to assign an IP to that session, not to the internal machine. Going back to the hotel analogy, imagine a desk clerk with mailboxes. Data traffic goes to the mailbox and is then delivered to the guest. That way, no junk mail gets through; in this case, junk mail would be specially crafted attacks against an internal computer designed to bypass firewalls. A firewall NAT'ing mitigates these attacks because it moderates all communication from inside to the outside.

AIR GAPS   Air gaps are the ultimate in firewall network protection. An air gap is literally a separation between computers containing nothing but air. That is, the machine is not on the network. Data have to be carried back and forth through the air gap by a person. The benefit to this is that no outsider can ever remotely access the air-gapped machine. The downside is that no one on the inside can reach the air-gapped machine through the network. Air gaps are typically only used with the most sensitive data. Data carried to the air-gapped machine may contain malicious code like a virus, but the air-gapped machine is 100 percent immune to network attacks. Unfortunately many security equipment vendors label devices as air gaps when they actually connect to the network; these are "virtual air gaps." Absolute protection only occurs when there is no electrical connection—virtual air gaps do not fulfill this requirement.

Limitations of Firewalls

Firewalls are powerful and increasingly versatile tools for managing risks on a computer network; however, they are not *the* single solution to network security. Firewalls have to be managed to allow for growth in network function while maintaining the highest level of protection. This requires interaction between the firewall administrator and other users of the network. In large organizations, this interaction is formalized in a security policy. A security policy requires updates as situations change, and it requires auditing to ensure that users and management are complying with the policy. The security policy tells the firewall administrator how to balance risks when configuring the firewall. It also allows the security administrator to plan other layers of security, if necessary, to cover the holes in the firewall made necessary by legitimate network functions.

Firewalls cannot stop improper use of legitimate services. This is why bastion servers are placed outside the secure perimeter of the network. Bastion servers are fully exposed to the Internet, unprotected by firewalls or network filters, and typically hardened against common attacks and vulnerabilities. Servers exist to provide interaction with people and systems outside the company; however, many network attacks exploit flaws in server software to gain unfettered access to the computer running the server software. If the server was inside the firewall, such malicious traffic could enter the secure perimeter. If the server is compromised, then the attacker would have a base of operations to explore the inside network.

Firewalls exist as part of an overall security strategy. They are not magical talismans that protect the network from all harm. Many users believe that the firewall will protect them; however, as we have seen in recent e-mail-based viruses and worms (see Chapter 4), this is not always so. Users surfing the Web from inside a firewall are still vulnerable to exploits written into the Web pages they access. There are remedies for these security risks not handled by firewalls, but they all exist as part of an overall layered security strategy.

Encryption

Bruce Schneier defines cryptography as "the art and science of securing messages."[26] Messages can be any data. Encryption is a technique of securing data by scrambling the data into apparent nonsense, but doing so in such a way that the message can be recovered by a person possessing a secret code called a key. The requirements for a good encryption scheme include protecting the classic elements of computer security discussed above: authenticity, integrity, and confidentiality. Availability is generally not facilitated by encryption. Encrypting data has the inherent effect of confidentiality. This comes into play most often when confidential data must be sent through an insecure medium. An encrypted message (i.e., the scrambled message) can be stored or transmitted to another point with a reasonable expectation of security—even if the medium used to transmit it is not secure (e.g., the Internet). Integrity can be assured through a similar technique called hashing. Hashing produces a unique signature of the original data—like a fingerprint. At the other end of the transmission, a new hash is calculated by the recipient of the data and compared to the sender's hash. If they match, the data have not been altered. A public key/private key system allows a user to authenticate data by matching a key—the only way to decode the data—with a well-known and publicly available key. This form of security is only as good as the secrecy of the key, but it offers a way to authenticate without being physically present (more about public key/private key systems below). Using these three techniques together provides a reasonable expectation that the message is private and unaltered.

To illustrate this process, imagine a check being mailed to a creditor. You create a transaction by filling in an amount to a preformatted check with all of your bank information already on it. You also fill in the receiver's name. You authenticate the instructions to your bank by signing the check. If there is any question as to who wrote the check, your signature can be checked against a signature card you filed when you opened the account. You place the check in an envelope to protect the confidentiality of your transaction. You then turn it over to the U.S. Postal Service and they deliver it. Evidence of tampering should be noticeable by the condition of the envelope. The elements of this transaction are as follows: authenticity—signature; confidentiality—envelope; and integrity—envelope. To conduct the same transaction over the Internet, you face different risks, but you still have tools to assist you.

To illustrate the online process, imagine that instead of writing and mailing a check, you log on to the bill payment section of your creditor's Web site. You enter your confidential bank information. Since you cannot sign a computer screen, you provide information that only you should know—a password. This password serves as your signature.[27] In the same way that your signature was verified by your presence in a bank with identification documents, your password is verified with identifying information when you start to do business with the online entity. Since only information is being exchanged, not a physical object like a signature on paper, confidentiality of your identifying information is imperative. The authenticity of your password is directly related to its confidentiality because anyone with the password would appear to be you. Both this information and the transaction details are protected with encryption. Finally, the integrity of the transaction details is guaranteed with a hash that accompanies the encrypted message. It is possible, although usually pointless, to blindly alter an encrypted message—a process called bit-flipping. A hash calculates a unique mathematical value for a message. When the message reaches its destination and is decrypted, a new hash is calculated. Any alteration of the message contents will cause the hashes not to match. The elements of this transaction are as follows: authenticity—password; confidentiality—encryption; and integrity—hash value. The transaction can be carried by the insecure Internet and retain a reasonable expectation of security.

A "reasonable expectation of security" does not mean absolute security. All encryption can be broken. "If the cost required to break an [encryption technique] is greater than the value of the encrypted data, it is probably safe."[28] The most essential feature of encryption is that scrambled data can be returned to a useful form by the data's intended user and cannot easily be returned to a useful form by others. Again, the concept of risk analysis can be applied to this security technique. The more valuable the information transmitted or the more determined a third party is to intercept the information, the more resources must be devoted to protecting it.

Encryption is used to store passwords on your home computer system and credit card numbers in "online wallets" and to secure e-commerce transactions. Modern encryption *can* be broken, but except for the most basic forms of encryption, like the encryption protecting Windows™ passwords, most criminals would find it immensely easier to look for other methods to get the data. While e-commerce may be protected as it crosses the Internet, credit information is often stored on unsecured computers at the merchant's site. It is important to remember that encrypted e-commerce data are decrypted at the other end. While e-commerce transactions are generally safe, few merchants have devoted the resources to securing their whole computer system.

USING PUBLIC KEY/PRIVATE KEY ENCRYPTION TO ENHANCE CONFIDENTIALITY   A public key and private key are parts of a matched pair of values. That is, they are mathematically related in such a way that no other value could be substituted for one of them. It is also impossible to predict the value of one based on the other. Thus, having access to a public key will not help an attacker (a person attempting to break the encryption). When a message is encrypted with one key, only the other can decrypt it. Thus, having access to a public key will not help an attacker decrypt a message encrypted with the public key. The idea of the key pair is that one key can be freely distributed while not compromising the other. When a key pair is generated, either one may become the public key. That does not need to be determined until it is actually distributed. Finally, having a document encrypted with either one of the keys does not necessarily help an attacker guess the key value used to encrypt it.

Public keys are often registered with a public key authority. Anyone wishing to send a confidential message to the key owner can use the public key to encrypt the message.

The resulting encrypted document can be sent across an insecure channel, like the Internet. The receiver simply uses the private key associated with the well-known public key to decrypt the message.

A malicious user intercepting the encrypted message cannot successfully decrypt the message with the public key.

The process of encrypting a document simply assures the recipient of the confidentiality of the document's contents.[29]

USING DIGITAL SIGNATURES TO ENHANCE AUTHENTICITY AND INTEGRITY   Another application of the public key/private key pair allows a user to authenticate a document with a "digital signature." Digital signatures use a hashing algorithm to create unique numeric value associated with the document. This value has two primary attributes. One, if the unaltered document is hashed again, it will produce the same hash value, and two, if the document is altered in any way, it will not produce the same value if hashed again. The problem with this method is that if the unencrypted original document is intercepted, it can be altered and a new hash value can be calculated based on the altered document and substituted for the old hash value. This means that the hash must be sent through a separate, secure mechanism or it must be cryptographically protected.

This is where the second step of the digital signature comes in. Once the hash value is calculated, it is encrypted with the sender's private key. Recall that having a document encrypted with the private key does not necessarily assist an attacker in trying to break the encryption or guess the key. To authenticate that the person claiming to have sent the message actually sent it, the signature is decrypted with the sender's public key. The sender's public key is known to be associated with the private key supposedly used to encrypt the message. If the signature decrypts properly, then the receiver knows that someone in possession of the supposed sender's private key sent the message; this is assumed to be the supposed sender.[30]

USING ENCRYPTION IN DAILY LIFE   Most users do not directly use tools that provide public key/private key encryption. Pretty Good Privacy (PGP) is one example of a common encryption package. It is commonly used to encrypt e-mail messages. In spite of the relative rarity of such encryption packages, most computer users today use encryption without knowing it. Web browsers have built-in encryption functions. Secure Web pages, such as shop cart checkout pages in e-commerce sites or any other secure information transfer page, use encryption to protect the transaction. This leads to an interesting problem with public key/private key encryption: It is very slow by computer standards. It is fine for small text files or very light graphics, but for wholesale secure transfer of information, it is simply inadequate. Symmetric key encryption is much faster, but it requires both parties to the transaction to have the same key; the key cannot be left unprotected to provide convenient authentication. The solution to this problem uses a hybrid of both symmetric key and public key/private key technology. A temporary symmetric key called a session key is generated for each data transfer "session." It is sent using a public key/private key exchange. The session key is simply information to be encrypted. Once both parties have the key, fast exchange of secure information is possible. As soon as the session is done, the session key can be discarded.

Encryption and hashing can be part of a risk management strategy to reduce threats to data authenticity, integrity, and confidentiality. The particular techniques discussed only indicate the possible uses of encryption. For example, a technology called IPsec (secure Internet protocol) utilizes cryptography to reduce threats to authenticity, integrity, and confidentiality of data as they travels on a network. IPsec is used to create secure cryptographic "tunnels" across the Internet so that eavesdroppers do not know where a packet is going after its next stop or what it contains. Without IPsec or similar measures, information traversing the Internet is vulnerable to even relatively unsophisticated eavesdropping attempts.[31] This and many other uses of cryptographic technology provide options to manage threats.

Password Discipline

The single greatest problem in computer security is password protection. Although there are some basic do's and don'ts, there are also sophisticated software programs that address the issue. Several approaches have been taken, including password-creation software, onetime password generators, and user authentication systems—like biometric devices. There is a variety of software programs that system administrators can use to in order to improve password security. Some programs force users to change their passwords on a regular basis, perhaps every month or few months, or even every week. Other programs automatically create random pronounceable passwords for users, such as "jrk^wud," which is pronounced "jerk wood." The user remembers that the ^ character is between two words. Such pronounceable passwords are subject to dictionary attacks by hackers, are easily remembered by users, and do not relate to user information (such as a child's first name or user Social Security number) that might be easily determined by an intruder. Other programs may force users to incorporate numbers, letters, and symbols into their passwords, making it more difficult to engage in dictionary attacks. When combinations of these protocols are in place, passwords are made even stronger, thereby increasing the overall strength of the network.

QUICK FACTS

As a general rule, the easier a password is for the owner to remember, the easier it is for an attacker to guess. Most Web sites now require a longer password with a mix of uppercase, lowercase, number and special characters. Others require a passphrase of three or more words and numbers, while others require the user to change their password on a monthly basis. These types of requirements may well help keep your private information safe and secure; however, they also place an onerous task on the user to remember the various passwords or passphrases for each site visited. Google released a list of the most common password types; all of which are considered insecure because they are too easy to guess (especially after researching an individual on social media, like Facebook or Twitter), and should be avoided:

- The name of a pet, child, family member, spouse, or significant other
- Anniversary dates and birthdays
- Name of a favorite hobby or sports team
- The word "password" or the numbers "123456" or "111111" or the combination "abc123"
- The words "querty," "master," "login," "welcome," or "starwars"

Sources: Google, Techlicious/Fox Van Allen @techlicious (2013-08-08). "Google Reveals the 10 Worst Password Ideas | TIME.com." Techland.time.com. See also Morgan Slain, "Worst Passwords for 2015." SplashData (January 19, 2016). Available at *https://www.teamsid.com/worst-passwords-2015/*

SECURITY VENDOR TECHNOLOGIES

RSA SecurID, from RSA, The Security Division of EMC, is perhaps the most popular onetime password generator, with over 3 million users in 5,000 organizations worldwide. SecurID identifies and authenticates each individual user on the basis of two factors: (1) something secret that user knows—a memorized personal identification number (PIN)—and (2) something unique that the user physically holds—the SecurID card. Under this system, a computer user, when logging on, first types in his or her PIN. The user may also be given a separate "duress PIN," which he or she would enter to indicate that they are being forced to access their system, and would trigger an alert and/or additional protection. Under normal circumstances, the user types in the number currently displayed on his or her SecurID card, which changes every 60 seconds. Each individual SecurID card is synchronized either with hardware or software on the computer system that the user is attempting to access. The result is a unique access code that is valid only for a particular user during a one-minute time period. Interestingly, in 2011, RSA experienced a three-pronged cyberattack that originated in China. A combination of social engineering and phishing allowed malware to be introduced to its networks; unspecified data were obtained as a result and the company suffered a $66 million loss. Ultimately, that event created an opportunity for software developers to create technology that runs on tablets and smartphones, which may eventually replace the SecurID cards altogether. Vendors Vasco Data Security International and Gemalto NV hold much of the market share as of 2013.[32]

Kerberos is a program developed at MIT by the Athena Project. It is a leading network and data encryption system. Cygnus Support, a Mountain View, California company, has developed Kerberos-based user-authentication software—Cygnus

Network Security (CNS)—that eliminates the need to use clear, unencrypted text passwords on a network. Recently, Kerberos has been updated and configured for use in mobile devices. In this system, an individual user is given an encryption key to encrypt and decrypt Kerberos passwords, log-ins, and other computer system transactions. When this individual wants to access the network, he or she will send a message to the Kerberos server. This computer sends back an encrypted package that can be read only with that user's secret key. This package also includes a temporary encryption key good for only that session on the computer. To prove his or her identity, the user then sends a message coded in the temporary encryption key back to the computer. The Kerberos computer then acknowledges the user's identity by sending a second encrypted message to him or her, which can be decoded only by using the temporary encryption key previously sent to him or her.

Kerberos is just one program that utilizes encryption and password technologies. Many other programs also create encrypted sessions between the user's computer and the destination computer, thus protecting passwords and other sensitive information from cybercriminals and cyberterrorists.

Symantec, the maker of Norton Utilities, is also a world leader in information security technologies. Focusing primarily on Internet security issues, Symantec offers a variety of security monitoring plans, management services, best practices, proactive protection methodologies, and educational services for enterprises and home users. Symantec routinely publishes white papers highlighting security issues, with authors eloquently pointing out that the Internet was developed primarily as an unregulated, open architecture.[33] This is an ideal environment for crime and terrorism where simply developed passwords may not be enough.

New technologies are altering the face of user identification. The use of tools such as digital fingerprint identification, retinal identification, and voice recognition greatly increases the accuracy of user identification, sometimes replacing passwords. In fact, a range of computers from various vendors are including some form of biometrics into the computer system, through the use of built-in cameras or fingerprint scanners. These features increase computer security by linking a user's unique physical attributes (those that do not change or cannot be easily altered) to known passwords or stored encryption keys. Biometrics do not provide absolute security; they make it increasingly difficult for intruders to guess passwords by adding another level of complexity to the password, but not making it harder for the user to remember the password. A retinal scan and a short password are effectively a 10,000- to 20,000-digit password. The longer the password is, the harder it is to guess.

Home Users

Cyberattacks have also focused on the home computer user. For instance, botnets infect and incorporate home computers into a broader network of compromised machines that can be used as a launch point for DDoS attacks, phishing, spam distribution, and theft. For instance, the Zeus Trojan or Zbot attacks in 2013 appeared to have been spread by fake Facebook pages. The Zeus malware infects a personal computer from initial log-in to the Facebook page, and targets information on banks and other financial institutions from the victim's browser. Once the victim logs into his or her financial Web site, the spyware is triggered and steals the login ID, name, Social Security number, address, and the like related to the account.[34] The Zeus Trojan (dubbed the "Eurograbber" because of its focused attacks in Italy, Germany, Spain, and the

Netherlands) has been responsible for infecting millions of personal computers resulting in nearly $50 million in losses to individuals throughout Europe. Like many international attacks, the malware is very stealthy and does not impact the normal operations of the PC (see Figure 14.1). In many cases, the user does not even know his or her PC is infected since the malware bypasses the onboard virus detector. The FBI reported that the Zeus infections were the result of a sophisticated group working out of Eastern Europe with ties to Russian and organized crime cartels (see Chapter 5).[35]

As a result, home users must also take computer security very seriously. As exemplified by the Zeus Trojan, it is important to note that the use of antiviral programs is not enough to provide total protection for a system. Thus, many computers and individuals can be victimized despite the presence and use of antivirus and other protective software programs. Aside from the routine backups and use of antiviral software, home users must periodically conduct maintenance on their machines. Using the analogy of a car, a person buys a car and then performs routine maintenance such as oil changes, brake replacement, tune-ups, and the like as the automobile is used. Similarly, people who purchase new personal computers need to conduct routine maintenance on their machines by updating their antiviral software on a regular basis, checking reports from their operating system Web site, and repairing software glitches through provided "patches" offered by a number of credible sources.

The personal computer is much more like an automobile that needs constant care and upkeep, rather than an appliance like a refrigerator that is simply plugged into the wall and will continue to function without much maintenance. For the most part, this is a user-awareness problem demanding a significant shift in attitude and philosophy on the part of literally billions of home users. Fortunately, all of the major operating system companies (e.g., Microsoft™, Linux™) provide well-developed Web sites that offer the latest information on problems and remedies. Software fixes and patches often require simply a stroke of the key to download a specific file from the Web site. Then too, the Computer Emergency Response Team (CERT®) at Carnegie Mellon University maintains a well-developed Web site that tracks and reports trends in computer viruses.[36] Established in 1988, the CERT® Coordination Center (CERT/CC) is a center of Internet security expertise, located at the Software Engineering Institute, a federally funded research and development center operated by Carnegie Mellon University. This site should be regularly visited by all computer users. In the next section, we look at the evolution of cybercrime and with an eye toward preventing new, sophisticated, multivector attacks impacting not only home users, but also businesses and government.

A RECAP OF THE EVOLUTION OF CYBERATTACKS

As we have already learned, cybercriminals used a variety of cyberattacks to facilitate the expansion of almost every traditional crime, including drug trafficking, black market commerce, money laundering, theft, piracy, stalking, fraud, espionage, and even terrorism. Through the evolution of technology, including programming languages and tools and the propagation of low-cost computers and/or network devised around the world, cybercriminals have identified inherent technical and social vulnerabilities and developed methods for infecting, compromising, and taking over computer systems at the personal, business, and government levels. Cyberattacks have evolved to keep pace with the technology.

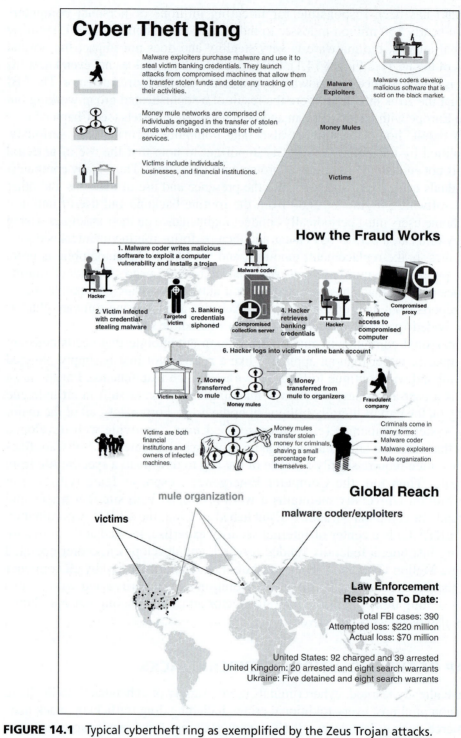

FIGURE 14.1   Typical cybertheft ring as exemplified by the Zeus Trojan attacks.

*Source: http://www.fbi.gov/news/stories/2010/october/cyber-banking-fraud/cyber-banking
-fraud-graphic*

The Early Attacks (1980–2000)

The traditional cyberattacks (see Figure 14.2) during this period were usually conducted from the public library or a university campus (when computers were not yet afford-able), and targeted specific organizations predetermined by the cybercriminal. The cybercriminal's objectives, which are not much different than today's, were access to financial accounts from large banks and access to classified information on govern-ment and military systems. The method of their attack, in the early 1980s, was to look for weaknesses in the perimeter of the network through understanding how the target's internal (private) systems communicate with the public Internet and thereby determin-ing what security controls are in place. If the target's internal systems can talk directly to the Internet (e.g., connecting to Google.com without network address translation), then it can be assumed that there are poor or nonexistent security controls in place to prevent the cybercriminal from attempting to compromise the target's internal systems. The process for determining this is considered, by today's standards, to be very loud, meaning that the cybercriminal is asking the target network a lot of questions (more than a benign Internet system would ask) and some of the questions are noticeably irrelevant to someone knowledgeable with valid business network traffic analysis (e.g., company network or security administrators we are familiar with today). The cybercriminal then launches attacks at the target operating systems (Microsoft Windows, IBM mainframe, etc.) to determine if any number of security weaknesses can be exploited (default passwords, open communication ports, database query capabilities, etc.). At this point, the cybercriminal has spent anywhere from 8 to 24 con-secutive hours attempting to achieve his goal; unless the target is a unsupported legacy system like Windows XP, in which case the system is almost instantly compromised. If the cybercriminal is successful in gaining access to financial accounts, classified data, etc., he or she will now begin stealing data or transferring funds. Seeing poten-tially malicious network traffic, in or out of the company, consistently for this duration of time would be another red flag in today's security conscious world, but during this

FIGURE 14.2 Typical cyberattack through the late 1990s.

time period the network and system administrators were not aware of malicious intent, for the most part, and furthermore did not know what to look for to identify an attack. In fact, it was most often that attacks on financial institutions during this period were identified by company personnel from the accounting/finance departments, not the technology personnel responsible for managing the networks or systems.

In the 1990s, this attack methodology evolved to include considerations for additional systems and technology being readily deployed and used during this period, notably Microsoft e-mail systems and wireless network capabilities. Also note that personal computers were becoming more affordable and most cybercriminals were capable of launching attacks from anywhere that had a phone line. As a result, cybercriminals developed new approaches to gaining access to information, data, and systems through the use of "social engineering" and wireless access point attacks. Wireless access point attacks were not very successful if the device was installed correctly; however, this new technology was not initially understood by consumers and the necessary security controls were not always implemented. Social engineering on the other hand is an attack on human nature and will likely be successful for the foreseeable future, socially persuading a company employee/system user to provide information that will further a cybercriminal's ability to achieve his or her goal (e.g., passwords, technical specification, name of the IT administrator). Social engineering is an aspect of cybercrime that will always evolve and likely never be fully mitigated (see Figure 14.3). In addition to the development of these two new attack vectors, another emerging trend during this period was that company personnel responsible for protecting the organization's computer systems and data were becoming more aware of the cyberthreat, and the industry began to develop and provide security-focused products and training to help protect against the cyberattack. A few of these security counter measures are firewalls and intrusion detection (late 1990s) and intrusion prevention (early 2000s) systems. A Firewall is a rule-based gateway between the public Internet and the company's private internal network. The Firewall can be configured to allow or prevent access into and out of the company network from specific computers, geographic regions of the world, specific

FIGURE 14.3 Evolution of cyberattacks.

users, specific types of network traffic, volume of traffic, access during certain times of the day, etc. These rules can be very granular or very generic; the important point is that there are now rules unknown to the cybercriminal that he must circumvent or defeat in order to achieve his objective. If the firewall is configured correctly and the business allows the technical administrator to define effective rules, the cybercriminal will likely be deterred. If the firewall does not discourage the cybercriminal and he continues his attack on the company, he may be detected by an Intrusion Detection System (IDS). The IDS is designed to passively identify specific types of network traffic that is usually considered anomalous, but through analysis can be determined to be malicious and a possible network attack. In either case, these systems (firewall and IDS) are only as good as the company employees responsible for monitoring their effectiveness and event logs.

The long story shortened, the period of technology development, deployment, and evolution between 1980 and the late 1990s allowed cybercriminals to perpetrate significant crimes mainly because the users of technology, the banks and other corporations, military, and government agencies did not recognize the cyberthreat, did not know how to identify/detect the attack, and/or the technology in itself was often not capable of defending against it (inherent security flaws). This begins to change, and cybersecurity controls and counter measures begin to evolve in the late 1990s, into the year 2000 and even today, in response to the growing threat of cybercrime.

Figure 14.3 suggests that the majority of cyberattack techniques matured very rapidly, but then as they were perfected have changed very little. Social engineering and the development of virus, worm, and other malware will continue to grow and adapt in response to the targeted attention being given to defend against these attack techniques.

Starting in the late 1990s, cybercriminals began to meet effective opposition in their attempts at compromising targeted systems. Cybersecurity technologies, including advancements in firewalls, intrusion detection, intrusion prevention, antivirus programs, and the automation of log monitoring for security specific events, were all becoming more effective in identifying and preventing cybercriminals from achieving their goals. In addition, cybersecurity-focused training organizations and cooperatives started to become more popular and were gaining notoriety across the technology industry; notably Carnegie Mellon's CERT program, which started in 1988 in response to the Morris Worm, is now globally recognized for its cybersecurity research and the SANS Institute has grown to become a global leader in cybersecurity training and certifications. Cooperative programs such as the development of the Cyber Defense Labs on the campus of the University of Texas at Dallas have also emerged as leading research institutes within the cyberworld. The industry appeared to be responding relatively well to the cybercrime threat and the myriad of cyberattack methodologies observed. However, with the new century came vastly new threats.

New Century Attacks (2000 to Present)

Until recently, the threat from cybercriminals and attacks was still underestimated and the success of cybercriminals continued to increase but were relatively marginalized and thwarted by simple awareness and newly developed antivirus, antimalware programs. However, in 2010, things started to change rather dramatically, with new attacks revealing a cooperative and complementary nature between actors and technology. Cybercriminals started working together not only in much more sophisticated

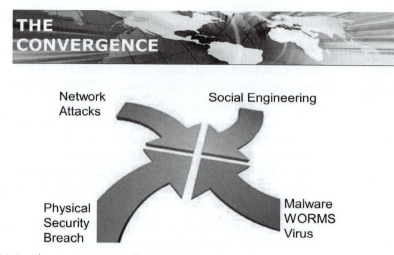

FIGURE 14.4   The convergence of cyber tradecrafts.

manners, but also with multiple new vectors—a convergence of criminal specialties within the cybercrime tradecraft (see Figure 14.4). This convergence was unexpected by computer security specialists and has presented a difficult threat to mitigate given its multilayer attack capabilities, including physical facility breach attacks, logical network and application attacks, human social engineering attacks, and the polymorphic nature (described later in this chapter) of the modern-day malware, including ransomware.

Cybercrime in the new century (2000 to present) has demonstrated rapid response to cybersecurity industry counter measures. Through cooperation and/or coordination between criminals specializing in different attack methodologies, cybercriminals are staying ahead of the industry's ability to detect and prevent the sophistication and complexity of these new attacks (which will continue until industry recognizes the need to converge physical, social, and network focused countermeasures). Where the traditional attacks from the 1980s and 1990s were targeting an organization's network perimeter and e-mail systems, the multivector attacks of today (see Figure 14.5) are highly specialized and highly successful and, by definition, approach a target from all possible angles (multiple vectors). Today's attack vectors include physically accessing target systems within the organization's facility, logically accessing the systems from the Internet or other trusted network (e.g., vendors), compromising an employee's account and accessing the system through his or her workstation, or infecting an internal system with malware that seeks out the target and establishes a foothold from which the cybercriminal can begin his or her attack from within the network. This multifaceted approach has proven effective against the sophistication of today's security countermeasures and the ability to identify and quarantine potentially malicious activity before the cybercriminal has the opportunity to gain access. As a result, cybercriminals have stopped banging on the door like they did in the 1980s; they are now quietly performing reconnaissance of the target organization, its employees, its business partners and vendors, and learning how the target operates. This reconnaissance activity alone can take weeks or months, compared to the 8–24 hours of the aggressive traditional attack methodology we saw 20 years ago. In addition, today's cybercriminals are conducting their own research, not just to find new ways to perpetrate crime, but also to reverse engineer the latest and greatest security countermeasures they are running up against in an effort

FIGURE 14.5 Typical multivector cyberattack today.

to understand how they work and identify ways to circumvent their capabilities. Cybercriminals then publicize their findings via social and/or technical Web sites and organizations. Infiltrating cybersecurity industry manufacturers is the next evolution, in which we believe cybercriminals have or will begin embedding malware at the hardware layer of security devices, including firewalls, antivirus appliances, and the basic building block of all computer systems—the central processing unit (CPU). The process may have already begun, as antivirus programs from the largest and most successful companies (e.g., Symantec Norton Anti-Virus, McAfee Antivirus) only detect 24 percent of the custom malware found on client's systems.[37] In a 2013 case involving *The New York Times*, Symantec's track record was worse still—just 1 out of 45 different pieces of malware planted on the *Times'* systems over the course of three months by Chinese hackers was identified, detected, and quarantined.[38]

In additional to the already advanced nature of today's cyberattack, cybercriminals are also extending their target possibilities beyond the brick and mortar of the organization, and are now including every aspect of technology that touches every employee, vendor, and trusted system that the organization has. Cybercriminals will look for every possible avenue to compromise every possible technology that has any possibility of breaching the desired access or even just one step closer. Today's cybercriminals will identify key personnel and perform cyberattacks at their home, set up fake social media profiles (e.g., Facebook or LinkedIn) to build rapport, and perform organizational reconnaissance to identify trusted vendors and suppliers and compromise their network to take advantage of any established trusted relationship. Despite these very successful ancillary attack vectors, the most damaging and successful attacks on an organization still come from someone on the inside—someone who already has access—someone on the inside of the target organization or someone within a trusted vendor or partner.

Figure 14.5 suggests that the multivector attacks perpetrated today consider a variety of possible attack vectors. Cybercriminals will begin with a modified (passive and quiet) traditional approach, in the event that the target organization has poor security controls, and then move on to more elaborate attack vectors, including Internet and social media reconnaissance, to identify organizational relationships and key employees, establishing fake social media profiles to build rapport; e-mailing malware under the guise of a legitimate attachment (e.g., happy hour invitation) resulting in a compromise of the employee's workstation; identifying the home address of key employees and attacking their home wireless networks to infect their work-laptop, which will then infect the organization's network when it is reconnected; identifying suppliers and vendors in the same manner as above in an attempt to compromise their network and leverage the trust between them and the target company; and lastly, though possible at any point during the attack, the cybercriminal may solicit an employee of the target organization and/or an employee of a trusted vendor/supplier to become a paid insider, providing the cybercriminal with direct access to the organization's systems and data. Coupling this new, multivector attack methodology with more sophisticated malware presents significant challenges for computer and cybersecurity specialists in the future.

BOX 14.2

Case Study in Multivector Attacks—TARGET Corporation

TARGET retail stores were hacked in 2013, the result of a multivector attack that included social engineering, malware, and various network attacks. In an analysis paper written by researchers at Virginia Tech University, computer scholars detailed the attacker's approach and tactics. According to the paper, attackers began with identifying companies that provide services to TARGET and began focusing on the heating and air conditioning (HVAC) provider—Fazio Mechanical Services. Fazio was socially engineered through the use of e-mail phishing attacks that contained malware payloads created by the hackers. Specifically, the malware that infected Fazio was designed to give the hackers complete control over the compromised computer systems. Once in control, hackers used Fazio's network connections into TARGET's HVAC systems to pivot their access from Fazio's network into TARGET's network. Hackers soon determined that TARGET did not effectively segment their HVAC network from their Point of Sale (POS) systems and began deploying POS-specific malware called BlackPOS. BlackPOS is designed to scan the memory stores of POS systems and collect all credit card data in real-time. During the collection, hackers began orchestrating their method for siphoning the data out of TARGET. Once sent outside of the TARGET network, hackers began aggregating the estimated 11GB of data on a server in Russia and listing the data for sale. The timeline for this attack began in September 2013 with the Fazio compromise and ended in December 2013 after TARGET identified the breach, informed the FBI and removed the malware infection. It took TARGET three days to begin alerting the breach, unfortunately it took TARGET security personnel an additional three days to respond to those security alerts; the six-day lag cost TARGET millions of dollars in direct loss and an unestimateable amount of bad public exposure.

Source: Xiaokui Shi, Ke Tian, Andrew Ciambrone, Danfeng Yao, "Breaking the Target: An Analysis of Target Data Breach and Lessons Learned," Department of Computer Science, Virginia Tech University, January 17, 2018, *https://arxiv.org/pdf/1701.04940.pdf*

Summary

We live in the "third wave" of the information society, and undoubtedly, abuses in information security resulting in computer crime and cyberterrorism will only grow in the future. Unfortunately, the losses suffered directly from these types of abuses may be only a part of overall economic devastation facing organizations. Indeed, the civil litigation resulting from the loss of privacy, denial or loss of service from partner-type corporations, and loss of reputation and key executives may comprise a much more lasting and severe economic loss to victims of computer crime and cyberterrorism. In addition, the individual committing these attacks will no longer be the relatively uneducated "crook" of the past. He or she may well be a very sophisticated criminal, a greedy inside employee, a highly motivated terrorist, or the *agent provocateur* from a rogue government. To be sure, the attacker will be attuned to the intricacies of mobile devices, Web applications, computer databases and the means to defeat information security systems within closed networks and open architecture systems like the Internet.

Risk analysis offers a continual strategy to assess and evaluate current systems and potential threats. The recommendations offered by risk analysis exercises often focus on the development of an aware organizational culture as well as the use of various security technologies: backup and redundant file systems, firewalls, encryption, and the use of passwords. Developing such programs only offers a first line of defense, as the computer hacker, vandal, or cyberterrorist is just one step behind in his or her ability to defeat the latest security measure. Information system security must be flexible, dynamic, and ever improving, characterized by an organizational culture that not only appreciates the issues associated with information security, but encourages and supports the types of work processes, upfront expenses, and awareness training consistent with change. There are no guarantees or immunities; security is not absolute and must be applied in layers.

Review Questions

1. What are the major principles of risk analysis? List the common steps in developing a risk analysis strategy.
2. Define the following terms in relation to information security: integrity, authenticity, confidentiality, and availability.
3. What is a firewall? Identify and explain some of the functions of a firewall.
4. What is TCP/IP?
5. What are the limitations of a firewall?
6. What is encryption and hashing, and how are they used to secure data and information?
7. How does a digital signature enhance authenticity and integrity of data?
8. How are new security technologies altering the face of user identification?

Critical Thinking Exercises

1. Go to www.WireShark.org and download the wireshark packet analysis tool. To determine which version to download, go to Control Panel, System, then About; system type will be either 32-bit or 64-bit. Once downloaded and installed, go to YouTube.com and view the packet analysis tutorial—https://youtu.be/r0l_54thSYU. What is a network protocol analyzer and why is it useful?

2. Go to http://www.passwordmeter.com/ and determine the strength of various passwords you may use or can think of, note your observations about the effect of constructing password variants. Why is it important to use sophisticated passwords and to change them frequently? Be honest, how many of you have used one of the "worst passwords" listed in this chapter?

Endnotes

1. HOLLINGER, R.C. (1997). *Crime, Deviance, and the Computer.* Brookfield, VT: Dartmouth Publishing Company.
2. LEVY, S. (1984). *Hackers: Heroes of the Computer Revolution.* New York: Dell Publishing; HAFNER, K. and LYON, M. (1996). *Where Wizards Stay Up Late: The Origins of the Internet.* New York: Touchstone.
3. A fire in the data center was the ultimate disaster. Spraying water onto running computers would destroy them as surely as fires. A "dry" chemical called Halon™ and later CO_2 fire suppression systems were, and still are, used to protect data centers.
4. Computers generate large amounts of heat. Heat adversely affects the operation of computers when it builds up. Even the earliest computer required massive refrigeration systems and special floor-vent air conditioning systems. Failure of the air conditioner meant failure of the computer.
5. BLOOMBECKER, B. (1990). *Spectacular Computer Crimes: What They Are and How They Cost American Business Half a Billion Dollars a Year.* Homewood, IL: Dow Jones-Irwin; PARKER, D.B. (1976). *Crime by Computer.* New York: Scribner.
6. LEVY, *Hackers.*

7. LOPER, D.K. (2000). "The Criminology of Computer Hackers: A Qualitative and Quantitative Analysis." *Dissertation Abstracts International* 61(8): AAT 9985422.

8. HAFNER, K. and MARKOFF, J. (1991). *Cyberpunk: Outlaws and Hackers on the Computer Frontier.* New York: Touchstone; SLATALLA, M. and QUITTNER, J. (1995). *Masters of Deception: The Gang that Ruled Cyberspace.* New York: HarperCollins Publishers; LITTMAN, J. and DONALD, R. (1997). *The Watchman: The Twisted Life and Crimes of Serial Hacker Kevin Poulsen.* Boston, MA: Little, Brown and Company; LITTMAN, J. (1996). *The Fugitive Game: Online with Kevin Mitnick.* New York: Little, Brown and Company; MUNGO, J. and CLOUGH, S. (1992). *Approaching Zero: The Extraordinary Underworld of Hackers, Phreakers, Virus Writers, and Keyboard Criminals.* New York: Random House.

9. SLATALLA and QUITTNER, *Masters of Deception.*

10. HOLLINGER, R.C. and LANZA-KADUCE, L. (1988). "The Process of Criminalization: The Case of Computer Crime Laws." *Criminology* 26: 101–126.

11. HAFNER and LYONS, *Where Wizards Stay Up Late.*

12. COMER, D.E. (1997). *The Internet Book,* 2nd ed. Upper Saddle River, NJ: Prentice Hall Inc.; BAASE, S. (2003). *A Gift of Fire: Social, Legal, and Ethical Issues in Computing,* 2nd ed. Upper Saddle River, NJ: Prentice Hall Inc.

13. HOWARD, J.D. (1997). "An Analysis of Security Incidents on the Internet 1989–1995." Doctoral dissertation, Carnegie Mellon University. Retrieved July 13, 1999, from *http://www.cert.org/research/JHThesis/;* LOTTOR, M. (January 1992). *Internet Growth (1981–1991)* (Request for Comments 1296). Menlo Park, CA: SRI. Retrieved July 13, 1999, from *http://www.nw.com/zone/rfc1296.txt*

14. HAFNER, K. (2001). *The Well: A Story of Love, Death and Real Life in the Seminal Online Community.* New York: Carroll & Graf.

15. Free Software Foundation. (2001). *Why We Exist.* Retrieved March 15, 2001, from *http://www.gnu.org/philosophy/philosophy.html*

16. The concept of an IRM plan was first introduced in the 1980s, as network systems first emerged. See CORBIN, D. (May 1988). "Strategic IRM Plan: User Involvement Spells Success." *Journal of Systems Management* 39(5): 12–16.

17. See KRAEMER, J. and DANZIGER, K. (January/February 1984). "Computers and Control in the Work Environment." *Public Administration Review* 44: 32–42; TAYLOR, R.W. (1989). "Managing Police Information." In D.J. KENNEY (ed.), *Police and Policing: Contemporary Readings.* New York: Praeger Press.

18. Much of this section has been adapted from TAYLOR, R.W. and LOPER, D.K. (2003). "Computer Crime." In C.R. SWANSON, N. CHAMELIN, and L. TERRITO (eds.), *Criminal Investigation,* 8th ed. New York: McGraw-Hill; SWANSON, C.R., CHAMELIN, N., TERRITO, L., and TAYLOR, R. (2009). *Criminal Investigation,* 10th ed. New York: McGraw-Hill.

19. RAID comes in many schemes. For other RAID configurations, see *http://www.whatis.com*

20. VACCA, J.R. (2006). *Guide to Wireless Network Security.* New York: Springer.

21. *Ibid.*

22. *Ibid.*

23. *Ibid.*

24. STEVENS, W.R. (1994). *TCP/IP Illustrated: The Protocols* (Vol. 1). New York: Addison-Wesley.

25. WAWARO, ALEX. (2012). "What Is Deep Packet Inspection?" *PC World.* Retrieved August 2, 2013, from *http://www.pcworld.com/article/249137/what_is_deep_packet_inspection.html*

26. SCHNEIER, B. (1996). *Applied Cryptography: Protocols, Algorithms, and Source Code in C,* 2nd ed. New York: John Wiley & Sons.

27. There are many other methods of online authentication, including third-party trust-based relationships, token-based authentication, and challenge hand-shake mechanisms, but simple passwords (preshared secrets) illustrate this point well enough.

28. SCHNEIER, *Applied Cryptography.*

29. *Ibid.*

30. *Ibid.*

31. KAUFMAN, E. and NEWMAN, A. (1999). *Implementing IPsec: Making Security Work on VPNs, Intranets, and Extranets.* New York: John Wiley & Sons Inc.

32. KHARIF, O. (2013). *EMC Losing Ground as Smartphones Displace RSA Tokens.* Bloomberg.com. Retrieved August 6, 2013, from *http://www.bloomberg.com/news/2013-03-27/emc-losing-ground-as-smartphones-displace-rsa-tokens.html*

33. GORDON, S. and FORD, R. (2003). "Cyberterrorism?" A white paper distributed by Symantec Corporation, Cupertino, California.

34. WESTERVELT, R. (May 24, 2013). "Zeus Malware Attacks Increase, Steals Account Credentials." *CRN.* See *http://www.crn.com/240155557/printablearticle.htm*

35. PERLROTH, N. (June 3, 2013). "Malware That Drains Your Bank Account Thriving on Facebook." *The New York Times.* See *http://bits.blogs.nytimes.com/2013/06/03/malware-that-drains-your-bank-account-thriving-on-facebook/?_r=0;* Federal Bureau of Investigation (October 1, 2010). Cyber Banking Fraud. See *http://www.fbi.gov/news/stories/2010/october/cyber-banking-fraud/cyber-banking-fraud*

36. See: *www.cert.org*

37. GREENBERG, A. (January 31, 2013). "Symantec Gets a Black Eye in Chines Hack of the New York Times." *Forbes.* See *http://www.forbes.com/sites/andygreenberg/2013/01/31/symantec-gets-a-black-eye-in-chinese-hack-of-new-york-times/*

38. *Ibid.*

Cyber Crime and Terrorism
A Forecast of Trends and Policy Implications[1]

CHAPTER OBJECTIVES

After completing this chapter, you should be able to

- Identify the future trends and issues the criminal justice system will have to contend with regarding cyber crime and cyber terrorism.

- Identify major high-technology "big data" trends

- Identify emerging cyberthreat or digital threat trends

- Discuss the areas of computer crime victimization that are growing in prevalence, magnitude, and frequency of occurrence.

- Describe the impact that cyber crimes and cyber terrorism are likely to have in the future.

- Identify and understand the eight general forecasts that experts believe are likely to occur in the area of computer crime.

- Understand what response the criminal justice system and other governmental agencies should adopt to deal with future issues in cyber crime and cyber terrorism.

THE IMPACT OF CYBER CRIME

Throughout this text, the authors have noted the significant problem of cyber crime and cyber terrorism, the motives and actors involved, and diverse agencies tasked with investigation and prosecution of these offenses. Taking this body of knowledge as a whole, it is important to consider how attacks and exploits in the digital realm will manifest themselves and what will constitute cyber crime in the future. This vision is highly dependent on the ways that computer technology shifts and changes with time as well as what constitutes a statutory crime in the future. For instance, federal law still holds that possession of marijuana on federal property remains a felony, and in Florida, for example, holding any amount of marijuana was a felony in the 1960s, but today it is only a misdemeanor for the possession of 20 grams or less (FL Criminal Code § 893.13(h)3).[2] In Colorado the possession of one ounce or less of marijuana was decriminalized in 1975 (CO Constitution Article XVIII, § 166(3).[3] More recently several other states (e.g., Oregon, Washington, and Alaska) have followed suit. On the Dark Web, marijuana and many other drugs are readily available (see Chapter 9). Given the steady increase of cyber crime since the 1970s and its pervasiveness today it is difficult to predict how laws may change in the future. What is clear and easy to forecast, is that cyber crime will continue to escalate and become more virulent than it is today.

Specifically, the hyperevolution of technology and networking that fuels e-commerce and communications are quickly co-opted or corrupted by cybercriminals. For example, the growth of wireless local area networks (WLANs) has not only increased mobile computing but also made networks easier to penetrate by outsiders. As noted in Chapter 4, hackers engage in war driving, where persons drive through a community with a wireless network card in a laptop computer activated in order to detect the presence of a wireless network. The "war drivers" then attempt to access the network—often successfully—and use this as a portal to the Internet. Less scrupulous users will also attempt to penetrate the network's computers—essentially a "drive-by hacking." Interestingly, wireless networks are fairly easy to penetrate because they are frequently "open" with no security, apparently to make it easier for the network's users; of course, this makes it easier for the intruder also.

Another technological trend is the increased availability of wireless microintegrated and multifunction devices that have increased storage and networking capacity. The most common illustrations of this are the integrated wireless telephone (i.e., smartphone) and tablets with full Internet connectivity capability. Given the types of information often kept in smartphones and tablets—ranging from credit card numbers to passwords to Social Security numbers and various types of account and financial information—the ability to access this information using a combination of hacking and phreaking skills within the device's operating system by intruders is a threat to be reckoned with. These devices also provide mobile attack platforms, as they can download applications and utilities that can be used to engage in hacking. For example, the Apple iPad has Internet connectivity and supports a variety of hacker tools, making it an excellent device to engage in covert mobile hacking from a coffee shop or private network. The presence of these devices, integrated with WLANs and combined with the growth of e-commerce and e-government, makes the probability of technological criminality even more pervasive.

Finally, there is a significant growth in the number of home computers using broadband access to the Internet. Generally speaking, whenever these computers are booted, they are connected to the Web, whether being used or not by the owner. Moreover, home computers are less likely to have security (such as a firewall), or if they have security, it is usually a form that is easier to penetrate. Hackers, using port scanners, can identify computers connected to the Web and can conceivably access personal and financial information. If, for example, a person manages his or her banking account and pays bills using a program such as QuickBooks, then the intruder could easily access those files and obtain a significant amount of information that could be used in frauds or other forms of identity theft. Essentially, the growth in capacity, speed, and ease of computerization and networking will also contribute to the speed of exploitation by offenders. The brief history of computer crime has shown that offenders are faster and more adaptable than law enforcement in using the technology.

With this in mind, this chapter will consider and explore the trends, needs, and issues related to cybercrime and terror in the future through the use of forecasts. The forecasts provided here were developed using inductive logic based on existing knowledge and trends within computer crime, criminal justice, and national security. Two important limitations to the forecasts are the lack of empirical data and the inability to be precise in anticipating incidents of computer crime. Forecasts of behavior—like weather forecasts—often lack pinpoint precision, but they can help prepare a response and minimize damage from a phenomenon. Using the small, but growing, knowledge of the incidence, methods, dispersion, character, and trends of computer crime, we can begin to make some assertions as to the future of computer crime and terror. The discussion provided here is not, however, based on scientifically categorized data, methodological controls, or rigorous analysis to explore the validity of typological constructs. In essence, the literature contains logical speculation and assumptions, but virtually no data or information collected and analyzed under controlled methods. It should be noted that these limitations are recognized by the authors, as is the problem of poor data sources and the lack of a uniform reporting system for computer-related crimes.

Other important factors limit the ability to analyze or collect valid and reliable quantitative data. One significant factor is the difficulty—and sometimes impossibility—of determining when a computer crime has occurred, for example, the undetected incursion of a system by a cracker or the undetected theft of intellectual property by an employee who copies files to removable media. Another factor is the tendency of businesses to not report computer-related crimes that have been detected. There are several reasons for this: In some cases, businesses view this simply as a "loss" or even an expense, but not a crime. In other cases, businesses hold the perspective that offenders will not be caught due to the difficulty of investigation, thus reporting the crime would be "wasted effort." Perhaps, however, one of the more fundamental reasons is the fear that publicity of computer crime victimization would undermine the confidence of the company's clients.[4]

BOX 15.1

Big Data Trends

Tableau is a Seattle-based software developer, in business since 2003. Highly regarded for its leading-edge work; Tableau is a recognized leader in the realm of data visualization, mapping techniques (plots latitude and longitude coordinates), geocoding, and more. Its origins trace to the late 1990s at Stanford University's Computer Science Department.

Accordingly, high technology's major breakthrough in 2016 was *big data*. Tableau recently projected several intriguing near-term big data trends that hold implications of potential significant consequences for law enforcement. The most powerful, and arguably the most significant trend is that big data will become faster and more approachable, hence, speeding up the development and use of an analytic software program called Hadoop.

Big Data is a term that evolved from an earlier phrase "information explosion" first used in 1941. In 1983, following a series of enabling and enhancing discoveries, "Tracking the Flow of Information," was published by *Science* magazine. It noted that by 1977 point-to-point media (think social media giants Facebook, Google, and Twitter) were growing more rapidly than broadcasting. And, by 1996 digital storage had

become more cost-effective for storing data than paper. In 1998 a conference paper "Big Data … and the Next Wave of Infrastress" suggested data and information were/are growing at "exponential rates." Information systems of massive volumes of data storage, both structured and unstructured, continue to emerge. The market's demand for fast analytical capabilities will not cease; it will grow. Government and business will seek this capability.

The only noted sticking point in this discussion, however, is that the vast majority of such analytics will be deemed to require "national security classification" by government and proprietary "intellectual property" status by business. Read here the growing demand for strong encryption; and issue that is already plaguing federal and state law enforcement digital investigations.

An urban legend holds that in reply to a reporter's question: Why do you rob banks? The infamous 1940s–1950s bank robber Willie Sutton reputedly replied: "That's where the money is." In the Information Age, the "money" is the data as foretold nearly three decades ago by futurist Alvin Toffler. But, gathering massive data, in and of itself, is not the significant issue. Rather the more problematic concern is how information is derived from the analyzed "big data." This trend strongly suggests that there will soon be a significant shift from *Single-Scene* to two other types of digital investigations: *Multiple-Scene* and *Network Crime Scenes* (see Chapter 12). This transference is likely to occur in the present decade.

Law enforcement administrators and cybercrime investigators would be well advised to heed the words of Professor Richard Hamming of the Naval Postgraduate School, "The purpose of computing is insight, not number." Implicit in his pithy statement is the notion that most organizations are better at storing than interpreting what they have collected and stored. Law enforcement has been especially excellent at collecting data, but as for analyzing their records and files; not so much, and that is where Hadoop steps-in.

Hadoop is the distributed computing and processing portion of a Web search engine called *Nutch,* originally developed in 2006 and subsequently transferred to Yahoo. Hadoop is an open-source, cross-platform framework for storing massive data and rapidly running multiple applications. In 2008, Yahoo released Hadoop as an open-source technology and it is now maintained by the nonprofit *Apachee Software Foundation*. Hadoop is critically important for several reasons: (1) Hadoop has a unique ability to store and rapidly process massive amounts of many kinds of data, (2) Hadoop offers enhanced computing power, (3) Hadoop is fault tolerant from hardware failure, (4) Hadoop offers flexibility of storing data as is, without the necessity to clean and/or process prior to storage, (5) Hadoop is inherently scalable, enabling growth by adding nodes, and most importantly, (6) Hadoop is low cost due to being open-source; and commodity hardware may be used to store large quantities of data.

One of the more interesting ways Hadoop is being used in the private sector is storage of data in its original or exact format. This should be particularly significant for law enforcement use. For example, managing large scale investigations, such as those involving a large terrorist strike, or an ongoing and sophisticated criminal cartel, or an extensive cyberattack on our infrastructure (e.g., multiple large banks, the national air traffic control system, several large sporting events) that involves multiple (hundreds or thousands) of subjects, persons of interest, victims, and witnesses over an extended period of time (several months or even years) are a perfect landscape for Hadoop.

Clearly, the trend to more involved, more advanced, and more sophisticated criminality has already been witnessed by our country. The message to law enforcement is also crystal clear—we can no longer afford the luxury of "catching-up" to more advanced criminals. We must begin now to prepare to train agents, detectives, and officers that can do a myriad of tasks; from advanced cyber investigations to data analytics relating to sophisticated criminal cartels that may be financially backed by a nation-state, to the analysis of intelligence information that may predict the next terrorist strike on our country.

Sources: Sookhak, M. *et al.* "Dynamic Remote Data Auditing for Securing Big Data Storage in Cloud Computing," *Information Sciences* (February, 2017) 380(20): 101–116, *http://www.sciencedirect.com/science/article/pii/S0020025515006581*; Press, G. "A Very Short History of Big Data," *Forbes*. Retrieved May 9, 2013, from *https://www.forbes.com/sites/gil;press/2013/05/09/a-very-short-history-of-big-data/#aa9161965a18*

Tableau, "Top 10 Big Data Trends for 2017," Seattle, WA: Tableau Software (2017), *https://www.tableau.com/asset/top-10-big-data-trends-2017*

Toffler, A. (1990) PowerShift. New York: Bantam Books; see also: Toffler, A. (1970) Future Shock; Toffler, A. (1980). The Third Wave

SAS (2017). "Bringing the Power of SAS to Hadoop," Cary, NC: SAS, *https://www.sas.com/enus/insights/big-data/hadoop.html*

Apache (2017). "What Is Apache Hadoop?" Houston, TX: Apache, *http://hadoop.apache.org*

Cornish, E. *The Study of the Future* (1977). New York: Routledge, *https://books.google.com'/books/about/The Study of the Future.html?id=UMbyiTSnsDOC*

Cornish, E. (2005). *Futuring*, Bethesda, MD: World Future Society World Future Society, *http://www.wfs.org*

Society of Police Futurists International, *http://www.policefuturists.org*

THE FUTURE OF CYBER CRIME AND CYBER TERRORISM: FORECASTS

Based on the analysis of information collected, eight primary forecasts related to computer crime have been developed for this chapter.

Forecast 1: Computer Crime Will Significantly Impact the Police and Courts

---

FORECAST

The number of offenses reported to the police involving computers and electronic storage media will continue to increase substantially, requiring changing priorities for resource allocation, new training for line officers and investigators, new police specialties, and new knowledge for prosecuting attorneys and judges.

Perhaps a keyword in this forecast is "require." The number of police agencies with a high-tech or computer crime unit has increased significantly over the last few years, but most of these agencies serve large urban populations.[5] In addition, prosecutors and judges are becoming increasingly well versed in computer crime and the unique law and vagaries inherent in these cases. That being said, it is still unknown how well state and local law enforcement agencies are equipped to handle these offenses.

For example, a study of forensic examiners found that they are regularly overworked and experience stress related to their work.[6] In fact, more than half of the individuals contacted felt that they did not have the workforce to complete their tasks at work.[7] The examiners felt that their work would be challenged by others and that there are other ways to accomplish their jobs. Additionally, examiners recognize that they need greater training to keep up with the rapid changes in computer technology.[8] Resources are always in demand within police agencies, but computer crime units appear to suffer disproportionately at this point in time due to the various resources needed to appropriately image and analyze digital evidence.

QUICK FACTS

The Institute for Information Security and Privacy (IISP) at Georgia Tech University recently issued *Emerging Cyber Threats, Trends and Technologies Report for 2017*. In their report, the authors identify the following forecast points:

- **Privacy, Democracy, and Security Square Off:** Those that are willing to give up some privacy and individual freedoms to attain more security in the homeland versus those that wish to maintain our democratic values.
- **Privacy and Technology Are on a Collision Course with No Clear Solution**
- **Insecure E-Voting Systems Emerge, but Crowdsourcing and Open-Source Software May Hold the Promise**
- **Ransonware Is on the Dramatic Rise:** Malware and Ransomware like the "WannaCry" and "Petya-Eternal Blue" exploit of 2017 that hit hundreds of thousands of computers worldwide. The latter Petya ransomware attacked, encrypted, and locked entire hard drives versus individual files. It was also primarily focused in Europe, Ukraine, Russia, and the United States.
- **Global Information Manipulation by Nation-States Is Now Widespread:** The problems of "fake news" become reality. In 2017, CNN retracted a story about President Trump aide Anthony Scaramucci meeting with Russian officials as "fake news." Although the three reporters that wrote the story for CNN were forced to resign, the incident was compounded by a video showing a prominent CNN producer lamenting that the network's Trump-Russia coverage had suffered a significant ratings drop, revealing that news networks were more interested in "ratings than accuracy."

- **Health Care Fraud Takes Off in the Absence of Good Defenses:** Today, health care fraud is one of the largest white-collar crimes toady (in terms of numbers of incidents as well as financial loss to victims).
- **When Trust Is Lost, "Smarts" Are Too:** The future portends rampant attacks on smart devices, such as tablets and cell phones, and most people are not ready for these attacks. Infrastructure attacks will greatly impact cities more than rural areas.
- **Dual-Use Technologies, such as Exploits and Encryption Will Come Under Governmental Scrutiny**
- **Demand for Security Professionals Will Dramatically Rise:** Colleges and universities will adapt to this change relatively rapidly to meet business and governmental demands.

Sources: Lee, W. and B. Rotoloni (2016). "2017: Emerging Cyber Threats, Trends, and Technologies Report," [of the Institute for Information Security and Privacy], Atlanta, GA: Georgia Tech University (September 28). Available at *http://www.iisp.gatech.edu/georgia-tech-releases-2017-outlook-emerging-cyber-threats*

Sherr, I. (2017). "WannaCry Ransomware: Everything You Need to Know," CNet (May 19). Available at *https://www.cnet.com/news/wannacry-wannacrypt-uiwix-ransomware-evervthing-you-need-to-know/*

Paul (2017). "Updated: Fatal Flaw Slows WannaCry Ransomware Spread, but Threats Remain," *The Security Ledger* (May 15). Available at *https://securityledger.com/2017/05/fatal-flaw-slows-wannacry-ransomware-but-threat-remains/*

Kirk, J. (2017). "Post-WannaCry, Microsoft Slams Spy Agency Exploit-Hoarding," *Data Breach* (May 15). Available at *http://www.bankinfosecurity.com/after-wannacry-microsoftcriticizes-spy-agency-practices-a-9918*; Anonymous (2017). "Global Ransomware Attack 'WannaCry' Still Infecting Organizations in 150+ Countries." Available at *http://pages.checkpoint.com/wannacry- ransomware1.html?gclid=CKT4hLOjo9QCFcFDhgodENEE8w*

A reasoned, analytic assessment documenting criminal incidents in a jurisdiction would give meaningful insight on which to make basic decisions. Ideally, a routinized data collection system—perhaps similar to the National Crime Victimization Survey managed by the U.S. Department of Justice, Bureau of Justice Statistics (BJS)—including computer crimes would be a useful planning tool. Such a survey was developed and implemented in the business community in 2005. The Bureau of Justice Statistics conducted the first National Computer Security Survey, drawing 7,818 responses from businesses around the country.[9] This study found that 67 percent of the businesses sampled experienced at least one cybercrime in 2005, with most of the sample experiencing a computer virus. Almost 90 percent of the respondents sustained some form of monetary loss, with most experiencing a loss of $10,000 or more.[10] However, only 15 percent of victimized businesses reported the event to law enforcement agencies. This suggests that businesses are still very unlikely to report a compromise or attack to law enforcement. Furthermore, it is important to consider that less than 25 percent of the businesses contacted actually participated in the survey.[11] Thus, there is a great deal of improvement needed in our understanding of the prevalence and incidence of cybercrime.

More useful, however, would be a system of collecting data on reported cyberoffenses by jurisdiction. This would permit crime analysis for a better understanding of jurisdiction-specific offenses, offenders, and targets. As we have learned with predatory crime, deployment of personnel and resources is most effective when based on crime analysis. There is hope, however, in the National Incident-Based Reporting System (NIBRS), which is a national criminal incident reporting system designed to replace the FBI's Uniform Crime Report (UCR). NIBRS reporting collects data from local law enforcement agencies on each incident reported to police, including persons involved, property taken, weapons and tools used, and other information, which is then aggregated to provide general trend data. There is some value in NIBRS for the assessment of computer crime, as officers can indicate whether a computer is used as an object in the crime and whether offenders used computer equipment to perpetrate the offense. This is a significant step forward for the documentation of computer crime, though it is important to note that this system is not in use in many agencies across the nation. As of 2012, 32 states were certified to provide data to NIBRS, and 3 additional states and the District of Columbia have individual agencies submitting NIBRS data.[12] Approximately 29 percent of the population is covered by NIBRS reporting, representing 27 percent of the nation's reported crime and 43 percent of law enforcement agencies.[13] As a result of its limited coverage, it may be some time before NIBRS data can provide insights into the scope of computer crimes nationwide.

Judicial, prosecutorial, and investigative officials as well as scholars and computer security specialists knowledgeable about cybercrime should perform a comprehensive review of criminal laws and procedure related to the unique character of computer crime. Additionally, hypothesized voids in a jurisdiction's penal code and anticipation of changes that may be required in response to technological evolution need to be conducted continually. Current computer crime laws will become dated and require expansion as greater integration of computers, telecommunications, and entertainment networks occurs. For example, the suicide of Megan Meier demonstrated the ways that computer crime laws may be uniquely applied in prosecutions. Lori Drew, the woman responsible for the creation of the fraudulent MySpace account that sent Megan hurtful messages, was prosecuted and convicted under the Computer Fraud and Abuse Act. Specifically, it was argued that she engaged in an act of unauthorized computer access because she violated the MySpace site's terms of service by creating a false account. Though the jury in this case found Drew guilty, many legal scholars questioned if this was an appropriate use of the law. The judge overturned the conviction ruling that applying the Computer Fraud and Abuse Act to Drew would mean anyone who violated a Web site's terms of service could be found guilty of a crime.[14] The judge reasoned that such an application of the Computer Fraud and Abuse Act **(18 U.S.C. § 1030) passed in 1984 and revised in 1996, changing the term "federal interest computer," with term "protected computer" making it less** unconstitutionally vague.[15] Thus, this is an excellent example of the ways that laws are developed, challenged, and pursued in relation to computer crime.

Similarly, with more databases, information systems, multimedia, and integration software, defining criminal offenses, and even distinguishing what is criminal and what is civil, will become more complex. Among other issues that may need to be reassessed are privacy issues, a redefinition of open records, changes in Freedom of Information law and processes, and new applications of liability law to law enforcement personnel.

New policies are needed to resolve questions of jurisdiction, the expenditure of resources in multijurisdictional investigations of network incursions, and multijurisdictional cooperation. Creative new policy areas must also be explored. For example, should a corporate computer crime victim be responsible for any costs of the investigation if the crime was due, in part, to inadequate computer security?[16] If so, how are these issues decided? Would the criminal justice system be better served if computer crime investigation and prosecution were privatized? Are state or regional computer crime units the best mechanism to deal with this problem? If so, how are they funded, and what are the boundaries of their jurisdiction? These and other policy issues must realistically be considered.

BOX 15.2

Responding to Computer Crime

The following scenario will describe the current typical response of law enforcement to computer crime. A business owner arrives at the office and discovers that locked filing cabinets have been broken into, and some documents have been destroyed and others stolen. The owner, suffering losses from the forced entry, damage, and theft, calls the police, reporting a burglary. A patrol officer responds to take an offense report; a crime scene technician may be called to search for and collect physical evidence. In all likelihood, a burglary detective will conduct a follow-up investigation by reviewing the evidence, interviewing the victim, checking leads from the burglary's *modus operandi*, and perhaps checking with informants. The police have a defined response procedure with personnel fully trained to report and investigate the crime.

Now, assume the same business owner calls the police to report that the office computer has been hacked, and some files have been destroyed and others stolen. What would the police response be? The losses are essentially the same, except that the first crime was physical, the second virtual. In the first case, the burglar may have used a crowbar on the door and the file cabinets; in the second case, the thief used only keystrokes.

When confronted with this scenario, one investigator said that many police departments would probably refer the victim to another agency. The investigator went on to say that he regularly received calls from victims outside of his jurisdiction saying they had been referred by another police department. These cases usually take a lower priority, which is likely to anger the citizen. What has made police agencies willing to respond immediately to a burglary, yet show hesitation and less than a full response to a computer crime? This is clearly inconsistent with the contemporary "customer-oriented" philosophy of community policing. Why should a virtual community be different from a physical community? Several factors apparently exist: Uncertainty of jurisdiction, lack of knowledge about computer crimes generally, and having a perspective that this is not a "real problem" are clear issues. Others include the lack of trained personnel who know the questions to ask and how to process a computer-based crime scene, the lack of knowledge and skill to analyze the computer forensically, and the lack of follow-up resources (such as informants) to "work" the case. While police officials would not consider denying a response to a burglary, they will deny a response to a computer crime.

Training and expertise development obviously go hand in hand. At a basic level, during preservice training related to criminal investigations, police officers need to be trained to regularly look for computers, smartphones, and removable storage media as evidence. They also need to know how to protect and collect cyberevidence as well as the elements of computer crimes and information needed in preparing reports of these offenses. At a more advanced level, training is needed for computer crime investigators—for example, understanding networks, tracing audit trails, dissecting telecommunications systems, tracing wireless transmissions, and associated other technical aspects that may be encountered. Similarly, if a police agency is large enough to have a crime laboratory, it is of sufficient size to warrant a trained computer forensic analyst. Essentially, the model used to investigate and forensically analyze evidence for physical crimes should also be used for virtual crimes. Similarly, judges and prosecutors need to have training on the character and unique aspects of computer crime in order to handle these cases fairly and effectively.

With these aspects of training, necessary expertise will be developed. Police agencies might also consider some changes in personnel management. Is it better to take a trained investigator and teach him/her the technical aspects of computers and networking or to employ a computer expert and teach that person about law, investigation, and criminal case development? Maybe a hybrid model would be better wherein nonsworn computer specialists are hired as in-house technical consultants assigned to computer crime investigations. Another aspect of expertise may lead to computer crime prevention specialists. Since there are clear methods—both technical and behavioral— that can be used to prevent cybercrime, the investment of expertise in this arena may be a functional addition to other crime prevention initiatives. Each jurisdiction must evaluate its needs and follow the avenue that best serves its goals.

Training new personnel and developing new expertise obviously lead to resource allocation issues. In all likelihood, most agencies are not going to be given generous new budget lines to address these issues. Where will the money come from? Realistically, resources will have to be redirected from other departmental programs. Difficult questions of resource redistribution must be undertaken with careful study. In any such redistribution, there are issues that go beyond finances, including "turf," vested interests, and other crime concerns. Changing and rapidly advancing technology also results in the need to keep training up to date, which can be quite costly.

The need to share expertise and resources in computer crime investigations appears inevitable for most law enforcement agencies. This sharing will likely extend beyond the interaction of government agencies and includes the need to work with the private sector. This raises some complicated issues related to the payment of expenses, privacy, and the parameters describing the types of cases and/or circumstances where external agencies and private companies are used. All aspects of these issues need to be fully explored and articulated in mutual aid pacts (where assistance between agencies is exchanged *quid pro quo*) and contracts (where financial reimbursement is provided.)

Forecast 2: Fraud and Identity Theft Will Be the Largest Computer Crime Problem Impacting the Police

---

FORECAST

The largest computer crime problem affecting local law enforcement representing the largest number of victims and the largest monetary loss will be Internet fraud, including fraud via identity theft/fraud.

This forecast should not be interpreted as diminishing other forms of computer crime. In fact, many computer crime cases investigated by local law enforcement are child pornography or exploitation related. However, given the current experiences and trends with e-commerce, online trading and banking, and a virtual buffet of other financial schemes coupled with the growth of personal computing, it appears fraud is the offense most likely to touch the largest number of community members. In 2014, 7 percent of the households in the United States, or about 17.6 million persons, experienced one or more types of identity theft victimization.[17] Two-thirds of these victims report a direct financial loss. The increase in identity theft from 2010 to 2014 was largely attributable to a significant increase in the misuse of existing credit card or bank accounts. This same cause appeared to be a significant factor through 2016.[18] Global financial loss of $21.8 billion due to all types of online fraud (e.g., identity theft, credit/debit card fraud, bank fraud) was reported in 2016.[19] Increasingly, local police agencies will receive complaints on these offenses with the expectation that reporting and an investigation will occur, just as would be the case of a noncomputer crime. As noted previously, most local law enforcement agencies are not able to comprehensively respond to and investigate Internet fraud cases due to the increased likelihood that the offenders reside in another state or nation, the complexity of the investigations, and the personnel resources needed to investigate these offenses.

With home Internet access becoming commonplace and more people using e-commerce resources to buy, sell, and trade money and goods, the probability of Internet fraud and identity theft has increased significantly. In fact, it is common to hear of companies experiencing a mass compromise of data, including customer passwords and credit card information, by computer hackers. The huge volume of data obtained in data breach cases demonstrates that consumers around the world can be affected by fraud through little fault of their own. Furthermore, the growth of carding markets, discussed in Chapter 6, allows computer criminals to buy and sell fraudulently obtained information and illustrates that an individual can become the victim of fraud several times over.[20]

Frauds—and other Internet-based crimes—will increase in the future simply because the massive size of the Internet makes monitoring or spotting potential fraudulent schemes difficult. For example, the recent economic downturn has facilitated opportunities for fraud. The merger of multiple national financial institutions has produced confusion over what company holds an individual's account. As a result, phishers and fraudsters send fraudulent e-mails stating that the consumer needs to provide the acquiring bank with their account information in order to keep the account active.[21] Such threats are not unique, but rather emphasize the ways that the Internet enables fraudsters to dynamically act on changes and world events to victimize consumers.

Even with technological monitoring techniques of keyword targeting, the size and dynamic character of the Internet presents major barriers. These barriers are aggravated by the difficulty of trans-jurisdictional investigations and communications. A fraud scheme targeting Americans, and operated by American criminals, may have a Web site based in a country such as Myanmar, which has virtually no Internet monitoring and only casual relations with U.S. law enforcement authorities. This will hamper investigations, and U.S. authorities can do little except provide warnings to citizens.

Finally, it is relatively easy to create a fraudulent enterprise on the Internet with minimal cost. Even sophisticated malicious software tools can be readily purchased through online black markets to facilitate fraud, as discussed in Chapter 7. As a result, the range of people who can create a virtual fraud is quite broad. Moreover, the inability to readily determine the authenticity of claims or organizations helps further the fraud. Recently, a range of fraudulent e-mails were circulated, claiming to contain tax refunds from the Internal Revenue Service or tracking information from Federal Express or the Postal Service. These schemes caught a number of victims because of the issue of authenticity.[22] This is particularly true when the scheme is related to alleged changes in technology-related businesses, such as Initial Public Offerings (IPOs), new mergers, or new products. Technology businesses and stocks continue to be profitable, which leads many people to feel a sense of urgency to complete a transaction while the opportunity is "hot." As a result, they frequently do not take the time to verify the offer's legitimacy. To further the appearance of legitimacy, the Web site may include fallacious quotes from recognized authorities and untrue statements of affiliations with respected businesses to lend further credence to the scheme's legitimacy.

The inherent character of the Internet and the expansion of the global economy, particularly related to technology issues, are fueling the growth of Internet fraud. The most effective tool for dealing with Internet fraud is prevention. The need to inform consumers of the potential for and character of fraud, notification of newly emerging fraud schemes, and precautions before investing or purchasing over the Internet are among the proactive approaches a local law enforcement agency may pursue. Delivery of this information could be from the police agency's Web page, creation of a listserv that describes newly discovered fraud schemes, and public service announcements. The Federal Trade Commission, FBI, the not-for-profit Anti-Phishing Working Group (APWG), and other entities are working to provide consumers with information to improve awareness of fraud. The significant point to note is that investigating Internet fraud is extraordinarily difficult, with a comparatively low rate of clearance. A comprehensive prevention strategy is the most efficacious approach to the problem.[23]

Forecast 3: Virtual Crimes Will Continue to Rapidly Increase

FORECAST

Virtual crimes against persons will increase at a faster rate compared with past years as a result of the significant expansion in networking, personal computing, and social networking sites. These hybrid crimes, which have coercive characteristics similar to those found in psychological warfare, will require new laws expressly to address the problem and new methodologies for investigation, prevention, and education.

Virtual crimes against persons encompass diverse behaviors; however, the common factors of these behaviors are (1) the use of networking and (2) a manifestation of social–psychological dynamics. Networking is a key factor because this is the medium through which the behavior is facilitated, most frequently by e-mail but also through social networking sites like Facebook, video- and photo-sharing sites, and Web site postings (particularly hate and pedophilia). The social–psychological factors take diverse forms. For example, cyberstalking and threats induce fear, while harassment can induce anger. Cyberbullying can produce depression, embarrassment, shame, or sadness. Hate messages can produce discriminatory behavior, and pedophilia can engender exploitation and intimidation. Interestingly, these behaviors are similar to the common law definition of assault. As a U.S. government report of the problem observed, "Make no mistake: This kind of harassment can be as frightening and as real as being followed and watched in your neighborhood or in your home."[24]

The manifestation of virtual crimes against persons is the product of several factors. For instance, virtual crimes against persons are easy and convenient. The offense may be committed immediately without leaving home, and gratification is instantaneous. The offender may also take action without physically confronting the victim. For instance, a person who posts a mean or hurtful message, picture, or video on a social networking site can harm another person without ever having to physically interact with that person. In turn, they may gain status from people within their virtual social network.

In all likelihood there are people who have a propensity to commit a retaliatory act of some form, but do not because of reluctance to confront another physically. It is therefore probable that some of those people would act on that propensity through networking. In fact, a national study of youth found that children are experiencing greater levels of online harassment, largely from their peers, and are increasingly engaging in harassing behaviors themselves.[25] Thus, the problem of person crimes online is likely to continue to increase.

Just as the offense may be committed without confrontation, it may also be committed with relative anonymity. The anonymity is obviously sought to protect the identity of the offender, but anonymity can add to the victim's fear. There are various techniques that may be used to maintain one's anonymity in networked communications, the easiest of which is sending threatening or harassing e-mail through a Web site that obfuscates the SMTP audit trail.[26] Also contributing to the anonymity of these virtual offenses is the fact that there is no physical evidence of the crime, such as a fingerprint on the paper of a threatening letter or DNA from saliva on an envelope. Neither are there voice nor handwriting specimens from the offender that may be used as evidence. Consequently, developing a criminal case that can meet the burden of proof in court becomes challenging.

One of the factors contributing to the growth of virtual crimes against persons is the increasing loss of privacy that is occurring through online sources. When greater personal information is available about an individual, it is easier for an offender to locate them. Even more problematic is the fact that individuals voluntarily provide details about themselves and their lives through social networking sites. Facebook and other social networking sites are especially popular among young people, and some youth readily share personal information, such as their address or school name with others online.[27] This simplifies the process of monitoring and tracking individuals online and off-line.

Moreover, if an offender provides personal information about the victim in a harassing message—such as a description and license number of the victim's car, a Social Security number, or information about the victim's family—then a cyberassault can become even more frightening. As the prevalence of these crimes increase, they must be analyzed to determine the adequacy of existing law and policy to deal with them effectively. While they may not always produce physical harm, the psychological damage, fear, and anxiety can be debilitating.

On a final note, the likelihood is strong that there will be an increase in "virtual workplace violence." A great deal of physical workplace violence appears to be retaliatory acts toward the organization and/or individuals who are perceived to have "wronged" the offender. It is clearly probable that employees with access to critical databases and/or information systems could vent their retaliation by the destruction or release of those files, as illustrated in the case of Edward Snowden and the National Security Agency. Similarly, harassment and the creation of a hostile work environment can now be accomplished electronically.

Forecast 4: The Threat from Computer Hacker Groups Will Increase

---

FORECAST

Computer hacker groups will continue to emerge in developing countries around the world, increasing the threat of malicious attacks motivated by religion, politics, and money.

The basis of this forecast lies in the increasing penetration of Internet connectivity around the world, coupled with the characteristics of the hacker subculture and the increased access to sophisticated hacker tools. As of July 1, 2016, there are over 3.6 billion Internet users around the world, an increase of more than 1 billion people since 2012 with the greatest number in Asia, Europe, and North America.[28] These continents have a substantial number of developed nations, though developing nations are increasingly gaining access to the Internet. In fact, the Middle East, Africa, and Latin America have also experienced significant growth in Internet connections since 2012.[29] These figures clearly illustrate the fact that soon most parts of the world will be online.

With this in mind, there is increasing evidence of hacker groups in emerging nations forming and connecting with others in developed nations. This is accomplished because of the borderless nature of the Internet. An individual with an interest in technology in Turkey or Costa Rica can search the Web to find groups that share common interests. That interest may be in using certain types of computers, cracking specific types of systems, supporting a specific cause—such as opposition to government controls on the Internet—or simply a self-selected group who feel their hacking skills are greater than others and who hack into challenging systems as a demonstration of their abilities. In furtherance of their common interest, they share techniques and may even agree on a specific plan to accomplish their hacking goals.

As a consequence, strong and established hacker communities can support and improve the skills of emerging hacker groups through guides, tutorials, software, and other materials. These resources can rapidly accelerate the skill and ability of a hacker and make it much easier for these individuals to engage in malicious attacks. Additionally, the free exchange of information can also lead hackers in established communities to borrow and find tools in emerging communities. For example, a study found that hacker tools to automate denial-of-service (DoS) attacks made in Guatemala, Argentina, and Chile were being used and advertised in hacker Web forums in Russia and China.[30] Additionally, this study found that a binding tool created by a hacker in France was quickly adopted by hacker groups in the Middle East and China. The emergence of malicious software and stolen data markets also allow hackers to buy and sell tools that may be beyond their ability to create on their own. As a result, the globalization of hacking will become a significant threat to networks around the world.

Given the diverse number of nations becoming active in the global hacker community, it is critical to consider how these hackers will use their skills. There is increasing evidence that hacker groups from Muslim majority nations are hacking to facilitate a religious or political agenda. For example, the publication of a cartoon satirizing the Prophet Mohammad in a Danish newspaper in 2005 led to a number of cyberattacks against different resources. By February 2006, Zone-h recorded almost 3,000 attacks against Danish Web sites, primarily by Turkish hackers. In addition, the al-Ghorabaa site coordinated a 24-hour DoS attack against *Jyllands-Posten,* the newspaper that first published the cartoons, and other newspapers in Denmark.[31] Other hackers may, however, be motivated by monetary gain and steal bank accounts and sensitive intellectual property in order to sell the information to others. Still others may have an interest in legitimate security applications of hacking and use their knowledge to benefit the larger community. It is important to note, however, that the variations in motivation will be difficult to discern based solely on country of origin.

As the hacker community expands around the globe, this will exacerbate the challenges faced by law enforcement agencies. Developing nations may not have laws in place against computer crimes, making prosecution unlikely and extradition complicated. The investigation, prosecution, and communication between law enforcement and intelligence organizations must also be better coordinated in order to effectively handle the changing landscape of threats.

Forecast 5: Organized Crime Groups Will Increasingly Adopt Computerization as a Criminal Instrument

---

FORECAST

Current organized crime groups will increasingly adopt computerization as a criminal instrument.

Interpol defines organized crime as any enterprise or group of persons engaged in a continuing illegal activity that has as its primary purpose the generation of profits and continuance of the enterprise regardless of national boundaries.[32] Key factors in this definition with respect to the forecast are that organized crime groups are *entrepreneurial* and that they exist to make a profit. Just like legitimate businesses, organized crime groups have consistently used methods that will enhance efficiency and effectiveness to achieve profits. Many methods are illegal—such as use of violence, corruption, or fraud—yet legal methods are also used, such as stock investments, purchase of real estate, and other principles common to legitimate businesses for distribution and marketing of a commodity. Globally, the character of organized crime is evolving into this entrepreneurial model. Traditional images of organized crime as a "Mafia-like" entity are dated, not reflecting the vast amount of organized criminal activity occurring around the world today. To neither recognize nor respond to this change is to perpetuate a myth. Law enforcement agencies must be proactive in devoting resources and attention to organized crime as entrepreneurial criminal enterprise. There is documented use of computerization by organized crime groups in several areas. As in the past, opportunistic organized crime groups will exploit any possible illegal avenues for increased profit. Several of these avenues are discussed below.

RECORD KEEPING   Evidence by law enforcement and intelligence organizations has found crime groups keeping computerized records in a manner similar to businesses, using spreadsheets and databases. Records that have been discovered include contraband shipment schedules; income and expenses of contraband or commodities; databases of conspirators and "customers"; locations, account numbers, and status of monetary transactions (typically, money being laundered); records of monetary transfers and payments; databases and "status" of bribed or vulnerable officials; and database dossiers of officials, conspirators, and others in whom the crime group has an interest.[33]

COUNTERFEIT CURRENCY AND DOCUMENTS   Computer technology has provided a revolution in the counterfeit currency and document business. Because of color scanners, color printers, sophisticated word processing and graphics software suites, and computer-driven color photocopiers, successful counterfeiting not only has significantly broadened but has also become much more difficult to detect. As an example, at one point the U.S. $100 bill was the most frequently counterfeited currency in the world. With computerized counterfeiting, the global market was becoming flooded with counterfeit $100 bills (particularly Central and Eastern Europe). As a result, the U.S. Treasury changed the bill's design and incorporated a watermark (like most of the rest of the world's currency) and other security factors. At the time of its release, it was announced by the Treasury Department that the new $100 bill was virtually impossible to counterfeit. Within a month of the new bill's introduction into circulation, good counterfeit copies surfaced in Eastern Europe. High-resolution color scanning of an original can even pick up the watermark and colors of fibers in the paper, which are, in turn, reproduced by high-resolution printers.

The same scanning process and graphics software are used for counterfeit passports. Counterfeiters maintain scanned masters of various passports in computer files and are then able to readily enter appropriate names, photographs, and identity information in the files to prepare a high-quality counterfeit.[34] Because the counterfeits are near the quality of legitimate documents and the process of creating the counterfeits is fast, the enterprise yields high profits. In fact, the online organized crime group the ShadowCrew sold identity documents through its Web forum as part of the resources available to engage in identity theft and fraud. In some cases, criminal enterprises offer a "package" to people who are illegally immigrating to Europe. One price includes the immigration documents, transportation, and an escort.

An additional technique in counterfeiting involves unique electronic devices and information to engage in fraud and theft. Specifically, hacker groups and computer fraudsters steal bank and credit account numbers, called dumps (outlined in Chapter 6). These dumps can be obtained online through a mass compromise, data breach, or phishing attack. This information can also be acquired in the real world through the use of electronic devices that capture the data obtained on a credit card's magnetic strip. These tools are called skimmers, as they skim information off of a card as it passes through the reader. In turn, the illegally acquired dumps can be placed onto blank plastic cards, called plastics, which can be used to make purchases in the real world. In fact, there are groups that sell counterfeit credit cards that have been printed and embossed to match the real thing.[35]

Another unique application of counterfeit technology has been found to make new certificates of origin and titles of stolen vehicles using the actual vehicle identification number (VIN) of the stolen auto. As with passports, master files of documents are scanned into a computer. They are then printed using the stolen vehicle's description and VIN along with the new "owner's" identification. Sophisticated auto theft rings operating from Poland to Morocco have used this method to ship luxury cars to the Mideast and Asia.

ILLEGAL IMMIGRATION   Evidence indicates that organized crime groups previously involved mostly in black market smuggling have created new processes to smuggle immigrants into Western countries with "appropriate" documentation, typically for a substantial fee. While computers play a comparatively smaller role in these enterprises, they nonetheless help expedite the scheme through the use of such processes as logistics and arrangements via e-mail, computer-forged immigration documents, and general record keeping related to this enterprise.

BLACK MARKET   Outside of its illegal commodities and avoidance of licensing and taxes, the black market operates much like any business. It is market driven; requires suppliers, transportation, and distribution networks; has a payroll; must remain competitive; and is obliged to keep its customers satisfied in order to maintain repeat clientele. Because of similarities to legitimate businesses, organized crime groups involved in the black market have increasingly begun to operate much like legitimate businesses. Such an evolution has occurred in the creation of malicious software production, which was discussed in Chapter 7.

Just as in any business, the black market needs to make its inventory descriptions known to both the "sales staff" and potential clients. Photographs, product descriptions, costs, inquiry processes, and related information for a wide variety of "commodities" have been found in computer files; in some cases, the files are accessible through a restricted server or Web site. Additionally, some black market merchandise (e.g., prescription medication) is readily available for order through the Internet (under the guise of a legitimate business), vastly expanding the enterprises' market and hence profits. In addition, computerization via networking provides increased anonymity to specific individuals in the criminal group. Then too, the Dark Web (see Chapters 5 and 9) continues to advance providing more clandestine and more sophisticated criminality.

COUNTERFEIT PRODUCTS The extent to which "traditional" organized crime is involved in this area is debatable; however, there is strong evidence that such groups are involved in the "marketing" and distribution of these products in what is referred to as the "fakes trade." While skilled craft workers have been quite successful in designing and manufacturing counterfeit products, one area that was frequently relied on by customs and corporate security investigators was product logos and subtle design and coloration characteristics to distinguish licensed products from counterfeit ones. This too is changing because of computer technology.

As in the case of counterfeit currency and documents, criminal enterprises have been using color scanners and computer-driven color printers to scan legitimate logos, product tags, and such things as "jackets" and labels for DVDs and software. Using the scanned images as masters, skilled printers are able to prepare these materials to legitimize the appearance of the counterfeit products. One corporate security director told the authors that while this process was an additional "wrinkle" for investigators to overcome, the intent of the counterfeiter was to make the product look more legitimate to the consumer. With packaging that makes the product appear authentic, the enterprise could sell more of their counterfeit products at higher prices and still undercut the legitimate manufacturer's sales.

SEXUALLY ORIENTED COMMERCE New criminal enterprises have emerged, largely consisting of intelligent young entrepreneurs who are familiar with the capabilities and potential of computers as a tool for sexual commerce. While these emerging groups may not fit neatly into traditional definitions of organized crime, they nonetheless are ongoing enterprises that are frequently violating the criminal law in order to gain a profit. A problem exists, however, because many activities of these groups fall into the gray area of law. Some of their activities may be lawful in their country of origin but unlawful in countries serving their clientele. Because of these legal ambiguities and the fact that sexual commerce is viewed as being less serious than other forms of crime, comparatively little attention is given to these groups.[36]

Using the Internet to arrange for prostitution is one of the more common enterprises. This includes not only logistical arrangements (i.e., appointments) but even payment by credit card using e-commerce protocols. The process is discreet and safer for both the "service provider" and "customer." In one case, a criminal enterprise using a server based in Amsterdam was arranging for prostitutes in both London and Frankfurt. Although the enterprise has been closed, it was difficult because of limitations inherent in dealing with multinational jurisdictions. One investigator stated that if the enterprise had been based in a non-European Union country, it would probably still be in operation.

ONLINE GAMBLING It is only natural that entrepreneurial criminals would turn to computerization—particularly the Internet—in order to expand their gambling operations and profits. A recent estimate indicates that online gambling revenues have significantly increased. The casino operators' online Web revenues in just two states account for $199.7 million in revenue in 2016.[37] The same source reports that New Jersey's revenues were $196.7 million, a 32.1 percent gain over 2015. Delaware's online gaming operators took in $3 million, a 62 percent "year-over-year increase." Interestingly, Nevada ceased reporting earnings as of February 2015.[38] On its face, the raw data might suggest a decline in overall revenues for the legitimate gambling industry. Intuition suggests otherwise. This is an online activity that warrants closer scrutiny and the undertaking of further research. While this amount reflects largely legitimate gaming, there are complicating factors. For example, the gaming may be lawful in the location where the gambling is based but unlawful in the jurisdiction of some of its customers. With the potential profits to be reaped combined with low overhead costs and comparative anonymity afforded by the Internet, the likelihood of criminal involvement in gambling will grow significantly, particularly in those locations where taxes and governmental regulation can be avoided through corruption or intimidation.

Accessibility to computerized gaming operations is increasingly available through the Internet through the use of virtual private network (VPN) access for security (largely from authorities) and to ensure payment for services. The expanded capacity for multimedia hardware and software is particularly fueling sites by enabling more effective simulation of video gaming machines. Typically the user must "join a club" to be given access to the site for gambling. Part of the membership ruse is to pay "dues," which are used as bets. Most typically gamblers supply a credit card number wherein they can purchase "units" to wager—units are essentially electronic poker chips. In some cases, when a member joins and is given his or her personal identification number, he or she can then make a deposit—either by wire or money order—to a front company, which serves as the "bank" for the gambling operation. All bets and communications are then conducted via the computer link. When the gambler wins, he or she is typically given credits, which can be used for further wagers, or he or she can request payment, typically through the front company, which serves as a bank. Credit card "credits" are not used for two reasons: (1) gamblers want their winnings quickly in a readily convertible form and (2) it is feared that the issuance of too many credits to a given card number would raise questions leading to investigation. Interestingly, one investigator said that the financial transaction accounting procedures for unlawful gaming operations were typically quite accurate and reliable. The reason is that the enterprise makes money from the "repeat business" of gamblers—if they cannot trust you, they will not bet their money.

IDENTITY THEFT AND FRAUD   As computers increasingly play a routine role in financial transactions, criminals are increasingly accessing them unlawfully to transfer funds, defraud, or steal information. The credit cards and financial information obtained through hacks and large database compromises mentioned earlier are commonly being used to engage in identity theft and fraud. Specifically, hackers sell the information they obtain to others, who in turn use the data to access bank accounts and steal money and make fraudulent purchases.

Criminal groups also recognize that stealing intellectual property has merit because it is a valuable commodity. Organized criminals have learned how to market stolen information for high profits and substantially less risk than more traditional illicit commodity trafficking. Theft of information such as trade secrets, new product specifications, product pricing plans, and customer lists has proven to be highly profitable. The cost to a business competitor to pay for this stolen information is far less than original research, development, and marketing. Increasingly active in this arena are criminal enterprises in Japan, the United States, France, and Germany. While these transactions typically do not have the violence and emotional daring associated with more traditional organized crime activities, the economic toll can be far higher.

A third form of fraud facilitated by computers is related to insurance and medical payments. The Florida Division of Insurance Fraud has discovered fraud through altered computer programs that underreport insurance agency incomes. Medical and pharmaceutical overpayments through Medicare/Medicaid have also been fraudulently made in many ways through the altering of computer records and, more commonly, the use of shell companies billing the government for medical services, equipment, and pharmaceuticals. While these forms of theft net significant amounts of money, they typically are not products of broad-based organized crime, although they frequently meet the technical definition of a criminal enterprise. Such offenses are difficult to detect, investigate, and prosecute. Moreover, they engender little emotional outcry from the public. As a result, they offer little risk and high profits—an appealing combination of factors for the entrepreneurial offender. The Health Care Fraud Unit (HCFAC) of the U.S. Department of Justice (USDOJ) has reported that nationwide health care expenditures are estimated to have exceeded $3 trillion in 2014. In that year over 2,100 defendants filed more than $6.5 billion in fraudulent claims resulting in over 1,200 defendants being sentenced to imprisonment.[39] The Healthcare Finance News' Running List reports, for example, that one Texas home health agency alone was charged with $13 million Medicare fraud.[40] This suggests a continuing increase in the direction and frequency of an upward incidence of health care and Medicare trend. For an-about-to-retire law enforcement officer with the requisite skill set (accounting and computer experience), this area of postretirement criminal investigation will surely prove to be a lucrative area to explore in the next few years.

TELECOMMUNICATIONS FRAUD   Telecommunications fraud is a particularly profitable area of computer-related crime that has many variations. Previously, individual criminal entrepreneurs committed these crimes, but they are increasingly being pushed out by organized crime groups because the profits are so high and the risk is so low. There are four types of telecommunications fraud in which criminal enterprises appear to be most involved. First is the theft of telephone credit card numbers, which can be gained by accessing computer records, some computerized voice mailboxes, and telephone billing files. Prime targets are large multinational corporations, because discovery of the fraudulent billings takes longer. The billing numbers are either sold "on the street" (using "pushers" in the same way as drug dealers) or, as is increasingly the case, sold to other crime groups for their use. In one case, stolen corporate telephone billing numbers from a U.S.-based multinational company were being sold to various drug trafficking groups, which in turn used the stolen numbers to make arrangements for drug transactions and shipments. Payment for the stolen numbers was cheaper than paying for numerous international calls, and it was more difficult for investigators to link the calls to their principal investigative targets.

The second type of telecommunications fraud, which has actually decreased, involves hacking into telecommunications "switches" (which are computers) for the purpose of routing calls and changing billing numbers. While individual hackers still break into switches, organized efforts to do this have largely stopped as a result of more aggressive security precautions by telecommunications carriers and comparatively little profit to be made.

The third area is the largest and fastest growing: wireless phone theft and fraud. This too was started by individuals and small groups but is increasingly involving organized crime groups. The process originally involved the capture of wireless electronic identification numbers (EINs) being transmitted from users' telephones. Using a device that detects and records the number, it could then be sold and programmed into a person's wireless phone. The number is typically usable for about one month before being detected as stolen. The fraudulent user would then need to purchase a new number.

In one study, interviewees stated that because of the large number of wireless (cell) telephones in use and the ease with which a large number of EINs could be captured, the process became one of "assembly line theft."[41] Essentially, a "client" pays a flat fee and receives a new billing number each month, or whenever the number he or she is using is canceled.[42] The "service provider" typically also has the computer equipment to readily reprogram the client's cell phone. Averaging about $30 a month ($60 if a "new" telephone is also obtained) with several hundred clients in a "territory" and several territories within a given geographic area, the profits can add up quickly and, again, with minimal risk.

The fourth type—which has increased significantly—is where organized crime groups have compromised private automatic branch exchanges (PABX) of companies to use telecommunications services for their own benefit.[43] A PABX is the heart of a digital telecommunications system that can include a company's internal phone system, its wireless network, voice mail, e-mail, and internal data network. A criminal enterprise using this system can call anywhere in the world without costs. Moreover, using a compromised system makes it more difficult for investigators to gain a wiretap order or to follow a trail of telephone calls. The growth of phreaking tools available on the Internet and the digital integration of voice and text on servers make this form of telecommunications increasingly accessible. Thus, unlawful use of a PABX not only constitutes a real monetary loss to the victim, it makes investigations of organized crime groups more difficult.

Forecast 6: Terrorist Groups Will Increasingly Use Global Networking

FORECAST

Terrorist groups will increasingly use global networking as a tool to accomplish their goals. This includes use of the Internet for recruitment, surreptitious communications, and coordination purposes as well as attempting to use network access to critical infrastructure systems to strike for their cause via the creation of chaos, disinformation, and file destruction—cyberterrorism.

Generally, critical infrastructure components include (1) the continuity of government services; (2) information and communications; (3) banking and finance; (4) electrical power, oil, and gas production/storage; (5) water supply; (6) public health services; (7) emergency services; and (8) transportation. Not surprisingly, most of these services in developed countries rely, in varying degrees, on computerization.

Experts argue that al Qaeda and other extremists are improving their ability to conduct cyberattacks on these critical infrastructure components. In fact, a book published by Mohammad Bin Ahmad As-Salim stated that individuals should engage in electronic jihad through the use of discussion boards for media operations and hacking attacks to strike out and attack against Web sites and information related to American, Jewish, and secular Web sites.[44]

Beyond unlawful intrusions designed to disrupt computer systems, virtually all types of extremist groups—international and domestic—are relying on computers for everything from communicating to spreading propaganda to fund-raising. It is reasonable to conclude that increasing numbers of these groups will, as computer skills and opportunities develop, become involved in some aspect of cyberterrorism or terroristic support. In light of these facts, what are the implications for state and local law enforcement with respect to cyberterrorism? The challenge seems daunting for a local police agency, yet given the omnipresence of computer networking and the ease with which one may digitally traverse the globe in nanoseconds, local police must accept this as a part of the challenge they face. As a consequence, examples of cyberterrorist activity may include use of information technology to organize and carry out attacks and support a group's activities and perception-management campaigns. For example, extremist groups participating in Jihad against the West have developed Web forums and sites to distribute manuals and tools for hacking and to promote and coordinate cyberattacks.

Clearly, the human tragedy of cyberterrorism has not yet approached that of traditional (physical) terror attacks. Yet the damage to assets, resources, and the fundamental principles of life in an open society for those who rely on such systems is significant. Indeed, *a successful cyberattack can make people begin to question the sanctity, security, and reliability of critical institutions on which we have daily reliance.* The proper functioning of our government and our banking systems are two important examples. A cyberattack would not need to be nationwide to generate such fear and lack of confidence in public institutions—the attack would only need to be publicized. Fear is irrational—a factor that terrorists rely on. If a cyberattack is successful, it can create chaos, which will translate to fear and eventual destruction of, or at least damage to, our critical infrastructure through distrust and failure to rely on institutions. Table 15.1 depicts different levels of seriousness of perpetrators committing similar types of Web intrusions. The legal implications based on motive,[45] as manifested by the character of the attacker, vary significantly.

TABLE 15.1 Characterizations of a Cyberattack

Perpetrator	Intrusive Act	Legal Interpretation
Computer cracker Hacktivist	Compromise a financial services Web site to steal sensitive information	Computer fraud, unauthorized access
	Defaces Web page of private company to promote a political belief	Criminal mischief or destruction of property
Racist group	Defaces Web page of a minority organization with racial epithets	Hate crime; possibly ethnic intimidation
Organized crime group	Sends out spam for a small company with low stock price to artificially increase the value, then sell its shares at the inflated price, with contributions going to the crime group	Theft by a continuing criminal enterprise; possibly RICO violation
al Qaeda/Islamic state	Attacks multiple banking Web sites, Web defacement to threaten future attacks against Americans; uses the Internet for propaganda, recruiting, training, and operational planning	Terrorism/terroristic threat

Forecast 7: The Character of Espionage Will Continue to Broaden

---

FORECAST

The character of espionage will continue to broaden into the arenas of information warfare, economic espionage, and theft of intellectual property.

A U.S. Department of Defense study on emerging threats to national security observed that the field of battle is increasingly moving away from political ideology and geographic control toward economic issues.[46] The essence of national security is to maintain the homeostasis of a country's sovereign principles and socioeconomic health. In a global economy punctuated by multinational corporations and international dependence, this homeostasis is inextricably related to economic stability.

In making a link between cybercriminality and national security, the Director of the U.S. Defense Intelligence Agency (DIA) observed:

> A growing array of state and non-state adversaries are increasingly targeting—for exploitation and potentially disruption or destruction—our information infrastructure, including the Internet, telecommunications networks, computer systems, and embedded processors and controllers in critical industries. Over the past year, cyberexploitation activity has grown more sophisticated, more targeted, and more serious. The Intelligence Community expects these trends to continue in the coming year.
>
> We assess that a number of nations, including Russia and China, have the technical capabilities to target and disrupt elements of the US information infrastructure and for intelligence collection. Nation states and criminals target our government and private sector information networks to gain competitive advantage in the commercial sector. Terrorist groups, including al-Qa'ida, HAMAS, and Hizballah, have expressed the desire to use cybermeans to target the United States. Criminal elements continue to show growing sophistication in technical capability and targeting and today operate a pervasive, mature online service economy in illicit cybercapabilities and services available to anyone willing to pay. Each of these actors has different levels of skill and different intentions; therefore, we must develop flexible capabilities to counter each. We must take proactive measures to detect and prevent intrusions from whatever source, as they happen, and before they can do significant damage.
>
> We expect disruptive cyberactivities to be the norm in future political or military conflicts … Such attacks have been a common outlet for hackers during political disputes over the past decade, including Israel's military conflicts with Hizballah and HAMAS in 2006 and 2008, the aftermath of the terrorist attacks in Mumbai last year, the publication of cartoons caricaturing the Prophet Mohammed in 2005 (and 2015), and the Chinese downing of a US Navy aircraft in 2001 (and increased information warfare from the PLA (Peoples Liberation Army - China), beginning in 2012).[47]

Global networking adds an important dimension to this problem. John Chambers, Chairman and CEO of Cisco Systems, a leader in producing networking hardware and software, stated, "The Internet levels the playing field between countries … regardless of size or political form of government, in a way that has never occurred before." Thus, the threat to national security is significantly increased as we move toward digital economies. This was demonstrated in a cyberconflict between Russia and Estonia in 2007. The removal of a war memorial in Estonia led hackers in Russia to engage in DoS attacks against Estonian embassies, government, and commercial Web sites.[48] Financial and communications systems were knocked off-line, leading to millions of dollars in losses for the Estonian people. These attacks clearly demonstrate the interrelated nature of security and economics in the digital age.

Government policies in Malaysia, Thailand, and Singapore are expressly developing technology centers to become major economic sectors of the global e-economy. A number of countries—notably Japan, China, and France—provide government support to businesses based in their countries through assistance with the surreptitious acquisition of intellectual property. In fact, examples of coordinated series of attacks on government and private industry contractor systems in the United States are becoming common today. Clearly, with the emergence of global networking and the digital economy, the greatest target threat for economic espionage is through cyberattacks on business networks rather than on government installations.

Forecast 8: Criminals Will Increasingly Use Technology-Based Instruments and Methodologies to Carry Out Attacks

FORECAST

Criminals, terrorists, nation-states, patriots, and anarchists will increasingly use technology-based instruments and methodologies, which can surreptitiously capture data/information or destroy technological communications, information processing, and/or storage appliances.

Part of the forecasting process is applying inductive logic to known facts. That logic is based on evidence and the reasonable extension of that evidence to a future state. The authors emphasize this point in the current forecast in light of three important factors. First, all of the technologies discussed in this forecast currently exist—in some cases, for at least two decades or more—yet they were not readily (or even feasibly) usable by criminals or terrorists because of technological complexities and/or limitations. Second, the exceptionally rapid evolution of computer-related technology and miniaturization of hardware and components in the past few years is making these offensive weapons more accessible and easier to use. These factors, coupled with the fiscal resources of criminal enterprises and "wealthy" terrorists,[49] make the development and use of these offensive weapons more probable. Third, the wide adoption of computers for communications, commerce, information distribution, and information management, and the integration of computer technology into everything from wireless telephones to automobiles magnify the potential impact electronic weapons can have on a business, government, or individuals.

Criminals will often take any step possible to gain an advantage over legitimate businesses and processes. For example, drug cartels have been found to use sophisticated weapons, surveillance devices, and intelligence techniques in order to maintain their competitive advantage in the drug trade, whether by undermining competition or attempting to corrupt officials. Since, as discussed previously, criminals are already taking advantage of computers and high-technology communications, it is reasonable to assume they will also adopt technologies that can surreptitiously capture information and/or incapacitate communications, surveillance, and information systems of government entities and businesses.

ELECTROMAGNETIC PULSE AND HIGH-ENERGY RADIO FREQUENCY The phenomenon known as an **E**lectro**M**agnetic **P**ulse (EMP) was discovered in the 1940s during the testing of nuclear weapons. Essentially, the EMP disabled electrical devices as a result of the massive electromagnetic field created by the nuclear blast. Research on this phenomenon led to the discovery that an EMP could also be produced by generating a high-energy radio frequency (HERF), typically by using a truck-sized device. The impact of a HERF electromagnetic emission is that any electronic "equipment can be irreversibly damaged or in effect electronically destroyed ... and may require complete replacement of the equipment."[50] Not only are computers and peripherals subject to destruction by HERF, but so are "...radios, satellites, microwave equipment, UHF, VHF, HF, and low band communications and television equipment."[51]

The HERF effect is real, with substantial research on its development as an electronic warfare tool in the United States, England, and Russia and speculated research on it as a weapon in China. The research is not focusing on creating an EMP, per se, but on accurate targeting and miniaturization.[52] Indeed, there has been development in the law enforcement community on the use of HERF as a less-than-lethal weapon that can be used to disable fleeing vehicles. There has also been a wide range of experimentation—typically unsuccessful—by hobbyists in developing homemade, handheld HERF devices. The probability is high that reliable, functional, and portable HERF devices will be developed in the short term. Just as weapons ranging from machine guns to surface-to-air missiles have found their way to organized crime groups and terrorists, so will HERF technologies. The destructive impact such weapons could have is evident, from disabling communications systems and computers in police cars to disrupting the computers of the New York Stock Exchange. The systems do not need to be hacked, nor does physical entry have to be gained—simply the transmission of a HERF is sufficient, which will not harm people but will destroy or disable every electrical device in its range from coffeepots to computers.

In addition to HERF, there is development of low-energy radio frequency (LERF) devices that are less damaging but can disrupt communications and data systems through "jamming" the signals. Whether used by a terrorist to disrupt air traffic control communications at a busy airport or by a speeder trying to disrupt radar, these devices could also have a significant impact in the future.

Fortunately, research has also explored promising ways to minimize the effects of HERF and LERF attacks (such as encasing computers in a wire mesh shroud, called a Faraday cage, to absorb the RF signal). The point to note is that EMP weapons are on the horizon and will eventually be in the hands of criminals. Plans for protecting assets, preventing attacks, recovering from attacks, and investigating offenders must be developed.

QUICK FACTS

A Faraday cage or Faraday shield is a series of continuous coverings of conductive material or a mesh of materials that block radio frequency interference (RFI). Named after the English scientist Michael Faraday, who invented the devices in 1836, the "cages" can even be woven into clothing in order to protect people from actual electric currents such as lightning strikes and electrostatic discharges. Today, the "cage" can be developed into a room (or series of rooms) to shield high-tech computer systems and data storage devices against electromagnetic pulse (EMP) attacks.

COMPROMISING ELECTRONIC EMANATIONS AND TEMPEST/EMISSIONS SECURITY (EMSEC)   The capture of compromising electronic emanations (CEE), which have been fully classified by the National Security Agency for several years, permits the surreptitious capture of electromagnetic signals emanating from computers. Also known as Van Eck phreaking in the hacking/phreaking community, the system works by capturing the computer's keystrokes, which are transmitted to the display (monitor). Each character (or keystroke) emits a unique characteristic that can be received with the proper equipment. By capturing these emanations, whatever was displayed on the target computer can also be read on the equipment of the CEE user.

The use of such devices for surveillance and espionage is obvious. A person with CEE equipment may be sitting outside a building surreptitiously capturing information from a target's computer. Just as there are privacy concerns with this technology, there are also concerns when CEE technology reaches the hands of criminals. Beyond gathering confidential information—such as intellectual property—information could be the basis for corruption, and could be used to blackmail, to undermine investigations, and to identify confidential informants or undercover personnel.

The implications for abuse of this technology are pervasive. What is the potential for this technology to become available for criminals? According to intelligence and law enforcement personnel interviewed in both Europe and Asia, the potential is quite high. One high-ranking police official in Asia told the authors that his organization has learned that wealthy drug traffickers in a neighboring country of the Golden Triangle had gained access to CEE equipment. While being used by criminals, the police official stated that his agency did *not* have this technology.

Electronic filters and interference devices can be defenses to Van Eck phreaking. However, at present, the CEE threat is not sufficiently severe to warrant widespread adoption of these defenses. Technological development of the systems and defenses are ongoing. Suffice it to note, there is a "dark side" to every technological development that will be exploited by criminals.

MALICIOUS SOFTWARE (MALWARE) Malicious software (or code) refers to viruses, worms, Trojan horses, logic bombs, and other "uninvited" software designed to disrupt a computer's operations or destroy files.[53] This software is widespread and widely available on the Internet, with new programs created regularly.[54] As noted in Chapter 7, malicious software is now sold and custom designed for individuals in online black markets, enabling participation in serious cybercrimes without the need for knowledge of computer systems. Bots, viruses, Trojan horse programs, and myriad other tools are all now a common component in computer and network attacks. What is more disconcerting is that these programs have shifted from demonstrations of curiosity and mischief to become tools designed to facilitate fraud, espionage, data theft, and network destruction.

In fact, one of the increasingly significant tools in the arsenal of attackers is spear phishing attack. This form of malware involves sending a fraudulent, yet convincing, e-mail to a targeted individual within an organization who has a position of authority or access to sensitive systems. Unlike traditional phishing schemes, however, the message appears to come from within the organization or an individual in a position of authority to increase the likelihood that the recipient will open the e-mail. In addition, the message will request information from the victim and request the individual to download or open a keylogger, spyware program, or some other type of malicious software to surreptitiously gather sensitive information. Spear phishing is less likely to be used by hackers, but rather "sophisticated groups out for financial gain, trade secrets, or military information."[55]

Malicious software has also been adapted by terror groups for the purposes of network attacks and destruction. The electronic jihad site al-Ghorabaa, for example, contained information on penetrating computer devices and intranet servers and stealing passwords, along with an encyclopedia on hacking Web sites and a 344-page book on hacking techniques.[56] Similarly, the forum Minbar ahl al-Sunna wal-Jama'a offered a hacking manual with details on infiltrating corporate and government networks, personal computers to steal information, and methods of intercepting sensitive information such as credit card numbers in transit.[57] Additionally, a hacker by the name of Younis Tsoulis, who used the handle Irhabi (Terrorist) 007, published a 74-page manual called *The Encyclopedia of Hacking the Zionist and Crusader Websites*.[58] This guide included instructions on how to hack and maintained a Web site that published details on vulnerable Web sites around the world. Tsoulis was arrested as a result of his actions and sentenced to 10 years in prison for inciting terrorist murder on the Internet. These examples demonstrate that malicious software is a particularly effective weapon to cause damage, disrupt network operations, steal data, and cause chaos and confusion. All of these effects would serve the goals of terrorists and criminals alike.

BOX 15.3

Policy Implications

Frankly, there is little that an operational-level law enforcement officer can do regarding policy. Little, not nothing. What police officers can do is provide policy-makers and administrators with information: (1) track record data about digital investigations (the pros and cons and what could/should have been handled differently); (2) create relevant information about state-of-the-art technological innovation; and (3) document how hardware and software enhancements could be used to increase identification, investigation, prosecution, and conviction of cybercriminals, by their agency.

An example of a policy change is the use of drones. In 2015 a Utah Sheriff's department—one of the earliest adopters—began using drones in search and rescue operations. More recently, an Indiana police department made use of a thermal imaging camera mounted on a drone to locate a man who had crashed his car after trying to evade a hot pursuit. In Maryland, a Sheriff's department drone located $400,000 worth of stolen construction equipment. Two states with the highest number of law enforcement agencies that have acquired drones are Texas and California.[64] Other states are not quite sure if or how to use drones.

Suggestive of the necessity for a major policy revision is information systems security. On January 25, 2017, U.K. Prime Minister Theresa May addressed the U.S. Congress. She observed that "the world is passing through a period of change—and in response to that change we can either be passive bystanders, or we can take the opportunity once more to lead." She added that we should not "return to the failed policies of the past." Further, in a keynote address at a Cybersecurity Conference sponsored by Boston College's Cybersecurity Policy and Governance Master's Program, then-FBI Director James Comey stated that "cyber threats are too fast, too big, and too widespread for any of us to address them alone." Two months later, with the announcement of the discovery of the "WannaCry" ransomware exploit, his words became prophetic. Comey further noted the wide array of "bad actors" using cybertactics, "terrorists have not turned to using the Internet as a tool of destruction in a way that logic tells us certainly will come in the future." He added "And we're not only worried about loss of data, but corruption of that data [data diddling], and lack of access to our own information." Of the FBI's 5-part strategy to address cyberintrusions, Comey's highest priority would be to enhance the "digital literacy" of state and local partners through training, equipment, and [more] task forces to make them more effective.

Sources: Glaser, A. (2017). "Police Departments Are Using Drones to Find and Chase Down Suspects," Recode (April6), *https://www.recode.net/2017/4/6/15209290/policefire-department-acquired-drone-us-flying-robot-law-enforcement*

Noble, A. (2015), "Drones Cleared for Takeoff in Virginia, but Law Enforcement Agencies Aren't Ready," *The Washington Times* (June 30), *http://www.washingtontimes.com/news/2015/jun/30/drones-cleared-for-takeoff-in-virginia-but-law-enf/*

CSPAN (2017). "Theresa May [British Prime Minister] Remarks at Congressional Republican Retreat," CSPAN.com (January 26). Washington, D.C., *https://www.c-span.org/video/?422831-1/british-prime-minister-theresa-may-addresses-congressional-republicans*

Comey, J.B. (2017). "Cyber Security," Keynote Address, Conference on CyberSecurity, Boston: Cyberscurity Policy and Governance Master's Degree Program, Boston College (March 8), *https://www.fbi.gov/news/stories/fbi-director-addresses-cyber-security-gathering*

Paul (2017). "Updated: Fatal Flaw Slows WannaCry Ransomware Spread, but Threats Remain," *The Security Ledger* (May 15), *https://securityledger.com/2017/05/fatal-flaw-slows-wannacry-ransomware-but-threat-remains/*

Fournier, C. (2017). Elided Branches Blog, *http://www.elidedbranches.com/2017/*; Weaver, C. (2016). "What Is Data Diddling?" CISSP Question of the Day (August 16), ITDOJO .com, *https://www.itdojo.com/cissp-question-of-the-day-8-16-2016/*

Comey, J.B. (2016). "The FBI's Approach to the Cyber Threat," (August 30). Symantec Government Symposium, Washington, D.C.: Federal Bureau of Investigation, *https://www.fbi.gov/news/speeches/the-fbis-approach-to-the-cyber-threat*

Summary

Organizations—public and private alike—must be made aware of the real threat posed by technology-related abuses and their impact on both crime and national security. One of the greatest challenges in this process is the willingness of organizations and people to be alert to changing criminal trends and devote resources to address emerging problems. As part of this change process, there must be development of new law and policy where voids exist. Policy should include regular development of both strategic and tactical intelligence as related to the integrated criminal and national security threats posed through computer crime and its evolution. Similarly, there must be a body of both civil and criminal law developed that expressly addresses the unique elements of cybercrime. This includes attending to the issues of transnational criminality and the ambiguities of attaching value to information and intellectual property. In addition, effective policy must address security, prevention, investigation, prosecution, and damage recovery of electronic property. There must also be a new standard of personnel development to ensure employees have skills necessary to deal with computer- and technology-related crime. These include knowledge of security issues, processes, and practices; investigative techniques; and the capacity to perform forensic analysis of electronic evidence.

Global crime issues require global strategies. In this regard, it would be advisable to have a transnational working group of police; national security; and relevant commerce, security, and regulatory groups to help guide efforts in the prevention, investigation, and prosecution of computer-related crime. Groups such as the Anti-Phishing Working Group, Infragard, and international partners such as the Netherlands-based Cyber Security Centre (EC3), of the European Union's Police (EUROPOL), and Infragard provide important assistance, though greater collaboration would improve the response from law enforcement, private industry, and academia. With the furious pace of technological development coupled with the global growth of e-commerce, networked computers are increasingly becoming as commonly used as the telephone. Dogmatism and traditional beliefs that "this is not a problem" must be set aside and replaced with an aggressive policy to address these trends.

To help remedy this dogmatism, there needs to be empirical data collection and analysis on computer criminality to define the problem more accurately, map trends, and fully understand the character of the offenses and offenders. National-level data collection has begun, and academic samples of computer crime offending and victimization are beginning to expand our understanding of these offenses. While exploration of hardware and software system protection is important, as is operational security of computers, research must go beyond this. Defining behaviorally based prevention, exploring the cybercrime equivalent of crime "hot spots," developing a catalog of best practices for investigation and prosecution of computer crime, and researching crime control methodologies in a fashion similar to predatory crime are all strategies where emerging research must focus. The National Institute of Justice and similar agencies have begun to produce such manuals, though constant updates are necessary to improve the law enforcement response to computer crimes. As with any forecast, neither a timetable nor certitude can be provided. A forecast is probabilistic; however, there is strong evidence supporting the evolution of cybercrime as described in this chapter. Further, to punctuate the importance that should be placed on looking ahead, exploring the feasibility of drawing upon scientifically based forecasting is endorsed. An excellent source for such forecasts is the Society of Police Futurists International (PFI).[59] PFIs goals are to:

- Encourage partnerships between law enforcement and applying the discipline of Futures Research.

- Develop information transfer concerning police futures research to its members.
- Develop, analyze, and interpret long range forecasts.
- Provide and promote education and training in the application of long range forecasting and the use of technology.
- Serve as a clearinghouse for the communication of innovative and proactive policing strategies.[60]

A willingness by public officials to openly explore the feasibility of these forecasts is clearly warranted in addressing the future of cyber crime and cyber terrorism.

Review Questions

1. What are the biggest problems facing the criminal justice system in the area of computer crime?
2. How is the hacker community changing with the spread of the Internet?
3. What types of computer crimes are going to become more prevalent in the future?

4. Describe the mechanisms and tactics terrorist organizations are likely to use in the future.
5. Which of the forecasts described in this chapter is most likely to come to pass? Which of the forecasts is least likely to come true? Why?

Critical Thinking Exercises

1. Creativity and imagination have propelled America and the world into the Information Age. Technology has improved the lives of millions. But, there is a dark side as well. Facilitated by high technology, growing global criminality signals the crucial importance of international cooperation. Hence, the proliferation of cyber crime and cyber terrorism require major change in the education and training of practitioners at all levels of government. Scour the Internet for training classes aimed at improving police and security personnel in this area. Look for programs that cross jurisdictional boundaries or are international in scope. Visit the Web site of your university or one nearby for classes focused on understanding and addressing the issues of cyber crime and cyber terrorism. Now, discuss how well we are doing to plan, prepare and bring about mechanisms to prevent or defeat the myriad of cyberthreats confronting our communities and our country.

Endnotes

1. This chapter was originally adapted from papers presented at the First Annual UNC-Charlotte Interdisciplinary Conference on Cybercrime, Charlotte, North Carolina, May 15–16, 2008, and CARTER, D.L. and KATZ-BANNISTER, A.J. "Computer Crime: A Forecast of Trends and Policy Implications." Paper presented at the 2003 meeting of the Academy of Criminal Justice Sciences. For the 4th edition (2018), our new author, William "Bill" Tafoya provided considerable updating and editing.

2. NORMAL (2017). "Florida Laws and Penalties." *http:l/norml .org/laws/item/florida-penalties*
3. NORMAL (2017). "Colorado Laws and Penalties." *http:l/ norml.org/lawslitem/coloradopenalties*
4. CARTER, D.L. and KATZ, A.J. (1999). "Computer Applications by International Organized Crime Groups." In L. MORIARITY and D.L. CARTER (eds.), *Criminal Justice Technology in the 21st Century*. Springfield, IL: Charles C. Thomas, Publisher. See also BROADHURST, R. *et al.* (2014). "An Analysis of the Nature of Groups Engaged in Cyber

Crime." *International Journal of Cyber Criminology* 8 (1), 1–20.

5. BRENNER, S.W. (2008). *Cyberthreats: The Emerging Fault Lines of the Nation State.* New York: Oxford University Press. See also WIENER, A. (2015). Virtual Crimes, Actual Threats: Deterring National Security Offenses Committed Through Cyberspace. *Journal of law and Cyber Warfare* 4(2). See: *https://papers.ssrn.com/sol3/papers.cfm?abstract_id=2576198*

6. HOLT, T.J. *et al.* (2017). "Examining the Impact of Organizational and Individual Characteristics on Forensic Scientists' Job Stress and Satisfaction." *Journal* of *Crime and Justice* 40(1): 34–39; BROWN, C.S. (2015). "Investigating and Prosecuting Cyber Crime: Forensic Dependencies and Barriers to Justice." *International Journal of Cyber Criminology* 9(1): 55.

7. WIENER, Virtual Crimes, Actual Threats.

8. TCHERNI, M. *et al.* (2016). "The Dark Figure of Online Property Crime: Is Cyberspace Hiding a Crime Wave?" *Justice Quarterly* 33(5): 890–911; LAGAZIO, M., SHERIF, N., and CUSHMAN, M. (2014). A Multi-Level Approach to Understanding the Impact of Cyber Crime on the Financial Sector. *Computers & Security* 45: 58–74

9. HARRELL, E. (2015). "Victims of Identity Theft, 2014." *Bureau of Justice Statistics Bulletin.* Washington, D.C.: U.S. Department of Justice. Available at *https:L/www.bjs.gov/content/pub/pdf/vit14.pdf*

10. MUTAWA, A. *et al.* (2016). "Forensic Investigation of Cyberstalking Cases Using Behavioural Evidence Analysis." *Digital lnvestigation* 16: S96–S103; LIVINGSTONE, S. and SMITH, P.K. (2014). "Annual Research Review: Harms Experienced by Child Users of Online and Mobile Technologies: The Nature, Prevalence and Management of Sexual and Aggressive Risks in the Digital Age." *Journal of Child Psychology and Psychiatry* 55(6), 635–654; ZETTER, K. (2009) "Judge Acquits Lori Drew in Cyberbullying Case, Overturns Jury." *Wired* (July 2). Available at *https://www.wired.com/2009/07/drewcourt/*

11. BURGARD, A. and SCHLEMBACH, C. (2013). "Frames of Fraud: A Qualitative Analysis of the Structure and Process of Victimization on the Internet." *International Journal of Cyber Criminology* 7(2): 112; KONRADT, C. *et al.* (2016). "Phishing: An Economic Analysis of Cybercrime Perpetrators." *Computers and Security* 58: 39–46.

12. FBI (2016). "UCR Program" Washington, D.C.: Federal Bureau of Investigation (April), see esp. NIBRS, *https://ucr.fbi.gov/ucr-program-quarterly/ucr-program-quarterly-april-2016*

13. FBI (2015). "National Incident-Based Reporting System." Washington, D.C.: Federal Bureau of Investigation, *https://ucr.fbi.gov/nibrs/2015*

14. *U.S. v. Lori Drew*—United States District Court, Central District of California—No. CR08-0582-6W.

15. MCCARTHY, T. and MICHAELS, S. (2009). "Lori Drew MySpace Suicide Hoax Conviction Thrown Out." *ABC News* (July 2), *http://abcnews.go.com/TheLaw/story?id=7977226*; ZETTER, K. (2008) "Lori Drew's Daughter 'Devastated' by Friend's Suicide but Doesn't Feel Responsible." *Wired*

(November 24), *https://www.wired.com/2008/11/defendants-daug/*; Facebook (2016) "Data Policy." (September 29), *https://_www.facebook.com/full* data use policy; USDOJ (2016). "Prosecuting Computer Crimes." Washington, D.C.: U.S/ Department of Justice, see esp. "Computer Fraud and Abuse Act," page 1, *https://www.justice.gov/sites/default/files/criminal-ccips/legacy/2015/01/14/ccmanual.pdf*; EFF (2013). "Computer Fraud and Abuse Act (CFAA)." San Francisco, CA: Electronic Frontier Foundation, *https://www.eff.org/issues/cfaa*

16. There is precedence for charging fees and placing responsibility on citizens. For example, many jurisdictions charge fines or service fees for police responses to false burglar alarms. See also GAO (1992). "Computer Security: DEA's Handling of Sensitive Drug Enforcement and National Security Information Is Inadequate." Document #: T-IMTEC-92-24 (September 30). Washington, D.C.: General Accounting Office, *http://www.gao.gov/products/T-IMTEC-92-24*; GAO (2017). "Cybersecurity: Actions Needed to Strengthen U.S. Capabilities." Document #: GAO-17-440T (February 14). Washington, D.C.: General Accounting Office, *https://www.gao.gov/products/*; VAN ZANDELHOFF, M. (2016). "The Biggest Cybersecurity Threats Are Inside Your Company." *Harvard Business Review* (September 19), *https://hbr.org/2016/09/the-biggest-cybersecurity-threats-are-inside-your-company*; WOLFF, J. (2016). "Why Computer Science Programs Don't Require Cybersecurity Classes." *Slate* (April 14), *http://www.slate.com/articles/technology/future_tense/2016/04/why_computer_science_programs_don_t_require_cybersecurity_classes.html*

17. LANGSTON, L. (November 2011). *Identity Theft Reported by Households, 2005–2010.* Washington, D.C.: Bureau of Justice Statistics. See also BJS (2015). "17.6 Million U.S. Residents Experienced Identity Theft in 2014." (September 27). Washington, D.C.: Bureau of Justice Statistics, *https://www.bjs.gov/content/pub/press/vit14pr.cfm*; FOLEY, L. *et al.* (2008). "Identity Theft: The Aftermath 2007." (May). San Diego, CA: Identity Theft Resource Center, *https://www.idtheftcenter.org/images/surveys_studies/Aftermath2007.pdf*

18. QuickBooks (2016). "4 Tips on How to Spot Fake Credit or Debit Cards." lntuit.com, *http://guickbooks.intuit.com/r/tech-review/4-tips-on-how-to-spot-a-fake-credit-or-debit-card/*

19. KIERNAN, J. (2017). "Credit Card and Debit Card Fraud Statistics." Washington, D.C.: Wallethub (February 17), *https://wallethub.com/edu/credit-debit-card-fraud-statistics/25725/*

20. SMITH, E. (2017). "What's Hiding in the Dark Web?" Truthfinder (April 4), *https://www.truthfinder.com/infomania/technology/deep-web-search/?utm_medium=social&utm_campaign=fbiaOrganic*; HOLT, T.J. *et al.* (2017). "Exploring the Subculture of Ideologically Motivated Cyber-Attackers." *Journal of Contemporary Criminal Justice, http://journals.sagepub.com/doi/abs/10.1177/1043986217699100*; HOLT. T.J. (2013). "Exploring the Social Organization and Structure of Stolen Data Markets." *Global Crime* 14(2–3): 155–174.

21. GIANDOMENICO, N. (2017). "What Is Spear-Phishing? Defining and Differentiating Spear-Phishing from Phishing." *Digital Guardian* (January 27), *https://digitalguardian.com/blog/*

what-is-spear-phishing-defining-and-differentiating -spear-phishing-and-phishing; DAVIS, J. (2016). *"Spear -Phishing Caused Majority of 2016 Cyberattacks, But Ransomware Is Rising." Healthcare IT News* (December 14), *http://www. healthcareitnews.com/news/spear-phishing-caused -majority-2016-cyberattacks-ransomware-rising*

22. LARSON, S. (2017). "Hackers Use FAFSA Application to Steal Tax Info." *Money* (April 7), *http://money.cnn.com/2017/04/07/ technology/hackers-irs-fafsa-data/index.html*; NSTP (2017). "Tax Professionals Warned of Various Scams: Urged to Be Wary of Schemes as Filing Season Deadline Approaches." NSTP Blog. Appleton, WI: National Society of Tax Professionals (April 15), *https://nstp.org/blog/tax -professionals-warned-various-scams-urged-wary-schemes -filing-season-deadline-approaches/*; IRS (2017). "Taxpayer Guide to Identity Theft." (February). Washington, D.C.: Internal Revenue Service, *https://www.irs.gov/uac/taxpayer -guide-to-identity-theft*

23. A good source of information on Internet fraud schemes can be found at the National Fraud Information Center: *www .fraud.org*. Information is also available through searching the U.S. Federal Trade Commission Web site: *www.ftc.gov*. See also APWG (2017). "Phishing Activity Trends Report, 4th Quarter, 2016." (February 23). Cambridge, MA: Anti-Phishing Working Group, *http://docs.apwg.org/reports/apwg _trends_report_q4_2016.pdf*; FTC (2017). "Online Businesses Could Do More to Protect Their Reputations and Prevent Consumers from Phishing Schemes." (March 3). Washington, D.C.: Federal Trade Commission, *https://www.ftc.gov/news -events/press-releases/2017/03/online-businesses-could-do -more-protect-their-reputations-prevent*; FBI (2017). "Internet Crime Complaint Center." Washington, D.C.: Federal Bureau of Investigation, *https://www.ic3.gov/crimeschemes.aspx*

24. U.S. Department of Justice (1999). *Cyberstalking: A New Challenge for Law Enforcement and Industry.* A report to the Vice President. *www.usdoj.gov/ag/cyberstalkingreport .htm.* See also FBI (2017). "Cyberbullying, 'Cyber Bully Rap,' Myron B. Thompson Academy." Video Transcript (October 3). Washington, D.C.: Federal Bureau of Investigation, *https://www.fbi.gov/video-repository/newss-mp4 -honolulu.mp4-cyberbullying.mp4/view*; PATCHIN, J.W., J.A. SCHAFER, and SAMEER H. (2013). "Cyberbullying and Sexting: Law Enforcement Perceptions." *FBI Law Enforcement Bulletin.* Retrieved June from *https:// leb.fbi.gov/2013/june/cyberbullying-and-sexting-law -enforcement-perceptions*

25. WOLAK, J., MITCHELL, K., and FINKELHOR, D. (2006). *Online Victimization of Youth: Five Years Later.* Washington D.C.: National Center for Missing and Exploited Children. See also CRC (2016). "New National Bullying and Cyberbullying Data." (October 10). *Cyberbullying Research Center, http:// cyberbullying.org/new-national-bullying-cyberbullying-data*; RICE, E. *et al.* (2015). "Cell Phone Internet Access, Online Sexual Solicitation, Partner Seeking, and Sexual Risk Behavior Among Adolescents." *Archives of Sexual Behavior* 44 (April): 3: 755–763, *https://link.springer.com/article/10.1007/s10508 -014-0366-3*; LIVINGSTONE, S. *et al.* (2014). "In Their Own Words: What Bothers Children Online?" *European Journal of Communication* 29(3): 271–288, *http://journals.sagepub.com/ doi/abs/10.1177/0267323114521045*; GOLDMAN, E. (2013). "Why Craigslist's 'Casual Encounters' Is a Bad Spot to Catch Predators." *Forbes.* Retrieved June 17 from *http://blog .ericgoldman.org/archives/2013/06/why_craigslists.htm*

26. The Simple Mail Transfer Protocol (SMTP) audit trail can give a wide range of information about the sender of e-mail: the sender's name, e-mail address, Internet service provider, e-mail client software, date, time, etc. There are Web sites that offer the service of hiding this information and sending an audit trail with e-mail that "can't be traced." For example, see *The Anonymizer, www.anonymizer.com* or *Hushmail, www.hushmail.com.*

27. PATCHIN, J. and HINDUJA, S. (2007). "What Kids Do on MySpace." *Technology and Learning* 27(7): 7. See also Facebook (2016) "Data Policy" [Regarding User Personal Information Sharing]. Menlo Park, CA: Facebook, *https://www. facebook.com/full_data_use_policy*

28. ILS (2017). "Internet Live Stats." [Individual users], InternetLiveStats.com, *http://www.internetlivestats.com/ internet-users/*

29. ILS (2017). "Internet Live Stats." [Countries], InternetLiveStats.com, *http://www.internetlivestats.com/ internet-users/*

30. HOLT, T.J. (2008). "Examining the Origins of Malware." Presented at the Department of Defense Cyber Crime Conference, Saint Louis, MO. See also BLAKE, A. (2017). "Russian Hackers Hit Election Systems in 39 States, Twice as Many as First Suspected." *The Washington Times.* Retrieved June 13, from *http://www.washingtontimes.com/news/2017/ jun/13/russian-hackers-targeted-election-systems-39-state/*; PHILLIPS, J. (2016). "Chinese Cybercriminals Go Global in Hacker Underground." *The Epoch Times.* Retrieved February 19 from *http://www.theepochtimes.com/n3/1970555-chinese -cybercriminals-go-global-on-hacker-underground/*

31. ULPH, S. (February 7, 2006). "Internet Mujahideen Refine Electronic Warfare Tactics." *Terrorism Focus* 3(5). Jamestown Foundation. See also Foreign Staff (2017). "Prophet Mohammed Cartoons Controversy" [*Jyllands-P https:// digitalguardian.com/blog/what-is-spear-phishing-defining -and-differentiating-spear-phishing-and-phishingosteri*, Denmark newspaper]. *The Telegraph* [UK Newspaper]. Retrieved June 5, from *http://www.telegraph.co.uk/news/ worldnews/europe/france/11341599/Prophet-Muhammad -cartoons-controversy-timeline.htm/*

32. FBI (2017). "Transnational Organized Crime." Washington, D.C.: Federal Bureau of Investigation, *https://www.fbi.gov/ investigate/organized-crime*; USAoWA (2017). "Six Arrested in Connection with Organized Criminal Ring Profiting from Prostitution Enterprise." (May 4). Seattle, WA: U.S. Attorney's Office, U.S. Department of Justice, *https://www.justice.gov /usao-wdwa/pr/six-arrested-connection-organized-criminal -ring-profiting-prostitution-enterprise*; Interpol (2012). "Organized Crime Enablers." (July). Geneva, Switzerland, *http://www3.weforum.org/docs/WEF_GAC_Organized CrimeEnablers_Report_2012.pdf*; LAVORGNA, A. (2015).

"Organized Crime Goes Online: Realities and Challenges. *Journal of Money Laundering Control* 18(2): 153–168.

33. SANDHU, H. (1999). "Underground Banking and Alternative Remittance Systems." *INTERPOL and Technology in Partnership.* London: Kensington Publications Limited. See also FinCEN (2017). "FinCen Penalizes California Bank for Egregious Violations of Anti-Money Laundering Laws." (February 27). Washington, D.C.: FinCEN, *https://www.fincen.gov/news/news-releases/fincen-penalizes-california-bank-egregious-violations-anti-money-laundering-laws*

34. The European Union passport is particularly popular for counterfeiters. See also Jasco (2017). "Fluorescence Detection of Counterfeit US Currency." Easton, MD: Fasco.com, *http://jascoinc.com/wp-content/uploads/2017/04/FP_01_02.pdf*

35. NW3C (2017). "Credit Card Fraud." Fairmont, WV: National White Collar Crime Center, *https://www.nw3c.org/docs/research/credit-card-fraud-2017.pdf*; SATANOVSKY, G. (2011). "How Counterfeit Credit Cards Are Created from ATM Skimmers." (January 17). FraudFighter.com, *https://blog.fraudfighter.com/bid/52994/How-Counterfeit-Credit-Cards-are-Created-From-ATM-Skimmers*; CBS Miami (2017). "3 Arrested for Trying to Use Fraudelent Credit Cards in Key Largo." (April 23). Miami, FL: CBS Miami, *http://miami.cbslocal.com/2017/04/23/three-arrested-for-trying-to-use-fraudulent-credit-cards-in-key-largo/*

36. OJJDP (2017). "OJJDP FY 2017 Internet Crimes against Children Task Force Program Support." (January 31) Office of Juvenile Justice and Delinquency Prevention, Washington, D.C.: U.S. Department of Justice, *https://www.ojjdp.gov/grants/solicitations/FY2017/ICACProgramSupport.pdf*; SUNDARESAN, S. *et al.* (2016). "Profiling Underground Merchants Based on Network Behavior." *Electronic Crime Research* (June), *2016 APWG* Sympo*sium* IEEE: 1–9.

37. TSAI, M.R. (2015). "Fantasy e-Sports: The Future Prospect of Fantasy Sports Betting Amongst Organized Multiplayer Video Game Competitions." *University of Nevada, Las Vegas Gaming Law Journal* 6: 393.

38. LegalGambling.com (2017). "State by State Online Gambling." *http://www.legalgamblingusa.com/states/index.html*; Casino.org (2017). "Complete Guide to USA Casino Gambling." *https://www.casino.org/us/guide/*

39. HHS (2017). "Health Care Fraud and Abuse Control Program: Annual Report for Fiscal Year 2016." Washington, D.C.: U.S. Department of Health and Human Services, *https://oig.hhs.gov/publications/docs/hcfac/FY2016-hcfac.pdf*

40. MCFSF (2017). "Medicare Fraud Strike Force: Strike Force Statistics." Washington, D.C.: U.S. Department of Health and Human Services, *https://oig.hhs.gov/fraud/strike-force/*

41. A telephone does not have to be in use, but simply turned on, in order to emit the EIN. See NANI, J. (2017). "Goshen Man Sold Counterfeit Cell Phones." *Times Herald-Record* newspaper, Middletown, NY (April 27), *http://www.recordonline.com/news/20170427/police-goshen-man-sold-counterfeit-cell-phones*; KANOWITZ, S. (2016). "How ID Can Move Out of the Wallet and Onto the Smartphone." (May 11) GCN.com, *https://gcn.com/articles/2016/05/11/digital-id.aspx?admgarea=TC_Mobile*

42. Traffickers in stolen wireless telephones and numbers recommend that a stolen number not be used over one month in case it is being traced by investigators. See RepublicWireless (2017). "I Would Like to Cancel Service to My Cell Phone …" (January 2). RepublicWireless.com, *https://community.republicwireless.com/thread/65274-hi-there-i-would-like-to-cancel-service-to-my-cell-phone-from-152017-2202017-i-would-like-it-re-activated-on-2212017ho*

43. ANDROULIDAKIS, I.I. (2016). VoIP and PBX Security and Forensics: A Practical Approach, 2nd ed. Geneva, Switzerland. Available at *https://books.google.com/books?id=OEsWDAAAQBAJ&pg=PA6&lpg=PA6&dq=PBAX+%26+organized+crime&source=bl&ots=GlUHspzJBW&sig=c51CoCU3rHg1LBDdhb0XywQJn7w&hl=en&sa=X&ved=0ahUKEwj385aEzL3UAhWIbiYKHVVZAXQQ6AEILzAD#v=onepage&q=PBAX%20%26%20organized%20crime&f=false*

44. BRANTLY, A. (2017). "Innovation and Adaptation in Jihadist Digital Security." *Survival.* 59(1): 79–102; JALATA, A. (2016). "AI-Qaeda: A Global Multinational Terrorist Network." *In Phases of Terrorism in the Age of Globalization.* London, England: Macmillan. 161–200; LEMIEUX, A.F. *et al.* (2014). "Inspire magazine: A Critical Analysis of Its Significance and Potential Impact Through the Lens of the Information, Motivation, and Behavioral Skills Model." *Terrorism and Political Violence* 26(2): 354–371; AWAN, I. (2014). "Debating the Term Cyber-Terrorism: Issues and Problems, *Internet Journal of Criminology*, 1–14.

45. Motive is typically not an element (i.e., part of the *corpus delecti*) of a crime; hence, while it can be presented in court, it is not required. Nonetheless, demonstrating the motive can aggravate or mitigate the actual crime charged as well as the severity of the penalty

46. When NATO began bombing Serbia in March 1999, Serbian hackers began a low-level campaign of harassment directed at the U.S. government and military groups involved in the NATO actions. The "Black Hand" hacker group and the "Serbian Angels" hacker group threatened to damage NATO computers in retaliation for the war against the Serbs. On March 29, the White House Web site was defaced by red letters reading "Hackerz wuz Here." It was speculated that anti-NATO activists were involved. On March 30, hackers damaged a NATO Web server, forcing it off-line for a short time. *Information Security* (December 1999), p. 26. See also DoD (2017). "Task Force on Cyber Deterrence." (February). Defense Science Board, Washington, D.C.: U.S. Department of Defense, *http://www.acq.osd.mil/dsb/reports/2010s/DSB-CyberDeterrenceReport_02-28-17_Final.pdf*

47. *http://www.dni.gov/testimonies/20090212_testimony.pdf*; see also CRS (2001). "China-U.S. Aircraft Collision Incident of April 2001: Assessment and Policy Implications." (October 10). Congressional Research Service Report RL30946, Washington, D.C.: U.S. Congress, *https://fas.org/sgp/crs/row/RL30946.pdf*

48. LANDLER, M. and MARKOFF, J. (May 29, 2007). "Digital Fears Emerge After Data Siege in Estonia." *The New York Times.* See also COLLIER, J. (2017). "Strategies of Cyber Crisis Management: Lessons from the Approaches of Estonia

and the United Kingdom." In Ethics and Policies for Cyber Operations, Geneva, Switzerland: Springer: 187–212.

49. The wealth amassed by drug dealers has purchased a wide array of sophisticated technology and the services of people—frequently intelligence personnel from the security services of the former Soviet bloc countries—to use these technologies to further their enterprises and avoid prosecution. Similar wealth has purportedly furthered terroristic acts, such as terrorism networks supported from Afghanistan by Osama Bin Laden. See MEOTTI, G. (2016). "Islamic Terrorists Not Poor and Illiterate, But Rich and Educated." (November 19). New York: Gatestone Institute, *https://www.gatestoneinstitute.org/9343/ terrorism-poverty-despair*

50. BURKE, S.E. and SCHNEIDER, E. (2015). "Who's Afraid of the Big Bas Pulse?" (July 2). Slate.com, *http://www.slate .com/articles/technology/future_tense/2015/07/emp_threats _could_an_electro_magnetic_pulse_weapon_wipe_out_the _power_grid.html*; Techopedia (2015). "High-Energy Radio Frequency Weapon (HERF)." Techopedia.com, *https://www .techopedia.com/definition/25107/high-energy-radio-frequency -weapon-herf*

51. *Shure (2016)* "What Is the Difference Between UHF and VHF Frequencies?" Shure.com, *http://shure.custhelp.com/ app/answers/detail/a_id/89/~/what-is-the-difference -between-uhf-and-vhf-frequencies%3F*

52. Miniaturization of a HERF weapon to a handheld size appears probable. As a comparison, a laptop computer that can be purchased today has more processing speed, more memory, and more diverse capacity (such as audio and video) than a state-of-the-art mainframe computer of 1980 that required an entire room with strict environmental controls to be housed. See KITADA, H. *et al.* (2017). "3D Packaging Technology to Realize Miniaturization/High-Density and High-Performance Servers." *Fujitsu Scientific Technology Journal* (February): 53(2): 15–22, *https://www.fujitsu.com/ global/documents/about/resources/publications/fstj/ archives/vol53-2/paper05.pdf*

53. DHRA (2017). "Emissions Security (TEMPEST)," Defense Human Resources Activity, Defense Personnel and Security Research Center, U.S. Department of Defense, Monterey, CA: PERSEC, *http://www.dhra.mil/perserec/osg/v3bugs /emissions.htm*

54. Norton (2017). "What Is Malware and How Can We Prevent It?" Mountain View, CA: Symentac, *https://us.norton.com /internetsecurity-malware.html*

55. O'BRIEN, T. (2005). "Gone Spear-Phishin." *The New York Times.* Retrieved May 4, 2008, from *http://www.nytimes .com/2005/12/04/business/yourmoney/04spear.html?_r=1& ex=1157083200&en=88dace68c6663bbb&ei=5070.* See also HALEVI, T. *et al.* (2015). "Spear-Phishing in the Wild: A Real-World Study of Personality, Phishing, Self-Efficacy, and Vulnerability to Spear-Phishing Attacks." *SSRN* (January 2), *https:// papers.ssrn.com/sol3/papers.cfm?abstract_id=2544742*

56. *Ibid.*; see also SCHELL, B.H. *et al.* (2005). *Encyclopedia of Hacking: Headline Makers, Hackers, Hack Attacks and Hacking Solutions.* Westport, CT: Greenwood Press, *http:// dl.acm.org/citation.cfm?id=1051025*

57. POOL, J. (October 11, 2005). "Technology and Security Discussions on the Jihadist Forums." Jamestown Foundation. See also al-Sunnah, Minbar Ahl al-Sunnah (2013). "They Massacred Tawhid Oh Ahi al-Sunnah in Lebanon." Beirut, Lebanon: 'Ā'ishah Media Center, *http://jihadology.net/ category/minbar-ahl-al-sunnah-wa-l-jamaah-in-lebanon/*

58. JAMESTOWN (March 4, 2008). "Hacking Manual by Jailed Jihadi Appears on Web." *Terrorism Focus* 5(9). Jamestown Foundation; STEWART, M. (2017). "Wellington Museum Trust Website Hacked by Pro-Palestine, Anti-Zionist Group." *Stuff* (February 10). Wellington, New Zealand newspaper, *http://www.stuff.co.nz/technology/89271506/wellington -museum-trust-website-hacked-by-propalestine-antizionist -group*; Anonymous (2012). "Hacking Group Threatens 'Crusade' Against Israel." *Independent* [UK] newspaper (February 2), *http://www.independent.co.uk/news/world/ middle-east/hacking-group-threatens-crusade-against -israel-6720039.html*

59. PFI (2017). "About PFI." Society of Police Futurists International, *http://www.policefuturists.org*

60. *Ibid.*

Index